Jürgen Zimmerer
From Windhoek to Auschwitz?

European Colonialism in Global Perspective

Edited by
Jürgen Zimmerer

Volume 1

Jürgen Zimmerer

From Windhoek to Auschwitz?

—

Reflections on the Relationship between Colonialism and National Socialism

DE GRUYTER
OLDENBOURG

Free access to the e-book version of this publication was made possible by the 36 academic libraries and initiatives that supported the open access transformation project in History.

With translations by Anthony Mellor-Stapelberg, Dr. Elizabeth Janik, Tosca Fischer, Dr. Elisabeth Hope Murray and Mark Osborne.

ISBN 978-3-11-075420-9
e-ISBN (PDF) 978-3-11-075451-3
e-ISBN (EPUB) 978-3-11-075460-5
ISSN 2941-3095
DOI https://doi.org/10.1515/9783110754513

This work is licensed under the Creative Commons Attribution 4.0 International License. For details go to https://creativecommons.org/licenses/by/4.0/.

Library of Congress Control Number: 2023940036

Bibliographic information published by the Deutsche Nationalbibliothek
The Deutsche Nationalbibliothek lists this publication in the Deutsche Nationalbibliografie; detailed bibliographic data are available on the internet at http://dnb.dnb.de.

© 2024 the author(s), published by Walter de Gruyter GmbH, Berlin/Boston
This book is published open access at www.degruyter.com.

Cover image: Ausstellung „Planung und Aufbau im Osten". Besichtigung durch Rudolf Hess, 1941. Am Ausstellungstisch vlnr: Rudolf Heß, Heinrich Himmler, SS-Obergruppenführer Martin Bormann, Konrad Meyer, N.N. über dem Modell eines Hauses; hinter Heß: SS-Hauptsturmführer Joachim Peiper, hinter Himmler: General Hermann Reinecke. Bundesarchiv/Agentur Scherl/Fotograf unbekannt
Typesetting: Integra Software Services Pvt. Ltd.
Printing and binding: CPI books GmbH, Leck

www.degruyter.com

Open-Access-Transformation in History

Open Access for excellent academic publications in the field of history: Thanks to the support of 36 academic libraries and initiatives, 9 frontlist publications from 203 can be published as gold open access, without any costs to the authors.

The following institutions and initiatives have contributed to the funding and thus promote the open access transformation in German linguistics and ensure free availability for everyone:

Dachinitiative „Hochschule.digital Niedersachsen" des Landes Niedersachsen
Universitätsbibliothek Bayreuth
Staatsbibliothek zu Berlin – Preußischer Kulturbesitz
Universitätsbibliothek Bern
Universitätsbibliothek Bielefeld
Universitätsbibliothek Bochum
Universitäts- und Landesbibliothek Bonn
Staats- und Universitätsbibliothek Bremen
Universitäts- und Landesbibliothek Darmstadt
Sächsische Landesbibliothek, Staats- und Universitätsbibliothek Dresden (SLUB)
Universitätsbibliothek Duisburg-Essen
Universitäts- und Landesbibliothek Düsseldorf
Albert-Ludwigs-Universität Freiburg – Universitätsbibliothek
Niedersächsische Staats- und Universitätsbibliothek Göttingen
Universitätsbibliothek der FernUniversität in Hagen
Staats- und Universitätsbibliothek Hamburg Carl von Ossietzky
Gottfried Wilhelm Leibniz Bibliothek – Niedersächsische Landesbibliothek, Hannover
Technische Informationsbibliothek (TIB)
Universitätsbibliothek Hildesheim
Universitäts- und Landesbibliothek Tirol, Innsbruck
Universitätsbibliothek Kassel – Landesbibliothek und Murhardsche Bibliothek der Stadt Kassel
Universitäts- und Stadtbibliothek Köln
Zentral- und Hochschulbibliothek Luzern
Universitätsbibliothek Mainz
Bibliothek des Leibniz-Instituts für Europäische Geschichte, Mainz
Universitätsbibliothek Marburg
Universitätsbibliothek der Ludwig-Maximilians-Universität München
Universitäts- und Landesbibliothek Münster
Bibliotheks- und Informationssystem (BIS) der Carl von Ossietzky Universität Oldenburg
Universitätsbibliothek Osnabrück
Universität Potsdam
Universitätsbibliothek Vechta
Universitätsbibliothek der Bauhaus-Universität Weimar
Herzog August Bibliothek Wolfenbüttel
Universitätsbibliothek Wuppertal
Zentralbibliothek Zürich

To Clara, Rebecca and Amélia

Contents

Glossary —— XIII

Preface to the English Edition —— XV

In Lieu of an Introduction

National Socialism from a Postcolonial Perspective: A Plea for the Globalisation of the History of German Mass Violence —— 3
    The Germans and Colonialism —— 3
    Towards a Global History of Mass Violence —— 6
    Deprovincialising German History —— 9
    National Socialism from a Postcolonial Perspective —— 13
    From Faith in Modernity and the Ideology of Progress to Colonial Apologetics —— 19

The War of Annihilation, the Racist Utopia and the Obsessive Delusion of Planning

The First Genocide of the Twentieth Century: The German War of Annihilation in South West Africa (1904–1908) and the Global History of Genocide —— 29
    Causes of the War —— 33
    The Course of the War —— 35
    The Decision for Genocide —— 37
    Von Trotha's 'Annihilation Proclamation' —— 40
    The War of Annihilation Against the Nama —— 43
    Concentration Camps —— 44
    The Camp on Shark Island and Annihilation through Neglect —— 46
    Colonialism, Racism and Genocide —— 49
    Genocide on the Frontier, Colonial Wars of Conquest and Annihilation —— 50
    The Second World War as a Colonial War —— 53
    Holocaust and Colonialism —— 54

Planning Frenzy: Forced Labour, Expulsion and Genocide as Elements of Population Economics in German South West Africa —— 57

Total Control? Law and Administration in German South West Africa —— 77
    Introduction —— 77
    Governmental and Administrative Utopia: Surveillance and Total Control —— 79
    Total Surveillance and Control on the Ground —— 86
    Negligent Officials and Uncooperative Settlers —— 91
    Africans on the Run; Inadequate Identification —— 96
    Conclusion —— 102

Germany's Racial State in Africa: Order, Development and Segregation in German South West Africa (1884–1915) —— 104
    The Founding of German South West Africa —— 105
    The German Governmental and Administrative Utopia —— 108
    Racial Segregation —— 111
    Definitions: Culturalistic v. Biologistic —— 113
    White 'Masters' – Black Servants —— 115
    Aporias of the Racial State —— 118
    The Society of Racial Privilege in German South West Africa and Its Significance in the Context of German History —— 119

The Herero and Nama War (1904–1908) in Global History

Colonialism and the Holocaust: Towards an Archaeology of Genocide —— 125
    Structural Similarity: 'Race' and 'Space' —— 131
    Genocides: Similarities and Differences —— 139
    Conclusion —— 152

The German Empire and Genocide: The Genocide Against the Herero and Nama in (German) History —— 154
    Genocide: The Meaning and History of a Term —— 154
    'Driven into the Desert' —— 158
    The Anti-Guerrilla Campaign and the War of Annihilation —— 165
    The Concentration Camps —— 167
    The Genocide in South West Africa and the Holocaust —— 171

Colonial Genocide? On the Use and Abuse of a Historical Category for Global History —— 175
    'Colonial Genocide': Some Reflections on the History of the Term —— 175
    Colonialism and National Socialism: Systematic Similarities —— 184
    The Archaeology of the Genocidal Impulse —— 187
    The Use and Abuse of Colonial Genocide as a Historical Category —— 196

From Germany's First Colonial Empire to Its Second

From Windhoek to Warsaw: The Society of Racial Privilege in German South West Africa – a Model with a Future? —— 201
    'Mixed' Marriages and Their Prohibition —— 202
    "Membership of the Native Race Is Determined by Descent" —— 207
    "A Sin against Racial Consciousness" —— 210
    "That Man Has Gone Completely Native; He Reeks of *pontok*" —— 213
    The Governmental and Administrative Utopia: A Society of Racial Privilege —— 217
    "Brutal Excesses of Whites Against Natives" —— 221
    From Windhoek to Warsaw —— 224

The Birth of the *Ostland* out of the Spirit of Colonialism: A (Post-)colonial Perspective on the Nazi Policy of Conquest and Annihilation —— 230
    (Post-)Colonial Perspectives —— 232
    The Reordering of the World —— 237
    Traditions of the 'War of Annihilation' —— 245
    Channels of Transmission: First-Hand Experience, Institutional Structures and the Collective Imagination —— 251
    Conclusion —— 261

In the Service of the Empire: Berlin University's Geographers from Colonial Sciences to *Ostforschung* —— 262
    'Armchair Explorers': Geography and the Educated Public in the 19th Century —— 269
    A Devotee of Colonialism: Ferdinand Von Richthofen —— 274
    Colonial Revisionism —— 280
    Expansion in the East —— 285
    Conclusion —— 292

Mass Violence: A German *Sonderweg*?

No German *Sonderweg* in 'Race Warfare': The Genocide against the Herero and Nama (1904–1908) —— 297

Archive Sources Referenced —— 317

Bibliography —— 319

Index —— 341

Glossary

Colonial and National Socialist language was full of racist, antisemitic and derogatory terms and phrases. In a study that concerns the perpetrators' mindsets and policies, it is almost impossible to avoid problematic and discriminatory language without substantially altering the meaning of the discourse – which would, if such a thing were at all possible, constitute a form of whitewashing insofar as it would mask the cruel intentions and racist mindsets of those perpetrators. The use of such terms and phrases is a form of quotation. This glossary explains key terms and their use in translation, and also points to the most blatant racist terms and why and how they have been used or translated in this text.

African: Term used for the colonised population, particularly in South West Africa. Often called *Eingeborene* ('natives' – see below) in colonial-era sources.

Black/White: Capitalised to emphasise that 'race' is not a biological category, but instead a social construct employed by colonisers to create a hierarchy among people.

district: *Bezirke* and *Distrikte* were administrative divisions in German South West Africa. For the sake of simplicity, both *Bezirk* and *Distrikt* are translated as 'district' in this work.

governmental and administrative utopia: *Herrschaftsutopie*. Trutz von Trotha's term for the conditions that German officials and the German military ultimately sought to realise.

***Großraumpolitik*, *Großraumwirtschaft*:** Related concepts for attempts to control, shape or exploit territories on a larger scale.

Herero and Nama War: Designation for the conflict as a whole from 1904 to 1908.

Herero: In accordance with general use in English, 'Herero' is used throughout this book not only as the singular but also as the plural form, rather than the technically more correct 'Ovaherero'.

***Lebensraum*:** 'living space', or the claim, based on expansionist and later fascist ideology, that Germans needed more land to settle on.

Nama: Referred to as *'Hottentotten'* ('Hottentots') in colonial-era sources. In accordance with general use in English, 'Nama' is used throughout this book not only as the singular but also the plural form, rather than the technically more correct 'Namaqua'.

'mixed': Because 'race' is not a biological category, but instead a social construct employed by colonisers to create a hierarchy among people, this term is placed in quotation marks to underscore that 'races' are not separate entities that can be 'mixed'.

'natives': *'Eingeborene'*, or the designation used by colonial officers for the African population of South West Africa, not including Black working migrants from the Cape Colony. To reflect the term's negative and racist implications, 'native' is placed in quotation marks throughout the book, unless it is part of a capitalised phrase or a longer quotation.

population economics: *Bevölkerungsökonomie*. German attempts to reorder the population and peoples of occupied territories.

'race' and 'space': See *Lebensraum* for the connection between these concepts.

'race': Placed in quotation marks to indicate that 'race' is not a biological category, but instead a social construct employed by colonisers to create a hierarchy among people.

resistance: In this book, resistance generally refers to deliberate actions against the German occupiers. Colonial-era sources referred to such actions as 'uprising' or 'rebellion'.

San: Referred to as 'Bushmen' (*Buschleute*) in colonial-era sources.

Schutzgebiet: The German colonies were officially called *Schutzgebiete*, or 'protectorates'. However, contrary to the use of the term 'protectorate' in British imperial history, the German *Schutzgebiete* had no status that distinguished them from colonies, and so the two terms are effectively interchangeable.

Schutztruppe: 'protection force', or the colonial army. The term's euphemistic meaning generally mirrors that of *Schutzgebiet*.

society of racial privilege: *rassische Priviliegengesellschaft*. A term for the new social order that the colonial government in South West Africa attempted to establish, which was to be based on a racist hierarchy and strict segregation.

Sonderweg: The often postulated 'special path' and a uniquely German approach to modernity.

'tribe': *Stamm*. A designation used by colonial officers for certain groups of the African population in South West Africa. The German term has connotations of backwardness, primitiveness and a lack of civilization, and it played an important part in constructing the colonised 'Other'. To reflect these negative implications, 'tribe' is placed in quotation marks throughout the book, unless it is part of a capitalised phrase or a longer quotation.

Volk: The people or 'nation', which, in a racist view of history and society, was understood to be a single composite organism, whose preservation and growth was to be safeguarded under all circumstances.

Preface to the English Edition

Books sometimes have a strange history, and *From Windhoek to Auschwitz?* is no exception. A first collection of my essays was published in German in 2011.[1] It brought together my writings in a debate among historians, about my own theses, that had been conducted in Germany since 2003. At that point, some of the essays were already a few years old. The dispute seemed to have ended in a truce, or even to have been mostly settled in my favour—although my antagonists from that time probably see this differently. My interpretation of the German war in eastern Europe after 1939 as a colonial war was largely accepted, and colonial crimes, especially those perpetrated by Germans, began to be more closely scrutinised. Even so, the degree to which the Holocaust itself was colonial in character remained a divisive question.

Seeking to assemble my reflections on this subject in one place, I compiled them in this book. I would have liked to accommodate the demand for an English translation, but other responsibilities and debates rose to the fore. Now the translation is complete, but little remains of the truce and interpretive consensus that existed in 2011.

Since 2020, debate over the colonial precedents of National Socialism has become the subject of a public controversy aimed at the heart of German memory politics. Talk of a 'new Historikerstreit' or 'Historikerstreit 2.0' is evidence of the intensity of this debate. In June 2021 even Jürgen Habermas, the intellectual doyen of the Federal Republic of Germany, felt called to weigh in on the relationship between colonialism and National Socialism, and on the need for a new and expanded German memory culture:

> Just as all historical facts can be compared with other facts, the Holocaust, too, can be compared with other genocides. But the meaning of the comparison depends on the context. The so-called Historikerstreit had to do with whether comparing the Holocaust with Stalinist crimes could absolve Germans born thereafter of their political responsibility [...] for Nazi mass crimes. [...] Today, under a different constellation, it is not about absolution from this responsibility, but instead about a shift in emphasis.[2]

---

1 Jürgen Zimmerer, *Von Windhuk nach Auschwitz? Beiträge zum Verhältnis von Kolonialismus und Holocaust*, Berlin 2011.
2 Jürgen Habermas, "Der neue Historikerstreit", *Philosophie Magazin* 60 (2021), pp. 10–11. See also the more comprehensive argumentation around these ideas in Jürgen Zimmerer, "Erinnerungskämpfe. Wem gehört die deutsche Geschichte?", in Jürgen Zimmerer, ed., *Erinnerungskämpfe. Neues deutsches Geschichtsbewusstsein*, Stuttgart 2023, pp. 11–37; and Jürgen Zimmerer, "Der Völkermord an den Herero und Nama und die deutsche Geschichte", in Zimmerer, *Erinnerungskämpfe*, pp. 55–79.

Open Access. © 2024 the author(s), published by De Gruyter. This work is licensed under the Creative Commons Attribution 4.0 International License.
https://doi.org/10.1515/9783110754513-204

With these words, Habermas immediately dismantled all objections that the debate's protagonists were seeking to deny German guilt. Only the eloquent matador of the first Historikerstreit in 1986 could have pronounced this judgment with such authority.

He not only refuted those critics who believed that asking about the pioneering role of colonialism for National Socialist crimes was an unacceptable relativisation of the Holocaust; he also recognised the debate's significance for a modern and more inclusive German memory politics in a society that had been shaped for decades by migration:

> Remembering our colonial history, which was repressed until only recently, is an important addition. This can also be helpful in another respect. The recent decades of immigration have not only enriched our culture; our own political culture must also expand so that adherents of other cultural life forms—with their own heritage and, in some cases, their own painful history—can also recognise themselves in it.[3]

One year earlier, the controversy around Cameroonian political theorist and historian Achille Mbembe drew public attention to this debate. Mbembe had long been a favored guest at scholarly conferences and cultural festivals in Germany. However, because of his alleged ties to the BDS (Boycott, Divestment and Sanctions) movement, he was accused—first, in leftist, or 'anti-German', circles and, soon thereafter, by the political establishment—of antisemitism and relativising the Holocaust, of equating National Socialist and Israeli crimes.[4]

Just a few weeks earlier, Michael Rothberg and I had criticised the "provinciality" of German memory that shone through in this debate, and which, in our eyes, leads to historical forgetting and failure in the self-critical engagement with the country's past. We believe that stigmatising all comparisons and the drawing of parallels and continuities between the Holocaust and other forms of mass violence leads to the separation of the Shoah from history, with far-reaching consequences. Insisting that nothing is comparable to the Holocaust blocks our ability to see important roots of National Socialist crimes. This reduces the moral force of 'never again', since singular events cannot be repeated. It also allows right-wing governments in Europe to cover up the thousands of ways that their own

---

[3] Habermas, "Der neue Historikerstreit", pp. 10–11.
[4] See Hajo Funke, "Der Streit um Achille Mbembe und die Frage der Deutungshoheit über die Geschichte", in Zimmerer, *Erinnerungskämpfe*, pp. 310–19.

citizens' ancestors were complicit. And it distorts the pluralism of public memory, thereby squandering the chance to develop a more inclusive memory culture.[5]

A few weeks later, A. Dirk Moses intensified this critique by identifying a "German catechism", according to which the 'sacralisation' of the Holocaust made criticising Israel impossible in German society and left no room in the discourse for people with Palestinian/Arab roots or identities.[6] In the months that followed, the debate revolved largely around the singularity of the Holocaust and around Israel. Rothberg's and my call for placing the Holocaust in context—including the genealogy of its prehistory and the multidirectional memory of its aftermath—were largely ignored, insofar as this context did not involve Israel or the Nakba associated with its founding.[7] In a sense, concentration of the (post-)colonial question on Israel followed the same logic as that of the 'anti-Germans' in the larger debate. The consequence of German history, they believed, was that only an affirmative position toward Israel was acceptable; the success in coming to terms with the past and with 'never again' could only be measured by this standard. This ignores the question of colonialism's role as one of the roots of National Socialist crimes.

Habermas recognised the fundamentally critical approach toward nationalism in the debate around the crimes of colonialism—an approach that was diametrically opposed to the affirmative nationalist intentions of Ernst Nolte and his apprentices. However, at the opening of the ethnological exhibitions at the Humboldt Forum in Berlin, Federal President Frank-Walter Steinmeier wisely avoided a broader assessment when he raised the subject of colonial crimes:

> I strongly believe that remembrance of the Shoah, that betrayal of all civilised values, is and remains quite singular in our national memory. It is a part of our identity. I say this not as a historian—that academic discipline holds its own specialist debates on singularity and comparability—but as Federal President.[8]

---

5 Michael Rothberg and Jürgen Zimmerer, "Enttabuisiert den Vergleich!", *Die Zeit* (31 March 2021), https://www.zeit.de/2021/14/erinnerungskultur-gedenken-pluralisieren-holocaust-vergleich-globalisierung-geschichte/komplettansicht, accessed 11 Sept. 2023.
6 A. Dirk Moses, "The German Catechism", *Geschichte der Gegenwart* (23 May 2021), https://geschichtedergegenwart.ch/the-german-catechism, accessed 11 Sept. 2023.
7 See, for example, Meron Mendel, *Über Israel reden. Eine deutsche Debatte*, Berlin 2023. Mendel recognises the problematic fusion of German memory politics with the political relationship to Israel, but he does not consider the significance of colonial precedents for understanding the Holocaust. See also Charlotte Wiedemann, "Über die Nakba sprechen lernen", *Geschichte der Gegenwart* (16 April 2023), https://geschichtedergegenwart.ch/ueber-die-nakba-sprechen-lernen/, accessed 11 Sept. 2023; and Wolfgang Benz, ed., *Erinnerungsverbot? Die Ausstellung 'Al Nakba' im Visier der Gegenaufklärung*, Berlin 2023.
8 Federal President Frank-Walter Steinmeier at the inauguration of the exhibitions of the Ethnological Museum and the Museum of Asian Art of the National Museums in Berlin, 22 September

Separating politics and scholarly debate, Steinmeier underscored the central distinction between remembrance and scholarly analysis, and—with a clear nod to Habermas—also subverted a transparent critique, which misuses the Holocaust to refute (post-)colonial criticism about the gaps in German memory culture. He thus acknowledged the colonial crimes in Namibia, after he himself had been unable or unwilling to push for this during his earlier term as foreign minister:

> There, in what was then called German South West Africa, at the beginning of the 1900s, Germany's so-called 'protective troops' committed the first genocide of that blood-soaked century. It took a long time, far too long, for Germany even to acknowledge this crime—an entire century. The crimes of the past still have an effect today. The suffering inflicted still marks the descendants of the victims; many of them still live in extreme poverty.[9]

By pointing to the blind spots of memory culture and drawing a connection to racism, Steinmeier detected a continuity that extended from the imperial era to the present day:

> The truth is that, when it comes to the colonial era, we Germans who are usually so historically conscious have far too many blank spaces! We have blind spots in our memory and our perception of ourselves. [...] Shining light into this darkness is a task not just for historians. The injustices that Germans committed in the colonial era concern us all as a society. [...] I firmly believe that we will only be able to understand and eradicate the deeper roots of everyday racism when we illuminate the blind spots of our memory, when we address our colonial history much more thoroughly than we have done to date![10]

However, Steinmeier was unwilling or unable to situate the Holocaust within this continuity. For him, the two historical eras remained separate spheres. He was thereby quite in sync with the disciplinary mainstream of national German history, which is why these debates remained mostly absent in widely reviewed works for general readers.[11]

In a radio debate, Norbert Frei explained this blind spot to me like so: Historians of contemporary Germany had left colonialism to people like me, because they themselves were not experts in the field. If they did not know the field, I asked, and thus could not assess lines of continuity or draw comparisons, how

---

2021: https://www.humboldtforum.org/wp-content/uploads/2021/09/Speech-of-Federal-President-Frank-Walter-Steinmeier.pdf, accessed 11 Sept. 2023.
9 Ibid.
10 Ibid.
11 One example is Birthe Kundrus, *"Dieser Krieg ist der große Rassenkrieg". Krieg und Holocaust in Europa*, München 2018. She does not mention the debates about connections between colonialism and National Socialism, although she herself participated in them—a sign of discursive silence and the relegation of debate to supposed niches.

could they so vehemently argue against the colonial precedents of National Socialist policy in every debate? He had no answer.[12]

Ill-equipped for undertaking an independent comparative analysis, he and others in the 'catechism debate' doubled down on the postulate of singularity, on the defamation of the opposing position and also its representatives, and in this way only kept affirming Moses's analysis anew.[13] In any case, there were fundamentally two separate debates in 'Historikerstreit 2.0': One was about the singularity of the Holocaust and its significance for German discourse about Israel, and the other asked about the colonial precedents of National Socialist crimes—and thus, ultimately, whether 'Auschwitz' was to be packed in a black box and extracted de facto from German history.

The first of these debates generated the most public interest and a swirl of media attention. However, for critically understanding the crimes themselves—and thus, for the possibility of a critical 'never again'—the second debate was decisive, as Habermas recognised:

> The controversy of past months essentially revolves around one argument: If one considers the colonial character of the aims of Hitler's racist war of annihilation against Russia, and if one observes the organised murder of the European Jews in this context in which it emerged, then in the German colonial administration's genocide of the Nama and Herero in southern Africa one already recognises those criminal features that recurred in the Holocaust, amplified and in a different way...[14]

By this point, of course, the controversy over the relationship between colonialism and National Socialism—at least, as a scholarly debate in Germany—was at least fifteen years old.[15] In essence, however, the debate is as old as the crimes

---

12 SWR2 Forum with Norbert Frei, Sybille Steinbacher, and Jürgen Zimmerer, 18 January 2022. See also A. Dirk Moses, "Deutschlands Erinnerungskultur und der 'Terror der Geschichte'", in Susan Neiman and Michael Wildt, eds, *Historiker Streiten. Gewalt und Holocaust – Die Debatte*, Berlin 2022, pp. 199-242, here p. 233.

13 See, for example, Dan Diner, Jürgen Habermas, Saul Friedländer, Norbert Frei and Sybille Steinbacher, eds, *Verbrechen ohne Namen. Anmerkungen zum neuen Streit über den Holocaust*, München 2022.

14 Habermas, "Der neue Historikerstreit", pp. 10–11.

15 This was when I published the first essays that subsequently appeared in this book's German edition. See Jürgen Zimmerer, "Holocaust und Kolonialismus. Beitrag zu einer Archäologie des genozidalen Gedankens", *Zeitschrift für Geschichtswissenschaft*, 51/12 (2003), pp. 1098–1119. An English version came out one year later, as "Colonialism and the Holocaust: Towards an Archaeology of Genocide", in A. Dirk Moses, ed., *Genocide and Settler Society: Frontier Violence and Stolen Indigenous Children in Australian History*, New York 2004, pp. 49–76. The essay appears under this title in this book.

themselves. The relationship between both historical phenomena—between the racist crimes of colonialism in general, and the racist and antisemitic crimes of National Socialist Germany—has occupied intellectuals since the Second World War: Hannah Arendt, Aimé Césaire, W. E. B. Du Bois, and Raphael Lemkin immediately come to mind. Shelley Baranowski, Timothy Snyder, Richard Overy, and A. Dirk Moses have more recently taken up the debates that commenced in Germany at the beginning of the new millennium.[16]

These debates were intense but largely conducted without the public excitement that has characterised the controversy of the last two years. In retrospect, I am struck by the degree of acceptance that my central thesis has found—that the German war against Poland, but especially against the Soviet Union, ought to be understood as a colonial war, a war of conquest and annihilation motivated by a racist worldview, in which the rules of 'civilised' warfare apparently did not apply to the Wehrmacht because it was fighting an 'uncivilised' opponent, constructed in a racist way.[17]

And yet, in order to discredit '**the** postcolonial position' (whereby the assumption of a monolithic 'postcolonial position' already demonstrates a lack of knowledge), a core part of my argument—identifying parallels in notions of *Lebensraum*, and in the means and strategies of colonisation—is presented as self-evident and separate from my argument as a whole. By suggesting that I have constructed a 'causality' between the genocide in Namibia and the Holocaust, and that I seek to use the fate of the Herero and the Nama to explain 'Auschwitz' in a monocausal way, my critics have set up a straw man that is all too easily toppled.[18] They ignore the fact that I myself have repeatedly disavowed a mono-

---

[16] Shelley Baranowski, *Nazi Empire: German Colonialism and Imperialism from Bismarck to Hitler,* Cambridge 2010; Timothy Snyder, *Bloodlands: Europe between Hitler and Stalin* New York 2012; Timothy Snyder, *Black Earth: The Holocaust as History and Warning,* New York 2015; Richard Overy, *Blood and Ruins: The Great Imperial War, 1931-1945,* London 2021; and A. Dirk Moses, *The Problems of Genocide: Permanent Security and the Language of Transgression,* Cambridge 2021.

[17] See, for example, Frank Bajohr and Rachel O'Sullivan, "Holocaust, Kolonialismus und NS-Imperialismus: Forschungen im Schatten einer polemischen Debatte", *Vierteljahrshefte für Zeitgeschichte* 70 (2022), pp. 191–202.

[18] So, for example, Michael Wildt at a symposium of the Hochschule für bildende Künste Hamburg, "Kontroverse documenta fifteen: Hintergründe, Einordnungen und Analysen". Although Wildt at least makes an effort to take postcolonial arguments seriously, he nevertheless lapses into the usual pattern: While acknowledging that the war unleashed "the genocidal violence of German settler colonialism", he simultaneously repeats the straw man argument of "direct continuities", without identifying its advocates. He ultimately calls for an "interwoven history of violence" (*Verflechtungsgeschichte der Gewalt*)—which is precisely what (post-)colonial history offers. See Michael Wildt, "Was heißt: Singularität des Holocaust", *Zeithistorische Forschungen/*

causal explanation.[19] It is unclear whether my critics have even made the effort to carefully read my studies and those of other colleagues.

If one acknowledges parallels in how the wars of annihilation were fought in South West Africa and in eastern Europe, and also in their aims to conquer *Lebensraum*, and if one seriously regards the results of Holocaust scholarship that has found "an evident connection between the Holocaust and other National Socialist mass crimes"[20]—then there must also be a connection between colonial violence outside Europe and genocidal violence within it.[21] That would be one path from "Windhoek to Auschwitz".

One can certainly adopt a critical stance toward the thesis of the 'final solution' as the result of a gradual radicalisation, particularly in conjunction with the events of the Second World War.[22] But in adopting such a stance, one discusses and criticises far more than 'only' colonial roots, because antisemitism thereby moves to the centre as almost the sole motive for unleashing deadly violence.[23] This also downplays other interpretations, such as Frank Bajohr's und Andrea Löw's observation about the murder of two million Soviet prisoners of war, and the planned 'dying off' of thirty million Slavs in the *Generalplan Ost*. Bajohr and Löw note that, "from the contemporary viewpoint of the perpetrators, the decision for the systematic mass murder of all European Jews might not have been an especially radical quantum leap."[24] My reflections on the colonial origins of the Holocaust can be situated in precisely this tradition. To my knowledge, the afore-

---

Studies in Contemporary History 19 (2022), pp. 128–147, https://zeithistorische-forschungen.de/1-2022/6022, accessed 11 Sept. 2023. Sybille Steinbacher's argument is similar in Friedlander, et al., *Verbrechen ohne Namen*.
19 See, for example, the final paragraph on p. 56.
20 Frank Bajohr and Andrea Löw, "Tendenzen und Probleme der neueren Holocaustforschung: Eine Einführung", in Frank Bajohr and Andrea Löw, eds, *Der Holocaust. Ergebnisse und neue Fragen der Forschung*, Frankfurt 2015, pp. 9-30, here p. 15.
21 I have explained my position repeatedly. See my responses to my critics—especially Birthe Kundrus, Stephan Malinowski, and Robert Gerwarth—in the first and last chapters of this book: "National Socialism from a Postcolonial Perspective: A Plea for the Globalisation of the History of German Mass Violence" (pp. 3–25 in this book), and "No German *Sonderweg* in 'Race Warfare': The Genocide against the Herero and Nama (1904–1908)" (pp. 297–316 in this book).
22 See Ulrich Herbert, ed., *Nationalsozialistische Vernichtungspolitik 1939–1945. Neue Forschungen und Kontroversen*, Frankfurt 1998.
23 For more on these debates, see Frank Bajohr, "Holocaustforschung – Entwicklungslinien in Deutschland seit 1945", in Magnus Brechtgen, ed., *Aufarbeitung des Nationalsozialismus. Ein Kompendium*, Göttingen 2021, pp. 122–42. Bajohr does not, however, discuss the (post-)colonial interpretation.
24 Bajohr and Löw, "Tendenzen und Probleme der neueren Holocaustforschung", p. 16.

mentioned approaches have never been accused of relativising the Holocaust, as postcolonial approaches have.

In a sense, the rejection of postcolonial approaches in analysing and explaining the Holocaust is the rearguard action of a German-centred historical discipline that, with odd self-complacency, has not apprehended international developments and debates. This rejection is the academic version of the journalistic, trivial provinciality in the present commotion around 'Historikerstreit 2.0'.[25] All this would be reason enough to make these collected essays accessible in English for an international audience. But there is also one more reason: The debate around German colonialism is taking place in the context of a fundamental shift in the Berlin Republic's core identity, including a new debate around Imperial Germany and its consequences for German history,[26] as is apparent also in the controversy around the Humboldt Forum. The reconstruction of the Berlin Palace, once the residence of the Hohenzollern family, is also an attempt to restore a connection with Prussian history before the catastrophe of 1914, when the imperial capital Berlin was a world centre of culture. The old, newly revived notion of Germany as the land of poets and thinkers (*Dichter und Denker*) is supposed to replace Germany's image as the land of judges and hangmen (*Richter und Henker*), thereby creating a new normality, even in the past, and putting it at the center of the new identificatory master narrative of the Berlin Republic. The debate surrounding colonial precedents and parallels for the crimes of the Third Reich runs counter to this positive reassessment.

New insights on German colonial history suggest that the imperial era must not be decoupled all too fundamentally from the German history of violence in the twentieth century. Doing so by emphasising the modernity of Imperial Germany ignores that it was precisely the modern elements of German colonial rule in South West Africa that enabled state-mandated racial segregation and strategies of ethnic cleansing and genocide. These modern elements included biopolitical concepts and thinking in categories such as the 'racial state', and designs for a modern economy across a large territory (*Großraumwirtschaft*) that disregarded African needs and rights. Modernity is also no argument against a continuity between Imperial Germany and the Third Reich. Rather, it is a constitutive element of this continuity, and also of the relationship between colonialism and National Socialism. If the Humboldt Forum can be understood as an attempt to renationalise and 'normalise' German historical identity by literally setting this identity in stone, then any emphasis on colonialism (and on the paths that led from colonial-

---

25 See Rothberg and Zimmerer, "Enttabuisiert den Vergleich!".
26 Eckart Conze, *Schatten des Kaiserreichs. Die Reichsgründung von 1871 und ihr schwieriges Erbe*, München 2020; and Eckart Conze, "'Fischer Reloaded?' Der neue Streit ums alte Kaiserreich", in Zimmerer, *Erinnerungskämpfe*, pp. 80–104.

ism to the war of annihilation against the Soviet Union and also to Auschwitz) is a rejection of this attempt. And so, at this particular moment, there may be renewed interest in my reflections on the relationship between colonialism and National Socialism. I am pleased to present these reflections here, also to facilitate international debate.

Publication and translation history

My first essay on the relationship between colonialism and the Holocaust was published in 2003. In the years thereafter, I kept responding to questions raised in the debate, introducing new arguments, deepening older ones. Some of the essays appeared in German, some in English, some were published in Germany, some internationally. In 2011 I compiled them in a collection entitled *Von Windhuk nach Auschwitz?* —a phrase that became synonymous with my theses, although usually without my very intentional question mark.

Now that the debate has reignited and acquired political relevance, the time at last seems right for the long planned English translation.

Its publication history is complicated. Individual chapters have multiple versions, in various lengths, as texts were sometimes shortened or edited for publication in German or English. For this collection, therefore, all texts were newly translated, largely on the basis of the original manuscripts, even when English versions already existed. This was also necessary for establishing consistent terminology. Because most of the chapters were initially published as stand-alone essays, there is some repetition among texts. Notes and scholarly references were largely kept as is, in part to document and preserve the character of the debate. However, a supplemental bibliography with important works published since 2011 was added to this edition.

Wherever possible, original English quotes are cited directly from English sources. In some cases, German quotes with published English translations have been newly translated for greater fidelity. Links and notes were updated as the need arose in the course of translation. Where certain expressions no longer seemed in step with contemporary usage, language was gently brought up to date.

Many colleagues and translators have contributed to this work over the years —some for longer, and some for shorter, periods of time. After Tosca Fischer, Mark Osborne, and Dr. Elisabeth Hope Murray, Anthony Mellor-Stapelberg assumed final responsibility for reworking and harmonising all of the texts—a task for which he was eminently suited after his outstanding work on *German Rule, African Subjects*. Dr. Elizabeth Janik translated the preface.

In different phases of the book, assistance with editing and organisation was provided by Mara Brede, Josefa Cassimo, Paula Dahl, Sina Hätti, Nils Lehmann, Zsuzsa Lummitsch, Cäcilia Maag, Arne Meinicke, Friederike Odenwald, Lara Mia Padmanaban, Dr. Nils Schliehe, and Dr. Kim Todzi. Dr. Julian zur Lage also kept track of the different versions and editions, and it is due to his organisational talents that this book was actually completed. I am grateful to my translators and colleagues at the University of Hamburg for their help and eloquence with words.

In Lieu of an Introduction

National Socialism from a Postcolonial Perspective: A Plea for the Globalisation of the History of German Mass Violence

The Germans and Colonialism[1]

Germans find colonialism a hard subject to tackle. For many years, it was disregarded at universities and repressed in the public consciousness. Although the subject has been brought back to mind in recent years, it is generally exoticised and treated as a mere banality.[2]

Hegel's well-known dictum that Africa does not have any history is apparently still believed by many people, at least in the sense that if Africa does have any history, this does not have any relevance to one's 'own' history, whether that is European or German. If taught at university level at all, colonial history has generally been and still is pushed aside into peripheral niches in terms of staff appointments. Although professorships and chairs for African, Asian and Latin American History or for Non-European History in general have been established here and there in recent decades, the result has been to make it even easier for other chairs designated as dealing with national history to focus solely on Germany. Even though this situation is gradually beginning to change, the significance of colonialism and globalisation for German history in particular is still

---

[1] The journal *Geschichte und Gesellschaft* ('History and Society') recently published an article criticising my theses (Vol. 33, 2007, No. 3). Its polemical tone appeared to be justified by the fact that it was placed in the 'debate' section: after all, when two people are debating it is normal for the tone to become more direct. However, the fact that my reply was not accepted for publication suggests an odd understanding of the academic culture of debate. I would like to take this opportunity to thank the *Zeitschrift für Geschichtswissenschaft* for allowing this debate to continue, regardless of its own position with regard to the content.

[2] The three-part television documentary 'Deutsche Kolonien' ('German Colonies', first broadcast by the ZDF from 8–22 November, 2005) may be taken as one example among many. Horst Gründer, the doyen of the field of colonial history in Germany, was responsible for both the film and the accompanying book: Gisela Graichen and Horst Gründer, eds, *Deutsche Kolonien. Traum und Trauma*, München 2005. However, this did not save either the book or the film from being kitschy or from a manner of presentation bordering on the apologetic. See also my detailed critique: Jürgen Zimmerer, "Warum nicht mal 'nen Neger? Menschenfresser und barbusige Mädchen: Ein ZDF-Film und ein Buch verkitschen und verharmlosen den deutschen Kolonialismus in skandalöser Weise" ["Why not put in a negro? Cannibals and bare-breasted girls: a ZDF film and book present a kitschy view of German colonialism that scandalously plays down its impact"], *Süddeutsche Zeitung* (23 November 2005).

Open Access. © 2024 the author(s), published by De Gruyter. This work is licensed under the Creative Commons Attribution 4.0 International License.
https://doi.org/10.1515/9783110754513-001

being wantonly underestimated. For example, one need only look at the generalised knee-jerk rejection of any postcolonial perspective on the history of the Third Reich, arising at best out of ignorance and at worst out of Eurocentricity and colonial apologetics. It is amazing to see the vehemence with which scholars have refused to consider any link between colonialism and Nazism, or have even branded such thinking as representing an underhand relativisation of the Holocaust. This makes one wonder what kind of idealised image of colonialism it is that is prevalent even in academic circles and that makes it appear almost obscene to attempt to determine structural similarities between the behaviour of German administrators in the colonies and in occupied Russia.

Before going into this in greater detail, I would first like to define the key coordinates of the project that I intend to refer to as 'the globalisation of the history of German violence'. This seems to be necessary as the debate is suffering under a cavalier refusal to acknowledge large parts of the relevant research and also a wilful distortion of its arguments.

Contrary to the claim that is constantly being repeated and which in itself is Germanocentric in its restrictiveness, this debate on the relationship between colonialism and National Socialism is not a reprise of the debate about a German *Sonderweg* (the often postulated 'special path' or 'different way'), nor is it a discussion that is primarily rooted in German history and therefore predominantly shaped by representatives of the German historians' guild. Rather, it is above all a debate about colonialism, its consequences and how it should be handled, both in the former colonies and in the former colonial powers. After all, it was none other than Aimé Césaire who concluded as early as 1950 that the factor that made the Holocaust appear so unbearable

> [...] is not the *humiliation of man as such*, it is the crime against the white man, the humiliation of the white man, and the fact that he [Hitler] applied to Europe colonialist procedures which until then had been reserved exclusively for the Arabs of Algeria, the coolies of India, and the blacks of Africa.[3]

Césaire here stands in the tradition of black intellectuals such as W. E. B. Du Bois, C. L. R James, George Padmore and Oliver Cox, all of whom concerned themselves with the relationship between fascism and colonialism. They saw the former not as an aberration of history but rather as the logical culmination of a European culture of extermination and exploitation that colonialism had given birth to. As early as 1947, W. E. B. Du Bois wrote:

---

[3] Aimé Césaire, *Discours sur le colonialisme* (1950), quoted according to Andrew Zimmerman, *Anthropology and Antihumanism in Imperial Germany*, Chicago 2001, p. 246: English edition *Discourse on Colonialism*, p. 13 ff.

> There was no Nazi atrocity – concentration camps, wholesale maiming and murder, defilement of women or ghastly blasphemy of childhood – which Christian civilization or Europe had not long been practicing against colored folk in all parts of the world in the name of and for the defense of a Superior Race born to rule the world.[4]

It was contemporaries of the Third Reich who looked to colonialism to explain its atrocities. As authentic expressions of those who had themselves suffered under these forms of violence, they deserve to be examined carefully and not simply swept aside with Eurocentric panache. Such a high-handed attitude, especially coming from the pens of the beneficiaries of colonialism and their descendants, can all too easily become apologetic itself. I shall return to this point below.

Thus Hannah Arendt, who examined imperialism in her book *The Origins of Totalitarianism* (1951),[5] was by no means the first to raise the question of a relationship between colonial and Nazi mass violence. She is, however, arguably the most influential of such authors, at least in the field of Holocaust research. She attempted to link colonialism and National Socialism in a fruitful way; whether her attempt was successful or convincing is a matter of continued debate.[6]

The debate about colonialism and National Socialism is not being conducted only in Germany and does not impinge only on research into National Socialism. It is time this was recognised in Germany too. We are now seeing decolonisation and globalisation producing the same effects in the historical field as they already have in the political and economic spheres: doubt is being cast on old certainties and scholars are being forced to adopt new perspectives. A tectonic shift is taking place in the study of history in its traditional westernised manifestations; the subject is becoming and must become global. If this is to be achieved, it is necessary both to solve the fundamental problem of developing concepts and ideas that will allow global history to be written in a way that is truly comprehensive in its scope, and also to answer the central question as to what the actual benefit of a global perspective is: what can be understood better with such a perspective than without it?

---

[4] W. E. B. Du Bois, *The World and Africa* (1947), quoted according to Robin Kelly, "A Poetics of Anticolonialism", *Monthly Review*, 51/6 (1999), http://www.monthlyreview.org/1199kell.htm, accessed 12 Jul. 2023.
[5] Hannah Arendt, *The Origins of Totalitarianism*, New York 1951.
[6] See also Richard H. King and Dan Stone, eds, *Hannah Arendt and the Uses of History. Imperialism, Nation, Race, and Genocide*, New York 2007.

Towards a Global History of Mass Violence

For the global history of mass violence, which will be the primary focus of what follows, this is easy to demonstrate: From Armenia to Rwanda, from the war against the Herero and Nama to the wars of succession in Yugoslavia, extreme violence is a hallmark – if not *the* hallmark – of the 20th century; a violence that is heavily charged with ideology and is exercised indiscriminately against combatants and civilians, against men, women and children. At the centre of these considerations stands the history of the Second World War: the total of 55 million deaths brought about by war and genocide marks this as the bloodiest decade by far[7] in world history. The task of incorporating the experiences of the Second World War into the framework of a global history of mass violence is one of the challenges that need to be met.

A global history of violence seeks to answer questions about the causes, forms and consequences of such extreme violence. In spite of its obvious importance, the global history of violence is marginalised in two respects: firstly, as mentioned above, because Global History is not adequately represented in academic circles, and secondly because the history of violence – and especially mass violence – is neglected within Global History.[8] However, if we wish to understand the 20th century we can no longer allow ourselves this luxury.[9]

Much the same applies to German history. Taking it out of its global context simply provincialises it. This is not merely Eurocentric; it also stands in the way of any fruitful approach from the outside to Germany's national history.[10] A postcolonial view of the conduct of the Second World War in the eastern European theatre, on the other hand, brings it out of its historical isolation and makes it fruitful for a global, integral analysis of the 20th century and beyond. This makes

---

[7] It is appropriate to refer to a 'decade' in view of the importance – which is often overlooked from a Eurocentric perspective – of the Asian theatre of war and the fact that the Japanese surrender certainly did not bring the dying to an end immediately.

[8] In its efforts to highlight the activity (agency) and the resistance of colonised people, research that is committed to a postcolonial perspective appears to have lost sight of the violent character of colonial mastery.

[9] This, however, does not yet even address the importance of an analysis of 20th century violence to the understanding and perhaps the prevention of violence in the 21st century. As an introduction to this topic, see Jürgen Zimmerer, "Environmental Genocide? Climate Change, Mass Violence and the Question of Ideology", *Journal of Genocide Research*, 9/3 (2007), pp. 349–352.

[10] Here I am referring to national history in the narrow sense; because of course German colonial history in Asia, Africa or the Pacific also forms part of German national history, just as Prussian rule over parts of what is now Poland is also certainly to be considered a part of German national history.

many points that otherwise seem incomprehensible much easier to understand. For the history of colonialism, on the other hand, a postcolonial perspective on the politics of German occupation and domination will afford valuable insights into the development, mode of operation and ultimate failure of racial ideologies and the conceptions of *Lebensraum* ('living space') at a crucial point in the development of European modernity.

The purpose of any postcolonial consideration of the Third Reich is to overcome the Eurocentric and to some extent Germanocentric view of the Second World War. It is not its aim to pursue the construction of a German *Sonderweg*, nor to relativise one phenomenon or enhance the significance of another.

Colonialism is an extremely complex phenomenon.[11] Its European variant alone[12] showed many different faces in the course of over five centuries, which demand to be taken seriously: European colonialism destroyed and built up, it brought death and medical progress, it brought slavery and education. European colonialism can neither be defined in terms of only one of these forms, nor can the motives, justifications and concrete actions of the Europeans and their descendants or the reactions of the indigenous populations be briefly summed up in any generalised way. It is therefore misleading even to refer simply to 'colonialism'. Colonialism cannot be turned into a dualistic horror story simply by stringing together a set of specific atrocities or of criminal personalities of the stature of a Pizarro or a Lothar von Trotha, any more than it can be transformed into a story of salvation by reference to certain persons whose biographies radiate virtue and achievement or to beneficial developments that it gave rise to. And under no circumstances should colonialism be assessed only in the light of its final phase, when the former colonial powers were desperately attempting at the eleventh hour to fulfil the promise of the 'civilising mission' by which they had justified their empire-building outside Europe. Nor may one, when attempting to arrive at a nuanced assessment of colonialism, ignore the settler colonies: because it was precisely in these, from South to North America, from New Zealand to Australia and on to South Africa, that the devastation and destruction of the indigenous cultures were the most far-reaching.

It is in these countries too that the debate concerning mass violence, especially as reflected in ethnic cleansing and genocide, is currently being conducted on a theoretically sophisticated level. This is the global context in which the de-

---

11 For an introduction to the topic in German, see Andreas Eckert, *Kolonialismus*, Frankfurt 2006; Jürgen Osterhammel, *Kolonialismus. Geschichte – Formen – Folgen*, München 1995; Wolfgang Reinhard, *Kleine Geschichte des Kolonialismus*, 2nd edn, Stuttgart 2008.
12 I do not have the space here to discuss non-European forms of colonialism, although they too would be well worth examining.

bate on the first genocide of the 20th century, committed against the Herero and the Nama in German South West Africa (1904–1908), is also being conducted. The fact that this is hardly noticed in Germany, but that the debate is constantly being (mis-)interpreted as a form of German self-absorption, is itself a result of the restrictive narrowness of perspective referred to above.

If the outbreaks of genocidal violence that occurred in Australia, North America and South Africa are analysed, they reveal parallels and structural similarities that are worth looking into. Settler colonialism – which is what we have to do with in all of these three cases – is the attempt to control the indigenous populations of largish geographical areas and reorganise their lives in ways determined by a foreign population that has penetrated the region from outside. Both the initial invasion and the subsequent occupation of foreign continents were justified by dividing humankind into higher 'races' with a 'destiny' to rule and lower 'races' that are subject to them. This doctrine of fundamental inequality was the only way in which the massive theft of land and the vast degree of exploitation that colonialism brought with it could possibly be justified.[13] All too often, groups of people who were considered to be at the bottom end of this ranking were imagined to be doomed 'races'. Helping this process along was regarded rather as doing one's bit to further the inevitable march of world history than as the brutal mass murder that it actually was.[14]

In this way, the ground was prepared for the exclusion of the indigenous population from the community of those "whom we are obligated to protect, to take into account, and to whom we must account",[15] and this was one of the major prerequisites for the initiation of genocide – the ideological prerequisite, so to speak, for turning quite normal people into mass murderers. In addition, considerable pressure was exerted by settlement, which intensified the competition for land; this too made genocidal violence more likely to occur in settler colonies than in plantation colonies:

---

[13] I have explored this point in more detail in Jürgen Zimmerer, "Holocaust und Kolonialismus. Beitrag zu einer Archäologie des genozidalen Gedankens", *Zeitschrift für Geschichtswissenschaft*, 51/12 (2003), pp. 1098–1119 (English version: "Colonialism and the Holocaust. Towards an Archaeology of Genocide", pp. 125–153 in this book).

[14] See, for example, Russell McGregor, *Imagined Destinies. Aboriginal Australians and the Doomed Race Theory, 1880–1939*, Victoria 1997; Saul Dubow, *Scientific Racism in Modern South Africa*, Cambridge 1995.

[15] Helen Fein, "Definition and Discontent: Labelling, Detecting, and Explaining Genocide in the Twentieth Century", in Stig Förster and Gerhard Hirschfeld, eds, *Genozid in der modernen Geschichte*, Münster 1999, pp. 11–21, here p. 20.

> Genocide has two phases: one, destruction of the national pattern of the oppressed group; the other, the imposition of the national pattern of the oppressor. This imposition, in turn, may be made upon the oppressed population which is allowed to remain, or upon the territory alone, after removal of the population and the colonization of the area by the oppressor's own nationals.[16]

The mechanism here described is precisely that of settler colonialism: the existing situation or "pattern" is suppressed or even eliminated and then replaced by a new one. It is therefore superfluous to ask whether the term 'genocide' can be applied to colonialism: genocide is colonial by nature. This was Raphael Lemkin's view too, as is shown by the above quotation, taken from his fundamental analysis of the Nazis' occupation policy in Eastern Europe, *Axis Rule in Occupied Europe*. The 'father' of the UN Genocide Convention[17] developed his concept explicitly with both of these phenomena in mind. Lemkin regarded the German occupation and extermination policies as being essentially colonial.

Deprovincialising German History

How important then is the colonial war in German South West Africa within the global history of genocidal violence? The answer is complex: on the one hand, of course, it involves the genocidal quality of settler colonialism – German South West Africa was after all the only German 'protectorate' that can be regarded, at least to a certain degree, as a settler colony – while on the other hand it represents a striking example of an outbreak of mass violence in German history. Colonial history is always both a part of the history of the colonised region and also part of the history of the colonising nation. It is precisely this that endows colonialism and the historical research into it with their global character. Within German history, the Holocaust and other Nazi crimes are among the most important points of reference. As the global history of (genocidal) mass violence also represents an important reference framework, this is a point where there is a meeting of interests between those studying national history and those investigating global aspects.

It is, though, little more than a truism that colonial genocide cannot be equated with the Nazi genocide: they were too different in the ways they were executed and in their choices of victims. Ultimately it is not possible to equate

---

16 Raphael Lemkin, *Axis Rule in Occupied Europe: Law of Occupation, Analysis of Government, Proposals for Redress*, Washington 1944, p. 79.
17 With regard to Raphael Lemkin, see Dominik J. Schaller and Jürgen Zimmerer, eds, *The Origins of Genocide. Raphael Lemkin as a Historian of Mass Violence*, London 2009.

one historical event with another; but it is nevertheless worthwhile comparing them, as it is not possible to define the specific, singular features of each without precisely detailing the features they have in common, which alone allow such a comparison to be made. This is precisely what comparative genocide research aims at. Any criticisms confusing comparison with equation which may be voiced in the course of such an analysis (and especially where such confusion is deliberate) are both polemical and ideological, or at least are neither scientifically nor intellectually honest.

What then is the relationship between the first genocide of the 20th century and the genocidal colonial violence of previous centuries? If we examine genocidal settler violence, we cannot fail to notice that on the North American and Australian frontiers the predominant factor was privatised violence exercised by individual persons or by groups of local settlers ganging together. At times these actions were sanctioned by the colonial authorities, at other times they were opposed by it. In general, the colonial state had neither the power nor any opportunity to control such behaviour on the spot in individual cases. The violence was correspondingly uncoordinated.[18]

Germany's war against the Herero and the Nama, on the other hand, was a turning point in respect of state organisation and bureaucratisation, as it represented a four-year-long, centrally directed colonial war of 'pacification' and genocide. The physical annihilation of the Herero and the Nama was not unintended 'collateral damage' as a by-product of the waging of a brutal war, as was the case in the Philippines more or less contemporaneously; rather, it was the objective of the war almost from the outset.[19] In addition, the war – the causes, progress and consequences of which cannot be described in detail here[20] – combined genocidal massacre with ethnic cleansing and extermination through neglect in camps. This

---

[18] I have examined this issue in detail in Zimmerer, "Holocaust und Kolonialismus" (English version: "Colonialism and the Holocaust", pp. 125–153 in this book).

[19] The thesis of situational radicalisation, recently taken up again by Isabel Hull, which to a great extent casts a veil over the ideological intentions of genocide, does not stand up to an empirical examination. On this subject, see Jürgen Zimmerer, "Annihilation in Africa: The 'Race War' in German Southwest Africa (1904–1908) and its Significance for a Global History of Genocide", *Bulletin of the German Historical Institute*, Washington 37/Fall (2005), pp. 51–57.

[20] For an introduction to the history of the war, see Jürgen Zimmerer and Joachim Zeller, eds, *Völkermord in Deutsch-Südwestafrika. Der Kolonialkrieg in Namibia (1904–1908) und seine Folgen*, Berlin 2003. As an introduction to its historiography, see Jürgen Zimmerer, "Colonial Genocide: The Herero and Nama War (1904– 1908) in German South West Africa and its Significance", in Dan Stone, ed., *The Historiography of Genocide*, London 2007, pp. 323–343.

too betrays a degree of ideological conviction and political centralisation that does not appear to have existed to the same extent in other colonial contexts.[21]

The genocide in South West Africa is important in German history in two respects. Firstly, it showed that fantasies of genocidal violence (and actions in realisation of those fantasies) existed in the German military and administration as early as the beginning of the 20th century. Secondly, it popularised this violence, leading to the spread of such fantasies of destruction and their legitimisation.[22]

Moreover, the occurrence of such genocidal practices in the military and in administration twice within a space of only 40 years is a clear indicator of the extent to which these practices were rooted in the structure and mentality of both organisations. This fact is sufficient in itself to raise the question of the connection between colonial and Nazi crimes. This is a complex relationship that the cliché of causality, which is as simplistic as it is polemical, cannot do justice to (any more than the related cliché of the *Sonderweg* can).

For the genocide in German South West Africa was two things: it was both an expression of a pre-existent genocidal tendency, and maybe even of a genocidal mentality, and also an intensifier and populariser of these tendencies. There is a path that connects Windhoek or the Waterberg to Auschwitz; but in the first place it did not begin in the Namibian uplands, and secondly it was not the only possible path that could have been followed. Of course there were other long-standing ideologies, especially anti-Semitism, anti-Bolshevism and anti-Slavism (a tradition which the myth of the colonisation of the East also forms part of) that played equally large or even larger roles in the initiation, form and legitimation

---

21 Comparative violence research is still too much in its infancy to be able to provide an answer to the question as to whether the German genocide was a procedure that was quite typical of the colonial wars of the time, or whether, as intentional genocide, it was an exceptional phenomenon. For initial considerations, see Jürgen Zimmerer, "Kein Sonderweg im Rassenkrieg. Der Genozid an den Herero und Nama 1904–08 zwischen deutschen Kontinuitäten und der Globalgeschichte der Massengewalt", in Sven-Oliver Müller and Cornelius Torp, eds, *Das deutsche Kaiserreich in der Kontroverse*, Göttingen 2008, pp. 323–340 (English version: "No German Sonderweg in 'Race Warfare': The Genocide against the Herero and Nama (1904–1908)", pp. 297–316 in this book). For an introduction to the international research, refer to the various articles in Dominik J. Schaller and Jürgen Zimmerer, eds, "Settlers, Imperialism, Genocide", *Journal of Genocide Research*, 10/2 (2008) (thematic issue), and in A. Dirk Moses, ed., *Empire, Colony, Genocide: Conquest, Occupation, and Subaltern Resistance in World History*, New York 2008.

22 For an introduction, see Jürgen Zimmerer, „Die Geburt des 'Ostlandes' aus dem Geiste des Kolonialismus. Die nationalsozialistische Eroberungs- und Beherrschungspolitik in (post-)kolonialer Perspektive", *Sozial.Geschichte. Zeitschrift für historische Analyse des 20. und 21. Jahrhunderts*, 19/1 (2004), pp. 10–43 (English version: "The Birth of the Ostland Out of the Spirit of Colonialism: A (Post)colonial Perspective on the Nazi Policy of Conquest and Annihilation", pp. 230–261 in this book).

of the Nazis' crimes. However, recognising the influence of these other factors does not negate the link to or the relevance of colonial history.

The ramifications of this relationship are in no way limited to the murderous and destructive policy of genocide. Rather, they also encompass, among other things, the first German attempt to found a 'racial state', a state and society organised on the basis of an ethnic hierarchy, as was attempted in German South West Africa. White Germans formed the 'master' class and Africans the lowest, the working class. These strata were kept strictly apart by segregation laws which also attempted to prevent sexual contacts by classifying them as *Rassenschande*, 'racial defilement'.[23] However, the racism that is expressed in this situation proves two things. Firstly, it shows that the binary structure of opposing concepts that made 'the African' into an unapproachable 'Other' was not limited to the years of war. What the German commander Lothar von Trotha described in his exterminatory rhetoric as a 'race war', in which Africans would "yield only to force" and which he was willing to pursue with 'blatant terrorism and even with cruelty' in order to annihilate "the rebellious tribes with rivers of blood",[24] was just as much a radical consequence of this way of thinking as were the permanent subjugation and the exploitation of the indigenous population. Secondly, the fundamental position occupied by racism in the structure of the colonial state and society in German South West Africa – quite independently of the question of genocide – also throws up the question of its relationship to the racial state of the Third Reich. 'Race' and 'territory', or 'race' and 'space', were crucial elements in both systems.

However, any statement declaring that a specific regime, in this case the Third Reich, is colonial by nature must be linked to the question as to how far this understanding can potentially help to explain *both* (settler) colonialism and its violent excesses *and* the crimes committed by the Third Reich.

As mentioned above, there is a lively international debate about colonial human rights violations, mass crimes and cases of genocide which is not restricted to the period prior to the Holocaust. Colonialism and the Third Reich do not follow on from one another; rather, colonialism preceded the Third Reich, ex-

---

[23] I have analysed this in great detail in Jürgen Zimmerer, *Deutsche Herrschaft über Afrikaner. Staatlicher Machtanspruch und Wirklichkeit im kolonialen Namibia*, Münster/Hamburg/London 2001 [English edition: *German Rule, African Subjects: State Aspirations and the Reality of Power in Colonial Namibia*, New York 2021].

[24] On this subject, see Jürgen Zimmerer, "The First Genocide of the Twentieth Century: The German War of Destruction in South West Africa (1904–1908) and the Global History of Genocide", in Doris L. Bergen, ed., *Lessons and Legacies, viii: From Generation to Generation*, Evanston 2008, pp. 34–64 (a revised version appears in this book on pp. 29–56).

isted parallel to it and outlasted it. The same holds true for the occurrence of genocidal violence. The post-Holocaust call of 'never again' found little resonance, especially in the states that emerged from the former European colonies. In Rwanda, to mention only the most infamous example, one of the most meticulously planned genocides in history took place within only three months in 1994: the fact that the 'technical' aspects of the use of machetes and knives were more reminiscent – at least to European minds – of an uncontrolled eruption of 'tribal violence' does nothing to alter this fact. For the events accompanying the partitioning of India or in Indonesia, Cambodia, East Timor, Biafra, Bosnia or Darfur, too, the classification as genocide has been suggested. Any attempt to explain these outbreaks of mass violence must refer back both to the Holocaust and also to the outbreaks of colonial violence in the decades and centuries before the crimes of the National Socialists.[25]

National Socialism from a Postcolonial Perspective

But how useful is a global and postcolonial perspective in analysing the Third Reich? Only a knowledge of what is generally the case allows one to identify what is unique. Talking in general terms about the singularity of certain occurrences does not throw light on them, but rather obscures them. The murder of whole population groups, for instance, is by no means unique in history; it has occurred and continues to occur relatively often.[26] The conquest and exploitation of largish territories has never been unusual either. Even the reorganisation of geographi-

---

[25] These include the cases of genocide in the final phase of the history of the Ottoman Empire: see Dominik J. Schaller and Jürgen Zimmerer, eds, *Late Ottoman Genocides: The Dissolution of the Ottoman Empire and Young Turkish Population and Extermination Policies*, London 2009; Hans-Lukas Kieser and Dominik J. Schaller, eds, *Der Völkermord an den Armeniern und die Shoah*, Zürich 2002.

[26] For an introduction, see the following general works: Boris Barth, *Genozid. Völkermord im 20. Jahrhundert: Geschichte – Theorien – Kontroversen*, München 2006; Adam Jones, *Genocide. A Comprehensive Introduction*, London 2006; Ben Kiernan, *Blood and Soil: A History of Genocide and Extermination from Sparta to Darfur*, New Haven 2007; Mark Levene, *Genocide in the Age of the Nation State*, 2 vols, London 2005; Michael Mann, *Die dunkle Seite der Demokratie. Eine Theorie der ethnischen Säuberung*, Hamburg 2007; Norman M. Naimark, *Flammender Hass. Ethnische Säuberungen im 20. Jahrhundert*, München 2004; Dominik J. Schaller, Boyadjian Rupen, Hanno Scholtz and Vivianne Berg, eds, *Enteignet – Vertrieben – Ermordet. Beiträge zur Genozidforschung*, Zürich 2004; Martin Shaw, *What is Genocide?*, Cambridge 2007; Jacques Semelin, *Säubern und Vernichten. Die politische Dimension von Massakern und Völkermorden*, Hamburg 2007; Eric D. Weitz, *A Century of Genocide. Utopias of Race and Nation*, Princeton 2003.

cal space, i.e. territory, on a 'racial' basis is not new: the history of colonialism provides countless examples.

Setting aside the purely technical aspects of the methods of conquest, exploitation and annihilation, what was new in the Nazi period were the criteria for the selection of the groups to be annihilated. This is where the Holocaust, the murder of the European Jews, differs from the violence used and the policy of destruction implemented against Poles, Russians and others. Although both 'the Slav' and 'the Jew' were derogated and caricatured in a way that fits neatly into the pattern of colonial Othering, the underlying rationale seems to have differed. This is despite the fact that both anti-Slavism and anti-Semitism have centuries-old traditions in Germany. In principle, anti-Slavism can be traced back to the colonisation of the East during the Middle Ages. 'The East' and its inhabitants were again and again portrayed as being 'primitive', 'underdeveloped', and the region as one that needed to be controlled and 'developed' – that is to say, colonised. Obviously, colonisation meant something different in the 12th century from what it meant in the late 19th or early 20th century; but the idea of a region being 'underdeveloped' or of a culture being 'primitive' is a constant theme running through history right back to the beginnings of Carolingian missionary efforts in the East, and fits in precisely with that binary structure of opposing concepts that served as a basis for overseas colonisation. Thus, the tradition of the colonisation of the East, which was also a factor that helped to shape the policies and worldview of the Nazis, does not in any way contradict the postcolonial interpretation: indeed, it vindicates it.

In the course of German history, imperial fantasies have been projected onto a variety of geographical locations: the open spaces of Russia's eastern plains, the Balkans, Africa and America. What they all had in common was that they were settlement fantasies: these areas were supposed to provide *Lebensraum* for the German people. Initially, these projects were not understood in a Malthusian or Social Darwinian sense; the impacts on the native populations, however, were ultimately similar. There was no room for them: they had to be driven out, subjugated or assimilated. This approach already came very close to cultural genocide. According to Lemkin, forced assimilation is also an act of genocide, whether it is of a cultural or a religious nature.[27]

If one regards eastern and overseas colonisation as two sides of the same (imperial) coin, then the First World War colonial experiment 'Ober Ost' also fits neatly into this tradition. What Hindenburg, Ludendorff and others created dur-

---

27 Lemkin, *Axis Rule in Occupied Europe*, p. 79.

ing their short time in power was a colonial structure.[28] Thus the simple objection that it was 'Ober Ost' – rather than German South West Africa – that provided, as it were, a dry run for the Nazi policies of expansion and subjugation, so that any colonial dimension may be disregarded, misses the point. 'Ober Ost' was just as much an expression of colonial fantasies as was the policy of conquest and subjugation carried out 25 years later.

Anti-Semitism too may well be viewed from a postcolonial standpoint, supplying as it does the image of an 'absolute Other' which in Fein's words is outside one's own moral sphere. This provided the basis for the dehumanisation in camps and ghettos during the Second World War that some historians see as a prerequisite for the mass murder. Anti-Semitism, however, is distinguished from anti-Slavism and from the traditional colonial racism seen in Africa, Asia, Australia or America by the idea of the existence of a global Jewish conspiracy. In the view of anti-Semites this conspiracy makes 'Jewry' especially dangerous, and therefore requires a global 'final solution'. Tied in, if not congruent, with this understanding is the implicit assumption of Jewish 'superiority' – a feature that is not to be found either in anti-Slavism or in colonial racism, in which the 'Other' was always seen as inferior. 'The Jew', by contrast, was considered to be an especially dangerous antagonist because of his 'superiority'. While anti-Slavism and colonial racism attribute superiority to the colonisers, to the Germans/Aryans, anti-Semitism attributes the role of the superior coloniser to the Jews and sees the Germans/Aryans as the colonised. After 1918 the latter did indeed perceive themselves as being subjected to occupation by foreign powers, humiliated and robbed of their national identity. After a period in which they had seen themselves as ideal colonisers, bringing benefits to the world by seeking to conquer it, they felt themselves tricked out of the rewards and prestige due to them for their pains and deprivations. Not only did the Treaty of Versailles determine that Germany was unfit to have colonies, thus justifying its being stripped of them: almost worse than that was the humiliation that France inflicted on Germany as a former colonial power by quite deliberately deploying African colonial troops in the French-occupied Rhineland. In a kind of 'reverse colonialism', the personified 'colonial Other', the 'Black' African, then became the master of the 'White' German. The phrase 'die schwarze Schmach am Rhein' – generally translated as 'the black horror on the Rhine', though 'disgrace' would be a more accurate translation than 'horror' – became a shorthand expression for this humiliation as well as a

---

[28] For the German experience in eastern Europe during the First World War, see Vejas Gabriel Liulevicius, *War Land on the Eastern Front. Culture, National Identity and German Occupation in World War I*, Cambridge 2000.

rallying cry against the political order after the First World War, which was threatening to turn the world upside down. This 'horror' or 'disgrace', further intensified by grossly exaggerated rumours about sexual relationships between occupying soldiers and German women, was felt far beyond the nationalist and right-wing scenes. In this, the sexualised fantasy of the formidable sexual potency of 'Black' masculinity came into disastrous contact with the biopolitical concept of a contamination of the 'body of the German people'. If in the colonies, and in German South West Africa in particular, there was a desire to prevent the emergence of a 'mixed population', since this would call into question the strict 'racial segregation' that colonial rule was founded on: the 'black horror' was regarded as a biopolitical attack on the genetic substance of the German 'race'. It was no mere accident that one of the first measures of racial policy implemented by the Nazi regime was the forced sterilisation of the 'Rhineland bastards'.[29]

The accusation of biopolitical colonisation of the 'body of the German people' could of course also be levied against the Jews. According to the *völkisch* manner of thinking the Jews were the oppressors and exploiters of the German nation, the colonisers of the 'Aryan race'. Anti-Semitic rhetoric referring for instance to 'alien elements in the Aryan race', to 'racial defilement' and 'racial contamination', displays this same biopolitical logic. Conspiracy theories associated with anti-Semitism – world domination by Jewish high finance and the exploitation of Germany by Jewish money magnates – even attribute a colonising role to the Jews. Seen through this prism, the struggle against Versailles and against 'international Jewry' was turned into a 'war of liberation' from colonialism.[30] However, whereas the 'danger' emanating from the 'black horror on the Rhine' still appeared containable, as it was visible, this seemed not to be the case with the Jews, which made them appear incomparably more threatening. 'The Jew' not only seemed 'superior', but was also invisible. And as we know to be the case from the colonial experience, laws and conflicts relating to segregation are all the more rigid, the less distinct the separation of the two groups is in everyday practice, whether because the 'Other' cannot easily be identified or because the population

---

[29] Christian Koller, *'Von Wilden aller Rassen niedergemetzelt': die Diskussion um die Verwendung von Kolonialtruppen in Europa zwischen Rassismus, Kolonial- und Militärpolitik (1914–1930)*, Stuttgart 2001; Reiner Pommerin, *Sterilisierung der Rheinlandbastarde. Das Schicksal einer farbigen deutschen Minderheit 1918–1937*, Düsseldorf 1979.

[30] One does not need to go as far as A. Dirk Moses, who recently interpreted the Holocaust as anti-colonial, subaltern genocide. A. Dirk Moses, "Empire, Colony, Genocide. Keywords and the Philosophy of History", in A. Dirk Moses, *Empire, Colony, Genocide: Conquest, Occupation, and Subaltern Resistance in World History*, New York 2008, pp. 3–54, here p. 37.

fails to uphold the prescribed segregation unless forced to do so by prohibitions or indoctrination.[31]

The application of colonial terminology and concepts to situations in the European sphere was not unfamiliar to contemporaries, as can be seen, for example, from the use of the term *Binnenkolonisation* – 'internal colonisation' – even in the days of the German Empire. At that time it was the eastern provinces of the Empire, which were inhabited predominantly by people of Polish origin, that were to be colonised and Germanised. In particular with regard to 'education to work', but also to various processes of cultural assimilation, concepts were prevalent that were also applied in the German overseas colonies in Africa and Asia.[32] What is important for the thesis presented here is an appreciation of the fact that colonial approaches and structures of argumentation existed independently of any specific geographical location and any sense of exoticism, and that 'German history', even if the application of the term is restricted to its European aspects, still demonstrates colonial traits.

There are repeated attempts to discredit the postcolonial view of the mass crimes committed under the Third Reich by pointing out that other European states had longer and more intensive experiences with colonialism than Germany had, but that no crimes of a magnitude comparable to those of the Third Reich were committed in them. From this, the conclusion is drawn that colonialism is a negligible factor in explaining mass violence. However, this simplistic argument on the one hand confuses continuity with causality, while on the other hand overlooking the important distinction that the question is not *why* the crimes of the Nazis took place in Germany, but rather *how* they came about and what the strategies were that were used to justify and support them. The postcolonial perspective does not explain – nor does it try to explain – why the Nazis came to power in Germany. Rather, it tries to explain the tradition that their programme of imperial conquest stood in and the role models they were able to draw on once they had decided to play the colonialism card again. The postcolonial view also tries to

---

31 German South West Africa is an outstanding example here as well, the 'racial segregation' propagated by the German colonial administration having initially had to be laboriously implemented against the resistance of a part of the German settler population. On this subject see Jürgen Zimmerer, "Deutscher Rassenstaat in Afrika. Ordnung, Entwicklung und Segregation in Deutsch-Südwest (1884–1915)", in Micha Brumlik, Susanne Meinl, and Werner Renz, eds, *Gesetzliches Unrecht. Rassistisches Recht im 20. Jahrhundert*, Frankfurt 2005, pp. 135–153 (English version: "Germany's Racial State in Africa: Order, Development and Segregation in German South West Africa (1884–1915)", pp. 104–121 in this book).
32 On this subject, see Sebastian Conrad, *Globalisierung und Nation im Deutschen Kaiserreich*, München 2006, pp. 74–123.

explain what patterns of justification were used to conceal the frequently invoked 'rupture in civilisation'.[33]

Such a postcolonial and global approach also provides an explanation for why so many Germans, completely "ordinary men",[34] participated so willingly in these crimes and why they did not exercise resistance, or exercise it more strongly. Colonialist conquest, administration and warfare were not perceived as something new, as the breaking of a taboo; rather they were felt to be something familiar, a recognised phenomenon that had been practised throughout the course of history. This also helped to give meaning to the events on an individual level.

The objection that German soldiers and the Nazi leadership had an erroneous view of colonialism does not hold water either. If Hitler, for example, could write that "The struggle for hegemony in the world will be decided in favour of Europe by the possession of Russia; that makes Europe the place that is more secure against blockade than anywhere else in the world. The territory of Russia is our India, and just as the English rule India with only a handful of people, so we will govern this colonial territory of ours",[35] this proves that the dictator's ideas were entrenched in colonialist discourse and thinking. This does not mean that he would have created a one-to-one copy of the style of British colonialism, nor does it even mean that he had any accurate picture of the state of affairs in India. But whether Hitler had a correct understanding of British colonialism is irrelevant to determining whether he was influenced by colonialist concepts. What is important is not so much any historical reality of colonialism, however that may have been defined, but rather the perception of such colonialism prevailing in Germany and particularly in the corridors of power of the regime and among its expert advisers.

As a mental construct and as a framework for claims to legitimacy, colonialism can to a great extent be detached from historical and contemporary examples. The reality is that just as anti-Semitism is able to develop its powerful impact effectively regardless of the fact that Jewish life and the Jewish identity are by no means realistically portrayed – indeed, just the opposite is the case – so the power of the colonial concept is effectively brought to bear even though di-

---

[33] Helmut Walser Smith, who is not otherwise linked to my theses in any way, has written of various 'vanishing points' that research has concentrated on: Helmut Walser Smith, *The Continuities of German History. Nation, Religion, and Race across the Long Nineteenth Century*, Cambridge 2008, pp. 13–38.
[34] Christopher R. Browning, *Ordinary Men. Reserve Police Battalion 101 and the Final Solution in Poland*, New York 1992.
[35] Hitler, 17 September 1941, in Adolf Hitler, *Monologe im Führerhauptquartier*, ed. Werner Jochmann, Hamburg 1980, pp. 60–64.

vorced from any portrayal of historical reality. But this construct too becomes real. How this works is shown by the example of a private soldier who, a few weeks after the attack on the Soviet Union, wrote home as follows:

> Marvellous as the successes are, great as the advance is [...], Russia on the whole is still a huge disappointment for the individual. There is nothing of culture, nothing of paradise [...] but only the absolute depths, filth, people who demonstrate to us that we will face a huge task of colonisation here.[36]

This disappointment did not put the brakes on the will to conquer, but rather justified it. Above all, visions of settler colonialism – however misconceived they may have been –provided those who committed crimes a legitimation even for their acts of violence: they could declare these deeds to be part of their 'colonising mission'. Colonialist ideas not only justify mass murder, but also allow the individual to deceive himself about his own terrible deeds.

From Faith in Modernity and the Ideology of Progress to Colonial Apologetics

In the light of the many arguments, the broad international debate and the fact that other connections between National Socialism and German history are acknowledged although they span far longer periods of time, the question arises as to why the role of colonialism as an inspiration and analytical framework has so often been denied, and why critics of a (post)colonial approach have not shied away either from personal defamation or from colonial apologetics.

It would be too simple to attribute the blame for this purely to the constraints of the discipline, in which it is supposedly only possible for an academic to make his mark at the expense of others. There is more at stake here: issues relating to 'progress' and the absence of historical 'development', and at bottom to the superiority of the western world.

From the critics' point of view, a general condemnation of any postcolonial perspective has the advantage that they can feel themselves to be on the safe side if they make sure they do not in any way deviate from the broadly accepted academic consensus. Arguments are then not examined too closely. It is precisely for this reason that statements regarding the postcolonial perspective allow conclusions to be drawn about the fundamental attitudes among those involved in the

---

[36] These were the words of a soldier of the 12th Airborne Regiment, 20 July 1941, quoted by Christian Gerlach, *Kalkulierte Morde. Die deutsche Wirtschafts- und Vernichtungspolitik in Weißrussland 1941–1944*, Hamburg 1999, p. 102.

discipline. And that is one of the reasons why it is well worth the effort to concern oneself with the debate in detail.

Fundamentally, the Hegelian position that there is an African (and colonial) 'Other' that lacks any history lives on in this debate. As well as the Germanocentrism that cannot permit any suggestion that the world outside may be significant for national history, a degree of uncritical belief in 'progress' is also implicit in it. Colonialism is once again highly regarded – and this is a phenomenon that can be observed internationally – as a modernising force. Viewed in this way, colonialism means 'civilisation' and 'progress', factors which in their turn brought about the rise of the 'west'.

The question as to why colonialism encountered opposition, generally leading to the application of more and more radical measures and the unleashing of violence, is completely ignored. Colonialism is reduced to its potential as a modernising force. This point of view is not only a form of apologia, but also completely ignores the tensions that characterise the relationship between modernity and violence, a relationship for which colonialism provides what can almost be regarded as a Weberian ideal type.

If the thesis formulated by Max Horkheimer and Theodor W. Adorno and by Zygmunt Bauman and others that there is a connection between modernity and the Holocaust evoked criticism, then this is even more so in the case of the connection between colonial violence and modernity, as it undermines even more seriously the foundations of western society. Even if it was possible to factor the Holocaust out of the universal history of modernity to some extent by restricting it to Germany and its particular history – the Germans themselves having succeeded in presenting the twelve disastrous years of the Third Reich as a mere aberration and expunging them from their national history – this procedure does not seem to work in respect of colonial violence. The modern world, the western world, is founded on colonialism, and as a result is discredited along with it in its central values. In a time that is seeing a new missionary zeal being propagated in the West in the aftermath of 9/11 and the associated war on terror, critiques of colonialism are no longer *en vogue*. Rather, positive examples from earlier times are invoked. This global political context helps to explain the vehemence with which every notion of there being a connection between colonialism and National Socialism is rejected.

In view of the numerous generalised condemnations of any attempt to view the Third Reich and its policies of exploitation, conquest and extermination from a postcolonial perspective, it is surprising that up to now such attempts have been met by only two serious counter-attempts at rebuttal – serious in that they use the tools of academic argumentation. Birthe Kundrus was involved in both.

After her polemic attempt[37] to suppress the debate even before it had really got under way by using both personal and factual defamation (accusations that the Holocaust was being relativised through comparison and equation with other events) had been met with broad resistance both from historians and from academics in related disciplines,[38] she followed it up with her lengthy article in 'WerkstattGeschichte'.[39]

Apart from many differences in matters of detail, the thing that above all divides Kundrus from the present author is her view of colonialism. Whereas in the one case, that of colonialism, Kundrus takes colonial discourse and rhetoric at their face value, in the other case, that of National Socialism, she calls for it to be evaluated almost exclusively on the basis of its social practice. Not only does this distort every comparative or relational perspective, it also leads to a playing down of the impact of colonialism. For example: Kundrus sees a fundamental difference between the Nuremberg race laws and the Windhoek race ordinances, in that the latter were not legislation enacted by the Reichstag parliament in Berlin, but only administrative regulations issued by colonial officials in Windhoek.[40] As a result, they would only have been valid and applicable within the colony. Kundrus gives the example that a Herero who travelled to Berlin would not have been subject to any official or legal disadvantages there, whereas in the Third Reich Jews could not be safe against stigmatisation or persecution anywhere where the German government's writ ran.

Apart from the fact that the formal legal distinction between laws and ordinances had no practical consequences in everyday life, the example of the Herero on his travels leads the reader up the garden path and ultimately only serves to put an unrealistic positive gloss on the colonial situation. After 1904 there was in fact no way in which Herero would have been able to travel freely to the 'mother

---

37 Birthe Kundrus, "Grenzen der Gleichsetzung. Kolonialverbrechen und Vernichtungspolitik", *Informationszentrum 3. Welt* (iz3w), 275/March (2004), pp. 30–33.
38 See for example Christoph Marx, "Entsorgen und Entseuchen. Zur Diskussionskultur in der derzeitigen namibischen Historiographie – eine Polemik", in Henning Melber, ed., *Genozid und Gedenken. Namibisch-deutsche Geschichte und Gegenwart*, Frankfurt 2005, pp. 141–161; Henning Melber, "How to Come to Terms with the Past: Re-visiting the German Colonial Genocide in Namibia", *Africa Spectrum* 40/2 (2005), pp. 139–148; Reinhart Kößler, "From Genocide to Holocaust? Structural Parallels and Discursive Conditions", *Africa Spectrum*, 40/2 (2005), pp. 309–317.
39 Birthe Kundrus, "Kontinuitäten, Parallelen, Rezeptionen. Überlegungen zur "Kolonialisierung" des Nationalsozialismus", *WerkstattGeschichte*, 43 (2006), pp. 45–62.
40 With regard to this argumentation see also Birthe Kundrus, "Von Windhoek nach Nürnberg? Koloniale 'Mischehenverbote' und die nationalsozialistische Rassengesetzgebung", in Birthe Kundrus, ed., *Phantasiereiche. Zur Kulturgeschichte des deutschen Kolonialismus*, Frankfurt 2003, pp. 110–131.

country'. If they had survived war and genocide within the boundaries of the German colony, then they were registered, issued with pass tokens and incorporated into a system of forced labour. Not only were they subject to limitations in their free choice of their places of residence and their freedom to trade, but they were even deprived of their freedom of movement.[41] Any Herero who wanted to leave the district he was registered as being resident in had to exchange his pass token (which bore a number and had to be worn in a clearly visible manner) for a travel pass at the local German police station, giving precise details of his travel route, and had to have this travel pass signed by the local office at his place of destination immediately on arrival there. The pass token and the travel pass could be inspected at any time by any White person. It may be true that a Herero or Nama would not have been persecuted within Germany itself; but his or her chances of reaching the ports of Swakopmund, Lüderitzbucht or Walvis Bay, never mind Hamburg or Bremen, without being discovered, severely punished and sent back, were virtually zero. Indeed, not a single case of the kind is known from the records.

What can this example teach us then, apart from the fact that there were subtle legal differences which led to Jews and Herero being treated differently? No serious academic claims that the treatment of the Herero and that of the Jews were the same. But it is impossible to deny that people of both groups were stigmatised and discriminated against because of their 'race', that sexual relations with Whites/Germans/'Aryans' were evaluated as *'Rassenschande'*, 'racial defilement' (in Nazi terminology) or as a 'sin against racial consciousness' (in the language current in German South West Africa) and that in both cases Germans or the part of the German nation living in German South West Africa were thus considered to be a biopolitical collective. Kundrus disputes this. Moreover, she even casts doubt on the consensus arrived at by historians of Africa over the past few years that the war waged by the German Empire against the Herero was genocide. Why does she claim, against all the historical evidence, that General von Trotha spared the lives of women and children in his Extermination Order of 2 October 1904, when in fact he explicitly ordered them to be driven back into the desert where they were to die of thirst?[42]

---

[41] I have gone into this in more detail in Jürgen Zimmerer, "Von Windhuk nach Warschau. Die rassische Privilegiengesellschaft in Deutsch-Südwestafrika – ein Modell mit Zukunft?", in Frank Becker, ed., *Rassenpolitik in den deutschen Kolonien*, Stuttgart 2004, pp. 97–123 (English version: "From Windhoek to Warsaw: The Society of Racial Privilege in German South West Africa – a Model with a Future?", pp. 201–229 in this book).

[42] This claim was made in a panel discussion at the Department of History of the University of Freiburg on 7 February 2008.

Is it really necessary and historically justifiable to play down the impact of colonialism in order to refute any link to the Third Reich? Is it not more important and more intellectually honest to take colonialism (and in this case above all settler colonialism) and National Socialism seriously as phenomena of extreme violence, and to investigate the connections, relationships and similarities, in order to better understand the differences? It may be that the reason why there is such a lack of appreciation of colonialism's potential for violence is that Hegel's dictum that African history is not important enough to merit any closer consideration still resonates in the background. In any case, it is a conspicuous fact that none of the critics of the postcolonial perspective are themselves historians of Africa, which may at least partly explain why they appear to take a bird's eye view of the matter.

It was also Hegel who saw the pinnacle of development in the modern European state, a 'development' that justified force and oppression for the 'greater good' of civilisation. Without a doubt, a certain degree of unquestioning faith in the state and in 'progress' that takes no notice of alternative forms of socialisation and political community, and consequently does not question the fundamental legitimacy of forced cultural change, is to be found in the debate outlined above.

Robert Gerwarth and Stephan Malinowski also seek to discredit the postcolonial perspective, though on a more sophisticated argumentative level, by presenting a more positive assessment of colonialism.[43] They try to do this by adopting two problematic intellectual approaches: the first being to completely ignore settler colonialism, and the second, which is linked to it, being to place a one-sided emphasis on colonialism's potential for promoting development. They speak of colonialism, but then deal only with 'indirect rule' on the one hand and with a few African and Asian intellectuals who they say were shaped by the 'school of colonialism' on the other. And so they see, in the fact that National Socialism neither knew the concept of 'indirect rule' nor planned to initiate any 'development' of the subjugated peoples, proof that National Socialism and colonialism were fundamentally different. Leaving aside the question as to whether or not Nazi plans for the satellite regimes of central, southeastern and western Europe corresponded to ideas of 'indirect rule': their argument fundamentally misses the core of the debate. It is settler colonialism that is the primary framework of reference for the Nazis' imperialistic ideas: Germans were to be settled in eastern Europe, and were to develop and control this *Lebensraum* (a central term in Nazi ideol-

---

[43] Robert Gerwarth and Stephan Malinowski, "Der Holocaust als kolonialer Genozid? Europäische Kolonialgewalt und nationalsozialistischer Vernichtungskrieg", *Geschichte und Gesellschaft*, 33 (2007), pp. 439–466.

ogy). Settler colonies like North America, Australia and New Zealand, which significantly are not mentioned by Gerwarth and Malinowski, did not experience 'indirect rule' (except as a temporary measure for tactical reasons), nor did they display the 'promise of development' that Gerwarth and Malinowski deem to be so characteristic. There exists neither a Native American Nehru, nor an Australian Kenyatta, nor a Ho Chi Minh from New Zealand. If one were to apply Gerwarth and Malinowski's criteria, one would come to the absurd conclusion that there were no echoes of colonialism in the histories of the United States, Canada, New Zealand or Australia.

It is also noticeable that the examples of successful 'development' put forward by Gerwarth and Malinowski are all cases taken from the final phase of colonialism, when the colonial powers, especially the United Kingdom, in the knowledge that the independence movements could no longer be stopped, attempted literally at the last minute to do something to window-dress their records.[44] Far less of this 'civilisatory' mission had been perceptible in earlier centuries.[45] To project this trait of development policy in the years following the First World War back into the past, however, is to view history with hindsight. Such an approach is based precisely on the kind of understanding of tradition and continuity that is held to be inadmissible in analysing National Socialism.

Above and beyond the desire to reject the postcolonial perspective at any cost, however, there appears to be another important motivation for the emphasis on the developmental characteristics of colonialism. Colonialism essentially shaped the modern world, and created the hegemonic position of 'the West' that prevailed right through to the beginning of the 21st century. Whereas National Socialism with all its crimes appears as a negative alternative model, colonialism has in recent years enjoyed a 'rediscovery', especially of its positive aspects, in part as a – positively perceived – precursor to globalisation.[46]

It is therefore seen as essential to repudiate every connection between colonialism and National Socialism, not only in order to ensure that National Socialism is not relativised but also to rescue a certain way of looking at colonialism.

---

[44] A responsibility of the colonial powers for their subjects overseas had been formulated at the latest by the peace conference at Versailles. Jürgen Zimmerer, "Von der Bevormundung zur Selbstbestimmung. Die Pariser Friedenskonferenz und ihre Auswirkungen auf die britische Kolonialherrschaft im Südlichen Afrika", in Gerd Krumeich, ed., *Versailles 1919: Ziele – Wirkung – Wahrnehmung*, Essen 2001, pp. 145–158.

[45] By contrast, the argument of the civilisatory mission had always played a prominent role in the justification for expanding colonial power. As an introduction, see Boris Barth and Jürgen Osterhammel, eds, *Zivilisationsmissionen. Imperiale Weltverbesserung seit dem 18. Jahrhundert*, Konstanz 2005.

[46] For instance, see Niall Ferguson, *Empire: How Britain made the Modern World*, London 2003.

Colonialism is subjected to a de facto whitewashing by placing a one-sided emphasis on the emancipatory elements of non-settlement colonialism (while almost completely ignoring settler colonialism). Pointing to "an ambivalence that was missing from National Socialism, but by contrast played a vital role in late European colonialism, regarding forced modernisation and development on the one hand, and violence and destruction on the other",[47] is in fact mere lip service: in reality, hardly any consideration is given to colonial violence, especially in settler colonialism. Misinterpretations of history, such as, for example, the judgment that von Trotha was recalled because of his violations of the law, whereas Nazi perpetrators were shielded by laws (the correct version being that von Trotha was incited from the highest level to exercise particular ruthlessness and was ultimately relieved of his command because he had not won the war quickly enough), imply an image of colonialism as a system that is under an obligation to respect minimum humanitarian requirements, and in which any crimes that may have been committed are to be regarded as regrettable 'operational glitches' or collateral damage. Not only is this approach revealingly reminiscent of the view that was typical of the post-war period in Germany of National Socialism as an 'operational glitch';[48] it also draws a veil over the systemically inherent potential for violence in colonialism. Anyone who presents the Nazi claim to be entitled to determine who had a right to live in the world and who not as being historically unique, without even mentioning the destructive potential of settler colonialism that resulted in the destruction of dozens of cultures, overlooks the fact that the racial hierarchies that deliberately encompassed the consequential 'disappearance' of entire peoples were a fundamental feature of settler colonialism. There was no other way of justifying the mass murder and robbery that settler colonialism basically was.

If, however, one takes the inherent excessive violence of settler colonialism seriously, then the postcolonial perspective on National Socialism can no longer be disparaged, but is rather explicitly demanded. This does not mean equating the Holocaust with other acts of mass violence and genocide, nor does it relativise it in any way. Rather, it opens up the way to a comprehensive analysis that helps us to understand both phenomena – settler colonialism and National Socialism – better.

---

47 Gerwarth and Malinowski, *Der Holocaust als kolonialer Genozid?*, p. 461.
48 Fritz Fischer, *Hitler war kein Betriebsunfall*, München 1998.

**The War of Annihilation, the Racist
Utopia and the Obsessive Delusion of Planning**

The First Genocide of the Twentieth Century: The German War of Annihilation in South West Africa (1904–1908) and the Global History of Genocide

I followed their tracks, which led me to a number of wells where I beheld terrible scenes. All around them lay heaps of cattle that had died of thirst, having reached the wells with their last remaining strength, but not having being able to drink in time. The Herero continued to flee before us into the *sandveld*. The terrible spectacle was repeated over and over again. The men had worked with feverish haste to dig wells, but the water had become more and more sparse, the waterholes scarcer and scarcer. They fled from one to the next, losing almost all their cattle and very many people. The nation was shrunk to meagre remnants which gradually fell into our hands, though both then and later some escaped through the *sandveld* into British territory. The policy of shattering the nation in this way was as foolish as it was cruel; many of them and their wealth of cattle could still have been saved if they had now been shown mercy and received back; they had been punished enough. I proposed this to General von Trotha; but he wanted them completely exterminated.[1]

This eyewitness account by Major Ludwig von Estorff provides first-hand documentation of the German policy of annihilation in South West Africa. Major Estorff was the commander of one of the cavalry units that pursued the Herero into the *sandveld* of the Omaheke desert after the Battle of Ohamakari (Waterberg) in August 1904. Although Estorff, as a career officer, had very probably seen his fair share of violence and cruelty, he was noticeably disturbed by what he had experienced on this occasion. When he wrote about cattle succumbing to thirst, he was writing in code: what he meant were dying human beings, men and women, children and old people. As we know from other sources, thousands of Herero died in the cruellest manner imaginable in the desert. They cut the throats of their cattle to quench their thirst with the blood and tried to squeeze the last drops of liquid out of the contents of their livestock's stomachs.[2]

---

1 Ludwig von Estorff, *Wanderungen und Kämpfe in Südwestafrika, Ostafrika und Südafrika 1894–1910*, ed. Christoph-Friedrich Kutscher, Wiesbaden 1968, p. 117.
2 For an introduction to the various aspects of the wars against the Herero and Nama see Jürgen Zimmerer and Joachim Zeller, eds, *Völkermord in Deutsch-Südwestafrika. Der Kolonialkrieg (1904–1908) in Namibia und seine Folgen*, Berlin 2003. References to further literature can also be found there. See also Jan-Bart Gewald, "Imperial Germany and the Herero of Southern Africa: Genocide and the Quest for Recompense", in Adam Jones, ed., *Genocide, War Crimes & the West, History and Complicity*, London 2004, pp. 59–77; Dominik J. Schaller, "'Ich glaube, dass die Nation als solche vernichtet werden muss': Kolonialkrieg und Völkermord in Deutsch-Südwestafrika 1904–907", *Journal of Genocide Research*, 6/3 (2004), pp. 395–430; Dominik J. Schaller, "Kolonial-

Von Estorff's is a remarkable testimony to one of the darkest chapters in German history: a chapter that has largely been expunged from Germany's public consciousness, having been overlaid by memories of the two World Wars with their millions of victims and, above all, by the inconceivable crimes of the Holocaust. But there was an additional reason why this chapter fell victim to collective colonial amnesia: namely because many Germans sought to set against the horrors of the Third Reich a more positive, indeed an immaculate picture of German history in the period prior to the monumental crime against humanity that the murder of the Jews represented. Yet events in German South West Africa, today's Namibia, during the years 1904–1908 reveal much about the destructive forces and the potential contempt for humanity that was already to be found in the military and bureaucratic institutions of Imperial Germany before the Nazis came to power.

In the minds of many people, however, no connection may be admitted to exist between colonial and Nazi practices of murder, since the thesis that the crimes of the Nazis were unprecedented can be used to exculpate German national history prior to 1933. Indeed, for a long time – before people came to forget that there had ever been such a thing – German colonial history had been held up as exemplary, humanely focused on 'educating' the 'Natives' to adopt civilisation. How and why it was possible for this false assessment (which appears to have been a late fruit of the resistance against the so-called 'colonial guilt lie', resistance which sought to counter and reject criticism of Germany's colonial record voiced by the victors of the First World War in the Versailles Peace Treaty) to be upheld for so long even in the Federal Republic after the Second World War, is an interesting phenomenon in itself.

Does examining the German genocide in Africa contribute to an understanding of the Holocaust? Anyone who is seeking simple answers to this question will be disappointed. There is no monocausal explanation for the crimes of the Nazis, nor is there any kind of straight line leading more or less automatically from German colonialism to the murder of the European Jews. Auschwitz was neither the logical consequence of the events in South West Africa, nor was it, viewed from a Windhoek perspective, inevitable. Auschwitz, to use that name as shorthand for the crimes of the Nazis, happened because the Nazis were in power in Germany and

---

krieg, Völkermord und Zwangsarbeit in Deutsch-Südwestafrika", in Dominik J. Schaller, Boyadjian Rupen, Hanno Scholtz and Vivianne Berg, eds, *Enteignet-Vertrieben-Ermordet. Beiträge zur Genozidforschung*, Zürich 2004, pp. 147–232; Reinhart Kößler and Henning Melber, "Völkermord und Gedenken. Der Genozid an den Herero und Nama in Deutsch-Südwestafrika 1904–1908", in Irmtrud Wojak and Susanne Meinl, eds, *Jahrbuch 2004 zur Geschichte und Wirkung des Holocaust*, Frankfurt/New York 1996, pp. 37–75.

because the majority of Germans clearly shared the antisemitic and racist attitudes of their leadership, or at least did not find it necessary or worth their while to oppose those attitudes. But nevertheless, a connection does exist between the colonial adventures of the Wilhelminian Empire and the crimes of the Nazis, both the Holocaust and the war of annihilation in the East. In the first place, colonial policy provides a clear illustration of the genocidal potential already present in parts of the bureaucracy and the military establishment. And secondly, colonialism in its culture of domination established a reservoir of practices that Nazi thugs were then able to draw on. Even where they did not adopt elements taken from this cultural reservoir directly (I have analysed elsewhere three lines of transmission of a colonial mindset: personal experience, institutional memory, and collective imagination),[3] Nazi perpetrators could, to a certain degree, subjectively feel legitimised in their actions by pointing to similarities with colonial practice. Intellectual familiarity with genocidal policy, racist thinking and ideas about population control and management derived from such practice was key to enabling a relatively large number of Germans, apparently without any great mental reservations, to play their part both in the Nazis' territorial occupations and in the war of annihilation. In particular, the positive connotations attached to European colonial rule at the time (and until well beyond the middle of the twentieth century) may well have helped to conceal the criminal nature of German rule from contemporaries. Intellectual familiarity with the expulsion and destruction of entire peoples, with resettlement and slavery to the benefit of German 'masters', and with the most brutal methods of 'combating partisans' and of annihilation through neglect, allowed perpetrators to contextualise events 'in the East' during the Second World War as a process of colonisation that was normal in a historical perspective. Anyone who so desired could therefore legitimise what he was experiencing.

The fact that in reality European colonial rule was not at all monolithic but took on a wide variety of forms does not affect these findings in any way. In the first place, the most important factor was not 'the reality', however defined, of colonialism but the ideas that people had of it during the Third Reich; and furthermore, German colonialism above all, and colonial rule in German South West Africa in particular, was marked by a terrible brutality. This brutality was widely known about in Germany, since one of the most conspicuous features of the genocide committed against the Herero and Nama was undoubtedly the fact that at the time nobody sought to conceal it. On the contrary, the events were popular-

---

[3] Jürgen Zimmerer, "The Birth of the 'Ostland' out of the Spirit of Colonialism: A Postcolonial Perspective on the Nazi Policy of Conquest and Extermination", *Patterns of Prejudice*, 39/February (2005), pp. 197–219 (pp. 230–261 in this book).

ised through countless memoirs, official reports and novels. They were, for example, presented quite openly in the official German military chronicle:

> This bold undertaking casts a brilliant light on the relentless energy of the German leadership during the pursuit of the defeated enemy. No effort, no deprivation was spared in order to rob the enemy of their last will to resist; like wild animals harassed half to death in the hunt, they were pursued from watering hole to watering hole, until they finally fell into a state of complete apathy, victims of the nature of their own country. The waterless Omaheke was to complete what German arms had started: the annihilation of the Herero nation.[4]

No words of pity, no words of regret. 'Mission accomplished', the reader was probably supposed to think. But the report is not entirely accurate. Though the Germans did indeed act extremely brutally, the campaign was not quite as victorious as the official historiography suggested.[5] The Herero had been successful in their resistance and several thousand of them survived the horror of the Omaheke. They managed to preserve the Herero nation and were able to restore or else build anew the political and cultural structures that had been destroyed. The image that the official chronicle conjures up of a German military machine proceeding with absolute precision and power is therefore misleading.[6]

---

[4] Kriegsgeschichtliche Abteilung I des Großen Generalstabs, *Die Kämpfe der deutschen Truppen in Südwestafrika*, 1, Berlin 1906/07, p. 211.

[5] Isabel Hull has recently depicted in great detail the many problems the German army faced in South West Africa. She provides empirical data to support the hypothesis of the 'weak' German army first put forward by Brigitte Lau. See Isabel V. Hull, *Absolute Destruction: Military Culture and the Practices of War in Imperial Germany*, Ithaca 2005, and Brigitte Lau, "Uncertain Certainties. The Herero-German War of 1904", in Brigitte Lau, *History and Historiography – 4 Essays in Reprint*, ed. Annemarie Heywood, Windhoek 1995, pp. 39–52. Although there can be no doubt that the image of the all-powerful German military machine is misleading and itself a product of colonial myth-building, I disagree with this argument in two respects: the question of ideology and the genocidal intent. Hull's argument neglects the ideology that influenced von Trotha's decisions in particular. And she ignores new archival evidence which shows that the genocidal policy was launched independently of military developments and logistical problems. See: Jürgen Zimmerer, "Das Deutsche Reich und der Genozid. Überlegungen zum historischen Ort des Völkermordes an den Herero und Nama", in Larissa Förster, Dag Henrichsen and Michael Bollig, eds, *Namibia – Deutschland. Eine geteilte Geschichte. Widerstand, Gewalt, Erinnerung*, Köln 2004, pp. 106–121. For a summary of the debate between Hull and myself see *Bulletin of the German Historical Institute*, Washington 37/Fall (2005).

[6] When Brigitte Lau argued against this misinterpretation, she threw out the baby with the bathwater. Completely misunderstanding the concept of genocide, she denied that it had occurred in Namibia, because she equated genocide with absolute power. Because of this, she regrettably came to be advanced as a key witness by all revisionists and representatives of the extreme right, who were only too keen to accept her denial that genocide had taken place. There is no

In addition, not everyone considered the policy of annihilation to be either successful or sensible. As is shown by the quotation at the beginning of this chapter, Major von Estorff, for example, was not of the opinion that the strategy of 'exterminating' the Herero had been successful, let alone sensible. Estorff stood out from among his fellow officers in that he was an 'old Africa hand', i.e. a soldier who had already been living and serving in German South West Africa prior to the war. The first governor, Theodor Leutwein, was such an 'old hand' as well, and he too criticised the strategy of his successor, Lieutenant General von Trotha. Leutwein was not, however, able to prevail with his views. Only a few months after the outbreak of the war he was more or less forced to resign, as he was seen as being too lenient toward the African population. Leutwein commented with great bitterness that several hundred million *Reichsmark* had been spent and several thousand soldiers deployed in order to ensure that of the three pillars of the German colonial economy – mining, cattle, and the African workforce – the second had been completely and the last-mentioned two-thirds destroyed. What had brought things to this catastrophic situation?

Causes of the War

Germany had made its entry onto the stage of formal colonial rule very late, because prior to 1871 it had lacked the national framework to do so. After the foundation of the Reich in 1871, however, an enthusiastic public demanded that Germany too must have its share in the partitioning of the globe. These voices eventually became so loud that in 1884 Chancellor Otto von Bismarck declared himself prepared to support the formal acquisition of colonies[7] – an idea that until then he had always rejected. Within only a few years, territories roughly corresponding to the present-day African states of Togo, Cameroon, Tanzania, Rwanda, Burundi and Namibia, as well as a few smaller possessions in the South Seas, were declared German *Schutzgebiete*, although this designation was a misnomer: they were colonies in all but name.[8] In view of the climatic conditions, only German South West Africa was considered suitable for the establishment of a settler colony, i.e. for permanent occupation by German settlers. This latter cir-

---

doubt that German troops committed genocide in Namibia, though without simultaneously exercising absolute power. Lau, "Uncertain Certainties".
7 For the various interpretations of Bismarck's decision to establish a formal colonial empire see Horst Gründer, *Geschichte der deutschen Kolonien*, 3rd edn, Paderborn 1995, pp. 51–62.
8 For an initial introduction to the histories of the various colonies see Gründer, *Geschichte der deutschen Kolonien*. Later, Kiaochow in China was added to the list.

cumstance fired the imaginations of a whole generation in Germany, and would prove decisive in shaping the further history of Namibia.[9]

Imperial Commissioner Heinrich Göring took formal possession of the colony with two fellow officials in 1885. However, this was little more than a symbolic act. It must have been clear to those responsible at home that they would never be able to establish a functioning administration in this vast territory with only three officials: a territory that towards the end of the nineteenth century was inhabited by an estimated 90,000 to 100,000 Ovambo, 70,000 to 80,000 Herero, 15,000 to 20,000 Nama, 30,000 to 40,000 Berg Damara and San and 3,000 to 4,000 Basters. Not until the first governor, Theodor Leutwein, took office in 1893 did the systematic establishment of German rule and the methodical build-up of a German administration commence. The increasing sophistication of the bureaucratic structures amply illustrates this process: In 1894 the colony was divided into three *Bezirke* (regions or districts), namely Keetmanshoop, Windhoek and Otjimbingwe. By 1903 this number had already doubled, and by 1914 there were sixteen *Bezirke* and autonomous *Distrikte*, which in their turn were divided into police station areas or 'police wards'.[10]

It was also Leutwein and his young administrative team who embarked on the implementation of a utopian vision for colonial rule, with the ultimate goal of building a model colonial state based on a racial ideology. Through a series of shifting alliances with African rulers such as Samuel Maharero and Hendrik Witbooi, to name only the two most important, the colonisers superficially secured the territory for the short term in an effort to convert the African societies into a 'black working class'; a status in which the Africans, though not completely without rights, would nonetheless face severe discrimination. It was the aim of the constant expansion of the German bureaucracy to establish White domination, the process being accompanied by the arrival in the colony of larger and larger numbers of settlers who regarded themselves as the 'master race'. Repeated in-

---

[9] Regarding the fantasies connected with 'South West' see for example Birthe Kundrus, *Moderne Imperialisten. Das Kaiserreich im Spiegel seiner Kolonien*, Köln/Weimar/Wien 2003.

[10] On this gradual intensification of the administrative presence see Jürgen Zimmerer, *Deutsche Herrschaft über Afrikaner. Staatlicher Machtanspruch und Wirklichkeit im kolonialen Namibia*, 3rd edn, Hamburg 2004, pp. 13–31, 112–118 [English edition: *German Rule, African Subjects. State Aspirations and the Reality of Power in Colonial Namibia*, New York 2021]. On the history of the bureaucracy see also Udo Kaulich, *Die Geschichte der ehemaligen Kolonie Deutsch Südwestafrika (1884–1914). Eine Gesamtdarstellung*, Frankfurt 2001. For a comparison of the history of colonial power structures from an African perspective see Jan-Bart Gewald, *Towards Redemption. A Socio-political History of the Herero of Namibia between 1890 and 1923*, Leiden 1996; and Gesine Krüger, *Kriegsbewältigung und Geschichtsbewußtsein: Realität, Deutung und Verarbeitung des deutschen Kolonialkriegs in Namibia 1904 bis 1907*, Göttingen 1999.

stances of Africans being defrauded, together with the murder and rape of individual Africans and increasing seizures of Herero land, ultimately led to war.[11]

The Course of the War

Academics are still at odds about who fired the first shot in 1904.[12] Much evidence, however, points to the escalation having been contributed to by provocations on the part of Lieutenant Zürn, the district chief of Okahandja. What is certain is that the attack by the Herero on 12 January was unexpectedly successful, partly because the German *Schutztruppe* was engaged in another, limited conflict in the south of the colony. Within only a few days the Herero had occupied the whole of central Namibia, with the exception of the military bases, and had plundered settlements and farms. Rumours that hundreds of German men, women and children had been murdered and mutilated spread like wildfire, and contributed to no small extent to the radicalisation of the war. It was later established that a total of 123 Germans had lost their lives during these initial raids; but that the Herero, following the orders of their leaders, had in fact deliberately spared women and children as well as missionaries and in some cases even conducted them to other German settlements.

The Herero did not, however, exploit their early successes to complete a quick victory over the Germans, who had taken refuge in their fortified positions. Instead, the latter were able to rally and summon reinforcements from Germany. Thanks to the rapid deployment of these troops the impending defeat was averted. A series of small skirmishes followed without a decisive victory on either side. The auxiliary forces arriving from Germany and also individual incensed settlers engaged in acts of retaliation and committed massacres that drove those Herero who had not yet been involved in the war to take up arms as well. Everywhere there was talk of

---

11 I have already, on multiple occasions, comprehensively analysed this vision of colonial rule and its consequences in more detail in Jürgen Zimmerer, *Deutsche Herrschaft* [English edition: *German Rule, African Subjects*, New York 2021]; Jürgen Zimmerer, "Der totale Überwachungsstaat? Recht und Verwaltung in Deutsch-Südwestafrika", in Rüdiger Voigt, ed., *Das deutsche Kolonialrecht als Vorstufe einer globalen 'Kolonialisierung' von Recht und Verwaltung* (Schriften zur Rechtspolitologie), Baden-Baden 2001, pp. 175–198; and Jürgen Zimmerer, "Der Wahn der Planarbeit: Vertreibung, unfreie Arbeit und Völkermord als Elemente der Bevölkerungsökonomie in Deutsch Südwestafrika", in Michael Mann, ed., *Comparativ*, 13/4 (2003), Special Issue: *Menschenhandel und unfreie Arbeit*, pp. 96–113 (English version: "Planning Frenzy: Forced Labour, Expulsion and Genocide as Elements of Population Economics in German South West Africa", pp. 57–76 in this book).
12 For a brief account of the course of the war see Jürgen Zimmerer, "Krieg, KZ und Völkermord in Südwestafrika. Der erste deutsche Genozid", in Jürgen Zimmerer and Joachim Zeller, eds, *Völkermord*, pp. 45–63.

"clearing up with them, hanging them, shooting them down to the very last man, with no mercy".[13] However, these were still uncoordinated individual actions, not a systematic strategy.

Nevertheless, a certain style of rhetoric was already developing that anticipated the forthcoming genocide. It was clearly reminiscent of Emperor Wilhelm II's infamous *Hunnenrede*, his 'Hun Speech', in which he had admonished troops on their way to China to crush the 'Boxer Rebellion' to act with particular brutality, drawing their inspiration from Attila's Huns. In the first few months of the war this kind of agitation became so strong that Leutwein was forced to step in to defuse the situation. Even though he too demanded the unconditional capitulation of the Herero, he warned against the "ill-considered voices [...] that now want to see the Herero completely annihilated". In his opinion, there were not only humanitarian considerations standing in the way of this. Apart from the fact that a nation of sixty to seventy thousand people "could not be exterminated just like that", Leutwein believed that the Germans still needed the Herero as "small-scale cattle breeders and particularly as labourers". He did, however, view it as a legitimate aim of the war for them to be rendered "politically dead", their social structures destroyed and their people forced into reservations that would be "only just sufficient for their needs". Individual "guilt" was not a decisive factor in these "punitive measures": even Africans who had not been involved in the war were explicitly to be forced to submit to disarmament and to "confinement in reservations".[14] Although Leutwein did not demand mass murder, it was his view as early as 23 February 1904, a mere forty days after the outbreak of hostilities, that the Herero no longer had any future as a people with political or social structures of their own. Though they had not (yet) been physically eliminated, in German planning the Herero were already "politically dead".

It is necessary to draw attention to a few misunderstandings that crop up repeatedly in interpretations of the history of the war and the postwar period. Political and military aims do not instantly become reality, and the giving of instructions and orders must not be confused with their actual execution, let alone their effectiveness. Just as the German settlers, soldiers and bureaucrats were not merely passive victims of their African adversaries during the first days of the war when the Herero had seized the initiative, but rather developed defensive strategies, so the Herero too reacted flexibly to developments once the colonial forces had started to

---

13 The missionary August Elger to the Rhenish Mission, 10 February 1904, quoted according to Horst Drechsler, *Südwestafrika unter deutscher Kolonialherrschaft. Der Kampf der Herero und Nama gegen den deutschen Imperialismus 1884–1915*, 2nd edn, Berlin 1984, pp. 146ff.
14 Governor's Office Windhoek to Colonial Department Berlin, 23 February 1904, quoted according to Drechsler, *Südwestafrika*, pp. 149f.

gain the upper hand. Neither the Herero nor the Nama were at any time passive victims. Nonetheless, the German forces displayed such brutality in South West Africa that they reduced the Herero's ability to act autonomously to a minimum. Though they continued to react in a skilful and indeed thoroughly successful manner to increasing German pressure, thus securing the survival of their nation, it is not admissible to play down the extremely repressive nature of German policy in an effort to emphasise this measure of autonomy.

Colonial rule is characterised, as post-colonial authors rightly stress, by a multitude of possible interactions, and relationships of power and domination certainly were the object of negotiation on occasions. A genocidal war of annihilation such as that waged in South West Africa by Imperial Germany, however, sought to eliminate the colonised Other. It represents one of the most extreme forms of inequality in domination relationships to be found anywhere in history. It is important, not least to preserve the victims' dignity in commemoration, to call a spade a spade and not to obscure the genocidal nature of these events by overemphasising a few individual cases of successful survival strategies or of flexible interaction on the part of some of the victims. The war meant death for tens of thousands of people. There was nothing to negotiate.

The Decision for Genocide

The decision by the authorities in Berlin not to allow the local commander of the *Schutztruppe*, Governor Theodor Leutwein, to lead the campaign was to prove decisive in the escalation of the war into the first genocide in German history. Instead, the task was conferred on Lieutenant General Lothar von Trotha, a protégé of the influential Chief of the General Staff, Count Alfred von Schlieffen. Von Trotha had already acquired a reputation for being a particularly ruthless officer during the colonial wars in German East Africa (1894–1897) and China (1900–01). He had no knowledge either of the country or of the people of South West Africa, but was obsessed with the idea of a coming 'race war'. Africans, he believed, would "yield only to force", and he was willing to exercise such force "with blatant terrorism and even with cruelty" and to "annihilate the rebellious tribes with rivers of blood."[15] Thus when von Trotha set foot on South West African soil he may not have known yet in precise detail how he would conduct the war from a tactical point of view; he did, however, already know how it would end: with destruction of the Herero. Local factors such as a situational radicalisation in re-

---

15 Trotha to Leutwein, 5 November 1904, quoted according to Drechsler, *Südwestafrika*, p. 156.

sponse to military developments like the Battle of Ohamakari (Waterberg) or the hostile natural conditions that took their toll on the German troops were merely of secondary importance.[16]

Even while he was still on his way to the colony, Trotha had declared martial law in South West Africa and empowered his officers to have all armed 'rebels' summarily shot. In his words:

   a. Every commanding officer is authorised to have coloured inhabitants of the territory who are caught in the act of carrying out treasonable activities against German troops, for example all rebels who are found under arms with belligerent intent, shot without any prior court proceedings, as has been customary practice in this war up to now.
   b. All other coloured inhabitants arrested by German military personnel on suspicion of having undertaken punishable activities will be sentenced by special field courts.
   c. The troops are to be instructed that any punitive measures against coloured people inflicted by troops acting on their own initiative will be met with the most severe punishments provided for under the general legal provisions on bodily harm, unlawful killing and murder, and that – outside combat situations – they are only permitted to make use of their weapons in self-defence or to prevent attempts to escape.[17]

The intention of this order was twofold. Firstly, von Trotha was attempting to impose order on the spontaneous illegal actions that had been occurring since the beginning of the war and that had led to downright massacres of Herero at the hands of incensed settlers and soldiers, i.e. to get the executions carried out by his soldiers under control. Secondly, while von Trotha's order did put a stop to the arbitrary actions of individuals, it instead turned massacres and terror into planned instruments of German warfare: whoever resisted the Germans would be shot. Without doubt, this represents an important step in the direction of radicalisation: where any prisoner was seen merely as a rebel acting illegally, rather than as an opposing belligerent of equal and equally honourable status, there was no imperative requiring that he should be afforded protection or fair and humane treatment. Such attitudes, types of behaviour and courses of action were typical of colonial wars.

---

[16] This seems to be the decisive difference between my interpretation and Isabel Hull's; she ignores ideology and intention in order to focus on the situational dimension, combined with structural characteristics of the German army's military organization. See Hull, *Absolute Destruction*.

[17] Proclamation made by von Trotha from on board the steamship *Eleonore Woermann*, June 1904. National Archives of Namibia, Windhoek (NAN) Zentralbureau des Gouvernements (ZBU) (Government Central Office): Geheimakten (Classified Documents) (IX.A.Vol.1, 1b).

When von Trotha arrived in Windhoek, Leutwein tried to dissuade him from pursuing his policy of annihilation. He attempted to persuade him to enter into peace negotiations with the Herero instead. Leutwein cited economic reasons for this course of action and pointed out that the Herero would be needed in the colony as labourers. Von Trotha merely replied that South West Africa was supposed to be a white settler colony, in which case the whites should do the work themselves. The opposing natures of two men's fantasies of colonial rule – Leutwein's colonial-economic vision and von Trotha's military-genocidal one – could not be more pointedly illustrated. Von Trotha prevailed. It is revealing that this discussion took place even before the Battle of Ohamakari (Waterberg). It shows that even at that point in time genocide was already a conceivable aim for von Trotha. Thus military developments did not give rise to his genocidal visions, but merely enabled him to make them a reality.

The battle that von Trotha was so longing for finally took place on 11 August 1904 at Ohamakari, where a large section of the Herero nation, apparently anticipating an offer of peace in the spirit of Leutwein's accustomed policy, had gathered with women, children and herds of cattle. Although this battle brought military victory to the *Schutztruppe*, the greater part of the Herero broke out of the encirclement and fled into the largely waterless *sandveld* of the Omaheke semi-desert in the east of the colony. At that point, the war had essentially been decided in military terms and the truly genocidal phase began, because the German troops now initiated a pincer movement, driving the Herero ahead of them in the direction of the Omaheke. Already at this juncture, terrible scenes must have unfolded: as the official history of the campaign reports, "Masses of sick and helpless men, women and children, having collapsed from exhaustion, lay parched with thirst [...] in the bush, apathetically awaiting their fate."[18] The German officer Captain Maximilian Bayer wrote that wherever the pursuing German units came upon Herero, summary executions took place: "Now and then, whenever our patrols came upon stragglers, shots were to be heard among the thorn bushes to the right and left."[19]

---

18 Kriegsgeschichtliche Abteilung I des Großen Generalstabs, *Die Kämpfe der deutschen Truppen*, 1, p. 203.
19 Maximilian Bayer, *Mit dem Hauptquartier in Südwestafrika*, Berlin 1909, p. 162.

Von Trotha's 'Annihilation Proclamation'

To the German military leadership it now seemed possible that the Omaheke could indeed "complete what German arms had started: the annihilation of the Herero nation", as was stated in the passage from the official war chronicle quoted above. German troops therefore systematically occupied all the known watering holes along the edges of the desert, and at the beginning of October, in his infamous Proclamation, von Trotha ordered that all returning Herero were to be shot:

> The Hereros have ceased to be German subjects.
> They have murdered and robbed, have cut off the ears and noses and other bodily parts of wounded soldiers, and are now too cowardly to want to go on fighting. I say to that people: Whoever delivers one of their *Kapteins* to one of my posts as a prisoner will be given 1,000 marks; whoever brings Samuel Maharero will be given 5,000 marks. But the Herero people must quit this country. If they do not, I will compel them to do so with the *Groot Rohr* [cannon].
> Within the borders of German territory, any Herero, with or without a firearm, with or without livestock, will be shot; nor will I give refuge to women or children any more. I will drive them back to their people or have them fired upon.[20]

Von Trotha then clarified that, for the sake of the reputation of the German soldier, this order to fire upon women and children was "to be understood in such a way that shots are to be fired over their heads, in order to force them to run away." He "definitely assume[d] that this Proclamation" would "lead to no further male prisoners being taken", but would not "degenerate into atrocities against women and children". They would "doubtless run away, if shots are fired over their heads a couple of times".[21] But there was nowhere they could run to except into the Omaheke, where thousands died of thirst as a consequence of this order.

Considering the military situation and the geographical location where this Proclamation was issued, it becomes obvious that genocide was indeed the objective. Though the talk was of 'driving out' or 'expelling' the people, the only possible escape was into the waterless area. This in itself would have been a particularly brutal course of action to adopt, even in a colonial war; but it would not yet have amounted to genocide. However, the passage in question serves merely as camouflage. If the Annihilation Proclamation is read in conjunction with a letter von Trotha wrote to the General Staff in Berlin two days later, its intentions are made plainer:

---

[20] Proclamation by von Trotha, Osombo-Wind[imbe], 2 October 1904. Bundesarchiv Berlin-Lichterfelde (BArch) Reichskolonialamt (Imperial Colonial Office) R 1001/2089, sheet 7af.
[21] Ibid.

The only question for me now is *how* the war with the Herero was to be brought to an end. The opinions on this subject of the Governor and some of the 'old Africa hands' on the one hand and myself on the other are diametrically opposed. For quite some time, there has been a desire on the part of the former to enter into peace negotiations, and they describe the Herero nation as being essential as labour for the future exploitation of the Territory. I am of a completely different opinion. I believe that the nation as such must be destroyed, or, if that should prove not to be possible by tactical actions, they must be expelled from the country operationally and by means of further individual actions. With the watering holes from Grootfontein to Gobabis having been occupied and the military convoys being constantly on the move, it is bound to be possible to track down those small groups of people who have begun moving back westwards and gradually finish them off.[22]

Researchers into genocide have established that in order to set in motion a war of annihilation, and in particular an act of genocide, certain processes of exclusion are necessary in order to prevent the perpetrator from coming to identify in any way with the victim. The potential victims must be dehumanised, they must be robbed of their human dignity and placed outside the sphere in which moral responsibility applies. They must be banished from the circle of those "whom we are obligated to protect, to take into account, and to whom we must account".[23] In the colonial situation, the ground was already prepared for this process by the racism that underpinned the system. It was further strengthened by the atrocity propaganda that accompanied the outbreak of the war: thus immediately after 12 January 1904 it was being said that the Herero had 'slaughtered' women and children and mutilated their victims. In his Proclamation von Trotha specifically made reference to this accusation in order to justify his policy of murder and expulsion. According to this logic, the Herero themselves were responsible for what was happening to them, due to the allegedly inhumane way they had conducted the war: they were the 'barbarians' and 'savages' standing opposite the 'civilised' and 'disciplined' German forces. The fact that almost without exception the Herero spared women and children, while many German soldiers deliberately waged war against them, may be pointed out here without any need for further comment.

Von Trotha's Annihilation Proclamation did not mark the beginning of the genocide, which was already in progress at that point. But it did help to legitimise it, and it provides proof that genocide was the intention of the German colonial forces. Von Trotha was serious about the need to annihilate the Herero. It was a

---

22 Von Trotha to the Chief of Staff of the Army, 4 October 1904, quoted according to Drechsler, *Südwestafrika*, p. 163.
23 Helen Fein, "Definition and Discontent: Labelling, Detecting, and Explaining Genocide in the Twentieth Century", in Stig Förster and Gerhard Hirschfeld, eds, *Genozid in der modernen Geschichte*, Münster 1999, pp. 11–21, here especially p. 20.

matter not just of breaking their military resistance, but of the mass murder of men, women and children, of combatants and non-combatants, of old and young; a mass murder that the responsible military leaders in Berlin looked upon as normal – as is shown by the quotation from the official war chronicle – and one that nobody even attempted to cover up. It is this deliberate waging of war against women and children as well, this intentional physical destruction of an entire people, that makes what happened in the colony genocide – the first genocide in German history.

After the Second World War, the United Nations established a legal definition of the term *genocide* as follows:

> any of the following acts committed with intent to destroy, in whole or in part, a national, ethnical, racial or religious group, as such:
> (a) Killing members of the group;
> (b) Causing serious bodily or mental harm to members of the group;
> (c) Deliberately inflicting on the group conditions of life calculated to bring about its physical destruction in whole or in part;
> (d) Imposing measures intended to prevent births within the group;
> (e) Forcibly transferring children of the group to another group.[24]

Using this definition as the basis of a historical analysis, the actions of von Trotha and the German forces must unambiguously be classified as genocide. Even the fact that Emperor Wilhelm II revoked von Trotha's Annihilation Proclamation a few weeks later does not change this finding. By that time, the crime had already been committed.[25]

Von Trotha's order was overturned in December 1904; but not because of humanitarian concerns. Rather, Berlin was afraid other countries could use it against the German Empire for propaganda purposes. But above all, military considerations demanded a change in strategy: the existing one was failing, defeated in the last instance by the sheer vastness of the land and by the epidemics of typhus and malaria that were rampant among the colonial troops, making it impos-

---

24 Article 2, United Nations, *Convention on the Prevention and Punishment of the Crime of Genocide*, 9 December 1948, printed in Frank Chalk and Kurt Jonassohn, *The History and Sociology of Genocide: Analyses and Case Studies*, New Haven 1990, pp. 44–49, here p. 44.
25 For an in-depth debate on the issue of the occurrence of the genocide see Zimmerer, "Das Deutsche Reich und der Genozid"; and Jürgen Zimmerer, "Kolonialer Genozid? Vom Nutzen und Nachteil einer historischen Kategorie für eine Globalgeschichte des Völkermordes", in Dominik J. Schaller, Boyadjian Rupen, Hanno Scholtz and Vivianne Berg, eds, *Enteignet-Vertrieben-Ermordet. Beiträge zur Genozidforschung*, Zürich 2004, pp. 109–128 (English versions: "The German Empire and Genocide: The Genocide Against the Herero and Nama in (German) History", pp. 154–174 in this book, and "Colonial Genocide? On the Use and Abuse of a Historical Category for Global History", pp. 175–197 in this book).

sible for the whole of the desert perimeter to be kept under observation for any length of time. Again and again, small groups of Herero managed to get through the German lines and secretly return to the *Schutzgebiet*. The danger they represented could only be eliminated by the procurement of their voluntary submission, linked to their internment until the end of the war.

The War of Annihilation Against the Nama

In the meantime, while actions against scattered pockets of Herero and "the whole misguided operation against that unhappy people" continued to "keep strong military forces tied down in a thankless task", as von Estorff wrote,[26] German troops had long been required elsewhere. In the south of the colony the Nama had now also taken up the struggle against the Germans. Some parts of the Nama nation had been bound by 'protection treaties' to provide military assistance to the Germans right up to the time of the Battle of Waterberg, but now turned against them.[27] In view of this new development, even the Chief of the General Staff Alfred von Schlieffen ultimately pleaded for a revocation of the Annihilation Order, though he did so without distancing himself from von Trotha's strategy, as he wrote to the Chancellor:

> His [Von Trotha's] intention to annihilate the whole nation, or to drive it out of the country, is a matter in which one can agree with him. [...] The race war that has broken out can only end with the annihilation or else the complete subjugation of the one party. But the latter course is one that cannot be sustained in the long term, given current attitudes. One is therefore able to approve of General v. Trotha's intentions; the only thing is that he does not have the power to implement them.[28]

One reason why he did not have this power was that the Nama were waging an extremely successful guerrilla war. They had recognised how difficult it had been for the colonial forces to pursue the fleeing Herero. Consequently, the latter avoided a set-piece battle and initiated a guerrilla war. Knowing the country better than the Germans did and possessing greater mobility, they were able to offset the advantages enjoyed by the more numerous and better equipped colonial troops. They were able to keep hostilities dragging on, tying down large forces and eventually wearing them out and overcoming them by attrition.

---

26 Estorff, *Wanderungen*, p. 117.
27 On the history of the Nama War, see also Andreas Heinrich Bühler, *Der Namaaufstand gegen die deutsche Kolonialherrschaft in Namibia von 1904–1913*, Frankfurt 2003.
28 Schlieffen to Bülow, 23 November 1904, quoted according to Drechsler, *Südwestafrika*, p. 166.

Against the Nama, as against the Herero, the Germans adopted a strategy of annihilation, systematically occupying watering holes in order to kill their opponents by thirst as they had done in the Omaheke. The deliberate destruction of the livelihoods of those who supported the guerrillas was a tactic that had been tried out in the time when von Trotha was serving in German East Africa. As early as the 1890s, when punitive expeditions were carried out against the Wahehe people, burning villages and crops and "to devour Mkwawa's [the leader of the Wahehe] land'", as Governor Eduard von Liebert called it,[29] were regarded as promising tactics. Likewise in the war against the Maji-Maji in German East Africa, which took place almost contemporaneously with the war against the Herero and the Nama, it was part of the colonial forces' tactics "to confiscate the opponent's possessions (livestock, provisions) and to devastate his villages and crops", as a military memorandum stated. The goal was to erode the crucial support for the guerrilla fighters among the population by destroying people's livelihoods and their infrastructure.[30]

As in the war against the Herero, so also in that against the Nama, the Germans exploited the hostile natural environment found in parts of the colony as a tactical instrument. As a result, the campaign once again turned into a war against women and children, whose deaths were at least accepted and condoned, if not positively pursued, as part of the strategy of annihilation.

Concentration Camps

At the same time, the Germans decided to set about 'cleansing' the country by means of mass internment. Thus von Trotha called on the Nama to surrender, because otherwise they might expect to meet the same fate as the Herero:

> To the rebellious Hottentots.
> The great and mighty German Emperor would like to show mercy to the Hottentot people, so that those who surrender of their own accord will be granted their lives. Only those who at the beginning of the rebellion murdered whites or gave orders that they should be

---

[29] Eduard von Liebert, *Neunzig Tage im Zelt – Meine Reise nach Uhehe Juni bis September 1897*, Berlin 1898, p. 33, quoted according to Martin Baer and Olaf Schröter, *Eine Kopfjagd. Deutsche in Ostafrika*, Berlin 2001, p. 57.

[30] *Militärpolitische Denkschrift über die Auswirkungen des Aufstandes,* Dar-es-Salaam, 1 June 1907, quoted according to Detlef Bald, *Afrikanischer Kampf gegen koloniale Herrschaft. Der Maji-Maji-Aufstand in Ostafrika*, in *Militärgeschichtliche Mitteilungen,* 19/January (1976), pp. 23–50, here p. 40. On the Maji-Maji Rebellion see also Felicitas Becker and Jigal Beez, eds, *Der Maji-Maji-Krieg in Deutsch Ostafrika, 1905–1907*, Berlin 2005.

murdered have, in accordance with the law, forfeited their lives. This I proclaim to you, and I further tell you that those few who will not submit will suffer what the nation of the Herero has suffered. In their delusion they believed they could wage a successful war against the mighty German Emperor and the great German people. I ask you, where is the Herero nation today, where are their chiefs today? Samuel Maharero, who once called thousands of cattle his own, has fled, hunted like a wild animal, across the British frontier. He has become as poor as the poorest of the *Veldherero* and no longer has any possessions. The other Big Men have fared the same, most of them having lost their lives, and so has the entire Herero nation. Some died of hunger and thirst in the *sandveld*, some were killed by the German cavalry, others were murdered by the Ovambo. The Hottentot people will meet no other fate if they do not surrender voluntarily and give up their weapons. You are to come to us with a white cloth on a stick and with all the inhabitants of your *werfs* [African settlements], and no harm shall befall you. You will be given work and food until the war is over, when the great German Emperor will order the territory anew. Anyone who from now on believes that this offer of mercy will not be applicable to him shall emigrate, because wherever he is found within German territory he will be fired on, until all such people have been annihilated. For the handing over of those guilty of murder, dead or alive, I set the following rewards: for Hendrik Witbooi 5,000 marks, for Stürmann [sic] 3,000 marks, for Cornelius 3,000 marks, for all other guilty leaders 1,000 marks.

Signed Trotha.[31]

Only from a superficial point of view can this call to capitulate be seen as representing an abandonment of the policy of annihilation. The decisive factor in judging the military leadership's intention is the fate that awaited the Nama in captivity. And in this respect it is completely justified to talk of a continuation of the existing murderous policy, because the camps the Nama were deported to themselves represented a further instrument in the war of extermination. They were part of a system of camps established across the whole *Schutzgebiet* immediately following the revocation of the Annihilation Proclamation. This system included 'collection camps', operated by the Missionary Society and used to bring scattered Herero and those who had been living in hiding under control, and concentration camps, established and operated by the military administration. As well as effecting the actual 'concentration' of the Herero and Nama to prevent them from supporting the combatants, these latter also served as labour camps, providing urgently needed labour to both private employers and state institutions. At the same time, it was hoped that the prisoners, by being 'educated to work' in the camps, could be disciplined and prepared for their new 'role' as labourers in the post-war period, as Governor von Lindequist wrote in 1906:

---

[31] Von Trotha, Proclamation to the Hottentots, 22 April 1905. Printed in: Kriegsgeschichtliche Abteilung I des Großen Generalstabs, *Die Kämpfe der deutschen Truppen*, 2, p. 186.

> Getting the Herero to work while they are prisoners of war is a very salutary matter for them, indeed they may regard themselves as being very fortunate in that they can learn to work before full freedom is restored to them, since otherwise they would probably continue to wander around the country avoiding work, and, since they have lost their entire cattle stocks, lead wretched lives.[32]

This conviction was accompanied by the idea of retribution. With regard to the conditions prevailing in the concentration camp at Swakopmund – which were by no means exceptional – Deputy Governor Hans Tecklenburg declared in 1905:

> The more the Herero people now experience the consequences of rebellion in terms of their own physical suffering, the less desire they will have to seek to repeat the rebellion for generations to come. Our military successes in themselves have made less of an impression on them. I expect the time of suffering they are now having to endure to have a more sustained effect, though in expressing this view it is by no means my wish to take up cudgels on behalf of Lieutenant General Trotha's Proclamation of 2 October of last year. From an economic point of view, though, the death of so many people does represent a loss.[33]

The Camp on Shark Island and Annihilation through Neglect

Conditions were even worse on Shark Island off Lüderitzbucht, which was the biggest of the prison camps. Both Herero and Nama were interned there and left to their fate, and once more the threshold to genocide was crossed. An eyewitness, the missionary Emil Laaf from Lüderitzbucht, described the conditions as follows:

> At that time there were about 2,000 Herero prisoners of war interned at the very far end of Shark Island. [...] As long as the people were in good health, they were given work by the forces or by other whites who lived nearby. They were allowed to leave Shark Island to go to work, but came back every evening. [...] As a result of the great hardships and deprivations that the prisoners had suffered while they were out in the *veld* they were very weak, and there was great misery and much sickness among them. And in addition to all that, they found the wet, harsh sea climate hard to endure at first; and in any case they had been completely taken away from their accustomed way of life. It was mainly scurvy and intestinal catarrh that people went down sick with, and a certain percentage died at that time. [...] On 7 September 1906 yet another large transport of prisoners of war arrived in Lüderitzbucht from the north. This time they were Hottentots of various tribes, predominantly Witboois and Bethany people who had surrendered to the Germans at Gibeon under the

---

[32] Governor's Office Windhoek to Colonial Department Berlin, 17.4.06, BArch R 1001/2119, sheets 42a–43b.
[33] Governor's Office Windhoek to Colonial Department Berlin, 3.7.05, BArch R 1001/2118, sheets 154a–155a.

leadership of Samuel Isaak, the deputy of *Kaptein* Hendrik Witbooi. Altogether, including women and children, they totalled 1,700 persons. Regrettably, a grave injustice was done to these people in transferring them to Lüderitzbucht, since it had been mutually agreed that these prisoners should be settled in Gibeon District once they had surrendered their weapons. So it was no wonder that they, and Samuel Isaak first and foremost, harboured a great grudge against the German government in their hearts. A period of great suffering and misery now began for these people. They were settled on the furthest tip of Shark Island.

Above all they did not get the food that the conditions demanded. The refined German flour they received was unsuitable for baking bread, and no unrefined flour from the Cape was brought in. They were given plenty of pulses, but had no way of cooking them. Fresh meat was an extreme rarity. When Samuel Isaak complained to the missionary Emil Laaf that they got so little meat and the latter advised him to look for the very popular shellfish on the beach, he replied: "We have collected them all already, there are none left."

> But even more than these miserable conditions, their isolation at the very far end of Shark Island played its part in destroying the people's will to live. They gradually became quite apathetic in the face of their wretched state. They were separated from the outside world by three high barbed-wire fences. [...]
> The number of the sick increased day by day. In order to keep the people profitably occupied, the tribes had initially been put to work on a major blasting operation, with a view to building a quay on the side facing Roberts Harbour. At first, almost five hundred men were employed on this blasting work. But within a short time this number had dwindled to such an extent that the blasting work had to be suspended. There was scarcely a *pontok* [hut] without one or more sick people in it. A hospital unit was set up in a few large rooms, created by hanging up sacks. But the rations provided were in no way adapted to the needs of the sick. The food was simply put down in front of the people suffering from scurvy, and then it was a matter of 'Eat it or die!' If a sick person had no sympathetic relative to help him, he could easily starve to death. [...] The mortality rate was horrifyingly high at that time. Sometimes as many as 27 people died on a single day. The dead were taken to the cemetery by the cartload.[34]

Not even the need for labour could move those responsible to see that the prisoners were better provided for; rather than do that, the risk was accepted that construction work might have to be suspended. The fact that there was also murderous intent lurking behind all of this is confirmed by a statement attributed by Emil Laaf to the responsible regional commander Berthold von Deimling. Replying to charges that conditions on Shark Island were unbearable and that the camp should be transferred to the mainland, where the climatic conditions were better, von Deim-

---

34 *Lüderitzbucht Chronicle* (Report on the period from the foundation until 1920, by the missionary Emil Laaf), Archives of the Evangelical Church in the Republic of Namibia, V 16, sheets 1–31, here sheets 21–26.

ling only declared cynically "that as long as he [Deimling] was in charge, no Hottentot would be allowed to leave Shark Island alive."[35] Thus although the Annihilation Proclamation had been revoked and von Trotha had been recalled to Germany in November 1905, there were clearly at least some parts of the officer corps who clung to his policy of extermination.

Conditions on Shark Island did not improve until Ludwig von Estorff was appointed commander of the *Schutztruppe*. Even before he assumed this position, he had been one of von Trotha's critics. He felt that his honour as an officer had been besmirched and therefore did not want to continue to take responsibility for 'executioner's duties of this kind', particularly as there were some among the prisoners whom he himself had promised when they had surrendered that they would be better treated.[36] In April 1907, therefore, he ordered the camp to be moved to the mainland, whereupon the mortality rate immediately declined sharply due to the better climatic conditions.

In the camp on Shark Island murder was committed through deliberate neglect. Victims were 'selected' solely on the basis of their actual or assumed ethnicity; 'crimes' or acts of resistance carried out personally by any individual played no role in the motives for internment. The intent was to destroy entire 'tribes', which in the view of the Germans were 'racial groups'. Therefore, this policy can be categorised under Article 2, Letter (c) of the United Nations Genocide Convention ("deliberately inflicting on the group conditions of life calculated to bring about its physical destruction in whole or in part") – to say nothing of the killing of individual members of the group (Letter (a)) or of the "causing of serious bodily or mental harm to members of the group" (Letter (b)) that also left their mark on the survivors. This widespread murder already displays the initial signs of a bureaucratisation of the process, because the inmates of the camp were counted and kept under surveillance. This bureaucratisation is also recognisable in the way deaths were handled administratively, for example in the death certificates with the entry "death by enfeeblement" filled in in advance.[37]

Even if conditions in the concentration camp on Shark Island were particularly horrific, prisoners died in massive numbers elsewhere as well. According to statistics collected by the colonial forces, a total of 7,682 inmates died between October 1904 and March 1907. This represents between 30 and 50 per cent of the total number of people interned. Even though the ending of the State of War had been declared on

---

35 *Lüderitzbucht Chronicle*, sheets 26ff.
36 Estorff to the Colonial Forces, 10 April 1907, BArch R 1001/2140, Sheet 88a ff.
37 Jan-Bart Gewald, "Herero and Missionaries. The Making of Historical Sources in the 1920s", in Wilhelm J. G. Möhlig (ed.), *Frühe Kolonialgeschichte Namibias 1880–1930*, Köln 2000; pp. 77–95, here p. 78.

31 March 1907, the captivity of prisoners of war was not formally ended until 27 January 1908, *Kaisers Geburtstag* (the birthday of Emperor Wilhelm II), when the last of the Herero and Nama were released.

Colonialism, Racism and Genocide

Studying the genocide committed on the Herero and the Nama is not an end in itself. Nor is it merely a contribution to Namibian history: it goes beyond that. It is significant both for German history and for the history of genocide in general.[38] When von Trotha spoke of a 'race war' that could end only with victory for one side and the destruction of the other, he was adopting a position within an area of discourse and concepts that was profoundly influenced by the colonial tradition: a view of the world in which genocide was no alien concept.

It is difficult to summarise the five-hundred-year history of European colonialism in just a few lines. Research conducted from a postcolonial standpoint in particular has in recent years drawn increased attention to the differences between various regions of the world and various periods of time, and has emphasised the importance of the situational context for the way relations between colonisers and colonised developed. Nonetheless, the history of colonialism is also a history of violent crimes committed on a mass scale.

However diverse the ways in which individual European colonial structures evolved over time, fundamental to them all was a binary coding of the world. Even though the justifications for European expansion and for European rule[39] over the indigenous peoples of the newly 'discovered' and conquered territories changed, whether it was the missionising of the 'heathen', the 'White Man's Burden' or a 'Manifest Destiny' that was advanced as legitimation, the emphasis on the rightness of one's own beliefs or on the conviction of having been chosen to fulfil this mis-

---

[38] Unfortunately the issue can only be discussed in a very cursory manner here. For a more detailed discussion and a more critical look at the literature on the topic see my arguments presented elsewhere: Jürgen Zimmerer, "Colonialism and the Holocaust. Towards an Archeology of Genocide", in A. Dirk Moses, ed., *Genocide and Settler Society: Frontier Violence and Stolen Indigenous Children in Australian History*, New York 2004 (a revised version appears in this book on pp. 125–153); Zimmerer, "Birth of the 'Ostland'" (pp. 230–261 in this book).

[39] The use of expressions such as 'Europeans', 'colonial masters' etc. should not be allowed to obscure the fact that these by no means formed a homogenous group with identical goals either. See also Stoler's instructive essay: Anna Laura Stoler, "Rethinking Colonial Categories: European Communities and the Boundaries of Rule", *Comparative Studies of Society and History*, 31 (1989), pp. 134–161.

sion always played an important role in the ideological preparation for exercising domination. True equality between the Europeans and the various 'Native' populations hardly ever existed. The pattern of binary opposition that underlay the perceived dichotomy between colonisers and the colonised, Christians and 'heathens', 'Blacks' and 'Whites', humans and 'less-than-humans', also brought about a homogenisation of the inherently disparate groups of both the rulers and the ruled. At the same time it established the distance between these two groups that was essential to the asymmetrical – i.e. colonial – exercise of power.

Social Darwinism, which became increasingly influential in the course of the nineteenth century, placed direct emphasis on the hierarchy among peoples and their competition with each other – in respect of both the relationship between the colonisers and the colonised and relations between the colonial powers themselves. It is within such a mindset that the concept of a 'race war' as envisioned by von Schlieffen, von Trotha and other members of the German colonial forces can be localised. The most drastic consequences of this dichotomy were manifested in the settler colonies, where the newly arrived Europeans – if they did not in the first place imagine the land to be empty of any human inhabitants at all – were of the opinion that they could embark on organising the land as they saw fit in order to bring 'order' to the 'chaos', without regard for indigenous settlement areas and economic spheres. The indigenous peoples who, contrary to the idea that was prevalent among Europeans, already lived there, only stood in the way of this endeavour. And if they were not willing to allow their labour to be exploited, they were either expelled or murdered. In the racist world view, this was the 'normal' course of events in world history. The existence of 'higher' races was taken for granted, and for these to occupy such a position logically required the existence of 'lower' races as well. And right at the bottom of this racial hierarchy were to be found those peoples who, according to the immutable laws of history, were doomed to perish. Helping this process along merely accelerated the inevitable.

Genocide on the Frontier, Colonial Wars of Conquest and Annihilation

Before indigenous people became victims of violence, they were dehumanised and robbed of their human dignity. How this dehumanisation of the 'Natives' manifested itself in individual perpetrators is illustrated by the practice, known from Australia, of 'shooting practice' – with Aborigines as targets. As an eyewitness reported in 1889: "There are instances when the young men of the station have employed the Sunday in hunting the blacks, not only for some definite purpose, but also for the sake of the sport."[40] This was possible because the Aborigines were not regarded as belonging to human society, as the description of this practice published in the newspaper The Queenslander also confirms:

> And, being a useless race, what does it matter what they suffer any more than the distinguished philanthropist, who writes in his behalf, cares for the wounded half-dead pigeon he tortures at his shooting matches. 'I do not see the necessity,' was the reply of a distinguished wit to an applicant for an office who remarked that 'he must live;' and we virtually and practically say the same to the blacks and with better reason.[41]

From this attitude it was but a small step to the murder of women and children. Placing Aborigines on the same level as animals that could be 'shot down' for sport was the plainest possible evidence of dehumanisation. In other cases, this function was fulfilled by the propagation of atrocity stories: Africans, Native Americans and Aborigines were accused of raping women and of (sexually) mutilating men. Thus the indigenous nations themselves were made to bear the blame for their own fate, because they had allegedly shown themselves to be 'animals' that it was therefore permissible to 'slaughter'. The Herero War and von Trotha's Proclamation are classic examples of this attitude.

Mass murder found even broader acceptance if individuals were able to justify it by claiming that they were protecting their own property. In 1889, for example, it was said of an Australian squatter: "He shot all the men he discovered on his run, because they were cattle killers; the women, because they gave birth to cattle killers; and the children, because they would in time become cattle killers."[42] Applying this logic, the murdering could only end with the complete extermination of the Aborigines. Similar arguments seeking to justify genocide are also known from North America: H. L. Hall, for example, an infamous murderer of Native Americans, rationalised the murder of small children with the saying that "nits make lice",[43] which had been well-known and applied to Native Americans since the time of King Philip's War (1675–1677).

Whereas the aforementioned squatter was a lone murderer, others went hunting together. In 1867, for example, readers of The Queenslander learnt about an act of reprisal carried out by several settlers jointly in retribution for real as well as imagined attacks by Australian Aboriginal People:

---

40 Quoted according to Alison Palmer, *Colonial Genocide*, Adelaide 2000, p. 44.
41 The Queenslander, 8 May 1880, https://trove.nla.gov.au/newspaper/article/20332884, accessed 12 Jul. 2023, see Palmer, *Colonial Genocide*, p. 45.
42 Quoted according to Palmer, *Colonial Genocide*, p. 43.
43 Quoted according to Ward Churchill, *A Little Matter of Genocide: Holocaust and Denial in the Americas 1492-Present*, San Francisco 1997, p. 229.

[...]in the present system by which blacks are shot down most ruthlessly for weeks and months after a case of murder or theft has been reported, and when many innocent are either killed in order that the guilty may possibly be included in the number, or so hunted about that the spirit of revenge is aroused in them[.][44]

Numerous examples of the slaughter of men, women and children by gangs of settlers or local militia can be found in North America as well as in Australia. The perpetrators justified such acts by pointing to real or imagined attacks by the 'savages'.[45] Especially on the frontier proper, it was private actions at the local level that predominated, precisely because this was by definition a mixed zone where the newly arrived settlers came into contact with the indigenous population, but where the Whites were initially not yet in the majority and official structures were lacking. In the course of time, however, specially recruited troops such as the Native Police of Queensland came to be deployed, which functioned as death squads with the task of 'cleansing' the frontier of Aborigines.

The genocidal wars of conquest and 'pacification' represent a further escalation of such frenzies of extermination, since they were more extensive military operations and accordingly required more organisation. The war that Imperial forces waged against the Herero and Nama in German South West Africa is the most important example of this. The fact that camps appear, and serve as spaces of death on a large scale underscores the degree of organisation of this genocide. Even if it has not been possible to clarify whether Kaiser Wilhelm ordered the genocide – von Trotha merely indicated that the Emperor had commissioned him to crush the 'rebellion' by whatever means – von Trotha was nonetheless unambiguously acting in the Emperor's name. He was the Kaiser's representative, and therefore the crimes committed in that context must be viewed as having been committed officially in the name of Germany. Von Trotha represented the German state, and this makes the war of annihilation into a criminal act perpetrated

---

44 The Queenslander, 23 February 1867, https://trove.nla.gov.au/newspaper/article/20312053/, accessed 12 Jul. 2023, see Palmer, *Colonial Genocide*, p. 43.

45 Most of the few studies that exist on this topic seek to fervently enlighten readers about the suffering of a particular group and they lobby for the recognition of that suffering: see, for example, Churchill, *A Little Matter of Genocide*, and David E. Stannard, *American Holocaust. The Conquest of the New World*, New York 1992. A. Dirk Moses demonstrates what an objective, scientific debate can accomplish: see A. Dirk Moses, ed., *Genocide and Settler Society: Frontier Violence and Stolen Indigenous Children in Australian History*, New York 2004. See especially his introduction to the problem of an activist vs. scientific perspective and the problem of the singularity of certain victims' experiences and the connected problems for scientific treatment. Lastly, also see A. Dirk Moses, "Conceptual Blockages and Definitional Dilemmas in the 'Racial Century': Genocides of Indigenous Peoples and the Holocaust", *Patterns of Prejudice*, 36/4 (2002), pp. 7–36; and Zimmerer, "Colonial Genocide?" (pp. 175–197 in this book).

by the state, which is one of the generally acknowledged identifying characteristics of genocide. Not least for this reason, the destruction of the Herero and Nama represents an important stepping up of the degree of radicalisation, lying between the genocides committed by settlers in the colonial context and the crimes of the Nazis.

The Second World War as a Colonial War

Compared to the gigantic battles and the millions of victims of the Second World War, the colonial war in South West Africa seems but a minor prelude to the barbarisms of the twentieth century. Nonetheless, the colonial war's numerous structural similarities to the Nazi "war of annihilation in the East" reveal that it is an important event not only in Namibian history, but in German history too. Many things that appear, when we look back at the Second World War, to be unimaginable breaches of taboos had already been common practice in German South West Africa.[46] If the underlying structure of the 'war in the East' – in other words, the grand design that lay behind the modern weapons and the armada of tanks and aircraft – is exposed, this 'war of annihilation' displays elements clearly reminiscent of colonial warfare, of "war[s] of destruction" incorporating "campaign[s] of annihilation", to use a term that is already to be found already in reports on the fighting in German East Africa, as it was pursued by, among others, the German colonial forces.[47]

---

[46] I have treated the structural similarities between colonialism and the German policy of occupation and extermination in the 'East' during the Second World War in depth in Zimmerer, "Birth of the 'Ostland'"; Jürgen Zimmerer, "Im Dienste des Imperiums. Die Geographen der Berliner Universität zwischen Kolonialwissenschaften und Ostforschung", *Jahrbuch für Universitätsgeschichte*, 7 (2004), pp. 73–100 (English version: "In the Service of the Empire: Berlin University's Geographers from Colonial Sciences to Ostforschung", pp. 262–293 in this book); Jürgen Zimmerer, "Von Windhuk nach Warschau. Die rassische Privilegiengesellschaft in Deutsch-Südwestafrika — ein Modell mit Zukunft?", in Frank Becker, ed., *Rassenmischehen—Mischlinge—Rassentrennung. Zur Politik der Rasse im deutschen Kaiserreich*, Stuttgart 2004, pp. 97–123 (English version: "From Windhoek to Warsaw: The Society of Racial Privilege in German South West Africa – a Model with a Future?", pp. 201–229 in this book). A connection between colonial rule in German South West Africa and the Third Reich had already been alluded to in Helmut Bley, *Kolonialherrschaft und Sozialstruktur in Deutsch-Südwestafrika 1894–1914*, Hamburg 1968; Drechsler, *Südwestafrika*; and Henning Melber, "Kontinuitäten totaler Herrschaft. Völkermord und Apartheid in Deutsch-Südwestafrika", *Jahrbuch für Antisemitismusforschung*, 1 (1992), pp. 91–116.

[47] Liebert, *Neunzig Tage im Zelt*, p. 33, quoted according to Thomas Morlang, "'Die Kerls haben ja nicht einmal Gewehre.' Der Untergang der Zelewski-Expedition in Deutsch-Ostafrika im August 1891", *Militärgeschichte*, 11/2 February (2001), pp. 22–28, 27.

Because although in formal terms the war against the Soviet Union was a regular war between European powers, it was the case right from the start that the Germans did not conduct it as such but as a war of plunder and destruction, which owing to the deliberate non-application of the international rules of war by the aggressor more closely resembled a colonial war than an 'ordinary' war inside Europe. Features of this were the denial to the adversary of the status of a legitimate belligerent of equal and equally honourable status, who even in defeat and captivity was entitled to a minimum of rights, and the racially driven willingness to let prisoners of war perish or to murder them outright. One only needs to think of the practice known as 'annihilation through neglect' by which millions of Russian prisoners of war were murdered during the Second World War.

Heinrich Himmler's order of the day of 1 August 1941 reads almost like a quotation from von Trotha's Proclamation. In it, Himmler ordered the massacre of the Pripet Marshes: "All Jewish men are to be shot, Jewish women driven into the swamps."[48] The intention was clear: very much like the Herero women and children who perished in the Omaheke, the Jewish women too would die, without any German soldier even having to lift his weapon. The attitude that paved the way for this crime also entailed a binary view of the world: there were only 'Aryans and Jews', 'Germans and Slavs', 'humans and subhumans'. Without this dichotomous opposition, identical in function to the colonial categorisation as 'civilised people' or 'savages', it would not have been possible to treat other human beings in such a cruel and inhuman way as then occurred.

Holocaust and Colonialism

However it would also be erroneous to view Nazi crimes, and particularly those of the Holocaust, as mere copies of colonial events, as postcolonial authors and activists have repeatedly maintained them to be, and continue to do so. In this respect the debate has taken on aspects of a competition between degrees of victimhood. It has been emphasised that in the process of colonising the Americas, multiple Holocausts occurred, an estimated hundred million deaths being manifoldly worse than six million deaths.[49] This emotionalised and politicised approach has damaged

---

[48] Quoted according to Christian Gerlach, "Deutsche Wirtschaftsinteressen, Besatzungspolitik und der Mord an den Juden in Weißrußland 1941–1943", in Ulrich Herbert, ed., *Nationalsozialistische Vernichtungspolitik 1939–1945. Neue Forschung und Kontroversen*, Frankfurt 1998, pp. 236–291, here p. 278.

[49] For an extreme example see Churchill, *A Little Matter of Genocide*; and Rosa Amelia Plumelle-Uribe, *Weisse Barbarei. Vom Kolonialrassismus zur Rassenpolitik der Nazis*, Zürich 2004.

rather than advanced research into the connection between colonialism and the Holocaust. To suggest such an equivalence is also an oversimplification, since the differences between events in the colonies and those in central and eastern Europe in the 1940s also demand to be clearly stated and defined.

One important difference, for example, is that the Jewish victims were drawn from the midst of German and European society, while the colonial victims had been viewed by their killers as subordinate from the onset. Basically, the Jews had first to be transformed into that 'absolute Other' that the colonised peoples already appeared to be, simply on account of the colour of their skin. The process of Othering, of binary coding, was similar, but in the case of the Jews the process of determining who were to become victims was completely different: centuries-old antisemitism allied itself with exterminatory racism of the colonialist pattern.

A further difference lies in the bureaucratisation of murder and thus in the role the state played in genocide, on the one hand in the colonial context and on the other hand in the Third Reich. It is precisely this systematic, almost industrialised murder – symbolised in an iconic fashion by barbed wire, heaps of discarded eye-glasses and mountains of bodies – for which the name Auschwitz stands, so that it has become a universally recognised chiffre for absolute evil. In the colonial state, which was far less centralised and bureaucratised, murder could not take such forms.

Nonetheless, bureaucratised and state-orchestrated killing is less a matter of a fundamental structural difference than of a difference in degree that is linked to the level of the state's historical development. Thus the massacres perpetrated by settlers and militias on the New England frontier were congruent with the weakness of state institutions there. As the State became more established, the instruments of genocide expanded in parallel; in Queensland and in the United States, for example, they were augmented by the Native Police or by military forces, through which the state itself committed mass murder. In the modern bureaucratised state, such as was beginning to take shape in South West Africa, concentration and prisoner-of-war camps were introduced as places of extermination. Active 'industrial' killing may not have been practiced there yet; but murder through neglect was already prevalent.

The crimes of the Nazis cannot be ascribed monocausally to the tradition of European colonialism: National Socialism was too complex and too eclecticist in its ideology and its policies for that. Nonetheless, to express the relationship in terms of the archaeology of economic population management and genocide, it must be said that colonialism served as an important source of ideas. Even the murder of the Jews, which – as already mentioned – sets itself off in many ways from other genocides, would scarcely have been possible if the ultimate breach of taboo that consists in thinking that other ethnic groups can simply be eliminated, and then acting accordingly, had not already occurred. And it had occurred in colonial times.

In the tradition of genocidal thought, another reason why colonialism occupies such a prominent place is because the themes of the 'discovery', conquest, 'opening up' and 'settlement' of the world had positive connotations, were disseminated throughout society and offered role models for the ambitious to emulate. At the same time, the similarity to colonialism helps us to understand why the expulsion and resettlement of Jews and Slavs, and in the last instance their murder, were perhaps not even perceived as being breaches of taboo. At the very least, colonial history offered the perpetrators of the Nazi crimes the possibility to exonerate themselves, and to deceive themselves in respect of the monstrosity of their own horrific acts.

Auschwitz marks the perverse culmination of state violence directed against both the state's own and also alien populations. The war against the Herero and Nama was an important step in this development and offered a portent, right at the beginning of the twentieth century, of what was yet to come. The genocide in German South West Africa is therefore neither simply a local event in the history of Namibia or of Germany, nor an isolated incident in colonial history. Rather, it is an event that stands out in a global history of violence that was to escalate and reach its zenith in the two world wars. It has often been asked whether there is a path connecting Windhoek and Auschwitz. I think there are many paths. Viewed from the Windhoek perspective, the Third Reich was by no means an inevitable consequence. But to pursue the same metaphor: of the numerous feeder routes that converged in the criminal policies of National Socialism, one originated in the colonies; and it was by no means an obscure or minor path.

Planning Frenzy: Forced Labour, Expulsion and Genocide as Elements of Population Economics in German South West Africa

> Expansion is everything. [...] I would annex
> the planets if I could.[1]
> (Cecil Rhodes)

Among the typical features that are used to characterise imperialism are inherent megalomania, conquest for conquest's sake and expansion as an end in itself. The same will to dominate and to rule was also manifest in the efforts to open up whole continents and to build railways from the Cape to Cairo or from Berlin to Baghdad. As the Earth was progressively 'explored', mapped and surveyed, the blank areas gradually vanished from the map, while people, animals and plants were organised into taxonomical systems.

After a long time in which debate was confined to the (foreign) policy and economic dimensions of imperialism, in recent years the influence of postcolonial theory has led to more serious consideration of the level of idealised constructs and imagined realities, and also of visions of the opening up of 'unknown' territories.[2] Despite this, postcolonial studies of the development of colonial discourse

---

[1] Quoted according to Hannah Arendt, The Origins of Totalitarianism, New York 1951, p. 124.
[2] With regard to classic imperialism research, see e.g. Wolfgang J. Mommsen, *Imperialismustheorien. Ein Überblick über die neueren Imperialismustheorien*, Göttingen 1980. The literature on postcolonialism now fills whole libraries. For an introduction see e.g.: Bill Ashcroft, Gareth Griffith and Helen Tiffin, *Key Concepts in Post-Colonial Studies*, London 1998; Dane Kennedy, "Imperial History and Post-Colonial Theory", *Journal of Imperial and Commonwealth History*, 24/3 (1996), pp. 345–363; Patrick Wolfe, "History and Imperialism. A Century of Theory, from Marx to Postcolonialism", *American Historical Review*, 102/2 (1997), pp. 388–420. The first steps in applying this research programme to Germany are being undertaken by Sebastian Conrad, Andreas Eckert and Albert Wirz: Sebastian Conrad, "Doppelte Marginalisierung. Plädoyer für eine transnationale Perspektive auf die deutsche Geschichte", *Geschichte und Gesellschaft*, 28 (2002), pp. 145–169; Andreas Eckert and Albert Wirz, "Wir nicht, die Anderen auch. Deutschland und der Kolonialismus", in Sebastian Conrad and Shalini Randeria, eds, *Jenseits des Eurozentrismus. Postkoloniale Perspektiven in den Geschichts- und Kulturwissenschaften*, Frankfurt 2002, pp. 372–392. For examples of literature devoted to idealised worlds under the banner of colonialism, see Kundrus, *Phantasiereiche*; Alexander Honold and Oliver Simons, eds, *Kolonialismus als Kultur. Literatur, Medien, Wissenschaft in der deutschen Gründerzeit des Fremden*, Tübingen/Basel 2002. For general information on utopian visions of the opening up of unknown territories, see Dirk van Laak, *Imperiale Infrastruktur. Deutsche Planungen für eine Erschließung Afrikas, 1880 bis 1960*, Paderborn 2004. On the relationship between geographers and colonialism, see Jürgen Zimmerer, "Wissenschaft und Kolonialismus. Das Geographische Institut der Friedrich-Wilhelms-Universität

and the colonialist mentality continue to be confined first and foremost to metropolitan discourses and the fantasies and visions of intellectuals, colonial writers for example. Fantasies can, however, also be found elsewhere, in both senses of that term: on the one hand in the colonies themselves, and on the other hand among the 'practitioners' of colonialism, the settlers, military officers and colonial civil servants.[3] Taking such visions into account does not merely lend a global dimension to analyses of the colonial mentality; it also creates links between them and the periphery-orientated research of recent years by which the history and development of indigenous societies was brought centre stage. Colonial histories are "entangled histories"[4] and call for a detailed examination of both sides. And the history of German South West Africa represents a particularly interesting example with regard to colonial fantasies of power and rule during the high imperialist age.

What I have written so far is already sufficient to indicate that I will be concentrating on the mentality of the German colonisers and the ways in which they acted. This approach appears to me to be historiographically justified, because while research into Namibian history has made significant progress in recent years above all in reconstructing African history,[5] it seems necessary to return to the German colonisers in order to assemble a complete picture of the colony as a place of interaction and communication.

---

vom Kaiserreich zum Dritten Reich", in Ulrich van der Heyden and Joachim Zeller, eds, *Kolonialmetropole Berlin. Eine Spurensuche*, Berlin 2002, pp. 125–130; Jürgen Zimmerer, "Im Dienste des Imperiums. Die Geographen der Berliner Universität zwischen Kolonialwissenschaften und Ostforschung", *Jahrbuch für Universitätsgeschichte*, 7 (2004), pp. 73–100 (English version: "In the Service of the Empire: Berlin University's Geographers from Colonial Sciences to Ostforschung", pp. 262–293 in this book).

3 I have attempted to pursue this in Jürgen Zimmerer, *Deutsche Herrschaft über Afrikaner. Staatlicher Machtanspruch und Wirklichkeit im kolonialen Namibia*, Münster/Hamburg/London 2001 [English edition: *German Rule, African Subjects. State Aspirations and the Reality of Power in Colonial Namibia*, New York 2021].

4 On the concepts of "entangled histories" and "shared histories" see: Sebastian Conrad and Shalini Randeria, "Einleitung. Geteilte Geschichten – Europa in einer postkolonialen Welt", in Sebastian Conrad and Shalini Randeira, eds, *Jenseits des Eurozentrismus*, pp. 9–49. I am deliberately applying these terms to the micropolitical situation in everyday colonial rule.

5 See e.g. Martti Eirola, *The Ovambogefahr. The Ovamboland Reservation in the Making – Political Responses of the Kingdom of Ondonga to the German Colonial Power 1884–1910*, Rovaniemi 1992; Jan-Bart Gewald, *Towards Redemption. A Socio-political History of the Herero of Namibia between 1890 and 1923*, Leiden 1996; Dag Henrichsen, *Herrschaft und Identifikation im vorkolonialen Zentralnamibia. Das Herero- und Damaraland im 19. Jahrhundert*, University of Hamburg 1997 (Ph.D. Thesis); Gesine Krüger, *Kriegsbewältigung und Geschichtsbewusstsein. Realität, Deutung und Verarbeitung des deutschen Kolonialkrieges in Namibia 1904–1907*, Göttingen 1999.

The objection has frequently been raised that any concentration on the 'White'/'German' side would evoke the image of passive Africans and their total domination, as was depicted in earlier historiography that sought to provide an apologia for colonialism. This seemed to be a particular danger with regard to German South West Africa, in the face of genocide and the rigid policies of control and subjugation.[6] However, this picture of German omnipotence is itself a result of inadequate research into the agents of colonial rule: a construction that is a peculiar mélange derived on the one hand from the colonial propaganda of the absolutely smooth manner in which German rule functioned and on the other from the attempt to destroy the idyllic and romantic vision of German colonialism by magnifying and so demonising the coloniser. For the image of omnipotence implies that the Germans were able to implement whatever policies they desired, and conversely, that whatever it was they implemented was also what they desired to implement. However, it is questionable whether this double equation is accurate.

Within the history of German South West Africa, the war against the Herero and Nama, the 100th anniversary of the outbreak of which fell in the year 2004, has doubtless received the most attention up until now.[7] The degrees of violence, brutality and ruthlessness with which the *Schutztruppe* waged this campaign, leading ultimately to the first genocide in German history, have resulted in this war being turned into a symbol for the failure of German colonialism as a whole. So for a long time research concentrated on the war and its causes. Consequently, the fact that the 'non-military' aspects of German colonial history were just as exemplary and paradigmatic for subsequent German history as the genocide itself was pushed into the background.

To the extent that the policies towards the African population pursued after the war were discussed at all, they were simply considered to be results of the war.[8] The postwar phase was thus separated off from the prewar period, and the history of South West Africa as a German colony was divided into three phases:

---

6 Cf. Brigitte Lau's remonstrances against the colonial war of 1904–1908 being labelled as genocide: Brigitte Lau, "Uncertain Certainties. The Herero-German War of 1904", in Brigitte Lau, *History and Historiography – 4 Essays in Reprint*, ed. Annemarie Heywood, Windhoek 1995, pp. 39–52.
7 For a recent summary of the extensive literature, see Jürgen Zimmerer and Joachim Zeller, eds, *Völkermord in Deutsch-Südwestafrika. Der Kolonialkrieg in Namibia (1904–1908) und seine Folgen*, Berlin 2003.
8 As an example, cf. Helmut Bley, *Kolonialherrschaft und Sozialstruktur in Deutsch-Südwestafrika 1894–1914*, Hamburg 1968, p. 193.

the establishment of German rule up to the outbreak of the colonial war of conquest (1884–1904), the genocidal war itself (1904–1908) and the postwar period (1908–1914). The last-mentioned was represented as a phase of pure destruction and stagnation, in which the "peace of the graveyard", as Horst Drechsler called it, prevailed.[9]

This, however, led to a fundamental continuity in German policy from the early years of the colony onwards being hidden from view: namely the attempt to create a model colonial state. This approach was supposed to avoid what were considered to be undesirable developments in modern society and so also to provide a suitable model for the motherland, the German Empire. This Wilhelminian colonial project was based on the idea that it was possible to plan every aspect of the economy of an extensive territory, including the measures of population economics required to make it as efficient as possible. Development and expansion, order and efficiency: these were the underlying principles. The key characteristic was a heavy emphasis on bureaucratic rule and the application of supposedly 'scientific' methods in Native Policy. The goal was to build an efficient economic system within a society of racial privilege, where the African population provided the workforce through which the colony's economic development could be pushed forward and raw materials extraction reliably pursued.[10] In this hubristic vision, the contradictions inherent in the system which led to the utopia of the society of racial privilege as a perfect model of order, with its planning frenzy and its delusion that everything could be planned, turning into a nightmare for the affected Africans were simply overlooked.

---

9 "Ruhe des Friedhofs", the title of a chapter in: Horst Drechsler, *Südwestafrika unter deutscher Kolonialherrschaft. Der Kampf der Herero und Nama gegen den deutschen Imperialismus 1884–1915*, 2nd edn, Berlin 1984, pp. 221–236. More recent research has sufficiently demonstrated that this picture of an African population broken by the war is inaccurate: there were both campaigns of direct resistance and also people who fled the colony or refused to submit to social or mental "re-education". What remained of Herero society reorganised itself and built up alternative self-help structures and support networks. See Gewald, *Towards Redemption*; Krüger, *Kriegsbewältigung und Geschichtsbewusstsein*; Philipp Prein, "Guns and Top Hats. African Resistance in German South West Africa 1907–1915", *Journal of Southern African Studies*, 20 (1994), pp. 99–121; Jürgen Zimmerer, "Der totale Überwachungsstaat? Recht und Verwaltung in Deutsch-Südwestafrika", in Rüdiger Voigt, ed., *Das deutsche Kolonialrecht als Vorstufe einer globalen 'Kolonialisierung' von Recht und Verwaltung* (Schriften zur Rechtspolitologie), Baden-Baden 2001, pp. 175–198 (English version: "Total Control? Law and Administration in German South West Africa", pp. 77–103 in this book).

10 For greater detail, see Zimmerer, *Deutsche Herrschaft* [English edition: *German Rule, African Subjects*].

This attempt – which the local colonial bureaucracy in the colony was the driving force behind – to completely reorder a territory covering an area approximately twice that of the German Empire is however of interest not only because it bears witness to the mentality of the Wilhelminian bourgeoisie and the alternation of its mindset between inferiority complex and megalomania, nor even only because it affords a particularly good example of the imperialistic credo that "everything is possible"; but also because it foreshadows future events. Almost half a century before the *Generalplan Ost* and similar concepts drawn up by German regional planners and experts were launched during the Second World War, in order to bring about a gigantic '*völkische Flurbereinigung*' – an 'ethnicity-based cleansing of the land' – which would have cleared the Slavic and Jewish populations out of areas of eastern Europe to make way for German/'Aryan' expansion – and before an economic system based on forced labour had been set up throughout Germany and its occupied territories, an attempt had been made in southern Africa to restructure populations in line with economic considerations and to set up a system of forced labour.[11] This is by no means intended to suggest complete identity between these events, and still less to relativise them. Rather, it is a matter of drawing attention to the structural similarities between German policies in South West Africa and Nazi rule in eastern Europe.[12] In both cases, the African population on the one hand and the Polish and Russian populations on the other

---

[11] In view of the wealth of literature on the Third Reich, there is space here only to refer to a few fundamental works: Ulrich Herbert, ed., *Nationalsozialistische Vernichtungspolitik 1939–1945. Neue Forschungen und Kontroversen*, Frankfurt 1998; Götz Aly and Susanne Heim, *Vordenker der Vernichtung. Auschwitz und die deutschen Pläne für eine neue europäische Ordnung*, Hamburg 1991; Götz Aly, '*Endlösung*'. *Völkerverschiebung und der Mord an den europäischen Juden*, Frankfurt 1995; Mechthild Rössler and Sabine Schleiermacher, eds, *Der 'Generalplan Ost'*, Berlin 1993; Czeslaw Madajczyk, ed., *Vom Generalplan Ost zum Generalsiedlungsplan*, München 1994; Mark Spoerer, *Zwangsarbeit unter dem Hakenkreuz. Ausländische Zivilarbeiter, Kriegsgefangene und Häftlinge im Deutschen Reich und im besetzten Europa 1939–1945*, Stuttgart/München 2001; Jan Erik Schulte, *Zwangsarbeit und Vernichtung: Das Wirtschaftsimperium der SS. O. Pohl und das SS-Wirtschafts-Verwaltungshauptamt 1933–1945*, Paderborn 2001.

[12] For a comparison of the colonial and National Socialist occupation policies, see Jürgen Zimmerer, "Die Geburt des 'Ostlandes' aus dem Geiste des Kolonialismus. Die nationalsozialistische Eroberungs- und Beherrschungspolitik in (post-)kolonialer Perspektive", *Sozial.Geschichte. Zeitschrift für historische Analyse des 20. und 21. Jahrhunderts*, 19/1 (2004), pp. 10–43 (English version: "The Birth of the 'Ostland' out of the Spirit of Colonialism: A Postcolonial Perspective on the Nazi Policy of Conquest and Extermination", pp. 230–261 in this book). On the relationship between colonialism and the Holocaust in general, see Jürgen Zimmerer "Colonialism and the Holocaust. Towards an Archeology of Genocide, in A. Dirk Moses, ed., *Genocide and Settler Society: Frontier Violence and Stolen Indigenous Children in Australia*, New York 2004, pp. 49–76 (a revised version appears in this book on pp. 125–153).

were viewed first and foremost as economic factors. Individual or collective self-determination was replaced by forcible external control, and it was the economic value of the individual to the occupiers that determined his or her right to live. In extreme cases, it also legitimised the neglect of these populations, even to the extent of their utter destitution or deliberate murder.

In German South West Africa, the experiment was undertaken of attempting to recreate an entire territory in accordance with the racial, economic and social ideas of a small group of civil servants. These had come to the territory, one of the most inhospitable areas of southern Africa, as representatives of a foreign power. And it did indeed require nothing less than the superabundant imagination of the nationalistic Wilhelminian bourgeoisie to turn this "sand strewer of a territory",[13] as Governor von Schuckmann once called it in a deliberate allusion to Prussia, into the pride of the German colonial movement. After all, this territory, only recently created in negotiations between the European colonial powers, covered an area of over 800,000 square kilometres, though it had a population of at most only 200,000 to 250,000 people.[14] This land was not of course empty of people, as colonial ideology liked to represent it; some areas of it, however, were not far from being so. Thanks to the climatic conditions, which appeared to be reasonably tolerable for White settlers, the phantasm of 'South West' as a settler colony was born.[15] However, even this expectation was disappointed; by 1915, the year of the South African conquest, only a meagre 15,000 Whites (mostly Germans) had settled in the colony.[16]

The Germans held political sway over the colony for only one generation before they were forced to hand South West Africa over to South Africa as a League of Nations Mandate.[17] Even so, under German colonial rule this southern African

---

[13] *Deutsches Kolonialblatt 1908*, pp. 467f, quoted according to Oskar Hintrager, *Südwestafrika in der deutschen Zeit*, München 1956, p. 100.
[14] Theodor Leutwein, *Elf Jahre Gouverneur in Deutsch-Südwestafrika*, 3rd edn, Berlin 1908, p. 11. With regard to the numbers generally, it must be said that they are based on very inexact estimates made by missionaries in the 1870s.
[15] For the discussions, conceptions and phantasms relating to German South West Africa, especially those prevalent in the Reich itself, see Birthe Kundrus, *Moderne Imperialisten. Das Kaiserreich im Spiegel seiner Kolonien*, Köln/Weimar/Wien 2003.
[16] A detailed overview of the progress of European settlement is given by Udo Kaulich, *Die Geschichte der ehemaligen Kolonie Deutsch-Südwestafrika (1884–1914). Eine Gesamtdarstellung*, Frankfurt 2001, p. 353.
[17] On this subject, see Jürgen Zimmerer, "Von der Bevormundung zur Selbstbestimmung. Die Pariser Friedenskonferenz und ihre Auswirkungen auf die britische Kolonialherrschaft im Südlichen Afrika", in Gerd Krumeich, ed., *Versailles 1919: Ziele – Wirkung – Wahrnehmung*, Essen 2001, pp. 145–158.

country underwent deeper and more rapid change than most other colonies, whether German ones or those of other colonial powers. The events that began in May 1885 with the arrival of Imperial Commissioner Heinrich Göring and just two other officials were to fundamentally transform the country. Thirty years later, the 'tribes' in the south and centre of the colony had been dissolved, the traditional economic and social structures of indigenous society largely destroyed and the greater part of the real property previously owned by Africans transferred into the possession of White farmers, mining companies or the colonial state. The African population had ceased to be free, economically independent inhabitants of their own land and had become dispossessed subjects of the German Empire, dependent on its representatives for the employment they needed in order to survive.[18]

These changes were the result of deliberate administrative action by the state in furtherance of the attempt described above to create a 'perfect' polity. The main cause, along with the genocidal war of 1904–1908, of the drastic consequences ensuing from the short period of German colonial rule was the *Herrschaftsutopie*, the utopian concept of the social order that the administration felt itself called upon to create and impose in South West Africa. This 'governmental and administrative utopia'[19] was essentially the work of the German colonial bureaucracy,[20] or rather, to be more exact, of a small group of top officials most of whom had already come to the colony with the first Governor, Theodor Leutwein, and had won their first colonial spurs building up and heading administrative districts before going on to climb the career ladder in Windhoek or Berlin. Of these, Friedrich von Lindequist, Angelo Golinelli and Hans Tecklenburg, with the later addition of Oskar Hintrager, were the most influential; and they were the people responsible for assuring that there was continuity in Native Policy.

---

18 On this subject, see Jürgen Zimmerer, *Deutsche Herrschaft* [English edition: *German Rule, African Subjects*]. In addition, an overview of the history of German South West Africa that concentrates heavily on the German side is that by Kaulich, *Deutsch-Südwestafrika*. He still follows the strict division of the history of German South West Africa into three phases that I reject. Not yet outdated on many issues are the classic works by Bley und Drechsler: Drechsler, *Südwestafrika unter deutscher Kolonialherrschaft*; Bley, *Kolonialherrschaft*.

19 The term *Herrschaftsutopie*, here translated as 'governmental and administrative utopia', is of enormous importance in this context. It is taken up from Trutz von Trotha and used to refer to the long-term regulation of the conditions of the indigenous population that the officials sought to achieve, as to them it represented an administrative ideal. On this subject, see Trutz von Trotha, *Koloniale Herrschaft. Zur soziologischen Theorie der Staatsentstehung am Beispiel des 'Schutzgebietes Togo'*, Tübingen 1994, p. 12.

20 Colonial civil servants are a professional group to whom far too little attention has been paid in research so far.

Their vision of how the state should function was derived from the model of the bureaucratic and centrally administered state that modern Germany represented, and its objective was to construct an efficient economic system on the basis of a society of racial privilege in which the institutions of government, the settlers and the African population each occupied its firmly assigned place. The indigenous population was to be comprehensively registered and kept under surveillance, integrated into the colony's economic system as cheap labour and re-educated to function as compliant workers through a process of social disciplining. In this way, it was assumed, the economic development of the colony could be pushed ahead with and the production of natural raw materials guaranteed, so that the *Schutzgebiet* would be able to develop into a settler colony in an orderly manner. The end result was intended to be a unified economic area in which the African people were distributed as workers in accordance with the needs of the colonial economy. The focus of the whole strategy was on planning and centralised direction.

The nature of this *Herrschaftsutopie* is concisely documented in Friedrich von Lindequist's so-called Native Ordinances of 1907. Forming the normative core of German Native Law, these ordinances provided for the establishment of a rigid system of control and surveillance and imposed an obligation on the African population to take up employment. Although they were promulgated by Theodor Leutwein's successor as civil governor, Friedrich von Lindequist, after the military victory over the Herero and the Nama, the essential provisions of these regulations all dated back to the time before 1904 and had been more or less ready and waiting in the office pigeonholes.

The first steps towards exercising control over the Africans, restricting their freedom of movement and exercising surveillance over their conditions of work had already been taken before the turn of the century. Even then, the objectives of these policies had been to force the Africans into employment, to establish their identities unambiguously and to monitor and control their movements. In 1892, only seven years after the establishment of the colony, the Colonial Department of the *Auswärtiges Amt* (Foreign Office) had made the first move towards implementing these ideas by accepting contracts of employment between government agencies and Africans only if they were made in written form.[21] Soon after, in 1894, von Lindequist issued an Ordinance for the district he administered, Otjimbingwe, concerning the general organisation of conditions of work for Afri-

---

21 Colonial Department to Imperial Commissioner, Windhoek, 5 May 1892, National Archives of Namibia, Windhoek (NAN), Central Office of the Colonial Governor (Zentralbureau des Gouvernements) (ZBU) W.III.N.1. Vol. 1, Sheet 1a f.

cans. This regulation not only included formal provisions for the regulation of working relationships between Africans and Whites, but also a passage that represented the first step towards the introduction of a compulsion to enter into employment. According to this passage, "persons who are not able to demonstrate that they are able to provide for themselves out of their own means or by undertaking work, and who roam around the country from place to place without working", were to be "assigned work by the police authorities against the provision of board, clothing or cash payment"; they could also be handed over to private employers.[22]

This measure introduced by von Lindequist immediately found Leutwein's approval: he saw in it a promising instrument to "relieve the very acute shortage of labour and to gradually accustom the unpropertied natives, in particular the Berg Damaras and the Hottentots, to working".[23] Leutwein himself was a proponent of forcing the Africans to enter into employment: in 1903, in a discussion on the issue of introducing a poll tax for Africans, he made the following statement:

> It would no doubt be a nice idea to compel the natives to work by means of this type of tax. But the nomadic lives led by our natives in this thinly populated territory stand in the way of this plan too. Only those few natives would be affected by the tax who have settled down either on the mission stations or where there are other white settlements. Instead of keeping them there, where it is to our advantage to have them, we would reawaken in them the longing to join up again with their fellow tribesmen who live more freely.[24]

---

22 Bezirksamt Otjimbingwe, *Verordnung betr. das Verhältnis der Arbeitgeber zu den Arbeitern* (Otjimbingwe District Office: 'Ordinance concerning the Relationship between Employers and Workers') [transcript], 3 July 1894, NAN ZBU W.IV.A.3. Vol. 2, Sheet 5a-7a, printed in *Die Deutsche Kolonial-Gesetzgebung (DKG). Sammlung der auf die deutschen Schutzgebiete bezüglichen Gesetze, Verordnungen, Erlasse und internationalen Vereinbarungen mit Anmerkungen und Sachregister* [German Colonial Legislation. A Collection of the Statutes, Ordinances, Decrees and International Agreements relating to the German *Schutzgebiete*, with Notes and an Index] (DKG), ed. Riebow, Gerstmeyer and Köbner, 2 (1893–97), p. 104. A notable feature of von Lindequist's District Police Ordinance is that it speaks of "workers" in a neutral manner throughout. Only from the context is it apparent that it is intended to apply to Africans: in the DKG, for example, it appears under the heading "Legal relationships with natives". Two years later, the District Office of Gibeon followed: "Bezirksamt Gibeon, Verordnung betr. Regelung der Dienstboten-Verhältnisse" ('Gibeon District Office, Ordinance concerning the Regulation of Master and Servant Relationships') [transcript], 23.3.96, NAN ZBU W.IV.A.3. Vol. 2, Sheet 41ea-41fa.
23 Imperial Administrator to Imperial Chancellor, 26 July 1894, NAN ZBU W.IV.A.3. Vol. 2, Sheet 2a-3a. (Leutwein's title was changed from "Imperial Administrator" ("Landeshauptmann") to "Governor" in 1898.)
24 Imperial Governor's Office Windhoek to Colonial Department, 26 September 1903, NAN ZBU W.II.I.1. Vol. 1, Sheet 1da-1ea.

It was only Leutwein's appreciation that he lacked the power necessary to enforce such measures, and thus that it was impractical to introduce either the tax or the compulsion to enter into employment, that persuaded him to distance himself from such a policy for the time being. He did state that further attention would be given at a later date to the matter of designing "a system for imposing taxation on the natives";[25] but he was pragmatic enough to know that his power and the strength of his troops were not yet adequate to implement such a plan. So at first, he relied on gaining the cooperation of influential African leaders.[26]

It was also out of the debate concerning employment contracts that the first suggestions for more comprehensive social disciplining and control of the African population emerged. In 1896, the District Officer of the Southern District in Keetmanshoop, Angelo Golinelli, spoke out in favour of making it compulsory for all employment contracts to be registered with the police. This was intended above all to make it easier to keep the Africans under surveillance, since every African employed by Whites would be given a numbered "service token" when he entered into his contract of employment, which would also identify the "issuing police authority":

> Every police station shall keep a list of the tokens issued, in which the date of issue, the name of the recipient and the file number of the contract of employment are to be entered. In this way the station will be in a position to exercise surveillance over the natives concerned and furnish them with a means of legitimisation. The native shall wear the service token attached to his clothing or his loincloth.

This was to allow the heads of the Districts "to get a picture of the work being performed by the natives belonging to their Districts and where necessary to intervene with a view to stimulating their desire to work". In order to promote "zeal in respect of work" state payments were to be granted to reward "long and faithful service with the same employer". Since it was in the government's interest "that the natives should be engaged in regular work and that their nomadic instincts should be subdued", employment contracts should have a term of at least one year.[27] In this way, elements that would come to form the foundations for the later monitoring and control system were outlined: namely service tokens and registers. Apparently it did not prove possible to establish uniform regulations governing the employment of African workers before the outbreak of war

---

25 Ibid.
26 This tactic, known under the name of "Leutwein's chiefs policy", is presented in detail in Bley, *Kolonialherrschaft*.
27 District Office Keetmanshoop to Imperial Governor's Office Windhoek, 28 August 1896, NAN ZBU W.IV.A.3. Vol. 2, Sheet 42aa-42ka.

in 1904; it was not until the promulgation of the Master and Servant Ordinance of 1907 that this area was regulated uniformly throughout the Territory.

As has been suggested above, it was not only the District Offices that were much preoccupied with the problem of exercising surveillance over the African population; so was the central colonial administration in Windhoek. There was a strong desire to be able to monitor and, ultimately, restrict the movements of every single 'Native'. Thus as early as August 1900, Leutwein had circulated for discussion – only within the Administration, of course – a draft Ordinance concerning a general pass and registration requirement for the African population. He intended to make it obligatory for every African "who crossed the boundaries of the area allotted to his tribe by the government", or who wanted to leave his place of residence if it was outside the 'tribal territory', to carry a pass. As well as details of the bearer, such as his or her place of residence and 'tribal affiliation', the pass would also give the reason for the journey, the name of the bearer's employer and the type of employment the bearer was engaged in. The police would be entitled to check the pass at any time, but above all, the issue of such a pass could be refused for were "reasons of security or other good cause".[28] Thus as well as providing for the surveillance of the indigenous population, this Ordinance would also have served to limit freedom of movement and thus to control the distribution of the available workforce: and in addition, anyone found away from his home without a pass could have been "taken into temporary police custody [...] and assigned work by the police authorities against the provision of board or cash payment".[29] As German rule became more established, suggestions were put forward (even though at first only in internal discussions) as to how direct measures against the Africans could be made more stringent. In 1900, during the debate on introducing the pass requirement, the District Office of Outjo suggested something that would, when implemented later, become the ultimate symbol of the German policy of subjugation and control: namely that in order to make it easier to control the Africans they should be issued with a "metal token to be worn visibly around the neck".[30]

---

[28] Imperial Governor's Office Windhoek, "Verordnungsentwurf betr. die Pass- und Meldepflicht der Eingeborenen" ("Draft Ordinance concerning Pass and Registration Requirements for Natives"), August 1900, NAN ZBU W.III.K.1. Vol. 1, Sheet 7a-8a.
[29] Ibid.
[30] District Officer Outjo to Imperial Governor's Office Windhoek, 21 December 1900, NAN ZBU W.III.B.1. Vol. 1, Sheet 7af. At first, this regulation was only to apply to new arrivals in each District. However, the proposal apparently went too far for the Governor's Office, as is shown by a large question mark drawn in the margin.

Ultimately, the colonial authorities were not able to put the Pass Ordinance into effect before the outbreak of the war against the Herero and the Nama. Only in the new political situation after the outbreak of war did some District Offices promulgate local pass regulations.[31]

It is not possible to deal with the genocidal war of 1904–1908 in detail here.[32] What is important to emphasise, though, is that it was neither a logical nor a necessary consequence of the German governmental and administrative utopia; rather, indeed, it stood in blatant contradiction to it. Triggered by the provocations of subordinate German officers,[33] it threatened to destroy the non-military utopia of the German colonial administration: firstly through the successes of the Herero, and later through the genocidal way the war was waged by the colonial forces under General Lothar von Trotha. The war of extermination ordered by

---

31 Thus the District Office of Swakopmund promulgated an Ordinance introducing a general pass requirement on 18 May 1904, Keetmanshoop followed on 7 October 1904, Grootfontein on 9 February 1905, Windhoek on 8 November 1905, Karibib on 16 January 1906, and later Outjo as well. Bestimmungen, betr. die Passpflicht der Eingeborenen im Bezirk Swakopmund ("Provisions concerning the Pass Requirement for Natives in Swakopmund District"), 18 May 1904, NAN ZBU W.III.K.1. Vol. 1, Sheet 53a-55a. Bestimmungen, betr. die Passpflicht der Eingeborenen im Bezirk Keetmanshoop ("Provisions concerning the Pass Requirement for Natives in Keetmanshoop District"), 7 October 1904, ibid, Sheet 62a-63b. Bestimmungen, betr. Passzwang für Eingeborene des Bezirks Grootfontein ("Provisions concerning Compulsory Passes for Natives in Grootfontein District") [transcript], 9 February 1905, ibid., Sheet 92af. Bestimmungen, betr. die Passpflicht der Eingeborenen im Bezirk Windhuk ("Provisions concerning the Pass Requirement for Natives in Windhoek District") [transcript, undated], ibid, Sheet 97a-98a. Bestimmungen, betr. die Passpflicht der Eingeborenen im Bezirk Karibib ("Provisions concerning the Pass Requirement for Natives in Karibib District") [transcript], 16 January 1906, ibid., Sheet 101a-103a [effective date: 1 February 1906]. District Office Outjo to Imperial Governor's Office Windhoek, 27 May 1907, ibid., Sheet 21a-24a.

32 For an overview of the war, see Zimmerer and Zeller, *Völkermord in Deutsch-Südwestafrika*; Henrik Lundtofte, "'I believe that the nation as such must be annihilated ...' – The Radicalization of the German Suppression of the Herero Rising in 1904", in Steven L.B. Jensen, ed., *Genocide: Cases, Comparisons and Contemporary Debates*, Copenhagen 2003, pp. 15–53; Jan-Bart Gewald, "Colonization, Genocide and Resurgence: The Herero of Namibia 1890–1933", in Jan-Bart Gewald and Michael Bollig, eds, *People, Cattle and Land: Transformations of a Pastoral Society in Southwestern Africa*, Köln 2001, pp. 187–225; Krüger, *Kriegsbewältigung*; Tilman Dedering, "'A Certain Rigorous Treatment of All Parts of the Nation ': The Annihilation of the Herero in German South West Africa, 1904", in Mark Levene and Penny Roberts, eds, *The Massacre in History*, New York 1999, pp. 205–222. On the question of whether this was a case of genocide and its position in history, see Jürgen Zimmerer, "Das Deutsche Reich und der Genozid. Überlegungen zum historischen Ort des Völkermordes an den Herero und Nama", in Larissa Förster, Dag Henrichsen and Michael Bollig, eds, *100 Jahre geteilte namibisch-deutsche Geschichte. Kolonialkrieg – Genozid – Erinnerungskulturen*, Köln 2004, pp. 106–121.

33 Gewald, *Towards Redemption*, pp. 178–191.

him threatened to annihilate the entire Herero nation, and later the Nama as well, although both peoples were – from the German point of view – key elements in the essential labour force. Theodor Leutwein, having been Governor for many years, knew what he was talking about when, in 1904, in the inflamed atmosphere of the first weeks of the war, he warned against those "ill-considered voices [...] that now want to see the Herero completely annihilated." For apart from the fact that in Leutwein's opinion a nation of 60,000 to 70,000 people "could not be exterminated just like that", he knew that the Herero would still be needed as "small-scale cattle breeders and particularly as labourers". Thus Leutwein was not primarily moved by philanthropic motives either: he too considered rendering the Herero "politically dead", destroying their political and social organisation and concentrating them in reservations that would be "only just sufficient for their needs" to be legitimate and reasonable war aims.[34]

This stance, which seems a curious one for Leutwein to have adopted, of seeking to 'protect' the African population for reasons of political or, in this case, economic pragmatism, and his call for the war to be conducted in such a way that the "the Herero nation be preserved", were not likely to persuade von Trotha. Indeed, von Trotha rejected the appeal with the comment that the Governor would have to allow him "to conduct the campaign as he saw fit".[35] He was deaf to economic arguments, because in his opinion German South West Africa should be a colony "in which a European can himself work to provide for his family".[36] Blinded by his idea of a "race war", he believed that Africans would "only yield to force"; and so he sought to annihilate "the rebellious tribes with rivers of blood".[37]

The outcome of this attitude was the genocide, which reached its initial climax when the Herero were forced to flee into the waterless *sandveld* of the Omaheke desert. The concentration camps were a further element in it; established throughout the territory to collect the surviving Herero, but also taking up thousands of deported Nama, they were intended to deprive the guerrilla fighters of support from the civilian population. Where the prisoners were not exterminated

---

[34] Leutwein to Colonial Department, 23 February 1904, quoted according to Drechsler, *Südwestafrika*, pp. 149f.
[35] According to a later report by a son of Leutwein's, quoted according to Drechsler, *Südwestafrika*, p. 155.
[36] Entry in von Trotha's diary, quoted according to Gerhard Pool, *Samuel Maharero*, Windhoek 1991, p. 265.
[37] Von Trotha to Leutwein, 5 November 1904, quoted according to Drechsler, *Südwestafrika*, p. 156.

by neglect, as was the case at least in the camp on Shark Island off Lüderitzbucht, both men and women were forced to work as forced labour.[38]

The concentration camp system also offered points of departure for the incorporation of all the surviving Herero and Nama into the surveillance and control system officially set up in 1907. To this extent, the war also accelerated the realisation of the non-military governmental and administrative utopia. The time seemed favourable, as a large proportion of the Herero and later of the Nama too had lost their lives, while others were refugees or captives, so that the opportunity presented itself to confiscate all the land that had been occupied by the defeated enemies and also any livestock they still had. Already at an earlier date, under Leutwein, available areas of land had been designated for White settlers, and these had been expanded more and more through treaties with Samuel Maharero and other chiefs. This process was accompanied by discussions between settlers, the Rhenish Mission and the government on how much land should be used for White settlement.[39] The target it was sought to achieve was that 75 per cent of the land should be declared to be government land, while the remaining 25 per cent should be left to the Africans.[40] However, such 'consideration' for the interests of the Africans proved to be no longer necessary. On the basis of the "Imperial Ordinance concerning the Sequestration of Native Assets in the Colony of South West Africa",[41] the entire land of the Herero and the Nama was brought into German ownership in two stages in 1906 and 1907.[42]

Expropriating the land and making it available for organised settlement were, however, only the first step. Farmers and entrepreneurs alike needed cheap African labour, a problem that – not least as a result of the war – was a factor inhibiting economic development right down to the end of German colonial

---

38 Presented in greater detail in Jürgen Zimmerer, "Kriegsgefangene im Kolonialkrieg. Der Krieg gegen die Herero und Nama in Deutsch-Südwestafrika 1904–1907", in Rüdiger Overmans, ed., *In der Hand des Feindes. Kriegsgefangenschaft von der Antike bis zum Zweiten Weltkrieg*, Köln 1999, pp. 277–294.
39 Drechsler, *Südwestafrika*, pp. 120–127.
40 Horst Gründer, *Geschichte der deutschen Kolonien*, Paderborn 1995, p. 118.
41 Kaiserliche Verordnung, betr. Einziehung des Stammesvermögens der Eingeborenen ("Imperial Ordinance concerning the Sequestration of Native Assets in the Colony of South West Africa"), 26 December 1905, Bundesarchiv Berlin-Lichterfelde R 1001/1220, Sheet 65a-66b. This Ordinance is printed in DKG 9 (1905), pp. 284–286.
42 Only the land of the Berseba Nama and the Bondelswarts was exempted from this. In addition, Ovaboland, the Caprivi Strip and the possessions of the Rehoboth Basters remained untouched. Compare also: Gründer, *Geschichte der deutschen Kolonien*, p. 122.

rule in 1915. Consequently, the need to settle the 'labour question' was a prominent issue in Native Policy after the war.[43]

Native Law was codified in von Lindequist's Ordinances of 1907, known collectively as the Native Ordinances. These regulations, consisting of the Pass, Control and Master and Servant Ordinances,[44] were the new straitjacket by which African society was to be reshaped, provided for the progressive imposition of social disciplining on the Africans, and laid the basis for a 'semi-free labour market', one which reduced the Africans to a pool of labour freely available to the colonial 'masters' as a result of a compulsion to enter into employment, but nevertheless – at least in theory – still allowed them a degree of freedom to choose their employers and to negotiate their wages.[45]

The basic prerequisite both for economic exploitation and for the protection of the *Schutzgebiet* against further 'Native uprisings' – another factor that ranked highly on the scale of priorities after the recent experiences of the war – was the registration and surveillance of the African population through the establishment of a seamless system of control that encompassed all aspects of life. The Administration was to be put in the position of being able to determine how many Africans were present in a particular District at any particular time, who they were, where they lived and whether and where they were employed. To achieve this, all Africans had to ensure that they were entered in Native Registers at their respective District Offices. In order to ensure that they could be unambiguously

---

[43] For instance, the number of additional workers required was estimated to stand at 15,000 in 1911, which was approximately 75 per cent of the working male African population of 23,227. See also Zimmerer, *Deutsche Herrschaft* [English edition: *German Rule, African Subjects*] p. 177.

[44] Verordnung, Kaiserliches Gouvernement Windhuk, betr. Maßregeln zur Kontrolle der Eingeborenen (Imperial Governor's Office, Windhoek: "Ordinance concerning Regulations for the Control and Surveillance of Natives"), 18 August 1907, NAN ZBU W.III.A.1. Vol. 1, Sheet 61a-62b; Verordnung, Kaiserliches Gouvernement Windhuk, betr. die Passpflicht der Eingeborenen (Imperial Governor's Office, Windhoek: "Ordinance concerning the Pass Requirement for Natives"), 18 August 1907, NAN ZBU W.III.A.1. Vol. 1, Sheet 63a-65b; Verordnung, Kaiserliches Gouvernement Windhuk, betr. Dienst- und Arbeitsverträge mit Eingeborenen (Imperial Governor's Office, Windhoek: "Ordinance concerning Employment and Service Contracts with Natives"), 18 August 1907, NAN ZBU W.III.A.1. Vol. 1, Sheet 66a-68a; Runderlass, Kaiserliches Gouvernement Windhuk, zu den Verordnungen, betr. die Kontrolle und Passpflicht der Eingeborenen sowie die Dienst- und Arbeitsverträge mit diesen (Imperial Governor's Office, Windhoek: "Circulated Decree accompanying the Ordinances concerning the Control of and Pass Requirement for Natives and Employment and Service Contracts with them"), 18 August 1907. All printed in: *DKG 11* (1907), p. 352–357.

[45] I have shown in greater detail in Zimmerer, *Deutsche Herrschaft* [English edition: *German Rule, African Subjects*] that the requirements laid down as norms in the Native Ordinances are by no means identical with the social and economic realities of everyday colonial life. I also explain the concept of the 'semi-free' labour market in more detail there.

identified, all individuals over seven years of age needed a pass, consisting of a metal token bearing the imperial crown and a registration number which had to be worn visibly around the neck and presented on demand to the police and to "any white person". As a pass was valid only in one District and bore a series of numbers that showed which District this was, it was possible to determine at any time if an African had left his home District. Anyone who wished to do this legally – for a limited period of time – had to obtain a travel pass from the responsible police station.[46] At his destination he then had to obtain confirmation of his arrival, specifying the time. Thus the Africans were under comprehensive surveillance, and were not to be allowed any freedom of movement.

By contrast to the forced labour practised during the war both in the concentration camps of the colonial forces and in labour camps set up by private companies,[47] in the period after the war the elements of direct compulsion were replaced by measures of a structural nature. Imprisonment, fetters and whips were (officially and in theory) no longer to be used to force the 'Natives' to work, but rather a sophisticated system in which rewards were balanced by direct or indirect compulsion. For this reason, the African population was prohibited from owning large livestock or riding animals.[48] Additionally, as the land of the Herero and the Nama had already been expropriated, the Africans essentially only had the option of hiring themselves out on farms, to the engineering companies building the railways, or in the diamond mines. Anyone who did not take up such work would in all probability be punished as a vagrant, a fate that threatened anyone found "roaming around [...] without any demonstrable means of support".[49]

In addition to the compulsion to take up employment, a further measure applied in the field of population economics was the control of the distribution of the population. By refusing to issue travel passes, the colonial administration could regulate the distribution of the African workforce, as people were simply prevented from moving away from any District where labour was in short supply. But an unbalanced concentration of Africans, for example on farms near to the graves of

---

[46] The only exemption from the travel pass obligation was if the African was travelling on behalf of or accompanied by his White employer: in this case, however, he required a letter of authority *(Begleitschreiben)* whose form and content corresponded to those of the travel pass.

[47] On this, see for example Gewald, *Towards Redemption*, pp. 220–224; Krüger, *Kriegsbewältigung*, pp. 126–135.

[48] Anyone who nevertheless wanted to possess animals needed explicit governmental approval; so the government could control the degree of economic independence of the African population, either limiting or promoting it as it saw fit.

[49] Verordnung, Kaiserliches Gouvernement Windhuk, betr. Maßregeln zur Kontrolle der Eingeborenen (Imperial Governor's Office, Windhoek: "Ordinance concerning Regulations for the Control and Surveillance of Natives"), 18 August 1907, NAN ZBU W.III.A.1. Vol. 1, Sheet 61a-62b.

their ancestors or other culturally important places, or else simply with particular employers, was not in tune with the concept of an economic utopia either. So in order to secure as even a distribution as possible of the African population across the country and thus on individual farms and in individual businesses, African settlements of more than ten families were prohibited.[50]

As practically all adult Africans had to work for Whites, a legal codification of employment relationships was necessary. At the same time, the Administration could use this to supplement the system of surveillance and control. One instrument to this end was the *Dienstbuch*, the Employment Logbook, which was prescribed for all employment contracts with a term of more than one month and was issued to the individual by the police, who also entered the conclusion of such contracts in the Native Register. The Employment Logbook had to contain the name, tribal affiliation and pass token number of the employee, but also the name of the employer, the date on which employment commenced, the term of the contract, the period of notice, and the "amount and type of remuneration to be granted to the native". The Logbook was therefore supposed to provide an unbroken sequence of information about the Africans' employment relationships and their availability for work, the 'willingness to work' so often invoked in colonial discourse. When the police issued the Employment Logbook they were supposed to ascertain "that the content of the contract had been made adequately comprehensible to the employee, and agreed to by him". To the displeasure of the farmers, this included instructing the Africans not only in respect of their duties, but of their rights as well.[51]

This provision, designed to protect the Africans, again indicates the ambivalent structure of the German governmental and administrative utopia, in which the 'semi-free' labour market combined rigorous control and the compulsion to take up employment with employees' rights intended to protect the 'Natives'. This was a very important matter for many officials; for such ostensibly protective elements in the system enabled them, subjectively, to feel reassured that they were neither the henchmen of commerce nor the executors of a ruthless policy of suppression, but to believe that they were in fact engaged in working to establish a balancing out of interests as between Europeans and Africans:

---

50 Employers who required more workers needed special permission from the Administration. Otherwise, larger settlements were legal only in the vicinity of the larger towns or cities.
51 For example, see the report of Gobabis District Office, where employers were rarely willing to make contracts of employment lasting longer than one month, as they feared the explanations that the Africans would be given by the police. District Office Gobabis to Imperial Governor's Office Windhoek, 31 October 1908, NAN ZBU W.III.A.3. Vol. 1, Sheet 42a.

> The Ordinance relating to Employment Contracts with natives is to be welcomed as a great step forward, in the interests both of the whites and of the natives themselves. [...] The native will lose the feeling of being practically a slave and deprived of all rights in respect of his employer, and if he is well treated and paid in accordance with his performance will do everything he can to keep his employer satisfied.[52]

This balancing out of interests was a central feature of the society of racial privilege, a socially hierarchical society in which the most important distinguishing feature was 'race'. According to the fictional narrative propagated by the Germans, it was supposed to give rise to a degree of stability in the relationship between Africans and Whites that could not be achieved through pure force. For this reason, White employers were also to be monitored: for the Administration had its doubts as to whether some of the settlers were really suited to pursuing the task of colonisation:

> It is absolutely essential that those whites who are responsible for supervising private werfs [Herero settlements] should themselves be subject to monitoring, since some of our settler material, coming mainly from very modest backgrounds at home, are easily inclined to exploit improperly any position of power granted to them.[53]

However inaccurate this analysis was – for in the *Prügelkultur*, the 'culture of fisticuffs' or 'culture of physical violence', that was emerging in South West Africa it was not only the socially marginalised who beat, whipped and boxed ears; it was rich and poor, aristocrats and commoners alike – statements such as "The introduction of the Employment Logbook and of contracts of employment serves the interests of both the employer and the employee in equal measure. This is the only way to prevent workers from running away and to protect them from abuse and exploitation"[54] should not merely be written off as colonialist propaganda. These comments stem from internal correspondence that was not meant to be disclosed to public scrutiny and that allows a profound insight into the self-image and the self-legitimisation strategies of the colonial officials. They saw themselves as bringers of 'civilisation' and as non-partisan judges over Africans and Europeans alike, agents of the social and economic transformation into a 'modern' society and an efficiently functioning economy who were committed to the general, i.e. White, public welfare. They saw Africans as culturally inferior, at a stage of development equivalent to that of a child and incapable of leading an indepen-

---

[52] District Office Swakopmund to Imperial Governor's Office Windhoek, 8 June 1907, NAN ZBU W.III.A.1. Vol. 1, Sheet 26b-27a.
[53] District Office Outjo to Imperial Governor's Office Windhoek, 27 May 1907, NAN ZBU W.III.A.1. Vol. 1, Sheet 21a-24a.
[54] Ibid.

dent life without a guardian, the colonial 'master'. He first had to be given an upbringing or education, and this could best be done in the service of the 'Whites', either as a domestic servant or houseboy, or else as a cheap labourer on farms, in the construction of the railways or in the mines. The ideology of the inferiority of the colonised peoples led to the officials failing to perceive any contradiction between their supposed task of 'raising up' the Africans and the economic benefits they gained from colonial rule. In particular, the protective provisions in the Native Ordinances served them as proof that they were fulfilling their duty of care with regard to the Africans. At the same time, however, it was their conviction of the superiority of their own culture, of their own tradition of administration, and their belief that in building up a 'modern' state they were acting in accordance with the laws of history, that led them to extend this administration to take in the indigenous population, without any regard for the consequences this gave rise to for the latter.[55]

It would of course be wrong to confuse the German governmental and administrative utopia, the utopia of absolute control over the African population and the total, all-round planning of their use as labour as envisaged by the colonial bureaucrats, with what came about as a result of how it was actually implemented in practice. The system failed for many reasons, which included refractoriness on the part of the Africans just as much as the refusal of the settlers to cooperate with the colonial authorities and the 'racial solidarity' of officials, judges and settlers when it was a matter of investigating crimes and offences against Africans. Thus the hopes of the German colonial administration that its sophisticated system of regulation would secure peace and order and also allow the Africans to enjoy at least a minimal degree of protection while they were gradually acclimatising to their new lives as dependent workers, were not fulfilled. Many officials turned a blind eye to the pronounced culture of physical violence that prevailed on the farms, on the railway construction sites and on the diamond fields. Those who wanted to take action against it were thwarted by the system. There was scarcely any judge who was willing to sentence a White person for mistreating Africans. White prosecution witnesses were hardly to be found, while testimony given by Black witnesses was simply not believed. In a colonial system that was rooted in the 'racial' hierarchy as between the colonisers and the colonised, there was no way in which the Africans' credibility deficit could be eliminated.

Even if the governmental and administrative utopia was unrealisable, it nevertheless has a significance going far beyond that for German South West Africa.

---

[55] With regard to this and to the failure of this utopia, see: Zimmerer, *Deutsche Herrschaft* [English edition: *German Rule, African Subjects*].

There were many colonial fantasies and dreams of a perfect world, but rarely was there such a systematic attempt to turn them into reality. In the service of a utopia deemed to be both rational and progressive, colonial administrators attempted to methodically reorder a whole country on a racial basis without any regard for the original inhabitants. It is the destructive potential that was released in the service of a form of development considered to be ideal and of an obsessive delusion that whatever it was one sought to achieve in this world, it was merely a matter of adequate planning, and that it was possible for thousands of people to be comprehensively monitored and controlled with their individual rights subordinated to the attainment of this utopia, which make the colonial experiment in German South West Africa an important episode in the history of population economics. Its shadow looms over the second German attempt to build a colonial empire in the years 1939–1945. And as in eastern Europe during the Second World War, those who played their part as servants of the occupying power were neither monsters nor psychopaths, but rather 'ordinary men', or better, 'ordinary bureaucrats'.

Total Control? Law and Administration in German South West Africa

Introduction

The arrival of Imperial Commissioner Heinrich Göring in May 1885 marked the official beginning of the process of establishing German colonial administration in the so-called *Schutzgebiet* of South West Africa. As early as the autumn of 1888, however, the representatives of Imperial Germany were forced to flee into the British territory of Walvis Bay in order to escape the Herero.[1] By the time the Germans surrendered to the South African invaders thirty years later, there were almost 15,000 Europeans living in the colony; the foundations for a settler society had been laid, the greater part of the land previously owned by Africans had become the property of farmers, mining corporations or the colonial state, the traditional economic and social structures of the indigenous societies had been largely destroyed, and the 'tribes' in the south and centre of the colony had been dissolved. The African peoples in those areas had changed from being free, economically self-sufficient inhabitants of their own land into dispossessed subjects of the German Empire, forced to undertake dependent labour for their survival. That such a rapid transformation could be effected in just one generation is a clear reflection of the nature of the German colonial state. This was set up so quickly that there was simply no time or opportunity to make adaptations to the system of colonial rule in order to take account of the disparate natures of the traditional societies that were subject to it; indeed, apart from a certain degree of restraint that was practised for tactical reasons during the early stages of colonialisation, no such adaptation was ever intended. Basically, the colonial administration that was in the process of being set up simply exported to Africa administrative structures, for which the imperial 'mother' country was the model. The colonial state was thus imposed on the German colonies from outside, and that more full-bloodedly than was the case in other countries' colonies.

The understanding of the state and of state administration possessed by the officials sent to South West Africa to establish colonial rule there was based on contemporary Germany; thus their intention was to build up an efficient economic system founded on a pre-modern idea of a society composed of different 'estates', in which the Administration, the settlers and the African population

---

1 For an overview of German colonial rule in South West Africa, see Horst Gründer, *Geschichte der deutschen Kolonien*, 3rd edn, Paderborn 1995, pp. 111–127.

each occupied the stations firmly assigned to them. The indigenous population was to be seamlessly registered and controlled, integrated into the colony's economic system as cheap labour and re-educated by a process of social disciplining to be compliant workers. It was assumed that this process would allow the economic 'development' of the colony to make rapid strides, with the exploitation of mineral deposits being facilitated and initial steps being taken towards the orderly development of a settler colony. The end result, it was assumed, would be a uniform economic area within which the African people would be evenly distributed, forming a workforce in line with the needs of the colonial economy. The most important instruments through which this fundamental transformation was to be effected were a bureaucratic administration and a newly created body of Native Law – the sum of those legal provisions that governed the relationships both between the State and its indigenous subjects and between the European[2] and the African populations.

A closer look at everyday colonial life reveals, however, that what was provided for by law did not correspond to the reality experienced by those who were subject to it. One cannot conclude merely from the fact that certain legal provisions existed that these were actually implemented. Thus any consideration that focuses exclusively on an analysis of the legislation and regulations will not do justice to the real historical situation. Any scholar who wishes not merely to present the declarations of intent emanating from the colonial authorities, but to paint a detailed picture of what life in the colonial state was like in practice – which is an essential precondition for any analysis of the effects of colonial rule – needs to inquire into the question of the degree to which each norm was in fact implemented.

This article will follow such an approach, taking as an example the regulations that aimed to control the African population; these measures were at the very heart of Native Policy, since without them it would not have been possible to realise the desired distribution of the labour force, or to enforce the obligation to take up employment, or to implement the measures for imposing social discipline on the Africans. The colonial bureaucracy too required an overview of the indigenous population in order to function. For this reason, after analysing the German governmental and administrative utopia, that is to say the long-term regulation of the conditions of the indigenous population in the direction of what the colo-

---

2 In this context, the term 'European' includes Afrikaners (also called Boers) who had migrated from South Africa.

nial officials regarded as an ideal state[3] and therefore devoted all their efforts to achieving, I will examine the degree to which it was implemented; for both the concept of the 'perfect' state and the failure, at least in part, to realise it in practice equally form part of the reality of German colonialism in South West Africa. In this way, the manner in which the control regulations were created, the visions of colonial rule associated with them and the difficulties involved in implementing them come together to provide an illuminating object lesson in the realities of law and administration in the German territory.[4]

Governmental and Administrative Utopia: Surveillance and Total Control

Tentatively though the German Empire's involvement in South West Africa had begun, with the dispatch of a mere three officials when the territory was first declared to be under German 'protection' in 1884, once Theodor Leutwein had assumed the office of Governor in 1893 the systematic development of a German administration began in earnest. The administrative structure was headed by the Governor, who at the same time was also Commander in Chief of the *Schutztruppe*, the colonial army. According to a plan for civil administration devised in 1894 by Leutwein and the then District Officer in Otjimbingwe, Friedrich von Lindequist, the *Schutzgebiet* was divided up into three *Bezirke* – regions or districts: Keetmanshoop, Windhoek and Otjimbingwe.[5] By 1903 their number had already increased to six.[6]

At the same time, the first measures for keeping the African population under surveillance were being discussed in the context of a debate on the introduction of a Master and Servant Ordinance (colloquially referred to in German as

---

3 The term 'governmental and administrative utopia' is used to translate Trutz von Trotha's expression 'Herrschaftsutopie': see Trutz von Trotha, *Koloniale Herrschaft. Zur soziologischen Theorie der Staatsentstehung am Beispiel des 'Schutzgebietes Togo'*, Tübingen 1994, p. 12.
4 For a comprehensive analysis of German Native Policy, the goals associated with it on the German side and their actual implementation in the everyday life of the colony, see Jürgen Zimmerer, *Deutsche Herrschaft über Afrikaner. Staatlicher Machtanspruch und Wirklichkeit im kolonialen Namibia*, Münster/Hamburg/London 2001 [English edition: *German Rule, African Subjects. State Aspirations and the Reality of Power in Colonial Namibia*, New York 2021]. This work also includes extensive bibliographical references, which in this text are therefore kept brief.
5 Gert Sudholt, *Die deutschen Eingeborenenpolitik in Südwestafrika. Von den Anfängen bis 1904*, Hildesheim 1975, p. 125.
6 On the development of the administration, see Walter Hubatsch, *Grundriß zur deutschen Verwaltungsgeschichte 1815–1945, 12 Bundes- und Reichsbehörden*, Marburg 1983, pp. 424–450.

the *Gesindeverordnung*). After von Lindequist had issued a "District Police Ordinance concerning the Relationship between Employers and Workers" in the summer of 1894,[7] and Gibeon District Office had followed suit with a similar regulation two years later,[8] Leutwein planned to introduce such an Ordinance for the entire colony in 1896. A response to his plans drawn up by Angelo Golinelli, the head of the Southern (Keetmanshoop) District, mentions on the one hand the aspect of protecting the Africans by providing for their employment contracts to be registered with the police, but on the other hand also the idea of keeping the African population under surveillance. This included every African employed by Europeans being issued with a numbered 'service token' when entering into a contract of employment, and registers were to be kept listing the tokens issued. And every African was to wear the service token "attached to his clothing or his loincloth" as a "means of legitimisation".[9] Although in the end it did not prove possible to establish uniform regulations governing the employment of African workers before the war, these provisions prefigured central aspects of the Master and Servant Ordinance of 1907.

Another issue which demonstrates the efforts of the German administrators to obtain a better overview and more control over the African population is that of a general pass and registration requirement. In August 1900 Leutwein had put forward for discussion a draft of an Ordinance that provided for every African "who crossed the boundaries of the area allotted to his tribe by the government", or who wanted to leave his place of residence if it was outside his 'tribal territory', to be required to be in possession of a pass. In addition to the date, the pass was to contain the name of the issuer, the name of the African, his 'tribal affiliation', his place of residence, his reason for leaving it, the type of employment he was engaged in and, where appropriate, the name of his employer and the authority or person to whom the pass was to be surrendered afterwards. The police

---

[7] Otjimbingwe District Office: "Verordnung betr. das Verhältnis der Arbeitgeber zu den Arbeitern" ("Ordinance concerning the Relationship between Employers and Workers"), 3 July 1894, NAN ZBU W.IV.A.3. Vol. 2, Sheets 5a–7a, reproduced in *Die Deutsche Kolonialgesetzgebung. Sammlung der auf die deutschen Schutzgebiete bezüglichen Gesetze, Verordnungen, Erlasse und internationalen Vereinbarungen mit Anmerkungen und Sachregister (German Colonial Legislation. A Collection of the Statutes, Ordinances, Decrees and International Agreements relating to the German Schutzgebiete, with Notes and an Index* – 'DKG'), published in 13 volumes, Berlin 1893–1910, here Vol. 2, p. 104.

[8] Gibeon District Office: "Verordnung betr. Regelung der Dienstboten-Verhältnisse" ("Ordinance concerning the Regulation of Master-Servant Relationships"), 23 March 1896, NAN ZBU W.IV.A.3. Vol. 2, Sheets 41ea–41fa.

[9] Keetmanshoop District Office to Imperial Governor's Office, Windhoek, 28 August 1896, ibid., Sheets 42aa–42ka.

would be entitled to inspect the pass at any time and it had to be surrendered to the named authority or person at the place of destination. The fact that the authorities could refuse the issue of such a pass for "reasons of security or other good cause" that were not more precisely specified, thereby restricting the Africans' mobility, points to the fact that the idea of controlling the distribution of the indigenous population across the colony was already in the air. The idea of forced labour is implicit in the proposals as well, as any Africans without a pass could be assigned to work for private European employers.[10] Indeed, a proposal by Outjo District Office that a provision should be added to the Ordinance whereby every African arriving in the District was to be furnished with a "metal token to be worn visibly around the neck", brought an additional factor into the discussion that anticipated the provisions of the Native Ordinances of 1907.[11] It was also proposed that any particular distinguishing features of the person concerned should be entered in the pass to facilitate identification, and also details of any punishments that the 'Native' had been subjected to previously, so that the police could impose harsher sanctions in the event of any repetition of an offence.[12]

Ultimately, the colonial authorities were not able to put the Pass Ordinance into effect before the outbreak of the Herero and Nama War. Only in the entirely different political situation after the outbreak of war did some District Offices promulgate local pass regulations. On 18 May 1904, for example, the Swakopmund District Office introduced a general pass requirement by decree,[13] and Keetman-

---

[10] Imperial Governor's Office Windhoek, "Verordnungsentwurf betr. die Paß- und Meldepflicht der Eingeborenen" ("Draft Ordinance concerning Pass and Registration Requirements for Natives"), August 1900, NAN ZBU W.III.K.1. Vol. 1, Sheets 7a–8a. The idea of a pass requirement was not new, however; Leutwein was merely trying to make a practice that was already customary in some districts binding throughout the *Schutzgebiet*. In Gibeon District the issue of a pass for travel outside the tribal territory was already customary: Gibeon District Office to Imperial Governor's Office Windhoek, 30 November 1900, NAN ZBU W.III.B.1. Vol. 1, Sheet 8a. In the Swakopmund District too, "letters of authority" (*Begleitscheine*) had already been issued: Swakopmund District Office to Imperial Governor's Office Windhoek, 5 November 1900, NAN ZBU W.III.B.1. Vol. 1, Sheets 5a–6a.

[11] At the time, however, this proposal apparently went too far for the Governor's Office, as is shown by a large question mark drawn in the margin of the document.

[12] Outjo District Office to Governor's Office Windhoek, 21 December 1900, NAN ZBU W.III.B.1. Vol. 1, Sheet 7a f.

[13] "Bestimmungen, betr. die Paßpflicht der Eingeborenen im Bezirk Swakopmund" ("Provisions concerning the Pass Requirement for Natives in Swakopmund District"), 18 May 1904, NAN ZBU W.III.K.1. Vol. 1, Sheets 53a–55a. See also: Swakopmund District Office to Imperial Governor's Office Windhoek, 8 June 1907, NAN ZBU W.III.A.1. Vol. 1, Sheets 26a–27a.

shoop followed suit on 7 October 1904.[14] Grootfontein District issued a Pass Ordinance on 9 February 1905,[15] Windhoek on 8 November 1905[16] and Karibib on 16 January 1906.[17] Outjo District Office also introduced a pass requirement.[18] Thus even prior to the Native Ordinances of 1907 there were regulations of this type in all Districts except Gibeon, Gobabis, Rehoboth and Okahandja.[19]

The Herero and Nama War then accelerated the development of the Big Brother-type surveillance state and shifted power in the colony in favour of the Germans. Although this development was of crucial importance, at this point a few brief remarks about the war will have to suffice.

The Africans' loss of ownership of what had been their land, which went hand in hand with the arrival of more and more European settlers, the deliberate humiliation of traditional leaders by the representatives of the colonial state, the breakdown of Herero social structures as a result of their being restricted to ever diminishing areas of land and the economic catastrophe of the rinderpest epidemic had all had a serious impact on the internal cohesion of Herero society. In addition, the settlers who were now entering the country in ever greater numbers increasingly conducted themselves as members of a 'master race', sought confrontation rather than coexistence and interfered with the property and in the

---

14 "Bestimmungen, betr. die Paßpflicht der Eingeborenen im Bezirk Keetmanshoop" ("Provisions concerning the Pass Requirement for Natives in Keetmanshoop District"), 7 October 1904, NAN ZBU W.III.K.1. Vol. 1, Sheets 62a–63b. See also: Keetmanshoop District Office to Imperial Governor's Office Windhoek, 10 June 1907, NAN ZBU W.III.A.1. Vol. 1, Sheets 28a–29a.
15 "Bestimmungen, betr. Paßzwang für Eingeborene des Bezirks Grootfontein" ("Provisions concerning Compulsory Passes for Natives in Grootfontein District"), 9 February 1905, NAN ZBU W.III.K.1. Vol. 1, Sheets 92a f.
16 "Bestimmungen, betr. die Paßpflicht der Eingeborenen im Bezirk Windhuk" ("Provisions concerning the Pass Requirement for Natives in Windhoek District") [undated], ibid., Sheets 97a–98a.
17 "Bestimmungen, betr. die Paßpflicht der Eingeborenen im Bezirk Karibib" ("Provisions concerning the Pass Requirement for Natives in Karibib District"), 16 January 1906, ibid., Sheets 101a–103a [effective date: 1 February 1906].
18 Outjo District Office to Imperial Governor's Office Windhoek, 27 May 1907, NAN ZBU W.III.A.1. Vol. 1, Sheets 21a–24a. The Ordinance is undated.
19 In many places, however, the local Pass Ordinances existed only on paper, or else were only implemented to a very limited extent. In Grootfontein, for example, the registration of the Africans soon had to be suspended again because not enough pass discs were available – a shortcoming that proved impossible to remedy until 1907. Grootfontein District Office to Imperial Governor's Office Windhoek, 26 August 1907, NAN ZBU W.III.A.1. Vol. 1, Sheets 69a–70a. In Outjo district too, the regulations could only be successfully implemented to a limited extent, since pass discs had only been issued to those 'Natives' settled in Outjo and to the Swartboois of Fransfontein, people who had already been listed in control registers. Outjo District Office to Imperial Governor's Office Windhoek, 27 May 1907, NAN ZBU W.III.A.1. Vol. 1, Sheets 21a–24a. In Windhoek District too, the Pass Requirement does not appear to have been implemented.

lives of Africans without the traditional African leaders having any chance of putting up effective opposition. The resulting discontent came to a head in 1904, when the Herero, and subsequently the Nama, rose up against the intruders. This was the beginning of a brutal colonial war which lasted until 1908, and which saw the German side overstep the boundary to deliberate genocide.[20] Even if no precise figures are available for the number of victims on the African side, they must certainly have amounted to tens of thousands. In addition, the traditional social and economic order was severely dislocated by flight and displacement. As far as the German administration was concerned, however, the war opened up the opportunity for it to realise its fantasies of control, as the tactical need to show consideration to the African 'tribes' which had previously governed Leutwein's policies no longer applied. The war was thus a catalyst, facilitating the implementation of ideas that had already been in the air in the pre-war period.

The first step towards the legal implementation of a Native Policy after the war took the form of the expropriation of the African population. The "Imperial Ordinance concerning the Sequestration of Native Assets in the Colony of South West Africa" of 26 December 1905 created the formal conditions for such expropriation to take place. It provided for the Governor to be able to sequestrate by decree the "tribal assets" of Africans "who had taken part in hostilities and belligerent acts against the Government, against non-Natives or against other Natives" or had "provided direct or indirect support" for such acts, whereby it was sufficient if only a part of the 'tribe' had participated in the acts concerned.[21] On 23 March 1906 Governor von Lindequist made use of this Ordinance for the first time to sequestrate the "movable and immovable" tribal assets of all Herero north of the Tropic of Capricorn and also of the Swartoobi Nama of Fransfontein and the Topnaar Nama of

---

20 On the war against the Herero and the Nama, see: Jürgen Zimmerer, "Kriegsgefangene im Kolonialkrieg. Der Krieg gegen die Herero und Nama in Deutsch Südwestafrika (1904–1907)", in Rüdiger Overmans, ed., *In der Hand des Feindes. Kriegsgefangenschaft von der Antike bis zum Zweiten Weltkrieg*, Köln 1999, pp. 277–294; Tilman Dedering, "The German-Herero War of 1904. Revisionism of Genocide or Imaginary Historiography?", *Journal of Southern African Studies*, 19 (1993), pp. 80–88; Tilman Dedering, "A Certain Rigorous Treatment of All Parts of the Nation. The Annihilation of the Herero in German South West Africa, 1904", in Mark Levene and Penny Roberts, eds, *The Massacre in History*, New York 1999, pp. 205–222; and Gesine Krüger, *Kriegsbewältigung und Geschichtsbewußtsein. Realität, Deutung und Verarbeitung des deutschen Kolonialkrieges in Namibia 1904 bis 1907*, Göttingen 1999.

21 "Kaiserliche Verordnung, betr. Einziehung des Stammesvermögens der Eingeborenen" ("Imperial Ordinance concerning the Sequestration of Native Assets in the Colony of South West Africa"), 26 December 1905, BArch R 1001/1220, Sheets 65a–66b, "Begründung der Verordnung" ("Grounds for the ordinance"), ibid., Sheets 67a–69a. The Ordinance is reproduced in: DKG, Vol. 9, pp. 284–286.

Sesfontein.²² On 8 May 1907 he repeated the procedure in respect of the Witbooi, Bethanie, Fransman and Veldskoendraer Nama, the Red Nation of Hoachanas and the Bondelswarts including the Swartmodder Nama.²³ For the Bondelswarts and the Stuurmann people, who in November and December 1906 had concluded respectively a submission agreement and a peace treaty with the Germans, the exceptions laid down in those treaties applied,²⁴ but this made no more than a minor difference to the overall extent of the expropriations. As a result, the land ownership situation was fundamentally transformed. All the 'tribal land' in South West Africa, except in Ovamboland and the 'Caprivi Strip' and with the exception of the land belonging to the Rehoboth Basters and the Berseba Nama, was now in German ownership.²⁵ Von Lindequist had almost completely realised his intention of doing away with "the independent existence of all the Native tribes who took part in the rebellion for all time", in order to "prevent any future unrest".²⁶

At the same time, also in the year 1907, the various considerations with regard to codifying into uniform regulations, to apply throughout the *Schutzgebiet*, the pre-war Native Policy that had been manifest in the local district regulations governing employment relations introduced in 1894 and 1896 and already mentioned above, and in the discussions relating to general pass and registration requirements in 1900, were brought together in three Native Ordinances.²⁷ These

---

22 Imperial Governor's Office Windhoek, "Bekanntmachung betr. Einziehung des Stammesvermögens der Herero, Swartbooi- und Topnaar Hottentotten", 23 March 1906, reproduced in: DKG, Vol. 10, pp. 142f. This became legally effective as of 7 August 1905. Imperial Governor's Office Windhoek, "Bekanntmachung, betr. Einziehung des Stammesvermögens der Herero, Swartbooi- und Topnaar Hottentotten", 8 August 1906: DKG, Vol. 10, p. 298.
23 Imperial Governor's Office Windhoek, "Bekanntmachung betr. Einziehung des Stammesvermögens der Witbooi- usw Hottentotten, sowie der Roten Nation und der Bondelszwarts – einschließlich der Swartmodder-Hottentotten", 8 May 1907, reproduced in: DKG, Vol. 11, pp. 233f. The sequestration became legally effective as of 11 September 1907. "Bekanntmachung, Kaiserliches Gouvernement Windhuk, betr. Einziehung des Stammesvermögens der Witbooi- usw. Hottentotten, sowie der Roten Nation und der Bondelszwarts – einschließlich der Swartmodder-Hottentotten", 11 September 1907, reproduced in: DKG, Vol. 11, pp. 370f.
24 Submission Agreement between Lieutenant Colonel von Estorff and the Bondelswart Hottentotts, concluded on 23 December 1906 with the approval of Colonel von Deimling, reproduced in: DKG, Vol. 11, p. 234. Peace negotiations between the German Government and Cornelius Stuurmann, concluded on 21 November 1906, reproduced ibid., p. 235.
25 Gründer, *Geschichte der deutschen Kolonien*, p. 122. Gründer's assessment is essentially correct: there were, however, still some (rare) cases of Africans owning private land.
26 Imperial Governor's Office Windhoek to Colonial Department, 25 April 1906, BArch R 1001/1220, Sheets 131a–134a.
27 Imperial Governor's Office Windhoek: "Verordnung betr. Maßregeln zur Kontrolle der Eingeborenen", 18 August 1907. NAN ZBU W.III.A.1. Vol. 1, Sheets 61a–62b; "Verordnung betr. die Paßpflicht der Eingeborenen", 18 August 1907. Ibid., Sheets 63a–65b; "Verordnung betr. Dienst- und

Control, Pass and Master and Servant Ordinances were an attempt to regulate all areas of the Africans' lives and to give the administration a comprehensive overview with regard to how many and what Africans were present in any given district at any given time, where they lived, whether they were in employment, and if so, where. For this purpose, every African had to be entered in a Native Register. A pass token, to be worn visibly, was intended to ensure that all Africans could be identified unambiguously. Africans who left their place of residence required a travel pass; it was not permitted either to employ them or furnish them with accommodation without such a pass. As Africans were prohibited from owning, without the explicit authorisation of the Governor, the large livestock or riding animals they would have needed to be economically independent, the only possibility that remained for them was to seek employment with Europeans, as they were otherwise in danger of being punished as 'vagrants'. To ensure that the Africans could be better kept under surveillance, and also to provide as efficiently as possible for an adequate supply of labour throughout the colony there was a provision that no more than ten families or individuals could live in any private *werf*, unless special permission was granted. This was designed to ensure an even distribution of the African population. Employment contracts had to be approved by the police, who issued an Employment Logbook that was supposed to include details of the wages paid, the term of the contract and any reasons for termination. This was intended on the one hand to protect the Africans against exploitation by their employers, but on the other hand also to supplement the system of surveillance.

In these Native Ordinances the governmental and administrative utopia of the colonial bureaucracy was made manifest: its supreme goal was to construct a new social order in South West Africa which can be best characterised as a society of racial privilege. The primary role of the Africans in it was to serve as a cheap source of labour; this was perceived by the colonial 'masters' as being imperative for economic development and for the construction of a settler colony. Yet on the German side the Native Ordinances were by no means regarded as being purely measures of subjugation; rather, they were perceived as an essential foundation for the restoration of 'peace and security'. The mere idea of an unregistered and uncontrollable indigenous population that was able to move around freely appeared to the German bureaucracy to be an incalculable threat, a feeling that was heightened after the outbreak of war by traumatic experiences on both

---

Arbeitsverträge mit Eingeborenen", 18 August 1907. Ibid., Sheets 66a–68a; "Runderlaß zu den Verordnungen, betr. die Kontrolle und Paßpflicht der Eingeborenen sowie die Dienst- und Arbeitsverträge mit diesen", 18 August 1907. These are reproduced in: DKG, Vol. 11, pp. 345–357.

sides. Accordingly, the only conceivable way forward – from a German perspective – was to register the Africans and integrate them into a narrowly defined legal system of obligations with only limited rights. The aim was not simply to ensure the uniform treatment of the African population, but to allow the bureaucracy to function at all. As every official action required a legal basis, it was not until the Native Ordinances had been put in place that there was – in the eyes of the officials – any basis at all for everyday dealings with Africans.

As has been shown, the three Native Ordinances represent the remote target point that German policy had had in its sights ever since the creation of the *Schutzgebiet* – a continuity that has been overlooked by academic research until now.[28] It is, however, crucial to an understanding of German colonial rule, or to put it more accurately, of German Native Policy, since it gives rise to a need to reevaluate the position occupied by the War of 1904–1908 within the history of German South West Africa. It does not, at least viewed in terms of the programmatic objectives being pursued by the colonialists, represent that crucial turning point in German colonial history it has always been viewed as in the past. And as a result, the policy of exerting total surveillance and control over the indigenous population, can be seen to have formed the very core of German colonial rule ever since 1894, when von Lindequist first considered how to regulate employment relationships.

Total Surveillance and Control on the Ground

The formulation and subsequent implementation of the Native Ordinances were accompanied by a further expansion of the German administration in the central and southern areas of the *Schutzgebiet*, the so-called Police Zone.[29] As a result, the

---

[28] The division of the history of German South West Africa into three periods proposed by Bley and Drechsler – the establishment of colonial rule up until the outbreak of the war of conquest (1884–1904), the genocidal war (1904–1907) and the post-war period (1907–1914) as the time of a completely new conception of Native Policy – is still predominant in academic writing today. However, neither is Bley's statement true that it is scarcely possible to derive the post-war situation from the initial policy approaches of the pre-war period, nor was there complete stagnation – what Drechsler termed "the peace of the graveyard" – after 1907. Helmut Bley, *Kolonialherrschaft und Sozialstruktur in Deutsch-Südwestafrika 1894–1914*, Hamburg 1968, p. 193; Horst Drechsler, *Südwestafrika unter deutscher Kolonialherrschaft. Der Kampf der Herero und Nama gegen den deutschen Imperialismus 1884–1915*, 2nd edn, Berlin 1984, pp. 221–236.
[29] The northern part of the *Schutzgebiet* was provisionally excluded from German administration in 1906. Imperial Governor's Office Windhoek, "Verordnung, betr. den Verkehr in und nach dem Amboland" ("Ordinance concerning Movements within and to Ovamboland" – the Ovambo-

number of autonomous Districts increased from six to sixteen between the years 1903 and 1914, partly through the carving up of the old large districts and partly through the conversion of former subsidiary districts into autonomous ones.[30] As far as the African population was concerned, the District Offices united the executive, legislative and judicial functions of government. The autonomous Districts were responsible to the Governor's Office in Windhoek, while the various police stations were subordinated to them.

In their executive capacity, the administrative authorities were supported by both the *Landespolizei*, the Territorial Police, and the *Schutztruppe*, the colonial military force. The latter was however primarily responsible for securing the colony against internal and external threats[31] and could therefore only be involved to a limited extent in the day-to-day surveillance of the Africans. Furthermore, a massive reduction in the force's manpower was put into effect immediately after the end of the war, its strength being cut from 3,988 men in the years 1907/08 to 2,431 in 1909 and 1,970 in the year 1912.[32] As a result, the Territorial Police became more and more important.

---

land Ordinance), 25 January 1906, reproduced in: DKG, Vol. 10, pp. 25–27. Imperial Governor's Office Windhoek, "Ausführungsverfügung zur Verordnung, betr. den Verkehr in und nach dem Amboland" ("Implementation Regulations to the Ovamboland Ordinance"), 25 January 1906, reproduced in: DKG, Vol. 10, pp. 27–30. In 1908 the same was done in respect of the Caprivi Strip. Imperial Governor's Office Windhoek, "Verordnung, betr. den Verkehr in und nach dem Caprivizipfel" ("Ordinance concerning Movements within and to the Caprivi Strip"), 16 October 1908, reproduced in: DKG, Vol. 12, pp. 436f. As well as these territories, the areas of Kaokoveld in the north-west and the Kalahari in the border region to the Cape Colony and the Bechuanaland Protectorate were also excluded from the administrative structure. Oskar Hintrager, *Südwestafrika in der deutschen Zeit*, München 1956, pp. 99f. Apart from financial considerations, the key factor was the realisation that enormous military resources would be required to occupy the areas outside the Police Zone.

30 Reichsministerium des Inneren, *Handbuch für das Deutsche Reich 41*, 1914, pp. 403f.

31 This included above all the immediate suppression of any renewed resistance and the defence of the *Schutzgebiet* in the event of war with the British. "Denkschrift über die Möglichkeit einer Verminderung der Schutztruppe für Deutsch-Südwestafrika und einer Verringerung der Ausgaben des Militär-Etats". Heydebreck, Commander of the *Schutztruppe*, to Imperial Colonial Office, 14 July 1912, NAN ZBU classified files IX.B. Vol. 1, Sheets 57a–79b; Theodor Seitz, *Vom Aufstieg und Niederbruch deutscher Kolonialmacht, 3: Die Gouverneursjahre in Südwestafrika*. Karlsruhe 1929, pp. 21f, p. 27.

32 Hintrager, *Südwestafrika in der deutschen Zeit*, p. 122. These figures apply only to German soldiers: the force was supplemented by African auxiliary troops, whose numbers amounted to 635 in 1910. Martti Eirola, *The Ovambogefahr. The Ovamboland Reservation in the Making. Political Responses of the Kingdom of Ondonga to the German Colonial Power 1884–1910*, Rovaniemi 1992, p. 274. In 1913/14 the strength of the force remained stable at 1,967 men.

The origins of the Territorial Police went back to an initiative of Theodor Leutwein's dating from the year 1900; he had seen that there was a need for a force that, unlike the military, was responsible to the civil administration. The proposals made in 1902 for the establishment of a police force separate from the military led to the setting up of the Territorial Police in 1905.[33] Whereas an establishment of 80 officers was envisaged in 1905, already in 1906 this number had been increased to 160. This expansion was all the more important in view of the massive reduction in the size of the military forces after the ending of the State of War on 31 March 1907 and their resulting imminent withdrawal from the places and military posts they had controlled until then. What is more, the introduction of the Native Ordinances, which was planned for August 1907, increased the staffing requirement enormously. This was reflected in the 1907 budget, which provided for the Territorial Police to be strengthened to 720 men.[34] This theoretical strength was, however, never achieved. The Territorial Police reached its maximum strength in 1912, with 569 policemen supplemented by an additional 370 African 'police servants', i.e. auxiliary policemen.[35] While there were a total of 69 police stations scattered across the colony in 1909, 33 of these were staffed by only two policemen and 19 others by only one; only nine stations had three police officers, and only eight had four or five. Although the number of stations had increased to 108 by 1914, staffed by a total of 393 men, the overall strength of the Territorial Police had fallen to 470 men; of these, on average a quarter were either on leave or sick at any given time.[36]

These police stations had to exercise surveillance over vast territories: in some cases the distance between them might be as much as 140 kilometres. And not all the policemen were available to keep check on the African population, since they were also responsible for policing the European community. It was not possible to exercise unbroken surveillance of the African population with the manpower available, especially as a considerable proportion of the population were still refugees or on the run. In addition, no proper infrastructure had yet

---

33 Imperial Governor's Office Windhoek, "Bestimmungen, betr. die Organisation der Landespolizei für das deutsch-südwestafrikanische Schutzgebiet", 1 March 1905, in: DKG, Vol. 9, pp. 64–69. On the history of the Territorial Police, see Hans Rafalski, *Vom Niemandsland zum Ordnungsstaat. Geschichte der ehemaligen Landespolizei für Deutsch-Südwestafrika*, Berlin [n.d.].
34 Rafalski, *Niemandsland*, pp. 56–61.
35 Reichskolonialamt, ed., *Die deutschen Schutzgebiete in Afrika und der Südsee. Amtliche Jahresberichte*, iv (1912/13), Berlin 1914, Report Section, p. 133.
36 Rafalski, *Niemandsland*, pp. 72–90.

been developed, and what there was had been totally disrupted by the war. However, although enormous difficulties ought to have been anticipated, the government planners paid no heed to them. Their self-imposed objective remained comprehensive control.[37]

In order to ensure uniform surveillance throughout the entire colony, it was intended that the registration and control of the indigenous population should follow a procedure developed by Windhoek District Office. Since Windhoek was among the administrative districts with the most developed and best equipped administrative apparatus, a study of that location tells us more about how the government envisaged that the surveillance of the indigenous population would take place in the future than it does about its actual implementation throughout the *Schutzgebiet*:

> As far as Windhoek District is concerned, the intention is to divide it up into individual 'police wards' *(Polizeischaften)*, within which the responsible police officer is to inspect all places where Natives live once a month. Every police ward will be allocated pass tokens with numbers of a particular series, which however is big enough to provide for any later growth in the Native population. This has the advantage that if a Native is stopped and checked it is possible to determine immediately which police ward he belongs to. [...] The Governor's Office will consult with the Commander of the *Schutztruppe* in order to ensure the support of the military authorities in any given area for the implementation of the Native control legislation.
>
> It is intended to prescribe that Native Registers should be kept not only at District Offices, but also at police stations and those military posts that are invested with police powers in respect of the Natives under their supervision. [...]
>
> Every time a Native is entered in the Native Register, enough space should be left for all changes of employer etc. to be entered subsequently. In order to ensure that the registers are always up to date the Natives are to be instructed that any births and deaths and any movements into or away from the area [...] are to be reported to the responsible police or military post immediately.
>
> It is considered by this office to be highly desirable that police station superintendents should submit monthly reports to their superior authorities on any changes in the numbers of Natives living in their areas, so that information is available at any time on the number and distribution of Native workers.[38]

---

37 Even the responses of the individual district heads to the Native Ordinances, written between May and August, largely remained silent on these issues. For an extensive analysis of the responses of the District Officers to the Native Ordinances see Zimmerer, *Deutsche Herrschaft über Afrikaner*, pp. 96–106 [English edition: *German Rule, African Subjects*, New York 2021].
38 Imperial Governor's Office Windhoek, "Rundschreiben an die Bezirks- und Distriktsämter", 13 May 1907. NAN ZBU W.III.A.1. Vol. 1, Sheets 15a–18a.

A sophisticated reporting system was designed to ensure that information from the individual Native Registers was collated and forwarded to the next higher level of the administration in each case, thereby furnishing the Governor's Office in Windhoek with a comprehensive picture of how the African population was distributed. To achieve this, the individual police stations were to report monthly or even weekly[39] to their local district offices, which in turn passed the information on to the autonomous district offices on a quarterly basis. These offices then summarised the returns and submitted them to the Governor's Office in Windhoek every six months.[40]

In order to obtain a complete overview of the African population, many of whom were employed on remote farms, the staff of the local police stations were to carry out patrols that took in these locations at regular short intervals – the intended frequency being once a month.[41] In addition to the inspections of "private *werfs*" [Herero settlements], the purpose of which was apparently only to allow the police to receive a report from the *werf* foreman, the police undertook "searches at three to six monthly intervals in order to identify any Africans who are unemployed or have run away from their places of work".[42] But apart from 'merely' searching for Africans, these checks also served the purpose of creating a climate of fear and evoking a feeling of total surveillance:

> The Natives in Swakopmund itself are continually kept under the impression, by frequent police inspections and unannounced checks of the werfs, that they are under constant observation as soon as they do anything to violate the Ordinances they are familiar with [the three Native Ordinances of 1907].
>
> For this reason it is no seldom occurrence that Natives themselves require their employers to register them with the police immediately, and will not take up their employment until they are in possession of the pass token or the Employment Logbook.[43]

Thus this feeling of being under constant observation had a profound impact on the African population. They knew the obligations imposed on them by the Native Ordinances, and due to the threat of punishment hanging over them they even

---

39 Lüderitzbucht District Office to Imperial Governor's Office Windhoek, 12 July 1907, ibid., Sheets 33a–36a.
40 Imperial Governor's Office Windhoek, "Runderlaß zu den Verordnungen, betr. die Kontrolle und Paßpflicht der Eingeborenen sowie die Dienst- und Arbeitsverträge mit diesen", 18 August 1907, reproduced in: DKG, Vol. 11, pp. 352–357.
41 Imperial Governor's Office Windhoek, "Rundschreiben an die Bezirks- und Distriktsämter", 13 May 1907, NAN ZBU W.III.A.1. Vol. 1, Sheets 15a–18a.
42 Windhoek District Office to Imperial Governor's Office Windhoek, 25 November 1908, NAN ZBU W.III.A.3, Vol. 1, Sheets 60a–69a.
43 Swakopmund District Office to Imperial Governor's Office Windhoek, 24 November 1908, ibid., Sheets 47a–51a.

insisted themselves that their employers should observe the regulations. But this also prepared the way for the pass token and the Employment Logbook to become a part of their own identity, thus leading to an internalisation of the identity attributes ascribed to them by the Germans, and in the case of the pass token reducing every individual person to a mere number.

No detailed research has yet been carried out regarding the consequences for the African population of this policy of instilling fear. What is certain is that the forcible intervention in the individual and the collective freedom of the Africans set in motion a process of social disciplining that brought about fundamental changes among the indigenous population. Even though a process of reconstruction did take place within African society after the war, this cannot disguise the fact that every African living in the centre or the south of South West Africa was confronted with a German administration that attempted to regulate the smallest detail of his or her existence. Of course there was resistance; and it was possible for the Africans to put themselves beyond the reach of the control mechanisms or to claim the rights that were also laid down for them in the Native Ordinances. However, when compared to a lifestyle that was self-determined or regulated only by the traditions of their own society, this was no more than a shadow of their former freedom. Secret attempts to revive their own traditions, attempts to flee or to exploit the protective mechanisms enshrined in Native Law were no more than pale substitutes for the pre-colonial conditions.[44] That independent African social structures did survive despite this difficult situation was facilitated by the fact that it proved impossible for the Germans to realise their governmental and administrative utopia in a perfect Big Brother state. This was due not only to the resistance exercised by the Africans, but also, as will be shown below, to the fact that the German administration was far removed from functioning perfectly. Moreover, some elements in the European population withheld the cooperation with the authorities that was imperative if such a system of control was to operate successfully.

Negligent Officials and Uncooperative Settlers

Even the first step, that of registering the Africans, began with a logistical disaster. In the autumn of 1907 there were no adequate quantities of pass tokens, registers, travel passes or Employment Logbooks available. When the additional materials

---

44 On this process of reconstruction in Herero society, see Krüger, *Kriegbewältigung*, pp. 123–194.

that were then ordered finally arrived in the colony in June 1908, it did not take long to find out that there were still far too few of them to meet even the District Offices' most urgent requirements.[45] At the same time, the officials were not particularly well motivated to implement the provisions of the Ordinances, which after all meant considerably more work for them. This could clearly be seen, for example, in the way reports were frequently submitted late. The Governor's Office was compelled to remind the District Offices time and time again of the importance of these reports, which were essential to the whole system of surveillance and control of the African population.[46] Reproved in such a manner, some of the District Officers admitted that they were overburdened with the implementation of the Ordinances, since the statistical details that were called for represented "a large amount of additional work" that would "keep a whole multitude of officials busy".[47] No such additional manpower was available, however. The officials also had to admit that communication between themselves and the police stations as the actual executive organs was not working, so that they had not received the necessary data from them.[48] Thus it became clear that it would not be possible for the clear overview of the situation of the Africans that the Native Ordinances were supposed to provide to be obtained in this way.

In some cases, the District Officers simply did not implement certain provisions of the Native Ordinances, even if it is difficult to make any general assessment of this factor since the officials concerned naturally did not leave any accounts of their own non-fulfilment of their duties on file. Only when the Governor's Office, for whatever reason, began to ask specific questions were the failings revealed. One such instance occurred in 1912 when the Governor's Office, in view of the lack of 'success' in mobilising workers, set about checking the implementation of Sec. 7 of the Control Ordinance (which made it necessary to obtain approval for more than ten families to live in a private *werf*) and obtaining detailed reports on the extent to which this had been enforced.[49] Okahandja District Office was caught completely off its guard and had to admit that this provision "has not been implemented here, since the big enterprises and farm operations have had

---

[45] Imperial Governor's Office Windhoek, "Rundschreiben an die Bezirks- und Distriktsämter", June 1908, NAN ZBU W.III.B.3. Vol. 1, Sheet 22a–23a.
[46] Imperial Governor's Office Windhoek, "Rundschreiben an die Bezirks- und Distriktsämter außer Lüderitzbucht und Zesfontein", 17 October 1908, NAN ZBU W.III.A.3. Vol. 1, Sheet 24a.
[47] Keetmanshoop District Office to Imperial Governor's Office Windhoek, 24 May 1909, ibid., Sheets 106a–107a.
[48] Windhoek District Office to Imperial Governor's Office Windhoek, 22 October 1908, ibid., Sheet 25a.
[49] Circulated Instruction, Imperial Governor's Office Windhoek, 20 January 1912, NAN ZBU W.III.B.4. Vol. 1, Sheet 2a.

more than ten families settled with them for many years already". In order to remedy this failure the District Officer announced that "a strict inspection" would be carried out, but was not in a position to say which enterprises or farms would be subjected to it. He promised to submit the results of the inquiries that were immediately ordered at a later date.[50] Two months later he then reported that he had instructed eleven farms "to immediately obtain the required authorisation".[51] Zealous declarations that particularly strict and rigorous control was now to be exercised were clearly intended to conceal earlier sins of omission. The District Officer of Maltahöhe tried to talk himself out of his embarrassing position by declaring that "in the few cases in this district where there are more than ten Native families living on a farm or other location, tacit authorisation has been granted". He further attempted to justify himself by stating that no case was known "in which an employer has kept more Natives on his farm than are required to meet his most urgent requirements".[52] In doing so he appears to have overlooked the fact that the objective of the Control Ordinance had been precisely to avoid allowing employers to decide on the number of their workers themselves.

However, an even more serious factor than this negligent behaviour on the part of the officials was the refusal of the European population to cooperate. They rated their own economic interests higher than the requirements of the control system, while at the same time loudly proclaiming how necessary that system was whenever they thought anybody might be listening. Just when the administration was attempting to use propaganda and to create a climate of fear in order to discipline the indigenous population, to the extent that they "as a general rule anxiously make every effort to always have their pass tags with them", their employers were actually inciting them to do just the opposite: in order to make it impossible for African servants to run away, "it was no rare occurrence" for employers to infringe the Ordinances by taking their pass tags off them and "so preventing them from leaving their service", as Windhoek District Office complained.[53] While the authorities were disseminating propaganda in an attempt to free the pass tokens and travel passes from the stigma of being instruments of repression, it was precisely as such that the settlers were using them. The Windhoek District Officer therefore

---

[50] Okahandja District Office to Imperial Governor's Office Windhoek, 13 February 1912, ibid., Sheet 6a.
[51] Okahandja District Office to Imperial Governor's Office Windhoek, 10 April 1912, ibid., Sheets 17a–18b.
[52] Maltahöhe District Office to Imperial Governor's Office Windhoek, 17 February 1912, ibid., Sheet 11a.
[53] Windhoek District Office to Imperial Governor's Office Windhoek, 25 November 1908, NAN ZBU W.III.A.3. Vol. 1, Sheets 60a–69a.

demanded that those Europeans who acted in this way should be punished, and complained that the European population was affording insufficient assistance, and that only reluctantly, to the implementation of the provisions on pass tokens and travel passes, and moreover was displaying a lack of interest in the "concerns of the Natives", as was "noticeable in particular in the way they perform those duties imposed on private individuals by the present Ordinance".[54]

The severe shortage of labour also led to individual employers abusing the privileges conferred on them by the Native Ordinances to get hold of workers illegally. Ironically enough, of all the provisions of the Pass Ordinance it was Sec. 4, under which Africans did not need a travel pass if they were travelling in the company of Europeans, which left a gap in the control system that was exploited by unscrupulous Europeans. District Officer Schenke of Swakopmund, for example, complained to the Governor's Office about cases in which

> [...] Native women have been abducted by white men without the knowledge of their masters. Similarly, it is often the case that Natives are recruited here by whites and travel to another place in their company without a travel pass. In such cases the police at the place of destination do not know whether the Natives who arrive without travel passes have terminated their previous employment in a proper manner or not, and in order to avoid any further repercussions have no option but to believe what the accompanying whites tell them.[55]

These Africans had slipped through a hole in the surveillance net, because even in respect of their identities the authorities had no other choice but to believe what they or the Europeans accompanying them said.

It was however the case that the ever more serious labour shortage had from the beginning not only led to such infringements of the law on the part of some Europeans, but also generated resentment among employers against the registration requirement. It cost working time, and some employers were apparently not prepared to pay this price for the implementation of the Control and Pass Ordinances. Even government employees joined in the protests. On 7 June 1907, for example, the Department of Works in Windhoek filed a complaint with the Governor's Office against the District Office there, which on the morning of that day, without any prior notice, had kept twenty-seven Africans who worked there away from work in order to register them. As a result they had come to work

---

54 Ibid.
55 Swakopmund District Office to Imperial Governor's Office Windhoek, 24 November 1908, ibid., Sheets 47a–51a.

an hour late, and the Department of Works was afraid that the enterprises to which it supplied workers would claim compensation for the lost working time.[56]

In this way the control measures came into conflict with the efforts of entrepreneurs to exploit every minute of the Africans' working time. The District Office's argument in its own defence that "such checks in the *werfs* occur only very rarely, and the Department of Works [could] easily put up with such a minor disruption of its operations" did not gain the sympathy of everybody in the Governor's Office, as a note written in the margin of the document testifies: "27 men means 27 working hours. I don't call that a minor disruption."[57]

The lack of a willingness to cooperate on the part of European employers was particularly apparent in relation to the Master and Servant Ordinance. The information contained in the Employment Logbook represented an important link in the unbroken chain of surveillance measures, since it was only this that enabled the Administration to obtain a complete overview of employment relationships. However, since the Ordinance provided for at least some of the basic rights of the African workers in relation to their employers to be explained to them when the Employment Logbook was issued, and some of the crucial conditions of the employment contract, such as its term and the amount and type of remuneration, were required to be set out in it in writing, it was boycotted by the employers. They agitated against the prescribed measures, and the overwhelming majority of them evaded the logbook requirement by avoiding the conclusion of employment contracts with a term of more than one month, for which a logbook was mandatory. "The reason is to be found in the fact that when the Native is issued with his Employment Logbook the police are required to explain not only his duties but also his rights to him. This point is not to the liking of many farmers", Gobabis District Office reported.[58] In Keetmanshoop,[59] Lüderitzbucht,[60] Karibib[61]

---

[56] Windhoek Department of Works to Imperial Governor's Office Windhoek, 7 June 1907, NAN ZBU W.III.B.2. Vol. 1, Sheet 5a.
[57] Ibid.
[58] Gobabis District Office to Imperial Governor's Office Windhoek, 31 October 1908, NAN ZBU W.III.A.3. Vol. 1, Sheet 42a.
[59] Keetmanshoop District Office to Imperial Governor's Office Windhoek, 24 May 1909, ibid., Sheets 106a–107a.
[60] Lüderitzbucht District Office to Imperial Governor's Office Windhoek, 1 July 1908, ibid., Sheets 7a–23a.
[61] Karibib District Office to Imperial Governor's Office Windhoek, 26 November 1908, ibid., Sheets 52a–59a.

and Bethanie[62] things were much the same.[63] In Gibeon, for example, only ninety-six of the 1,768 Africans employed there in August 1908 had an employment contract with a term of more than one month.[64] This was a situation in which no improvement was noticeable anywhere in the territory over the following years. Thus it was the case that far from displaying the identity of interests as between the bureaucracy and the settlers that is so often invoked,[65] the latter not only held out against the implementation of a minimum degree of protection for African workers, but also threw spanners into the works of the entire control system.

Africans on the Run; Inadequate Identification

Right from the start, the Native Ordinances had aimed to encompass not merely those Africans living in larger centres of population, those who were prisoners of war and those who were employed by Europeans, but all Africans living in the *Schutzgebiet*, including "Herero, Berg Damara and Bushmen living wild in the mountains, on the *veld* and in the bush".[66] Especially after the Herero and Nama War, the existence of thousands of refugees made this appear to be one of the most urgent tasks facing the Administration. However, the provisions of the Native Ordinances did not offer any satisfactory way of resolving this situation. In 1911, therefore, the Governor's Office had renewed recourse to a procedure that had already been practised during the war, and proposed the setting up of collection points:

> In order to get the Natives who are still wandering around in the *veld* to take up a settled existence and to register themselves, it appears necessary to send out police patrols to collect these Natives up again and bring them to collection points.

---

[62] Bethanie District Office to Imperial Governor's Office Windhoek, 10 January 1910, ibid., Sheets 131a–133a.
[63] Only Grootfontein District Office reported that it was the Master and Servant Ordinance that "had best proved itself by a long chalk", since both sides had recognised the advantages accruing to them from it. Grootfontein District Office to Imperial Governor's Office Windhoek, 24 October 1908, ibid., Sheets 43a–44a.
[64] Gibeon District Office to Imperial Governor's Office Windhoek, 23 October 1908, ibid., Sheets 33a–34b.
[65] This identity of interests is suggested by Drechsler in his chapter on the period after the Herero and Nama War, when he writes in a generalised way of "German imperialism" having turned the Africans into forced labourers. See e.g. Drechsler, *Südwestafrika unter deutscher Kolonialherrschaft*, pp. 221f.
[66] Grootfontein District Office to Imperial Governor's Office Windhoek, 26 August 1907, NAN ZBU W.III.A.1. Vol. 1, Sheets 69a–70a.

> At these collection points, which would be best located close to a police station and must be under the supervision of a police officer, these Natives should construct their *werf* under the direction of a foreman and be assigned to farmers as workers should there be any demand.[67]

This proposal already in itself bears witness to a realisation, gradually taking shape, that the fugitives could not be tracked down through force alone. This impression is confirmed by the responses of various District Officers to the proposal. They were disillusioned by the success, or lack of it, of the Native Ordinances, but were divided about how to proceed further. Windhoek District Office, for example, feared that the provision of free meals would even create an incentive for other Africans to run away from their places of work:

> If they were now to be accommodated at a collection point and given food at the State's expense, then no doubt they would have nothing against this in principle. Because to not work and nevertheless be given food is something that suits the Natives fine. [...] The Natives run away from their masters, throw away their pass tags, move away noiselessly into a different District and present themselves at the assembly point there as having been living out on the *veld* since the war.[68]

The fact that Grootfontein District Office suggested the exact opposite, since the view there was that among the San in particular the "thirst for freedom [...] is unconquerable", and that they could only be attracted to a settled existence by the lure of free rations and above all of tobacco,[69] is a clear indication that the District Officers were increasingly coming to feel themselves to be at their wits' end.

It was certainly true that the many inaccessible places of refuge could not be systematically and permanently kept under surveillance either by the police or by the military. Although the District Offices repeatedly reported that Africans had been found and brought in, such 'successes' occurred more or less by chance, as the District Officer of Karibib openly admitted:

> In this District, however – and predominantly, as has already repeatedly been reported elsewhere, in the thinly populated mountainous and inaccessible areas in the south-west of the District – there are indeed individual Natives and occasionally also smallish bands of vagrant Natives wandering around in the *veld*. But these are almost exclusively runaway *Bambusen* [African army servants] or workers who are all to a greater or lesser extent accused

---

[67] Imperial Governor's Office Windhoek, Circulated Instruction to District Offices and Police Stations, 26 January 1911, NAN ZBU W.III.B.5. Vol. 1, Sheets 8a f.
[68] Windhoek District Office to Imperial Governor's Office Windhoek, 14 February 1911, ibid., Sheets 9a–10a.
[69] Grootfontein District Office to Imperial Governor's Office Windhoek, 16 February 1911, ibid., Sheet 12a.

of having committed some offence or other and therefore will not give themselves up voluntarily under any circumstances. How extraordinarily difficult it is to lay hands on them has been demonstrated by numerous mounted patrols, some of them patrols of this District's police, some of them strong combined patrols of this and the adjoining Districts, most of which however did not produce any results.[70]

The Africans were obviously taking advantage of the division of the *Schutzgebiet* into administrative areas, and were "almost always to be found close to the District boundaries, so that if they are pursued they can vanish into the neighbouring District".[71] Much the same situation prevailed on the external borders of the colony as well, the borders with British territory having already proved porous during the 1905–07 guerrilla war.

If the Native Commissioner in the Windhoek administration, Kurt Streitwolf, nevertheless called for a stepping up of the number of mounted patrols by the military, whose task it would be to 'clean up' the *sandveld*, the open arid area where the greater part of the free Africans were presumed to be holding out most of the time, this amounted to an involuntary admission that the previous efforts to exercise control and surveillance over the Africans had failed. Prone though he was to come out with statements such as "The more ruthlessly we proceed against the Natives out in the *veld*, the more successful we will be. Not only will we gain hundreds of workers, but we will also put an end to the desertions by Natives who are already working",[72] these could not conceal the fact that the Native Ordinances were not fulfilling their primary purpose of preventing the continued existence of an uncontrolled African population and the desertion of their workplaces by urgently needed workers.

How wrong Streitwolf was in his forecast that a policy of ruthless severity would serve to stem the flight of the Africans is demonstrated by the course taken by the debate on how to control the Africans in the years 1912 and 1913: it became more and more extreme in particular with regard to the matter of how Africans were to be identified, which right from the beginning had been one of the main obstacles to implementing the Ordinances. As early as March 1911, as a result of the numerous complaints he had received, Governor Theodor Seitz had to admit that "the identification of the Natives is made extraordinarily difficult by

---

70 Karibib District Office to Imperial Governor's Office Windhoek, 15 February 1911, ibid., Sheets 11a f.
71 Okahandja District Office to Imperial Governor's Office Windhoek, 8 March 1911, ibid., Sheets 18a f.
72 Imperial Governor's Office Windhoek, Dept. F (Native Affairs) to Governor, 6 May 1911, ibid., Sheets 26a–27b.

arbitrary changes of name".[73] This had been preceded by a complaint from Pastor Johannes Olpp, the head of the Rhenish Mission in South West Africa, that "the Natives have a penchant for giving themselves additional names, which is further reinforced by the fact that masters too often confer new names on their servants. This makes it very difficult, and in some cases impossible, to keep track of who is who."[74] The solution proposed in response by a clerical officer in the Governor's Office named von Schwerin testifies unambiguously to the desperate situation of the control measures introduced with such great enthusiasm in 1907:

> For this reason, a name register for Natives is now to be set up at the District Offices, which every Native in the District is to be entered in and which is to be kept constantly up to date. In the case of unbaptised Natives, the surname and first name are to be entered; in the case of baptised Natives, the surname and the Christian name given at baptism. The Natives should be specially instructed at the time when this entry is made that from that time on it is forbidden for them to use any other name. A penalty must be laid down for deliberately using a false name.[75]

Since these very measures had already been provided for in the Control Ordinance of 1907, von Schwerin was basically demanding that the registration of the African population should be begun all over again. Thus precisely the lack of respect for the individuality and the personality of the Africans on the part of European employers, who were both able to give their workers whatever names they liked and also to change those names arbitrarily, proved to be a serious factor detracting from the functionality of the control system. Olpp himself now gave more concrete details of what was happening: it was often the case that employers who had several servants with the same name would summarily change their names, not infrequently simply because the employer did not like the worker's actual name, or because he thought it was too long.[76]

Olpp's complaints were apparently justified, for Governor Seitz saw a need for action:

> I therefore [because of the complaints of inadequate identification] earnestly desire that all means should be applied to ensure that the Native retains the name he has once taken, and furthermore that the master should not simply give his Native some other name. If the master has several Natives with the same name, then he would be well advised to add a number

---

73 Imperial Governor's Office Windhoek, Circulated Instruction to District Offices, 29 March 1911, NAN ZBU W.III.B.1. Vol. 1, Sheet 26a.
74 This is how the clerical officer von Schwerin reported Olpp's complaint. Imperial Governor's Office Windhoek, internal memorandum, 24 January 1911, ibid., Sheets 21a–22b.
75 Imperial Governor's Office Windhoek, internal memorandum of von Schwerin's, 24 January 1911, ibid.
76 Pastor Olpp to Imperial Governor's Office Windhoek, 13 March 1911, ibid., Sheets 24a f.

to the name in order to distinguish them. In the Native Registers the Native's own name and the name of his father is always to be noted in addition to the number of the pass token, so that the custom of using family names as surnames will gradually become established among the Natives.[77]

In this respect as well, it was the behaviour of the European employers that undermined the effectiveness of administrative control. Although they themselves were the ones largely to blame for the fact that measures to 'control' the African population were no more than partly successful, they refused to find any fault in their own conduct, but instead merely applied themselves to raising demands for ever stricter measures. These demands not only express the colonisers' contempt for their fellow human beings, but are also indicative of the ineffectiveness of the policies pursued until then.

Facing increasing pressure from public opinion, the Administration decided to make the control system even stricter. In April 1912 the Governor's Office therefore recommended that "every Native who is found without a pass token is to be punished for contravening the Pass Ordinance".[78] This was obviously intended to prevent Africans who had run away from their places of work from talking themselves out of the situation by claiming never to have been registered. On 29 March 1912 the Governor's Office then circulated to all District Offices an "Instruction for Undertaking Physical Descriptions", and again ordered on 25 June 1912: "On all official identity documents, passes etc. for Natives, the holder's right thumbprint is always to be impressed, so that identification is possible."[79] Thus five years after the introduction of the pass requirement it was at last becoming generally recognised that this was the only way "to provide for the certain identification of a person", since the "easily exchangeable pass token does not ensure this."[80] However, the farmers' representatives were far from convinced that this measure would be successful, and in the months that followed the Farmers' Associa-

---

77 As an example, Seitz gave "Isaak (son of) Christian (i.e. Christiansen)". Imperial Governor's Office Windhoek, Circulated Order to District Offices, 29 March 1911, NAN ZBU W.III.B.1. Vol. 1, Sheet 26a.
78 Imperial Governor's Office Windhoek to Outjo District Office, 9 April 1912, NAN ZBU W.III.B.1. Vol. 1, Sheet 30a.
79 Imperial Governor's Office Windhoek, Circulated Instruction to District Offices, 25 June 1912, ibid., Sheet 34a et seq. This contains the reference to the Instruction of 29 March 1912. Why the Instruction had to be repeated is not known.
80 Ibid.

tions of Waterberg,[81] Gobabis[82] and Okahandja demanded that "Natives who display a propensity to run away should be identified by a tattoo".[83] They justified this by insisting that it was the only way in which effective control would be possible, since "as has been highlighted in the press on various occasions, runaways throw their pass tokens away and if captured claim never to have worked for a farmer".[84] The Administration in Windhoek rejected this measure, however, pointing out that no colonial nation made use of such methods. In addition, it was feared that it would "stir up great unease among the Natives and be met with great resistance", and that "the implementation of this measure would be exploited at home by elements hostile to colonialism to justify wild agitation".[85]

The farmers refused to be placated, however, and took the matter up repeatedly in the Territorial Council. Since "the pass requirement for Natives that has existed up until now has proved unsuccessful" they demanded not only tattooing but also "in order to improve surveillance, a strict requirement for registration of residence and a poll tax".[86] The Governor remained unyielding in the matter of tattooing, but promised at least to consider issuing an Ordinance concerning a requirement for Africans to register their places of residence;[87] however, this never seems to have reached the stage of implementation.

Six years after the promulgation of the Native Ordinances, the Colonial Government was practically at a loss with regard to how it might be possible to prevent Africans from deserting their workplaces and how to track down those who were in hiding. On the one hand, the labour shortage demanded that recruiting should be more comprehensive; but on the other hand, the Colonial Government could not bring itself to adopt all too barbarous methods. The only thing that was certain was there was no way in which watertight surveillance of the Africans could be achieved with the control measures introduced in 1907. The outbreak of

---

[81] Waterberg Farmers' Association to Imperial Governor's Office Windhoek, 2 February 1913, ibid., Sheet 37a.
[82] Gobabis Farmers' Association to Imperial Governor's O Windhoek, 9 February 1913, ibid., Sheet 39a.
[83] Okahandja Agricultural Association to Imperial Governor's Office Windhoek, 16 December 1912, ibid., Sheet 35a.
[84] Gobabis Farmers' Association to Imperial Governor's Office Windhoek, 9 February 1913, ibid., Sheet 39a.
[85] This reasoning is that of Outjo District Office. That these remarks also reflected the opinion of the Colonial Government can be deduced from the comment "very true" in the margin. Outjo District Office to Imperial Governor's Office Windhoek, 4 March 1913, ibid., Sheet 29a.
[86] Grootfontein Farmers' Association to Territorial Council, 1 September 1913, ibid., Sheet 41a.
[87] Imperial Governor's Office Windhoek to Grootfontein Farmers' Association, 24 November 1913, ibid., Sheet 42a. A local registration ordinance had been in effect in Windhoek District since 1913.

the First World War in 1914 and the surrender of German South West Africa a year later meant that any further planning was in vain.

Conclusion

When one contemplates the development of the 'total' surveillance and control of the indigenous population, the thing that strikes one is the enormous gap between the supposedly binding legal framework and the reality, between the aspirations of the rulers and the stark limitations on the possibility of actually implementing them. From the very outset, German Native Policy was geared towards the creation of a 'model' colonial state best characterised as a society of racial privilege. The African population was assigned the role of a pool of cheap labour which simply needed to be comprehensively mobilised and efficiently deployed in the colonial economy. If this aim was to be realised, it was essential that the Africans should be comprehensively registered and subjected to a system of continuous control.

Native Law was no more than the tool by which the programme of colonial policy was implemented. It did not codify African common law, but rather served to impose European ideas of rulership or domination on the Africans in their daily lives. At the same time, it was only through these legal instruments that the actions of state officials were legitimised and a basis established for the uniform treatment of the African population in all districts of the Police Zone and for the proper functioning of the bureaucratic state administration.

In view of the inadequate human resources that were available and the vast area covered by the colony, however, this goal was illusory from the very outset, a mere expression of the utopian nature of German colonial policy. Although the early years of German colonial rule were much influenced by pragmatic considerations concerning how to deal with Africans who were far superior both numerically and in military terms, the German administration was at the same time engaged in setting up a legal and administrative framework that would enable this colonial policy programme to be implemented. Even at the time when it was still de facto necessary for Governor Leutwein to enter into agreements with African leaders in order to secure the very survival of German colonial rule, he and his administrative staff were already drafting regulations that went far beyond mere survival and anticipated the three Native Ordinances of 1907 that were the core of German Native Policy. The German victory in the Herero and Nama War, as a result of which the Herero and Nama were eliminated as factors in the power politics of the colony, appeared to provide the opportunity to implement these policies. But even then, their seamless implementation still proved impossible. The realisation of a perfect Big Brother state with total surveillance and control failed – due to the negligence of the Administration, the lack of sufficient willingness to cooperate among the European population, the sheer vastness of the country, and the resistance of the Africans.

However, even this incomplete realisation of the German governmental and administrative utopia brought about a radical change in the living conditions of the indigenous population; a change which meant that by the end of German colonial rule economic and social conditions in the colony had been utterly transformed. The repercussions of this are still being felt today.

Germany's Racial State in Africa: Order, Development and Segregation in German South West Africa (1884–1915)

Like European colonialism in general, German colonialism in particular continues to have about it a whiff of the olde-worlde, the quaint, the exotic and the faraway. For most Germans, terms like 'Africa', 'Natives' or 'colonies' invoke images of a European civilising mission, of self-sacrificing missionaries, bold conquerors and fearless explorers. Where the topic is 'colonial society', it is practically only 'White' society that is meant; and where this mental disposition prevails the African exists only as the object of the 'civilising' task to be performed by the 'White man'. All of this applies especially to Namibia, the only one of the former German colonies, or *Schutzgebiete* as they were officially called, that even today is home to a German-speaking minority which is more than insignificant in numbers. Tourism is booming there, and many people book a holiday in this southern African country precisely because it is still possible to use German there when one goes shopping or orders a meal in a restaurant. Of the colonial crimes that were committed there in the name of Germany, the genocide against the Herero and the Nama is the only one that is remembered – and even that has been the case only since 2004. The racism that the German colonial administration pursued in everyday life has, by contrast, been completely forgotten, even though it made German South West Africa an important precursor not only of the later apartheid regime in South Africa, but also of the racial policies of the Third Reich.[1]

An essential trait of modern colonialism, especially settler colonialism, is the binary distinction between the rulers and the ruled, the colonisers and the colonised. A certain territory was to be settled, regardless of the fact that there were

---

[1] On racial policies in German South West Africa in general, see Jürgen Zimmerer, *Deutsche Herrschaft über Afrikaner. Staatlicher Machtanspruch und Wirklichkeit im kolonialen Namibia*, 3rd edn, Hamburg 2004, pp. 94–109 [English edition: *German Rule, African Subjects. State Aspirations and the Reality of Power in Colonial Namibia*, New York 2021]. I have considered the relationship between the society of racial privilege in South West Africa and the Nazi policy of domination in: Jürgen Zimmerer, "Von Windhuk nach Warschau: Die rassische Privilegiengesellschaft in Deutsch-Südwestafrika – ein Modell mit Zukunft?", in Frank Becker, ed., *Rassenmischehen – Mischlinge – Rassentrennung. Zur Politik der Rasse im deutschen Kaiserreich*, Stuttgart 2004, pp. 97–123 (English version: "From Windhoek to Warsaw: The Society of Racial Privilege in German South West Africa – a Model with a Future?", pp. 201–229 in this book). Henning Melber was also among the first scholars to point out the relationship between the apartheid regime and Nazism: see Henning Melber, "Kontinuitäten totaler Herrschaft. Völkermord und Apartheid in Deutsch-Südwestafrika", *Jahrbuch für Antisemitismusforschung*, 1 (1992), pp. 91–116.

Open Access. © 2024 the author(s), published by De Gruyter. This work is licensed under the Creative Commons Attribution 4.0 International License.
https://doi.org/10.1515/9783110754513-005

people already living there. These were to be subjugated, displaced, and in some cases even exterminated. This was motivated and even ideologically justified through racism, the division of people into 'higher races', destined to rule, and 'lower races', destined to be subject to them. At the lowest end of this scale were groups that were considered 'doomed races' (having been left behind by 'cultural evolution' and so being seen by the self-proclaimed more advanced 'races' as being no longer viable in the modern world), who were predestined to perish, or rather, who were to be deliberately murdered.[2] Even in those cases where the objective was not mass murder, but the integration of the indigenous population into the colonial economy as cheap labour (cases where the 'Natives' were to be 'educated to work'), there was never any attempt to create a partnership on a basis of equality as between the existing population and the newly arrived colonists. German South West Africa is the best example of this in the German colonial empire, as it was the first attempt to establish a 'racial state', i.e. to construct the colonial community on the basis of 'racial' affiliation as the colonialists saw it.

The Founding of German South West Africa

Germany had made its entrance onto the stage of formal colonial rule very late; for a long time it lacked the framework of a strong central state necessary for a policy of imperial expansion.[3] The establishment of the German Empire served to

---

[2] I have discussed the connection between colonialism and extermination extensively in Jürgen Zimmerer, "Kolonialer Genozid? Vom Nutzen und Nachteil einer historischen Kategorie für eine Globalgeschichte des Völkermordes", in Dominik J. Schaller, Boyadjian Rupen, Hanno Scholtz and Vivianne Berg, eds, *Enteignet-Vertrieben-Ermordet. Beiträge zur Genozidforschung*, Zürich 2004, pp. 109–128. (English version: "Colonial Genocide? On the Use and Abuse of a Historical Category for Global History", pp. 175–197 in this book); and Jürgen Zimmerer, "Holocaust und Kolonialismus. Beitrag zu einer Archäologie des genozidalen Gedankens", *Zeitschrift für Geschichtswissenschaft*, 51/12 2003, pp. 1098–1119 (English version: "Colonialism and the Holocaust: Towards an Archaeology of Genocide", pp. 125–153 in this book). On colonial racism and the colonial racial hierarchy, see also Russell McGregor, *Imagined Destinies. Aboriginal Australians and the Doomed Race Theory, 1880–1939*, Victoria 1997; Saul Dubow, *Scientific Racism in Modern South Africa*, Cambridge 1995.

[3] Colonialism as a mental disposition and an enthusiasm for colonialism had however both enjoyed a relatively long history in Germany. For an overview, see Sebastian Conrad, "Doppelte Marginalisierung. Plädoyer für eine transnationale Perspektive auf die deutsche Geschichte", *Geschichte und Gesellschaft*, 28 (2002), pp. 145–169; Andreas Eckert and Albert Wirz, "Wir nicht, die Anderen auch. Deutschland und der Kolonialismus", in Sebastian Conrad and Shalini Randeria, eds, *Jenseits des Eurozentrismus. Postkoloniale Perspektiven in den Geschichts- und Kulturwissenschaften*, Frankfurt 2002, pp. 372–392; Hans Fenske, "Imperialistische Tendenzen in Deutschland

remedy this lack. An enthusiastically pro-colonial public thereupon began to demand that Germany too must have its share in the partitioning of the globe. These voices eventually became so insistent that in 1884 Chancellor Otto von Bismarck was persuaded to perform a U-turn in his colonial policy. Up until then he had always rejected the idea of establishing colonies, as he saw them on the one hand as an albatross around the country's neck in respect of foreign policy, and on the other hand as entailing incalculable costs – both financial and in terms of human resources. Now, though, he declared himself prepared to support the formal acquisition of colonies.[4] Within only a few years, territories roughly corresponding to the present-day African states of Togo, Cameroon, Tanzania, Rwanda, Burundi and Namibia, as well as a few smaller possessions in the South Seas, were declared German *Schutzgebiete*, although this designation was a misnomer.[5] In view of the climatic conditions only German South West Africa was considered suitable for the establishment of a settler colony, i.e. for permanent occupation by German settlers. This latter circumstance fired the imaginations of a whole generation in Germany,[6] and contributed to certain features of German rule which were to prove to be harbingers of future developments, including in the further course of German history.

Imperial Commissioner Heinrich Göring took formal possession of the colony with two fellow officials in 1885. However, this was little more than a symbolic act. It must have been clear to those responsible at home that they would never be able to establish a functioning administration in this vast territory with only three officials: a territory that towards the end of the nineteenth century was inhabited by an estimated 90,000–100,000 Ovambo, 70,000–80,000 Herero, 15,000–20,000 Nama, 30,000–40,000 Berg Damara and San and 3,000–4,000 Basters.[7] In 1893,

---

vor 1866. Auswanderung, überseeische Bestrebungen, Weltmachtträume", *Historisches Jahrbuch*, 97/98 (1978), pp. 336–383; Hans Feske, "Ungeduldige Zuschauer. Die Deutschen und die europäische Expansion 1815–1880", in Wolfgang Reinhard, ed., *Imperialistische Kontinuität und nationale Ungeduld im 19. Jahrhundert*, Frankfurt 1991, pp. 87–140. Russell Berman, *Enlightenment or Empire: Colonial Discourse in German Culture*, Lincoln 1998; Susanne Zantop, *Kolonialphantasien im vorkolonialen Deutschland, 1770–1870*, Berlin 1999.

4 What exactly it was that induced Bismarck to take this step continues to be a matter of dispute among academics. For a summary, see Horst Gründer, *Geschichte der deutschen Kolonien*, Paderborn 1995, pp. 51–62.

5 For an initial introduction to the histories of the various colonies, see: Gründer, *Geschichte der deutschen Kolonien*. Kiauchow in China was added to the list later on.

6 Regarding the fantasies connected with 'South West' see for example: Birthe Kundrus, *Moderne Imperialisten. Das Kaiserreich im Spiegel seiner Kolonien*, Köln/Weimar/Wien 2003.

7 The details given by Theodor Leutwein for the year 1892 are based on very rough estimates made by travellers, colonial officials and missionaries, and give more of an indication of the pro-

with the arrival of Theodor Leutwein, who was later appointed the first Governor, the systematic establishment of German rule and the methodical build-up of a German administration began in earnest. The increasing complexity of the bureaucratic structures amply illustrates this process. In 1894 the territory was divided into three *Bezirke* (regions or districts), namely Keetmanshoop, Windhoek and Otjimbingwe; by 1903 this number had already doubled, and by 1914 there were sixteen *Bezirke* and autonomous *Distrikte*, which in their turn were divided into police station areas or 'police wards'.[8]

It was also Leutwein and his young administrative team who embarked on the implementation of a utopian vision for colonial rule with the ultimate goal of building a model colonial state based on a racial ideology. Through a series of shifting alliances with African rulers such as Samuel Maharero and Hendrik Witbooi, to name only the two most important, the colonisers superficially secured the territory for the short term, with the aim of converting the African societies into a 'Black working class'; a status in which the Africans, though not completely without rights, nonetheless suffered severe discrimination.[9]

The constant expansion of the German administration, the pronounced 'master race' attitude of the settlers who began to arrive in the colony in larger and larger numbers, and which manifested itself in repeated instances of murder, rape and fraudulent dealing, and last but not least in the increasingly prevalent seizures of Herero land, ultimately led to the Herero and Nama War, which broke out on 12 January 1904.

This is not the place to analyse the war and the genocide in detail.[10] The following must suffice: the war with its tens of thousands of victims on the African

---

portionate strengths of the various ethnicities than of the actual sizes of their populations. Theodor Leutwein, *Elf Jahre Gouverneur in Deutsch-Südwestafrika*, 3rd edn, Berlin 1908, p. 11.

8 On this gradual intensification of the administrative presence, see Zimmerer, *Deutsche Herrschaft*, pp. 13–31, 112–118 [English edition: *German Rule, African Subjects*]. On the history of the bureaucracy, see also Udo Kaulich, *Die Geschichte der ehemaligen Kolonie Deutsch-Südwestafrika (1884–1914). Eine Gesamtdarstellung*, Frankfurt 2001.

9 On the 'governmental and administrative utopia' or 'utopia of dominance' see Zimmerer, *Deutsche Herrschaft* [English edition: *German Rule, African Subjects*]. The 'divide and rule' policy is described by Horst Drechsler, *Südwestafrika unter deutscher Kolonialherrschaft. Der Kampf der Herero und Nama gegen den deutschen Imperialismus 1884–1915*, 2nd edn, Berlin 1984; and especially in Helmut Bley, *Kolonialherrschaft und Sozialstruktur in Deutsch-Südwestafrika 1894–1914*, Hamburg 1968.

10 I have done so in detail elsewhere: Jürgen Zimmerer, "Das Deutsche Reich und der Genozid. Überlegungen zum historischen Ort des Völkermordes an den Herero und Nama", in Larissa Förster, Dag Henrichsen and Michael Bollig, eds, *Namibia-Deutschland. Eine geteilte Geschichte. Widerstand, Gewalt, Erinnerung*, Köln 2004, pp. 106–121 (English version: "The German Empire and

side, with its forced migration and internal displacement, gave the German administrators the opportunity to accelerate the realisation of their visions of domination, as the tactical need to show consideration for the African 'tribes' no longer applied. The war was thus a catalyst, facilitating the implementation of ideas that had already been in the air in the pre-war period. It is important to emphasise, however, that all the subsequent measures towards the setting up of a society of racial privilege had already been considered and to some extent already initiated before the outbreak of war in 1904. The war was therefore not the cause of a radicalisation of German policy, leading it in the direction of the creation of a racial state. Rather, it simply offered the opportunity to implement extreme positions that had already been put forward in the pre-war years.[11]

The German Governmental and Administrative Utopia

The Germans' utopian vision of colonial rule was derived from the model of the bureaucratic and centrally administered state that modern Germany represented, and its goal was the construction an efficient economic system on the basis of a society of racial privilege in which the institutions of government, the European settlers and the African population each occupied their firmly assigned place. The indigenous population was to be comprehensively registered and kept under surveillance, integrated into the colony's economic system as cheap labour and re-educated to function as a compliant workforce through a process of social disciplining. In this way, it was assumed, the economic development of the colony could be

---

Genocide", pp. 154–174 in this book). An introduction with an overview of the relevant literature can be found in Jürgen Zimmerer and Joachim Zeller, eds, *Völkermord in Deutsch-Südwestafrika. Der Kolonialkrieg in Namibia (1904–1908) und seine Folgen*, Berlin 2003. Since then further books have been published: Jan-Bart Gewald, "Imperial Germany and the Herero of Southern Africa: Genocide and the quest for recompense", in Adam Jones, ed., *Genocide, War Crimes, and the West: Ending the Culture of Impunity*, London 2003; Reinhart Kößler and Henning Melber, "Völkermord und Gedenken. Der Genozid an den Herero und Nama in Deutsch-Südwestafrika 1904–1908", in Irmtrud Wojak and Susanne Meinl, eds, *Völkermord und Kriegsverbrechen in der ersten Hälfte des 20. Jahrhunderts*, Frankfurt etc. 2004, pp. 37–75; Dominik J. Schaller, "Kolonialkrieg, Völkermord und Zwangsarbeit in Deutsch-Südwestafrika", in Dominik J. Schaller, Boyadjian Rupen, Hanno Scholtz and Vivianne Berg, eds, *Enteignet–Vertrieben–Ermordet, Beiträge zur Genozidforschung*, Zürich 2004, pp. 147–232; Dominik J. Schaller, "'Ich glaube, dass die Nation als solche vernichtet werden muss': Kolonialkrieg und Völkermord in Deutsch-Südwestafrika 1904–1907", *Journal of Genocide Research*, 6/3 (2004), pp. 395–430.
11 I have furnished demonstrations of this continuity in: Zimmerer, *Deutsche Herrschaft*, pp. 56–109 [English edition: *German Rule, African Subjects*].

pushed ahead with and the extraction of minerals guaranteed, so that the *Schutzgebiet* would be able to develop into a settler colony in an orderly manner.[12] The end result was intended to be a unified economic area across which the African people were to be distributed as workers in such a way as to meet the needs of the colonial economy. The focus of the whole strategy was on planning and centralised direction.

Native Law was codified in von Lindequist's so-called Native Ordinances of 1907, consisting of the Pass, Control and Master and Servant Ordinances.[13] These regulations were the new straitjacket by which African society was to be reshaped; they provided for the progressing social disciplining of the Africans and laid the basis for a 'semi-free labour market', one which reduced the Africans to a pool of labour freely available to the colonial masters as a result of a compulsion to enter into dependent employment, but nevertheless – at least in theory – still allowed them a degree of freedom to choose their employers and to negotiate their wages.

An essential prerequisite both for this economic exploitation and for the protection of the colonialists against further 'Native uprisings' – another factor that ranked high on the scale of priorities after the recent experiences of the war – was the registration and surveillance of the African population through the establishment of a seamless system of control that encompassed every aspect of their lives. The Administration was to be put in the position of being able to determine how many Africans were present in a particular District at any given time, who they were, where they lived and whether and how they were employed. To

---

12 On this, see Jürgen Zimmerer, "Planning Frenzy: Forced Labour, Expulsion and Genocide as Elements of Population Economics in German South West Africa", pp. 57–76 in this book. I have also documented the failure of this utopian vision in Jürgen Zimmerer, "Der totale Überwachungsstaat? Recht und Verwaltung in Deutsch-Südwestafrika", in Rüdiger Voigt, ed., *Das deutsche Kolonialrecht als Vorstufe einer globalen 'Kolonialisierung' von Recht und Verwaltung*, Baden-Baden 2001, pp. 175–198 (English version: "Total Control? Law and Administration in German South West Africa", pp. 77–103 in this book).

13 Imperial Governor's Office Windhoek: "Verordnung betr. Maßregeln zur Kontrolle der Eingeborenen" ("Ordinance concerning Measures for the Control of the Natives"), 18 August 1907, NAN ZBU W.III.A.1. Vol. 1, Sheets 61a–62b; "Verordnung betr. die Paßpflicht der Eingeborenen" ("Ordinance concerning the Pass Requirement for Natives"), 18 August 1907, ibid., Sheets 63a–65b; "Verordnung betr. Dienst- und Arbeitsverträge mit Eingeborenen" ("Ordinance concerning Contracts of Service or Employment with Natives"), 18 August 1907, ibid., Sheets 66a–68a; "Runderlaß zu den Verordnungen, betr. die Kontrolle und Paßpflicht der Eingeborenen sowie die Dienst- und Arbeitsverträge mit diesen" ("Circulated Decree accompanying the Ordinances concerning the Control of and the Pass Requirement for Natives and Contracts of Service or Employment with them"), 18 August 1907. For a detailed analysis, see Zimmerer, *Deutsche Herrschaft*, pp. 84–94 [English edition: *German Rule, African Subjects*].

achieve this, all Africans had to ensure that they were entered in Native Registers kept at their local District Offices. In order to enable them to be unambiguously identified, all individuals over seven years of age needed a 'pass', consisting of a metal token bearing the Imperial crown and a registration number, which had to be worn visibly around the neck and shown on demand to the police and "any white person". As a pass was valid only in one District and bore a sequence of numbers that showed which District this was, it was supposed to make it possible to determine at any time whether an African had left his or her home district. Anyone who wished to do this legally – for a limited period of time – had to obtain a travel pass from the police station under whose jurisdiction they fell. At their destination they then had to obtain confirmation of their arrival, specifying the time. Thus the Africans were under comprehensive surveillance, and were not to be allowed any freedom of movement.

Moreover, the African population was prohibited from owning riding animals or other large livestock. As the Herero and the Nama had already had their land expropriated, the Africans essentially had no other option than to hire themselves out as farm labourers, to the engineering companies building the railways or in the diamond mines. Anyone who nevertheless did not take up such work would in all probability be punished as a 'vagrant', a fate that threatened anyone found "roaming around [...] without any demonstrable means of support".[14]

In addition to the compulsion to take up employment, a further measure introduced in the field of population economics was the control of the distribution of the population. By refusing to issue travel passes the colonial administration could regulate the distribution of the African workforce, as people were simply prevented from moving away from any District where labour was in short supply. But an unbalanced concentration of Africans, for example on farms near to the graves of their ancestors or other culturally important sites, or else simply with particular employers, was not in tune with the vision of an economic utopia either. So in order to secure as even a distribution as possible of the African population across the country and thus also on individual farms and in individual businesses, African settlements of more than ten families were prohibited.

As practically all adult Africans had to work for Whites, a legal codification of employment relationships was necessary. At the same time, the Administration could use this to supplement the system of surveillance and control. One instrument to this end was the *Dienstbuch*, the Employment Logbook, which was pre-

---

[14] Verordnung, Kaiserliches Gouvernement Windhuk, betr. Maßregeln zur Kontrolle der Eingeborenen (Imperial Governor's Office, Windhoek: "Ordinance concerning Regulations for the Control and Surveillance of Natives"), 18 August 1907, NAN ZBU W.III.A.1. Vol. 1, Sheet 61a-62b.

scribed for all employment contracts with a term of more than one month and was issued to the individual by the police, who also entered the conclusion of such contracts in the Native Register. The Employment Logbook had to contain the name, 'tribal affiliation' and pass token number of the employee, but also the name of the employer, the date on which employment commenced, the term of the contract, the period of notice, and the "amount and type of remuneration to be granted to the Native". The Logbook was therefore supposed to provide an unbroken sequence of information about the Africans' employment relationships and their availability for work, the 'willingness to work' so often invoked in colonial discourse.

Racial Segregation

The heated atmosphere prevailing at the outbreak of war in 1904, when settlers throughout the colony were crying out for revenge and retribution, provided the Administration with the opportunity to effect a change of course in another matter as well – a change of course it had previously been unable to implement due to resistance from Berlin. In response to an enquiry from a District Office as to whether it was permitted to register the marriages of two soldiers in the colonial army to African women, Deputy Governor Hans Tecklenburg instructed all register offices "not to conclude such marriages until further notice", since they were "undesirable [...] in view of their legal, political and social consequences".[15]

Although the Colonial Department in Berlin had decreed as late as 1899 that such marriages were admissible, it was now possible for the colonial administration, under the impact of the war, to achieve what Theodor Leutwein had failed to achieve: to give legal effect to the drawing of a line between 'Black' and 'White', between 'Native' and 'Non-Native'.[16] For even Leutwein, the first Governor of the *Schutzgebiet*, had deemed 'mixed marriages' to be less than desirable, because not only any children born of such marriages but also the African spouse herself would be able to gain German nationality.

The question regarding the permissibility of 'mixed marriages', and especially regarding the status of the children born of relationships between White men and African women, the so-called 'people of mixed-race', was an important

---

[15] Imperial Governor's Office Windhoek, Circulated Order to Register Offices, 23 September 1905, NAN ZBU F.IV.R.1., Sheet 22a.
[16] A general overview of the racial politics in the German colonial empire is to be found in Becker, *Rassenmischehen*.

issue; the Whites who migrated to South West Africa were predominantly men, so that there was a glaring gender imbalance.[17] It was above all the missionaries who, applying a culturalistic definition of 'Native', argued in favour of the recognition of 'mixed marriages', and even of their active encouragement, as the believed that the "gradual development of a new race, standing between the [...] Natives on the one hand and the outsiders with their higher nature on the other" would "work a marvellous transformation of the wretched conditions that exist at the present time. People of mixed race, endowed with a new level of drive and with almost unlimited opportunities to further improve themselves, will be in a position to open up their far-off countries completely to the German nation."[18]

However, this 'culturalistic' attitude, which assumes assimilation and gradual advancement to a position of equality, did not go down particularly well with those who bore political responsibility on the spot, as it did not fit in with their vision of the model racial state they aspired to create, resting as it did on a clear division between the colonisers and the colonised. This vision seemed to be at risk, as Tecklenburg wrote in 1903, a year before the outbreak of the war:

> Panzlaff's Hottentot woman is now taking up a lot of space alongside our German ladies at the festivities of the Soldiers' and Marksmen's Associations, although still without managing to form much in the way of relationships with them. This would change if two or three more such women were to gain admittance to the circle. [...] So we have no other alternative than to get legislation in place while there is still time that will erect a strong barrier between non-Natives and Natives, even if this represents a hard blow to some mixed-race individuals or people married to mixed-race individuals, and it initially leads to something of an increase in the number of illegitimate children.[19]

---

17 As of 1 January 1903 there were 4,640 Whites living in South West Africa, of whom 3,391 were men. Leutwein, "Elf Jahre Gouverneur", p. 232. Lora Wildenthal has recently quite rightly pointed out that there was not a shortage of women at all, there were plenty of African women; only that they were of the wrong skin colour or "race". See: Lora Wildenthal, "German Women for Empire, 1884–1945", Durham 2001, p. 6. The colonial administration and circles of enthusiasts for colonialism in Germany tried to remedy this by deliberately encouraging single women of marriageable age to go to South West Africa. On this subject, see: Karen Smidt, "'Germania führt die deutsche Frau nach Südwest'. Auswanderung, Leben und soziale Konflikte deutscher Frauen in der ehemaligen Kolonie Deutsch-Südwestafrika 1884–1920. Eine sozial- und frauengeschichtliche Studie", University of Magdeburg 1995 (Ph.D. Thesis).
18 Rhenish Missionary Society, "Denkschrift betr. die Schließung von Ehen zwischen Weißen und Farbigen in den deutschen Schutzgebieten" ("Memorandum on the Conclusion of Marriages between Whites and Coloured Persons in the German Protectorates") [transcript], 1887, NAN ZBU F.IV.R.1., Sheets 3a–6b.
19 Report by Tecklenburg [transcript], 24 September 1903, NAN ZBU F.IV.R.1., Sheets 61ca–61ea.

During the war it then seemed that those responsible were not able to wait any longer;[20] and Tecklenburg issued an Ordinance prohibiting "mixed marriages". In September 1907, Windhoek District Court reinforced this position by retrospectively declaring even marriages that had already been validly entered into to be null and void. This was a highly questionable procedure from the point of view of legal theory, since retroactive legislation was then and still is today incompatible with the principles of the rule of law. It demonstrated, however, that the colonies existed in a legal sphere of their own, separate even from that of the German Empire itself.[21]

Definitions: Culturalistic v. Biologistic

The shift in the definition of the term 'Native', of what constitutes the 'Other', was to prove crucial in the further course of Namibian, South African (apartheid) and German history. During the early years of colonial rule, a culturalistic definition for these terms predominated. Assimilation was rewarded and 'mixed marriages' were regarded positively, as is demonstrated in a memorandum of the Rhenish Mission:

> Such people of mixed race, who have been brought up by their white fathers and so are able to count themselves, and like to count themselves, as being in every respect part of the 'white' community, will strengthen the German element in the *Schutzgebiet*, and that increasingly as time goes by; and increasingly as time goes by, the Native population, whose leading families are related by marriage to the settlers, will truly feel themselves happy and at ease as subjects of the German Empire and enjoying its protection.[22]

Tecklenburg's complaint about 'Hottentot women' who mingled with the Germans at marksmen's fairs basically provides evidence of this. They may not have been completely integrated, but they were in relationships with German men and took part in social life. Their entry ticket was their assimilation.

---

20 The rapid increase in the number of Afro-German children as a result of rape and the forced prostitution of African women now made the issue seem even more urgent. On the matter of the 'mixed-race question' see Frank Becker, "Soldatenkinder und Rassenpolitik. Die Folgen des Kolonialkriegs für die Mischlinge in Deutsch-Südwestafrika (1904–1913)", *Militärgeschichtliche Zeitschrift*, 63/1 (2004), pp. 53–77.
21 On the status of the colonies under international law, see Harald Sippel,"'Im Interesse des Deutschtums und der weißen Rasse', Behandlung und Rechtswirkungen von 'Rassenmischehen' in den Kolonien Deutsch-Ostafrika und Deutsch-Südwestafrika", *Jahrbuch für afrikanisches Recht*, 9 (1995), pp. 123–159.
22 Rhenish Missionary Society, *Denkschrift* [transcript], 1887, NAN ZBU F.IV.R.1., Sheets 3a–6b.

All of this was now changed by a judgment in which Windhoek District Court decreed that 'Natives' were "all the blood members of a primitive people, including the progeny of native women that they have borne to men of the white race, even if there should have been miscegenation with white men over a period of several generations. As long as descent from a member of the primitive people can be proven, the descendant is, by virtue of his blood, a Native."[23]

The confirmation of this judgment by the Superior Court of South West Africa[24] meant that the principle of descent had finally established itself in a legally binding manner in the definition of who was a 'Native', so that the cultural concept of 'race' was replaced by a biologistic one. The degree of assimilation was no longer the key criterion. Basically, indeed, assimilation was not possible any more anyway, as the biologistic interpretation of the concept of the 'Other' closed the boundary between the two sides, preventing any crossing. There naturally continued to be relationships between German men and African women, but in terms of the social construct the 'races' were segregated from each other.

Yet why did this problem suddenly seem so urgent after the turn of the century? There are two closely interwoven answers to this question. On the one hand, this was just the time at which the idea of 'race' as a biological concept was gaining much more widespread acceptance, and finding adherents especially among a certain part of the population – interestingly enough, often people with a rather higher standard of education – who wanted to "protect [...] the ranks of the Europeans against being mixed with coloured blood",[25] as they were afraid that otherwise the settler population would 'go Native', or 'go kaffir', to use the local idiom. This was, after all, a process that was regarded as being demonstrated by history, as could supposedly be seen in the "deterioration of the European race in the former Spanish and Portuguese colonies in America and in Portugal's African possessions", as Tecklenburg wrote later.[26] Or, as the missionary Carl Wandres formulated it a few years later in the course of a discussion as to how one could also prevent extramarital sexual relations:

> Mixed marriages are not only undesirable, but are truly immoral and a slap in the face for Germanness. [...]
>
> Mixed marriages are always a sin against racial consciousness. A nation that sins against its own honour in this way definitely sinks to a lower level and, as can be seen from the Latin nations, is not capable of carrying out any thorough colonisation. [...]

---

23 Judgment of Windhoek District Court, 26 September 1907 [transcript of 25 April 1908], NAN ZBU F.IV.R.1., II-37a–40b [spec. pag.]. Original of the judgment in NAN GWI 530 [R 1/07], 23a–26a.
24 Judgment of Windhoek Superior Court, 10 November 1909, NAN ZBU F.IV.R.1., Sheets 52a–55a.
25 Report by Tecklenburg [transcript], 24 September 1903, NAN ZBU F.IV.R.1., Sheets 61ca–61ea.
26 Tecklenburg to Colonial Department, 23 October 1905, NAN ZBU F.IV.R.1., Sheets 24a–34a.

> As far as people of mixed race are concerned, we have to say on the basis of widespread experience that these people are a calamity for our colony. These pitiable creatures are almost all very severely impaired genetically. All that is to be seen among them are lies and deceit, sensuosity and stupid pride, an inclination to dishonesty and to alcoholism, and last but not least they are almost without exception syphilitic. And it could scarcely be otherwise, since their fathers are not good for very much, and their mothers for nothing at all.[27]

On the other hand, the 'people of mixed race' did actually call into question one of the constitutive principles of the colonial state, resting as it did upon the binary distinction between 'White' and 'Black', between 'Native' and 'non-Native', between 'masters' (i.e. members of the 'master race') and 'servants'. If this boundary were to become blurred, then confusion and ambiguity would threaten and ultimately endanger German rule. For as Tecklenburg put it:

> Males of mixed race will be liable to serve in the forces, will be capable of occupying public offices, and will be beneficiaries of the right to vote, which is likely to be introduced at some time in the future, and of other rights attached to nationality. These consequences are extremely alarming and in view of the present situation in German South West Africa they represent a grave danger. They will not only compromise the maintenance of the purity of the German race and of German civilisation to a major extent, but also put the white man's entire position of power in jeopardy.[28]

White 'Masters' – Black Servants

Perhaps even more strongly than was the case in other colonies, the German governmental and administrative utopia in South West Africa was based on the distinction between 'Natives' and 'non-Natives'. In such a society of racial privilege there was a need for a precise definition of who belonged to the privileged and who to the disadvantaged 'race'.[29]

This governmental and administrative utopia rested on a legal and administrative system that displayed a discriminatory dichotomy. While for Europeans, or more precisely for all Whites, a separation of powers existed as between the

---

27 The missionary Carl Wandres, "Bemerkungen über Mischehen und Mischlinge aus der Praxis für die Praxis" ("Remarks on Mixed Marriages and Mixed-Race People, from Practical Experience for Practical Application") [transcript, n.d.], NAN ZBU F.IV.R.1., Sheets 143b–145b.
28 Tecklenburg to Colonial Department, 23 October 1905, NAN ZBU F.IV.R.1., Sheets 24a–34a.
29 I have gone into this in detail in Zimmerer, *Deutsche Herrschaft* [English edition: *German Rule, African Subjects*].

executive and the judicial branches of government – in addition to four Imperial Courts there was a Superior Court that acted as a Court of Appeal – this was not the case for the 'Natives'. For them, the district officials were prosecution, judiciary and executive all rolled in one. From 1910 onwards a Native Administration with a Native Affairs Department and Native Commissioners was established alongside the classic district administrations.

The three Native Ordinances of 1907, which represented the regulatory foundation for the society of racial privilege, did not only introduce an obligation to enter into employment and a system of complete overall surveillance, they did not only initiate a process of social disciplining, but they also elevated every White person to the status of an overseer of the Africans. For example, the passes which the Africans had to wear visibly around their necks had to be shown to any White on demand, and the Whites took on crucial tasks in the sophisticated system of reporting. Whites were superior, so they had to be saluted; when an African met a White person, the African had to stand aside. What this linking of real and symbolic subordination could lead to, this mingling of private economic superiority as employers with the function of an official authority in the surveillance system, was manifest in the so-called *väterliches Züchtigungsrecht* – ‚parental powers of physical chastisement'. The settlers claimed for themselves this right to physically chastise their workers, as these were considered to be at a stage of development equivalent to that of children and therefore to need a 'firm hand'. By giving their sanction to this as a common law right, the courts opened the doors wide for the development of a *Prügelkultur*, a general culture of physical violence. This led to an extreme brutalisation of relations between Whites and Africans. In 1912 the Governor was seriously worried by the "alarming increase" in the number of "brutal excesses of whites against natives", in some instances even involving police officers, since he was afraid that such cases, in which individuals "rage against the Natives with the violence of madness, and see their White skins as giving them carte blanche to commit brutal crimes", would arouse "feelings of hatred among the Natives" which were bound "sooner or later, to the extent that no determined measures are taken to remedy them, to lead to a renewed desperate rebellion on the part of the Natives, and thus to the economic ruin of the country".[30]

In order to avoid becoming victims of this inhuman treatment, many African workers would try to escape from the farms they were employed on. In doing so,

---

30 Circulated Order, Imperial Governor's Office Windhoek, 31 May 1912, NAN ZBU W.III.R.1. Vol. 1, Sheets 7a–8a.

however, they violated some important provisions of the Native Ordinances of 1907, namely the requirement to pursue employment and the condition that they might only leave their place of residence – that is to say their place of employment – with the express permission of the Administration. If they quit their service before the expiry of their contracts "without good reason in accordance with law", they could, upon an application from their masters, be forced to continue their employment (in the dry bureaucratic language of the Native Ordinances) "through measures of compulsion imposed on the part of the authorities". The country was regularly crisscrossed by military patrols searching for fugitives. The labour shortage became a dominant issue during the post-war period: as a large proportion of the Herero and the Nama had been massacred by the Germans during the war from 1904–1908, there was unsurprisingly a shortage of workers afterwards.[31] While some sections of the German colonial administration attempted to improve the lot of the Africans by pursuing a more restrained policy and granting them minimum rights, the farmers relied on pure violence: the degree to which the farmers' attitudes were governed by a contemptuous disregard for the human dignity of their employees can be seen from the fact that in 1912 various Farmers' Associations demanded that "Natives who display a propensity to run away should be identified by a tattoo".[32] Although the Government ultimately rejected these demands, since "no [...] colonial nation makes use of such measures",[33] which moreover might "stir up major unrest among the Natives and be met with great resistance", and furthermore "would be exploited at home by elements hostile to colonialism to justify wild agitation",[34] this example nevertheless shows a radicalisation of thought in the field of Native Policy, with ideas being put forward which a generation later, when the State was no longer restrained by any inhibitions whatsoever, would be applied millions of times over.

---

31 On the importance of the 'labour question' see Zimmerer, *Deutsche Herrschaft*, pp. 176–242 (English edition: *German Rule, African Subjects*).
32 Okahandja Agricultural Association to Imperial Governor's Office Windhoek, 16 December 1912, NAN ZBU W.III.B.1. Vol. 1, Sheet 35a.
33 Imperial Governor's Office Windhoek, to a farmer named von Gossler, Chairman of the Agricultural Association of Okahandja, 31 December 1912, NAN ZBU W.III.B.1. Vol. 1, Sheet 36a.
34 Outjo District Office to Imperial Governor's Office Windhoek, 4 March 1912, NAN ZBU W.III.B.1. Vol. 1, Sheet 29a.

Aporias of the Racial State

However, the administration's endeavours to put the society of racial privilege on a more stable foundation by granting the African population a minimum degree of 'protection' also failed,[35] mainly due to the internal self-contradictions within the racial state: the surveillance of these protective measures that the Administration and the courts were supposed to exercise was ineffective, as both judges and administrative officers showed solidarity with the European settlers and entrepreneurs.

If a White was to be punished for the 'maltreatment of Natives', he had to be sentenced under due process of law. This hardly ever happened, however, and if it did, the penalties imposed were ridiculously light. For it was as a rule impossible to find any White witnesses who were prepared to speak against the accused, while Black ones would "simply not be believed, whereas the most dubious statements made by whites under oath would be given credence", as the Lüderitzbucht District Officer complained."And so the whole affair would end with a glowing acquittal, and there could be no more thankless task than to represent the prosecuting authorities in such cases."[36] In a society as strongly characterised by racism as this colonial one, the Africans' 'lack of credibility', itself an emanation of the racist system, could not be eliminated. If an official shared the view that nothing Africans said was to be believed, it was scarcely to be expected that he would help them to obtain justice. Even in the courts, they were not believed. To give the Africans any chance of being treated equally by the courts, the colonial situation itself – that is to say, the way the colonised were discriminated against in all aspects of everyday life – would have had to have been set aside. But nobody who formed part of the camp of the colonisers wanted that.

The society of racial privilege extends far beyond ethnic segregation as an end in itself or as the means of implementing diffuse ideological concepts of 'racial purity'. It refers to a social order that is designed to be permanent and is based on a biological hierarchisation encompassing all aspects of life. The members of the 'races' concerned were to be brought to an internalisation of their positions in this hierarchy through measures of social disciplining. Direct force was

---

[35] The influence of the State Secretary for the Colonies, Bernhard Dernburg, who is referred to again and again in this connection in research, is hugely overestimated. The measures for the 'protection' of the 'Natives' had already been discussed in connection with the Native Ordinances of 1907 and dated back to the period before the Herero and Nama War. When Dernburg intervened to modify the text of the Ordinances, he most often made them more stringent.

[36] Lüderitzbucht District Office to Governor's Office Windhoek, 21 April 1913, NAN ZBU W.III.R.2. Vol. 1, Sheets 156a–159a.

to be rendered superfluous, being replaced by a structural compulsion that would no longer be perceptible as such. This is not the least of the reasons why the mental deformations set in train by this situation turned into a legacy that outlasted the actual phase of colonialism for so long.

The Society of Racial Privilege in German South West Africa and Its Significance in the Context of German History

German South West Africa was Germany's first attempt to establish a society of racial privilege, a racist state. Only 35 years later, an attempt was made to construct a social system in Europe that rested upon similar principles. Once again the context was a colonial one, since the aim was to settle territory and undertake measures of land reclamation, with Germans forming the 'master race' there, to use an expression of the German colonial 'pioneer' Carl Peters.

Any examination of the Nazis' plans and visions for their 'Eastern Empire', of the motives underpinning their *Lebensraum* policy and of their ideas with regard to the future interaction between the new German 'master class' and the Slav underclass will reveal echoes of colonialism at every turn.[37]

The parallels with colonial history were perfectly clear to those responsible on the German side, starting with Hitler himself:

> The struggle for hegemony in the world will be decided in favour of Europe by the possession of Russia; this will make Europe the place that is more secure against blockade than anywhere else in the world. [...] The Slavic peoples on the other hand are not destined to lead independent lives of their own. [...] The territory of Russia is our India, and just as the English rule India with only a handful of people, so we will govern this colonial territory of ours. We will supply the Ukrainians with headscarves, glass bead necklaces as jewellery, and all the other things that appeal to colonial peoples.[38]

Regardless of whether Hitler had a proper grasp of British colonial rule in India and elsewhere – India of all places was by no means a settler colony such as he

---

[37] I have explored this in more detail elsewhere; here, a few sketched outlines must suffice: Zimmerer; "Holocaust und Kolonialismus", (English version: "Colonialism and the Holocaust", pp. 125–153 in this book, and Jürgen Zimmerer, "Die Geburt des'Ostlandes' aus dem Geiste des Kolonialismus. Ein postkolonialer Blick auf die NS – Eroberungs- und Vernichtungspolitik", *Sozial.Geschichte. Zeitschrift für die historische Analyse des 20. und 21. Jahrhunderts*, 19/1 (2004), pp. 10–43 (English version: "The Birth of the 'Ostland' out of the Spirit of Colonialism: A (Post)colonial Perspective on the Nazi Policy of Conquest and Annihilation", pp. 230–261 in this book).
[38] Hitler, 17 September 1941, Adolf Hitler, *Monologe im Führerhauptquartier*, ed. Werner Jochmann, Hamburg 1980, pp. 60–64.

imagined the German *Lebensraum* in the east would become – he was most definitely impressed by the prestige of British colonial rule and the techniques by which it was implemented. What is more important in relation to what we are interested in here is the discursive structure Hitler uses, his recourse to the world of the British Empire as he imagined it in order to illustrate his own goals.

Similar mechanisms are repeatedly found in descriptions of the 'barren' eastern lands, in the manner in which both common soldiers and high Nazi officials tried to put their experience of 'the East' into words. Whether it was Hitler speaking of this "primeval world" (*Urwelt*) which one "only needed to see" in order to know "that nothing happens here if one does not assign people the work they have to do" and concluding that "The Slav is a born slave, they are a mass crying out for a master";[39] or a soldier writing home from Russia that "there is nothing of culture, nothing of paradise [to be seen here]; but only the absolute depths, filth, people who demonstrate to us that we will face a huge task of colonisation here":[40] it was colonial history, or what colonial history was imagined to be, that was drawn upon for the purposes of comparison. It served to endow what was unexpected, what was foreign, with meaning. Colonial attributions helped to cast the cloak of a civilising mission over conquest. Himmler's secretary Hanns Johst, who travelled with the *Reichsführer SS* through Poland during the winter of 1939/40, wrote:

> The Poles are not a state-building people. They lack even the most basic prerequisites. I have travelled all over the country at the side of the *Reichsführer* SS. A country which has so little feeling for the essence of settlement that it is not even up to the task of creating a village of any style has no claim to any sort of independent political status within Europe. It is a country crying out to be colonised![41]

Seen as lacking any cultural abilities of their own, the Polish, Ukrainian and Russian populations could only win the right to survive in the function of servants, or rather slaves, to the Germans; there was no hint of their being granted equal entitlement. Segregated legally and socially from the Germans, the 'Natives' of Eastern Europe were above all assigned the role of servants and a labour force for the 'ruling class' constituted by the German 'master race'. It was this function as a workforce that essentially gave rise to any right to survive they might have;

---

39 Hitler, 17 September 1941, Hitler, *Monologe*, p. 63.
40 These are the words of a soldier in the 12th Airborne Regiment, 20 July 1941, quoted according to: Christian Gerlach, *Kalkulierte Morde. Die deutsche Wirtschafts- und Vernichtungspolitik in Weißrußland 1941–1944*, Hamburg 1999, p. 102.
41 Hanns Johst, *Ruf des Reiches – Echo des Volkes!*, München 1940, p. 94, quoted according to: Michael Burleigh, *Die Zeit des Nationalsozialismus. Eine Gesamtdarstellung*, Frankfurt 2000, p. 515.

just as in German South West Africa Theodor Leutwein had tried to divert General von Trotha from his genocidal plans by drawing attention to the need for labour in the colony.

Germans and Poles were subject to different legal systems, this dual jurisdiction being ultimately based on the criterion of 'racial' affiliation. But preferential treatment within this society of racial privilege was not restricted to formal law; rather, the *situation coloniale* permeated all spheres of social interaction. Just as Europeans were favoured always and everywhere in South West Africa, so in Eastern Europe the Germans formed the apex of the social hierarchy. If Hitler was able to say of the Ukraine, "Our Germans – this is the main thing – must form a closed community, like a fortress; outside the main centres, even the lowest stable boy must stand above any of the natives";[42] then this attitude is ultimately based on a similar vision of a society of racial privilege.

It is this mental disposition to create a social hierarchy on the basis of biology that indicates a common mindset in the two cases. This does not represent the formulation of any causality or any irreversible *Sonderweg* leading from German South West Africa to occupied eastern Europe. Rather, German South West Africa furnished the necessary experience of the utopia of a racial state to be made the object of development and total control, experience that could be drawn upon once again when the conquest of Poland and the Soviet Union presented Nazi administrators and planners with the opportunity to implement their ideas of utopian population economics on the grandest possible scale.[43]

Within the field of post-colonial studies it has long been advocated that academics should no longer regard colonialism only as a one-way street, understood merely in terms of the export of specific behaviours from the European 'home' countries to the non-European regions; but rather should also examine how developments in Europe and in the overseas colonies affected, spurred on and radicalised each other. The society of racial privilege in the former German South West Africa is an important starting point for such an undertaking.

---

42 Hitler, 17 September 1941, Hitler, *Monologe*, pp. 62f.
43 It will be a task for researchers in the coming years to explore and set out in detail the ways in which this knowledge was passed on. I myself have analysed the factors of personal experience, preservation in institutional archives and collective imagination in Zimmerer, "Geburt des 'Ostlandes'" (English version: "Birth of the 'Ostland'", pp. 230–261 in this book).

The Herero and Nama War (1904–1908) in Global History

Colonialism and the Holocaust: Towards an Archaeology of Genocide

The German war against Poland and the USSR was without doubt the biggest war of colonial conquest in history. Never before had so many people and resources been mobilised by a conqueror, never before had the war aims been so wide in their scope. Unprecedented, too, was the deliberately planned murder of such a large number of people, or at least the conscious acceptance of the likelihood of their deaths. All of this with the objective of conquering *Lebensraum* in the East, a colonial empire to which the Germans claimed to be entitled and that reached far beyond the Ural Mountains.[1]

The parallels with colonial history were perfectly clear to those responsible on the German side, starting with Hitler himself:

> The struggle for hegemony in the world will be decided in favour of Europe by the possession of Russia; this will make Europe the place that is more secure against blockade than anywhere else in the world. [...] The Slavic peoples on the other hand are not destined to lead independent lives of their own. [...] The territory of Russia is our India, and just as the English rule India with only a handful of people, so we will govern this colonial territory of ours. We will supply the Ukrainians with headscarves, glass bead necklaces as jewellery and all the other things that appeal to colonial peoples.[2]

But although Hitler himself thus invoked the British Empire as a model, the Third Reich and its expansionist endeavours are not generally considered by the academic world from the perspective of the history of colonialism, either because scholars instinctively regard colonialism as being a term relating to certain geographical regions outside Europe, or else because they have a mistaken and inadequate conception of what colonialism is. In fact, historical research has largely ignored structural similarities and direct references between the two. Instead, study of the Nazis' colonial enthusiasm has been restricted to the investigation of plans to win back the German empire in Africa; which has produced the negative conclusion that Hitler did not appear to be at all enthusiastic about the idea of possessing a colonial empire. This misses the point that the concrete geographical

---

[1] I would like to thank John Docker, Clara Ervedosa, Jan-Bart Gewald, Christian Gerlach, Christoph Marx, A. Dirk Moses, Armin Nolzen and Eric D. Weitz for their constructive criticisms and valuable advice. For an overview of the enormous literature on the German war against the USSR, see Rolf-Dieter Müller and Gerd Überschär, *Hitlers Krieg im Osten 1941–1945: Ein Forschungsbericht*, Darmstadt 2000.
[2] Hitler, 17 September 1941, in Adolf Hitler, *Monologe im Führerhauptquartier*, ed. Werner Jochmann Hamburg 1980, pp. 60–64.

location for a German colonial empire had long since changed, moving from the south to the east.[3] This shift is evinced, as a prominent example, in the slogan 'Nation without Space' *(Volk ohne Raum).*[4] Hans Grimm's novel of that name may have been set in South Africa; but its title was later used to sum up the essence of German attempts to gain territory in eastern Europe.

Although Hannah Arendt argued as long as half a century ago that imperialism was the precursor of National Socialism, her thesis was basically not at the time followed up by others.[5] Apart from the criticism of her conception of totalitarianism, the reason for this neglect is presumably also to be found in the rapidly expanding scholarship both on colonialism and on National Socialism, each of which now fills whole libraries. As a result, our understanding of both the Third Reich and colonialism has changed so enormously that any comparison has now of necessity to be placed on an entirely new foundation. Furthermore, experts on colonialism have tended not to be interested in the crimes of the Nazis, preferring to leave these to historians of Germany and eastern Europe, while researchers into National Socialism – used to dealing with vast armies, millions of victims and perpetrators and war as it is conducted between modern states – did not for a long time seem to take the colonial conquest of the world seriously. Although there have been plenty of studies that have traced the Nazi expansion policy back to the German Empire of 1871 – as exemplified by the Fischer controversy on Germany's war aims in the First World War[6] – or which categorise that Empire and German colonialism as fascist or proto-fascist,[7] as yet no one has attempted to systematically portray the Nazi policy of expansion and occupation in the East as being colonial by nature.[8]

---

[3] See Klaus Hildebrand, *Vom Reich zum Weltreich: Hitler, NSDAP und koloniale Frage 1919–1945*, München 1969; Jan Esche, *Koloniales Anspruchsdenken in Deutschland im Ersten Weltkrieg, während der Versailler Friedensverhandlungen und in der Weimarer Republik (1914 bis 1933)*, Hamburg 1989. By contrast, Alexandre Kum'a N'dumbe III, *Was wollte Hitler in Afrika? NS-Planungen für eine faschistische Neugestaltung Afrikas*, Frankfurt 1993, exaggerates Africa's importance to Hitler.

[4] Hans Grimm, *Volk ohne Raum*, München 1926.

[5] Hannah Arendt, *The Origins of Totalitarianism*, New York 1951.

[6] Fritz Fischer, *From Kaiserreich to Third Reich*, London 1986; Fritz Fischer, *Germany's aims in the First World War*, New York 1967; Fritz Fischer, *War of illusions: German Policies from 1911 to 1914*, London 1975. On the controversy surrounding his thesis, see John A. Moses, *The Politics of Illusion*, London 1975.

[7] Peter Schmidt-Egner, *Kolonialismus und Faschismus: Eine Studie zur historischen und begrifflichen Genesis faschistischer Bewußtseinsformen am deutschen Beispiel*, Gießen 1975.

[8] Mark Mazower's plea for a closer examination of the colonial roots of Nazi policy seems to have gone largely unheard. See his "After Lemkin: Genocide, the Holocaust and History", *The Jewish Quarterly*, 5/Winter (1995), pp. 5–8. In his *Dark Continent: Europe's Twentieth Century*, London 1998, Mazower suggests that the reason there was such outrage in Europe over Nazi atrocities was that

The problem of the relationship between colonialism and National Socialism is highly political and emotional, for the matter of the singularity of the Holocaust and the relationship between Nazi crimes and previous or subsequent collective mass murders has long since ceased to be an issue only among academic historians, having also taken on a philosophical dimension that touches on intimate questions of identity.[9] Whereas proponents of the singularity thesis regard comparisons as a blasphemous mockery of the Holocaust's victims, its opponents – raising an analogy to the accusation of Holocaust denial – argue that the singularity thesis amounts to a denial of all other genocides.[10]

Above all, the issue of colonial genocide is disturbing, in part because it increases the number of mass murders regarded as genocide, and in part too because it calls into question the assumption that the Europeanisation of the globe was a modernising – and as such positive – project. It is even more difficult to bring about a recognition of colonial genocide among the members of former settler com-

---

the Nazis treated other Europeans like 'Natives'; but he does not go into the connection systematically. The best-known consideration of the connection between colonial mass murders and the Holocaust is that by Sven Lindqvist. But as neither his understanding of European colonialism in Africa nor that of the German policy of annihilation in the East goes beyond extremely simplistic descriptions, the questions he poses are more important than the answers he gives: Sven Lindqvist, *Exterminate all the Brutes*, London 1997. Much the same applies to Ward Churchill, who even speaks of the National Socialists imitating the colonial conquest of North America: Ward Churchill, *A Little Matter of Genocide: Holocaust and Denial in the Americas, 1492–Present*, San Francisco 1997. Richard L. Rubinstein also touched on this idea as early as 1987: Richard L. Rubinstein, "Afterword: Genocide and Civilization", in Isidor Wallimann and Michael N. Dobkowski, eds, *Genocide and the Modern Age: Etiology and Case Studies of Mass Death*, 2nd edn, Syracuse 2000, pp. 283–298, especially p. 288. Hillgruber too writes that the Nazis had intended to reduce large parts of eastern Europe to the status of colonies with a view to exploiting and settling them, but he does not analyse the relationship with colonialism in any greater detail either: Andreas Hillgruber, *Hitlers Strategie. Politik und Kriegführung 1940–41*, München 1982, p. 567.

9 On this subject, see also Daniel Levy and Natan Sznaider, *Erinnerung im globalen Zeitalter: Der Holocaust*, Frankfurt 2001; Norman G. Finkelstein, *The Holocaust Industry*, London 2000; Peter Novick, *The Holocaust in American Life*, Boston/New York 1999.

10 See also Lilian Friedberg, "Dare to Compare: Americanizing the Holocaust", *American Indian Quarterly*, 24/3 (2000), pp. 353–380; David E. Stannard, "'Uniqueness as Denial: The Politics of Genocide Scholarship", in Alan S. Rosenbaum, ed., *Is the Holocaust Unique? Perspectives on Comparative Genocide*, Oxford 1996, pp. 163–208; A. Dirk Moses, "Conceptual Blockages and Definitional Dilemmas in the 'Racial Century': Genocide of Indigenous Peoples and the Holocaust", *Patterns of Prejudice*, 36/4 (2002), pp. 6–37; Jürgen Zimmerer, "Kolonialer Genozid? Vom Nutzen einer historischen Kategorie für eine Globalgeschichte der Massengewalt", in Dominik J. Schaller, Boyadjian Rupen, Hanno Scholtz and Vivianne Berg, eds, *Enteignet-Vertrieben-Ermordet. Beiträge zur Genozidforschung*, Zürich 2004 (English version: "Colonial Genocide? On the Use and Abuse of a Historical Category for Global History", pp. 175–197 in this book).

munities, as it would undermine that very view of the past on which national identity is built. That is why it has been so difficult for Australian conservatives, and first and foremost among them Prime Minister John Howard, to recognise the genocide committed against the Indigenous Australians.[11] And while former US President Bill Clinton has been able in the meantime to apologise in Africa for the crimes of slavery, both these crimes and the extermination of the Native Americans continue to be denied public commemoration within the US.[12] Similarly, the then German President Roman Herzog refused to apologise for the genocide committed against the Herero and Nama peoples during his visit to Namibia in 1998.[13]

At the same time, victim groups and their representatives insist on the crimes against their peoples being acknowledged as genocide precisely for the reason, among others, that genocide is regarded as absolutely the worst crime committed by humanity, and because the use of the term implicitly creates a connection to the Holocaust; that is to say, it places the mass crime concerned, in terms of its moral repugnance, on the same level as the murder of more than six million Jews by the Nazis. This is demonstrated by book titles such as "The American Holocaust",[14] "American Indian Holocaust",[15] "The Herero Holocaust"[16] or "The Black Holocaust".[17]

---

[11] See also: A. Dirk Moses, "Coming to Terms with Genocidal Pasts in Comparative Perspective: Germany and Australia", *Aboriginal History*, 25 (2001), pp. 91–115.

[12] See also Stannard, *Uniqueness as Denial*; Churchill, *A Little Matter of Genocide*. For the blank spaces in American commemorative culture generally, see: James W. Loewen, *Lies across America: What our Historic Sites Get Wrong*, New York 2000. On the issue of compensating entire peoples for genocide and slavery, see: Elazar Barkan, *Völker klagen an. Eine neue international Moral*, Düsseldorf 2002.

[13] "Kein Pardon für Herero-Morde", *Die tageszeitung* (5 March 1998). See also: "Herzog lobt die Beziehungen zu Namibia", *Frankfurter Allgemeine Zeitung* (5 March 1998); "Herzog will Deutsch in Namibia stärken", *Süddeutsche Zeitung* (7 March 1998). The German Foreign Minister Joschka Fischer repeated this position during his visit to Windhoek in October 2003: Ulrike Winkelmann, "Keine Entschuldigung, keine Entschädigung", *Die tageszeitung* (10/11 January 2004).

[14] David E. Stannard, *American Holocaust: The Conquest of the New World*, Oxford/New York 1992.

[15] Russell Thornton, *American Indian Holocaust and Survival: A Population History since 1492*, London 1987.

[16] Jeremy Silvester, Werner H. Illebrecht and Casper Erichsen, "The Herero Holocaust? The Disputed History of the 1904 Genocide", *The Namibian Weekender* (20 August 2001).

[17] Black History Resource Working Group in conjunction with the Race Equality Management Team, ed., *Slavery: An Introduction to the African Holocaust, with Special Reference to Liverpool, 'Capital of the Slave Trade'*, 2nd edn, Liverpool 1997; Thomas Mordekhai, *Vessels of Evil: American Slavery and the Holocaust*, Philadelphia 1993. There are now also museums and societies that commemorate the "Black Holocaust", such as "America's Black Holocaust Museum" and "The Black Holocaust Society" in Milwaukee, Wisconsin. See www.blackwallstreet.freeservers.com, accessed 12 Jul. 2023.

But the inflationary use of the term creates problems for scholarly and academic engagement with the history of genocide. Its application to very diverse cases of mass murder in history and in the present day, cases which differ vastly in respect of their historical backgrounds, the concrete ways in which they proceeded, and the character, number and intention of the perpetrators, robs it of its analytical precision and power to distinguish, and thus of its usefulness in historical analysis. Not every case of mass mortality brought about by outsiders constitutes a case of genocide.

Basically, the academic debate within the fields of Holocaust and Genocide Studies about the proper definition of genocide reflects the positions mentioned above – either stressing or denying the singularity of the Holocaust.[18] Whereas Israel W. Charny, for example, defines genocide very broadly as "the mass killing of substantial numbers of human beings, when not in the course of military action against the military forces of an avowed enemy, under conditions of the essential defenselessness and helplessness of the victims",[19] Steven T. Katz, seeking to limit the concept to the Nazi murder of the Jews, would like to see it applied only to "the actualization of the intent, however successfully carried out, to murder in its totality any national, ethnic, racial, religious, political, social, gender or economic group, as these groups are defined by the perpetrator".[20] Both definitions appear to be largely useless for any consideration of a universal historical nature, since they make sensible comparison difficult. A working definition is needed that neither excludes an event from historical consideration, nor diminishes the horror of the deliberate murder of entire peoples within a general history of mass killings.

The 1948 United Nations Genocide Convention still seems to offer the best and most widely accepted working basis. It defines genocide as

> any of the following acts committed with intent to destroy, in whole or in part, a national, ethnical, racial or religious group, as such:

---

[18] For a brief overview of the stages in the development of Genocide Studies, see Frank Chalk and Kurt Jonassohn, "Genozid: Ein historischer Überblick", in Mihran Dabag and Kristin Platt, eds, *Genozid und Moderne*, i: *Strukturen kollektiver Gewalt im 20. Jahrhundert*, Opladen 1998, pp. 294–308. See also Myriam Gessler, *Die Singularität des Holocaust und die vergleichende Genozidforschung: Empirische und theoretische Untersuchung zu einem aktuellen Thema der Geschichtswissenschaft*, University of Bern 2000 (M.A. thesis).
[19] Quoted according to Helen Fein, "Definition and Discontent: Labelling, Detecting and Explaining Genocide in the Twentieth Century", in Stig Förster and Gerhard Hirschfeld, eds, *Genozid in der modernen Geschichte*, Münster 1999, pp. 11–21, 17.
[20] Steven T. Katz, *The Holocaust in Historical Perspective*, i: *The Holocaust and Mass Death before the Modern Age*, Oxford 1994, p. 131.

(a) Killing members of the group;
(b) Causing serious bodily or mental harm to members of the group;
(c) Deliberately inflicting on the group conditions of life calculated to bring about its physical destruction in whole or in part;
(d) Imposing measures intended to prevent births within the group;
(e) Forcibly transferring children of the group to another group.[21]

Thus the focus is on the intentions of the perpetrators. Raphael Lemkin, the intellectual father of the definition of genocide, speaks of a "coordinated plan of different actions aiming at the destruction of essential foundations of the life of national groups, with the aim of annihilating the groups themselves."[22] Helen Fein calls it a "sustained purposeful action by a perpetrator to physically destroy a collectivity directly or indirectly".[23]

If this yardstick is applied, then it is true that many cases of mass death commonly regarded as genocide are removed from the list: neither in the practice of slavery nor in the deaths of millions of members of the American First Nations who were above all the victims of diseases introduced by the conquerors is there an evident intention to annihilate. Nonetheless, cases of genocide can be shown to have taken place in North America, Australia, and southern Africa, and these will form the focus of the comparative analysis that follows. This is not to suggest that there may not have been further instances of genocidal massacres; it is simply the case that the examples discussed here seem to be the most fruitful for an investigation of structural similarities and connections with National Socialism. It goes without saying that, as Stig Förster and Gerhard Hirschfeld, for example, formulated, "it cannot be a matter of weighing up cases of genocide and numbers of victims against each other".[24] Neither is it a matter of completely equating or denying specific historical features of the various cases: every case of genocide or mass murder organised by a society or a state is singular in important respects. Rather, in the sense of pursuing an 'archaeological' study of the ideas of genocide and population economics (*Bevölkerungsökonomie*), it is a matter of exploring the historical roots of the readiness to uproot whole populations in pursuit of one's own requirements, or even ultimately simply to kill them. In this respect, European colonialism is an important historical starting point, since it and the Nazi

---

21 Article 2, United Nations, *Convention on the Prevention and Punishment of the Crime of Genocide*, 9 December 1948, reproduced in Frank Chalk and Kurt Jonassohn, *The History and Sociology of Genocide: Analyses and Case Studies*, New Haven 1990, pp. 44–49, here p. 44.
22 Raphael Lemkin, *Axis Rule in Occupied Europe: Law of Occupation, Analysis of Government, Proposals for Redress*, Washington 1944, p. 79.
23 Helen Fein, *Genocide: A Sociological Perspective*, London 1990, p. 24.
24 Stig Förster and Gerhard Hirschfeld, "Einleitung", in Stig Förster and Gerhard Hirschfeld, eds, *Genozid in der modernen Geschichte*, Münster 1999, pp. 5–10, here p. 7.

policy of expansion and murder rest on fundamentally similar concepts of 'race' and 'territory', or 'race' and (living) 'space'. The following section explores the structural similarity of the two concepts in terms of both the formulation of their content and their function within the historical phenomena of colonialism and National Socialism respectively, while a second section asks questions regarding the conditions under which genocide took place in colonialism and in National Socialism, and addresses the similarities and differences between the two cases.

Structural Similarity: 'Race' and 'Space'

In considering the various phenomena that gave shape to Nazi policy in Eastern Europe – the war of annihilation, the occupation policy and the genocide – one constantly finds oneself faced by two concepts that link these phenomena together.[25] The first is racism, which is the unifying thread of divergent aspects of Nazi ideology and practice;[26] the second is *Großraumpolitik* (policy of large space) with its associated 'economy of annihilation'.[27]

Racism in this context does not mean simply the attribution of various characteristics to different 'races' and the consequent determination of a level of value for each within an assumed ethnic hierarchy, but a conception of the world "that is applied both internally and externally and can be defined as the comprehensive 'biologisation of social relationships'".[28] Seen under this aspect, the victims of the forced sterilisation policy, of the policy of exterminating 'life not

---

25 Among the sheer unending mass of literature, I would like just to mention a few of the more recent works which I have drawn on particularly for the following discussion: Ulrich Herbert, ed., *National Socialist Extermination Policies: Contemporary German Perspectives and Controversies*, New York 2000; Götz Aly and Susanne Heim, *Vordenker der Vernichtung: Auschwitz und die deutschen Pläne für eine neue europäische Ordnung*, Hamburg 1991; Götz Aly, *'Final Solution': Nazi Population Policy and the Murder of the European Jews*, London/New York 1999; Christian Gerlach, *Kalkulierte Morde: Die deutsche Wirtschafts- und Vernichtungspolitik in Weißrußland, 1941–1944*, Hamburg 1999; Christian Gerlach, *Krieg, Ernährung, Völkermord: Forschungen zur deutschen Vernichtungspoltik im Zweiten Weltkrieg*, Hamburg 1998; Dieter Pohl, *Nationalsozialistische Judenverfolgung in Ostgalizien, 1941–1944: Organisation und Durchführung eines staatlichen Massenverbrechens*, München 1996; Thomas Sandkühler, *'Endlösung' in Galizien: Der Judenmord in Ostpolen und die Rettungsinitiativen von Berthold Beitz*, Bonn 1996.
26 See Michael Burleigh and Wolfgang Wippermann, *The Racial State. Germany, 1933–1945*, Cambridge 1991.
27 See Aly and Heim, *Vordenker der Vernichtung*; Aly, *'Final Solution'*.
28 Ulrich Herbert, "Traditionen des Rassismus", in Ulrich Herbert, ed., *Arbeit, Volkstum, Weltanschauung. Über Fremde und Deutsche im 20. Jahrhundert*, Frankfurt 1995, pp. 11–29, here p. 13.

worthy of life' (*lebensunwertes Leben*), the Soviet prisoners of war and the Jews were all victims of the same inhuman ideology.[29]

In this racist view of history and society, the *Volk* (the people/the nation), was understood to be a single composite organism, whose preservation and growth was to be ensured under any circumstances. Eugenic measures like breeding and at the same time the 'purging' of 'contaminations' and 'pathological conditions' from the 'body of the nation' were intended to guarantee the survival of the German *Volk* and its rise to ascendency in a struggle for existence understood in terms of social Darwinism.[30] But what a *Volk*, whose greatness lay in the number of its 'racially healthy' members appeared to need above all was sufficient territory – *Lebensraum*. Thus the idea of the presumed need for 'sufficient' space to live in was directly linked to the ideology of 'race'. It incorporated ideas both of economic self-sufficiency and of a territory for Germans to settle – a territory that was supposed to exist in Poland and Russia, and where they would find the space they supposedly lacked.[31]

Both concepts, 'race' and 'space', were also at the heart of colonialism. The settler colonies above all created large-scale spatial economies (*Großraumwirtschaften*), being characterised, as was the later German occupation policy in the East, by their efforts to take possession of and develop an enormous dependent territory. An essential element in the concept was the assumption that this would not entail any partnership as between equals, but rather the subjugation, or on occasion even the annihilation, of the original inhabitants. This policy was motivated and also justified by racism, i.e. by the division of humankind into higher 'races', destined to rule, and lower 'races', destined to be subjugated. At the lowest end of the scale

---

[29] This is clearly evident from the fact that the practice of 'euthanasia' was first applied to 'undesirable elements' and the 'disabled', and then also used in concentration camps, and that Himmler later made use of its practitioners, in view of their 'experience' as murderers, when the mass murder of the Jews began. Michael Burleigh, *The Third Reich: A New History*, London 2000, pp. 345–381.

[30] There is a relatively large body of literature on this issue. See Michael Burleigh, *Death and Deliverance. Euthanasia in Germany c. 1900–1945*, Cambridge 1994; Peter Weingart, Jürgen Kroll and Kurt Bayertz, *Rasse, Blut und Gene. Geschichte der Eugenik in Deutschland*, Frankfurt 1988. On the international context, see Stefan Kühl, *Die Internationale der Rassisten. Aufstieg und Niedergang der internationalen Bewegung für Eugenik und Rassenhygiene im 20. Jahrhundert*, Frankfurt 1997; Stefan Kühl, *The Nazi Connection. Eugenics, American Racism, and German National Socialism*, New York 1994.

[31] For a striking example of the settlement policy, see Wendy Lower's interesting article on the Hegewald Project, Himmler's demonstration model of active settlement policy by the SS. However, Lower uses the term "colonial" more or less synonymously with "settlement": Wendy Lower, "A New Ordering of Space and Race: Nazi Colonial Dreams in Zhytomry, Ukraine, 1941–1944", *German Studies Review*, 25 (2002), pp. 227–254.

were groups that were seen as being doomed to destruction, or that were to be deliberately murdered.[32]

Of course, European colonialism experienced various stages of development and assumed different forms in its 500-year history. Even the justification for European expansion and rule over the indigenous populations of the newly 'discovered' and conquered territories changed. But whether it was a question of missionary endeavours to convert the 'heathen', of the 'White Man's Burden' or the 'Manifest Destiny': even if there were shifts in the forms of legitimation, an emphasis on the truth of one's own beliefs or on one's own status as a recipient of divine favour was always the ideological prerequisite for an extension of colonial domination. Social Darwinism, as it gained influence in the course of the nineteenth century, then directly emphasised the 'racial hierarchy' and the idea of competition between nations, both in respect of the relationship between the colonisers and the colonised and also between the colonial powers themselves. This biologistic interpretation of world history – the conviction that one's own nation needs to secure space, territory, in order to ensure its survival – is one of the fundamental parallels between colonialism and the expansionist policies of the Nazis.[33]

The space won by 'discovery' and conquest then had to be 'developed' and 'civilised', for in the perception of the colonisers it was 'savage', chaotic and dangerous.[34] Particularly in the settler colonies the land was regarded as being 'unpopulated',[35] and the settlers believed they could transform it according to their own ideas, supposedly bringing order to chaos without paying any regard to indigenous communities and economies. Cities were founded; roads and later railways were constructed, and the land was surveyed and recorded in land registers.[36]

---

32 See for example: Russell McGregor, *Imagined Destinies. Aboriginal Australians and the Doomed Race Theory, 1880–1939*, Melbourne 1997; Saul Dubow, *Scientific Racism in Modern South Africa*, Cambridge 1995. For a comparison of eugenic and racist discourses in Australia and Germany, even if direct influence is not proven, see Tony Barta, "Discourses of Genocide in Germany and Australia: A Linked History", *Aboriginal History*, 25 (2001), pp. 37–56.
33 Woodruff D. Smith's conclusions are similar: Woodruff D. Smith, *The Ideological Origins of Nazi Imperialism*, Oxford 1986. See also Charles Reynolds, *Modes of Imperialism*, Oxford 1981, pp. 124–171.
34 See for example Albert Wirz, "Missionare im Urwald, verängstigt und hilflos: Zur symbolischen Topografie des kolonialen Christentums", in Wilfried Wagner, ed., *Kolonien und Missionen*, Hamburg 1994, pp. 39–56; Johannes Fabian, *Out of Our Minds: Reason and Madness in the Exploration of Central Africa*, Los Angeles 2000.
35 See for example John K. Noyes, *Colonial Space. Spatiality in the Discourse of German South West Africa, 1884–1915*, Chur 1992.
36 On the ordering of the American West, which was perceived as resembling a featureless ocean that first needed to have a structure imposed on it by surveying, see: Stefan Kaufmann, "Naturale Grenzfelder des Sozialen: Landschaft und Körper", in Monika Fludernik and Hans-

Similarly, the Nazi conquerors regarded the East as an enormous *tabula rasa* that could be recreated in a new form according to their own conceptions, as an arena in which spacial planners and population economists, engineers and economic planners could give free rein to their imaginations.[37] One only needs to think of the megalomaniac plans for the building of an autobahn network reaching deep into Asia, with *Germania*, the new capital of the Reich, at its hub.

Even in their own descriptions of the situation they found in eastern Europe, the German conquerors drew on colonial history as a point of reference. For example, a member of the German 12th Airborne Regiment reported a few weeks after the attack on the Soviet Union:

> Marvellous as the successes are, great as the advance is [...], Russia on the whole is still a huge disappointment for the individual. There is nothing of culture, nothing of paradise [...] but only the absolute depths, filth, people who demonstrate to us that we will face a huge task of colonisation here.[38]

Joachim Gehrke, eds, *Grenzgänger zwischen Kulturen*, Würzburg 1999, pp. 121–136. On the German tradition of opening up remote areas of the earth, see Dirk van Laak, *Imperiale Infrastruktur. Deutsche Planungen für eine Erschließung Afrikas, 1880 bis 1960*, Paderborn 2004.

37 A vigorous debate has arisen in recent years on the participation of scientists and experts generally in Nazi crimes. See: Franz-Rutker Hausmann, *Deutsche Geisteswissenschaft im Zweiten Weltkrieg: Die 'Aktion Ritterbusch' (1940–1945)*, Dresden 1998; Michael Fahlbusch, *Wissenschaft im Dienst der nationalsozialistischen Politik? Die 'Volksdeutschen Forschungsgemeinschaften' von 1931–1945*, Baden-Baden 1999; Winfried Schulze and Otto Gerhard Oexle, eds, *Deutsche Historiker im Nationalsozialismus*, Frankfurt 1999. With regard to the question of scholarship concerning, and planning for, the East, see Bruno Wasser, *Himmlers Raumplanung im Osten*, Basel 1993; Mechtild Rössler, *'Wissenschaft und Lebensraum': Geographische Ostforschung im Nationalsozialismus, Ein Beitrag zur Disziplingeschichte der Geographie*, Berlin 1990; Michael Burleigh, *Germany Turns Eastwards: A Study of Ostforschung in the Third Reich*, Cambridge 1988; Mechtild Rössler and Sabine Schleiermacher, eds, *Der 'Generalplan Ost'*, Berlin 1993; Czeslaw Madajczyk, ed., *Vom Generalplan Ost zum Generalsiedlungsplan*, München 1994; Aly and Heim, *Vordenker der Vernichtung*; Aly, *'Final Solution'*. Specifically on the role of scholarship in colonialism and on the academic continuity between colonialism and National Socialism, see Jürgen Zimmerer, "Wissenschaft und Kolonialismus: Das Geographische Institut der Friedrich-Wilhelms-Universität vom Kaiserreich zum Dritten Reich", in Ulrich van der Heyden and Joachim Zeller, eds, *Kolonialmetropole Berlin: Eine Spurensuche*, Berlin 2002, pp. 125–130; Jürgen Zimmerer, "Im Dienste des Imperiums. Die Geographen der Berliner Universität zwischen Kolonialwissenschaften und Ostforschung", *Jahrbuch für Universitätsgeschichte*, 7 (2004), pp. 73–100 (English version: "In the Service of the Empire: Berlin University's Geographers from Colonial Sciences to Ostforschung": pp. 262–293 in this book).

38 A soldier of the 12th Airborne Regiment, 20 July 1941, quoted according to Gerlach, *Kalkulierte Morde*, p. 102.

The impression of the eastern lands as being "primitive, barren and backward",[39] which Christian Gerlach has identified as underlying many accounts relating to Belarus, meant that from the German point of view there was a need for the whole country to be comprehensively 'modernised' and reorganised, without any regard for its existing social, political and economic structures. And it was precisely this comprehensive reorganisation that was interpreted by those involved in it as colonisation. The then chief state planning officer for East Prussia, Ewald Liedecke, for example, who later performed the same function in the *Reichsgau* (administrative division) of Danzig-West Prussia, commented as early as 1939 on the issue of how the pre-existing settled and cultivated areas were to be handled:

> In restructuring German territory we cannot follow in the footsteps of the Poles and base an area of German settlement on the Polish pattern of settlement and land division. Rather than taking such a half-hearted approach, a process of total colonisation is required, one that encompasses the entire area, redistributes it and resettles it in accordance with German conceptions.[40]

But the sense of entitlement to rule over the conquered territories was derived not only from the allegedly 'underdeveloped' state of the land, but also from the supposed backwardness and immaturity of the inhabitants. According to Hitler, one "only needed to see this primeval world" in order to appreciate "that nothing happens here if one does not assign people the work they have to do. The Slav is a born slave, they are a mass crying out for a master."[41]

And Himmler's secretary Hanns Johst, who travelled through Poland with the *Reichsführer SS* in the winter of 1939/40, was no doubt reflecting his boss's ideas as well when he wrote:

> The Poles are not a state-building people. They lack even the most basic prerequi-sites. I have travelled all over the country at the side of the *Reichsführer* SS. A country which has so little feeling for the essence of settlement that it is not even up to the task of creating a village of any style has no claim to any sort of independent political status within Europe. It is a country crying out to be colonised![42]

---

39 Gerlach, *Kalkulierte Morde*, p. 102.
40 Ewald Liedecke, *Kolonisatorische Aufgaben der Raum-Ordnung im Nordosten des Deutschen Reiches*, Königsberg, 1 September 1939, quoted according to Michael A. Hartenstein, *Neue Dorflandschaften: Nationalsozialistische Siedlungsplanung in den 'eingegliederten Ostgebieten', 1939–1944*, Berlin 1998, p. 79.
41 Hitler, 17 September 1941, in Hitler, *Monologe*, p. 63.
42 Hanns Johst, *Ruf des Reiches: Echo des Volkes!*, München 1940 p. 94, quoted according to: Michael Burleigh, *Die Zeit des Nationalsozialismus. Eine Gesamtdarstellung*, Frankfurt 2000, p. 515.

The parallels to colonialism are however not limited just to the ideological justification of conquest and domination; they are also evident in the techniques the colonial power used to enforce its rule. Except in the settler colonies, where there was a gradual shift in the proportion of Europeans to the indigenous population, a small elite of colonial administrators and military personnel ruled over a far more numerous local population that lacked any opportunity to participate in government. The colonisers and the colonised were subject to different legal systems, and this 'dual legal system' rested on racial criteria. The advantageous status of Europeans in this society of racial privilege[43] was however not confined to matters of formal law. The *situation coloniale* permeated all spheres of social interaction between colonisers and colonised. Europeans occupied a privileged position at all times and in all places. They had their own schools and kindergartens and their own counters at post offices and in other government agencies. In German South West Africa this constant subjugation was evident, for example, in the fact that Africans were obliged to salute every White person, and were forbidden to ride horses or walk on pavements. In occupied Poland, too, Poles had to display appropriate humility towards all Germans by making way for them on pavements, raising their hats to them and saluting. They were prohibited from attending cinemas, concerts, exhibitions, libraries, museums or theatres, and from owning bicycles, cameras or radios.[44] To be sure, this everyday discrimination pales into insignificance in comparison with the mass murder that was being committed at the same time, but it nevertheless provides an indication of an often-overlooked strand of tradition in German policy in the occupied eastern territories.

This idea of a society of racial privilege basically also underlies Hitler's statement that "Our Germans – this is the main thing – must form a closed community, like a fortress; outside the main centres, even the lowest stable boy must stand above any of the natives."[45] Though this only applied, of course, to that part of the local population whose very right to live was recognised at all.

Neither in colonialism nor in National Socialism was the different treatment of Germans and non-Germans, of 'Whites' and 'non-Whites', merely laid down in law and in everyday life: rather, active steps were taken to avoid any 'mixing' of the populations. But the problem of maintaining this distance between the privileged

---

43 On this concept, see Jürgen Zimmerer, *Deutsche Herrschaft über Afrikaner. Staatlicher Machtanspruch und Wirklichkeit im kolonialen Namibia*, Münster/Hamburg/London 2001, pp. 94–109 [English translation: *German Rule, African Subjects: State Aspirations and the Reality of Power in Colonial Namibia*, New York, 2021, pp. 111–126].
44 Burleigh, *The Third Reich*, pp. 450f.
45 Hitler, 17 September 1941, in Hitler, *Monologe*, pp. 62–63.

upper and the non-privileged lower strata was particularly acute in the settler colonies, where there was a relatively large number of European residents. People of 'mixed' descent (*Mischlinge*), who, like their parents, to some extent blurred the boundaries between the 'races', were seen as a potential threat. Thus attempts were made to prevent their coming into existence at all, to which end, beginning in the English colonies in North America, 'mixed' marriages were forbidden in more and more places. In German South West Africa, for example, Deputy Governor Hans Tecklenburg forbade all 'mixed' marriages, on the grounds that "it is an old fact of experience, evident not only in Africa, that where the white man lives together permanently with a member of the lower race he does not draw her up to his level, but is drawn down to hers; he 'goes native' or 'goes kaffir'".[46] Any transgression against the prohibition of sexual relations was branded as "a sin against racial consciousness", as the Protestant missionary Carl Wandres put it.[47] It is not difficult to see in this a parallel with the Nazi concept of *Rassenschande* ('racial defilement') and the racial laws of the Third Reich: the Nuremberg Laws of 1935 for example forbade both marriages with Jews and "extramarital intercourse between Jews and citizens of German or kindred blood."[48]

---

46 Tecklenburg to Colonial Department Berlin, 23 October 1905, NAN F.IV.R.1., Sheets 24a–34a.
47 The missionary Carl Wandres in a memorandum *Bemerkungen über Mischehen und Mischlinge aus der Praxis für die Praxis* (1912), NAN F.IV.R.1., sheets 143b–145b. For the example of German South West Africa, see Zimmerer, *Deutsche Herrschaft*, pp. 94–109 [English translation: *German Rule, African Subjects*, pp. 111–126].
48 *Law for the Protection of German Blood and of German Honour*, 15 September 1935, reproduced in Walther Hofer, ed., *Der Nationalsozialismus: Dokumente, 1933–1945*, new revised edn, Frankfurt 1982, p. 285. See also Saul Friedländer, *Nazi Germany and the Jews*, i, *The Years of Persecution, 1933–1939*, New York 1997, pp. 145–164; Cornelia Essner, *Die 'Nürnberger Gesetze' oder die Verwaltung des Rassenwahns 1933–1945*, Paderborn 2002. The connections – including in terms of the people involved – between colonial and Nazi racism are also pointed out by Ehmann: Annegret Ehmann "From Colonial Racism to Nazi Population Policy: The Role of the so-called 'Mischlinge'", Michael Berenbaum and Abraham J. Peck, eds, *The Holocaust and History: The Known, the Unkown, the Disputed, and the Reexamined*, Washington 1998, pp. 115–133. Birthe Kundrus recently attempted to disprove any connection between colonial and Nazi race policy: Birthe Kundrus, "Von Windhoek nach Nürnberg? Koloniale 'Mischehenverbote' und die nationalsozialistische Rassengesetzgebung", Birthe Kundrus, *Phantasiereiche. Zur Kulturgeschichte des deutschen Kolonialismus*, Frankfurt 2003, pp. 110–131. But her argument is not convincing. The supposed openness and heterogeneity of Wilhelminian discourse in relation to Africans – if they existed at all – were no more than apparent. In the hegemonial discourse such as was reflected notably in colonial practice, no such openness existed. On this, see Jürgen Zimmerer, "Von Windhuk nach Warschau. Die rassische Privilegiengesellschaft in Deutsch-Südwestafrika – ein Modell mit Zukunft?", Frank Becker, ed., *Rassenmischehen – Mischlinge – Rassentrennung. Zur Politik der Rasse im deutschen Kolonialreich*, Stuttgart 2004, pp. 97–123 (English version: "From Wind-

The notion of the freedom to reshape colonised territory at will presupposed an indigenous population that was deprived of all rights and reduced to being at the disposal of the colonial masters, so that it could be used in accordance with their interests. This manifested itself in two ways: the forced recruitment of labour and the arbitrary resettlement of the indigenous population. The recruitment of labour took a number of different forms. In the Congo, for instance, able-bodied men were literally hunted down; women and children were taken as hostages to force the men to come out of hiding, and whole villages were destroyed if they failed to meet quotas for the provision of workers.[49] In South West Africa, by contrast, recruitment was ensured after 1907 by the promulgation of the Native Ordinances, and was implemented, or at least overseen, by the colonial administration. With the aid of a system of surveillance probably unique in the history of colonialism,[50] the Africans were to be completely integrated into the colonial economy as labour. Even if this constituted a 'semi-free labour market' rather than a system of forced labour, behind this practice stood the notion of an indigenous population completely at the disposition of the colonial state.[51] This was carried to the extent that larger African settlements were forbidden in order to ensure an even distribution of labour across the whole country.

The National Socialist economy also recruited forced labour in every occupied country and deported the workers to Germany.[52] The German armaments industry, for example, relied to no small extent on slave labour, and the forcible

---

hoek to Warsaw. The Society of Racial Privilege in German South West Africa – a Model with a Future?", pp. 201–229 in this book).

49 Adam Hochschild, *Schatten über dem Kongo. Die Geschichte eines der großen fast vergessenen Menschheitsverbrechen*, Stuttgart, 2000, pp. 165–99; Samuel Henry Nelson, *Colonialism in the Congo Basin, 1880–1940*, Athens (Ohio) 1994.

50 Jürgen Zimmerer, "Der totale Überwachungsstaat? Recht und Verwaltung in Deutsch-Südwestafrika", in Rüdiger Voigt, ed., *Das deutsche Kolonialrecht als Vorstufe einer globalen 'Kolonialisierung' von Recht und Verwaltung*, Baden-Baden 2001, pp. 175–198 (English version: "Total Control? Law and Administration in German South West Africa", pp. 77–103 in this book).

51 On this, see Jürgen Zimmerer, "Der Wahn der Planbarkeit. Unfreie Arbeit, Zwangsmigration und Genozid als Elemente der Bevölkerungsökonomie in Deutsch-Südwestafrika", *Comparativ*, 13/4 (2003), pp. 96–113 (English version: "Planning Frenzy: Forced Labour, Expulsion and Genocide as Elements of Population Economics in German South West Africa", pp. 57–76 in this book); Zimmerer, *Deutsche Herrschaft*, pp. 126–175 [English translation, *German Rule, African Subjects*, pp. 159–230].

52 Gerlach, *Kalkulierte Morde*, pp. 449–502. See also the classic study by Ulrich Herbert, *Hitler's Foreign Workers: Enforced Foreign Labor in Germany under the Third Reich*, Cambridge/New York 1997.

removal of workers from their home areas could easily assume forms that are familiar from reports from the Congo.[53]

The arrogant assumption of the colonial 'masters' that the indigenous population were at their absolute disposition, in accordance with their own economic and security requirements, had been manifested even earlier in other colonies in the utter lack of scruple with which they were prepared to resettle local populations in response to economic needs, to cram them into reserves or to expel them completely from the colonial territory. Whether in the reservations of North America or those of German South West Africa, the common thread was that any people deemed to be undesirable as components of the new colonial society were simply physically removed. Not surprisingly, the land to which they were to be resettled was almost without exception unsuitable, indeed unusable.

That the economic and social decline that all too often ensued in such cases was intended or at least readily accepted suggests that genocidal inclinations played a role in this as well, at least in part. The German plans for eastern Europe, though of course conceived on a much larger scale and providing for the resettlement of millions of people and the cramming of Jews in particular into 'reservations', may have borrowed from these colonial precedents. At the very least, the fact that a policy of creating reservations was familiar to the perpetrators as a 'normal' practice in dealing with indigenous populations may well have contributed to the lack of any proper perception of the criminal nature of such a policy.[54]

Genocides: Similarities and Differences

The most radical consequence of a policy of conquest and settlement based on the concepts of 'race' and 'space' was genocide, i.e. the murder of people considered to be enemies, 'superfluous' or a 'hindrance' to one's own economic development.

This section attempts to explore the relationships between genocidal moments in colonialism and in National Socialism. It will seek to demonstrate how genocidal tendencies developed on the colonial frontier and how, in their degree of organisation and with regard to the responsible groups of perpetrators, they gradually came to resemble the crime of modern bureaucratic genocide typically perpetrated by states. However, it is first necessary briefly to establish a differen-

---

[53] For examples of this sort of forced recruitment see Michael Burleigh, *The Third Reich*, p. 551–54.
[54] Similarly, Gerlach argues that the so-called territorial plans made the "rupture in civilisation" a gradual one. See Gerlach, *Krieg, Ernährung, Völkermord*, pp. 258–299, especially p. 262.

tiation between what is to be understood as genocide in a colonial and in a Nazi context respectively.

In the Third Reich, genocidal policies arose in such a concentrated fashion and were directed against so many different groups of victims within such a short space of time that the genocides can justifiably be seen as one of the main characteristics, if not *the* main characteristic, of National Socialism. Although they were all emanations of the same policy aimed at achieving a racist utopia, the Nazi genocides committed against the various categories of victims can be differentiated according to their motives and the methods of destruction employed. Such a differentiation is necessary if comparisons are to be drawn with genocides committed in colonial contexts, since over and above all the similarities differences are also apparent.

Jews were to be completely exterminated, because they were regarded as occupying the very lowest rung on the ladder of the new 'racial hierarchy' and were not to be accorded any chance of survival in the racist utopia of the future. They allegedly posed a worldwide threat that had to be combated everywhere; they were regarded as 'parasites' in the body of the nation (*Volkskörper*) that had to be destroyed.[55] The latter applied also to the Sinti and Roma,[56] as well as to 'antisocial elements' and to the 'handicapped'; these groups were however not regarded as a global threat or deemed to form part of a worldwide conspiracy.[57]

Nonetheless, the methods of destruction were shared by all victim groups. In accordance with the intention to annihilate them radically and systematically, the genocide committed against the Jews was bureaucratically organised and carried out in a quasi-industrialised manner with techniques adopted from the so-called 'euthanasia campaign'. These policies were also applied to homosexuals and to Sinti and Roma. As it is this aspect – in the form of the universally-known gas chambers and crematoria – that has shaped our perception of Nazi crimes generally, it is necessary to emphasise that many Jewish and also Sinti and Roma victims were killed in mass shootings and in summary executions associated with campaigns against 'partisans'.[58] Murder through gas was the culmination of a

---

[55] See Friedländer, *Nazi Germany and the Jews*, i, pp. 73–112.
[56] The German term generally used as the equivalent of the English 'Gypsies' covers two ethnic groups: the Sinti, traditionally living in Germany, and the eastern European Roma.
[57] On the individual groups, see Michael Zimmermann, *Rassenutopie und Genozid. Die nationalsozialistische 'Lösung der Zigeunerfrage'*, Hamburg 1996; Burleigh, *Death and Deliverance*; Wolfgang Ayaß, *'Asoziale' im Nationalsozialismus*, Stuttgart 1995; Ernst Klee, *'Euthanasie' im NS-Staat. Die 'Vernichtung lebensunwerten Lebens'*, Frankfurt 1983; Hans-Walter Schmuhl, *Rassenhygiene, Nationalsozialismus, Euthanasie*, Göttingen 1987.
[58] See, for example, Ruth Bettina Birn, "Zweierlei Wirklichkeit? Fallbeispiele zur Partisanenbekämpfung", in Bernd Wegner, ed., *Zwei Wege nach Moskau. Vom Hitler-Stalin Pakt zum 'Unter-*

process that began with arbitrary shootings and local killings; and many murders, as Christian Gerlach has shown with regard to the shooting of Jews in Belarus in the summer of 1941, had economic motives. Like Poles and Russians, Jews were deliberately killed in order to ensure the supply of provisions for the German Army in the occupied territories. To create a surplus for the German troops, the consumption of the local population had to be reduced.

In the "greatest murder plan in history" the Nazis deliberately intended to allow up to thirty million people to starve to death in order to use the food that would thus be saved to supply both the German Army and the Reich.[59] At the same time, the number of people in the occupied territories was to be reduced by expelling local inhabitants to the east, with the future area of German settlement being protected by a 'strip of scorched earth' (*Brandstreifen*). All foodstuffs were to be transported out of this area, which was to extend eastwards from the line Bakuto–Stalingrad–Moscow–Leningrad – the limit of the German settlement area – as far as the Urals, so that all life was to be destroyed.[60]

The mass murders were also related to the general settlement policy. In a Europe-wide attempt at 'ethnic disentanglement' (*ethnischer Entflechtung*), the Germans to be settled in those occupied territories were to come from areas such as South Tyrol, Bessarabia or the Bukovina where they comprised ethnic minorities. In a "policy of ethnic dominos", these people were to be allocated areas from which Polish farmers, for example, had been expelled, while they in turn would take the place of Jews who were to be deported to the margins of the area of German rule. As this ultimately proved impossible due to the military situation, the readiness to commit mass murder grew.[61]

Mass murder was committed not only in the concentration camps but also in prisoner-of-war camps and in the ghettos of the occupied territories. The fate of Russian prisoners of war lies somewhere between industrialised annihilation and genocidal massacre. They were initially interned and subjected to bureaucratic administration, but then killed through intentional neglect – a policy that was also genocidal, since it was because of their Russian ethnicity that the victims

---

nehmen Barbarossa', München 1991, pp. 275–290. For German anti-partisan warfare in general, see Philip Warren Blood, *Bandenbekämpfung: Nazi Occupation Security in Eastern Europe and Soviet Russia 1942–45*, Cranfield University 2001 (Ph.D. Thesis).
59 Christian Gerlach, "Deutsche Wirtschaftsinteressen, Besatzungspolitik und der Mord an den Juden in Weißrußland, 1941–1943", in Ulrich Herbert, ed., *Nationalsozialistische Vernichtungspolitik 1939–1945. Neue Forschung und Kontroversen*, Frankfurt 1998, pp. 263–291, here p. 268.
60 Gerlach, *Kalkulierte Morde*, p. 53.
61 Götz Aly, "'Jewish Resettlement': Reflections on the Political Prehistory of the Holocaust", in Herbert, ed., *National Socialist Extermination Policies*, pp. 53–83; Aly, *'Final Solution'*.

were left to die.[62] There was no such policy of annihilation in camps with British, French or American prisoners of war.

In addition to this bureaucratically organised form of murder embracing millions of people, there were also genocidal massacres. In my understanding, these include both mass shootings, carried out on orders from above, and also killings in the course of operations against partisans.[63] These latter also form part of the planned policy of genocide, since the 'cleansing' of whole areas of land and the deliberate murder of, for example, children and old people in the process indicate that these measures also had a broader dimension relating to questions of population economics.[64]

It is notable that the individual groups of victims cannot be strictly distinguished according to the ways in which they were murdered. Non-Jewish Poles and Russians were also killed by gassing, Jews and also Sinti and Roma were also shot or starved to death in camps and ghettos. What they have in common, however, relates to the killers. All of them killed as representatives and with the approval of their state, whether in the role of occupation soldiers, members of firing squads, supervisors in concentration or prison camps or members of staff in planning units, ministries or universities charged with the advance planning.

At first sight, the crimes of the National Socialists and the genocides committed in the colonies are distinguished from each other by one important criterion, namely that their implementation and bureaucratic organisation were in the hands of organs of the state. However, the present author's position is that this is a difference in degree but not in essential structures, since under closer examination many of those genocides can be identified as being crimes committed by the state, and also display strong bureaucratic elements.

---

62 On prisoners of war, see the classic study: Christian Streit, *Keine Kameraden. Die Wehrmacht und die sowjetischen Kriegsgefangenen, 1941–1945*, Stuttgart 1978.

63 On this, see Gerlach, *Kalkulierte Morde*, pp. 859–1,054.

64 It should be pointed out that supporters of the 'singularity thesis' reject the use of the term 'genocide' if the fates of several groups of victims are considered together. For Steven T. Katz, for example, the Sinti and Roma were not victims of genocide, but were gassed in Auschwitz because they had typhoid. On this, see Fein, *Definition and Discontent*, p. 15. The same is also true of Yehuda Bauer, who, while he accepts 'genocide' as an all-embracing term, introduces the expression 'Holocaust' as a special category for the murder of the Jews: "The conclusion to draw is that one ought to differentiate between the intent to destroy a group in a context of selective mass murder and the intent to annihilate every person of the group. To make this as simple as possible, I would suggest retaining the term *genocide* for 'partial' murder and the term *Holocuast* for total destruction" (emphasis in orginial). Yehuda Bauer, *Rethinking the Holocaust*, New Haven 2001, pp.10 f. And he argues that "up until now 'total destruction' had been the intention only in the case of the Jews, so that the Holocaust had no precursors, but was 'unprecedented'."

Other than in the case of National Socialism, which was genocidal in its very core, the individual cases of genocide in the history of European colonialism are more difficult to identify, despite the fact that the 500 years since the 'discovery' of America have been shaped by violence, suffering and oppression. Mass deaths accompanied the Europeans' penetration of the interiors of America, Africa, Asia and Australia, and indigenous states and peoples were destroyed. In all probability, no other period in human history saw the destruction of so many cultures as did the sixteenth and seventeenth centuries. But the overwhelming majority of those who died were the victims either of imported diseases, or of forced labour, or of the propagation of Christianity by the sword. The victims' suffering was certainly just as great as in cases of intentional annihilation, and yet one cannot speak of genocide in these colonial cases, as the destruction of entire peoples was not intended. Indeed, the colonial economies needed the indigenous populations in order to exploit their labour.[65] The same is true of slavery, which does not constitute genocide, despite the fact that it impacted an estimated 24 million African men and women, about half of whom were transported to America and the Caribbean where they had to perform forced labour under the most inhuman conditions.[66] After all, an intention to exploit the Africans' labour and an intention to destroy them physically would have been self-contradictory, though this is not intended to exclude a willing acceptance of their being worked to death in some cases. These conclusions apply to the other continents as well.[67]

Nonetheless, there were genocidal moments in the process, when the desire to consider the original inhabitants of a country to be 'less than human' (*Untermenschen*) and to eliminate them rather than simply dispossessing them shone through in various places. Such cases mainly concern the settler colonies of North America, Australia, New Zealand and southern Africa. This is no coincidence, since it was only where it was possible or seemed desirable to replace the indigenous peoples with a new population that the genocidal idea could gain traction,

---

[65] Cf. Gründer, who rejects the notion of colonial genocide, even if he does not deny that in a few cases there were genocidal orders, massacres or consequences. Horst Gründer, "Genozid oder Zwangsmodernisierung? Der moderne Kolonialismus in universalgeschichtlicher Perspektive", in Mihran Dabag and Kristin Platt, eds, *Genozid und Moderne*, i: *Strukturen kollektiver Gewalt im 20. Jahrhundert*, Opladen 1998, pp. 135–51.

[66] Seymour Drescher, "The Atlantic Slave Trade and the Holocaust: A Comparative Analysis", in Alan S. Rosenbaum, ed., *Is the Holocaust Unique? Perspectives on Comparative Genocide*, Oxford 1996, pp. 65–86, especially pp. 66f.

[67] A contrary position regarding Australia and America is held by Churchill, *A Little Matter of Genocide*; Stannard, *American Holocaust*; and Tony Barta, "Relations of Genocide: Land and Lives in the Colonization of Australia", in Isidor Wallimann and Michael N. Dobkowski, *Genocide and the Modern Age: Etiology and Case Studies of Mass Death*, 2nd edn, Syracuse 2000, pp. 237–251.

with the process of settlement taking on a genocidal dynamic and mass murder being used to create space for new settlement.

The ideological basis for such events could be furnished by either secular or millennial utopian thinking. It was the dream of the Promised Land, of the White settler colony, of the unpopulated *tabula rasa* that could be reshaped in accordance with one's own ideas of civilisation, or the identification of one's own life with a divine, historic or civilising mission, that could create a readiness to commit mass murder if necessary.[68]

The combination of a pronounced sense of calling, the conviction of belonging to a 'chosen race', as is expressed in the doctrine of the 'Manifest Destiny', with the readiness to regard Native Americans as 'non-believers' or even to view them as vermin, is characteristic of this genocidal impetus and can already be found among the New England Puritans. The author of a poem entitled 'Some Meditations', probably Captain Wait Winthrop, prophesied as early as 1675 that God would destroy the Narragansett people, who had just taken on the New England militia in the 'Great Swamp Fight':

> O *New England*, I understand, with thee God is offended:
> And therefore He doth humble thee, till thou thy ways hast mended
>
> Repent therefore, and do no more, advance thy self so High
> But humbled be, and thou shalt see these Indians soon will dy.
>
> A Swarm of Flies, they may arise, a Nation to Annoy,
> Yea Rats and Mice, or Swarms of Lice a Nation may destroy.
> [...]
> And now I shall my Neigbours all give one word of Advice,
> in Love and Care do you prepare for War, if you be wise.
>
> Get Ammunition with Expedition your Selves for to defend,
> And Pray to God that He His Rod will please to suspend.[69]

Sir Jeffery Amherst, commander of the British troops in North America, stood in the same tradition when he initiated biological warfare against members of the Delaware Nation by having his officers give them blankets contaminated with smallpox: 'You will Do well to try to Innoculate the Indians by means of Blanketts,

---

[68] On the significance for genocide of utopian concepts of the re-creation of the world and of mankind, see Omer Bartov, "Utopie und Gewalt. Neugeburt und Vernichtung der Menschen", in Hans Maier, ed., *Wege in die Gewalt: Die modernen politischen Religionen*, Frankfurt 2000, pp. 92–120.
[69] Quoted according to Chalk and Jonassohn, *History and Sociology of Genocide*, p. 194.

as well as to try Every other method that can serve to Extirpate this Execrable Race."[70]

In the nineteenth century, the religiously based concept of being 'chosen' gradually gave way to a Social Darwinian and biological view of history based on the concept of 'race'. For Lieut. General Lothar von Trotha, commander-in-chief of the German troops in the war against the Herero in South West Africa (1904–1908) and the man primarily responsible for the first German genocide, the destruction of the enemy was an absolutely essential measure in a 'race war' that in his opinion could only end with one of the belligerent parties being annihilated. Von Trotha's view was that Africans would "yield only to force", and it was his intention to exercise this force "with blatant terrorism and even with cruelty" and annihilate "the rebellious tribes with rivers of blood";[71] for as he saw it, a war in Africa could not be conducted "in accordance with the rules of the Geneva Convention."[72] Von Trotha also clearly articulated the connection between the settler colony and genocide. When the long-serving Governor Theodor Leutwein attempted to dissuade the newly-arrived general from mass murder by arguing that the Herero were needed as labourers, von Trotha answered that South West Africa was the one colony "in which a European can himself work to provide for his family".[73]

Whether it was by emphasising the indigenous population's status as 'unbelievers', by equating them with vermin, or by characterising them as an 'enemy race', the ground for genocide was prepared by scare propaganda. In each case this placed the indigenous population outside the "universe of obligation", i.e. outside of that group "whom we are obligated to protect, to take into account, and to whom we must account": an exclusion that is an essential precondition for genocide, the mental disposition, so to speak, to make mass murderers out of otherwise ordinary people.[74] How this dehumanisation of the indigenous inhabitants manifested itself in individual perpetrators is illustrated by the practice, known from Australia, of 'shooting practice' – with Australian Aboriginal people as targets. As an eyewitness reported in 1889: "There are instances when the young

---

70 Quoted according to a facsimile of Amherst's original letter, to be found under https://people.umass.edu/derrico/amherst/34_41_114_fn.jpeg, accessed 12 Jul. 2023, see Chalk and Jonassohn, *History and Sociology of Genocide*, p. 177.
71 Von Trotha to Leutwein, 5 November 1904, quoted according to Horst Drechsler, *Südwestafrika unter deutscher Kolonialherrschaft. Der Kampf der Herero und Nama gegen den deutschen Imperialismus, 1884–1915*, 2nd edn, Berlin 1984, p. 156.
72 "Politik und Kriegsführung", in *Der Deutschen Zeitung*, 3 February 1909, as quoted according to: Gerhard Pool, *Samuel Maharero*, Windhoek 1991, p. 293.
73 Von Trotha's diary, quoted according to Pool, *Samuel Maharero*, p. 265.
74 Helen Fein, *Definition and Discontent*, p. 20.

men of the station have employed the Sunday in hunting the blacks, not only for some definite purpose, but also for the sake of the sport."[75]

This was only possible because Australian Aboriginal people, including women and children, were not regarded as belonging to human society; as is demonstrated in The Queenslander:

> And, being a useless race, what does it matter what they suffer any more than the distinguished philanthropist, who writes in his behalf, cares for the wounded half-dead pigeon he tortures at his shooting matches. 'I do not see the necessity,' was the reply of a distinguished wit to an applicant for an office who remarked that 'he must live;' and we virtually and practically say the same to the blacks and with better reason.[76]

From this attitude it was but a small step to the murder of women and children, especially if one was able to justify the act with the protection of one's own property, as one Australian squatter did of whom it was reported in 1889:

> He shot all the men he discovered on his run, because they were cattle killers; the women, because they gave birth to cattle killers; and the children, because they would in time become cattle killers.[77]

Justifications of the murder of women and children in order to interrupt the biological reproductive process are also found in North America. H. L. Hall, an infamous murderer of Native Americans, justified the slaughter of babies with the saying well known since the time of King Philip's War (1675–1677) that "a nit would make a louse". The slogan was popularised by Colonel John Milton Chivington, who himself claimed: "My intention is to kill all Indians I may come across".[78]

Some scholars argue that individual intention to exterminate a population does not constitute genocide unless it becomes state policy.[79] The UN Convention leaves open the question as to who and how many people must belong to the group of perpetrators. What is important here is that the issue of the role of the state points to a significant difference between colonial and Nazi genocides. For whereas the murder of Jews, Sinti and Roma, Poles and Russians was orchestrated from the centre and carried out by organs of the state, this type of state

---

75 Quoted according to Alison Palmer, *Colonial Genocide*, Adelaide 2000, pp. 44.
76 The Queenslander, 8 May 1880, https://trove.nla.gov.au/newspaper/article/20332884, accessed 12 Jul. 2023, see Palmer, *Colonial Genocide*, p. 45.
77 Quoted according to Palmer, *Colonial Genocide*, p. 43.
78 Quoted according to Churchill, *A Little Matter of Genocide*, p. 229; Stannard, *American Holocaust*, p. 131, n. 123.
79 Helen Fein, "Genozid als Staatsverbrechen: Beispiele aus Rwanda und Bosnien", in *Zeitschrift für Genozidforschung 1* (1999), pp. 36–45; Chalk/Jonassohn, *The History and Sociology of Genocide*, p. 23.

involvement was rarer in the colonial context. Particularly right on the frontier, private actions at a local level were predominant; this was after all by definition the mixed zone where contact between new arrivals and local populations predominantly occurred, and where the Whites were at least initially not yet in the majority and state structures were lacking.[80]

This is why in most cases the planned murder of Native Americans and Australian Aboriginal people cannot be traced back to the highest state representatives even within the colonies, let alone to London or later, in the American case, to Washington. Often it was local army or militia commanders or bands of settlers who took matters into their own hands. Hence different situations prevailed from settlement to settlement and from colony to colony, and hence, too, orders for the protection of the 'natives' often went unheeded. The colonial states lacked the power and the means to control the behaviour of their citizens. Even in the case of the murder of Herero and Nama in German South West Africa (1904–1908), where there is no doubt that an 'annihilation order' existed, it did not originate from the highest representatives of the state, the Emperor or the Chancellor. Its initiator was General von Trotha, the local military commander.[81]

But does it make sense, in a historical comparison of mass murders, to conceive of the state as the bureaucratic and centralised institution in the particularly highly developed form that it was in the Third Reich? Should we not rather historicise our conception of the state?[82] If we apply a historical concept of the state that is appropriate to colonial contexts, rather than one based on the ideal type of the modern state, then the differences between colonial and Nazi genocides do not appear so great. The colonial state was by and large a pre-modern and not yet or not completely bureaucratised state that relied heavily on the influence of intermediate authorities. And it was these, the heads of local communities, parish officers and local military commanders, who represented the state at this grass-roots level and had the power – at least symbolically – to legitimise actions on its behalf. Even if what these local leaders said was in fact not legally binding, they provided a basis on which perpetrators could feel justified in their

---

[80] For a compelling description of the frontier as a territory outside the jurisdiction of the state, see Stefan Kaufmann, "Der Siedler", in Eva Horn, Stefan Kaufmann and Ulrich Bröckling, eds, *Grenzverletzer. Von Schmugglern, Spionen und anderen subversiven Gestalten*, Berlin 2002, pp. 176–201.
[81] Jürgen Zimmerer, "Kriegsgefangene im Kolonialkrieg: Der Krieg gegen die Herero und Nama in Deutsch Südwestafrika (1904–1907)", in Rüdiger Overmans, ed., *In der Hand des Feindes: Kriegsgefangenschaft von der Antike bis zum Zweiten Weltkrieg*, Köln 1999, pp. 277–294.
[82] On the development of the modern state as it originated in Europe and spread throughout the world, see Wolfgang Reinhard, *Geschichte der Staatsgewalt. Eine vergleichende Verfassungsgeschichte Europas von den Anfängen bis zur Gegenwart*, München 1999.

actions, or even duty bound to perform them. For them to constitute a state-perpetrated crime in the colonial context, it is not necessary to demonstrate a chain of command stretching back to the centres of colonial power, which ultimately means the colonial offices back in Europe.

Accordingly, the biological attack on the Delaware mentioned above was legitimised by the state through Sir Jeffery Amherst's order; and in the same sense the genocide committed against the Herero and Nama was committed officially in the name of the German state, since von Trotha, as military commander-in-chief and later also as Governor was the Emperor's representative in South West Africa. The importance of intermediate levels of command has basically also been confirmed by the latest research into National Socialism: a detailed analysis of the decision-making processes in German-occupied Eastern Europe has recently gone a long way to discrediting the notion of a chain of command from the top to the bottom, emphasising instead the importance of local initiatives.[83]

The question of the state's role in the commission of genocide is, however, also important with regard to the forms of mass murder: genocidal massacres do not require a large degree of organisation, whereas quasi-industrial extermination in camps presupposes a 'modern', centralised and bureaucratised state. As has been shown above, both massacres and death camps are found in National Socialism, whereas in the colonial context massacres or other strategies with relatively low organisational requirements clearly predominated. Whether in the Pequot War in New England, in the conflict with the Round Valley people, or at the Sand Creek Massacre, examples of the butchering of men, women, and children by bands of settlers or local militia can readily be found. Punitive expeditions carried out by settlers in reprisal for actual or alleged attacks by Australian Aboriginal people, such as those reported by The Queenslander in 1867, also belong in this category:

> [...] in the present system by which blacks are shot down most ruthlessly for weeks and months after a case of murder or theft has been reported, and when many innocent are either killed in order that the guilty may possibly be included in the number, or so hunted about that the spirit of revenge is aroused in them[.][84]

Over time, special army and police units were established for precisely this purpose. The Third Colorado Cavalry, which was responsible for the massacre of the

---

[83] See Herbert, *National Socialist Extermination Policies*; Gerlach, *Kalkulierte Morde*.
[84] The Queenslander, 23 February 1867, https://trove.nla.gov.au/newspaper/article/20312053/, accessed 12 Jul. 2023, see Palmer, *Colonial Genocide*, p. 43.

Cheyenne at Sand Creek, was set up specially to fight the indigenous population.[85] The Native Police of Queensland were also state units, in this case composed of Australian Aboriginal people from other parts of the country under the command of White officers. As "mobile death squads aimed at eradicating Aborigines", they 'cleansed' the 'frontier' in Queensland of the indigenous population in order to make room for an increasing number of settlers and their livestock.[86]

A further, heightened form of these campaigns of annihilation was the genocidal war of conquest and pacification, a larger military action requiring a correspondingly higher level of organisation. The most important example of this was the war waged by German imperial troops against the Herero and Nama in German South West Africa between 1904 and 1908, which represents an important link between colonial genocide and the crimes of the Nazis.[87]

Sparked in January 1904 by an attack by the Herero, this conflict soon far exceeded the dimensions of previous warlike episodes in the German colony.[88] This

---

[85] Chalk and Jonassohn, *The History and Sociology of Genocide*, pp. 199–201. The background was a conflict between Native Americans and settlers, who however managed to involve the state in their struggle. The regiment deployed consisted of volunteers engaged for a fixed period of time. The force they used was thus legitimised by the state.

[86] Quoted according to A. Dirk Moses, "An Antipodean Genocide? The Origins of the Genocidal Moment in the Colonization of Australia", *Journal of Genocide Research*, 2 (2000), pp. 89–106, here p. 102.

[87] I have included some initial considerations of this matter in Jürgen Zimmerer, "Die Geburt des 'Ostlandes' aus dem Geiste des Kolonialismus. Die nationalsozialistische Eroberungs- und Beherrschungspolitik in (post-)kolonialer Perspektive", *Sozial.Geschichte. Zeitschrift für historische Analyse des 20. und 21. Jahrhunderts*, 18/1 (2004), pp. 10–43 (English version: "The Birth of the Ostland Out of the Spirit of Colonialism: A (Post)colonial Perspective on the Nazi Policy of Conquest and Annihilation", pp. 230–261 in this book). Some mention of the links between German colonial rule in German South West Africa and the 'Third Reich' have already been made in Drechsler, *Südwestafrika unter deutscher Kolonialherrschaft*; Helmut Bley, Kolonialherrschaft und Sozialstruktur in Deutsch-Südwestafrika 1894–1914, Hamburg 1968; Henning Melber, "Kontinuitäten totaler Herrschaft. Völkermord und Apartheid in Deutsch-Südwestafrika", *Jahrbuch für Antisemitismusforschung*, 1 (1992), pp. 91–116.

[88] Various aspects of the war and its outcome are covered in Jürgen Zimmerer and Joachim Zeller, *Völkermord in Deutsch-Südwestafrika. Der Kolonialkrieg (1904–1908) und seine Folgen*, Berlin 2003. On the war, see also Zimmerer, *Deutsche Herrschaft*, pp. 31–55 [English translation: *German Rule, African Subjects*]; Jan-Bart Gewald, *Towards Redemption: A Socio-Political History of the Herero of Namibia between 1890 and 1923*, Leiden 1996, pp. 178–240; Helmut Walser Smith, "The Logic of Colonial Violence: Germany in Southwest Africa (1904–1907); the United States in the Philippines (1899–1902)", in Hartmut Lehmann and Hermann Wellenreuther, eds, *German and American Nationalism. A Comparative Perspective*, Oxford 1999, pp. 205–231; Tilman Dedering, "The German-Herero War of 1904: Revisionism of Genocide or Imaginary Historiography?", *Journal of Southern African Studies*, 19 (1993), pp. 80–88; Tilman Dedering, "'A Certain Rigorous Treatment of All Parts of the Nation': The Annihilation of the Herero in German South West Africa,

was in part due to the extraordinary success of the Herero, who within a few days brought German rule to the verge of collapse, and in part to the German reaction. The General Staff in Berlin sent an expeditionary corps and removed the long-serving governor, Theodor Leutwein, replacing him with General Lothar von Trotha, who pursued a genocidal policy from the outset. The 'race war' he conducted culminated on 2 October 1904 in von Trotha's infamous Annihilation Proclamation. Having ordered that a chain of picket posts should be set up to seal off the Omaheke Desert, into which the Herero had fled following the only large battle of the war at Ohamakari (Waterberg), von Trotha proclaimed:

> The Hereros have ceased to be German subjects.
>
> They have murdered and robbed, have cut off the ears and noses and other bodily parts of wounded soldiers, and are now too cowardly to want to go on fighting. I say to that people: Whoever delivers one of their *Kapteins* to one of my posts as a prisoner will be given 1,000 marks, whoever brings Samuel Maharero will be given 5,000 marks. But the Herero people must quit this country. If they do not, I will compel them to do so with the *Groot Rohr* [cannon].
>
> Within the borders of German territory, any Herero, with or without a firearm, with or without livestock, will be shot; nor will I give refuge to women or children any more. I will drive them back to their people or have them fired upon.

He clarified this in an 'order of the day' stating that for the sake of the 'good reputation' of the German soldier, the order

> to fire upon women and children is to be understood in such a way that shots are to be fired over their heads, in order to force them to run away. I definitely assume that this Proclamation will lead to no further male prisoners being taken, but will not degenerate into atrocities against women and children. They will doubtless run away, if shots are fired over their heads a couple of times.[89]

1904", in Mark Levene and Penny Roberts, eds, *The Massacre in History*, New York 1999, pp. 205–222; Gesine Krüger, *Kriegsbewältigung und Geschichtsbewußtsein. Realität, Deutung und Verarbeitung des deutschen Kolonialkriegs in Namibia 1904 bis 1907*, Göttingen 1999; Henrik Lundtofte, "'I believe that the nation as such must be annihilated ...' – The Radicalization of the German Suppression of the Herero Rising in 1904", in Steven L.B. Jensen, ed., *Genocide: Cases, Comparisons and Contemporary Debates*, Copenhagen 2003, pp. 15–53.

89 Proclamation by von Trotha, Osombo-Wind[imbe] [transcript], 2 October 1904, Bundesarchiv Berlin-Lichterfelde (German Federal Archive, Berlin Lichterfelde), R 1001/2089, Sheet 7a f. I have discussed the significance of this proclamation and the genocidal German policy in general in Jürgen Zimmerer, "Das Deutsche Reich und der Genozid. Überlegungen zum historischen Ort des Völkermordes an den Herero und Nama", in Larissa Förster and Dag Henrichsen, eds, *100 Jahre geteilte namibisch-deutsche Geschichte: Kolonialkrieg – Genozid – Erinnerungskulturen*, Köln 2004, pp. 106–121.

But there was nowhere they could run to except into the desert, where thousands died of thirst in consequence of this order.

When the Nama started their war of resistance only a few days later – a very successful guerrilla war, which almost defeated the German army – they too became the target of the German strategy of annihilation.[90] Their food and particularly their sources of water were actively destroyed.

In addition to deaths in battle, expulsion into the waterless Omaheke desert, and the destruction of the necessities of life, the Germans also used camps to deliberately exterminate the indigenous population. Prisoner-of-war camps were established across the country between 1904 and 1908, and after the lifting of the Annihilation Order, Herero and Nama men, women and children were interned in them. Huge numbers of people died in these "concentration camps", as they were called at the time,[91] the most notorious of which were in Swakopmund and on Shark Island near Lüderitz.[92] In total, from October 1904 to March 1907 between 30 and 50 per cent of the internees died – 7,682 prisoners.[93] While disease and weakness caused by the privations of war were certainly a factor in this mass mortality, deliberate neglect was also significant. The responsible commander, Berthold von Deimling, refused to improve the state of the Shark Island camp by moving it to the mainland. For as long as he was in command, he said, no African would be allowed to leave the island alive. Even the need for forced labour, which would have required the prisoners' nutrition to be improved, could not bring him to alter his position. Instead, building projects already begun at Lüderitz were stopped.[94]

A superficial consideration would suggest that the Second World War, with its tank battles and carpet bombing, had nothing in common with this sort of colonial guerrilla war. And yet, on closer inspection, the war against the Herero and Nama reveals clear parallels with the 'war of annihilation' waged in the East from 1941 to 1945. These parallels deserve closer consideration, for the two wars are separated by only forty years, so that it is possible to speak of the 'war of racial annihilation'

---

[90] In his Proclamation of 22 April 1905, von Trotha threatened the Nama with the same fate as the Herero should they not surrender. Published in: *Kämpfe der deutschen Truppen*, Vol. 2, p. 186.

[91] The term "concentration camp" was first used by the Spanish during their campaign in Cuba in 1896, later by the Americans in the Philippines, the British in South Africa, and the Germans in South West Africa. See Andrzej J. Kaminski, *Konzentrationslager 1896 bis heute: Geschichte-Funktion-Typologie*, München 1996; Joël Kotek and Pierre Rigoulot, *Le siècle des camps*, Paris 2000.

[92] Zimmerer, *Kriegsgefangene im Kolonialkrieg*.

[93] These are the numbers provided by the army. See Drechsler, *Südwestafrika unter deutscher Kolonialherrschaft*, p. 213.

[94] Zimmerer, *Kriegsgefangene im Kolonialkrieg*, pp. 291–292.

(Rassen- und Vernichtungskrieg) as having a certain military tradition. Although the war against the Soviet Union was formally an 'ordinary' war between European powers, the Germans did not, from the beginning, wage it as such, but as a predatory war of plunder and destruction which, through the deliberate non-application of the laws of warfare by the aggressor resembled a colonial war more than the type of war 'usually' waged within Europe. In the conventional European war, the enemy was recognised as a legitimate opponent of equal status who was entitled to at least some basic rights even in defeat and captivity. In the colonial war, however, this status was denied, and the victors were prepared to leave prisoners to perish or to murder them directly on the basis of their race. The massacres that took place during the 'anti-partisan campaigns' are reminiscent of the practice, common in colonial warfare, of combating guerrillas with punitive and retributive expeditions. Himmler's order of the day of 1 August 1941, in which he ordered the massacre of the Pripet Marshes, reads almost like a quotation from von Trotha's Proclamation: "All Jewish men are to be shot, Jewish women driven into the swamps."[95] The intention was clear: very much like the Herero women and children in the Omaheke, the Jewish women too would die without any German soldier even having to lift his weapon. That Hitler was also familiar with the colonial strategy of 'driving them into the desert' is clear from his comment in October 1941, when – in connection with his prophecy that the Jews would be eradicated – he refused to countenance the possibility that he might be urged to display greater moderation by objectors declaring "But we cannot chase them into the swamp!"[96]

Conclusion

The structural similarity between colonialism and National Socialism goes beyond the line of continuity from the Herero War, however. With its key concepts of 'race' and 'space', the Nazi policy of expansion and annihilation stands firmly in the tradition of European colonialism, a tradition also recognisable in the Nazi genocides. Yet it would be wrong to see the Third Reich's murderous policies in the East as being merely a copy of the conquests of the Americas, Australia or southern Africa. Rather, they constitute an extremely radicalised variant.

Particularly with regard to its readiness to wipe out whole peoples, European colonialism stood at the beginning of a development of particular notions of

---

[95] Quoted according to Gerlach, *Deutsche Wirtschaftsinteressen*, p. 278.
[96] Hitler, 25 October 1941, in Hitler, *Monologe*, p. 106.

space and race that found their culmination in the 'hunger plan' of 1941, the genocidal massacres aimed at suppressing partisans, and the organised mass gassings.

Colonial genocides do not constitute a fundamentally different category from the Nazi genocides. They were merely earlier and less organised, less centralised and less bureaucratised forms of genocide. Ultimately, the various colonial manifestations of genocide can also be recognised in the Nazis' policies of murder, exemplified by genocidal massacres of partisans and the practice of eradication through deliberate neglect. The main difference between the two lies in the different roles played by the state, due to the far lower level of centralisation and bureaucratisation in the colonial state. Thus the Nazis' bureaucratised and state-orchestrated killing is to be seen less as a fundamental structural departure than as a difference in degree that is linked to the level of the state's historical development. While massacres perpetrated by settlers and militia on the New England frontier corresponded to the weakness of state institutions there at the time, as the state became more firmly established the instruments of genocide expanded in parallel. In Queensland or North America, for example, they were augmented by the Native Police or the army, through which the state itself committed mass murder. In states with a modern administration such as was already beginning to take shape in South West Africa, concentration and prisoner-of-war camps were introduced as places of extermination. Active 'industrialised' killing may not have been practised there yet; but murder through neglect was already prevalent.

The crimes of the Nazis cannot, to be sure, be traced back monocausally to the tradition of European colonialism: National Socialism was too complex and too eclecticist in its ideology and policies for that. Nonetheless, to express the relationship in terms of an archaeology of population economics (*Bevölkerungsökonomie*) and genocide, it must be said that colonialism served as an important source of ideas. Even the murder of the Jews, which is distinguished from other genocides by its motive – the notion of eradicating a worldwide conspiracy – would scarcely have been possible if the ultimate breach of taboo that consists in thinking that other ethnic groups can simply be eliminated, and then acting accordingly, had not already occurred. Another reason why colonialism occupies such a prominent place in this tradition of genocidal thought is that the themes of the 'discovery', conquest, opening up and settlement of the world acquired positive connotations, were disseminated throughout society and offered role models for the ambitious to emulate. At the same time, the similarity to colonialism helps us to understand why the expulsion and resettlement of Jews and Slavs, and in the last instance their murder, were perhaps not even perceived as being breaches of taboo. At the very least, colonial history offered the perpetrators of the Nazi crimes the possibility to exonerate themselves, and to deceive themselves in respect of the monstrosity of their own horrific acts.

The German Empire and Genocide: The Genocide Against the Herero and Nama in (German) History

Genocide: The Meaning and History of a Term[1]

Genocide is a relatively new term, but a much older crime. It was first defined during the Second World War by the Polish-Jewish lawyer Raphael Lemkin in his ground-breaking study *Axis Rule in Occupied Europe*. During his exile in the United States, Lemkin came to an important realisation derived from his personal experience of the crimes of the National Socialists and from the knowledge he had gained studying the Turkish mass murder of Armenians during the First World War: namely, that certain cases of mass violence could not be encompassed by the existing instruments of international criminal law, let alone punished by them. For this reason, he created a new term: "New concepts require new terms. By 'genocide' we mean the destruction of a nation or of an ethnic group."[2]

After the end of the Second World War, Lemkin's definition became the basis of the Genocide Convention adopted by the UN in 1948. In this document, genocide is defined as

> any of the following acts committed with intent to destroy, in whole or in part, a national, ethnical, racial or religious group as such:

---

[1] For a closer examination of some these issues, see my discussion in Jürgen Zimmerer, "Krieg, KZ und Völkermord in Südwestafrika. Der erste deutsche Genozid", in Jürgen Zimmerer and Joachim Zeller, eds, *Völkermord in Deutsch-Südwestafrika. Der Kolonialkrieg (1904–1908) in Namibia und seine Folgen*, Berlin 2003, pp. 45–63; Jürgen Zimmerer, "Holocaust und Kolonialismus. Beitrag zu einer Archäologie des genozidalen Gedankens", *Zeitschrift für Geschichtswissenschaft*, 51/12 (2003), pp. 1098–1119, English translation: "Colonialism and the Holocaust. Towards an Archaeology of Genocide", in Dirk A. Moses, ed., *Genocide and Settler Society. Frontier Violence and Stolen Indigenous Children in Australia*, New York 2004, pp. 49–76 (a revised version appears in this book on pp. 125–153).

[2] Raphael Lemkin, *Axis Rule in Occupied Europe: Law of Occupation, Analysis of Government, Proposals for Redress*, Washington 1944, p. 79. More on the origin and meaning of the term genocide can now also be found in Jürgen Zimmerer, "Kolonialer Genozid? Vom Nutzen und Nachteil einer historischen Kategorie für eine Globalgeschichte des Völkermordes", in Dominik J. Schaller, Boyadjian Rupen, Hanno Scholtz and Vivianne Berg, eds, *Enteignet – Vertrieben – Ermordet. Beiträge zur Genozidforschung*, Zürich 2004 (English version: "Colonial Genocide? On the Use and Abuse of a Historical Category for Global History", pp. 175–197 in this book); A. Dirk Moses, "The Holocaust and Genocide", in Dan Stone, ed., *The Historiography of the Holocaust*, London 2004.

Open Access. © 2024 the author(s), published by De Gruyter. This work is licensed under the Creative Commons Attribution 4.0 International License.
https://doi.org/10.1515/9783110754513-007

(a) Killing members of the group;
(b) Causing serious bodily or mental harm to members of the group;
(c) Deliberately inflicting on the group conditions of life calculated to bring about its physical destruction in whole or in part;
(d) Imposing measures intended to prevent births within the group;
(e) Forcibly transferring children of the group to another group.[3]

Since then, the term has achieved an unprecedented degree of currency, and is now used to categorise phenomena that are thoroughly diverse in nature. The term "Holocaust", often used as a synonym for "genocide" is applied in areas as wide-ranging as environmental protection issues and economic crises. Nowadays one can read of "environmental Holocausts",[4] or of a "Holocaust on your plate" as a plea for animal rights.[5] The Australian Prime Minister John Howard spoke of the economic crisis of the late 1990s as an "economic holocaust" that Australia had come through pretty well.[6] Used in slogans such as "The American Holocaust",[7] the "American Indian Holocaust",[8] "The Black Holocaust"[9] or "The Herero

---

[3] United Nations: *Convention on the Prevention and Punishment of the Crime of Genocide*, Article 2, 9 December 1948, as reproduced in Frank Chalk and Kurt Jonassohn, *The History and Sociology of Genocide: Analyses and Case Studies*, New Haven 1990, pp. 44–49, here p. 44.

[4] See, for example, S. K. Chadha, ed., *Environmental Holocaust in Himalaya*, New Delhi 1989; Mike Davis, *Late Victorian Holocausts: El Niño famines and the making of the Third World*, London 2001. Interestingly enough, the book was published in German under the less sensational title *Die Geburt der Dritten Welt (The Birth of the Third World)*, Berlin 2003.

[5] In March 2003 the animal protection organization PETA (People for the Ethical Treatment of Animals) drew vehement criticism, especially from Jewish groups, when as part of an advertising campaign entitled "Holocaust on your Plate" it placed pictures of children behind barbed wire in a Nazi concentration camp alongside a picture of pigs in a cage. Brian Willoughby, "PETA Sparks Outrage with Holocaust Comparison", 23 March 2003, https://www.alternet.org/2003/03/peta_sparks_outrage_with_holocaust_comparison, accessed 12 Jul. 2023.

[6] "Transcript of the Prime Minister, the Hon. John Howard MP, Address to the Tasmanian Division, State Council Dinner, Burnie Civic Centre, Burnie, 6 November 1998", *Prime Minister of Australia, News Room*, https://pmtranscripts.pmc.gov.au/release/transcript-10972, accessed 12 Jul. 2023.

[7] David E. Stannard, *American Holocaust. The Conquest of the New World*, Oxford/New York 1992.

[8] Russel Thornton, *American Indian Holocaust and Survival. A Population History since 1492*, London 1987.

[9] Black History Resource Working Group in conjunction with the Race Equality Management Team, ed., *Slavery: An Introduction to the African Holocaust; with Special Reference to Liverpool, 'Capital of the Slave Trade'*, 2nd edn, Liverpool 1997; Thomas Mordekhai, *Vessels of Evil: American Slavery and the Holocaust*, Philadelphia 1993. There are now also museums and societies that

Holocaust",[10] the term serves to characterise colonial mass violence and mass suffering. The terms "genocide" and "Holocaust" are no doubt among the few such buzzwords from the field of history that are understood globally. Victims of such crimes in particular are prone to use the terms "Holocaust" or "genocide" in order to tap into the worldwide outrage over the fate of the Jews in the Third Reich – an outrage that is not matched to the same extent with regard to mass crimes committed under colonialism[11] – to gain audiences for their own causes.[12] This is evinced by the way the term "genocide" has been replaced by "Holocaust", which was originally applied only to the murder of the European Jews. At the same time, this is also one of the reasons why the use of these two terms in colonial history has generated such bitter controversy. From the perspective of the 'perpetrator society' – in the colonial context, that is White settler society – the admission that cases of genocide did take place in the colonies fundamentally calls into question the assumption that the Europeanisation of the world was a progressive project, precisely because it would implicitly associate it with the crimes of the Nazis.[13]

The term 'genocide' was also applied very early on to the German war against the Herero and Nama in German South West Africa,[14] and quickly unleashed in-

---

commemorate the "Black Holocaust", such as "America's Black Holocaust Museum" and "The Black Holocaust Society" in Milwaukee, Wisconsin.

10 Jeremy Silvester, Werner Hillebrecht and Casper Erichsen, "The Herero Holocaust? The Disputed History of the 1904 Genocide", *The Namibian Weekender* (20 August 2001).

11 On this subject, see (for example) the complaints of Stannard and Churchill: David E. Stannard, "Uniqueness as Denial: The Politics of Genocide Scholarship", in Alan S. Rosenbaum, ed., *Is the Holocaust Unique? Perspectives on Comparative Genocide*, Oxford 1996, pp. 163–208; Ward Churchill, *A Little Matter of Genocide: Holocaust and Denial in the Americas 1492-Present*, San Francisco 1997.

12 See, for example, the reparations claim of the Herero before the court of the District of Columbia, United States. The "First Amended Complaint" explicitly listed "Violations of International Law, Crimes Against Humanity, Genocide, Slavery and Forced Labor". The grounds of the action refer repeatedly to the relevance of the act of genocide under criminal law. Statement of complaint by the "Herero People's Reparations Corporation" before the Superior Court of the District of Columbia, 18 Sept. 2001.

13 I have depicted the political dimensions of this problem, and in particular those relating to the politics of remembrance, in greater detail in: Jürgen Zimmerer, "Colonial Genocide? On the Use and Abuse of a Historical Category for Global History", pp. 175–197 in this book.

14 As Dominik J. Schaller has recently been able to demonstrate by analysing writings of Lemkin about the Herero War that had previously been largely neglected, Lemkin himself saw von Trotha's policies as fulfilling the criteria for being regarded as genocidal. On this subject, see Dominik J. Schaller, "Kolonialkrieg, Völkermord und Zwangsarbeit in Deutsch-Südwestafrika", in Dominik J. Schaller Boyadjian Rupen, Hanno Scholtz and Vivianne Berg, eds, *Enteignet – Vertrieben – Ermordet. Beiträge zur Genozidforschung*, Zürich 2004, pp. 147–232. This thesis was then brought to more general attention by Horst Drechsler, *Südwestafrika unter deutscher Kolonial-*

tense controversy.[15] The fact that the issue as to whether genocide was committed during the War of 1904–1908 is so hotly contested also raises the question of the place this conflict occupies in German and in international history; that is to say, in short, of its historical localisation. This question becomes all the more pressing when the temporal proximity to the Holocaust and the fact that it was Germans who were the perpetrators in both cases are taken into account; factors that in turn suggest that the genocide against the Herero and the Nama played a role as a precursor to the crimes of the Third Reich. I will therefore attempt below to clarify whether the term 'genocide' can meaningfully be applied at all to the events in German South West Africa between 1904 and 1908, and which of those events in particular may be regarded as having been genocidal in nature. In my closing remarks, I will then add reflections on the positioning of the genocide against the Herero and Nama in the history of genocide in general, and thus also on its relationship with the Holocaust.

The inflationary use of the term 'genocide' as outlined above makes it necessary to ascertain its true meaning if we wish to establish 'genocide' as a category that is viable for use in historical analysis. Several such categorisations have already been made.[16] I base my definition on that of the UN Convention inspired by Lemkin, as it seems to me to be the most widely acknowledged. In Lemkin's own words:

---

herrschaft. Der Kampf der Herero und Nama gegen den deutschen Imperialismus 1884–1915, 2nd edn, Berlin 1984, p. 20.

15 For a summary of the arguments of those who criticise the thesis that genocide occurred, see Brigitte Lau, "Uncertain Certainties. The Herero-German War of 1904", in Brigitte Lau, *History and Historiography – 4 Essays in Reprint*, ed. Annemarie Heywood, Windhoek 1995, pp. 39–52. A good overview of the debate is given by Tilman Dedering, "The German-Herero War of 1904. Revisionism of Genocide or Imaginary Historiography?", *Journal of Southern African Studies*, 19 (1993), pp. 80–88. The following have appeared more recently: Henrik Lundtofte, "'I believe that the nation as such must be annihilated ...' – The Radicalization of the German Suppression of the Herero Rising in 1904", in Steven L. B Jensen, ed., *Genocide: Cases, Comparisons and Contemporary Debates*, The Danish Center for Holocaust and Genocide Studies 2003, pp. 15–53; Jan-Bart Gewald, "Colonization, Genocide and Resurgence: The Herero of Namibia 1890–1933", in Michael Bollig and Jan-Bart Gewald, eds, *People, Cattle and Land: Transformations of a Pastoral Society in Southwestern Africa*, Köln 2001, pp. 187–225; Alison Palmer, *Colonial Genocide*, Adelaide 2000; Tilman Dedering, "A Certain Rigorous Treatment of All Parts of the Nation: The Annihilation of the Herero in German South West Africa, 1904." in Mark Levene and Penny Roberts, eds, *The Massacre in History*, New York 1999, pp. 205–222.

16 On this subject, see: Dirk A. Moses, "Conceptual Blockages and Definitional Dilemmas in the 'Racial Century': Genocides of Indigenous Peoples and the Holocaust", *Patterns of Prejudice*, 36/4 (2002), pp. 7–36; Zimmerer, *Colonialism and the Holocaust*.

> Generally speaking, genocide does not necessarily mean the immediate destruction of a nation [...] It is intended rather to signify a coordinated plan of different actions aiming at the destruction of essential foundations of the life of national groups, with the aim of annihilating the groups themselves. [...] Genocide is directed against the national group as an entity, and the actions involved are directed against individuals, not in their individual capacity, but as members of the national group.[17]

The decisive factor is therefore the intention of the perpetrators. There needs to be a will to 'exterminate' a certain group defined by the perpetrators. Equally, there needs to be actual action, i.e. the initiation of the genocidal process, but not necessarily its completion. This means that the murder of a relatively small number of people is sufficient if the reason they were murdered is that they belonged to a certain group. It is not the number of victims that determines whether genocide has taken place. Thus the repeated attempts by revisionists to demonstrate lower and lower numbers of victims in order to refute allegations that genocide was committed against the Herero and Nama lead nowhere. In establishing whether genocide took place, it is irrelevant whether 50,000 to 70,000 or 'only' 10,000 to 20,000 Herero were killed.

For acts of genocide in the colonial context, this is a significant point, since in comparison with the Holocaust, perceived by many as the archetypal model of genocide, the numbers of victims are often relatively small.[18] The aura of a large number (of victims) is a powerful one, but at the same time gives rise to the danger that smaller ethnicities, which find it difficult enough in any case to attract the attention of the public and the interest of historians engaged in research, will be disregarded. The importance of 'intention', on the other hand, demands that we should focus on the motives and actions of the perpetrators.

'Driven into the Desert'

In the case of the Herero War, a crucial document pointing to the genocidal intentions of those responsible on the German side is the infamous Proclamation or 'Annihilation Order' issued on 2 October 1904 by General Lothar von Trotha, the Commander in Chief of the German colonial forces:

---

17 Lemkin, *Axis Rule*, p. 79.
18 On the other hand, many North American genocide researchers claim that the colonisation of North and South America involved the biggest genocide – also in numerical terms – in history, with up to 100 million deaths. On this subject, see: Stannard, *American Holocaust*, or Ward Churchill, who even speaks of the Nazis having imitated the colonial conquest of North America: Ward Churchill, *A Little Matter of Genocide. Holocaust and Denial in the Americas 1492-Present*, San Francisco 1997.

> The Hereros have ceased to be German subjects.
> They have murdered and robbed, have cut off the ears and noses and other bodily parts of wounded soldiers, and are now too cowardly to want to go on fighting. I say to that people: Whoever delivers one of their *Kapteins* to one of my posts as a prisoner will be given 1,000 marks; whoever brings Samuel Maharero will be given 5,000 marks. But the Herero people must quit this country. If they do not, I will compel them to do so with the *Groot Rohr* [cannon].
> Within the borders of German territory, any Herero, with or without a firearm, with or without livestock, will be shot; nor will I give refuge to women or children any more. I will drive them back to their people or have them fired upon.[19]

In an Order of the Day of the same date, he sought to clarify this by stating that for the sake of the reputation of the German soldier the order to "fire upon women and children is to be understood in such a way that shots are to be fired over their heads, in order to force them to run away. I definitely assume that this Proclamation will lead to no further male prisoners being taken, but will not degenerate into atrocities against women and children. They will doubtless run away, if shots are fired over their heads a couple of times."[20]

As this text unambiguously demonstrates, it was von Trotha's intention to permanently expel the Herero from the colony. How exactly he imagined that could be brought about is not revealed in the Proclamation text itself, which only states that he intended to expel the Herero and to have any Herero shot who nevertheless remained within the *Schutzgebiet*. Though such a mass expulsion would in itself have been a particularly brutal course of action to adopt, even by the standards of a colonial war, it would still not have been sufficient to amount to genocide. However, the passage in question serves merely as camouflage. For if the Proclamation is read in conjunction with a letter that von Trotha wrote to the General Staff in Berlin two days later, his intentions become plainer:

> Now the only question for me was *how* the war with the Herero was to be brought to an end. The opinions on this subject of the Governor and some of the 'old Africa hands' on the one hand and myself on the other are diametrically opposed. For quite some time, there has been a desire on the part of the former to enter into peace negotiations, and they describe the Herero nation as being essential as labour for the future exploitation of the territory. I am of a completely different opinion. I believe that the nation as such must be destroyed, or, if that should prove not to be possible by tactical actions, they must be expelled from the country operationally and by means of further individual actions. With the watering holes

---

19 Proclamation by von Trotha, Osombo-Wind[imbe], 2 October 1904, Bundesarchiv Berlin-Lichterfelde (BArch), Imperial Colonial Office R 1001/2089, Sheets 7a f. This is a transcript of the original document. Other transcripts of the Proclamation are to be found in the Bundesarchiv/Militärarchiv Freiburg and in the National Archives of Namibia in Windhoek.
20 Ibid.

from Grootfontein to Gobabis having been occupied and the military convoys being constantly on the move, it is bound to be possible to track down those small groups of people who have begun moving back westwards and gradually finish them off.[21]

Against the background of the concrete historical situation in which the Proclamation was issued, it can be seen that 'expulsion' and 'murder' were essentially one and the same thing.

When precisely von Trotha made the decision to commit genocide cannot be determined. What is certain, however, is that he had no knowledge either of the country or of its people,[22] but was obsessed with the idea that this conflict was a 'race war' and so right from the start planned a military operation that can only be described as a war of extermination.[23] Von Trotha himself maintained that he had not been given any instructions or directives at the time of his appointment; he had merely been called upon by Emperor Wilhelm II to quell the uprising by

---

21 Von Trotha to the Chief of the General Staff of the Army, 4 October 1904, quoted according to Drechsler, *Südwestafrika*, p. 163.

22 Born on 3 July 1848 as the son of a Prussian officer, he too joined the army and took part in the Austro-Prussian and Franco-Prussian Wars. Between 1894 and 1897 he was the Commander of the colonial forces in German East Africa, where he gained military renown through his suppression of the 'Wahehe Rising'. Thereafter he took part voluntarily, as Commander of the First East Asian Infantry Brigade, in the campaign to suppress the Boxer Rising in China. See Gerhard Pool, *Samuel Maharero*, Windhoek 1991, pp. 260 f.

23 By the middle of the 19th century at the latest, the idea that not only would 'higher races' subjugate 'lower' ones, but that the latter were also 'doomed', was thoroughly widespread, and not only in Germany. For examples, see the following: Russell McGregor, *Imagined Destinies. Aboriginal Australians and the Doomed Race Theory, 1880–1939*, Victoria 1997; Saul Dubow, *Scientific Racism in Modern South Africa*, Cambridge 1995. Dan Stone has also recently pointed out similar attitudes among German anthropologists on the sidelines of the war against the Herero and Nama: Dan Stone, "White Men with Low Moral Standards? German Anthropology and the Herero Genocide", *Patterns of Prejudice*, 35/2 (2001), pp. 33–45. The same holds true for the vision of a battle of annihilation. For initial systematising reflections on the significance of the military campaign in China, see: Susanne Kuß, "Deutsche Soldaten während des Boxeraufstandes in China: Elemente und Ursprünge des Vernichtungskrieges", in Susanne Kuß and Bernd Martin, eds, *Das Deutsche Reich und der Boxeraufstand*, München 2002, pp. 165–181. For a general exposition of the history of 'total war' and its origins, see the "Total War" conference series organised by Manfred F. Boemeke, Roger Chickering, Stig Förster and Jörg Nagler, which explicitly concerns itself with the exploration of the "Road to Total War": Stig Förster and Jörg Nagler, eds, *On the Road to Total War: The American Civil War and the German Wars of Unification, 1861–1871*, New York 1997; Manfred F. Boemeke, Roger Chickering and Stig Förster, eds, *Anticipating Total War. The German and American Experiences, 1871–1914*, Cambridge 1999; Roger Chickering and Stig Förster, eds, *Great War – Total War, Combat and Mobilization on the Western Front, 1914–1918*, Cambridge 2000; Roger Chickering and Stig Förster, eds, *The Shadows of Total War: Europe, East Asia, and the United States, 1919–1939*, New York 2003.

any means necessary".[24] His own ideas as to how that was to be done were revealed in a letter to the colony's Governor, Theodor Leutwein: as he believed Africans would "yield only to force", he was willing to exercise such force "with blatant terrorism and even with cruelty". He wanted to "annihilate the rebellious tribes with rivers of blood".[25] This letter having been written four weeks after the issue of the 'Annihilation Order', there is no reason to doubt that von Trotha was totally serious about its content.

This course of action had been embarked on in June 1904, when von Trotha, who was still on his way to the *Schutzgebiet* – and so certainly not in the heat of battle or in view of any personal experience of military difficulties or reverses – issued orders from his ship which empowered his officers in South West Africa to have all armed 'rebels' shot immediately on the basis of summary proceedings:

a) Every commanding officer is authorised to have coloured inhabitants of the territory who are caught in the act of carrying out treasonable activities against German troops, for example all rebels who are found under arms with belligerent intent, shot without any prior court proceedings, as has been customary practice in this war up to now.
b) All other coloured inhabitants arrested by German military personal on suspicion of having undertaken punishable activities will be sentenced by special field courts.
c) The troops are to be instructed that any punitive measures against coloured people inflicted by troops acting on their own initiative will be met with the most severe punishments provided for under the general legal provisions on bodily harm, unlawful killing and murder, and that outside combat situations they are only permitted to make use of their weapons in self-defence or to prevent attempts to escape.[26]

The intention of this order was twofold. Firstly, von Trotha was attempting to impose order on the spontaneous illegal actions that had been occurring since the beginning of the war and that had led to downright massacres of Herero at the hands of incensed settlers and soldiers, and had in their turn caused Herero who until then had not participated in the war to join in the fighting. At the same time, however, while von Trotha's order did put a stop to the arbitrary actions of individuals, it instead turned massacres and terror into planned instruments of German warfare: whoever resisted the Germans would be shot. Without any doubt, this meant that at that time, if not before, the first step was taken along the road to a war of annihilation and to genocide: for where any member of the

---

24 Quoted according to Lundtofte, *"I believe ..."*, p. 28.
25 Von Trotha to Leutwein, 5 November 1904, quoted according to Drechsler, *Südwestafrika*, p. 156.
26 Proclamation made by von Trotha on board the steamship *Eleonore Woermann*, June 1904, National Archives of Namibia, Windhoek (NAN), Imperial Governor's Office (ZBU) classified files, IX.A. Vol. 1, Sheet 1b.

enemy forces was seen merely as a rebel acting illegally, rather than as an opposing belligerent of equal and equally honourable status, it was no longer possible for him to be afforded protection or fair and humane treatment. And such attitudes and behaviour were typical of colonial wars.[27]

Researchers into genocide have established that in order to set in motion a war of annihilation, and in particular an act of genocide, certain processes of exclusion are necessary in order to prevent the perpetrator from coming to identify in any way with the victim. The potential victims must be dehumanised, they must be robbed of their human dignity and placed outside the sphere in which moral responsibility applies. They must be banished from the circle of those "whom we are obligated to protect, to take into account, and to whom we must account", as Helen Fein writes.[28] In the colonial situation, the ground had already been prepared for this process by the racism that underpinned colonial rule; and this situation was further reinforced by the atrocity propaganda that accompanied the outbreak of the war. Thus immediately after 12 January 1904 it was being said that the Herero had 'slaughtered' women and children and mutilated their victims.[29]

In his Annihilation Order von Trotha specifically made reference to these rumours in order to justify his policy of murder and expulsion. According to this logic, the Herero were themselves to blame for their fate, as they were 'barbarians' and 'savages' in contrast to the 'civilised' and 'disciplined' German army they faced. The fact that the Herero demonstrably spared women and children while German soldiers deliberately waged war against them may be pointed out here without further comment.

The truly genocidal phase of the war began after the setback suffered by the Germans at the Battle of Ohamakari (Waterberg), when von Trotha, having failed to prevent the majority of the Herero from escaping his attempted encirclement, deliberately forced them into the waterless regions in the eastern part of the colony. German troops pursuing the fleeing Herero initiated a pincer movement, driving them in the direction of the *sandveld*, the sandy waste of the Omaheke

---

27 On this subject, see Jürgen Zimmerer, "Kriegsgefangene im Kolonialkrieg. Der Krieg gegen die Herero und Nama in Deutsch-Südwestafrika (1904–1907)", in Rüdiger Overmans, ed., *In der Hand des Feindes. Kriegsgefangenschaft von der Antike bis zum Zweiten Weltkrieg*, Köln 1999, pp. 277–294.
28 Helen Fein, "Definition and Discontent: Labelling, Detecting, and Explaining Genocide in the Twentieth Century", in Stig Förster and Gerhard Hirschfeld, eds, *Genozid in der modernen Geschichte*, Münster 1999, pp. 11–21, here especially p. 20.
29 On these atrocity rumours, see also Gesine Krüger, *Kriegsbewältigung und Geschichtsbewußtsein: Realität, Deutung und Verarbeitung des deutschen Kolonialkriegs in Namibia 1904 bis 1907*, Göttingen 1999, pp. 104–115.

Desert.[30] Already at this juncture, terrible scenes must have unfolded: as the official history of the campaign reports, "Masses of sick and helpless men, women and children, having collapsed from exhaustion, lay parched with thirst [...] in the bush, apathetically awaiting their fate."[31] The German officer Captain Maximilian Bayer wrote that wherever the pursuing German units came upon Herero, summary executions took place: "Now and then, whenever our patrols came upon stragglers, shots were to be heard among the thorn bushes to the right and left."[32]

By this time at the latest, the idea had taken root within the German military command that the Omaheke Desert could "complete what German arms had started: the annihilation of the Herero nation", as the consequences of this policy are described in the official war chronicle quoted above.[33] It was in this situation, in which German troops were also systematically occupying the waterholes, that von Trotha issued the Annihilation Order quoted above. His war aim, the extermination of the Herero or their expulsion into the desert, was therefore by no means merely a feverish fantasy. Rather, it was the expression of a policy that was already in progress, since he already knew that the Herero were confined to the largely waterless *sandveld* of the Omaheke Desert, while his troops had closed off the edges of the desert in order to prevent the Herero from returning to the waterholes. In von Trotha's view, there was no escape for the Herero men, objects as they were of the General's Proclamation. They were shot or died of thirst. At the same time, however, the passage in the Proclamation that women would not be targeted became meaningless, because they too had no other choice but to flee into the desert, where the same fate awaited them as the men.

There are plentiful eye-witness accounts from German soldiers as to how the extermination unfolded.[34] Ludwig von Estorff, who had been one of the critics of von Trotha's policy of extermination even before the Battle of Ohamakari (Waterberg), may serve as one example among many. This is how he described the scene facing the pursuing German troops:

> I followed their tracks, which led me to a number of wells where I beheld terrible scenes. All around them lay heaps of cattle that had died of thirst, having reached the wells with their last remaining strength, but not having being able to drink in time. The Herero contin-

---

30 On this pursuit action, see: Lundtofte, Henrik, *"I believe ..."*, pp. 33–38.
31 Kriegsgeschichtlichen Abteilung I des Großen Generalstabes, *Die Kämpfe der deutschen Truppen in Südwestafrika*, 2 vols, Berlin 1906/07, Vol. 1, p. 203, see Lundtofte, *"I believe ..."*, p. 38.
32 Maximilian Bayer, *Mit dem Hauptquartier in Südwestafrika*, Berlin 1909, p. 162, see Lundtofte, *"I believe ..."*, p. 35.
33 *Die Kämpfe der deutschen Truppen*, p. 211.
34 On this subject, see Krüger, *Kriegsbewältigung*, pp. 73–103.

ued to flee before us into the *sandveld*. The terrible spectacle was repeated over and over again. The men had worked with feverish haste to dig wells, but the water had become more and more sparse, the waterholes scarcer and scarcer. They fled from one to the next, losing almost all their cattle and very many people. The nation was shrunk to meagre remnants which gradually fell into our hands, though both then and later some escaped through the *sandveld* into British territory. The policy of shattering the nation in this way was as foolish as it was cruel; many of them and their wealth of cattle could still have been saved if they had now been shown mercy and received back; they had been punished enough. I proposed this to General von Trotha; but he wanted them completely exterminated.[35]

In their distress, some of the Herero cut the throats of their cattle to quench their thirst with the blood, or squeezed the last remnants of moisture out of the content of the stomachs of dead animals.[36] But many could not save themselves even in this way; thousands died, even though no precise figure can be given for the number of the victims.[37]

If we follow the definition of genocide set out in the UN Convention quoted above, using it as a category for historical analysis as is done also in respect of the murder of the European Jews by the Germans, then the way von Trotha and the German army proceeded is to be identified unambiguously as a case of genocide. Both the crucial requirement for genocide – the intention – and its execution are undeniably present, the latter both in respect of direct murder (Letter (a) of the UN Convention) and of expulsion into the desert (Letter (c)). The fact that Emperor Wilhelm II revoked von Trotha's Annihilation Order a few weeks later, for fear of its being exploited in anti-German propaganda and also because of new developments in the military situation, does not make any material difference. The crime had already been committed by then.

The fact that humanitarian considerations were not a primary factor in the decision to revoke von Trotha's order is confirmed by the Chief of the General Staff, Alfred von Schlieffen, who on the occasion of the revocation explicitly emphasised once again that he shared von Trotha's genocidal attitudes:

---

35 Ludwig von Estorff, *Wanderungen und Kämpfe in Südwestafrika, Ostafrika und Südafrika 1894–1910*, ed. by Christoph-Friedrich Kutscher, Windhoek 1979, p. 117.
36 Pool, *Samuel Maharero*, p. 282.
37 In view of the lack of any exact figures either for the pre-war population of the Herero – estimates vary between 70,000 and 100,000, though this does not yet take account of the number of victims of the rinderpest epidemic and its consequences – or for the post-war population, estimated at 17,000 to 40,000, no exact assessment of the losses during the war can be made. There are not even any precise figures with regard to the strength of the German colonial forces; however, the number of soldiers involved in the military operations was probably between 14,000 and 19,000. For more information on the various estimates and the problem of determining reliable figures, see: Lau, *Uncertain Certainties*, pp. 43–46.

His [von Trotha's] intention to annihilate the whole nation, or to drive it out of the country, is a matter in which one can agree with him. [...] The race war that has broken out can only end with the annihilation or else the complete subjugation of the one party. But the latter course is one that cannot be sustained in the long term, given current attitudes. One is therefore able to approve of General v. Trotha's intentions; the only thing is that he does not have the power to implement them.[38]

The Anti-Guerrilla Campaign and the War of Annihilation

The genocidal strategy was however not restricted either to the war against the Herero or to the phases of actual combat. It was also implemented in the war against the Nama, and was practised in the concentration camps as well. As is commonly known, the Nama under Hendrik Witbooi attacked the Germans in October 1904, although prior to the Battle of Ohamakari (Waterberg) they had provided military support to the German colonial forces. This volte-face was decisively occasioned by demands that were being raised particularly in settler circles, now that there were strong forces present in the region, for the Nama too to be disarmed and permanently subjugated.[39] Learning from the mistakes of the Herero – the Nama had recognised what great difficulties the German troops had experienced in pursuing the fleeing Herero – they avoided a set-piece battle and initiated a guerrilla war. Knowing the country better than the Germans did and possessing greater mobility, they were able to offset the advantages enjoyed by the more numerous and better equipped colonial troops; thus they were able to keep hostilities dragging on, tying down large forces and eventually wearing them out and overcoming them by attrition.[40]

In order to defeat the Nama, German troops had to be withdrawn from the centre of the *Schutzgebiet*, where the genocidal strategy with its requirement for an enormous number of troops, the "whole misguided operation against that unhappy people", in von Estorff's knowledgeable formulation, continued to "keep strong military forces tied down in a thankless task".[41]

---

38 Von Schlieffen to von Bülow, 23 November 1904, quoted according to Drechsler, *Südwestafrika*, p. 166.
39 Drechsler, *Südwestafrika*, p. 172.
40 Von Estorff, *Wanderungen*, pp. 116–120. For more on the conflict with the Nama see also Werner Hillebrecht, "Die Nama und der Krieg im Süden", in Jürgen Zimmerer and Joachim Zeller, eds, *Völkermord. Der Kolonialkrieg (1904–1908) in Namibia und seine Folgen*, Berlin 2003, pp. 121–132.
41 Von Estorff, *Wanderungen*, p. 117.

Against the Nama, as against the Herero, the Germans adopted a strategy of annihilation, systematically occupying watering holes – as they had done in the Omaheke – in order to kill their opponents by thirst. The deliberate destruction of the livelihoods of those who supported the guerrillas was a tactic that had already been tried out 'successfully' in German East Africa at a time when von Trotha was serving there. As early as the 1890s, when punitive expeditions were being carried out against the Wahehe people, burning villages and crops and "devour Mkwawa's [the leader of the Wahehe] land'", as Eduard von Liebert, the Governor of German East Africa, called it,[42] had been regarded as promising tactics. Likewise in the war "to suppress the Maji-Maji rebellion", which was taking place in German East Africa almost contemporaneously with the war against the Herero and the Nama in South West Africa, it was part of the colonial army's tactics "to confiscate the opponent's possessions (livestock, provisions) and to devastate his villages and crops",[43] in order to erode the crucial support for the guerrilla fighters among the population by destroying people's livelihoods and their infrastructure.

As in the war against the Herero, so also in that against the Nama, the Germans exploited the hostile natural environment found in parts of the territory as a tactical instrument. As a result, this campaign too turned into a war against women and children, whose deaths were, at the very least, accepted and condoned, if not perhaps even positively pursued, as part of the strategy of annihilation. At the same time, the policy embraced a 'purging' or 'cleansing' of the land through mass internment. Von Trotha called upon the Nama to surrender, as otherwise they might expect to meet the same fate as the Herero:

> To the rebellious Hottentots.
>
> The great and mighty German Emperor would like to show mercy to the Hottentot people, so that those who surrender of their own accord will be granted their lives. Only those who at the beginning of the rebellion murdered whites or gave orders that they should be murdered have, in accordance with the law, forfeited their lives. This I proclaim to you, and I further tell you that those few who will not submit will suffer what the nation of the Herero has suffered. In their delusion they believed they could wage a successful war against the mighty German Emperor and the great German people. I ask you, where is the Herero nation today, where are their chiefs today? Samuel Maharero, who once called thousands of

---

[42] von Liebert, "Neunzig Tage im Zelt – Meine Reise nach Uhehe Juni bis September 1897", Berlin 1898, p. 33, quoted according to Martin Baer and Olaf Schröter, *Eine Kopfjagd. Deutsche in Ostafrika*, Berlin 2001, p. 57.

[43] *Militärpolitische Denkschrift über die Auswirkungen des Aufstandes*, Dar-es-Salaam, 1 June 1907, quoted according to Detlef Bald, "Afrikanischer Kampf gegen koloniale Herrschaft. Der Maji-Maji-Aufstand in Ostafrika", *Militärgeschichtliche Mitteilungen*, 19/1 (1976), pp. 23–50, here p. 40. On the Maji-Maji Rebellion see also Felicitas Becker and Jigal Beez, eds, *Der Maji-Maji-Krieg in Deutsch-Ostafrika, 1905–1907*, Berlin 2005.

cattle his own, has fled, hunted like a wild animal, across the British frontier. He has become as poor as the poorest of the *Veldherero* and no longer has any possessions. The other Big Men have fared the same, most of them having lost their lives, and so has the entire Herero nation. Some died of hunger and thirst in the *sandveld*, some were killed by the German cavalry, others were murdered by the Ovambo. The Hottentot people will meet no other fate if they do not surrender voluntarily and give up their weapons. You are to come to us with a white cloth on a stick and with all the inhabitants of your *werfs* [African settlements], and no harm shall befall you. You will be given work and food until the war is over, when the great German Emperor will order the territory anew. Anyone who from now on believes that this offer of mercy will not be applicable to him shall emigrate, because wherever he is found within German territory he will be fired on, until all such people have been annihilated. For the handing over of those guilty of murder, dead or alive, I set the following rewards: for Hendrik Witbooi 5,000 marks, for Stürmann [sic] 3,000 marks, for Cornelius 3,000 marks, for all other guilty leaders 1,000 marks.

Signed: Trotha.[44]

It is only superficially that this call to capitulate appears to represent an abandonment of the policy of annihilation. The decisive factor in judging the military leadership's intention is the fate that awaited the Nama in captivity. And in this respect it is justified to talk of a continuation of the existing murderous policy, because the camps the Nama were deported to themselves represented a further instrument in the war of extermination. They were part of a system of camps established across the whole colony immediately following the revocation of the Annihilation Order. This system included 'collection camps', operated by the Mission and used to bring scattered Herero and those who had been living in hiding under control, and concentration camps, established and operated by the military administration.

The Concentration Camps

The concentration camps – the term was used as early as January 1905 by Chancellor Bernhard von Bülow[45] – were set up 'behind the lines' to take people off the hands of the collection camps, and to function as internment camps where

---

44 Von Trotha, Proclamation to the Nama, 22 April 1905, reproduced in Kriegsgeschichtliche Abteilung I des Großen Generalstabs, *Die Kämpfe der deutschen Truppen in Südwestafrika*, ii, Berlin 1906/07, p. 186.

45 Following the revocation of von Trotha's Annihilation Order, Chancellor von Bülow suggested that "Herero who gave themselves up", including women and children, should with the assistance of the Missionary Society be "accommodated in concentration camps in different areas of the territory" and forced to perform "labour under surveillance". Bülow to Imperial Governor's Office Windhoek, 13 January 1905, BArch, R 1001/2087, Sheets 116a–117a. Previously, the term

'tribes' from the area affected by the guerrilla war could be incarcerated, in order to deprive the combatants of the support they enjoyed among the civilian population. This in itself makes clear the difference between these concentration camps and ordinary prisoner-of-war camps. At the same time it is a further indication of the fact that this was a war directed against entire peoples, since the camps were deliberately intended to serve as places of internment not only for combatants, but also for women, elderly men and children. To an extent they were also labour camps, providing urgently needed labour to both private employers and state institutions. While smaller employers would pick up prisoners from the camps every day to work for them, larger enterprises such as the Woermann shipping company even set up camps of their own.[46] At the same time, it was hoped that the prisoners, through being 'educated to work' in the camps, could be disciplined and prepared for their new 'role' as labourers in the post-war period.[47] Coupled with this there was also a spirit of retribution, as Deputy Governor Hans Tecklenburg wrote:

> The more the Herero people now experience the consequences of rebellion in terms of their own physical suffering, the less desire they will have to seek to repeat the uprising for generations to come. Our military successes in themselves have made less of an impression on them. I expect the time of suffering they are now having to endure to have a more sustained effect, though in expressing this view it is by no means my wish to take up cudgels on behalf of Lieutenant General Trotha's Proclamation of 2 October of last year. From an economic point of view, though, the death of so many people does represent a considerable loss.[48]

The largest prison camp was located on Shark Island off Lüderitzbucht, and it was here that the line between murder and genocide was clearly crossed. An eye-

---

"concentration camp" had been used by the Spanish as early as the war in Cuba in 1896, and turned up again two years later during the American war in the Philippines. The expression gained worldwide familiarity during the South African War (1899–1902). An overview of the history of concentration camps is given by Andrzej J. Kaminski, *Konzentrationslager 1896 bis heute. Geschichte – Funktion – Typologie*, München 1990; Joël Kotek and Pierre Rigoulot, *Das Jahrhundert der Lager. Gefangenschaft, Zwangsarbeit, Vernichtung*, Berlin/München 2001.

46 Jan-Bart Gewald, *Towards Redemption. A Socio-political History of the Herero of Namibia between 1890 and 1923*, Leiden 1996, pp. 220–222.

47 For more on this and on the post-war order, see Zimmerer, Jürgen, *Deutsche Herrschaft über Afrikaner. Staatlicher Machtanspruch und Wirklichkeit im kolonialen Namibia*, Münster/Hamburg/London 2001 [English translation: *German Rule, African Subjects. State Aspirations and the Reality of Power in Colonial Namibia*, New York 2021]. A summary is also to be found in Jürgen Zimmerer, "Der koloniale Musterstaat? Rassentrennung, Arbeitszwang und totale Kontrolle in Deutsch-Südwestafrika", in Jürgen Zimmerer and Joachim Zeller, *Völkermord in Deutsch-Südwestafrika. Der Kolonialkrieg in Namibia (1904–1908) und seine Folgen*, Berlin 2003, pp. 26–41.

48 Governor's Office Windhoek to Colonial Department Berlin, 3 July 1905, BArch R 1001/2118, Sheets 154a–155a.

witness, the missionary Emil Laaf from Lüderitzbucht, described the conditions as follows:

> At that time there were about 2,000 Herero prisoners of war interned at the very far end of Shark Island. [...] As long as the people were in good health, they were given work by the forces or by other whites who lived nearby. They were allowed to leave Shark Island to go to work, but came back every evening. [...] As a result of the great hardships and deprivations that the prisoners had suffered while they were out in the *veld* they were very weak, and there was great misery and much sickness among them. And in addition to all that, they found the wet, harsh sea climate hard to endure at first; and in any case they had been completely taken away from their accustomed way of life. It was mainly scurvy and intestinal catarrh that people went down sick with, and a certain percentage died at that time. [...] On 7 September 1906 yet another large transport of prisoners of war arrived in Lüderitzbucht from the north. This time they were Hottentots of various tribes, predominantly Witboois and Bethany people under the leadership of Samuel Isaak, *Kaptein* Hendrik Witbooi's deputy, who had surrendered to the Germans at Gibeon. Altogether, including women and children, they totalled 1,700 persons. Regrettably, a grave injustice was done to these people in transferring them to Lüderitzbucht, since it had been mutually agreed that these prisoners should be settled in Gibeon District once they had surrendered their weapons. So it is no wonder that they, and Samuel Isaak first and foremost, harboured a great grudge against the German government in their hearts. A period of great suffering and misery now began for these people. They were settled on the furthest tip of Shark Island. [...]

Above all they did not get the food that the conditions demanded. The refined German flour they received was unsuitable for baking bread, and no unrefined flour from the Cape was brought in. They were given plenty of pulses, but had no way of cooking them. Fresh meat was an extreme rarity. When Samuel Isaak complained to the missionary Emil Laaf that they got so little meat and the latter advised him to look for the very popular shellfish on the beach, he replied: "We have collected them all already, there are none left."

> But even more than these miserable conditions, their isolation at the very far end of Shark Island played its part in destroying the people's will to live. They gradually became quite apathetic in the face of their wretched state. They were separated from the outside world by three high barbed-wire fences. [...]
>
> The number of the sick increased day by day. In order to keep the people profitably occupied, the tribes had initially been put to work on a major blasting operation, with a view to building a quay on the side facing Roberts Harbour. At first, almost five hundred men were employed on this blasting work. But within a short time this number had dwindled to such an extent that the blasting work had to be suspended. There was scarcely a *pontok* [hut] without one or more sick people in it. A hospital unit was set up in a few large rooms, created by hanging up sacks. But the rations provided were in no way adapted to the needs of the sick. The food was simply put down in front of the people suffering from scurvy, and then it was a matter of 'Eat it or die!' If a sick person had no sympathetic relative to help him, he could easily starve to death. [...] The mortality rate was horrifyingly

high at that time. Sometimes as many as 27 people died on a single day. The dead were taken to the cemetery by the cartload.[49]

Not even the need for labour could move those responsible to see that the prisoners were better provided for; rather than do that, the construction work was suspended. Criticism of the conditions came above all from representatives of the Church. Eventually, impelled by the degree of misery they had witnessed, two missionaries, Emil Laaf and Hermann Nyhof, succeeded in arranging a meeting with the Commandant of Lüderitzbucht, Captain von Zülow, during which they were able to persuade him that it was absolutely essential to improve the catastrophic conditions. According to Laaf's account, von Zülow then asked Colonel Berthold von Deimling, the Commander of the Southern Division of the colonial forces, if it would not be better to move the prisoners away from Shark Island and intern them on the mainland, as "in his opinion, they no longer had any will to live". The answer he received was that "as long as he [Deimling] was in charge, no Hottentot would be allowed to leave Shark Island alive".[50] Thus although the Annihilation Order had been revoked and von Trotha had been recalled to Germany in November 1905, there were evidently elements among the officers who clung to his policy of extermination.

In the camp on Shark Island, murder was committed through deliberate neglect. The selection of victims was solely based on their actual or assumed group identity; 'crimes' or acts of resistance carried out personally by any individual played no role in the grounds for their internment. The intent was to destroy entire 'tribes', which in the German understanding were 'racial groups'. Therefore, this policy can be deemed to be genocidal under Letter (c) of the United Nations Genocide Convention ("Deliberately inflicting on the group conditions of life calculated to bring about its physical destruction in whole or in part") – to say nothing of the killing of individual members of the group (Letter (a)) or of "causing serious bodily or mental harm to members of the group" (Letter (b)), which also left its mark on the survivors. This widespread murder already displays the initial signs of a bureaucratisation of the process, because the inmates of the camp were counted and kept under surveillance. This bureaucratisation is also recognisable

---

49 *Lüderitzbucht Parish Chronicle* (Report on the period from the foundation to 1920, by the missionary Emil Laaf), Archives of the Evangelical Church in the Republic of Namibia, V. 16, Sheets 1–31, here Sheets 21–26.

50 *Lüderitzbucht Parish Chronicle,* Sheets 26 ff. In each month from October 1906 to March 1907 between 143 and 276 prisoners died. All in all, 1,032 out of 1,795 prisoners died during this period; of the 245 survivors who were men, only 25 were still capable of working, while the rest "could only get about on crutches", as von Estorff wrote in a report. Von Estorff to the Colonial Forces, 10 April 1907, BAB R 1001/2140, Sheet 88a f.

in the way deaths were handled administratively, for example in the death certificates with "death by enfeeblement" already printed on them in advance as the cause of death.[51]

Thus although this genocidal policy was initiated by von Trotha, he cannot be alone held responsible for its implementation. In his method of combating guerrilla opponents he stood in a very distinct tradition of German counter-insurgency that was also to be found in other German colonies. There too, the goal was to destroy the basis of life for the opposing civilian population, in order to prevent them from supporting the enemy combatants. But the fact that this non-combatant population itself thereby became a target for the German forces, and that even after the elimination of the guerrilla threat its members were doomed to certain death by being provided with inadequate rations or being displaced into arid regions, represents a crossing of the boundary line into genocide in this case as well. The genocide against the Herero may possibly be more obviously recognisable as such than that against the Nama; but for the latter too, internment on Shark Island, for example, also generally meant certain death – and that for one reason only: namely that they were Nama.

The Genocide in South West Africa and the Holocaust

Compared to the massive battles and the millions of victims of the Second World War, with its acts of genocide and the implementation of a strategy of annihilation on a gigantic scale by the German side, the colonial war in South West Africa seems but a minor prelude to the barbarisms of the twentieth century. Nonetheless, the colonial war's numerous structural similarities to the Nazi 'war of annihilation in the East' reveal that the colonial war against the Herero and the Nama is an important event in history, and not only in Namibian history but in German history too. Many things that appear, when we look back at the Second World War, to be unimaginable breaches of taboos had already been common practice in German South West Africa.[52] If the underlying structure of the 'war in the East' – in other words, the grand design that lay behind the modern weapons and the armada of tanks and aircraft – is exposed, this 'war of annihilation' displays

---

51 Jan-Bart Gewald, "Herero and Missionaries. The Making of Historical Sources in the 1920s", in Wilhelm J. G. Möhlig, ed., *Frühe Kolonialgeschichte Namibias 1880–1930*, Köln 2000, pp. 77–95, here p. 78.
52 I have presented the structural similarities between colonialism and the German policy of occupation and extermination in the 'East' during the Second World War in depth in Jürgen Zimmerer, "Die Geburt des 'Ostlandes' aus dem Geiste des Kolonialismus. Die nationalsozialistische

elements clearly reminiscent of colonial warfare, of "war[s] of destruction", incorporating "campaign[s] of annihilation", such as had already been waged by, among others, the German colonial forces.[53] Because although in formal terms the war against the Soviet Union was a regular war between European powers, it was the case right from the start that the Germans did not conduct it as such but as a war of plunder and conquest, which thanks to the deliberate non-application of the international law of war by the aggressor more closely resembled a colonial war than an 'ordinary' war inside Europe. Features of this were the denial to the adversary of the status of a legitimate belligerent of equal and equally honourable status, who even in defeat and captivity was entitled to a minimum of rights, and the racist willingness to let prisoners of war perish or to murder them outright.[54] As we have seen, there had already been arbitrary shootings, summary executions of prisoners and mass murder by starvation, thirst and disease in South West Africa.

Taking into consideration the high degree of interest in the war in German South West Africa within the German Empire, and the enormous popularity[55] of war memoirs and novels extending well beyond the middle of the 20th century, which established a place for the war in the collective memory, one may well speak of a 'tradition of warfare'. And as the period that lay between the war in South West Africa and the Second World War was less than 40 years, the absence of any connection would be more surprising than its existence.

The genocide in German South West Africa is also important in the prehistory of the Holocaust. The very terms used, terms such as 'concentration camp' and 'genocide', themselves indicate a link to the mass crimes committed under the

---

Eroberungs- und Beherrschungspolitik in (post-)kolonialer Perspektive", *Sozial.Geschichte. Zeitschrift für historische Analyse des 20. und 21. Jahrhunderts*, 19 (2004), pp. 10–43 (English version: "The Birth of the 'Ostland'", pp. 230–261 of this book).

53 These expressions originate from Eduard von Liebert, who used them to describe the tactic of destroying the basic necessities of life in the struggle between the German colonial forces and the Wahehe in German East Africa: Eduard von Liebert, *Neunzig Tage im Zelt. Meine Reise nach Uhehe Juni bis September 1897*, Berlin 1898, p. 33, here quoted according to Thomas Morlang, "'Die Kerls haben ja nicht einmal Gewehre'. Der Untergang der Zelewski-Expedition in Deutsch-Ostafrika im August 1891", in *Militärgeschichte*, 11/2 (2001), pp. 22–28, here p. 27.

54 On this subject, see the classic study by Christian Streit, *Keine Kameraden. Die Wehrmacht und die sowjetischen Kriegsgefangenen 1941–1945*, Stuttgart 1978.

55 Regarding the way the war was handled in literature, see Medardus Brehl, "'Das Drama spielt sich auf der dunklen Bühne des Sandfeldes ab.' Die Vernichtung der Herero und Nama in der deutschen (Populär-)Literatur", in Jürgen Zimmerer and Joachim Zeller, eds, *Völkermord. Der Kolonialkrieg (1904–1908) in Namibia und seine Folgen*, Berlin 2003, pp. 86–96.

Third Reich.[56] And although one needs to be on one's guard against overhasty comparisons, there are indeed structural similarities between the genocide against the Herero and Nama on the one hand and the Holocaust on the other, similarities which are worthy of being afforded closer consideration. In a general history of genocide in modern times, the colonial war in German South West Africa stands as a significant half-way house between the massacres committed on the American and Australian frontiers by groups of settlers and local militia[57] and the mass murder conducted with quasi-'industrialised' methods in the Third Reich. It represents an intermediate link between earlier acts of genocide with a low degree of state organisation and the fully bureaucratised crimes of the Nazis.

The objection has repeatedly been raised that the Holocaust differs from all other mass murders in history because of the role played in it by the State. However, this is a grossly over-simplified and essentially ahistorical view of the matter. Of course it is true that the role played by the State in colonial acts of genocide differs from the role it played in the Holocaust. This, though, is hardly surprising; because the State was far less firmly established in America and Australia, for example, during the period of colonial settlement, than it was in Germany between 1933 and 1945. If, however, one does not take the centralised and bureaucratised state of the Third Reich as the yardstick, but rather bears in mind the historical stage that the State had arrived at in each case, then the apparently fundamental differences turn into merely differences of gradation: the precise form of the murdering may change, depending on the degree of bureaucratisation of the state that carries it out or has it carried out, but there remains as a common factor the readiness to exterminate groups of people defined by the 'perpetrators'. This ultimate breach of taboo, not only to imagine exterminating entire ethnicities but actually to set about doing it, was first carried out in the colonies. This also contributed to making the Holocaust conceivable and possible, however disparate the motives for the murder of Jews or of Sinti and Roma, of homosexuals or the disabled, may have been. The Holocaust therefore represents an extremely radicalised variant of actions of a type that had already been practised in the colonial context.

---

56 The relationship between genocide in the colonial context and the Holocaust can only be depicted very sketchily here. I have analysed it in greater detail elsewhere: Zimmerer, "Holocaust und Kolonialismus" (English version: "Colonialism and the Holocaust", pp. 125–153 in this book); Zimmerer, "Kolonialer Genozid?" (English version: "Colonial Genocide?", pp. 175–197 in this book).
57 On the concept of the 'frontier' see: Stefan Kaufmann, "Der Siedler", in Stefan Kaufmann, Eva Horn and Ulrich Bröckling, eds, *Grenzverletzer. Von Schmugglern, Spionen und anderen subversiven Gestalten*, Berlin 2002, pp. 176–201; Christoph Marx, "Grenzfälle: Zu Geschichte und Potential des Frontierbegriffs", *Saeculum*, 54/1 (2003), pp. 123–143.

The most conspicuous differences from earlier cases of genocide in Africa, Australia or America are to be found in the methods of mass murder employed. Whereas the genocide in the American New England states primarily took the form of massacres committed by settlers or local militias, as early as the 19th century the State itself came to the fore in the United States or in the Australian State of Queensland in the guise of the army or the Native Police. The genocide against the Herero and the Nama is then to be regarded as a further intensified form of the genocidal war of conquest and pacification, in that largish formations of troops under a unified senior command structure were deployed for a longish period of time. At the same time, the beginnings of a bureaucratised form of extermination can be seen in the camps: admittedly not yet in the active, 'industrialised' form of killing practised after 1941 in the Nazi extermination camps, but already existent in the form of murder through neglect. Even under the Third Reich, more people were killed by shooting and starvation than through 'industrialised' killing in the seemingly clinically clean gas chambers, even though it is these that have become the archetypal symbol of Nazi genocide. It is this bureaucratised form of murder for which the name 'Auschwitz' essentially stands as a shorthand expression. The fact that this name has become lodged in the global memory of humanity has caused the link between genocide and the modern administrative state to become anchored in our collective awareness as well. Essentially, however, this gets in the way of any clear view of similar approaches and precursor events in the colonial context.

Auschwitz marks the perverse culmination of state violence directed against both the state's own and also alien populations. The war against the Herero and Nama was a decisive step in the development that ultimately produced this, and offered a portent, right at the beginning of the twentieth century, of what was yet to come. The genocide in German South West Africa is therefore neither simply a local event in the history of Namibia or of Germany, nor an isolated incident in colonial history. Rather, it is an event that stands out in a global history of the unleashing of that violence that was to culminate in the two World Wars.

Colonial Genocide? On the Use and Abuse of a Historical Category for Global History

'Colonial Genocide': Some Reflections on the History of the Term

> New conceptions require new terms. By 'genocide' we mean the destruction of a nation or of an ethnic group. [...] Generally speaking, genocide does not necessarily mean the immediate destruction of a nation, except when accomplished by mass killings of all members of a nation. It is intended rather to signify a coordinated plan of different actions aiming at the destruction of essential foundations of the life of national groups, with the aim of annihilating the groups themselves. [...] Genocide is directed against the national group as an entity, and the actions involved are directed against individuals, not in their individual capacity, but as members of the national group.[1]

It was the mass murder of the Armenians and the concerted crimes of the National Socialists that Raphael Lemkin had in mind in 1944 when he developed his new concept, 'genocide', which found its way into the UN Convention on the Prevention and Punishment of the Crime of Genocide a few years later.[2] Since then, the term 'genocide' has achieved an unprecedented degree of recognition as a word denoting a certain kind of criminal behaviour; it has long since moved beyond the realm of jurisprudence and has become a term used in political polemics as well. Bitter disputes have been conducted concerning singularity, comparability and continuity. Particularly for Jewish survivors and their descendants, the fact of having been victims of genocide – many would say of the first-ever genocide – has become a part of their identity; and this needs to be taken into account by anyone using the word. The term 'genocide' is highly charged – emotionally, historically and philosophically. In fact, the term is to some extent so overloaded that this detracts from its usefulness as a category of academic analysis. Despite this, I do not believe that the term should be avoided; but I do believe that terminological clarification is necessary. The following analysis therefore concentrates on the functionality of the category of genocide and its fitness for purpose; and that particularly when it is used with the prefix 'colonial'.

So is 'colonial genocide' a separate category of its own? Is it a meaningful expression? And what consequences does such a category have for a political culture

---

1 Raphael Lemkin, *Axis Rule in Occupied Europe: Law of Occupation, Analysis of Government, Proposals for Redress*, Washington 1944, p. 79.
2 Regarding the origin and meaning of the term genocide, see also A. Dirk Moses, "The Holocaust and Genocide", in Dan Stone, ed., *The Historiography of the Holocaust*, London 2004.

of commemoration or remembrance? To answer these questions, it is necessary to take a brief look at the areas of semantics and remembrance culture that the term 'colonial genocide' relates to.

A consideration of the inherent appellative structure of the term, i.e. of the chain of associations that are evoked when the term 'genocide' is used, will lead to the conclusion that it creates a connection between certain forms of mass murder and the Holocaust, the attempted complete extermination of the European Jews; that is to say a crime that in the meantime has become, in people's general awareness, a globally understood shorthand term for pure evil, for the worst crime in the history of humankind. At the same time, the term "Holocaust" is currently also being applied, again as a shorthand term that really is understood throughout the world, to ecological and economic dangers, in an attempt to portray them as particularly threatening. One can read about an "Environmental Holocaust",[3] or about the "Holocaust on your Plate" as a plea against intensive animal husbandry.[4] The former Australian Prime Minister John Howard spoke of an "economic holocaust", referring to the economic crisis of the late 1990s, even though, he said, Australia had come through it pretty well.[5]

This global understandability and moral connectivity has made the term 'genocide' very attractive to representatives of the victims of other mass crimes as well. It may therefore be observed that in such contexts there is an insistence on the term genocide precisely because it implies a connection to the Holocaust, i.e. it is used to express the view that in terms of its moral reprehensibility the mass crime concerned is on a par with the murder of over six million Jews by the Nazis. The same holds true for uses of the term "Holocaust" in which the semantic link emerges even more clearly: slogans such as "American Holocaust",[6] "Ameri-

---

[3] See for example S. K. Chadha, ed., *Environmental Holocaust in Himalaya*, New Delhi 1989; Mike Davis, *Late Victorian Holocausts. El Niño famines and the making of the Third World*, London 2001. Interestingly enough, this latter book was published in German under the less sensational title *Die Geburt der Dritten Welt* (*The Birth of the Third World*), Berlin 2003.
[4] In March 2003, the animal protection organisation PETA (People for the Ethical Treatment of Animals) drew vehement criticism, especially from Jewish groups, when as part of an advertising campaign entitled "Holocaust on your Plate" it placed pictures of children behind barbed wire in a Nazi concentration camp alongside a picture of pigs in a cage. Brian Willoughby, "PETA Sparks Outrage with Holocaust Comparison", 23 March 2003, https://www.alternet.org/2003/03/peta_sparks_outrage_with_holocaust_comparison, accessed 12 Jul. 2023.
[5] "Transcript of the Prime Minister, the Hon. John Howard MP, Address to the Tasmanian Division, State Council Dinner, Burnie Civic Centre, Burnie, 6 November 1998", *Prime Minister of Australia, News Room*, https://pmtranscripts.pmc.gov.au/release/transcript-10972, accessed 12 Jul. 2023.
[6] David E. Stannard, *American Holocaust. The Conquest of the New World*, Oxford/New York 1992.

can Indian Holocaust",[7] "Herero Holocaust"[8] or "Black Holocaust",[9] to name just a few examples taken from the colonial arena, demonstrate the point.

At the same time, it is precisely for this reason that the application of the term 'genocide' to the colonial context is so explosive: because its use also suggests a content-related connection. Positions in this area are extremely emotionalised, as the term touches on the issue of the uniqueness of the Holocaust. The question of its singularity, its comparability and the relationship between Nazi crimes and earlier or even subsequent collective mass murders has long since ceased to be an issue only among academic historians, having also taken on a philosophical dimension that touches on intimate questions of identity.[10] Whereas proponents of the singularity thesis regard the making of any comparisons as a blasphemous mockery of the Holocaust's victims, its opponents – raising an analogy to the accusation of Holocaust denial – argue that the singularity thesis amounts to a denial of all other cases of genocide.[11]

This is not the place to hold a debate about singularity and the legitimacy of comparisons; this has already been done many times.[12] Essentially, it is a question that cannot be decided academically. In the context under consideration here, the issue of the pros and cons of a separate category of 'colonial genocide', an important factor is that for a long time many Holocaust researchers ignored the exis-

---

[7] Russell Thornton, *American Indian Holocaust and Survival. A Population History since 1492*, London 1987.
[8] Jeremy Silvester, Werner Hillebrecht and Casper Erichsen, "The Herero Holocaust? The Disputed History of the 1904 Genocide", *The Namibian Weekender* (20 August 2001).
[9] Black History Resource Working Group in conjunction with the Race Equality Management Team, ed., *Slavery: An Introduction to the African Holocaust; with Special Reference to Liverpool, 'Capital of the Slave Trade'*, 2nd edn, Liverpool 1997; Thomas Mordekhai, *Vessels of Evil: American Slavery and the Holocaust*, Philadelphia 1993. There are now also museums and societies that commemorate the "Black Holocaust", such as "America's Black Holocaust Museum" and "The Black Holocaust Society" in Milwaukee, Wisconsin.
[10] On this subject, see Daniel Levy and Natan Sznaider, *Erinnerung im globalen Zeitalter: Der Holocaust*, Frankfurt 2001; Peter Novick, *The Holocaust in American Life*, Boston/New York 1999.
[11] On this subject, see Lilian Friedberg, "Dare to Compare. Americanizing the Holocaust", *American Indian Quarterly*, 24/3 (2000), pp. 353–380; David E. Stannard, "Uniqueness as Denial: The Politics of Genocide Scholarship", in Alan S. Rosenbaum, ed., *Is the Holocaust Unique? Perspectives on Comparative Genocide*, Oxford 1996, pp. 163–208.
[12] See, for instance: Thomas W. Simon, "Genocides: Normative Comparative Studies", in Margot Levy, ed., *Remembering the Future. The Holocaust in an Age of Genocide*, i: History, pp. 91–112; Doris L. Bergen, "Rivalry, Indifference or Solidarity? Jews and 'Other Victims' in Studies of the Holocaust and Comparative Genocide", in Margot Levy, ed., *Remembering the Future. The Holocaust in an Age of Genocide*, i: History, pp. 29–42; Gavriel D. Rosenfeld, "The Politics of Uniqueness: Reflections on the Recent Polemical Turn in Holocaust and Genocide Scholarship", *Holocaust and Genocide Studies*, 13/1 (1999), pp. 28–61.

tence of any earlier or later occurrences of genocide. For reasons that are to be sought in their individual philosophies of history and their own biographies, it was almost impossible for many historians to accept any comparative approach to the problem of genocide. Leading researchers such as Yehuda Bauer or Steven T. Katz adhered to the singularity of the Holocaust in that they (initially) reserved the term 'genocide' for the attempted extermination of the European Jews.[13]

This stance is understandable, since the trauma of the Holocaust – as Dirk Moses, drawing upon the theories of Emile Durkheim, points out – expresses itself in the survivors (partially) through the sacralisation of the victims. This was often the only way in which they could make sense of the horrific crime they had experienced. The sacralisation of Jewish victims, however, has as its corollary the 'profanisation' or 'secularisation' of other victims of Nazi and other mass crimes. This does not necessarily exclude a recognition of the sufferings of other groups and individuals in particular cases – a point it is important to raise against those critics who make accusations of inadequate sensitivity towards indigenous victims, and also against the trite thesis that such scholars are merely seeking to instrumentalise the Holocaust in order to serve their own private interests[14] – but it is nonetheless a barrier to any meaningful comparison. The sacred and the profane cannot be compared.

Nevertheless, even one of the most vehement advocates of the thesis of singularity, Yehuda Bauer, has not been able to completely withstand the pressure to recognise other cases of genocide as well. In the meantime, therefore, he has adopted a mediatory position, accepting – superficially at least – the generic use of the term genocide:

> It [the Holocaust] is, on the one hand, a genocide and must be compared with other genocides; that universal dimension of comparability should concern everyone, from Kamchatka to Tasmania and from Patagonia to the Hudson Bay. On the other hand, it is a unique genocide, with unprecedented – and, so far, unrepeated – characteristics.

These, according to Bauer, were to be found predominantly in the motivation of the perpetrators, because so far only the murder of the European Jews had been characterised by the attempt to achieve complete physical extermination:

> The conclusion to draw is that one ought to differentiate between the intent to destroy a group in a context of selective mass murder and the intent to annihilate every person of the

---

13 For more on this and the following, see A. Dirk Moses, "Conceptual Blockages and Definitional Dilemmas in the 'Racial Century': Genocides of Indigenous Peoples and the Holocaust", *Patterns of Prejudice*, 36/4 (2002), pp. 7–36.
14 See, for instance, Norman G. Finkelstein, *The Holocaust Industry*, London 2000.

group. To make this as simple as possible, I would suggest retaining the term *genocide* for 'partial' murder and the term *Holocaust* for total destruction.[15]

In this way, Bauer accepts a common category only superficially, and then immediately calls it into question again through a new differentiation. The message seems to be that while there have been many genocides, there has been only the one Holocaust. This naturally raises the question as to what academic sense and purpose this categorisation has; the new duality of genocide and holocaust is no different from the old one which declared that there had been many mass murders but only one case of genocide.

In order to avoid any misunderstanding: a plea for a category 'genocide' that would make comparison possible is not to be seen as countenancing any kind of moral relativisation. It cannot be a matter of "weighing up cases of genocide and numbers of victims against each other";[16] nor of drawing equivalences between specific historical cases, or of denying them; all cases of genocide or of mass murder organised by society or the state are singular in important respects. However, drawing comparisons makes it possible to search in a concerted way for causes, for traditions preparing the way for the event, or for mindsets that facilitated it; and – surely what most people will hope – for ways of preventing any repetition.

It is therefore necessary in comparative historical genocide research to have categories that do not in themselves already anticipate the results of a comparative investigation. It is for this reason that I am doubtful about the value of the historical category 'colonial genocide', involving as it does the danger that it will fulfil a similar function to Bauer's essentially epistemological distinction between genocide and holocaust, namely that of detaching mass crimes committed in the colonial context from the history of the Holocaust. For even if there has recently seemed to be a growing interest in colonial violence and in mass murder and genocide committed in that context, and attempts are being made to explore the significance of colonialism for a history of mass violence, these have not yet gained entry into the collective awareness of Europe. Mark Mazower's summary of the different reactions of Europeans to Nazi and colonial crimes still holds true:

> I think there may have [...] been a widely-held unspoken assumption that the mass killing of African or American peoples was distant and in some senses an 'inevitable' part of progress while what was genuinely shocking was the attempt to exterminate an entire people in Eu-

---

15 Yehuda Bauer, *Rethinking the Holocaust*, New Haven/London 2001, pp. 10f. (emphases in original).
16 Stig Förster and Gerhard Hirschfeld, "Einleitung", in Stig Förster and Gerhard Hirschfeld, eds, *Genozid in der modernen Geschichte*, Münster 1999, pp. 5–10, here p. 7.

rope. This assumption may rest upon an implicit racism, or simply upon a failure of historical imagination.[17]

Moreover, another reason for the silence maintained with regard to colonial crimes, or for their marginalisation in historiography and people's conceptions of history, may have been that they did not fit in with the image of the moral superiority of 'the West'. The Australian historian Dirk Moses formulated this as follows:

> Another reason is the fact that the regimes responsible for upholding human rights and the moral universalism on which they are based – the nation-states of 'the west' – profitted enormously from imperialism or owe their very existence to their projects of settlement. 'Colonial genocide' or the 'genocide of indigenous peoples' necessarily poses thorny questions today regarding the dark past or provenance of these societies.[18]

In the former settler communities it is also especially difficult to acknowledge that there were occurrences of colonial genocide because this would undermine that very view of the past that national identity is built on. This is why Australian Prime Minister John Howard refused to recognise the violent history of the colonisation of his country;[19] and it is why, although the American President Bill Clinton apologised in Africa for the crime of slavery, in the United States itself there is no official commemoration of the 'eradication' of the Native Americans.[20] Similarly, the German President Roman Herzog declined to provide an apology for the genocide committed against the Herero and Nama peoples that was demanded during his visit to Namibia in 1998.[21] And these are just three examples among many. Above and beyond the question of the guilt of the nation concerned, this is in each case a touchstone of its attitude towards the history of colonialism as a

---

17 Mark Mazower, "After Lemkin: Genocide, the Holocaust and History", in *The Jewish Quarterly*, 5/Winter (1994), pp. 5–8; quoted according to Moses, "Conceptual blockages", p. 8f.
18 Moses, "Conceptual blockages", p. 9.
19 On this subject, see Jürgen Zimmerer, "Die Zeugen der Massaker. Ein Historikerstreit über die Aborigines in Australien", *Süddeutsche Zeitung* (24 February 2003). As regards historical awareness in Australia in general, see A. Dirk Moses, "Coming to Terms with Genocidal Pasts in Comparative Perspective: Germany and Australia", *Aboriginal History*, 25 (2001), pp. 91–115.
20 On this subject, see: Stannard, "Uniqueness as Denial"; Ward Churchill, *A Little Matter of Genocide. Holocaust and Denial in the Americas 1492 to the Present*, San Francisco 1998. On the blank spaces in the American culture of commemoration in general, see James W. Loewen, *Lies across America. What our Historic Sites Get Wrong*, New York 2000. On the issue as to whether entire nations should be paid compensation for genocide and slavery, see Elazar Barkan, *Völker klagen an. Eine neue internationale Moral*, Düsseldorf 2002.
21 "Kein Pardon für Herero-Morde", *die tageszeitung* (5 March 1998). See also: "Herzog lobt die Beziehungen zu Namibia", *Frankfurter Allgemeine Zeitung* (5 March 1998); "Herzog will Deutsch in Namibia stärken", *Süddeutsche Zeitung* (7 March 1998).

whole, since any acceptance of the claim that genocide took place in the colonies represents a fundamental calling into question of the assumption that the Europeanisation of the earth was a project that furthered 'progress'.

Compared with the long-term prevalence of this denial that mass crimes were committed under colonialism, and the repression of any awareness of them in favour of a romantic transfiguration of the colonial past, it is certainly progress that colonial genocide is now spoken and written about at all; as a category, however, it merely perpetuates the differentiation between the Holocaust and other cases of genocide. It is for this reason that I argue for the abandonment of colonial genocide as a historical category. It does not exist and never has: there is only genocide, which however, it goes without saying, has been committed with varying motives and varying degrees of intensity.

My thesis is admittedly only meaningful if it can be successfully proved that the term genocide can be applied to events as varied as the North American 'Indian Wars', the massacres of Australian Aboriginal people, the war against the Herero and the crimes of the Nazis. It should be remembered that the term colonial genocide was introduced in the academic field not least in order to take account of the apparently utterly irreconcilable differences between the crimes committed under the Third Reich and earlier mass crimes.

Difficulties arise immediately simply in the search for a suitable definition of what genocide entails, because the opposing positions – the emphasis on the singularity of the Holocaust and the direct opposite – are essentially both reflected in the academic debate accompanying the quest for an accurate definition.[22] Whereas Israel W. Charny, for instance, defines genocide very broadly as "the mass killing of substantial numbers of human beings, when not in the course of military action against the military forces of an avowed enemy, under conditions of the essential defenselessness and helplessness of the victims",[23] Steven T. Katz, seeking to limit the concept to the Nazi murder of the Jews, would like to see it applied only to "the actualization of the intent, however successfully carried out, to murder in its totality any national, ethnic, racial, religious, political, social, gen-

---

[22] For a brief overview of the stages of development in genocide research, see Frank Chalk and Kurt Jonassohn, "Genozid – Ein historischer Überblick", in Mihran Dabag and Kristin Platt, eds, *Genozid und Moderne*, i: *Strukturen kollektiver Gewalt im 20. Jahrhundert*, Opladen 1998, pp. 294–308. See also Myriam Gessler, *Die Singularität des Holocaust und die vergleichende Genozidforschung. Empirische und theoretische Untersuchung zu einem aktuellen Thema der Geschichtswissenschaft*, University of Bern 2000 (M.A. thesis).

[23] Quoted according to: Helen Fein, "Definition and Discontent: Labelling, Detecting, and Explaining Genocide in the Twentieth Century", in Stig Förster and Gerhard Hirschfeld, eds, *Genozid in der modernen Geschichte*, Münster 1997, pp. 11–21, here p. 17.

der or economic group, as these groups are defined by the perpetrator".[24] Neither of these two concepts seems to me to be suitable for use in an examination of global history. A working definition is needed that neither excludes an event from historical consideration, nor diminishes the horror of the deliberate murder of entire peoples within a general history of mass killings.[25]

I shall base my arguments below on the United Nations Genocide Convention, as it seems to offer the most widely accepted working basis. In 1948, it defined genocide as:

> any of the following acts committed with intent to destroy, in whole or in part, a national, ethnical, racial or religious group, as such:
> (a) Killing members of the group;
> (b) Causing serious bodily or mental harm to members of the group;
> (c) Deliberately inflicting on the group conditions of life calculated to bring about its physical destruction in whole or in part;
> (d) Imposing measures intended to prevent births within the group;
> (e) Forcibly transferring children of the group to another group.[26]

As was made clear in Lemkin's definition quoted at the beginning of this chapter, the decisive factor is intention. It is necessary to demonstrate the will to 'exterminate' the persecuted group, a "sustained purposeful action by a perpetrator to physically destroy a collectivity directly or indirectly", as Helen Fein expressed it.[27]

If this yardstick is applied, then it is true that many cases of mass deaths commonly regarded as genocide are removed from the list: neither in the practice of slavery nor in the deaths of millions of Native Americans who were above all victims of diseases introduced by the conquerors is there an evident intention to annihilate. Nonetheless, cases of genocide can be shown to have taken place in North America, Australia, southern Africa and elsewhere.

---

24 Steven T. Katz, *The Holocaust in Historical Perspective*, i: *The Holocaust and Mass Death before the Modern Age*, Oxford 1994, p. 131.
25 A. Dirk Moses has recently argued in a very stimulating way that Lemkin's definition does not encompass only mass murder. See Moses, "Holocaust and Genocide". Nevertheless, I shall concentrate here on the act of murder, not in order to exclude other manifestations of genocide, but rather because in my opinion it is a crucial feature of Nazi genocide that mass murder was actually carried out. And for the sake of the argument as set out here I shall accept the Holocaust as being paradigmatic of genocide, even though I am aware that there are also contrary standpoints.
26 Article 2, "Convention on the Prevention and Punishment of the Crime of Genocide", United Nations, 9 December 1948. Printed in Frank Chalk and Kurt Jonassohn, *The History and Sociology of Genocide. Analyses and Case Studies*, New Haven/London 1990, pp. 44–49, here p. 44.
27 Helen Fein, *Genocide: A Sociological Perspective*, London 1990, p. 24.

Before moving on, however, allow me to offer a further theoretical argument: the UN Convention is little help in determining who might be considered as the perpetrator, because ultimately the exterminatory intention of an individual person, for instance, does not yet constitute genocide, at least insofar as this individual is not, thanks to his authority as a representative of the state, in a position to make his own xenophobia the basis for the actions of a state executive organ. Many genocide researchers, such as Helen Fein, therefore assume that genocide is a state crime.[28]

I believe it was the difficulty in finding proof of intention and in tracing the causality of genocidal massacres back to state authorities, that have made colonial genocide so attractive in the academic field as a category in its own right. The images that are set so firmly and iconically in all our minds of the 'final solution to the Jewish question' ordered by Adolf Hitler and other leading Nazis and of mass murder organised bureaucratically by Eichmann and his lieutenants and then perpetrated quasi-industrially in the concentration camps have made direct comparisons with other cases of genocide that took place outside Europe difficult. For while the murder of Jews, of Sinti and Roma and of Russians was centrally directed and implemented by state authorities, this type of state involvement is harder to find in the colonial context. This is especially true out on the 'frontier', where private action at the local level predominated, as this was by definition precisely the mixed zone where contact between the new arrivals and the local population occurred, but where the 'Whites' were initially not yet in the majority and in particular there was a lack of established state structures.[29] The establishment of a separate category of colonial genocide appeared to offer a way out of this dilemma.

I shall attempt to demonstrate below that this is not necessary. My arguments are based on the observation that colonialism and the Nazi policy of conquest and extermination possess a large measure of systematic similarity, as the concepts of 'race' and 'space' were fundamental to both.[30]

---

[28] Helen Fein, "Genozid als Staatsverbrechen. Beispiele aus Rwanda und Bosnien", *Zeitschrift für Genozidforschung*, 1 (1999), pp. 36–45. Fein speaks of the perpetrators as a "political elite that either controls the state or intends to seize power in the state": ibid. p. 38. Thus the state remains the point of reference for determining the perpetrators.

[29] For a gripping account of the frontier as a state-free zone, see Stefan Kaufmann, "Der Siedler", in Stefan Kaufmann, Eva Horn and Ulrich Bröckling, eds, *Grenzverletzer. Von Schmugglern, Spionen und anderen subversiven Gestalten*, Berlin 2002, pp. 176–201. On the same subject see also Christoph Marx, "Grenzfälle: Zu Geschichte und Potential des Frontierbegriffs", *Saeculum*, 54/1 (2003), pp. 123–143.

[30] I have depicted the systematic similarities between the two in more detail in Jürgen Zimmerer, "Die Geburt des 'Ostlandes' aus dem Geiste des Kolonialismus. Die nationalsozialistische

Colonialism and National Socialism: Systematic Similarities

In considering Nazi policy in Eastern Europe in its various guises[31] – the war of annihilation, the occupation policy and the genocide – one constantly finds oneself faced by two concepts that link these phenomena together. The first is racism,[32] in the sense of a comprehensive biologisation of all aspects of life, which is the thread that unifies divergent aspects of Nazi ideology and practice; the second is *Großraumpolitik* (policy of large space) in association with an 'economy of annihilation'.[33] In a racist view of history and society, the 'nation', the *Volk*, was understood to be a single composite organism, whose preservation and growth was to be safeguarded under all circumstances.[34] But what a nation whose greatness lay in the number of its 'racially healthy' members seemed to need above all was sufficient territory – 'living space'. Thus the idea of the need for sufficient space to live in was directly linked to the ideology of 'race'. It incorporated ideas both of economic self-sufficiency and of a territory for Germans to settle – a territory that was supposed to exist in Poland and Russia, where the Germans thought they could find the 'living space' they supposedly lacked.

These two concepts 'race' and 'space', were also at the heart of colonialism. The settler colonies above all created large-scale spatial economies (*Großraumwirtschaften*), being characterised, as was the later German occupation policy in the East, by

---

Eroberungs- und Beherrschungspolitik in (post-)kolonialer Perspektive", *Sozial.Geschichte. Zeitschrift für historische Analyse des 20. und 21. Jahrhunderts,* 1 (2004), pp. 10–43 (English version: "The Birth of the 'Ostland' out of the Spirit of Colonialism", pp. 230–261 in this book).

31 Among the sheer unending mass of literature, I would like just to mention a few of the more recent works which I have drawn on particularly for the following remarks: Ulrich Herbert, ed., *National Socialist Extermination Policies: Contemporary German Perspectives and Controversies,* New York 2000; Götz Aly and Susanne Heim, *Vordenker der Vernichtung. Auschwitz und die deutschen Pläne für eine neue europäische Ordnung,* Hamburg 1991; Götz Aly, *'Final Solution': Nazi Population Policy and the Murder of the European Jews,* London/New York 1999; Christian Gerlach, *Kalkulierte Morde: Die deutsche Wirtschafts- und Vernichtungspolitik in Weißrußland, 1941–1944,* Hamburg 1999. References to further literature can be found there.

32 See Michael Burleigh and Wolfgang Wippermann, *The Racial State: Germany 1933–1945,* Cambridge 1991; Ulrich Herbert, "Traditionen des Rassismus", in Ulrich Herbert, *Arbeit, Volkstum, Weltanschauung. Über Fremde und Deutsche im 20. Jahrhundert,* Frankfurt 1995, pp. 11–29.

33 On this subject, see Aly and Heim, *Vordenker der Vernichtung*; Aly, *Endlösung*.

34 There is a relatively large amount of literature on this issue. See Michael Burleigh, *Death and Deliverance. Euthanasia in Germany c.1900–1945,* Cambridge 1994; Peter Weingart, Jürgen Kroll and Kurt Bayertz, *Rasse, Blut und Gene. Geschichte der Eugenik in Deutschland,* Frankfurt 1988. On the international context, see Stefan Kühl, *Die Internationale der Rassisten: Aufstieg und Niedergang der internationalen Bewegung für Eugenik und Rassenhygiene im 20. Jahrhundert,* Frankfurt 1997.

their efforts to take possession of and 'develop' an enormous dependent territory. The population living there was not perceived as a partner with equal rights; rather, a racial hierarchy was established in which a clear distinction was made between the colonisers as higher beings, destined to rule, and the colonised as 'lower races', subject to the colonisers. Regardless of whether it was the proselytising of the 'heathen', the 'White Man's Burden' or the 'Manifest Destiny', what all of these legitimising concepts shared in practice was that the colonisers were positioned at the top of the hierarchy and the colonised at the bottom, even if in the everyday experience of colonial contact and colonial rule it was not possible, or not intended, to implement this at all times, or everywhere, or with equal rigidity. At the lowest end of the scale were groups that were seemingly doomed to destruction, or that were to be deliberately murdered.[35] Even if the justifications for European rule underwent change and development during the 500-year history of European colonialism, which is here presented only in the abbreviated form of an 'ideal type',[36] this did not impact the fundamental dichotomy. Colonialism's 'asymmetrical relationships of dominance' could go to the extreme of bringing about the physical annihilation of the indigenous population, to say nothing of the psychological depredations. Social Darwinism, as it gained influence in the course of the 19th century, then directly emphasised the racial hierarchy and the concept of competition between nations, both in respect of the relationship between the colonisers and the colonised and also as between the colonial powers themselves. This biologistic interpretation of world history – the conviction that one's own nation needed to secure space, territory, in order to ensure its survival – is then also one of the fundamental parallels between colonialism and the expansionist policies of the Nazis.[37] The foreign land, perceived by the colonisers as

---

[35] See for example: Russell McGregor, *Imagined Destinies. Aboriginal Australians and the Doomed Race Theory, 1880–1939*, Victoria 1997; Saul Dubow, *Scientific Racism in Modern South Africa*, Cambridge 1995.

[36] For an initial overview of colonial history, see Jürgen Osterhammel, *Kolonialismus. Geschichte, Formen, Folgen*, München 1995; Wolfgang Reinhard, *Kleine Geschichte des Kolonialismus*, Stuttgart 1996.

[37] Smith comes to similar conclusions: Woodruff D. Smith, *The Ideological Origins of Nazi Imperialism*, Oxford 1986. See also Charles Reynolds, *Modes of Imperialism*, Oxford 1981, pp. 124–171. Ehmann too refers to the connection – even in terms of the persons involved – between colonial and Nazi racism. Annegret Ehmann, "Rassistische und antisemitische Traditionslinien in der deutschen Geschichte des 19. und 20. Jahrhunderts", in Sportmuseum Berlin, ed., *Sportstadt Berlin in Geschichte und Gegenwart*, Berlin 1993, pp. 131–145. Kundrus's attempt to disprove any relationship between colonial and Nazi racial policies is unconvincing. The openness and heterogeneity of the Wilhelminian discourse on Africans that she postulates were at best merely apparent: in the hegemonic discourse as it was reflected in colonial practice no such openness existed. Birthe Kundrus, "Von Windhoek nach Nürnberg? Koloniale 'Mischehenverbote' und die nationalsozialistische Ras-

savage and chaotic and (at least in some cases) as being empty of people, was reordered, surveyed, recorded in land registers and opened up for exploitation, usually without any regard for pre-existing structures.[38]

Similarly, the Nazi conquerors regarded the East as an enormous *tabula rasa* that could be recreated in a new form according to their own conceptions, as an arena in which spatial planners and population economists, engineers and economic planners could give free rein to their imaginations.[39] They regarded it as a colonial territory, placing themselves in the tradition of the colonial conquest and opening up of the world. For example, a member of the German 12th Airborne Regiment reported a few weeks after the invasion of the Soviet Union:

> Marvellous as the successes are, great as the advance is [...], Russia on the whole is still a huge disappointment for the individual. There is nothing of culture, nothing of paradise [...] but only the absolute depths, filth, people who demonstrate to us that we will face a huge task of colonisation here.[40]

From the German point of view there was a need for the whole country to be comprehensively 'modernised' and reorganised, without any regard for its existing social, political and economic structures. And it was precisely this comprehensive reorganisation that was interpreted by those involved in it as colonisation.

---

sengesetzgebung", in Birthe Kundrus (ed.), *Phantasiereiche. Zur Kulturgeschichte des deutschen Kolonialismus*, Frankfurt 2003, pp. 110–131.

38 On the ordering of the American West, which was perceived as resembling a featureless ocean that first needed to have structures imposed on it by surveying, see Stefan Kaufmann, "Naturale Grenzfelder des Sozialen: Landschaft und Körper", in Monika Fludernik and Hans-Joachim Gehrke, eds, *Grenzgänger zwischen Kulturen*, Würzburg 1999, pp. 121–136. On the German tradition of opening up remote areas of the Earth, see Dirk van Laak, *Imperiale Infrastruktur. Deutsche Planungen für eine Erschließung Afrikas, 1880 bis 1960*, Paderborn 2004.

39 For example, see Bruno Wasser, *Himmlers Raumplanung im Osten*, Basel 1993; Mechtild Rössler, 'Wissenschaft und Lebensraum'. *Geographische Ostforschung im Nationalsozialismus. Ein Beitrag zur Disziplingeschichte der Geographie*, Berlin 1990; Michael Burleigh, *Germany turns Eastwards. A Study of Ostforschung in the Third Reich*, Cambridge 1988; Mechtild Rössler and Sabine Schleiermacher, eds, *Der 'Generalplan Ost'*, Berlin 1993; Czeslaw Madajczyk, ed., *Vom Generalplan Ost zum Generalsiedlungsplan*, München 1994; Aly and Heim, *Vordenker der Vernichtung*; Aly, *Endlösung*. For more on the role of academics in colonialism and the continuity between colonialism and National Socialism on an academic level, see Jürgen Zimmerer, "Im Dienste des Imperiums. Die Geographen der Berliner Universität zwischen Kolonialwissenschaften und Ostforschung", *Jahrbuch für Universitätsgeschichte*, 7 (2004), pp. 73–100 (English version: "In the service of the Empire", pp. 262–293 in this book); Jürgen Zimmerer, "Wissenschaft und Kolonialismus. Das Geographische Institut der Friedrich-Wilhelms-Universität vom Kaiserreich zum Dritten Reich", in Ulrich van der Heyden and Joachim Zeller, eds, *Kolonialmetropole Berlin. Eine Spurensuche*, Berlin 2002, pp. 125–130.

40 A soldier of the 12th Airborne Regiment, 20 July 1941, quoted according to Christian Gerlach, *Kalkulierte Morde*, p. 102.

The then chief state planning officer for East Prussia, Ewald Liedecke, for example, who later performed the same function in the *Reichsgau* (administrative division) of Danzig-West Prussia, commented as early as 1939 on the issue of how the pre-existing settled and cultivated areas were to be handled:

> In restructuring German territory we cannot follow in the footsteps of the Poles and base an area of German settlement on the Polish pattern of settlement and land division. Rather than taking such a half-hearted approach, a process of total colonisation is required, one that encompasses the entire area, redistributes it and resettles it in accordance with German conceptions.[41]

The sense of entitlement to rule over the conquered territories was derived from the allegedly 'underdeveloped' state of the land and from the supposed 'backwardness' of the people who lived there. According to Hitler, one needed "only to see this primeval world" ("*Urwelt*") in order to appreciate "that nothing happens here if one does not assign people the work they have to do. The Slav is a born slave, they are a mass crying out for a master."[42] And Himmler's secretary Hanns Johst, who travelled through Poland with the *Reichsführer SS* in the winter of 1939/40, was no doubt reflecting his boss's ideas as well when he wrote:

> The Poles are not a state-building people. They lack even the most basic prerequi-sites. I have travelled all over the country at the side of the *Reichsführer* SS. A country which has so little feeling for the essence of settlement that it is not even up to the task of creating a village of any style has no claim to any sort of inde-pendent political status within Europe. It is a country crying out to be colonized.[43]

The Archaeology of the Genocidal Impulse

Genocide, i.e. the murder of people considered to be enemies, superfluous or a hindrance to one's own development, was the most extreme consequence of a policy of conquest and settlement based on the concepts of 'race' and 'space'. This policy of murder and the destruction of alien cultures has a long tradition in colonial-

---

41 Ewald Liedecke, *Kolonisatorische Aufgaben der Raum-Ordnung im Nordosten des Deutschen Reiches*, Königsberg 1 September 1939, quoted according to Michael A. Hartenstein, *Neue Dorflandschaften. Nationalsozialistische Siedlungsplanung in den 'eingegliederten Ostgebieten' 1939 bis 1944*, Berlin 1998, p. 79.
42 Hitler, 17 September 1941, quoted according to Adolf Hitler: *Monologe im Führerhauptquartier. Die Aufzeichnungen Heinrich Heims*, ed. Werner Jochmann, Hamburg 1980, p. 63.
43 Hanns Johst, *Ruf des Reiches – Echo des Volkes!*, München 1940, p. 94, quoted according to Michael Burleigh, *Die Zeit des Nationalsozialismus. Eine Gesamtdarstellung*, Frankfurt 2000, p. 515.

ism.[44] Nonetheless, one should be on one's guard against describing every massacre as genocide. Although the 500 years of post-Columbian history have been characterised by violence, suffering and subjugation, which have also brought about mass mortality among indigenous populations, this process was, for the most part, not genocidal.[45] The attitudes and actions of the Europeans were racist and violent, but they were not originally intended to bring about the destruction of existing ethnicities. The overwhelming majority of those who died were the victims either of unknowingly imported diseases, or of forced labour, or of the propagation of Christianity by the sword. This does not alter the degree of the victims' personal suffering; it does not reduce it, nor does it, in the cases of forced labour or Christianisation, minimise the guilt of the perpetrators; and yet one cannot speak of genocide in these cases as the destruction of entire populations was not intended. Indeed, the colonial economy needed the indigenous population in order to exploit their labour.[46]

Nevertheless, cases of genocide did occur, mainly in settler colonies, and they certainly displayed features matching those of the genocide perpetrated by the Nazis. These are to be regarded as systematic similarities, though admittedly manifesting themselves in quite different forms. I would like to demonstrate these similarities in terms of three factors which in my opinion are to be regarded as being particularly typical of the mass crimes of the Nazis:
1. the mental predisposition towards committing mass murder,
2. the role of the State as perpetrator,
3. the bureaucratisation of the process of extermination.

Most cases of genocide occurred in the settler colonies of North America, Australia and southern Africa. This was no coincidence, since it was only where it seemed desirable to replace the indigenous peoples with a new population that the genocidal impulse could be realised to a particularly high degree, so that the process of settlement developed a genocidal momentum, and mass murder then

---

44 I have explored this in detail in: Jürgen Zimmerer, "Colonial Genocide and the Holocaust. Towards an Archaeology of Genocide", in A. Dirk Moses, ed., *Genocide and Settler Society: Frontier Violence and Stolen Indigenous Children in Australia*, New York 2004, pp. 49–76.
45 An opposing view with regard to Australia and America is represented by Churchill, *A Little Matter of Genocide*; Stannard, *American Holocaust*; Tony Barta, "Relations of Genocide: Land and Lives in the Colonization of Australia", in Isidor Wallimann and Michael N. Dobkowski, eds, *Genocide and the Modern Age. Etiology and Case Studies of Mass Death*, 2nd edn, Syracuse 2000, pp. 237–251.
46 For more on this cf. Gründer, who rejects the thesis of colonial genocide while not denying that certain situations led to genocidal orders or massacres or other genocidal consequences. Horst Gründer, "Genozid oder Zwangsmodernisierung? Der moderne Kolonialismus in universalgeschichtlicher Perspektive", in Mihran Dabag and Kristin Platt, eds, *Genozid und Moderne*, i: *Strukturen kollektiver Gewalt im 20. Jahrhundert*, Opladen 1998, pp. 135–151.

in its turn created space for further settlement. The ideological basis for such a mental predisposition could be furnished by either secular or millenarianist utopian thinking. It was the dream of the Promised Land, of the White settler colony, of the unpopulated *tabula rasa* that could be reshaped in accordance with one's own understanding of what civilisation is, or the identification of one's own life with a divine, historic or civilising mission that could create a readiness to commit mass murder if necessary.[47]

The combination of a pronounced sense of calling, the conviction of belonging to a chosen 'race', as is expressed in the doctrine of the 'Manifest Destiny', with the proclivity to view the Indians with contempt, even as vermin, or as heathen nations whose destruction God himself would help to bring about, is already apparent among the New England Puritans. In 1675, in a poem entitled "Some Meditations", a certain "W.W." – often identified as Wait Winthrop, son of the Governor of Connecticut – called for the destruction of the Narragansett Indians, who had just defeated a New England militia:

> O *New England*, I understand, with thee God is offended:
> And therefore He doth humble thee, till thou thy ways hast mended
>
> Repent therefore, and do no more, advance thy self so High
> But humbled be, and thou shalt see these Indians soon will dy.
>
> A Swarm of Flies, they may arise, a Nation to Annoy,
> Yea Rats and Mice, or Swarms of Lice a Nation may destroy.
> [...]
> And now I shall my Neigbours all give one word of Advice,
> in Love and Care do you prepare for War, if you be wise.
>
> Get Ammunition with Expedition your Selves for to defend,
> And Pray to God that He His Rod will please to suspend.[48]

A similar mentality is also betrayed by the way the British forces conducted biological warfare against the Native Americans only a hundred years later, as the war was waged indiscriminately against men, women and children.[49] And this

---

[47] On the significance for genocide of utopian concepts of the re-creation of the world and of mankind, see: Omer Bartov, "Utopie und Gewalt. Neugeburt und Vernichtung der Menschen", in Hans Maier, ed., *Wege in die Gewalt. Die modernen politischen Religionen*, Frankfurt 2000, pp. 92–120.
[48] Quoted according to Chalk and Jonassohn, *History and Sociology of Genocide*, p. 194.
[49] An overview of the literature on biological warfare in Australia and North America is provided by: Norbert Finzsch, *Late 18th Century Genocidal Practices in North America and Australia: A Comparison*, Canberra 2003 (Humanities Research Centre, Australian National University, Work in Progress Lecture), https://web.archive.org/web/20030731085250/http://www.uni-koeln.de/phil-fak/histsem/anglo/html_2001/Finzsch/Lecture.pdf, accessed 12 Jul. 2023.

was not 'collateral damage', but a planned objective of British strategy. For instance, Sir Jeffery Amherst, the commander-in-chief of the British forces in North America, explicitly encouraged his officers, in addition to distributing blankets contaminated by smallpox, to "try Every other method that can serve to Extirpate this Execrable race".[50]

In the nineteenth century, the religious reasoning of belonging to the 'elect', of having been chosen to fulfil a divine mission, gradually gave way to a Social Darwinian view of history based on the biological concept of 'race'. For Lieutenant General Lothar von Trotha, commander-in-chief of the German troops in the war against the Herero and Nama in South West Africa (1904–1908) and the man responsible for the first German genocide, the extermination of the enemy was an absolutely essential measure in a 'race war' that in his opinion could only end with one of the belligerent parties being annihilated. Von Trotha's view was that Africans would "yield only to force", and it was his intention to exercise this force "with blatant terrorism and even with cruelty" and annihilate "the rebellious tribes with rivers of blood";[51] for after all, he declared, a war in Africa could not be conducted "in accordance with the rules of the Geneva Convention".[52]

This genocidal mentality was not restricted to individual actions carried out, more or less, by the State – for officers too did no more than merely exhibit certain racial attitudes of their time – but could also find expression in 'private' actions. How this dehumanisation of the indigenous inhabitants manifested itself in individual perpetrators is illustrated by the practice, known from Australia, of 'shooting practice' – with Australian Aboriginal people as targets. As an eyewitness reported in 1889:

> There are instances when the young men of the station have employed the Sunday in hunting the blacks, not only for some definite purpose, but also for the sake of the sport.[53]

This was only possible because the Australian Aboriginal people were viewed as not belonging to human society, as is demonstrated in a reader's letter to *The Queenslander*:

---

[50] Quoted according to a facsimile of Amherst's original letter, to be found under https://people.umass.edu/derrico/amherst/34_41_114_fn.jpeg, accessed 12 Jul. 2023, see Chalk and Jonassohn, *History and Sociology of Genocide*, p. 177.

[51] Von Trotha to Leutwein, 5 November 1904, quoted according to Horst Drechsler, *Südwestafrika unter deutscher Kolonialherrschaft. Der Kampf der Herero und Nama gegen den deutschen Imperialismus 1884–1915*, 2nd edn, Berlin 1984, p. 156.

[52] "Politik und Kriegführung", in *Die Deutsche Zeitung*, 3 February 1909, quoted according to Gerhard Pool, *Samuel Maharero*, Windhoek 1991, p. 293.

[53] Quoted according to Alison Palmer, *Colonial Genocide*, Adelaide 2000, p. 44.

And, being a useless race, what does it matter what they suffer any more than the distinguished philanthropist, who writes in his behalf, cares for the wounded half-dead pigeon he tortures at his shooting matches. 'I do not see the necessity,' was the reply of a distinguished wit to an applicant for an office who remarked that 'he must live;' and we virtually and practically say the same to the blacks and with better reason.[54]

From this attitude, it was but a short step to the murder of women and children. Equating the Australian Aboriginal people with animals that could be shot for sport like pigeons was equivalent to banishing them from the "universe of obligation", the realm of those "whom we are obligated to protect, to take into account, and to whom we must account".[55]

In other cases, this function was fulfilled by downright atrocity propaganda. Africans, Native Americans and Australian Aboriginal people were accused of raping women and (sexually) mutilating men. Thus the indigenous populations themselves were made to take the blame, in that they had shown themselves to be 'animals' and could therefore 'legitimately' be 'slaughtered'. Mass murder found even broader acceptance if it could be justified by the need to protect one's own property, as one Australian squatter did of whom it was reported in 1889:

> He shot all the men he discovered on his run, because they were cattle killers; the women, because they gave birth to cattle killers; and the children, because they would in time become cattle killers.[56]

According to this logic, the murdering could only end with the complete 'extermination' of the Australian Aboriginal people. Similar patterns of genocidal argumentation are also familiar from North America. H. L. Hall, an infamous murderer of Native Americans, justified the slaughter of babies with the saying well known since the time of King Philip's War (1675–1677) that "a nit would make a louse". This slogan was popularised by Colonel John Milton Chivington, who himself claimed: "My intention is to kill all Indians I may come across".[57]

While the aforementioned squatter murdered alone, others went 'hunting' together. For instance, one reads in *The Queenslander* in 1867 about punitive expeditions carried out by bands of settlers in reprisal for actual or alleged attacks by Australian Aboriginal people:

---

54 The Queenslander, 8 May 1880, https://trove.nla.gov.au/newspaper/article/20332884, accessed 12 Jul. 2023, see Palmer, *Genocide*, p. 45.
55 Fein, "Definition and Discontent", p. 20.
56 Quoted according to Palmer, *Colonial Genocide*, p. 43.
57 Churchill, *A Little Matter of Genocide*, p. 229; Stannard, *American Holocaust*, p. 131, n. 123.

[...] in the present system by which blacks are shot down most ruthlessly for weeks and months after a case of murder or theft has been reported, and when many innocent are either killed in order that the guilty may possibly be included in the number, or so hunted about that the spirit of revenge is aroused in them[.][58]

This raises the question of the perpetrators. Who were they, who can be held responsible? As described above, the question of the state character of these mass murders touches upon an essential element in the definition of genocide. Measured against the paradigm of the Nazi crimes, none of the cases of Euro-indigenous mass murder constitutes a case of genocide as the order to commit it cannot be traced back to the imperial authorities of the European state concerned, or, later, to the capital of the settler colony. In general it was bands of settlers or local militia or army commanders who did the dirty work. It was therefore possible for different situations to prevail from settlement to settlement and from colony to colony, and for that reason too, orders issued with a view to protecting the indigenous population often went unheeded. The colonial state lacked the power and the means to control the behaviour of its own citizens. Even in the case of the murder of the Herero and Nama in German South West Africa, where the existence of an Annihilation Order is incontrovertible, this did not originate from the highest representatives of the State, the Emperor or the Chancellor. Its initiator was General von Trotha, the local military commander-in-chief.[59]

But does it make sense, in a historical comparison of mass murders, to conceive of the state as the bureaucratic and centralised institution that it was in the Third Reich, and that in a particularly highly developed form? Would it not be more appropriate to historicise the concept of the state?[60]

If we apply a historical concept of the state that is appropriate to colonial contexts, rather than one based on the ideal type of the modern state, then the differences between colonial genocide and that committed by the Nazi no longer appear so great. The colonial state was by and large a pre-modern and not yet or not fully centralised state, and one that relied heavily on intermediate authorities. And it was these, the heads of local communities, of civil or ecclesiastical parishes, or local militia commanders, who represented the state at this grass-roots

---

58 The Queenslander, 23 February 1867, https://trove.nla.gov.au/newspaper/article/20312053/, accessed 12 Jul. 2023, see Palmer, *Colonial Genocide*, p. 43.
59 Jürgen Zimmerer, "Kriegsgefangene im Kolonialkrieg. Der Krieg gegen die Herero und Nama in Deutsch-Südwestafrika (1904–1907)", in Rüdiger Overmans, ed., *In der Hand des Feindes. Kriegsgefangenschaft von der Antike bis zum Zweiten Weltkrieg*, Köln 1999, pp. 277–294.
60 On the development of the modern state as it originated in Europe and spread across the world, see: Wolfgang Reinhard, *Geschichte der Staatsgewalt. Eine vergleichende Verfassungsgeschichte Europas von den Anfängen bis zur Gegenwart*, München 1999.

level and had the power – at least symbolically – to legitimise actions on its behalf. Even if what these local leaders said was strictly speaking not legally binding, it provided a basis on which perpetrators could feel justified in their actions, or even duty bound to perform them. For such actions taken in the colonial context to be regarded as state-perpetrated crimes, therefore, it is not necessary to demonstrate a chain of command stretching back to the centres of colonial power, which ultimately means the Colonial Offices back in Europe.

Accordingly, the biological attack on the Delaware Indians mentioned above was legitimised by the state through Sir Jeffery Amherst's order; and in the same sense the genocide committed against the Herero and Nama was committed officially in the name of the German state, since von Trotha, as military commander-in-chief and later also as Governor, was the Emperor's representative in South West Africa.

The question of the state's role in the commission of genocide leads to the question of the form the mass murders took, and ultimately to the degree of bureaucratisation. Genocidal massacres do not, after all, require a high degree of organisation, whereas quasi-industrialised extermination in concentration camps presupposes a 'modern', centralised and bureaucratic state. In the colonial context, massacres or other strategies with relatively low organisational requirements clearly predominated. Whether in the Pequot War in New England or in the conflict with the *Round Valley Indian Tribes*, examples of the butchering of men, women, and children by bands of settlers or local militia can readily be found.

Over time, special army and police units were gradually established for precisely this purpose. The Third Colorado Cavalry, which was responsible for the massacre of the Cheyenne at Sand Creek, was set up specially to fight the 'Indians'.[61] The Native Police of Queensland were also state units, in this case composed of Australian Aboriginal people drawn from other parts of the country, under the command of White officers. As "mobile death squads aimed at eradicating Aborigines",[62] they 'cleansed' the frontier in Queensland of the local population in order to make room for an increasing number of settlers and their livestock.

A further, heightened form of these campaigns of annihilation is represented by the genocidal war of conquest and 'pacification', a military campaign on a

---

61 Chalk and Jonassohn, *History and Sociology of Genocide*, pp. 199–201. The background was a conflict between the Native Americans and the settlers, who however managed to involve the state in their struggle. The regiment deployed consisted of volunteers who were engaged for a fixed period. In this way, the violence that they used was legitimised by the state.
62 Palmer, quoted according to: A. Dirk Moses, "An Antipodean Genocide? The Origins of the Genocidal Moment in the Colonization of Australia", *Journal of Genocide Research*, 2 (2000), pp. 89–106, here p. 102.

larger scale requiring a correspondingly higher degree of organisation. The most important example of such a war is that waged by the German Empire against the Herero and the Nama in South West Africa. It represents a crucial connective link between Euro-indigenous genocide and the crimes of the Nazis.[63]

This is because on the one hand it constitutes a case of military genocide, i.e. the use of a relatively large number of regular troops integrated into a hierarchical command structure; and on the other hand because it displays the transition to a bureaucratic form of extermination. The view frequently expressed in certain circles that this war was a perfectly 'normal' military operation is utterly wide of the mark.[64] The Herero and Nama War was waged by the Germans from the very outset with complete disregard for the international law of war. It attained to its genocidal quality through the dispatch to the *Schutzgebiet* of General Lothar von Trotha, who at the behest of the General Staff in Berlin replaced the long-serving Governor, Theodor Leutwein, and conducted a 'race war'.[65] Clear

---

[63] On this subject, see Jürgen Zimmerer, "Colonialism and the Holocaust. Towards an Archeology of Genocide", in A. Dirk Moses, ed., *Genocide and Settler Society: Frontier Violence and Stolen Indigenous Children in Australian History*, New York 2004, pp. 49–76. The connection between German colonial rule in German South West Africa and the Third Reich has already been pointed out to some extent by Drechsler, *Südwestafrika unter deutscher Kolonialherrschaft*; Helmut Bley, *Kolonialherrschaft und Sozialstruktur in Deutsch-Südwestafrika 1894–1914*, Hamburg 1968; Henning Melber, "Kontinuitäten totaler Herrschaft. Völkermord und Apartheid in Deutsch-Südwestafrika", *Jahrbuch für Antisemitismusforschung*, 1 (1992), pp. 91–116.

[64] For instance, see the readers' letters in the *Frankfurter Allgemeine Zeitung* from Dr. Hans-Rudolf Horn, "Schwarze Legende vom Herero-Genozid", *Frankfurter Allgemeine Zeitung* (12 November 2002) and Prof. Hartmut Fröschle, "Ein normaler Kolonialkrieg, kein Genozid", *Frankfurter Allgemeine Zeitung* (11 November 2002) in response to my article, "'Wir müssen jetzt 'krassen Terrorismus üben'. Von der Unterdrückung zur Ausrottung: Der Krieg gegen die Herero und Nama in Deutsch-Südwestafrika als Erbe der deutschen Kolonialzeit und die Klage auf Entschädigung", *Frankfurter Allgemeine Zeitung* (2 November 2002). Christoph Marx quite correctly labels these revisionist objections as "a barrage of colonial apologetics": Christoph Marx, "Kolonialapologetisches Sperrfeuer", *Frankfurter Allgemeine Zeitung* (23 November 2002).

[65] Various aspects of the war have now been summarised in Jürgen Zimmerer and Joachim Zeller, eds., *Völkermord in Deutsch-Südwestafrika. Der Kolonialkrieg (1904–1908) in Namibia und seine Folgen*, Berlin 2003. See also Jürgen Zimmerer, *Deutsche Herrschaft über Afrikaner. Staatlicher Machtanspruch und Wirklichkeit im kolonialen Namibia*, Münster/Hamburg/London 2001, pp. 31–55 [English edition: *German Rule, African Subjects: State Aspirations and the Reality of Power in Colonial Namibia*, New York/Oxford 2021, pp. 35–58]; Jan-Bart Gewald, "Colonization, Genocide and Resurgence: The Herero of Namibia 1890–1933", in Michael Bollig and Jan-Bart Gewald, eds, *People, Cattle and Land: Transformations of a Pastoral Society in Southwestern Africa*, Köln 2001, pp. 187–225; Gesine Krüger, *Kriegsbewältigung und Geschichtsbewusstsein: Realität, Deutung und Verarbeitung des deutschen Kolonialkrieges in Namibia 1904 bis 1907*, Göttingen 1999.

proof of von Trotha's genocidal intention is provided by the proclamation known as the Annihilation Order, under which he set up a chain of picket posts to seal off the largely waterless *sandveld* of the Omaheke desert into which the Herero had fled, having previously escaped from encirclement by the army at the Battle of Omahakari (Waterberg) and having been literally driven into the arid region by the *Schutztruppe*. Von Trotha's proclamation declared:

> The Hereros have ceased to be German subjects.
> They have murdered and robbed, have cut off the ears and noses and other bodily parts of wounded soldiers, and are now too cowardly to want to go on fighting. I say to that people: Whoever delivers one of their *Kapteins* to one of my posts as a prisoner will be given 1,000 marks, whoever brings Samuel Maharero will be given 5,000 marks. But the Herero people must quit this country. If they do not, I will compel them to do so with the *Groot Rohr* [cannon].
> Within the borders of German territory, any Herero, with or without a firearm, with or without livestock, will be shot; nor will I give refuge to women or children any more. I will drive them back to their people or have them fired upon.[66]

As a result of this policy, thousands of men, women and children were consigned to wretched deaths.

In a global history of genocide, the history of the concentration camps is at least equally important. After the revocation of the Annihilation Order, surviving Herero were brought to such camps, as were the Nama, who had also entered the war in the meantime. These camps fulfilled a variety of functions. As well as the actual 'concentration' of the Herero and Nama to prevent them from supporting guerrilla fighters, they also served as labour camps, providing urgently needed labour to both private employers and state institutions. At the same time it was

---

[66] Proclamation by von Trotha, Osombo-Wind[imbe], 2 October 1904, Federal Archives Berlin-Lichterfelde (BArch), Imperial Colonial Office R 1001/2089, Sheets 7af. This is a transcript of the original document. Other copies of the Proclamation can be found in the Federal Archives/Military Archives Freiburg and in the National Archives of Namibia in Windhoek. For more on the question of genocide, see Jürgen Zimmerer, "Das Deutsche Reich und der Genozid. Überlegungen zum historischen Ort des Völkermordes an den Herero und Nama", in Larissa Förster und Dag Henrichsen, eds, *100 Jahre geteilte namibisch-deutsche Geschichte: Kolonialkrieg – Genozid – Erinnerungskulturen*, Köln 2004, pp. 106–121 (English version: "The German Empire and Genocide", pp. 154–174 in this book); Jürgen Zimmerer, "Krieg, KZ und Völkermord in Südwestafrika. Der erste deutsche Genozid", in Jürgen Zimmerer and Joachim Zeller, eds, *Völkermord in Deutsch Südwestafrika. Der Kolonialkrieg (1904–1908) in Namibia und seine Folgen*, Berlin 2003, pp. 45–63; Henrik Lundtofte, "'I believe that the nation as such must be annihilated ...' – The Radicalization of the German Suppression of the Herero Rising in 1904", in Steven L. B. Jensen, ed., *Genocide: Cases, Comparisons and Contemporary Debates*, Copenhagen 2003, pp. 15–53; Zimmerer, *Colonialism*. Earlier debates are summarized by Tilman Dedering, "'A Certain Rigorous Treatment of All Parts of the Nation'. The Annihilation of the Herero in German South West Africa, 1904", in Mark Levene and Penny Roberts, eds, *The Massacre in History*, New York 1999, pp. 205–222.

hoped that the prisoners, through being 'educated to work' in the camps, could be disciplined and prepared for their new 'role' as labourers in the post-war period. To some extent there were cases of deliberately withholding food from the prisoners, i.e. of extermination through neglect, so that it is possible in individual cases to speak of a continuation of the genocidal policy. At the same time, these camps marked the transition to the bureaucratisation of extermination, because the inmates of the camps were counted and kept under surveillance. This is also demonstrated by the existence of blank death certificates with "death by enfeeblement" already printed on them in advance.[67]

The Use and Abuse of Colonial Genocide as a Historical Category

The crimes of the Nazis cannot, to be sure, be ascribed monocausally to the theory and practice of European colonialism: National Socialism was too complex and too eclecticist in its ideology and policies for that. Nonetheless, to express the relationship in terms of an archaeology of *Bevölkerungsökonomie* (population economics) and genocide, it must be said that colonialism served as an important source of ideas. In their central concepts of 'race' and 'space' the Nazi policies of expansion and extermination display astonishing structural similarities to European colonialism. With regard to the history of the mass crimes of the Nazis, this means directing attention to a previously neglected strand of historical tradition. In this way, precursors and patterns can be identified. Nevertheless, it would be a mistake to see the Third Reich's murderous policies in the East as being merely a copy of the conquests of America, Australia or southern Africa. Rather, they constitute an utterly extreme variant.

Using colonial genocide as a category draws attention to this precursor role, making clear that some elements that may appear unique from a narrow point of view often actually correspond to an earlier practice already applied in the colonial context. This is the great advantage of the term.

The disadvantage of setting up colonial genocide as an independent category lies in the danger of semantically detaching cases of genocide that occurred in the colonial context from the history of intra-European genocide, and thus of perpetuating the supposed antithesis between European and non-European history. In

---

67 Jan-Bart Gewald, "Herero and Missionaries. The Making of Historical Sources in the 1920s", in Wilhelm J.G. Möhlig, ed., *Frühe Kolonialgeschichte Namibias 1880–1930*, Köln 2000, pp. 77–95, here p. 78.

order to avert the danger of this Eurocentric narrowing of perspective, it appears sensible to me to avoid introducing new sub-divisions of the category of genocide.

Euro-indigenous genocide does not represent any fundamentally different category from National Socialist genocide, but rather simply earlier, less organised, less bureaucratised and less centralised forms of the same phenomenon. At this point, therefore, I need to correct my statement that there was no colonial genocide. It would be more correct to say that all genocide has been colonial.

From Germany's First Colonial Empire to Its Second

From Windhoek to Warsaw: The Society of Racial Privilege in German South West Africa – a Model with a Future?

> I have repeatedly encountered *Bambusen* [African army servants] alone on horseback; I urge all authorities to strictly ensure that Natives do not appear on the street on horseback unless accompanied by whites – signed Langer, Major

In September 1906, the senior officer of the Windhoek garrison wrote to the Imperial Governor's Office to express his concern at this outrageous conduct.[1] The Governor's Office reacted promptly, and only a few days later circulated the following instruction to all offices of the Administration:

> Native servants (*Bambusen*) are only allowed to ride government horses when accompanied by their masters. Every official who has charge of horses must ensure compliance with this order and is responsible for such compliance.[2]

This may sound like a trifle, even a laughing matter, and in a sense it is. Nonetheless, it reveals some of the principles that were central to the society of racial privilege as it shaped the interaction between African subjects and colonial masters in the former German colony of South West Africa. Precisely because the matter it relates to is essentially a triviality, it lays bare the fundamental character of the racial state: manifesting itself not only in the fields of politics and administration but also in those of business and culture, this social system radiated a powerful symbolism that left no scope for any readiness, or indeed any ability, to admit of any exceptions, even in the smallest detail.

The example of the 'Native servants on horseback' highlights the subordination of the 'Natives' to the officials. The former are servants, the latter are masters who keep themselves personal servants following the pattern of the military officers' batmen. But why should a 'Native' not be permitted to ride a horse? Because he could not possibly be allowed the extra height he gained from being 'mounted', and certainly not if this placed him 'above' any Whites who might be standing nearby on a lower level. This would symbolically overturn the socio-political order. For the society of racial privilege was founded precisely upon this strict separation of the 'races', on the binary coding of all areas of life. It represents at

---

[1] Major Langer, Windhoek Garrison, to the Governor's Office, Windhoek, 25 September 1906, National Archives of Namibia, Windhoek (NAN), Central Office of the Governor (ZBU) W.III.A.1, Vol. 1, Sheet 1a.
[2] Hintrager, Circular Order, 23 October 1906, NAN ZBU W.III.A.1, Vol. 1, Sheet 1c.

∂ Open Access. © 2024 the author(s), published by De Gruyter. [CC BY] This work is licensed under the Creative Commons Attribution 4.0 International License.
https://doi.org/10.1515/9783110754513-009

one and the same time both real subjugation and the repression that is implicit in colonial discourse based on the construct of the 'Other', the colonised, itself a construct invented by the colonisers – by those who are allowed to ride horses and above all are able to forbid others from riding. Despite this, in a country the size of German South West Africa it is not possible to prohibit the 'Native' from riding entirely; after all, the White man does not want to have to do without his servant when he is travelling. But he is not allowed to ride by himself, but only in the company of his 'master', whose presence symbolically re-establishes the hierarchical order.

At the same time, the correspondence quoted above demonstrates that it was not possible to implement such a prohibition by a simple stroke of the pen, that merely issuing the prohibition did not guarantee that it would be observed. The complaint relates precisely to the fact that African servants were riding horses in defiance of the prohibition, and could be seen to be doing so "repeatedly". They were breaking the prohibition, and showing their will to resist even in this trivial respect.

'Mixed' Marriages and Their Prohibition

The 'Native servant alone on horseback' who was such a headache for the German administration in 1906 is only a minor example of the kind of society of racial privilege that the Administration was seeking to construct in South West Africa.[3] Essentially it is the same attitude that lies at the root of this trifle on the one hand and of an issue with far more serious implications on the other, which Deputy Governor Hans Tecklenburg warned about in 1903 when he wrote:

---

3 I have described the history of German Native Policy and the German governmental and administrative utopia in greater detail in Jürgen Zimmerer, *Deutsche Herrschaft über Afrikaner: Staatlicher Machtanspruch und Wirklichkeit im kolonialen Namibia*, 3rd edn, Hamburg 2004 [English edition: *German Rule, African Subjects. State Aspirations and the Reality of Power in Colonial Namibia*, New York 2021]; Jürgen Zimmerer, "Der totale Überwachungsstaat? Recht und Verwaltung in Deutsch-Südwestafrika", in Rüdiger Voigt, ed., *Das deutsche Kolonialrecht als Vorstufe einer globalen 'Kolonialisierung' von Recht und Verwaltung*, Baden-Baden 2001, pp. 175–198 (English version: "Total Control? Law and Administration in German South West Africa", pp. 77–103 in this book); Jürgen Zimmerer, "Der koloniale Musterstaat? Rassentrennung, Arbeitszwang und totale Kontrolle in Deutsch-Südwestafrika", in Jürgen Zimmerer and Joachim Zeller, eds, *Völkermord in Deutsch-Südwestafrika. Der Kolonialkrieg in Namibia (1904–1908) und seine Folgen*, Berlin 2003, pp. 26–43. These works also include detailed references to and an analysis of the research literature. I shall therefore refer below only to a number of fundamental and more recent works and source references.

Panzlaff's Hottentot woman is now taking up a lot of space alongside our German ladies at the festivities of the Soldiers' and Marksmen's Associations, although still without managing to form much in the way of relationships with them. This would change if two or three more such women were to gain admittance to the circle. [...] So we have no other alternative than to get legislation in place while there is still time that will erect a strong barrier between non-natives and natives, even if this represents a hard blow to some mixed-race individuals or people married to mixed-race individuals, and it initially leads to something of an increase in the number of illegitimate children.[4]

Here again, the Deputy Governor was outraged by the open breaching of the 'race barriers', the blurring of the distinction between 'Black' and 'White'. Two years later, therefore, in 1905, he ordered a complete U-turn in the previous policy of assimilation.[5]

---

[4] Report by Tecklenburg [transcript], 24 September 1903, NAN ZBU F.IV.R.1., Sheets 61ca–61ea.

[5] The history of the ban on 'mixed marriages' has already been presented numerous times, whereby the majority of authors have limited themselves to the discursive level, or else focus on the development of the applicable rules and legislation. Here I shall mention only the most important sources, from which it is easy to access older literature as well. For a summary of the current state of research, see Wolfram Hartmann, "'... als durchaus unerwünscht erachtet ...'. Zur Genese des 'Mischehenverbotes' in Deutsch-Südwestafrika", in Larissa Förster, Dag Henrichsen and Michael Bollig, eds, *Namibia-Deutschland. Eine geteilte Geschichte. Widerstand, Gewalt, Erinnerung*, Köln 2004, pp. 182–193. Sippel analyses the ban from the point of view of legal history: Harald Sippel, "'Im Interesse des Deutschtums und der weißen Rasse'. Behandlung und Rechtswirkungen von 'Rassenmischehen' in den Kolonien Deutsch-Ostafrika und Deutsch-Südwestafrika", *Jahrbuch für afrikanisches Recht*, 9 (1995), pp. 123–159. Wildenthal positions the ban in the context of general endeavours in the colonial women's movement to improve the social standing of White women through an emphasis on 'racial purity': Lora Wildenthal, *German Women for Empire, 1884–1945*, Durham 2001, esp. pp. 86–107. Walgenbach places the ban in the metropolitan context of the Empire, and taking the journal *Kolonie und Heimat* as an example analyses the ban on 'mixed' marriages in connection with the creation of the construct of 'whiteness' as part of the settler identity: Katharina Walgenbach, "Zwischen Selbstaffirmation und Distinktion: Weiße Identität, Geschlecht und Klasse in der Zeitschrift 'Kolonie und Heimat'", in Carsten Winter, Andreas Hepp and Tanja Thomas, eds, *Medienidentitäten – Identität im Kontext um Globalisierung und Medienkultur*, Köln 2003, pp. 136–152. Becker analyses the question more pronouncedly in the context of the colony itself, by thematising the attitude of the Missionary Society to 'mixed' marriages: Frank Becker, "Kolonialherrschaft, Rassentrennung und Mission in Deutsch-Südwestafrika", in Frank Becker, Thomas Großbölting, Armin Owers and Rudolf Schlögel, eds, *Politische Gewalt in der Moderne*, Münster 2003, pp. 133–163. Closer consideration of aspects of the image of the African that were crucial to the concepts of 'race', 'defilement' and 'degeneration' is to be found in Schubert: Michael Schubert, *Der schwarze Fremde. Das Bild des Schwarzafrikaners in der parlamentarischen und publizistischen Kolonialdiskussion in Deutschland von den 1870er bis in die 1930er Jahre*, Stuttgart 2003. Kundrus too analyses the issue of 'mixed' marriages on the basis of German colonial discourse and fantasies: Birthe Kundrus, *Moderne Imperialisten. Das Kaiserreich im Spiegel seiner Kolonien*, Köln

The topic of 'racial mixing', of sexual relations between Europeans and Africans, had preoccupied the colonial administration right from the start; it was above all men who migrated to the colony, so that there was a conspicuous 'shortage' of European women.[6] Many of the unmarried men entered into relationships with African women. Although they essentially looked down on them as being members of an "inferior race", as Carl Gotthilf Büttner noted, the shortage of White women caused them to push this fact to one side. In addition, marriage to African women, who generally came from the leading families, offered numerous economic advantages.[7] On the one hand, many of these women contributed substantial dowries, often in the form of land ownership; while on the other hand, the support given to the wife by her relations represented valuable assistance from an economic point of view.

At that time, such relationships were not yet regarded as a particularly significant problem. Sexual relations with African women were not stigmatised, but appear to have been largely regarded as 'necessary' for the wellbeing of the men, as

---

2003, pp. 219–279. For a general view of the problem of 'mixed' marriages in the colonies, see Franz-Josef Schulte-Althoff, "Rassenmischung im kolonialen System. Zur deutschen Kolonialpolitik im letzten Jahrzehnt vor dem Ersten Weltkrieg", *Historisches Jahrbuch*, 105 (1985), pp. 52–94; Cornelia Essner, "'Wo Rauch ist, da ist auch Feuer'. Zu den Ansätzen eines Rassenrechts für die deutschen Kolonien", in Wilfried Wagner, ed., *Rassendiskriminierung, Kolonialpolitik und ethnisch-nationale Identität*, Münster 1992, pp. 145–160; Cornelia Essner, "Zwischen Vernunft und Gefühl. Die Reichstagsdebatten von 1912 um koloniale 'Rassenmischehe' und 'Sexualität'", *Zeitschrift für Geschichtswissenschaft*, 45/6 (1997), pp. 503–519; Kathrin Roller, "'Wir sind Deutsche, wir sind Weiße und wollen Weiße bleiben' – Reichstagsdebatten über koloniale 'Rassenmischung'", in Ulrich van der Heyden and Joachim Zeller, eds, *Kolonialmetropole Berlin. Eine Spurensuche*, Berlin 2002, pp. 73–79. What was hitherto lacking was a contextualisation of German racial policy as a component of German Native Policy and the German governmental and administrative utopia. I have attempted this in Zimmerer, *Deutsche Herrschaft* (English edition: *German Rule*.) The following analysis is based on this.

6 On 1 January 1903, for instance, there were 4,640 Whites living in South West Africa, of whom 3,391 were men. Theodor Leutwein, *Elf Jahre Gouverneur in Deutsch-Südwestafrika*, 3rd edn, Berlin 1908, p. 232. Lora Wildenthal has recently quite rightly pointed out that there was by no means any lack of women; there were plenty of African women, but they were simply of the 'wrong' skin colour or 'race'. On this subject, see Wildenthal, *German Women*, p. 6. The colonial administration and pro-colonial circles in Germany tried to remedy this by deliberately encouraging women of marriageable age to emigrate to South West Africa. On this subject, see also Karen Smidt, *'Germania führt die deutsche Frau nach Südwest'. Auswanderung, Leben und soziale Konflikte deutscher Frauen in der ehemaligen Kolonie Deutsch-Südwestafrika 1884–1920. Eine sozial- und frauengeschichtliche Studie*, University of Magdeburg 1995 (Ph.D. Thesis).

7 Memorandum of the Rhenish Missionary Society, "Denkschrift betr. die Schließung von Ehen zwischen Weißen und Farbigen in den deutschen Schutzgebieten" [transcript], 1887, NAN ZBU F.IV.R.1., Sheets 3a–6b.

more or less normal manifestations accompanying the process of settlement, as can also be seen in the failure of the German administrative and judicial institutions to take any effective action in the face of the ever-increasing number of African women being subjected to rape.

The debate was initially much more focused on the question as to whether 'mixed' marriages should be permitted, and especially on that of the status of the children born out of relationships between White men and African women, who were direct personifications of trespasses against the 'racial barriers'. Büttner in particular, in the name of the Rhenish Missionary Society, was in favour of permitting legally binding marriage. He refused to countenance extramarital relations for moral reasons and was concerned about the consequences of the widespread practice whereby, after a period of time, men simply departed from the colony again, leaving their partners and children behind. Büttner argued in favour of 'mixed' marriages in such cases as an economic opportunity, as the people involved were potential consumers of German goods.

Although he was unconvinced by arguments regarding the "moral, political and economic consequences", as he presumed the number of such marriages that were likely to occur would be small, the first Imperial Commissioner, Heinrich Göring, did concede the admissibility of marriages between Whites and African women, while believing that the best thing would be for such marriages "to be neither restricted nor encouraged".[8] Governor Theodor Leutwein was already much more strongly opposed to the practice, wanting to prevent the legal recognition of such relationships and conceding only the possibility of a church ceremony for them. Under the Act on the Acquisition and the Loss of Confederation and State Nationality of 1 June 1870, all "children born in wedlock to a German man acquire the nationality of the father by birth, even if this takes place abroad",[9] – and thus even if the mother was an African.[10] Children born out of wedlock, on the other hand, acquired the nationality of the mother. In the case of a legally valid marriage, the wife also acquired the nationality of the husband; but Leutwein nevertheless wanted such 'mixed-race' children to be regarded as illegitimate, as he considered "the promotion of such marriages" to be "not in the interests" of the colony, and hoped to create a deterrent effect. It was after all the case, he maintained, that some Germans had indeed been put off marry-

---

8 Göring to Imperial Chancellor, 17 September 1887, NAN ZBU F.IV.R.1., Sheets 7a–8b.
9 "Gesetz über die Erwerbung und den Verlust der Bundes- und Staatsangehörigkeit", 1 June 1870. This was actually a law of the North German Confederation, which was taken over into Imperial German law a year later. It is reproduced in Theodor Meyer, *Reichs- und Staatsangehörigkeitsgesetz*, Berlin 1914, pp. 235–272, here pp. 237 and 242.
10 The Colonial Department informed Leutwein of this. Colonial Department Berlin to Governor's Office Windhoek, 17 August 1897, NAN ZBU F.IV.R.1., Sheets 14a–15b.

ing African women when it was made clear to them that their children would be considered to be 'bastards'.[11]

The Colonial Department in Berlin was however not willing to accept Leutwein's unilateral position, but stuck to its own view that "a marriage can be entered into in the *Schutzgebiet* of South West Africa [...] even if only one of the bridal couple is a non-Native."[12] This made it possible for 'mixed' marriages to be entered into in a civil ceremony. The wife and children of such marriages automatically acquired German citizenship and were therefore removed from the sphere of applicability of the nascent Native Law.

The Administration in the colony was however not prepared to let things rest there. Even though a mere 42 'mixed' marriages in all had been concluded in the time up to 1 January 1903, Leutwein and others saw in them a threat to the 'German character' of the colony. The opportunity to ban 'mixed' marriages, even against the will of Berlin, arose during the upheavals following the outbreak of war in 1904. There were about 1,000 soldiers from the colonial forces who wanted to settle in the colony after completing their service, and some of them intended to marry African women. This conferred a degree of urgency on the matter which served as an excuse to implement a ban on 'mixed' marriages even without the consent of the Colonial Department in Berlin, which had foiled Leutwein's previous attempts in this respect.

When in September 1905 a District Officer inquired if it would be in order for him, in two cases, to conduct weddings between soldiers and 'Baster' women, the aforementioned Hans Tecklenburg, who had headed the civil administration under von Trotha's military regime during the Herero War, circulated an order to all register offices instructing them "not to conclude such marriages until further notice", since they were to be regarded as "undesirable [...] in view of their legal, political and social consequences".[13] Although the Colonial Department in Berlin had declared such marriages to be admissible as recently as 1899, the impact of the war was such as to enable the Administration to force through what Theodor Leutwein had failed to achieve: the drawing of a statutory line between 'Black' and 'White', between 'Native' and 'non-Native'. The concept of a 'race war' that was being propagated just at that time by Lothar von Trotha, the commander of the *Schutztruppe*, which had been expanded by massive reinforcements from

---

11 Leutwein to Colonial Department Berlin, 22 August 1898, NAN ZBU F.IV.R.1., Sheets 15b–17a.
12 Colonial Department Berlin to Governor's Office Windhoek, 3 August 1899, NAN ZBU F.IV.R.1., Sheets 21af. Panzlaff had applied to the Colonial Department for its authorisation of his civil marriage to Magdalena van Wyk, a 'Baster'.
13 Circulated Order, Governor's Office Windhoek, 23 September 1905, NAN ZBU F.IV.R.1., Sheet 22a.

'home', provided a suitable environment for this move. In September 1907 Windhoek District Court followed Tecklenburg's line and retroactively declared marriages that had previously been validly entered into to be null and void.[14]

"Membership of the Native Race Is Determined by Descent"

More important than the detailed background of this decision is what the court had to say about how to define a 'Native', a question that had, until this point, not been specified in law. In the early years of the colony, a culturalistic definition had clearly predominated. Assimilation was rewarded and 'mixed' marriages were seen as positive, as Büttner's memorandum already quoted above shows:

> Such people of mixed race, who have been brought up by their white fathers and so are able to count themselves, and like to count themselves, as being in every respect part of the 'white' community, will strengthen the German element in the *Schutzgebiet*, and that increasingly as time goes by; and increasingly as time goes by the Native population, whose leading families are related by marriage to the settlers, will truly feel themselves happy and at ease as subjects of the German Empire and enjoying its protection.[15]

Windhoek District Court, however, had now decided the question in favour of a racist biological position, defining 'Natives' as:

> all blood members of a primitive people, including the progeny of native women that they have borne to men of the white race, even if there should have been miscegenation with white men over a period of several generations. As long as descent from a member of the primitive people can be proven, the descendant is, by virtue of his blood, a Native.[16]

---

14 Judgment of Windhoek District Court, 26 September 1907 [executed copy dated 25 April 1908], NAN ZBU F.IV.R.1., Sheets II-37a–40b. Original of the judgment in NAN Gericht Windhuk (GWI) 530 [R 1/07], Sheets 23a–26a.
15 Rhenish Missionary Society, "Denkschrift" [transcript], 1887, NAN ZBU F.IV.R.1., Sheets 3a–6b. According to Kathrin Roller, this is not an official statement of the position of the Rhenish Mission, but rather the personal opinion of Carl Gotthilf Büttner. The high regard in which 'mixed marriages' appear to be held in this text is, she maintains, by no means representative of the entire mission. Kathrin Roller, "Mission und 'Mischehen', Erinnerung und Körper – geteiltes Gedächtnis an eine afrikanische Vorfahrin. Über die Familie Schmelen-Kleinschmidt-Hegner", in Larissa Förster, Dag Henrichsen and Michael Bollig, eds, *Namibia-Deutschland. Eine geteilte Geschichte. Widerstand, Gewalt, Erinnerung*, Köln 2004, pp. 194–211.
16 Judgment of Windhoek District Court, 26 September 1907 [executed copy dated 25 April 1908], NAN ZBU F.IV.R.1., Sheets II-37a–40b. Original of the judgment in NAN Gericht Windhuk (GWI) 530 [R 1/07], Sheets 23a-26a.

Two years later, Windhoek Superior Court confirmed this decision on appeal.[17] Thus through the adoption of a definition of the 'Native' based on the principle of descent, the idea of 'race' as being a question of the level of civilisation was replaced definitively and in a legally binding manner by one based on biology. The degree of assimilation was no longer the criterion. Basically it was no longer possible for it to remain so anyway, as the biologisation of the concept of the 'Other' meant that the boundary between the two sides was closed, and any crossing of it prevented. There continued, of course, to be relationships between German men and African women, but in terms of the social construct the 'races' were segregated from each other.

Contrary to the publicly asserted justification for anchoring racial segregation in law, which argued on the basis of the unbridgeable, since indeed racial, differences between the individual 'races', one of the main reasons why such an unassailable legal grounding appeared necessary to Tecklenburg and others was that the differences were in fact not always so easy to determine in everyday life. One could not always simply recognise with the naked eye who was a European and who was a 'Native'. Even the 'lifestyle' aspects that were often put forward, i.e. the distinctions in levels of 'culture' or 'civilisation', often did not help here either, as is shown by laments from German settlers of good standing about other Germans from low social backgrounds or about 'Boers' who had 'gone native'. This was made evident by a few spectacular cases of people who had lived as 'Whites' and were then suddenly classified as 'Natives' and thus assigned to a completely different legal sphere.

One example of this was the case of the trader Willy Krabbenhöft of Keetmanshoop, who in 1910 had been sentenced to pay a fine of 20 *Reichsmark* by Keetmanshoop District Court on a charge of causing damage to property, and had then appealed to the Superior Court. The Superior Court quashed the sentence on the grounds that Willy Krabbenhöft was a 'Native', since it had been discovered during the trial that his mother was the daughter of a Scotsman and a 'bastard girl', as the court called her, that is to say a woman of 'mixed' descent from the Cape Colony. The fact that his parents had been married in a register office changed nothing. The court explained its reasoning as follows:

> Membership of the native race is determined by descent, whether on the paternal or the maternal side or both. People of mixed race, as opposed to members of the pure white race, belong to the coloured tribes and are natives. This is not dependent on the degree of consanguinity with any native. As long as descent can be proved, membership of the native race is established. It cannot be ignored that this principle, applied with complete consistency, may

---

17 Judgment of Windhoek Superior Court, 10 November 1909, NAN F.IV.R.1., Sheets 52a–55a.

result in hardship. The admixture of native blood (!) may over the course of generations become so infinitesimal that one can barely still speak of native ancestry; it would perhaps be useful to legally define the degree of kinship from which, given exclusively white reproduction thereafter, membership of the native race would cease. The Court cannot however determine this border on its own initiative, and must therefore, at least at present, identify all those as natives whose descent from natives is still demonstrable and known to the living, and not just through documentation. This is undoubtedly so in the case of the Defendant, whose grandmother is still fully a member of the well-known Baster family of Kluthe. [...] And finally, insofar as the Defendant has pointed out that the military accepted him as a volunteer in 1903, and that he served in the forces until 1906, i.e. that he was treated as a national of the *Reich* by the military authorities, this would only have led to the Defendant losing his quality of being a native if the military had been the authority responsible for determining whether a person is a native or not. This, however, is not the case, and there does not appear to have been any precise examination of the question. Therefore the Defendant is deemed to be a native, and as such, hard though it may be for him considering his position in life up until now and his level of education, must be subject to the separate native jurisdiction.[18]

The court did, however, assure Krabbenhöft that it was still possible for him to apply for naturalisation.

Much the same thing happened just two years later to Ludwig Baumann, a graduate civil engineer and scion of the distinguished Kleinschmidt missionary family. As the executor of an acquaintance's will he had embezzled money, resulting in a two-year prison sentence handed down by Swakopmund District Court. When Baumann appealed to the Superior Court in Windhoek, it quashed this sentence, but on grounds that were disastrous for Baumann: the court found that, as had become clear during the proceedings before the lower court, "he is descended on the maternal side from a native woman". The consequences were clear: "The Defendant, as the great-grandchild of a native woman, is thus to be regarded as a native and as such, hard as it may be for him in view of his educational achievements and his position in life up until now, must be subject to native jurisdiction."[19]

The main reason why this hit the persons affected so hard was that classification as 'Natives' transferred them to the legal sphere of Native Jurisdiction, resulting in the loss of their most essential individual rights. Within the colony, the legal spheres of 'non-Native' and 'Native' jurisdiction were strictly separated to the point where a dual legal system prevailed. Not only was participation of any kind in political processes excluded; so was the private ownership of land or live-

---

[18] Grounds of the judgment, Krabbenhöft appeal proceedings, Windhoek Superior Court, 26 January 1911, NAN ZBU F.IV.R.2. Vol. 2, Sheets 54a–58a.
[19] Grounds of the judgment, Baumann appeal proceedings [transcript], Windhoek Superior Court, 12 March 1913, NAN ZBU F.IV.R.2., Vol. 3, Sheets 36a–37b.

stock. Freedom of movement was restricted and an obligation to seek employment imposed: both of these matters fell under the provisions of Native Law, as determined especially in the three Lindequist Native Ordinances of 1907. It was this separation that formed the foundation of the society of racial privilege the German bureaucrats were bent on constructing.

"A Sin against Racial Consciousness"

'Mixed' marriages and 'persons of mixed race' were however deemed undesirable not only because of their implications for the political power structure, but also from the point of view of 'racial hygiene'. The protagonists of a biological concept of 'race' sought to "protect [...] the ranks of the Europeans against being mixed with coloured blood",[20] as they feared that any mixing of the 'races' would lead to more and more of the population 'going native', or 'going kaffir' as the local idiom expressed it. It was after all said to be "an old fact of experience, evident not only in Africa, that where a white man lives together permanently with a woman of a lower race he does not draw her up to his level, but is drawn down to hers". Similarly, "experience teaches us that such relationships do not improve the race, but debase it: the offspring are as a rule physically and morally weak, they unite in themselves the bad qualities of both parents and by their nature take more after the native mother in their language and behaviour than after the White father." What happened if one did not pay attention to the 'race' question could be seen in the "deterioration of the European race in the former Spanish and Portuguese colonies in America and in Portugal's African possessions."[21]

As a consequence of this logic of binary opposition, critical attention was drawn not only to legal marriages and the question of the citizenship of 'persons of mixed race', but to their very existence in itself. Thus all sexual contacts became a matter of concern to the colonial authorities and their supporters; as the missionary Carl Wandres formulated in a memorandum:

> Mixed marriages are not only undesirable, but are truly immoral and a slap in the face for Germanness [...]
>
> Mixed marriages are always a sin against racial consciousness. A nation that sins against its own honour in this way definitely sinks to a lower level and, as can be seen from the Latin nations, is not capable of carrying out any thorough colonisation. [...]

---

20 Report by Tecklenburg [transcript], 24 September 1903, NAN ZBU F.IV.R.1., Sheets 61ca–61ea.
21 Tecklenburg to Colonial Department Berlin, 23 October 1905, NAN F.IV.R.1., Sheets 24a–34a.

> As far as people of mixed race are concerned, we have to say on the basis of widespread experience that these people are a calamity for our colony. These pitiable creatures are almost all very severely impaired genetically. All that is to be seen among them are lies and deceit, sensuosity and stupid pride, an inclination to dishonesty and to alcoholism, and last but not least they are almost without exception syphilitic. And it could scarcely be otherwise, since their fathers are not good for very much, and their mothers for nothing at all.[22]

In an intensifying process of interventionism, the toleration of 'mixed' marriages under Göring was succeeded by a first attempt to restrict them under Leutwein and their banning under Tecklenburg, until in the end all sexual relations came under scrutiny. Initially, the target of this attack was the White father. He was to be socially ostracised and punished for his lack of 'racial consciousness' by being deprived of his rights of citizenship. Thus the *Selbstverwaltungsverordnung* (Local Self-Government Ordinance) of 1909, which was designed to afford the German population of South West Africa a limited degree of political involvement in the administration of the colony through the election of District and Regional Councils and a Territorial Council, simply excluded all men who lived with African women from the right to vote for or to be elected to these bodies.[23] As "experience shows" that these men were "drawn down by such marriages", it appeared to be justified for them to be "treated under public law as being disqualified from voting". The Imperial Colonial Office claimed that this measure was "in harmony with the views of the majority of the white population of the *Schutzgebiet*, who regard those whites who are married to native women as having forfeited something of the reputable standing they would otherwise enjoy".[24]

---

22 Wandres, "Bemerkungen" , NAN F.IV.R.1., Sheets 143b–145b. Similar ideas were also popularised by various journals in the Empire: see, for example, Walgenbach, "Zwischen Selbstaffirmation und Distinktion", pp. 144f.

23 Imperial Chancellor, "Verordnung betr. die Selbstverwaltung in Deutsch-Südwestafrika", 28 January 1909, reproduced in DKG, Vol. 13 (1909), pp. 19–34. For more on local self-government, see Helmut Bley, *Kolonialherrschaft und Sozialstruktur in Deutsch-Südwestafrika 1894–1914*, Hamburg 1968, pp. 223–256, here pp. 223–234; also: Hansjörg Michael Huber, *Koloniale Selbstverwaltung in Deutsch-Südwestafrika. Entstehung, Kodifizierung und Umsetzung*, Frankfurt 2000.

24 Imperial Colonial Office Berlin to Imperial Governor's Office Windhoek, August 1908, Federal Archive Berlin Lichterfelde (BArch) R 1001/2057, Sheets 118a–122a. In fact, though, the attitude of the settlers in South West Africa to this issue was far from being as clear-cut and unequivocal as the Imperial Colonial Office tried to make out. Among the men disqualified under the Local Self-Government Ordinance there were settlers who enjoyed high regard. They defended themselves against the stigmatisation and were supported in this by other citizens. Moreover, by constantly making submissions to the highest levels of the Administration the men concerned succeeded in keeping the issue on the boil, so that in the end even the Reichstag was forced to devote time to the problem. For examples, see Bley, *Kolonialherrschaft und Sozialstruktur.*

This measure apparently bore little fruit: for as Deputy Governor Oskar Hintrager explained in a letter to the Imperial Colonial Office two years later, it was essential for the measures concerned to be strictly implemented in the "already very bastardised colony". He feared that if the Administration sought to accommodate those who were "forgetful of their race", it would only encourage others to imitate them in this issue, which involved "nothing less than the maintenance of racial purity and racial consciousness".[25]

With Hintrager himself being forced to acknowledge that there were "still regrettably lax attitudes on the part of the settlers in this respect", and therefore to announce that more stringent measures would be forthcoming, in May 1912 Governor Theodor Seitz once again intensified his struggle against extramarital sexual relationships between White men and African women by extending the stigmatisation and social ostracism of the father of a 'mixed-race' child to the mother as well, and promulgating an Ordinance Concerning the Mixed-Race Population.[26] This made it mandatory for the births of children whose fathers were 'non-Natives' but whose mothers were 'Natives' to be recorded in special registers at the District Offices. While these register entries, containing the name, 'tri' affiliation, status or occupation and pass number of the mother – no details of the father were asked for[27] – were still completely in the tradition of the way illegitimate German children were registered within Germany itself,[28] Section 3 of the Ordinance was clearly directed towards criminalising such relationships:

> Where the extramarital cohabitation of a non-native man with a native woman gives rise to a public nuisance, the police may require them to separate, and to the extent that the period set for compliance expires without such compliance, may enforce such a separation. In the same way, the immediate ending of a contract of employment and the removal of the

---

[25] In concrete terms, this related to the proposal by which Governor Bruno von Schuckmann attempted to calm the fury of settlers who were married to African women, namely that the Local Self-Government Ordinance should be amended to the effect that the Governor could admit exceptions. Imperial Governor's Office Windhoek to Imperial Colonial Office Berlin, 20 June 20 1910, BArch R 1001/2059, Sheets 44a–47b.

[26] Imperial Governor's Office Windhoek, *Verordnung über die Mischlingsbevölkerung*, 23 May 1912, NAN ZBU F.IV.R.1., Sheets 128a et seq.

[27] Only in cases of 'mixed' marriages, which in fact no longer legally existed, or if it was the father himself who reported the birth were his personal details to be recorded as well. Circulated Decree, Imperial Governor's Office Windhoek to DOs, 19 July 1912, NAN ZBU F.IV.R.1., Sheets 146a et seq.

[28] Imperial Chancellor, Instruction relating to the Act of 4 May 1870, *Gesetz betr. die Eheschließung und die Beurkundung des Personenstandes von Bundesangehörigen im Ausland*, reproduced in DKG, Vol. 1 (up to 1892), pp. 58–79.

mother of a half-white child may be required if the father of the child is the employer or a relative or employee of the employer who forms part of his domestic community.[29]

In order to enhance the social disciplinatory impact on African women, Hintrager instructed Registrars to conduct the registration proceedings in such a way that they would have the effect of "deterring the coloured mothers [...] through the disgrace involved" and make them aware of the fact that it was "a transgression against their nation to become involved with a white man".[30]

Especially under Section 3 of the Ordinance, private and intimate matters were dragged out into the public domain and every White person was given the task of supervising the sexual behaviour of his or her fellows. There was a certain logic behind this: if sexuality and reproduction were made a matter of public concern, if they were regarded as a contribution to the health or the endangerment of an abstract *Volkskörper* ('body of the nation'), then they were no longer private matters. At the same time, it threw the door wide open for denunciations of any kind, which could now be represented as acts performed in the interests of the nation. With Native Law having already ascribed to every White person a supervisory and police function in respect of every African, the Whites were now also subjected to mutual social control.

"That Man Has Gone Completely Native; He Reeks of *pontok*"

The employment of African women and girls as domestic servants provided a cloak for many sexual encounters. It was one of the contradictions of German Native Policy that while all African women, like the men, were required to work, it was a matter of common knowledge "that in these cases the girls, with few exceptions, are used for sexual intercourse and thus spoilt for work of any kind"[31] and that "almost every white man who is not married procures himself a native woman to have sexual intercourse with".[32] The Windhoek Native Commissioner was also well

---

[29] Imperial Governor's Office Windhoek, *Verordnung über die Mischlingsbevölkerung*, 23 May 1912, NAN ZBU F.IV.R.1., Sheet 128a f.
[30] Ibid.
[31] Native Commissioner Ebeling, Warmbad, to Governor's Office Windhoek, 6 May 1914, NAN ZBU W.IV.A.5. Vol. 1, Sheet 8a.
[32] District Office of Grootfontein to Governor's Office Windhoek, 6 May 1914, NAN ZBU W.IV.A.5. Vol. 1, Sheet 6a.

enough informed to report "that sexual intercourse takes place between a large proportion of the unmarried employers and their female servants".[33]

So even after the promulgation of the various Ordinances aimed at furthering racial segregation, relationships between White men and African women were still commonplace. The local officials were well aware of this, but generally did not see any possibility of taking action against such behaviour, or any occasion to do so. As with the implementation of the rigid Native Policy in general,[34] how the 'mixed marriage' question was handled depended on the personal attitudes of the officials concerned.[35] Nonetheless, the latent threat of sanctions, and the fact that any official was in a position to be able to take action against a sexual relationship whenever he felt inclined to do so, definitely represented a substantial intrusion into the private lives of all those affected.

In general it is hard to gain any meaningful insights into the day-to-day cohabitation of African women and White men, as it largely took place away from the public view. Such cases only became a matter of record when state authorities got involved. One such case related to the trader Feodor Stelzner and an African girl known to us only by the name Amanda.

On 27 May 1914, Stelzner complained to the Imperial Government in Windhoek that he had been forbidden by the police officer stationed in Usakos to employ the sixteen-year-old Amanda, whom he knew from a previous job, as an assistant in his store there. Instead, he claimed, she was to be forced to work for someone else against her will. Police Sergeant Knickrehm, to whom he had complained, had informed him that he was not going to get the girl back, even if it was her own wish to remain with him; to which Stelzner had replied: "A. does not have a will of her own any more." Stelzner was of the view that Amanda could not be denied the right to work for him; he did not want to have any other 'Natives', people he did not know.[36]

---

33 Native Commissioner Bohr to Governor's Office Windhoek, 22 July 1914, NAN ZBU W.IV.A.5. Vol. 1, Sheet 23a.
34 I have described how differently the individual colonial officials used the discretion they possessed under Native Law in Zimmerer, *Deutsche Herrschaft*, pp. 126–242 [English translation *German Rule*, pp. 159–294].
35 Detailed research into this is still lacking. Henrichsen provides an interesting case study on one such relationship: Dag Henrichsen, "Heirat im Krieg. Erfahrungen von Kaera Ida Getzen Leinhos", in Jürgen Zimmerer and Joachim Zeller, eds, *Völkermord in Deutsch-Südwestafrika. Der Kolonialkrieg in Namibia (1904–1908) und seine Folgen*, Berlin 2003, pp. 160–168. Further research will however be needed to determine whether this was merely a one-off case, or whether it can be viewed as being representative of a larger number of 'mixed' marriages.
36 Feodor Stelzner, Usakos, to Governor's Office Windhoek, 28 May 1914, NAN ZBU W.III.N.2. Vol. 1, Sheets 35–41.

Knickrehm, who was then called upon to report to the Governor's Office on the case, explained his decision on the basis of the sexual relationship between Stelzner and Amanda, which needed to be put a stop to. Right at the beginning of his justification, he spoke at length about "the immoral life led by the Complainant":

> Stelzner, now a man of 25, has indulged in intimate relations with native women for about 6–7 years, which has cost him a great deal of the respect due to him as a white man from the reputable white population. He begat four mixed-race children with a recently deceased Herero woman called 'Sucko'. It was a few years ago that the offence evoked by this intercourse with the native woman reached its peak among the population at large. Brawls occurred in which Stelzner was consistently the party that came off worse. Very often, whites whose word can be relied on observed events that constituted a public nuisance, and in some individual cases they also informed the police in confidence. However, they stopped short of filing any formal complaints, in order not to expose themselves to unpleasant talk, which they would otherwise not have been able to avoid. No-one wanted to be the first to bring a public accusation. There was still a certain amount of sympathy for Stelzner, whose character even today displays a lot of childlike traits.[37]

This account does not rest upon Knickrehm's own observations, he wrote, but had been communicated to him, and was now confirmed again, by his predecessors. In the previous year, Stelzner had then got to know Amanda when he took over the running of the store and restaurant in Johann-Albrechtshöhe for a person named Zingel:

> With time, a relationship developed between the two which went far beyond the degree of what was permissible and once again cast Stelzner in a negative light. This relationship attracted the particular attention of the railway crossing keeper and his wife, who made some very derogatory remarks about it. Zingel himself explained to me that he had received information regarding Stelzner's conduct towards natives – and especially towards Amanda – from people whose credibility was beyond doubt.[38]

As a result, Stelzner lost his job. An aspect of his behaviour that was regarded as particularly scandalous was the way he openly called the 'racial hierarchy' into question, allowing Amanda to be served by other 'Natives' and permitting her to make use of the areas of the house reserved for Whites.

> Stelzner had the table on the veranda of the restaurant laid for Amanda and himself, and the two had breakfast there together. Other natives waited on them. Moreover, Amanda had been witnessed sitting on the sofa while Stelzner knelt in front of her with his arms around her legs, imploring and beseeching her not to leave him. In addition, the two had

---

[37] Police Sergeant Knickrehm to Governor's Office Windhoek, 3 July 1914, NAN ZBU W.III.N.2. Vol. 1, Sheets 46a–49a.
[38] Ibid.

danced together to music from the gramophone in full view of other natives. These last incidents sound rather improbable or exaggerated, but they presumably represent only a small proportion of several similar cases.[39]

When Amanda changed her job of her own accord, Sergeant Knickrehm's report continued, Stelzner had gone after her and begged her employer to transfer Amanda back into his service. With regard to this conversation, the "woman, who was otherwise very restrained in her manner of speaking and very scrupulous about telling the truth [...] expressed herself most disparagingly" and was very indignant. Subsequently he went to the local tavern:

> During his conversation with the proprietor's wife he also brought up the topic of his motherless mixed-race children and sorrowfully bewailed the way Amanda was being withheld from him. With tears in his eyes he unburdened himself to the woman in such a way that when she wanted to tell me about it soon afterwards all she could bring out was a single 'pooh', and the spontaneous utterance: 'That man has gone completely native, he reeks of *pontok* [hut]!'[40]

In consultation with Karibib District Office, therefore, Knickrehm had refused Stelzner's plea to send Amanda back into his service. He declared that any giving way would "represent full endorsement of their earlier relationship". Stelzner's claim that Amanda did not have a free will of her own any more had, according to Knickrehm, been misinterpreted; what he had been referring to was the fact that Amanda still had a father, who was also against her being employed by Stelzner. The Governor's Office dismissed Stelzner's complaint.[41]

What is striking is the amount of detail about Stelzner's and Amanda's private lives that was known to the police, even if it is impossible to distinguish how much was based on precise information and how much on rumour or malicious gossip. The whole weight of prejudice against such relationships is summed up in the remark that Stelzner "reeked of *pontok*", as a way of expressing the process of 'going native' so often invoked by Tecklenburg, Wandres and others as an ever-present danger. But the image of self-neglect and backwardness it evoked was only one reason for the fear of 'mixed' marriages and 'people of mixed parentage'. The possibility that precisely the opposite might also occur seemed equally unsettling.

Transgressions against the 'purity of the race' appeared threatening not only because of the imagined 'pollution' of the 'body of the German nation': rather, the

---

39 Ibid.
40 Ibid.
41 Governor's Office Windhoek to Feodor Stelzner, Usakos [draft], 31 July 1911, NAN ZBU W.III.N.2. Vol. 1, Sheet 50a.

very existence of people of, in particular, 'mixed race' actually called into question a constitutive principle of the colonial state, which rested upon the binary distinction between 'White' and 'Black', 'Native' and 'non-Native', 'master (race)' and 'servant'. If this boundary became blurred, then confusion and uncertainty loomed, threatening ultimately to jeopardise German rule altogether, because, according to Tecklenburg:

> Males of mixed race will be liable to serve in the forces, will be capable of occupying public offices, and will be beneficiaries of the right to vote, which is likely to be introduced at some time in the future, and of other rights attached to nationality. These consequences are extremely alarming and in view of the present situation in German South West Africa they represent a grave danger. They will not only compromise the maintenance of the purity of the German race and of German civilisation to a major extent, but also put the white man's entire position of power in jeopardy.[42]

The "maintenance of the purity of the German race" and the "white man's entire position of power" could not be separated from one another. The ban on 'mixed' marriages and the measures taken to prevent sexual relations of any kind between the 'races' were attempts to compel people to observe and uphold a boundary between the colonisers and the colonised, one which in this binary form had only been created by the colonial laws themselves. Any transgression was thus perceived as a threat to the system of colonial rule, one that called into question the utopian conception of the society of racial privilege.

The Governmental and Administrative Utopia: A Society of Racial Privilege

In South West Africa perhaps even more strongly than in other colonies, the German governmental and administrative utopia, meaning the ideal-typical construct of what the colonial state and its society would look like if the German colonial bureaucracy were able to implement its theoretical conceptions without having to pay any regard to power politics and without effective resistance either from Africans or from Germans, was based on the distinction between 'Natives' and 'non-Natives'. Ideological concepts of 'race' and considerations relating to power politics need to be seen in context and in their mutual interdependency; they were conditional upon each other. Racial segregation did not represent an end in itself or an erratic block unconnected to other aspects of colonial policy; rather, it was a funda-

---

[42] Tecklenburg to Colonial Department Berlin, 23 October 1905, NAN ZBU F.IV.R.1., Sheets 24a–34a.

mental pillar in the model colonial state that the administrators were seeking to realise. Since the days of Theodor Leutwein, the goal of this utopia of development and exploitation had been the construction of an efficient economic system whose functionality was to be ensured through the establishment of a society of racial privilege in which the institutions of government, the European settlers and the African population would each occupy their firmly assigned place. The African population was to be comprehensively registered and kept under surveillance, integrated into the colony's economic system as cheap labour and re-educated to function as a compliant workforce through a process of social disciplining. In this way, it was assumed, the economic development of the colony could be pushed ahead with and the extraction of minerals guaranteed, so that the territory would be able to develop into a settler colony in an orderly manner. The end result was intended to be a unified economic area across which the African people were to be distributed as workers in such a way as to meet the needs of the colonial economy.

The core of this colonial Native Law consisted of the three Native Ordinances of 1907: the Control Ordinance, the Pass Ordinance and the so-called Master and Servant Ordinance, by which for the first time every individual African was subjected directly to German laws and ordinances and placed under the control of a bureaucratic and centralised Administration.[43] This was an attempt to regulate all spheres of African life and to give the Administration an overview of how many and which Africans were resident in any particular Region or District at any given time, where they lived and if and where they were employed. For this purpose, all Africans had to be entered in a Native Register. A pass token, to be worn visibly, was designed to ensure that all Africans could be unambiguously identified. Moreover, anyone who needed to leave his or her place of residence was required to be in possession of a travel pass. As opposed to the forced labour practised during the war, both in the concentration camps of the colonial forces and in the labour camps set up by private companies,[44] in the period after the war the elements of direct compulsion were replaced by measures that were structural in nature. It was no longer imprisonment, fetters and whips that were to be used to force the 'Natives' to work, but rather a sophisticated system of rewards and direct or indirect compulsion. Since the Africans no longer owned any

---

43 For more detail, see: Zimmerer, *Deutsche Herrschaft* [English translation: *German Rule*].
44 See, for example, Jan-Bart Gewald, *Towards Redemption. A Socio-political History of the Herero of Namibia Between 1890 and 1923*, Leiden 1996, pp. 220–224; Gesine Krüger, *Kriegsbewältigung und Geschichtsbewußtsein: Realität, Deutung und Verarbeitung des deutschen Kolonialkrieges in Namibia 1904–1907*, Göttingen 1999, pp. 126–135. As an introduction to the war in general, see Jürgen Zimmerer and Joachim Zeller, eds, *Völkermord in Deutsch-Südwestafrika. Der Kolonialkrieg (1904–1908) in Namibia und seine Folgen*, Berlin 2003.

land – they had been expropriated as early as 1906/07[45] and were now also prohibited from owning riding animals or other large livestock[46] – they had no other option than to hire themselves out – as farm labourers, to the engineering companies building the railways or in the diamond mines. Anyone who nevertheless did not take up such work was to be punished as a vagrant. Free choice of one's place of residence was abolished, and a special permit from the colonial authorities was required for African settlements consisting of more than ten families. This served the purpose of making it possible for the African population to be better monitored and for the entire colony to be supplied as efficiently as possible with a labour force.

As practically all adult Africans had to work for Whites, a legal codification of working relationships was necessary. Instruments to this end were a *Dienstbuch* (Employment Logbook), and contracts of employment. The former contained the 'working biography' of each individual and was supposed to provide an unbroken sequence of information about the African's employment relationships and his availability for work, i.e. the 'willingness to work' so often invoked in colonial discourse. Contracts of employment between workers and employers had to be approved by the police. On handing out an Employment Logbook, the police were to verify "that the content of the contract had been made adequately comprehensible to the employee, and agreed to by him". To the displeasure of the farmers, this encompassed instructing the Africans with regard not only to their duties, but to their (minimal) rights as well.[47]

This last provision, like others offering 'protection for the natives' in general, was overshadowed by the repressive character of Native Policy as a whole, and nonetheless formed an integral part of the society of racial privilege. It afforded German officials an illusory confirmation that they were not merely the cat's paws of business or executors of a ruthless policy of oppression, but that rather they were doing their part in achieving a balance of interests between Europeans and Africans:

---

45 On this subject, see Zimmerer, *Deutsche Herrschaft*, pp. 57–68 [English edition: *German Rule*, pp. 72–83].
46 Anyone who nevertheless still sought to possess animals was required to obtain explicit governmental approval; so that the government was able to control, restrict or promote the degree of economic independence of the African population.
47 As an example see the report of Gobabis District Office, where employers rarely made contracts of employment for longer than a month as they feared the explanations of their rights that the Africans would be entitled to receive from the police. Gobabis District Office to Governor's Office Windhoek, 31 October 1908, NAN ZBU W.III.A.3. Vol. 1, Sheet 42a.

> The Ordinance relating to Employment Contracts with natives is to be welcomed as a great step forward, in the interests both of the whites and of the natives themselves. [...] The native will lose the feeling of being practically a slave and deprived of all rights in respect of his employer, and if he is well treated and paid in accordance with his performance will do everything he can to keep his employer satisfied.[48]

In the internal logic of the largely hermetic world of colonialist attitudes inhabited by the officials involved, the Native Ordinances were by no means seen merely as measures of subjugation; rather, they truly believed them to be instruments that could bring about a long-term 'reconciliation' between the interests of the different 'races'. After all, they were seen as a way of teaching the 'Natives' to work, which in its turn was regarded as a basic prerequisite for any development towards a higher level of civilisation. True, they had to work for very low wages and their rights were restricted as compared to those of the Whites, but this corresponded to what was assumed to be their 'nature', their level of 'development'. This colonial logic could only function if justification could be found for discrimination and subjugation as such, and to this end the 'racial' distinctions were emphasised. To do this, though, it was necessary to make a strict differentiation, a precise definition. Violations of the 'racial boundaries' called this intellectual construct into question, thereby endangering more than merely the 'purity of the race'.

Discrimination also extended to the realms of the law, the administration and the police. The society of racial privilege was based on a dual legal and administrative system. Whereas, for example, the separation of powers as between the executive and judicial branches of government existed for Europeans, or rather for all Whites (apart from the four Imperial District Courts, there was also a Superior Court to hear appeals), this was not the case for the 'Natives'. For them, the Regional or District Officers were prosecutors, judges and penal authorities all rolled into one. This was why the Superior Court rejected the appeals in the cases of Krabbenhöft and Baumann. From 1910 onwards, a separate Native Administration with an Office of Native Affairs and Native Commissioners was set up.

In addition, the three Native Ordinances of 1907 not only led to the compulsion to take up employment and a system of unparalleled surveillance, but also elevated every White to the rank of a supervisor over the African population. The newly introduced pass tokens, for example, which had to be worn visibly around the neck, were to be shown to any White person upon request. In the sophisti-

---

[48] Swakopmund District Office to Governor's Office Windhoek, 8 June 1907, NAN ZBU W.III.A.1. Vol. 1, Sheets 26b–27a.

cated system of registration, too, Whites took on several crucial tasks. Thus not only did the boundary between the colonial authorities and the settler population become blurred, but the settlers themselves became increasingly conscious of being part of the legal or law enforcement systems, and ultimately even of standing above them.

"Brutal Excesses of Whites Against Natives"

The possible consequences of this were shown in the so-called 'parental powers of physical chastisement'. The settlers claimed for themselves the right to inflict corporal punishment on their African workers, as in respect of their state of personal development they were considered to be the equivalent of children and to need a 'firm hand'. The courts, by acknowledging this 'right of chastisement' as one hallowed by custom, opened the doors wide for a general culture of corporal punishment. Although it was forbidden to inflict punishment in such a way as to cause damage to the health of the person concerned,[49] any assessment of whether this was the case was clouded by the racial stereotypes that were shared by officials and settlers. According to these, Africans were not affected by physical punishment due to their "lower level of civilisation"; and their different type of skin, being "particularly hardened and largely insensitive", meant that "even when they are more severely punished" they would suffer "at the most superficial abrasions of the skin".[50]

Such beatings eventually got so out of hand that the Government and the representatives of the settlers complained in the *Landesrat* (Territorial Council) that the "brutal excesses of whites against natives", which in some individual cases even policemen were involved in, were increasing in number "to an alarming extent, and are often not expiated before the courts in a manner that satisfies the natives' own sense of justice", so that the Africans "would lose faith in the impartiality of our administration of justice".[51]

---

[49] For a discussion of and the application of the 'parental right of chastisement', see Martin Schröder, *Prügelstrafe und Züchtigungsrecht in den deutschen Schutzgebieten Schwarzafrikas*, Münster 1997, pp. 101–120.
[50] Governor's Office Windhoek to Imperial Colonial Office Berlin, 30 December 1907, quoted according to: Horst Gründer, ed., '… *da und dort ein junges Deutschland gründen'. Rassismus, Kolonien und kolonialer Gedanke vom 16. bis zum 20. Jahrhundert*, München 1999, p. 279.
[51] Circular Order, Governor's Office Windhoek, 31 May 1912, NAN ZBU W.III.R.1. Vol. 1, Sheets 7a–8a.

And indeed it was the case that in the rare instances in which settlers were prosecuted, generally only ridiculously light sentences were imposed. Thus it was in the case of the farmer Friedrich Schneidewind who in 1912 was sentenced to two years and three months in prison by Windhoek District Court for inflicting bodily harm resulting in death and grievous bodily harm. He was found guilty of having, on 18 December 1911, threatened an African woman called Goras, who allegedly was not doing her work, with the *sjambok*, a type of heavy horsewhip, whereupon she ran away. He then pursued her with his dogs, caught up with her after some 600–800 metres and drove her back, "striking her repeatedly with the sjambok":

> In doing so he shoved her violently several times, so that she fell very heavily. When he got close to the ox cart he first grabbed the girl, who was lying completely exhausted on the ground, by the left foot and dragged her a distance of 20 m, then placed an ox strap around her neck, dragged her by it another 12 m or so to the cart and tied her firmly to it. When she tried to crawl into the shadow of the cart, he pulled her back into the sun [The occurrence took place in December, i.e. at the height of summer]. Finally he threw several heavy rocks at her, striking her on the thigh and on the upper arm. This was in the morning. She died in the afternoon, at about 4 o'clock. It was later possible to determine from the body that an upper arm and several ribs were broken.[52]

Such were the findings of the court. Nevertheless, extenuating circumstances were allowed, since the accused person had been suffering from *Jähzorn* (an outbreak of violent temper).

This was not the only such case. The conditions that prevailed on the farms, on railway construction sites and in the mines are further illustrated by the sarcastic letter that the farmer and retired captain Georg Engelhard wrote to the Government in 1913, in which he ironically inquired:

> There are cases known to me in which whites, without being in any employment relationship with a particular black person, have fallen upon the latter totally without cause and beaten him, without the black person being able to have any idea of why. In such cases, is the black person allowed, before he dies, to defend himself or to hold the white person fast until other whites come to protect him, or must he wait until after his death has occurred or he has fallen into a state of unconsciousness? Am I allowed to force the wife of one of my workers to work without giving her any food or wages or any other remuneration? Am I considered legally to be her master? May I hit her on the head if in my – incontrovertible – opinion she carries out my orders too slowly?[53]

---

[52] Judgment of Windhoek District Court against Friedrich Schneidewind; proceedings of 19 July 1912, NAN ZBU W.III.R.2. Vol. 1, Sheets 130a–132a.
[53] Georg Engelhard to Governor's Office Windhoek, 7 April 1913, NAN ZBU W.III.R.2. Vol. 1, Sheets 151a f. Emphases (underlinings) inserted in the original by a clerical officer in the Governor's Office.

The government clerk responsible for replying to this letter was evidently not receptive to this ironic tone, and answered tersely: "The Governor's Office does not regard itself as being under any obligation to respond to inquiries of a purely theoretical nature. You are recommended to report any occurrences of the type you describe to the competent court with a view to prosecution."[54]

The brutality of the farmers was matched by the mildness and indulgence of the courts. If a White man was to be punished for the 'maltreatment of natives', he first had to be sentenced under due process of law. This hardly ever happened, however, and if it did, the penalties imposed were ridiculously light. For it was as a rule impossible to find any White witnesses who were prepared to speak against the accused, while Black ones would "simply not be believed, whereas the most dubious statements made by whites under oath would be given credence", as the Lüderitzbucht District Officer complained. "And so the whole affair would end with a glowing acquittal, and there could be no more thankless task than to represent the prosecuting authorities in such cases."[55] In a society as strongly characterised by racism as the colonial one, it was impossible to eliminate the racist assumption that Africans lacked credibility.

The claim of the settlers to be entitled to do whatever they liked even with the actual bodies of the 'Other' is also demonstrated in the demand raised by farmers in 1912 that "natives who display a propensity to run away should be identified by a tattoo".[56] Al-though the Government ultimately rejected these demands, since "no [...] colonial nation makes use of such measures",[57] and moreover, they might "stir up major unrest among the natives and be met with great resistance", and furthermore "would be exploited at home by elements hostile to colonialism to justify wild agitation",[58] this example still demonstrates what kinds of measures were deemed to be conceivable in certain circles in the colony.[59]

---

54 Governor's Office Windhoek to Engelhard, Ferdinandshöhe Farm near Omaruru, 16 April 1913, NAN ZBU W.III.R.2. Vol. 1, Sheet 153a.
55 Lüderitzbucht District Office to Governor's Office Windhoek, 21 April 1913, NAN ZBU W.III.R.2. Vol. 1, Sheets 156a–159a.
56 Okahandja Farmers' Association to Governor's Office Windhoek, 16 December 1912, NAN ZBU W.III.B.1. Vol. 1, Sheet 35a.
57 Governor's Office Windhoek to a farmer named von Gossler, Chairman of the Okahandja Farmers' Association, 31 December 1912, NAN ZBU W.III.B.1. Vol. 1, Sheet 36a.
58 Outjo District Office to Governor's Office Windhoek, 4 March 1912, NAN ZBU W.III.B.1. Vol. 1, Sheet 29a.
59 For more detail on this debate and on the context in which it was conducted, see Zimmerer, *Deutsche Herrschaft*, pp. 146–148 [English edition: *German Rule*, pp. 180–183].

As has been made clear in this section, the idea of the society of racial privilege extends far beyond ethnic segregation as an end in itself or as the means of implementing diffuse ideological concepts of 'racial purity'. It refers to a social order that is designed to be permanent and is based on a biological hierarchisation encompassing all aspects of life. The members of the 'races' concerned were to be made to internalise their positions in this hierarchy by measures of social disciplining. In this way, direct force was supposed to be rendered superfluous, being replaced by a structural compulsion that would no longer be perceptible as such. This is not the least of the reasons why the mental deformations set in train by this situation gave birth to a legacy that outlasted the actual phase of colonialism for so long. This society of racial privilege is not just a discursive formation, but also a cultural, social and communicative practice that permeated the relationships between the colonisers and the colonised at all levels. It is essential to be able to keep all these different levels in view in their entirety in order to understand the impact of colonialism on everyday life and its still persisting consequences. Taking this as a starting point, the question then arises as to how far these ideas continue to play a role.

From Windhoek to Warsaw

It has recently been argued very aggressively that it was a very long way from Windhoek to Nuremberg, and that it is therefore not possible to establish a connection between the German colonial experience and the crimes of the Nazis.[60] In my opinion, this judgment is based on two errors in perception. Firstly, it fails to take account of how racial segregation was actually practised in society and therefore presents a picture of a relatively open discourse; and secondly, it seeks parallels in the wrong places.

As has been shown earlier, there was very little to be seen of any heterogeneity and openness in the cultural image of the 'African Other' during the last 15 years of German colonial rule. Even though there were divergent views in Germany as to

---

60 Birthe Kundrus, "Von Windhoek nach Nürnberg? Koloniale 'Mischehenverbote' und die nationalsozialistische Rassengesetzgebung", in Birthe Kundrus, ed., *Phantasiereiche. Zur Kulturgeschichte des deutschen Kolonialismus*, Frankfurt 2003, pp. 110–131; Birthe Kundrus, *Moderne Imperialisten*, pp. 277–279. Annegret Ehmann instead points to the connection – including in terms of the persons involved – between colonial and Nazi racism: Annegret Ehmann, "Rassistische und antisemitische Traditionslinien in der deutschen Geschichte des 19. und 20. Jahrhunderts", in Sportmuseum Berlin, ed., *Sportstadt Berlin in Geschichte und Gegenwart*, Berlin 1993, pp. 131–145.

who was a 'Native' and how 'Natives' should be treated, ultimately it was the hegemonic discourse of the German colonial bureaucracy in Windhoek that was decisive, since that was the discourse of those actively involved. Equipped with a relatively homogenous and consistent image of the 'Native', but also determined by the demands of power politics in the governmental and administrative utopia that they sought to create, i.e. in a society of racial privilege, a small group of highly influential colonial officials succeeded in bringing about the practical realisation of their ideas. These sought to prevent any transgression of the boundaries between the colonisers and the colonised. But the establishment of a social hierarchy along racial lines brought with it not only differing treatment, but generally also severe disadvantage. Even if in individual cases an attitude of paternalistic benevolence towards the African population was to be found, the Native Policy system as it was put into practice under the conditions of colonial rule and in everyday colonial life often mutated into brutal exploitation and subjugation, which in its most extreme manifestation could even go as far as sadistic murder.

However mistaken it would be to reduce German colonialism to the exploitation of the colonised and to see a sadist and an exploiter in every colonial official, it would be equally wrong to distil a paternalistically benevolent image of colonial rule from the opinions and programmatic writings of a few colonial propagandists and fantasists, most of whom had never even been in Africa.

A Herero man or a Nama woman living in German South West Africa at the beginning of the 20th century will not have gained any sense of there being an open – German – discourse. Their everyday life was controlled by the Native Policy of their colonial 'masters'. It is true that the latter never succeeded in transforming them into the compliant objects of colonial policy that they imagined them as being or becoming. They were able to find loopholes in various ways, and they had wills and ideas of their own which they deployed in opposition to those of their colonisers, to cultivate their own cultural traditions;[61] but their opportunities to live their own lives and their options for action were severely restricted. Admittedly, the racial legislation did not apply 'back home' in Germany itself,[62] so that Africans travelling there were not legally discriminated against; but the fact is that from 1904 onwards practically no African managed to travel to Germany, and even the number of those who had managed to get there in earlier years and from other German colonies was tiny. By contrast, the number of Afri-

---

[61] On this subject, see the studies by Gewald and Krüger: Gewald, *Towards Redemption*; Krüger, *Kriegsbewältigung und Geschichtsbewusstsein*.
[62] Kundrus, *Moderne Imperialisten*, pp. 278f.

cans who suffered repression and exploitation on the farms, in the mines and in the private households of South West Africa amounted to many thousands.

If, however, one bases a historical comparison on real practice in society rather than on colonialist discourse, then Nuremberg (that is to say the Nuremberg Race Laws) is not the right place, or at least not the only place, that it is worth while searching for similarities in. One must also look at the way things developed under the German occupation of eastern Europe: here too, German rule was based on a strict racial distinction between the occupiers and the occupied. If one takes not Nuremberg but Warsaw as the point of comparison – or indeed almost any other region in eastern Europe that was occupied by the Germans during the Second World War and was subjected to the Germans' plans for a complete reordering of society, politics and population economics,[63] then the similarities are easier to recognise. Unfortunately I do not have the time or space here to go into the relationship between colonialism and National Socialism overall, as I have done in more detail elsewhere;[64] so I will restrict myself to just a few remarks concerning the society of racial privilege in the 'East'.

Taking a look at the practical implementation of occupation behind the actual front line, we can see that in occupied Poland too, a small elite of German civil servants and military personnel ruled over a much larger Polish population who were practically excluded from any opportunity to play a role in politics. Germans and Poles were assigned to the jurisdiction of different legal systems; this 'dual

---

[63] Among the sheer unending mass of literature, I would like just to mention a few of the more recent works: Ulrich Herbert, ed., *National Socialist Extermination Policies: Contemporary German Perspectives and Controversies*, New York 2000; Götz Aly and Susanne Heim, *Vordenker der Vernichtung. Auschwitz und die deutschen Pläne für eine neue europäische Ordnung*, Hamburg 1991; Götz Aly, *'Final Solution': Nazi Population Policy and the Murder of the European Jews*, London and New York 1999; Christian Gerlach, *Kalkulierte Morde: Die deutsche Wirtschafts- und Vernichtungspolitik in Weißrußland, 1941–1944*, Hamburg 1999; Christian Gerlach, *Krieg, Ernährung, Völkermord. Forschungen zur deutschen Vernichtungspolitik im Zweiten Weltkrieg*, Hamburg 1998; Dieter Pohl, *Nationalsozialistische Judenverfolgung in Ostgalizien 1941–1944. Organisation und Durchführung eines staatlichen Massenverbrechens*, München 1996; Thomas Sandkühler, *'Endlösung' in Galizien. Der Judenmord in Ostpolen und die Rettungsinitiativen von Berthold Beitz*, Bonn 1996; Bernhard Chiari, *Alltag hinter der Front. Besatzung, Kollaboration und Widerstand in Weißrußland 1941–1944*, Düsseldorf 1998.

[64] I have attempted this in Jürgen Zimmerer, "Holocaust und Kolonialismus. Beitrag zu einer Archäologie des genozidalen Gedankens", *Zeitschrift für Geschichtswissenschaft*, 51/12 (2003), pp. 1098–1119 (English version: "Colonialism and the Holocaust", pp. 125–153 in this book); Jürgen Zimmerer, "Die Geburt des 'Ostlandes' aus dem Geiste des Kolonialismus. Ein postkolonialer Blick auf die NS-Eroberungs- und Vernichtungspolitik", *Sozial.Geschichte. Zeitschrift für die historische Analyse des 20. und 21. Jahrhunderts*, 1 (2004), pp. 10–43 (English version: "The Birth of the 'Ostland' out of the Spirit of Colonialism", pp. 230–261 in this book).

legal system' rested upon the criterion of 'race', whereby it is no longer necessary at this point to emphasise the purely constructed nature of the racial categories used. However, preferential treatment within this society of racial privilege was not limited to the area of formal law. The *situation coloniale* permeated all spheres of social interaction. Just as Europeans were always and everywhere favoured in South West Africa, so too in eastern Europe the Germans were to form the apex of the social hierarchy. Just as, for example, in German South West Africa the permanent situation of subjugation was demonstrated symbolically in the prohibition on riding horses described at the beginning of this chapter, in the obligation to greet every White person, or in the prohibition on walking on the pavements, so in the General gouvernement Poles had to show an appropriate degree of deference towards every German by making room for them on the pavements, by taking their hats off and by saluting them. They were prohibited from attending cinemas, concerts, exhibitions, libraries, museums or theatres, and from owning bicycles, cameras or radios.[65] If Hitler, talking about the Ukraine, once said: "Our Germans – this is the main thing – must form a closed community, like a fortress; outside the main centres, even the lowest stable boy must stand above any of the natives",[66] this is essentially a view of a social order based on 'race' similar to that of the society of racial privilege in South West Africa.

Similarities also exist with regard to the evaluation of the respective 'Native' populations. The value attributed to them derived from their degree of usefulness to the occupiers, but above all from their function as a labour force. Segregated legally and socially from the Germans, the 'Natives' of Eastern Europe were assigned above all the roles of servants and labourers for the German 'master class'. It was this function as a labour force that essentially gave them their right to live. As has already been demonstrated above by reference to the three Native Ordinances, it was the Africans' function as a labour force that stood in the foreground in German South West Africa too. What distinguished the two occupation situations, that in

---

[65] Michael Burleigh, *Die Zeit des Nationalsozialismus. Eine Gesamtdarstellung*, Frankfurt 2000, p. 518. On this *situation coloniale*, now see also David Furber, *'Going East'. Colonialism and German Life in Nazi-Occupied Poland*, University of New York at Buffalo 2003 (dissertation), pp. 5f. Furber shows how it was only by emphasising their common Germanness and the colonial task they shared in the 'East' that the German occupiers were able to establish a distance between themselves and the Poles, to whom they were essentially more similar than they would have liked to admit. This discursive colonisation of the 'Other' as well as of the conquered terrain also represents an important parallel to colonial rule outside Europe. I have covered this subject in more detail in Zimmerer, "Geburt des 'Ostlandes'" (English version: "The Birth of the 'Ostland'", pp. 230–261 in this book).
[66] Hitler, 17 September 1941, Adolf Hitler, *Monologe im Führerhauptquartier*, ed. and with a commentary by Werner Jochmann, Hamburg 1980, p. 63.

Africa and that in eastern Europe, from each other was the idea that the Africans would in time adapt to their role, and thereby attain to an enhanced level of civilisation. Even though this was empty talk in the day-to-day reality of the colony, which was dominated by brutal exploitation, it was nonetheless never abandoned as an objective of colonialism. During the Second World War, the Germans no longer made this effort towards the Poles or the Russians, or whoever else they were prepared to allow to continue to exist purely as a helot class. There was no longer any trace of a cultural mission or of an educational function; or where such a mission was used as an argument, it applied to the terrain, to the area available for development, not to the local inhabitants. Some suggestion of this had already been perceptible in certain radical voices in South West Africa which had applauded the genocide against the Herero and the Nama; the development of the infrastructure was indeed conducted without any regard for the people living there.[67]

The German colonial empire was not the same as the occupation of eastern Europe during the Second World War, and what happened in it did not have to lead inevitably to the criminal regime of the Third Reich. Nonetheless, around and shortly after the turn of the century ideas were articulated and, far more importantly, put into practice, which were then to be found again a generation later in a similar or more radical form. These included the belief that a society could be built up on a foundation of 'race' and the idea of adopting a eugenic policy to protect your own group from biological 'contamination'. There was no one-way street leading from South West Africa to the occupied eastern territories; looked at from the Windhoek perspective, the German colonial experience did not inevitably lead to the Third Reich; however, to maintain the metaphor, of the numerous roads that came together in the criminal policies of the Nazis, one began in the colonies, and it was by no means the least important. The colonial experience provided a cultural reservoir from which the perpetrators of the Nazi crimes could help themselves.[68]

What impact does this have on the writing of history from a global point of view? The society of racial privilege was limited neither to the German colonial territories, nor to colonies outside Europe. Taking it seriously as a conceptual

---

[67] On this subject, see Jürgen Zimmerer, "Der Wahn der Planbarkeit: Vertreibung, unfreie Arbeit und Völkermord als Elemente der Bevölkerungsökonomie in Deutsch-Südwestafrika", *Comparativ*, 13/4 (2003), pp. 96–113 (English version: 'Planning Frenzy: Forced Labour, Expulsion and Genocide as Elements of Population Economics in German South West Africa', pp. 57–76 in this book).

[68] A direct continuity between the persons concerned can be proved only in individual cases. However, there are numerous other channels of reception through which this knowledge of the practice of dominance were transmitted, such as, for example, personal experience, institutional memory and the collective imagination. I have sketched this out in: Zimmerer, "Geburt des 'Ostlandes'" (English version: "The Birth of the 'Ostland'", pp. 230–261 in this book).

basis for the comparative investigation of foreign rule across the centuries and across continents would make a valuable contribution to overcoming the Eurocentric constriction of the term 'colonial rule'. Put into practice consistently, this would fulfil a central demand of the representatives of post-colonial studies, who have long pleaded for the history of colonial rule to be viewed not merely as a one-way street in which the non-European world was moulded in accordance with the European model and European concepts, but rather for it to be investigated how developments in Europe and overseas mutually influenced, spurred on and radicalised each other. To explore the paths that led from Windhoek to Warsaw, even if they did not necessarily all lead via Nuremberg, would not only link non-European and European history together, but would also help to prevent historiography from once again constructing an image of the colonial as existing in 'a special hermetic world', in "an exotic sphere all of its own".[69]

---

[69] A demand that this should be done has come recently from Jürgen Osterhammel: Jürgen Osterhammel, "Krieg im Frieden. Zu Form und Typologie imperialer Interventionen", in Jürgen Osterhammel, *Geschichtswissenschaft jenseits des Nationalstaats. Studien zu Beziehungsgeschichte und Zivilisationsvergleich*, Göttingen 2001, pp. 283–321, here p. 286.

The Birth of the *Ostland* out of the Spirit of Colonialism: A (Post-)colonial Perspective on the Nazi Policy of Conquest and Annihilation

> No doubt the temptation, and the danger, do exist that partial measures, such as the expansion of agricultural operations, the amalgamation of locations or the occasional creation of new settlements, will be adopted in an attempt to enlarge farming operations in line with German requirements (which is the way the farming community is being restructured throughout the entire area at present), or, in particular individual cases, by setting up new operations of sufficient size. But the result would be dubious in planning terms and culturally worthless, because in restructuring German territory we cannot follow in the footsteps of the Poles and base an area of German settlement on the Polish pattern of settlement and land division. Rather than taking such a half-hearted approach, a process of total colonisation is required, one that encompasses the entire area, redistributes it and resettles it in accordance with German conceptions. And it must be accepted as a side-effect that where necessary, so-called economic assets such as may have been created by investment in buildings and farm installations will have to be sacrificed in the higher interests of reshaping the area on definitively German lines.[1]

What Ewald Liedecke, the Nazis' chief state planning officer for East Prussia, set out on 1 September 1939, the day on which Germany invaded Poland, as being the fundamental principle according to which the not yet conquered territories in 'the East' were to be restructured, was destined to become one of the characteristic features of German rule in eastern Europe: the complete remodelling of the conquered territories in economic, political and demographic terms.[2] This, together with the inhuman exploitation of the local population, the brutal 'pacifica-

---

[1] Ewald Liedecke, *Kolonisatorische Aufgaben der Raum-Ordnung im Nordosten des Deutschen Reiches* (Königsberg 1.Sept.39), Manuscript BA, R 113/41, 'Streng vertraulich' ('Strictly confidential'), quoted according to Michael A. Hartenstein, *Neue Dorflandschaften. Nationalsozialistische Siedlungsplanung in den 'eingegliederten Ostgebieten' 1939 bis 1944*, Berlin 1998, p. 79.

[2] From among the abundance of the endless mass of literature on this subject, only a few of the more recent works can be mentioned here: Ulrich Herbert, ed., *Nationalsozialistische Vernichtungspolitik 1939–1945. Neue Forschungen und Kontroversen*, Frankfurt 1998; Götz Aly and Susanne Heim, 'Vordenker der Vernichtung'. *Auschwitz und die deutschen Pläne für eine neue europäische Ordnung*, Hamburg 1991; Götz Aly, '*Endlösung*'. *Völkerverschiebung und der Mord an den europäischen Juden*, Frankfurt 1995; Christian Gerlach, *Kalkulierte Morde. Die deutsche Wirtschafts- und Vernichtungspolitik in Weißrußland 1941–1944*, Hamburg 1999; Christian Gerlach, *Krieg, Ernährung, Völkermord. Forschungen zur deutschen Vernichtungspolitik im Zweiten Weltkrieg*, Hamburg 1998; Dieter Pohl, *Nationalsozialistische Judenverfolgung in Ostgalizien 1941–1944. Organisation und Durchführung eines staatlichen Massenverbrechens*, München 1996; Thomas Sandkühler, '*Endlösung*' *in Galizien. Der Judenmord in Ostpolen und die Rettungsinitiativen von Berthold Beitz*, Bonn

---

∂ Open Access. © 2024 the author(s), published by De Gruyter. This work is licensed under the Creative Commons Attribution 4.0 International License.
https://doi.org/10.1515/9783110754513-010

tion' policy and the genocide committed in the occupied territories, was a major cause of the catastrophic degree of destruction in 'the East'. Together with the size of the armies on both sides, the vastness of the conquered territories and the brutality of the fighting, these factors give the war of conquest and annihilation the appearance of something that had never been seen before.[3]

In White Russia (Belarus) alone, a quarter of the population died during the four years of German occupation, and 30 per cent were made homeless. The number of factories was reduced by 85 per cent and industrial capacity fell by 90 per cent. The quantity of livestock declined by 80 per cent, and the amount of arable land was almost halved. As Christian Gerlach has noted: "White Russia's economic development was set back by decades, and the region continued to bear the marks of war for a very long time."[4]

Statistics like these, and the degree of the suffering that lies behind them and that millions of people had to endure, are so inconceivable that they have led many to regard the war as having been a crime of apocalyptic dimensions, an unprecedented breach of taboo as compared with everything that had gone before it. By emphasising the uniqueness of the Nazi genocide, people feel that they are on the one hand demonstrating the degree of respect owed to the victims, while at the same time reducing the burden of guilt weighing upon their own history by identifying a defined period, a number of years of criminality, that can be excised from history like a cancerous growth. Perhaps what is at stake even more than the redemption of national history is the preservation of the grand universal historical narrative of the dawning, development and consummation of the Enlightenment and of modernity. Couching the debate in the language of the breach of taboos suggests that the crimes of National Socialism are separated from the modern tradition by an impenetrable wall.[5]

1996; Bernhard Chiari, *Alltag hinter der Front. Besatzung, Kollaboration und Widerstand in Weißrussland 1941–1944*, Düsseldorf 1998.

3 For an overview of the literature on the German war against the Soviet Union, see Rolf-Dieter Müller and Gerd Überschär, *Hitlers Krieg im Osten 1941–1945. Ein Forschungsbericht*, Darmstadt 2000.

4 Christian Gerlach, *Kalkulierte Morde. Die deutsche Wirtschafts- und Vernichtungspolitik in Weißrußland 1941–1944*, Hamburg 1999, p. 11.

5 The fateful relationship between Modernity and the Holocaust was gone into by Zygmunt Bauman: Zygmunt Bauman, *Modernity and the Holocaust*, Ithaca 1989; Zygmunt Bauman, *Modernity and Ambivalence*, Cambridge 1991. For an overview of the various interpretations see: A. Dirk Moses, "Structure and Agency in the Holocaust: Daniel J. Goldhagen and his Critics", *History and Theory*, 2 (1998), pp. 194–219. On the 'profound contradictions of modernity that made Auschwitz possible', see also Bartov's enlightening overview "Antisemitism, the Holocaust, and

At the same time, however, it increases the urgency of the question as to how such events could ever have come to pass; and above all as to how quite "ordinary men"[6] could be transformed into mass murderers, how they could be led to commit breaches of recognised taboos. But perhaps this is the wrong question to ask: perhaps the fundamental structures of the policies implemented between 1939/41 and 1944 were much more familiar to contemporaries than is generally appreciated.

The aim of this essay is not to equate German war crimes with those of earlier generations or other countries, and still less to weigh them up against those of others. Rather, it is to make the case that the Nazi atrocities required prior mental preparation: as is the case with the strategies and tactics of the Nazi manner of waging war,[7] so too the way the occupied territories were administered during the Second World War had its precursors. Revealing these does not exculpate the guilty in any way, but it does make an important contribution to explaining how such events could have come to happen, and why so many Germans condoned or accepted them, or at least raised no vocal opposition to them.

(Post-)Colonial Perspectives

The decisive factor in being able to identify precursors and the sources of ideas and traditions is where it is one is looking for them. And in this respect, the Eurocentric perspective of academic research has blocked its view in one crucial direction. Even simply the general use of the term 'occupation' is enough to reveal a constriction of the geographical outlook that obstructs the view of the global dimension of the events and structures, and so serves to avoid the need to use a term which, as is argued in the following text, would afford a better description of the aims and intentions of the National Socialists, namely 'colonial rule'.

Reinterpretations of National Socialism", in Omer Bartov, *Murder in Our Midst. The Holocaust, Industrial Killing and Representation*, New York 1996, pp. 53–70.

6 Christopher R. Browning, *Ordinary Men: Reserve Police Battalion 101 and the Final Solution in Poland*, London 2001.

7 With regard to this, refer to the conference series 'Total War', organized by Manfred F. Boemeke, Roger Chickering, Stig Förster and Jörg Nagler, which also explicitly attempts to explore the 'Road to Total War'. See the conference documentation: Stig Förster and Jörg Nagler, eds, *On the Road to Total War: The American Civil War and the German Wars of Unification, 1861–1871*, New York 1997; Manfred F. Boemeke, Roger Chickering and Stig Förster, eds, *Anticipating Total War. The German and American Experiences, 1871–1914*, Cambridge 1999; Roger Chickering and Stig Förster, eds, *Great War – Total War, Combat and Mobilization on the Western Front, 1914–1918*, Cambridge 2000.

The term 'occupation' is used to refer to a situation in which, generally in the course of military conflict, foreign troops come to be stationed in conquered territories. In order to secure the territory, the conqueror will establish an administrative machinery above, alongside or in place of the established local administration. The latter will then be more or less thoroughly restructured and adapted to meet the victor's needs. But fundamentally, in the eyes of both the occupiers and the occupied, it will be a matter of rule by foreign outsiders only for a limited period of time. A second term for this, alongside 'occupation', is 'colonial rule': although this does not always denote the outcome of military conflict, it too indicates, in common with 'occupation', the existence of a foreign administration. But the difference is that in this case there is no time limit on such foreign rule, or at least, if there is it will not be reached until a very long time in the future. The aims associated with colonial rule are longer term, and generally – intentionally or unintentionally – lead to a profound political, economic and social restructuring of the subjugated communities.

Under the prevailing linguistic convention, the difference between colonial rule and military occupation is clearly defined. The first term is applied in respect of lands and territories outside Europe; where Europe is concerned 'occupation' is the preferred term. Whereas the former encompasses as an ideological basis the concept of a civilising mission, often allied to a sense of racial superiority, the latter is based – at least officially – on military exigences and events. This, however, not only perpetuates the distinction that prevails on all sides between developments within Europe and those outside it, but also deprives research of a useful perspective from which to investigate the development of the ideas that lie at the root of both European military history and of the history of foreign occupation during the Second World War.

For if one considers the changes mentioned above – whether they were actually implemented or were only prospective – that the Nazis envisaged carrying out in the territories of the Soviet Union in particular, it becomes clear that they amounted fundamentally to the imposition of colonial rule. As defined all-embracingly by Wolfgang Reinhard, the latter is "the control exercised by one nation over another, foreign, nation, exploiting the differences in their levels of economic, political and ideological development".[8] If this formulation is broadened to include also 'intentional' developmental differences, i.e. the creation of such differences where they had not previously existed, in order to deliberately maintain a state of underdevel-

---

8 Wolfgang Reinhard, *Kleine Geschichte des Kolonialismus*, Stuttgart 1996, p. 1. He himself, however, did not have Nazi policies in Eastern Europe in mind either.

opment in certain territories and their inhabitants, then the definition will also embrace the intentions of Nazi policy in 'the East'.

If consistently and thoroughly implemented, an investigation of the colonial elements in Nazi rule also meets one of the central demands of postcolonial studies, whose proponents argue that colonial history should not be regarded as a one-way street in which the non-European world was shaped in accordance with European models and ideas, but rather that developments inside and outside Europe should be examined for evidence that they mutually influenced, drove forward and radicalised each other.[9] This approach not only reveals links between non-European and European history, but also does away with the impression that the colonial existed in "a special hermetic world", that constituted an "exotic sphere all of its own",[10] the persistence of which is doubtless a shortcoming of the studies so far undertaken from a postcolonial point of view. What Jürgen Osterhammel has recently claimed with regards to the history of international relations can be formulated for topics such as war, violence, power, domination and state administration: they are still mostly ignored. But however important works on the history of consumerism and the like may be (these being topics that postcolonial studies prefer to concern themselves with, to the extent that they depart at all from the sphere of the imaginations and discourses, the interactions and repercussions of colonialism are by no means restricted to (everyday) cultural factors.

In this article, therefore, I will attempt to set out on a search for traces in the fields of the history of ideas, administration and military activities, from which parallels can be drawn between the concept of 'occupation' as associated with the Nazis on the one hand, and European colonial rule on the other, and to analyse the National Socialist regime in eastern Europe using the tools of colonial historiography. I am not concerned to reconstruct in detail German occupation policy in any

---

[9] For an introduction to this complex of problems, see Bill Ashcroft, Gareth Griffith and Helen Tiffin, *Key Concepts in Post-Colonial Studies*, London 1998; Dane Kennedy, "Imperial History and Post-Colonial Theory", *Journal of Imperial and Commonwealth History (1996)*, pp. 345–363; Patrick Wolfe, "History and Imperialism. A Century of Theory, from Marx to Postcolonialism", *American Historical Review*, 102/2 (1997), pp. 388–420. The first steps towards applying this research programme to Germany are being taken by Sebastian Conrad, Andreas Eckert and Albert Wirz: Sebastian Conrad, "Doppelte Marginalisierung. Plädoyer für eine transnationale Perspektive auf die deutsche Geschichte", in *Geschichte und Gesellschaft 28*, (2002), pp. 145–169; Andreas Eckert and Albert Wirz, "'Wir nicht, die Anderen auch.' Deutschland und der Kolonialismus", in Sebastian Conrad and Shalini Randeria, eds, *Jenseits des Eurozentrismus. Postkoloniale Perspektiven in den Geschichts- und Kulturwissenschaften*, Frankfurt 2002, pp.372–392.

[10] Jürgen Osterhammel, "Krieg im Frieden. Zu Form und Typologie imperialer Interventionen", in Jürgen Osterhammel, *Geschichtswissenschaft jenseits des Nationalstaats. Studien zu Beziehungsgeschichte und Zivilisationsvergleich*, Göttingen 2001, pp. 283–321, here p. 286.

specific region. Rather, I seek to reveal fundamental structures of dominance, exploitation and murder. Examples are therefore chosen from diverse locations and from different phases of the German occupation. My focus is on the German administration in eastern Europe, or more precisely in Poland and parts of the Soviet Union. The German occupation of western Europe is not covered by this study, as its practices differed, in some respects substantially, from what happened in 'the East'. The extent to which colonial structures might also be found to have existed in occupied western Europe would be the subject of a separate investigation.[11]

But the German occupation of eastern Europe was not static either: the face it presented when the war began in Poland was different from what was apparent after the Battle of Stalingrad, to name just two dates at random. In order to focus on the similarities between colonialism and National Socialism that are of interest here, I will analyse the nature of the governmental and administrative utopia[12] that motivated and legitimised the actions taken in both cases, while leaving the situational context aside. In a first step I will point out structural similarities between the historical phenomena of colonialism and of the Nazi policies of conquest and rule, in order then to illustrate this through examples such as the 'society of racial privilege', the utopian pursuit of infrastructure projects, and the practice of the war of annihilation. In a third section I will then put forward some considerations on the transmission of colonial ideas, motifs and concepts. Since the ideas presented here are not to be understood as being conclusive remarks, the whole will remain deliberately lightly sketched.

Amazingly, right down to this day not a single systematic study of the relationship between colonialism and National Socialism has been undertaken,[13]

---

[11] In his recent publication of the 'Stuckart Memorandum' of 14 June 1940 on German plans for redrawing the western border with France, Peter Schöttler has pointed out that there were also plans for partition and resettlement on a major scale in respect of western Europe. Peter Schöttler, "Eine Art 'Generalplan West'. Die Stuckart-Denkschrift vom 14. Juni 1940 und die Planungen für eine neue deutsch-französische Grenze im Zweiten Weltkrieg", *Sozial.Geschichte. Zeitschrift für historische Analyse des 20. und 21. Jahrhunderts* 3 (2003), pp. 83–131.

[12] For an explanation of this concept see Trutz von Trotha, *Koloniale Herrschaft. Zur soziologischen Theorie der Staatsentstehung am Beispiel des 'Schutzgebietes Togo'*, Tübingen 1994, p. 12. I have made use of the concept myself in Zimmerer, Jürgen, *Deutsche Herrschaft über Afrikaner. Staatlicher Machtanspruch und Wirklichkeit im kolonialen Namibia*, Münster/Hamburg/London 2001 (English edition: *German Rule, African Subjects. State Aspirations and the Reality of Power in Colonial Namibia*, New York 2021).

[13] Established experts on colonialism are apparently not interested in the crimes of the Nazis and prefer to leave these to those engaged in German or eastern European history, whereas researchers into National Socialism, accustomed as they are to dealing with huge armies, victims and perpetrators numbered in their millions, and the way modern states wage war against each other, seem for a long time not to have taken the colonial conquest of the world seriously. Al-

even though Hannah Arendt raised this as an issue no less than fifty years ago.[14] At most, there are some publications that comment on Hitler's 'colonialistic' plans

---

though Mark Mazower claimed that the reason the Europeans were so enormously outraged by the Nazis was because they treated Europeans like 'Natives', he does not explore this connection systematically. Cf. Mark Mazower, *Dark Continent. Europe's Twentieth Century*, London 1998, p. xiii. In this work he follows the positions adopted at an early date by postcolonial authors such as Aimé Césaire or Franz Fanon, who saw in Fascism a form of colonialism turned inwards. On Césaire, see David Furber, *'Going East': Colonialism and German Life in Nazi-Occupied Poland*, Dissertation, University of New York in Buffalo 2003, pp. 5f. On Fanon, see Robert Young, *White Mythologies. Writing History and the West*, London/New York 1990, pp. 7f. The postulation of a connection between colonial mass murders and the Holocaust that has achieved the widest currency so far is that of Sven Lindqvist; but as neither his portrayal of European colonialism nor that of the German policy of annihilation in eastern Europe goes beyond simplistic descriptions, the questions he poses are more significant than his answers: Sven Lindqvist, *Exterminate all the Brutes*, translated from the Swedish by Joan Tate, London 1997. Much the same applies to Ward Churchill, who even speaks of the National Socialists imitating the colonial conquest of North America: Ward Churchill, *A Little Matter of Genocide: Holocaust and Denial in the Americas, 1492 to the Present*, San Francisco 1997. This thesis is one that Richard L. Rubinstein had already outlined as early as 1987: cf. Richard L. Rubinstein, "Afterword: Genocide and Civilization", in Isidor Wallimann and Michael N. Dobkowski, *Genocide and the Modern Age: Etiology and Case Studies of Mass Death*, 2nd edn, Syracuse 2000, pp. 283–298, here p. 288. The fact that the importance of the colonial experience for the history of European violence was gradually discovered in the course of the twentieth century is demonstrated by, among others, the recently published books by Dan Diner and Volker Berghahn, in which at least a few remarks are devoted to the role of colonialism as a precursor to Europe's history of violence in the twentieth century. Dan Diner, *Das Jahrhundert verstehen. Eine universalhistorische Deutung*, München 1999; Volker Berghahn, *Europa im Zeitalter der Weltkriege. Die Entfesselung und Entgrenzung der Gewalt*, Frankfurt 2002.
14 Hannah Arendt, *The Origins of Totalitarianism*, New York 1951. This is also postulated by Eckert and Wirz, "Wir nicht, die Anderen auch", p. 385, who pose the question: 'Why has the expansionism in eastern Europe, which had been discussed and put into practice since the nineteenth century, so far scarcely been interpreted as a part of German colonialism?' How fruitful the application of the conceptual instruments of colonial history to the Nazi occupation of eastern Europe can be is demonstrated by David Furber in bis recently completed doctoral thesis *Going East*. In his account of everyday life under German rule and those who upheld it, particularly the lower and middle levels of officialdom, Furber makes an important contribution to an understanding of how the German civil administrators organized their lives in 'the East', what the motivation was that drove them to make themselves available for this task, and what strategies they invoked to derive meaningfulness from their activities. These did indeed demonstrate considerable congruences with the colonial experiences of people of other nationalities in the African and Asian colonies. However, my approach goes farther than this, since I deliberately extend my analysis to include population economics, the war of annihilation and genocide, these being areas in which many people see the decisive characteristics of Nazi rule over eastern Europe. In addition, I attempt to put names to concrete channels of reception for colonial fantasies and conceptions.

for the East; but in these cases the notion of 'colonising' is mainly used as a synonym for 'settlement', without any real comparison being undertaken.[15]

At the time, however, people certainly understood 'colonialism' to mean more than simply Germans setttling there; they were thoroughly aware of the parallels between German plans and the colonial empires of history. To Hitler, the parallels were obvious:

> The struggle for hegemony in the world will be decided in favour of Europe by the possession of Russia; this will make Europe the place that is more secure against blockade than anywhere else in the world. [...] The Slavic peoples on the other hand are not destined to lead independent lives of their own. [...] The territory of Russia is our India, and just as the English rule India with only a handful of people, so too we will govern this colonial territory of ours. We will supply the Ukrainians with headscarves, glass bead necklaces as jewellery, and all the other things that appeal to colonial peoples. [...] In any case, my goals are not immoderate; basically these are all areas that were previously settled by Germanic peoples. The German *Volk* is to expand, to grow into this territory.[16]

Obviously, Hitler's use of the word 'colonial' is not enough in itself to demonstrate Nazism's structural similarity to colonialism. Nevertheless, the quotation contains references to the two concepts that stand at the centre of both National Socialism and colonialism and also serve to link the two: namely 'race' and 'space'.

The Reordering of the World

Any enquiry into the concepts that represented the foundations on which the various aspects of the Nazi regime in eastern Europe were built – the war of annihilation, the policy of occupation and the genocide – inevitably leads one to the ideas of 'race' and 'space'. In the National Socialists' view of history and society, the *Volk* – the nation or the people – was understood as an organic entity whose preservation and expansion had to be secured by any means. But what this *Volk*, whose greatness was measured by the number of its 'racially pure' members,

---

[15] On the synonymous use of the words 'colonial' and 'settlement', see for example Lower's interesting article on the Hegewald Project, Himmler's showpiece project in the field of active settlement policy: Wendy Lower, "A New Ordering of Space and Race: Nazi Colonial Dreams in Zhytomyr, Ukraine, 1941–1944", *German Studies Review* 25 (2002), pp. 227–254. On the same subject, Hillgruber had already written that the Nazis had intended to reduce large parts of eastern Europe to the status of colonies, with the aim of exploiting and resettling them. Cf. Andreas Hillgruber, *Hitlers Strategie. Politik und Kriegführung 1940–1941*, München 1982, p. 567.
[16] Hitler, 17 September 1941, in Adolf Hitler, *Monologe im Führerhauptquartier*, ed. Werner Jochmann Hamburg 1980, pp. 60–64.

lacked above all was sufficient *Lebensraum* – 'living space' or 'territory'. Thus the concept of 'space' was directly linked to the ideology of 'race'. It encompassed ideas both of economic self-sufficiency and of settlement of the occupied areas by *Volksgenossen* (i.e. ethnically 'pure' Germans).[17]

Both concepts, ethnicity and territory, or 'race' and 'space', were also at the heart of colonialism. Colonial empires – and sometimes even individual colonies – formed unified economic systems stretching over vast areas (*Grossraumökonomie*), and were characterised by their efforts to take possession of and develop a more than merely sizeable area of dependent territory. A vital element in enabling the colonial powers to exercise control over such territories was the assumption that the relationship with the local inhabitants would not entail any partnership as between equals, but rather the subjugation, or on occasion even the annihilation, of the original inhabitants. This policy was motivated and also justified by racism, i.e. by the division of humankind into the categories of superior races, destined to rule, and lower races, destined to be subjugated by them. At the lowest end of this scale were groups that were considered to be doomed to destruction, or that were to be deliberately murdered.[18]

Of course, European colonialism experienced various stages of development and assumed different forms in the course of its five-hundred-year history.[19] Even the justifications for European expansion and rule over the indigenous populations of the newly 'discovered' and conquered territories changed.[20] But whether it was a question of missionary endeavours to convert the 'heathen', of the 'White Man's Burden' or the 'Manifest Destiny': even if there were shifts in the forms of legitimation, an emphasis on the correctness of one's own beliefs or on one's own status as

---

17 On racism as an element uniting the divergent aspects of Nazi ideology, see Michael Burleigh and Wolfgang Wippermann, *The Racial State. Germany 1933–1945*, Cambridge 1991; and on planning policy for the reorganization of large areas of territory, with the associated 'economy of annihilation', see Aly and Heim, *Vordenker der Vernichtung*, and Aly, *'Final Solution': Nazi Population Policy and the Murder of the European Jews*, London/New York 1999.
18 For a more extensive treatment of this topic, see Jürgen Zimmerer, "Colonialism and the Holocaust. Towards an Archeology of Genocide", in A. Dirk Moses, ed.: *Genocide and Settler Society: Frontier Violence and Stolen Indigenous Children in Australia*, New York 2004, pp. 49–76 (a revised english version appears on pp. 125–153 in this book). Todorov too points out the importance of the construct of inequality between colonizers and the colonized in the mass murder of the latter: Tzvetan Todorov, *Die Eroberung Amerikas. Das Problem des Anderen*, Frankfurt 1985, p. 177.
19 For an initial overview of colonial history see: Jürgen Osterhammel, *Kolonialismus. Geschichte, Formen, Folgen*, München 1995; Reinhard, *Kleine Geschichte des Kolonialismus*.
20 The use of terms like 'Europeans', 'colonists' etc. is not intended to obscure the fact that that these do not refer to homogeneous groups of people, all with the same aims and interests. On this, see the instructive article by Ann Laura Stoler, "Rethinking colonial categories: European communities and the boundaries of rule", *Comparative Studies in Society and History*, 31 (1989), pp. 134–161.

a recipient of divine favour was always the ideological prerequisite for colonial conquest and expansion. Genuine equality seldom existed between Europeans and the indigenous population. It is true that the content and meaning of these notions varied, but the important element in this context is the underlying 'structure of asymmetrical argumentation', as Reinhart Koselleck, for example, has pointed out: Hellenes/barbarians, Christians/heathens, superhuman/subhuman, human/nonhuman, culminating in the purely formal distinction of friend/enemy, as formulated by Carl Schmitt.[21] Postcolonial theorists have emphasised that this binary encoding of the world is the central prerequisite for any form of colonial domination.[22] It homogenises the fundamentally disparate groups of both the rulers and the ruled, and at the same time creates a distance between the two groups, a distance that is necessary for the asymmetrical exercise of power by the colonisers.[23]

In the course of the nineteenth century, the spread of the influence of Social Darwinism gave rise to a direct emphasis on notions of hierarchy and competition between nations, not only as between the colonial masters and the colonised, but also as between the colonial powers themselves. This 'biologistic' interpretation of world history, the belief in the need to secure sufficient space to ensure one's own people's survival, is one of the fundamental parallels between colonialism and Nazi expansionist policies.[24]

The colonial territories won by 'discovery' and conquest then had to be developed and 'civilised': for in the perception of the colonisers they were savage, cha-

---

[21] On this, see Reinhart Koselleck, "Zur historisch-politischen Semantik asymmetrischer Gegenbegriffe", in Reinhart Koselleck, *Vergangene Zukunft. Zur Semantik geschichtlicher Zeiten*, Frankfurt 1989, pp. 211–259.
[22] For an introduction to this concept, see the article on 'binarism' in Bill Ashcroft, Gareth Griffin and Helen Tiffin, *Key Concepts*, pp. 23–27.
[23] Furber shows how it was the German occupiers who, by emphasizing a common German heritage and the colonial task facing them in 'the East', actually created distance between themselves and the Poles, to whom they were fundamentally more similar than they liked to admit. Furber, *Colonialism*. There can be no doubt that this colonization of 'the Other' through discourse, like that of the conquered territories themselves, presents an important parallel to colonial rule outside Europe.
[24] Similar conclusions can be found in Woodruff D. Smith, *The Ideological Origins of Nazi Imperialism*, Oxford 1986; see also Charles Reynolds, *Modes of Imperialism*, Oxford 1981, pp. 124–171. Ehmann too points to the connection – also through specific people involved – between colonial and Nazi racism: Annegret Ehmann, "Rassistische und antisemitische Traditionslinien in der deutschen Geschichte des 19. und 20. Jahrhunderts", in Sportmuseum Berlin, ed., *Sportstadt Berlin in Geschichte und Gegenwart. Jahrbuch 1993 des Sportmuseums Berlin*, Berlin 1993, pp. 131–145. Kundrus recently attempted to refute any relation between colonial and Nazi racial policy in Birthe Kundrus, "Von Windhoek nach Nürnberg? Koloniale Mischehenverbote und die nationalsozialistische Rassengesetzgebung", in Birthe Kundrus, ed., *Phantasiereiche. Zur Kulturgeschichte des deutschen Kolonialismus*, Frankfurt 2003, pp. 110–131. Her argumentation is not wholly con-

otic and dangerous.[25] Particularly in the settler colonies the land was regarded as being 'unpopulated',[26] and the settlers believed they were entitled to transform it according to their own ideas, bringing order to 'chaos' without paying any regard to indigenous communities and economies. Towns were established, roads and later railways were constructed, and the land was surveyed and recorded in an orderly fashion in land registers.[27]

Similarly, the Nazi conquerors regarded 'the East' as a vast *tabula rasa* that needed to be recreated according to their own conceptions, as an arena in which regional developers, demographers, engineers and economic planners could give free rein to their imaginations. One only needs to think of the megalomaniac plans for the building of an autobahn network reaching deep into Asia, with *Germania*, the new capital of the Reich, at its hub.[28]

Even in their own descriptions of the situation they found in eastern Europe, the German conquerors drew on colonial history as a point of reference. For example, as a member of the German 12th Airborne Regiment reported only a few weeks after the attack on the Soviet Union:

> Marvellous as the successes are, great as the advance is [...], Russia on the whole is still a huge disappointment for the individual. There is nothing of culture, nothing of paradise [...] but

---

vincing, however, because the alleged openness and heterogeneity of the colonial discourse in imperial Germany on which she bases her argument was, if it existed at all, only apparent. In the hegemonial discourse as it was also reflected in the practice of colonial rule no such openness existed.

25 See for example Albert Wirz, "Missionare im Urwald, verängstigt und hilflos: Zur symbolischen Topografie des kolonialen Christentums", in Wilfried Wagner, ed., *Kolonien und Missionen*, Hamburg 1994, pp. 39–56; Johannes Fabian, *Out of Our Minds: Reason and Madness in the Exploration of Central Africa*, Los Angeles 2000.

26 See for example John K. Noyes, *Colonial Space. Spatiality in the Discourse of German South West Africa 1884–1915*, Chur 1992.

27 On the aspect of the ordering of the American West, which was perceived as a featureless ocean that first had to be surveyed in order to be given structure, see Stefan Kaufmann, "Naturale Grenzfelder des Sozialen. Landschaft und Körper", in Monika Fludernik and Hans-Joachim Gehrke, eds, *Grenzgänger zwischen Kulturen*, Würzburg 1999, pp. 121–136. On the German tradition of exploration of the world, see Dirk van Laak, *Imperiale Infrastruktur. Deutsche Planungen für eine Erschließung Afrikas 1880 bis 1960*, Paderborn 2004.

28 On the issue of research relating to eastern Europe and spatial planning there, see: Bruno Wasser, *Himmlers Raumplanung im Osten*, Basel 1993; Mechthild Rössler, 'Wissenschaft und Lebensraum'. *Geographische Ostforschung im Nationalsozialismus. Ein Beitrag zur Disziplingeschichte der Geographie*, Berlin 1990; Michael Burleigh, *Germany turns Eastwards. A Study of Ostforschung in the Third Reich*, Cambridge 1988; Mechthild Rössler and Sabine Schleiermacher, eds, *Der 'Generalplan Ost'*, Berlin 1993; Czeslaw Madajczyk, ed, *Vom Generalplan Ost zum Generalsiedlungsplan*, München 1994; Aly and Heim, *Vordenker der Vernichtung*; Aly, *Endlösung*.

only the absolute depths, filth, people who demonstrate to us that we will face a huge task of colonisation here.[29]

The perception of conditions as being "primitive, barren and backward",[30] which Christian Gerlach has found to underlie many accounts relating to White Russia (Belarus), meant that from the German point of view there was a need for the whole country to be comprehensively modernised and reorganised, without any regard for its existing social, political and economic structures. And it was precisely this comprehensive reorganisation that was interpreted by those involved in it as colonisation.

But the sense of entitlement to rule over the conquered territories was derived not only from their underdevelopment, but also from the supposed backwardness and immaturity of the inhabitants. According to Hitler, one "only needed to see this primeval world" (*"Urwelt"*) in order to appreciate "that nothing happens here if one does not assign people the work they have to do. The Slav is a born slave, they are a mass crying out for a master."[31] And Himmler's secretary Hanns Johst, who travelled through Poland with the *Reichsführer SS* during the winter of 1939/40, was no doubt reflecting his boss's ideas as well when he wrote:

> The Poles are not a state-building people. They lack even the most basic prerequisites. I have travelled all over the country at the side of the *Reichsführer* SS. A country which has so little feeling for the essence of settlement that it is not even up to the task of creating a village of any style has no claim to any sort of independent political status within Europe. It is a country crying out to be colonised[32]

Similarly, African and American 'Natives' were deemed to be devoid of any capacity for state-building and, thus, for having their own history. Since they – in contrast to the image of the Slavic peoples prevailing in the Third Reich – were at least in theory ascribed the ability to undergo development, they were imagined as being like children, needing a master, a guardian to look after them. Or as Hegel formulated it,

> The Negro, as has already been observed, represents natural man in his completely wild and untamed state. [...] It is the lack of self-control that is typical of the Negro character. This condition is not susceptible to any development or education, and as we see them today, so they have always been. [...] Africa [...] plays no part in the history of the world; it

---

29 A serviceman of the 12th Airborne Regiment, 20 July 1941, quoted according to Gerlach, *Kalkulierte Morde*, p. 102.
30 Ibid.
31 Hitler, 17 September 1941, quoted according to Adolf Hitler: *Monologe im Führerhauptquartier. Die Aufzeichnungen Heinrich Heims*, ed. Werner Jochmann, Hamburg 1980, p. 63.
32 Hanns Johst, *Ruf des Reiches: Echo des Volkes!*, München 1940 p. 94, quoted according to: Michael Burleigh, *Die Zeit des Nationalsozialismus. Eine Gesamtdarstellung*, Frankfurt 2000, p. 515.

cannot exhibit any forward movement or development. [...] What we properly understand by Africa is the state of being without history, without development, of still being completely captive to its purely natural conditions, and which here merely had to be presented as standing on the threshold of World History.[33]

Thus the ideology of the European civilising mission could be used as an all-embracing justification for not only the conquest and colonisation of foreign peoples, but also for their exploitation, for example through forced labour. Accordingly, the French, on taking over Togo from the Germans who had introduced 'tax labour' there, that is to say forced labour in lieu of the payment of tax due, regarded this measure as a positive one, in view, among other things, of the fact that the Africans needed a 'firm hand':

> Tax labour is necessary, even indispensable [...] Besides the material advantages it offers a further significant moral benefit. The Native, who has always lived under the care of somebody else, [...] needs to have the feeling that he is under the care of capable and sensible people, of a just and benevolent administration that will watch over him and his people and protect him from 'rogues' and 'villains'; and this moral and political benefit of tax labour is rendered effective precisely by the opportunity it gives the administrative officers to let the Natives experience the efficiency with which they go about their work, and to make contact at least once a year with those groups of the population still living in very remote areas.[34]

The parallels with colonialism are not, however, limited to ideological justifications of conquest and rule, but are also evident in its very practice. In the colonies, a small elite of colonial administrators and military officers ruled over a much larger indigenous population that had barely any opportunity to participate in the political system.[35] The colonisers and the colonised lived under two different legal systems, to one or the other of which one was assigned on the criterion of racial identity.[36] The influence of colonial images on Nazi occupation policy is demonstrated for example by the fact that the *Ostministerium* (Ministry for the

---

[33] Georg Wilhelm Friedrich Hegel, *The Philosophy of History*, translated from the German by J. Sibree, New York 1956, pp. 93, 98f.
[34] Captain Sicre, 'Monographie du cercle de Sokode', 29 September 1918, quoted according to Trutz von Trotha, *Koloniale Herrschaft*, p. 358.
[35] The settler colonies form an exception, since alongside the state officials they attracted an ever-expanding population of 'White' settlers, which shifted the balance of numbers. But the fact that the indigenous population generally enjoyed scarcely any opportunities to be involved in political processes applies to these colonies as well.
[36] See the contributions in Rüdiger Voigt, ed., *Das deutsche Kolonialrecht als Vorstufe einer globalen 'Kolonialisierung' von Recht und Verwaltung*, Baden-Baden 2001.

East) in Berlin was described as a 'territorial ministry' explicitly modelled on the British India Office.[37]

Preferential treatment within this 'society of racial privilege'[38] did not, however, arise solely out of the formal colonial legal system. The *situation coloniale* was evident in all areas of social interaction between colonisers and colonised. Europeans were advantaged everywhere and all the time; they had their own schools and kindergartens as well as separate counters at post offices and other public offices. In German South West Africa, for example, this permanent symbolic subjection was expressed in the fact that Africans were not allowed to ride horses, were forced to salute all Whites and were forbidden to walk on the footpath. In occupied Poland too, Poles had to display appropriate humility before all Germans by making way for them on footpaths, raising their hats and saluting. They were banned from attending cinemas, concerts, exhibitions, libraries, museums or theatres; nor were they permitted to own bicycles, cameras or radios.[39] Fundamentally, it is this concept of a 'society of racial privilege' that also underpins the following statement of Hitler's: "Our Germans – this is the main thing – must form a closed community, like a fortress; outside the main centres, even the lowest stable boy must stand above any of the natives."[40] This, of course, applied only to that part of the indigenous population that was recognised as enjoying any right to live at all.

Although the 'Natives' of eastern Europe were socially and legally divided off from the Germans, in their function as workers they were integrated into the economy of the Third Reich; indeed, the potential as labour that they embodied was the basis of their right to go on living.[41] Here, too, there are colonial precedents. The enslavement of millions of Africans and their transportation to America and the Caribbean stands out as the most obvious precursor to the National Socialists' forced labour system. No doubt it would be too much of an oversimpli-

---

[37] This is an assessment drawn from the *Reichspropagandaministerium* in Chef Sipo/SD, Command Staff, Information Sheet No. 3 (undated, 1942), Federal Archives Military Archives Freiburg SF-01/28985, sheet 142; quoted according to Gerlach, *Kalkulierte Morde*, p. 157.
[38] With regard to this concept, see Zimmerer, *Deutsche Herrschaft über Afrikaner*, pp. 94–109 (English edition: *German Rule, African Subjects,* New York 2021 pp. 111–126).
[39] Burleigh, *The Third Reich*, pp. 450f. On the *'situation coloniale'*, see Furber, *Going East*.
[40] Hitler, 17 September 1941, in Hitler, Monologe, p. 62f.
[41] On the system of forced labour see, in addition to Ulrich Herbert's classic study *Hitler's Foreign Workers: Enforced Foreign Labor in Germany under the Third Reich,* Cambridge 1997, and also the following: Mark Spoerer, *Zwangsarbeit unter dem Hakenkreuz. Ausländische Zivilarbeiter, Kriegsgefangene und Häftlinge im Deutschen Reich und im besetzten Europa 1939–1945,* Stuttgart/München 2001; Jan Erik Schulte, *Zwangsarbeit und Vernichtung: Das Wirtschaftsimperium der SS. O. Pohl und das SS-Wirtschafts-Verwaltungshauptamt 1933–1945,* Paderborn 2001.

fication to see in colonialism only a way to get hold of 'Native' labour; the indigenous population also played the roles of potential soldiers, possible consumers of European goods, or objects of missionary endeavour; but nevertheless, a variety of forms of forced labour and the recruiting of workers for the benefit of the colonial economy are factors that consistently accompany the history of European domination of large parts of the earth from 1492 onwards.[42]

And precisely in the case of German colonial rule in South West Africa, the paradigmatic case linking colonialism and National Socialism,[43] this aspect plays a central role. One should not be deceived by the degree of bureaucratisation accompanying the Nazis' mobilisation of labour resources: labour recruitment procedures in the colonies too could be legally highly formalised.[44] In German occupied Russia, by contrast, workers were procured by being actually hunted down,[45] in a manner that rather evokes associations with the Congo.[46]

The idea that land and land use could be remodelled ad lib. corresponded to the way the indigenous peoples were deprived of their rights and suffered degradation, right down to the level of being a disposable mass which could be made use of in the interests of the colonial masters.[47] If the 'Natives' could not be uti-

---

[42] See the thematic number *'Menschenhandel und erzwungene Arbeit'* (ed. Michael Mann), of the periodical *Comparativ*, 4 (2003).

[43] On the concept of the 'semi-free labour market' planned for South West Africa, which was based on a compulsion to take employment, see Zimmerer, *Deutsche Herrschaft über Afrikaner*, pp. 126–175 (English edition: *German Rule, African Subjects*, New York 2021, pp. 159–210). The link between German colonial rule in South West Africa and the Third Reich had already been touched on by Horst Drechsler, *Südwestafrika unter deutscher Kolonialherrschaft. Der Kampf der Herero und Nama gegen den deutschen Imperialismus 1884–1915*, 2nd edn, Berlin 1984; Helmut Bley, *Kolonialherrschaft und Sozialstruktur in Deutsch-Südwestafrika 1894–1914*, Hamburg 1968; Henning Melber, "Kontinuitäten totaler Herrschaft. Völkermord und Apartheid in Deutsch-Südwestafrika", *Jahrbuch für Antisemitismusforschung*, 1 (1992), pp. 91–116.

[44] In German South West Africa, for example, an attempt was made to erect a system of total control and mobilization that was probably unique in the history of colonialism: one based on the idea that the indigenous population should be made totally available for the benefit of the colonial state. On this, see Jürgen Zimmerer, "Der totale Überwachungsstaat? Recht und Verwaltung in Deutsch-Südwestafrika", in Voigt, ed., *Das deutsche Kolonialrecht*, pp. 175–198 (English version: "Total Control? Law and Administration in German South West Africa", pp. 77–103 in this book).

[45] For examples of this kind of forced recruiting, see Burleigh, *The Third Reich* pp. 551–554.

[46] Adam Hochschild, *Schatten über dem Kongo. Die Geschichte eines der großen fast vergessenen Menschheitsverbrechen*, Stuttgart 2000, pp. 165–199.

[47] In respect of German South West Africa, I have described this in greater detail in Jürgen Zimmerer, "Der Wahn der Planbarkeit: Vertreibung, unfreie Arbeit und Völkermord als Elemente der Bevölkerungsökonomie in Deutsch-Südwestafrika", *Comparativ*, 4 (2003) (English version: "Planning Frenzy: Forced Labour, Expulsion and Genocide as Elements of Population Economics in German South West Africa", pp. 57–76 in this book).

lised in this way where they had originally lived, or if their labour was not required there, the colonial rulers showed from very early on that where it was a matter of fulfilling their own economic requirements they had no scruples about resettling them in reservations or expelling them completely from the territory occupied by the colonisers. Whether it was the reservations for indigenous peoples in North America or the reservations in South West Africa: what they all had in common was that people who had come to be regarded as being out of place in the new – colonial – society were simply removed from its territory, the area it was planned to resettle them in consisting almost without exception of unproductive land.[48] The fact that the German plans for eastern Europe, albeit on a much larger scale, also assumed that millions of people would be resettled, and that Jews of all people were herded together in 'reservations', represents a continuation of this tradition. At any rate, the fact that the policy of establishing reservations was familiar as a more or less 'normal' way of dealing with 'Natives' in all probability contributed to the failure of the German perpetrators to fully register the extent of the criminal nature of the policies being implemented.[49]

Traditions of the 'War of Annihilation'

But parallels with colonialism, in particular with German colonialism, are not only to be found in the 'civil' aspects of the Nazi occupation of the East. They are also evident in the war of conquest and in the 'pacification' conflicts themselves. If one uncovers the structures, i.e. the tactics, lying behind modern weaponry with its armadas of tanks and aircraft, it will be found that the 'war of annihilation' displays features that are clearly reminiscent of colonial wars, of "war(s) of destruction", including the "campaign[s] of annihilation"[50] such as were also waged by the German *Schutztruppe*, the colonial army. For although the war

---

48 A brief overview of cases of resettlement in North Amerika is given by Jürgen Heideking, *Geschichte der USA*, 2nd edn, Tübingen 1999, pp. 137–139 and 193–196. An overview of the policy of reservations in South West Africa under South African rule is given by Jan-Bart Gewald, *'We Thought we Would be Free ...'. Socio-Cultural Aspects of Herero History in Namibia 1915–1940*, Köln 2000, pp. 36–65.
49 Gerlach argues similarly when he puts forward the thesis that the so-called territorial plans resulted in a gradual radicalisation. Christian Gerlach, 'Nachwort' in *Krieg, Ernährung, Völkermord*, p. 262.
50 These expressions stem from Eduard von Liebert, who used them to describe the tactic of destroying the essentials for life employed by the *Schutztruppe* in its fight against the Wahehe in German East Africa: Eduard von Liebert, *Neunzig Tage im Zelt. Meine Reise nach Uhehe Juni bis September 1897*, Berlin 1898, p. 33, quoted according to Thomas Morlang, "'Die Kerls haben ja nicht einmal Gewehre.' Der

against the Soviet Union was, on the formal level, a 'normal' war between European powers, in fact it was from the beginning fought by the Germans not as such, but as a war of predation (*Raubkrieg*) which, through the deliberate suspension of the international law of war on the part of the aggressors, took on a form more like a colonial war than the form of war 'usually' fought within Europe. This included denying the enemy the status of a legitimate and equal opponent who, even when defeated or captured, was still entitled to a modicum of rights, and a willingness to leave prisoners of war to perish on the basis of their race or even simply to murder them without any more ado.[51]

Summary shootings and other executions of prisoners and mass murder through hunger, disease and dehydration also occurred during colonial wars. In German South West Africa, for example, Herero and Nama prisoners of war, including women and children, were incarcerated in 'concentration camps' (the name they were called by at the time) in which the mortality rate was 30–50 per cent, and were deliberately left to die from lack of food and accommodation unfit for human habitation.[52] 'Annihilation through deliberate neglect' was the term for the same practice, although on a much larger scale, through which millions of Russian prisoners of war were murdered during the Second World War.

Parallels to the 'war of annihilation in the East' are also to be found in the operations to combat partisan activities in the colonies; massacres and the destruction of all essentials for life of people who supported the guerrillas formed part both of the standard practice of colonial wars and the tradition of punitive and retributive expeditions. As early as the punitive campaigns against the Wahehe in German East Africa in the 1890s, it was considered a highly promising tactic to destroy villages and fields with fire, and thereby "to devour Mkwawa's [the leader of the Wahehe] land", as Governor Eduard von Liebert called it.[53] During the Maji-Maji War in German East Africa (1905–6), as in the war against the

---

Untergang der Zelewski-Expedition in Deutsch-Ostafrika im August 1891", *Militärgeschichte*, 11/2 (2001), pp. 22–28, here p. 27.
51 On the treatment of POWs in general, see the classic study by Christian Streit, *Keine Kameraden. Die Wehrmacht und die sowjetischen Kriegsgefangenen 1941–1945*, Stuttgart 1978.
52 This is analysed in detail in Jürgen Zimmerer, "Kriegsgefangene im Kolonialkrieg. Der Krieg gegen die Herero und Nama in Deutsch-Südwestafrika (1904–1907)", in Rüdiger Overmans, ed., *In der Hand des Feindes. Kriegsgefangenschaft von der Antike bis zum Zweiten Weltkrieg*, Köln 1999, pp. 277–294.
53 Von Liebert, *Neunzig Tage im Zelt*, p. 33, quoted according to Martin Baer and Olaf Schröter, *Eine Kopfjagd. Deutsche in Ostafrika*, Berlin 2001, p. 57.

Herero and Nama that was being waged simultaneously in South West Africa (1904-8), it was also a standard practice of the colonial forces "to confiscate the opponent's possessions (livestock, provisions) and to devastate his villages and crops",[54] in order to destroy the infrastructure and all the necessities of life, and so to deny the guerrillas the support they needed among the population. During the Second World War, the German army designated 'dead zones' in which to 'combat gangs'; these areas were then encircled by strong forces which systematically destroyed the villages that lay within them and the infrastructure that was vital for the people who lived there to be able to carry on their lives.[55]

Both this colonial manner of combating partisans with a strategy of destruction and the way prisoners were deliberately allowed to perish through neglect were an integral part of these wars waged against whole populations, including women and children. They were part of the 'race war' (*Rassenkrieg*) as propagated, for example, by General Lothar von Trotha,[56] the Commander in Chief of the German forces in the war against the Herero and Nama, who thanks to his copious experience of war in the colonies enjoyed the protection of General von Schlieffen, Chief of the General Staff of the German army; a war that he believed would be ended only by the complete annihilation of one of the warring parties. He therefore also conducted his campaign against the Herero, and later against the Nama – campaigns that can be viewed as being paradigmatic for the Nazi war of annihilation (*Vernichtungskrieg*) – along these lines.[57]

---

[54] Military policy memorandum on the consequences of the Rising, Dar-es-Salaam, 1 June 1907, quoted according to Detlef Bald, "Afrikanischer Kampf gegen koloniale Herrschaft. Der Maji-Maji -Aufstand in Ostafrika", *Militärgeschichtliche Mitteilungen*, 19/1 (1976), pp. 23–50, here p. 40.

[55] Gerlach, *Kalkulierte Morde*, pp. 859–1055. On German anti-partisan warfare in general, see also Philip Warren Blood, *Bandenbekämpfung: Nazi Occupation Security in Eastern Europe and Soviet Russia 1942–45*, Cranfield University, Bedfordshire 2001 (Ph.D. Thesis).

[56] Born on 3 July 1848 as the son of a Prussian officer, he too joined the army and took part in the Austro-Prussian and Franco-Prussian wars. Between 1894 and 1897 he was the commander of the *Schutztruppe* in German East Africa, where he gained military renown through his suppression of the Wahehe rising. Thereafter he took part voluntarily, as commander of the First East Asian Infantry Brigade, in the campaign to suppress the Boxer rising in China. See Pool, *Samuel Maharero*, Windhoek 1991, pp. 260f. Although von Trotha unquestionably played a key role in the way the Namibian War developed into genocide, regrettably no biography of him exists. Undoubtedly, the lack of any investigation of his socialization and of the nature of his military background represents a distressing gap in research into the radicalization of warfare in the twentieth century.

[57] See Jürgen Zimmerer, "Krieg, KZ & Völkermord. Der erste deutsche Genozid", in Jürgen Zimmerer and Joachim Zeller, eds, *Völkermord in Deutsch-Südwestafrika. Der Kolonialkrieg (1904–1908) in Namibia und seine Folgen*, Berlin 2003, pp 45–63; Jürgen Zimmerer, "Das Deutsche Reich und der Genozid. Überlegungen zum historischen Ort des Völkermordes an den Herero und Nama", in Larissa Förster and Dag Henrichsen, eds, *100 Jahre geteilte namibisch-deutsche Geschichte. Kolonialk-*

As Africans would "yield only to force", von Trotha set out to exercise such force using "blatant terror and even with cruelty" and to annihilate "the rebellious tribes in rivers of blood".[58] After all, as he wrote later, a war in Africa simply could not be fought "'in accordance with the rules of the Geneva Convention".[59] The clearest expression of von Trotha's genocidal policy was the notorious 'Order to Shoot All Herero' (also known as the Anihilation Order) of 2 October 1904, with which, after the Battle of the Waterberg, the only sizeable battle of the war, when the Hereros fled into the Omaheke desert, he ordered that the area should be sealed off by a cordon of guard posts:

> The Hereros have ceased to be German subjects.
>
> They have murdered and robbed, have cut off the ears and noses and other bodily parts of wounded soldiers, and are now too cowardly to want to go on fighting. I say to that people: Whoever delivers one of their *Kapteins* to one of my posts as a prisoner will be given 1,000 marks; whoever brings Samuel Maharero will be given 5,000 marks. But the Herero people must quit this country. If they do not, I will compel them to do so with the *Groot Rohr* [cannon].
>
> Within the borders of German territory, any Herero, with or without a firearm, with or without livestock, will be shot; nor will I give refuge to women or children any more. I will drive them back to their people or have them fired upon.[60]

Von Trotha then issued a clarification in an Order of the Day, that for the sake of the reputation of the German soldier, the "order to fire upon women and children" was "to be understood in such a way that shots are to be fired over their heads, in order to force them to run away." He "definitely assume[d] that this Proclamation" would "lead to no further male prisoners being taken", but would not "degenerate into atrocities against women and children". They would "doubtless run away, if shots are fired over their heads a couple of times".[61] But the only place they could run to was into the desert, where thousands died of thirst as a consequence of this order.

In the official historical description of the war, this reads as follows:

> [L]ike wild animals harassed half to death in the hunt, they were pursued from watering hole to watering hole, until they finally fell into a state of complete apathy, victims of the

---

rieg – Genozid – Erinnerungs-kulturen (*Ethnologia* Vol. 24), Köln 2004, pp. 106–121 (English version: "The German Empire and Genocide", pp. 154–174 in this book).
58 Letter from von Trotha to Leutwein, 5 November 1904, Bundesarchiv Berlin-Lichterfelde R-1001/2089, quoted according to Horst Drechsler, *Südwestafrika*, p. 156.
59 Von Trotha in *Die Deutsche Zeitung*, 3 February 1909, quoted according to Pool, *Maharero*, p. 293.
60 Proclamation by von Trotha, Osombo-Wind[imbe] [transcript], 2 October 1904, BArch, R 1001/2089, sheet 7af.
61 Ibid.

nature of their own country. The waterless Omaheke was to complete what German arms had started: the annihilation of the Herero nation.[62]

The intention to destroy an entire people and the official announcement of this having been fulfilled could hardly be expressed more clearly.[63]

Von Trotha's strategy of 'driving them into the desert' became proverbial, and echoes of it are still to be found coming from Hitler. In October 1941, for instance, in connection with his prophecy that the Jews would be annihilated, Hitler refused to allow the possibility that anyone seeking to persuade him to adopt a more moderate stance might put forward the objection that "We can't just drive them into the marshes!"[64] Heinrich Himmler's Order of the Day of 1 August 1941 reads almost like a quotation from von Trotha's 'Order to Shoot All Herero'. In it, Himmler ordered the massacre of the Pripet Marshes: "All Jewish men are to be shot, Jewish women driven into the swamps."[65] The intention was clear: very much like the Herero women and children who perished in the Omaheke, the

---

62 Kriegsgeschichtliche Abteilung I des Großen Generalstabs, *Die Kämpfe der deutschen Truppen in Südwestafrika*, 2 vols, Berlin 1906/07, Vol. 1, p. 211.
63 For a summary of the conduct of the Herero War, see Zimmerer and Zeller, *Völkermord in Deutsch-Südwestafrika*. See also Jan-Bart Gewald, *Towards Redemption: A Socio-Political History of the Herero of Namibia between 1890 and 1923*, Leyden 1996, pp. 178–240; Helmut Walser Smith, 'The Logic of Colonial Violence: Germany in Southwest Africa (1904–1907), the United States in the Philippines (1899–1902)', in Hartmut Lehmann and Hermann Wellenreuther, eds, *German and American Nationalism. A Comparative Perspective*. Oxford 1999, pp. 205–231; Gesine Krüger, *Kriegsbewältigung und Geschichtsbewußtsein: Realität, Deutung und Verarbeitung des deutschen Kolonialkriegs in Namibia 1904 bis 1907*, Göttingen 1999. Explicitly on the question of genocide: Zimmerer, "Das Deutsche Reich und der Genozid"; Zimmerer, "Colonialism and the Holocaust"; Jürgen Zimmerer, "Kolonialer Genozid? Möglichkeiten und Grenzen einer historischen Kategorie für eine Globalgeschichte des Völkermordes", in Dominik J. Schaller, Boyadjian Rupen, Hanno Scholtz and Vivianne Berg, eds, *Enteignet – Vertrieben – Ermordet. Beiträge zur Genozidforschung*, Zürich 2004, pp. 109–128 (English versions of these three articles by Zimmerer are to be found as Chaps 6–8 in this book); Jan-Bart Gewald, "Colonization, Genocide and Resurgence: The Herero of Namibia 1890–1933", in Jan-Bart Gewald and Michael Bollig, eds, *People, Cattle and Land: Transformations of a Pastoral Society in Southwestern Africa*, Köln 2001, pp. 187–225; Alison Palmer, *Colonial Genocide*, Adelaide 2000; Tilman Dedering, "The German-Herero War of 1904: Revisionism of Genocide or Imaginary Historiography?" *Journal of Southern African Studies*, 19 (1993), pp. 80–88; Tilman Dedering, "'A Certain Rigorous Treatment of All parts of the Nation.' The Annihilation of the Herero in German South West Africa, 1904", in Mark Levene and Penny Roberts, eds, *The Massacre in History*, New York 1999, pp. 205–22; Gunter Spraul, "Der 'Völkermord' an den Herero", *Geschichte in Wissenschaft und Unterricht*, 39 (1988), pp. 713–739.
64 Hitler, 25 October 1941, in Hitler, *Monologe*, p. 106.
65 Christian Gerlach, "Deutsche Wirtschaftsinteressen, Besatzungspolitik und der Mord an den Juden in Weißrußland 1941–1943", in Ulrich Herbert, ed., *Nationalsozialistische Vernichtungspolitik 1939–1945. Neue Forschung und Kontroversen*, Frankfurt 1998, pp. 236–291, here p. 278.

Jewish women too would die, without any German soldier even having to raise his weapon.

The objection has repeatedly been raised that the Holocaust is distinguished from all other mass murders in history by the role played in it by the state. This, however, is an excessively abbreviated and fundamentally ahistorical view. The role played by the state in the colonial genocides was certainly different from the one it played in the Holocaust.[66] This is unsurprising, however, since the state's presence was far 'weaker' in North America and Australia during their colonisation by settlers than it was in Germany between 1933 and 1945. If, however, instead of the bureaucratic and centralised state apparatus of the Third Reich one takes as a yardstick the level of development of the state in the relevant historical period in each case, then the differences no longer appear fundamental, but rather a matter of degree: the forms of murder may change – depending on the level of bureaucratisation of the state that commits or orders the murders – but the common factor remains: the readiness of the 'perpetrator' to destroy distinct groups of people. This ultimate breach of taboo – to not only contemplate the annihilation of whole ethnic communities but to actually act accordingly – was first committed in the colonies. This fact also contributed to making the Holocaust thinkable and doable, however different the motives for murdering Jews, Gypsies, homosexuals or people with disabilities may have been. Even the murder of the Jews, which is distinguished from other genocides in terms of its motive – namely, anti-Semitism and the elimination of a supposed Jewish world conspiracy – would scarcely have been possible if the ultimate taboo breach, that of being able to think that other ethnicities could simply be destroyed, and then to act accordingly, had not already taken place earlier. The Holocaust thus represents an extreme, radicalised version of a form of behaviour that was by no means new in the colonial context. A historicised concept of the state, however, also helps to explain the difference in the forms that mass murder took in the colonies and in eastern Europe under German occupation. The bureaucratised form of murder, which is what Auschwitz fundamentally stands as the universally recognisable symbol of, requires as a precondition the thoroughly and efficiently organised administrative apparatus of a centralised government. There was no such administrative organisation in the colonies. As the example of German South West Africa shows, with the increase in the degree of organisation the first beginnings of a bureaucratised form of annihilation also appeared in the camps, even though active, 'industrial' killing such as was practised in the Nazi extermination camps after 1941 did not yet exist. And at this point it is also important to recall

---

[66] On this and the following remarks, see Zimmerer, "Colonialism and the Holocaust" and Jürgen Zimmerer, "Kolonialer Genozid?".

that even during the Third Reich, more people perished as victims of execution by shooting or from being allowed to starve to death than were suffocated in the apparently 'industrial' gas chambers.

Channels of Transmission: First-Hand Experience, Institutional Structures and the Collective Imagination

The structural similarities between colonialism and National Socialism allow the expansionist policies of the Third Reich to be seen as a part of colonial history. This connection immediately raises the question of how colonial ideas and experiences were transmitted to the decision-makers and those who executed their decisions in Nazi Germany. Although there is still an extraordinary lack of research into this area, three channels of transmission – first-hand experience, institutional structures and the collective imagination – can be distinguished, which will be sketched out in the following.

First-hand experience is the most obvious channel, but at the same time the most difficult one to trace, especially since up until now no prosopographical study has been undertaken, either with regard to the German colonial administrators and military personnel or the settlers. Nonetheless, such experience can be demonstrated in the cases of some individuals who fought against the Herero: for example Hermann Ehrhardt (of the *Marinebrigade* Ehrhardt, a de facto *Freikorps*),[67] Ludwig Maercker (of the *Freikorps* Maercker),[68] Wilhelm Faupel (of the *Freikorps* Görlitz/Faupel),[69] Franz Xaver Ritter von Epp (*Freikorps* and the Office of Colonial Policy of the NSDAP – the Nazi Party),[70] Paul von Lettow-Vorbeck (the 'Hero of East Africa', who participated in the Kapp Putsch), the Settlement Com-

---

67 Hagen Schulze, *Freikorps und Republik, 1918–1920*, Boppard am Rhein 1969, p. 257.
68 Ehmann, *Rassistische und antisemitische Traditionslinien*, p. 143.
69 On this, see Oliver Gliech, "Wilhelm Faupel. Generalstabsoffizier, Militärberater, Präsident des Ibero-Amerikanischen Instituts", in Reinhard Liehr, Günther Maihold and Günter Vollmer, eds, *Ein Institut und sein General. Wilhelm Faupel und das Ibero-Amerikanische Institut in der Zeit des Nationalsozialismus*, Frankfurt 2003, pp. 131–279, especially 176–94. Faupel was later active together with Rudolf Böhmer, a former District Officer of Lüderitzbucht in German South West Africa, and with Lübbert, a former head of the Chamber of Mines there, in the 'Volksbund für Arbeitsdienst' (Popular League for Labour Service) and the 'Gesellschaft zum Studium des Faschismus' (Society for the Study of Fascism), organisations which served in the first case to prepare the dissemination of Nazi ideology and in the second case to promote the adoption of Italian-style Fascism in Germany.
70 On the biography of Epp, see Katja Wächter, *Die Macht der Ohnmacht. Leben und Politik des Franz Xaver Ritter von Epp (1868–1946)*, Frankfurt 1999.

missioner for South West Africa, Paul Rohrbach (journalist),[71] and the Governor of South West Africa and later head of the Imperial Colonial Office, Friedrich von Lindequist. Of these, von Lettow-Vorbeck, Rohrbach and von Lindequist were mainly active as journalistic writers and propagandists.[72] Directly involved in the administration of the occupied territories was Dr Viktor Boettcher, *Regierungspräsident* (head of the regional administration) in Posen im Warthegau (Posnań), who had been Deputy Governor of Cameroon before the First World War.[73]

But it would also be wrong to assume that there is a straight path leading from enthusiasm for colonialism and experience in the German colonies to enthusiasm for National Socialism. For some of these people, their involvement with colonialism found their fulfilment after 1918 in 'colonial revisionism', i.e. the campaign for the restoration of the former colonies to Germany; while this movement had many points of intersection with the *völkisch* (nationalist-identitarian) movement, it was not identical with it,[74] even though, as has been sketched out above, a fundamental readiness to countenance territorial expansion was one of the prerequisites for the Nazi policy of conquest. Furthermore, rejection of the measures regarding the colonies set out in the Treaty of Versailles was also well-established among parts of the political left or of political expressions of Catholicism, both of which were critical in their attitudes to National Socialism. Others became critics of colonialism or even pacifists due to their experiences in colonial campaigns and/or the First World War. This includes a number of members of the colonial

---

71 On the biography of Rohrbach see Walter Mogk, *Paul Rohrbach und das 'Größere Deutschland'. Ethischer Imperialismus im Wilhelminischen Zeitalter. Ein Beitrag zur Geschichte des Kulturprotestantismus*, München 1972.

72 This list does not include the 'colonial revisionists', i.e. those who engaged in practical, political or journalistic activities to promote the re-establishment of Germany's colonial empire in Africa. A list of such people would be many times longer than that of the group mentioned.

73 Furber, *Colonialism*.

74 On colonial revisionism see Jens Ruppenthal, *Die Kolonialfrage in der Politik der Weimarer Republik. Der Kolonialrevisionismus in der deutschen Außenpolitik von 1919 bis 1926*, University of Kiel 2002 (M.A. Thesis); Jan Esche, *Koloniales Anspruchdenken in Deutschland im Ersten Weltkrieg, während der Versailler Friedensverhandlungen und in der Weimarer Republik (1914 bis 1933)*, Hamburg 1989. For extensive coverage of the relationship between colonial revisionism and the Nazi party, see Klaus Hildebrand, *Vom Reich zum Weltreich – Hitler, NSDAP und koloniale Frage 1919–1945*, München 1969. On the issue of the plans for a colonial empire in Africa put forward during the Third Reich, see also Karsten Linne, *Weiße 'Arbeitsführer' im 'Kolonialen Ergänzungsraum'. Afrika als Ziel sozial- und wirtschaftspolitischer Planungen in der NS-Zeit*, Münster 2002. How the measures in respect of the colonies adopted by the Paris Peace Conference were arrived at is dealt with in Jürgen Zimmerer, "Von der Bevormundung zur Selbstbestimmung. Die Pariser Friedenskonferenz und ihre Auswirkungen auf die britische Kolonialherrschaft im Südlichen Afrika", in Gerd Krumeich, ed., *Versailles 1919: Ziele – Wirkung – Wahrnehmung*, Essen 2001, pp. 145–158.

forces, such as Berthold von Deimling, already mentioned above, who had served as a general during the First World War but later became a virulently ostracised pacifist;[75] and Hans Paasche, who even earlier, after the Maji-Maji War in German East Africa, submitted his resignation in disgust at the conduct of the German campaign, was committed to a Berlin 'lunatic asylum' during the First World War, and afterwards participated in the revolutionary Soldiers' Soviet in Berlin; he was subsequently murdered in May 1920.[76]

The example of the volunteer units known as *Freikorps* demonstrates how the experience of violence in the colonies, which has frequently been identified as a determining factor in the unbridled brutality displayed by the *Freikorps* in the conflicts they were involved in,[77] could also be passed on to others. In this case it is a matter of indirect or derivative experience, such as can also be transmitted through personal networks or teacher-student relationships. An example of this would be the racial anthropologist Eugen Fischer, whose post-doctoral thesis (*Habilitation*) was concerned with the *Rehobother Bastards und das Bastardisierungsproblem beim Menschen*, ("The Rehoboth Bastards and the Problem of Bastardisation in Humans") that is to say with an ethnic group in German South West Africa. He later became the founder-director of the *Kaiser Wilhelm Institut für Anthropologie, menschliche Erblehre und Eugenik* (Kaiser Wilhelm Institute of Anthropology, Human Heredity and Eugenics), and from 1933–35 was President (*Rektor*) of Berlin University.[78] Such careers can be found quite often in the field of medicine, and indeed of science in general. Ernst Rodenwaldt, Otto Reche, Philalethes Kuhn and Theodor Mollison, too, combined experience of this kind in the

---

75 On Deimling's career after the First World War see Christoph Jahr, "Berthold von Deimling. Vom General zum Pazifisten. Eine biographische Skizze", *Zeitschrift für die Geschichte des Oberrheins*, new version 142 (1994), pp. 359–387; Christoph Jahr, '"Die reaktionäre Presse heult auf wider den Mann." General Berthold von Deimling (1853–1944) und der Pazifismus', in Wolfram Wette, ed., *Pazifistische Offiziere in Deutschland 1871 bis 1933*, Bremen 1999, pp. 131–146.
76 Werner Lange, *Hans Paasches Forschungsreise ins innerste Deutschland. Eine Biographie*, Bremen 1995.
77 As it was for example by Dan Diner. Diner, *Das Jahrhundert verstehen*, pp. 52f. Theweleit pointed out the connection between the colonial military, the *Freikorps* and the National Socialists at an early date: Klaus Theweleit, *Männerphantasien*, Frankfurt 1977.
78 On Fischer, see the overview in Kathrin Roller, "Der Rassenbiologe Eugen Fischer", in Ulrich van der Heyden and Joachim Zeller, eds, *Kolonialmetropole Berlin. Eine Spurensuche*, Berlin 2002, pp. 130–134 and 302; Niels C. Lösch, *Rasse als Konstrukt. Leben und Werk Eugen Fischers*, Frankfurt 1997; Bernhard Gessler, *Eugen Fischer (1874–1967). Leben und Werk des Freiburger Anatomen, Anthropologen und Rassenhygienikers bis 1927*, Frankfurt 2000.

colonies with ardent enthusiasm for the National Socialist cause and active participation in its racial and extermination policies.[79]

A kind of opposite case, as it were, to Fischer and his colleagues, who were active in teaching, is represented by Richard Walther Darré, who was a student at the German Colonial School in Witzenhausen, and during the Third Reich was appointed head of the *SS Rasse- und Siedlungshauptamt* (SS Race and Resettlement Office), which was responsible among other things for the 'racial' assessments of eastern European children who were 'capable of being re-Germanised'.[80]

Also worth mentioning here are the graduates from the institutions established to train future colonial officials; their subsequent 'careers' have not been examined so far. Among these institutions, in addition to the already mentioned Colonial School in Witzenhausen and the *Hamburger Tropeninstitut* (Hamburg Tropical Institute),[81] there was the *Koloniale Frauenschule* (Women's Colonial School) in Rendsburg. The training for life in the colonies that this institution imparted was the kind of practical knowledge that was also desirable for the 'campaign in the East', a fact that made it possible for the colonial schools to justify the existence, even after the Battle of Stalingrad when the prospect of direct involvement with colonies receded further and further into the distance. The *Koloniale Frauenschule*, for instance, offered Russian as an elective subject, and ultimately established a second campus in Potok Zloty and sent some of its students to the East.[82]

---

79 Ehmann, *Rassistische und antisemitische Traditionslinien*. On colonial medicine in general, see Wolfgang Uwe Eckart, *Medizin und Kolonialimperialismus. Deutschland 1884–1945*, Paderborn 1996. Also to be found in the same context is the former medical missionary Friedrich Hay, who in the time when he was active in Togo became a witness to human experiments aimed at producing a substance that would be effective against smallpox, leprosy and sleeping sickness – if he was not even involved in them himself, as has been reconstructed by Christine Wolters. He himself, on the basis of the racist world view he had acquired in Africa, was an early supporter of the NSDAP (Nazi Party); and his son would later propagate a drug for use against tuberculosis manufactured by his father's company, trials of which had been carried out in Sachsenhausen concentration camp. Even if they were not themselves actively involved, father and son apparently had no qualms about furthering medical 'advances' at the expense of other people. Christine Wolters, 'Dr. Friedrich Hey (1864–1960). Missionsarzt und Bückeburger Unternehmer', in Hubert Höing, ed., *Strukturen und Konjunkturen. Faktoren in der schaumburgischen Wirtschaftsgeschichte*, Bielefeld 2004.
80 On Darré, see Gustavo Corni, "Richard Walther Darré´ – Der 'Blut-und-Boden' Ideologe", in Ronald Smelser, Enrico Syring and Rainer Zitelmann, eds, *Die braune Elite: 21 weitere biographische Skizzen*, 4th edn, Darmstadt 1999, pp. 15–27.
81 On this, see Stefan Wulf, *Das Hamburger Tropeninstitut 1919 bis 1945. Auswärtige Kulturpolitik und Kolonialrevisionismus nach Versailles*, Berlin 1994.
82 Linne, *Weiße Arbeitsführer*, p. 180.

Such initiatives were welcomed by the German state and the Nazi Party. Not only were former settlers from the German Empire's colonies in Africa preferred settlers in the East, where their 'pioneer qualities' could be usefully employed,[83] but there was also a great demand for trained specialists. Franz Xaver Ritter von Epp, for example, the Director of the Nazi Party's Colonial Policy Office, called upon colonial experts to volunteer for 'the East':

> As the Director of the Colonial Policy Office I urge all colonial planters and experts from the German colonies or other tropical regions who have registered with my Office for future employment in our colonies, now to make themselves and their expertise available for the duration of the war, for practical tasks in the southern part of the occupied territories in the East. [...] Those who prove themselves there are assured of preferential consideration for the colonies in the future.[84]

And it was not only governmental institutions that started to turn their attention eastward. German companies experienced in doing business in Africa also became more and more involved there, as their traditional business with overseas trading partners had been put on hold since the outbreak of war.[85] Immediately after the invasion of Poland German 'colonial' companies received preferential treatment there, as they could already, among other things, boast experience in trading with 'primitive' societies.

Alongside the personal continuities, institutional continuity also played a decisive role. Apart from the military academies, about which we unfortunately know nothing at all with regard to their processing and passing on of tactical experience gained in the colonial wars,[86] universities and individual academic disciplines were also among the major transmission channels for colonial ideas and experience. In addition, they have been gaining in importance since academic research has started to emphasise the participation of science in the Third Reich's 'race' and 'space' policies. But whereas the involvement of individual researchers in National

---

83 Furber, *Colonialism*.
84 Letter from von Epp to the head of the Deko Group, Weigelt, 20 November 1941, BArch, R 1501, No. 27191, sheets. 99 f; quoted according to Karsten Linne, "Deutsche Afrikafirmen im 'Osteinsatz'", *1999. Zeitschrift für Sozialgeschichte des 20. und 21. Jahrhunderts* 16/1 (2001), pp. 49–90, here p. 88.
85 Ibid.
86 With regard to the United Kingdom, we know more: Colonel Callwell's manual, which was mandatory reading in anti-guerrilla warfare training, ran through several editions after its first appearance in 1896 and also dealt with experience gained in colonial wars (including among others the Herero war). Charles E. Callwell, *Small Wars. Their Principles and Practice*, London 1896.

Socialist policies is now beginning to be examined in detail,[87] in-depth studies of the different disciplines have for the most part been left aside, so that diachronic analyses of particular subjects over longer periods of time remain rather few and far between.[88] But academic theories and opinions are not formed in a vacuum; they are imbedded in contexts of both synchronic and diachronic discourse.

---

[87] A whole number of academic disciplines were directly or indirectly involved in the restructuring of 'race' and 'space' in Eastern Europe as well as in Germany itself: Eugenics, Medicine, Biology and Social Sciences in the one case, Geography, Economics, Transportation and Engineering in the other. Then there were Law and the Humanities, which played their part both in racial legislation and ethnic history and also in new international law and the history of settlement. Academics readily provided legitimation both for racial policy and territorial planning, were involved in shaping concepts and readily lent their expertise to racial hygiene measures, serving as advisors in the military and civil administrations of the occupied territories. On this matter, see the more recent literature, in which comprehensive bibliographical references to the large volume of older literature are also to be found: Michael Fahlbusch, *Wissenschaft im Dienst der nationalsozialistischen Politik? Die 'Volksdeutschen Forschungsgemeinschaften' von 1931 to 1945*, Baden-Baden 1999; Rössler and Schleiermacher, eds, *'Generalplan Ost'*; Bruno Wasser, *Himmlers Raumplanung im Osten*, Basel 1993; Czeslaw Madajczyk, ed., *Vom Generalplan Ost zum Generalsiedlungsplan*, München 1994; Martin Burkert, *Die Ostwissenschaften im Dritten Reich. Teil I: Zwischen Verbot und Duldung. Die schwierige Gratwanderung der Ostwissenschaften zwischen 1933 und 1939*, Wiesbaden 2000; Uwe Mai, *'Rasse und Raum'. Agrarpolitik, sozial- und Raumplanung im NS-Staat*, Paderborn 2001. An overview in respect of Racial Hygiene and Euthanasia in the Third Reich is provided by the following works: Ernst Klee, *'Euthanasie' im NS-Staat. Die 'Vernichtung lebensunwerten Lebens'*, Frankfurt 1983; Hans-Walter Schmuhl, *Rassenhygiene, Nationalsozialismus, Euthanasie*, Göttingen 1987. On the role of Geography in the Third Reich, see Michael Fahlbusch, Mechthild Rössler and Dominik Siegrist, *Geographie im Nationalsozialismus. 3 Fallstudien zur Institution Geographie im Deutschen Reich und der Schweiz*, Kassel 1989; Mechthild Rössler, *'Wissenschaft und Lebensraum'. Geographische Ostforschung im Nationalsozialismus. Ein Beitrag zur Disziplingeschichte der Geographie*, Berlin 1990. Mathias Schmoeckel concerns himself with the contribution made by the field of Law in *Die Grossraumtheorie. Ein Beitrag zur Geschichte der Völkerrechtswissenschaft im Dritten Reich, insbesondere der Kriegszeit*, Berlin 1994. On Technology in the Third Reich in general, see for example Jeffrey Herf, *Reactionary Modernism. Technology, Culture and Politics in Weimar and the Third Reich*, Cambridge 1984; Monika Renneberg and Mark Walter, eds, *Science, Technology and National Socialism*, Cambridge 1994; Peter Lundgreen, ed., *Wissenschaft im Dritten Reich*, Frankfurt 1985. On the Humanities in general, see Franz-Rutker Hausmann, *'Deutsche Geisteswissenschaft' im Zweiten Weltkrieg. Die 'Aktion Ritterbusch' (1940–1945)*, Dresden 1998. On the role played by Historians, see: Winfried Schulze and Otto Gerhard Oexle, eds, *Deutsche Historiker im Nationalsozialismus*, Frankfurt 1999; Ingo Haar, *Historiker im Nationalsozialismus. Deutsche Geschichtswissenschaft und der 'Volkstumskampf' im Osten*, Göttingen 2000.

[88] One exception to this is the field of Racial Hygiene, on which there is a comparatively broad range of research: Michael Burleigh, *Death and Deliverance. Euthanasia in Germany c.1900–1945*, Cambridge 1994. Peter Weingart, Jürgen Kroll and Kurt Bayertz, *Rasse, Blut und Gene. Geschichte der Eugenik in Deutschland*, Frankfurt 1988. On the international context, see Stefan Kühl, *Die*

It is also important to reconstruct these lines of tradition by which content was transmitted, in order to understand where academics came across those concepts that they then passed on to those in power. Here as well, an important point of reference is the colonial research that had been pursued since the end of the nineteenth century, as prior to 1933 this had been the prominent showcase for population studies.[89] Already in the Kaiserreich, scientists had readily entered government service and the prevailing colonial euphoria, thus sharpening the profiles of their own disciplines. The discipline of Geography, for example, exploited the colonial enthusiasm of a broad section of the bourgeoisie to gain social prestige and to establish itself as being on a level with the more venerable academic disciplines.[90] Geographers such as the Berlin Professor Ferdinand von Richthofen, one of the doyens of his discipline, deliberately sought to influence the competition for research funding with the argument that it was geographers who could best make concrete knowledge available that could be made use of in the development of the colonies. His successor as occupant of the Chair in Berlin, Albrecht Penck, was not only the founder of the field of *Kulturbodenforschung* (research into the cultivation of land), as which he also performed valuable service to the Third Reich's eastern expansion, but was also journalistically active after 1933 in support of both *Volkstum* (ethnicity) policies and 'colonial revisionism'.[91]

Internationale der Rassisten. Aufstieg und Niedergang der internationalen Bewegung für Eugenik und Rassenhygiene im 20. Jahrhundert, Frankfurt 1997.
89 Unfortunately, the current state of research on this topic is extremely unsatisfactory. As an introduction, see the articles on various academic disciplines in van der Heyden and Zeller, eds, *Kolonialmetropole Berlin;* and in Pascal Grosse, *Kolonialismus, Eugenik und bürgerliche Gesellschaft in Deutschland, 1850–1918*, Frankfurt 2000. The academic disciplines that dealt explicitly with the colonised peoples, such as African Studies and Ethnology, belong in this context; on this, see Christoph Marx, *'Völker ohne Schrift und Geschichte'. Zur historischen Erfassung des vorkolonialen Schwarzafrika in der deutschen Forschung des 19. und frühen 20. Jahrhunderts*, Stuttgart 1988; and Sara Pugach, *Afrikanistik and Colonial Knowledge. Carl Meinhof, the Missionary Impulse and the Development of African Studies in Germany 1887–1919*, Ph.D. thesis, University of Chicago, 2000. Research into this field has already advanced further in other colonial powers such as Britain or France. On this, and also on the debate concerning 'orientalism', which also belongs in this context, see: Jürgen Osterhammel, "Wissen als Macht: Deutungen interkulturellen Nichtverstehens bei Tzvetan Todorov und Edward Said", in Eva-Maria Auch and Stig Förster, eds, *'Barbaren' und 'Weiße Teufel'. Kulturkonflikte in Asien vom 18. bis 20. Jahrhundert*, Paderborn 1997.
90 On this, see Jürgen Osterhammel, "Die Wiederkehr des Raumes: Geopolitik, Geohistorie und historische Geographie", *Neue Politische Literatur*, 43 (1998), pp. 374–396.
91 On Geography between colonialism and Nazism, see Jürgen Zimmerer, "Im Dienste des Imperiums. Die Geographen der Berliner Universität zwischen Kolonialwissenschaften und Ostforschung", in Andreas Eckert, ed., *Universitäten und Kolonialismus, Jahrbuch für Universitätsgeschichte*, 7, special issue (2004), pp. 73–99 (English version: "In the Service of the Empire", pp. 262–293 in this book); Jürgen Zimmerer, "Wissenschaft und Kolonialismus. Das Geographische Institut der Friedrich-Wilhelms-

It is thus not too far-fetched to pose the question as to whether there were also overlaps in content between the two.

Geography is however only one of the disciplines that need to be investigated, since it made use of knowledge from so many different areas. 'Political geography' alone, for instance, as is shown by its division into the sub-disciplines of 'colonial population science', 'colonial economics and production', 'colonial settlement and transport geography', 'colonial ethnology', 'colonial governance' and 'comparative governance of the great colonial empires', was concerned with 'racial research', tropical medicine, the exchange of commodities between colonies, colonial production, the processes of economic exchange between the home country and the colony, but also with issues of 'cultural mixing', colonial settlement and conditions in other colonies.[92] All these subjects still need to be researched on their own individual accounts, in particular with regard to what options were discussed under those headings in respect of the development and exploitation of large areas of territory and their inhabitants. Even if the conclusions these scientists came to perhaps did not directly anticipate those reached by their successors a generation later, they surely shaped their disciplines in a way that made it possible for later scientists to take up where they had left off.[93]

The transmission of colonial ideas and attitudes did not, however, take place only through the dissemination of the concrete personal experiences of individuals who had served in the colonies or who had worked in institutions that were concerned with 'overseas' affairs but, almost more importantly, by being propagated

---

Universität vom Kaiserreich zum Dritten Reich", in van der Heyden and Zeller, eds, *Kolonialmetropole Berlin*, pp. 125–130.

92 On this, see Klaus Kost, *Die Einflüsse der Geopolitik auf Forschung und Theorie der Politischen Geographie von ihren Anfängen bis 1945. Ein Beitrag zur Wissenschaftsgeschichte unter besonderer Berücksichtigung von Militär und Kolonialgeographie*, Bonn 1988, pp. 193–234.

93 More detailed analyses exist only for Colonial Medicine, Engineering and Geopolitics. On Medicine, see Eckart, *Medizin und Kolonialimperialismus*. On Engineering, see Dirk van Laak, *Imperiale Infrastruktur*. On Geopolitics, see Jürgen Osterhammel, "Raumerfassung und Universalgeschichte im 20. Jahrhundert", in Gangolf Hübinger, Jürgen Osterhammel and Erich Pelzer, eds, *Universalgeschichte und Nationalgeschichten*, Freiburg 1994, pp. 51–72. See also the articles in Irene Diekmann, Peter Krüger and Julius H. Schoeps, eds, *Geopolitik. Grenzgänge im Zeitgeist, 1890–1945*, 2 vols, Potsdam 2000. On Haushofer, see Bruno Hipler, *Hitlers Lehrmeister. Karl Haushofer als Vater der NS-Ideologie*, St. Ottilien 1996; Hans-Adolf Jacobsen, *Karl Haushofer. Leben und Werk*, 2 vols, Boppard am Rhein 1979; and Frank Ebeling, *Geopolitik. Karl Haushofer und seine Raumwissenschaft 1919–1945*, Berlin 1994.

through monuments,[94] in schools,[95] and by early films,[96] lecture tours, exhibitions and literature.[97] People such as Paul von Lettow-Vorbeck and Paul Rohrbach, who were able to skilfully transform their own colonial experiences into (lucrative) journalistic success, stand for the importance, which is not to be underestimated, of the media in the dissemination of colonial notions.[98] A wide range of colonial literature developed,[99] which included, for example, such diverse texts as (to name only an arbitrary selection) Paul von Lettow-Vorbeck's *Heia Safari*,[100] Margarethe von Eckenbrecher's *Was Afrika mir gab und nahm. Erlebnisse einer deutschen Freu in Südwestafrika*,[101] or Maximilian Bayer's *Mit dem Hauptquartier in Südwestafrika*,[102] i.e. examples of memoirs and of fictional and semifictional texts. The most famous of them all was doubtless Gustav Frenssen's *Peter Moors Fahrt nach Südwest*,[103] the

---

94 On this, see Joachim Zeller, *Kolonialdenkmäler und Geschichtsbewußtsein. Eine Untersuchung der kolonialdeutschen Erinnerungskultur*, Frankfurt 2000.

95 See, for example, Willi W. Puls, *Der koloniale Gedanke im Unterricht der Volksschule*, Leipzig 1938; Johannes Petersen, *Der koloniale Gedanke in der Schule. Sinn, Aufgabe und Wege kolonialer Schularbeit*, Hamburg 1937.

96 On early colonial films, see Wolfgang Fuhrmann,"'Nashornjagd in Deutsch-Ostafrika' – Die frühe Kolonialfilmindustrie", in van der Heyden and Zeller, *Kolonialmetropole Berlin*, pp. 184–188. See also Jörg Schöning, ed., *Triviale Tropen. Exotische Reise- und Abenteuerfilme aus Deutschland 1919–1939*, München 1997.

97 From an early date onwards, photographs and even films from the colonies and heroic graphic representations of scenes from the colonial wars appeared. On these, see Joachim Zeller, "Orlog in Deutsch-Südwestafrika. Fotografien aus dem Kolonialkrieg 1904 bis 1907", *Fotogeschichte. Beiträge zur Geschichte und Ästhetik der Fotografie*, 85/86 (2002), pp. 31–44.

98 On this, see also the texts collected in Kundrus, ed., *Phantasiereiche*.

99 For an overview and detailed bibliographies, see Joachim Warmbold, *'Ein Stückchen neudeutsche Erd' ...' Deutsche Kolonialliteratur. Aspekte ihrer Geschichte, Eigenart und Wirkung dargestellt am Beispiel Afrikas*, Frankfurt 1982; Sibylle Benninghoff-Lühl, *Deutsche Kolonialromane 1884–1914 in ihrem Entstehungs- und Wirkungszusammenhang*, Bremen 1983; Amadou Booker Sadji, *Das Bild des Negro-Afrikaners in der Deutschen Kolonialliteratur (1884–1945). Ein Beitrag zur literarischen Imagologie Schwarzafrikas*, Berlin 1985; and Rosa B. Schneider, *'Um Scholle und Leben'. Zur Konstruktion von 'Rasse' und Geschlecht in der deutschen kolonialen Afrikaliteratur um 1900*, Frankfurt 2003.

100 Paul von Lettow-Vorbeck, *Heia Safari! Deutschlands Kampf in Ostafrika*, Leipzig 1920.

101 Margarethe von Eckenbrecher, *Was Afrika mir gab und nahm. Erlebnisse einer deutschen Frau in Südwestafrika*, Berlin 1907. By 1940 an eighth edition had already appeared.

102 Maximilian Bayer, *Mit dem Hauptquartier in Südwestafrika*, Berlin 1909.

103 Gustav Frenssen, *Peter Moors Fahrt nach Südwest*, Berlin 1906. See also Rolf Meyn, 'Abstecher in die Kolonialliteratur. Gustav Frenssens "Peter Moors fährt nach Südwest"', in Kay Dohnke and Dietrich Stein, eds, *Gustav Frenssen und seine Zeit. Von der Massenliteratur im Kaiserreich zur Massenideologie im NS-Staat*, Heide 1997, pp. 316–346. See also Medardus Brehl, 'Vernichtung als Arbeit an der Kultur. Kolonialdiskurs, kulturelles Wissen und der Völkermord an den Herero', in *Zeitschrift für Genozidforschung*, 2 (2000), pp. 8–28; Medardus Brehl, '"Das Drama

best-selling German young peoples' book up until 1945. Hans Grimm's *Volk ohne Raum*[104] also enjoyed a real boom during the 1930s and 1940s. It was regarded as a modern classic by the Nazis, was compulsory reading in German schools, and was the only book by a German author to represent the category of 'German Literature' at the Chicago World's Fair of 1934.[105]

This unreal version of colonial history as viewed through the literary imagination, which also embraced (despite its not being strictly speaking colonial history) the westward expansion of the United States, that is to say the phantasmagoria of the 'Wild West' (one only has to think of Karl May)[106] forms as much of a backcloth to the Nazis' eastern European colonial fantasies as real history does. It contributed to the conquerors' self-image as the bearers of civilisation, in contrast to whom the Polish and Russian populations were viewed as 'savages' who could either be 'trained' to be servants, or else could be 'resettled' or 'removed' so that the land could be more efficiently utilised.

Throughout history, colonial adventurers have also felt motivated to go and live 'out in the wild', in order to be able to pursue a lifestyle that was or had become unaffordable at home. Hence, a lifestyle mirroring that of the aristocracy or the country gentry was exported, for example, to Africa. During the Nazi period a *Herrenmenschentum* ('master race' attitude) that had been cultivated in this way returned to Europe. The binary distinctions of 'White' and 'Black', 'Natives' and 'non-Natives', 'masters' (i.e. members of the master race) and 'servants', 'human' and 'subhuman', 'worthy to live' and 'unworthy to live', were in themselves profoundly colonial. The way the 'colonial' concept was shaped into discourse also contributed to this manner of thinking in dichotomies, which doubtless also existed in areas unrelated to colonialism, being disseminated throughout broad sectors of the population.

---

spielt sich auf der dunklen Bühne des Sandfeldes ab.' Die Vernichtung der Herero und Nama in der deutschen (Populär-)Literatur", in Zimmerer and Zeller, eds, *Völkermord in Deutsch-Südwestafrika*, pp. 86–96.
104 Hans Grimm, *Volk ohne Raum*, München 1926.
105 Jürgen Hillesheim and Elisabeth Michael, *Lexikon nationalsozialistischer Dichter. Biographien – Analysen – Bibliographien*, Würzburg 1993, pp. 211–222, here p. 211.
106 On the importance of Karl May in German popular culture see, for example, Rolf-Bernhard Essig and Gudrun Schury, 'Karl May', in Etienne François and Hagen Schulze, eds, *Deutsche Erinnerungsorte*, Vol. 3, 2nd edn, München 2002, pp. 107–121.

Conclusion

Both in the days of the German Empire and in the subsequent decades, the German population's awareness of colonial history, including the conquest of and dominion over large parts of the world by the British, the French, the Spanish, the Portuguese, the Belgians, the Dutch and so on, was much stronger than is generally assumed. This knowledge was disseminated in places that included colonial societies, geographical societies and political parties; but also popular novels and magazines and university lectures. Consequently, even the man in the street is likely to have picked up some notion, in one form or another, of such concepts as 'racial society' and 'mixed marriage', expulsion and resettlement on reservations, 'ailing races doomed to disappear' or poor 'Natives' with 'untutored minds' and without any history or ability to make advances in civilisation, even if those notions stem only from reports of successes in the 'mission to the heathen' and appeals for donations to support it.

By rendering this aspect of German history largely invisible, both in general and also especially when investigating the roots of National Socialism, we forgo an essential viewpoint that can contribute towards some understanding of Nazi policy in 'the East'. But if we take seriously this thread of tradition in German history, which has so far been neglected, we can identify precursors and become aware of models. Some things that from the constricted – European – viewpoint appear to be without parallel turn out to be variations – though admittedly extremely radicalised variations – on earlier practices that had already been applied in the colonial context.

A truly global history of foreign occupation, whether military or political, should abandon the Eurocentric distinction between occupation in Europe and colonial rule overseas, and see Nazi policies in the conquered areas of Poland and the Soviet Union in the tradition from a global historical perspective that they form part of: the tradition of colonial rule. Both German and European history could only benefit from such a global perspective.

In addition, this demonstration of the existence of a long tradition of racist and population-economical thinking helps towards an understanding of how it could be that such a relatively large number of Germans appear to have been willing to participate in the Nazi military occupation and the war of annihilation without too many scruples. Precisely the positive connotations that were attached to European colonialism until well past the middle of the twentieth century are likely to have played their part in making the criminal nature of the German occupation invisible to from contemporary witnesses; while for others they may have served as convincing evidence for the fact that brutal action against 'gangs' (i.e. groups of partisans), resettlement and a slave economy had accompanied the colonising process everywhere, and were therefore legitimate.

In the Service of the Empire: Berlin University's Geographers from Colonial Sciences to *Ostforschung*

Anyone who perceives the increasing importance of German trade and German shipping along these coasts [of China] and gives consideration to the extent to which both still have scope for growth will inevitably find it painful how little political weight Prussia carries in the countries of eastern Asia.[1] [...] The acquisition of such an extraordinarily favourably located seaport [on the island of Chusan] would be of great importance especially at this present moment in time, since the almost certainly imminent opening of major coal mines and the prospect of railways being constructed in China, although this, it is true, is still further away, herald a considerable upturn in all areas, and especially in the development of commercial interests, of a magnitude that cannot as yet be predicted. [...] The harbour can be fortified without great difficulty and transformed into a secure naval station, which would then control access to northern China and Japan in a way no other location could rival. [...] As I have made bold to approach Your Excellency, even though Your Excellency is not acquainted with me, I further give myself the honour of naming His Excellency Count zu Eulenburg as a reference, to whose one-time mission to eastern Asia I was attached as a geologist. I am presently continuing my travels in China that I began at that time, primarily for scientific purposes. Should Your Excellency wish to command further reports from me, I place myself most respectfully at your disposal. I would count myself fortunate to be able to employ my small powers in such a way as to make myself useful to my Fatherland.[2]

These are the words of the then still largely unknown explorer and geographer Ferdinand von Richthofen, writing to introduce himself to the Chancellor of the North German Confederation, Otto von Bismarck, in 1869.[3] As is generally known, fifteen more years would pass before the newly unified German Empire acquired

---

[1] I would like to extend most sincere thanks to Clara Ervedosa, Armin Nolzen, A. Dirk Moses, Dominik J. Schaller and Dirk van Laak for their valuable suggestions and critique. I bear sole responsibility for any errors.
[2] Ferdinand von Richthofen, "Denkschrift an den Kanzler des Norddeutschen Bundes, Bismarck, über ein preußisch-deutsches Engagement in Asien", 2 January 1869 [transcript], reproduced in: Horst Gründer, ed., "... *da und dort ein junges Deutschland gründen*". *Rassismus, Kolonien und kolonialer Gedanke vom 16. bis zum 20. Jahrhundert*, München 1999, pp. 59–62.
[3] For a critical assessment of Richthofen, including with regard to his contribution to German colonialism, see Jürgen Osterhammel, "Forschungsreise und Kolonialprogramm. Ferdinand von Richthofen und die Erschließung Chinas im 19. Jahrhundert", *Archiv für Kulturgeschichte*, 69 (1987), pp. 150–195. Dirk van Laak, *Imperiale Infrastruktur. Deutsche Planungen für eine Erschließung Afrikas, 1880 bis 1960*, Paderborn 2004.

∂ Open Access. © 2024 the author(s), published by De Gruyter. [CC BY] This work is licensed under the Creative Commons Attribution 4.0 International License.
https://doi.org/10.1515/9783110754513-011

its first colonies and another eighteen before it actually established a base in East Asia with the occupation of Kiaochow.

At this time, Ferdinand von Richthofen had long been one of the most influential figures in German geography. As a professor, he was head of the Department of Geography at the Friedrich Wilhelm University in Berlin, one of the most important teaching and research institutes for geography in Germany.[4] Both von Richthofen's career and the development of geographical research at the Friedrich Wilhelm University are illustrative of the dramatic rise in importance that geography experienced as an academic discipline in the 19th century. As late as 1871 there were only two Chairs of Geography in the newly established Reich. In schools, geography was not even a subject in its own right, and at the universities it was mainly taught as an ancillary discipline to other subjects by their respective professors. Three years later, the Prussian government decided to establish Chairs of Geography at all its universities; ten years later it was being taught in all schools.[5]

This upsurge in the popularity and importance of the subject was closely linked to political developments in Germany, especially the growing enthusiasm for colonialism that finally led in 1884–1885 to German South West Africa, German East Africa, Cameroon, Togo and various island groups in the South Seas being formally proclaimed German *Schutzgebiete* (colonies). However, colonial fantasies, interest in travelogues and in the 'discovery' of foreign lands and cultures had a much older tradition in Germany: colonialism is not restricted to formal colonial rule.[6]

---

4 Apart from the Department of Geography (*Geographisches Seminar*) that was established upon the appointment of von Richthofen, there was also an older Geography Unit (*Geographischer Apparat*), which had originated with Carl Ritter, and was renamed Department of Political and Historical Geography (*Seminar für Staatenkunde und Historische Geographie*) in 1922. See Norman Balk, *Die Friedrich-Wilhelms-Universität zu Berlin*, Berlin 1926, pp. 125–131; Jürgen Zimmerer, "Wissenschaft und Kolonialismus. Das Geographische Institut der Friedrich-Wilhelms-Universität vom Kaiserreich zum Dritten Reich", in Ulrich van der Heyden and Joachim Zeller, eds, *Kolonialmetropole Berlin. Eine Spurensuche*, Berlin 2002, pp. 125–130.

5 Franz-Josef Schulte-Althoff, *Studien zur politischen Wissenschaftsgeschichte der deutschen Geographie im Zeitalter des Imperialismus*, Paderborn 1971, p. 14, 120.

6 On this see, for example: Susanne Zantop, *Kolonialphantasien im vorkolonialen Deutschland, 1770–1870*, Berlin 1999; Russell A. Berman, *Enlightenment or Empire. Colonial Discourse in German Culture*, Lincoln 1998; Sara Friedrichsmeyer, Sara Lennox and Susanne Zantop, eds, *The Imperialist Imagination. German Colonialism and Its Legacy*, Ann Arbor 1998. For a theoretical discussion of postcolonial theories using Germany as an example, see Sebastian Conrad, "Doppelte Marginalisierung. Plädoyer für eine transnationale Perspektive auf die deutsche Geschichte", *Geschichte und Gesellschaft*, 28 (2002), pp. 145–169; Andreas Eckert and Albert Wirz, "Wir nicht, die Anderen auch. Deutschland und der Kolonialismus", in Sebastian Conrad and Shalini Randeria, eds, *Jenseits des Eurozentrismus. Postkoloniale Perspektiven in den Geschichts- und Kulturwissenschaften*, Frankfurt 2002, pp. 372–392.

Geographers were able to exploit this interest to promote the establishment of their subject as an academic discipline.[7] A relationship that can be regarded as truly symbiotic between the emerging academic field and the growing enthusiasm for colonialism in Germany[8] offered geographers the opportunity to demonstrate the subject's practical value, which in turn was reflected in enhanced social esteem, the creation of posts at universities and easier access to research funds. Although there were certainly also geographers who were critical of colonialism, the vast majority of them doubtless shared the enthusiasm for Germany's new prestige in the international political arena, as expressed in the acquisition of an overseas empire, with the rest of the country's nationalistically-minded bourgeoisie.[9] Additionally, they exploited Germany's growing international standing, as demonstrated by, amongst other things, the increasing importance of foreign trade, to lead their subject out of the shadow of historical studies and to ensure its institutionalisation. This cooperation took on formal aspects once the German Empire had indeed acquired its colonies: geographers became members of the Colonial Council and political advisers, they trained colonial civil servants and provided the academic foundations required for practical work in the colonies.

The history of this mutual interdependency is of interest with regard not only to the history of the discipline of geography, but also to that of German colonialism and of European expansion in general. On the one hand, it shows how widely colonial fantasies were entertained by the educated middle classes, and thus offers an example of how personal interests and national inferiority complexes could be combined into collective emotions and a search for the nation's "place in the sun".[10] On the other hand, it also provides evidence of a more rational element at the core of the colonial euphoria. Colonial undertakings were the playgrounds not just of adventure-seeking loners, failed aristocrats and sons of the bourgeoisie at

---

[7] On this, see Schulte-Althoff, *Studien*; Jürgen Osterhammel, "Raumerfassung und Universalgeschichte im 20. Jahrhundert", in Gangolf Hübinger, Jürgen Osterhammel and Erich Pelzer, eds, *Universalgeschichte und Nationalgeschichten. Ernst Schulin zum 65. Geburtstag*, Freiburg 1994, pp. 51–72.

[8] For a more detailed discussion of the origins and motives of the German colonial movement, see Horst Gründer, *Geschichte der deutschen Kolonien*, 3rd edn, Paderborn 1995, pp. 25–62. On early demands for a German colonial empire, see Hans Fenske, "Ungeduldige Zuschauer. Die Deutschen und die europäische Expansion 1815–1880", in Wolfgang Reinhard, ed., *Imperialistische Kontinuität und nationale Ungeduld im 19. Jahrhundert*, Frankfurt 1991, pp. 87–140.

[9] A differentiated discussion of the terminology (expansion, empire, etc.) can be found in: Jürgen Osterhammel, "Expansion und Imperium", in Peter Burschel, Mark Häberlein, Volker Reinhard, Wolfgang J. Weber and Reinhard Wendt, eds, *Historische Anstöße*, Berlin 2002, pp. 371–392.

[10] In von Bülow's memorable phrase. See Klaus Hildebrand, *Das vergangene Reich. Deutsche Außenpolitik von Bismarck bis Hitler*, Stuttgart 1995, p. 193.

loggerheads with their families and in search of wealth, power, adventure and sexual gratification, or of unscrupulous trading companies greedy for profit; but also of seriously-minded officials and of the explorers and researchers who were seen as the very epitome of modern-day European rationality.[11] The *Schutzgebiete* also always served as fields for research and for the trying out of new, rational and scientific methods of exploitation and 'development'.

The colonial project of the Wilhelminian era, which took on its most distinctive form in German South West Africa, was an attempt to bring about a modern utopia, orientated towards modern ideas of the state and the economy, which attempted to avoid the supposed 'undesirable developments' in modern society while striving to create a model colonial state that could proudly bear comparison with the imperial 'mother country'. The opening up of 'undeveloped' areas, their 'development', the establishment of 'order and efficiency': these were the underlying principles. The key characteristic was a heavy emphasis on bureaucratic rule and the application of supposedly 'scientific' approaches to Native Policy. The aim was to build an efficient economic system and a society of racial privilege in which the African population provided the labour, which factors were supposed to accelerate the economic 'development' of the colony and guarantee the extraction of raw materials.[12] However, in order for this to be implemented, information was required about the land and people and about available transportation routes and natural resources, and there needed to be possibilities for settlement, areas suitable for cultivation by Europeans, and a supply of trained skilled workers. In short, the administration needed the universities as training centres and academics to collect and organise data. In view of this situation, it is all the more remarkable that there is hardly any literature concerning the relationship between colonialism and academic research.

Geography was the quintessential colonial science; this is not intended to suggest that all its results or research were geared solely towards the exploration and 'development' of overseas territories, but that of all the sciences geography was the one able to offer most to the process of European expansion. Like medi-

---

11 The fact that the travellers emphasised their own rationality in this way was itself a construct, born out of the experience of their own physicality and emotionality, is clearly shown in Johannes Fabian, *Out of our minds. Reason and madness in the exploration of Central Africa*, Los Angeles 2000.
12 On this subject and the failure of this utopia in colonial practice, see Zimmerer, Jürgen, *Deutsche Herrschaft über Afrikaner. Staatlicher Machtanspruch und Wirklichkeit im kolonialen Namibia*, Münster/Hamburg/London 2001 [English edition: *German Rule, African Subjects. State Aspirations and the Reality of Power in Colonial Namibia*, New York 2021].

cine[13] and engineering,[14] the discipline trained specialist staff for service overseas; like eugenics,[15] it furnished ideological and (pseudo-)scientific justifications for colonial exploitation and the establishment of a racist hierarchy in the political and legal systems. In its sub-systems of 'Colonial Population Studies', 'Colonial Economic Production', 'Colonial Settlement and Infrastructure', 'Colonial Typology', 'Colonial Historical Geography' and 'Comparative Studies of Colonial Empires', 'Political Geography' was concerned with racial research, geomedicine and tropical diseases, trade in colonial commodities, colonial economic production, processes of economic exchange between the metropolis and the colony, and also questions concerning the 'intermingling' of cultures, colonial settlement and conditions in other colonies.[16] It therefore took up the discoveries of other disciplines and converted them into knowledge that could be applied in the exercise of colonial rule.

Unfortunately, German historians have up until now rather neglected this complex of problems.[17] In respect of the second attempt at building a German empire in modern times, namely the National Socialist policy of *Lebensraum* ('living space'), however, the situation is different. The research that has been and is being carried out into the involvement of academics in the policies of conquest and extermination has, especially in recent years, been extremely controversially debated. While the initial focus was on the doctors, clinics and 'population experts' involved in the euthanasia programme,[18] the spotlight soon moved on to the policy of occupation in eastern Europe and the murder of the European Jews.[19] It turned out that academics from a wide range of disciplines, as diverse

---

13 See Wolfgang Uwe Eckart, *Medizin und Kolonialimperialismus. Deutschland 1884–1945*, Paderborn 1996.
14 See Laak, *Imperiale Infrastruktur*.
15 See Pascal Grosse, *Kolonialismus, Eugenik und bürgerliche Gesellschaft in Deutschland, 1850–1918*, Frankfurt 2000.
16 See Klaus Kost, *Die Einflüsse der Geopolitik auf Forschung und Theorie der Politischen Geographie von ihren Anfängen bis 1945. Ein Beitrag zur Wissenschaftsgeschichte unter besonderer Berücksichtigung von Militär und Kolonialgeographie*, Bonn 1988, pp. 193–234.
17 An exception in Germany is provided by Jürgen Osterhammel, who has been pleading for years for a stronger consideration of geography. In particular, see Osterhammel, "Raumerfassung". With regard to the British Empire it is now possible to refer to Felix Driver, *Geography Militant: Cultures of Exploration and Empire*, Oxford 2001.
18 On this subject, see the articles in the series of journals *Beiträge zur nationalsozialistischen Gesundheits- und Sozialpolitik*, Berlin 1985ff. Peter Weingart, Jürgen Kroll and Kurt Bayertz, *Rasse, Blut und Gene. Geschichte der Eugenik in Deutschland*, Frankfurt 1988.
19 See: Götz Aly and Susanne Heim, *Vordenker der Vernichtung. Auschwitz und die deutschen Pläne für eine neue europäische Ordnung*, Hamburg 1991; Michael Burleigh, *Germany turns Eastwards. A Study of Ostforschung in the Third Reich*, Cambridge 1988.

as eugenics, medicine and biology,[20] social studies, geography,[21] economics, transportation and engineering,[22] jurisprudence[23] and the humanities,[24] all supported the Nazis in their planned re-ordering of Europe. Academics willingly provided legitimation for the racial and spatial planning policies, participated in the development of these concepts and served as expert assessors of measures of 'racial hygiene' and expert advisers to the military and civil administrative staffs in the occupied areas.[25]

However closely, in empirical terms, the works referred to manage to depict the contribution of academics to occupation and war, they nevertheless display a tendency to neglect the historical contexts that those academics were embedded in. Academic or scientific insights and attitudes do not develop in a vacuum; rather, they are embedded in the context of synchronic or diachronic debates, in academic networks and in networks linking the academic world to society or the political arena. But whereas historical research has made some progress in revealing the involvement of academics and other 'experts' in the Nazi policies of conquest and extermination, this is much less the case in respect of those lines of

---

20 On racial hygiene and euthanasia in the Third Reich, see Ernst Klee, 'Euthanasie' im NS-Staat. Die 'Vernichtung lebensunwerten Lebens', Frankfurt 1983; Hans-Walter Schmuhl, Rassenhygiene – Nationalsozialismus – Euthanasie, Göttingen 1987.

21 For further information regarding the role of geography in the Third Reich, see Michael Fahlbusch, Mechthild Rössler and Dominik Siegrist, Geographie im Nationalsozialismus. 3 Fallstudien zur Institution Geographie im Deutschen Reich und der Schweiz, Kassel 1989; Mechthild Rössler, 'Wissenschaft und Lebensraum'. Geographische Ostforschung im Nationalsozialismus. Ein Beitrag zur Disziplingeschichte der Geographie, Berlin 1990.

22 For example, see Jeffrey Herf, Reactionary Modernism. Technology, Culture and Politics in Weimar and the Third Reich, Cambridge 1984; Monika Renneberg and Mark Walter, eds, Science, Technology and National Socialism, Cambridge 1994; Peter Lundgreen, ed., Wissenschaft im Dritten Reich, Frankfurt 1985.

23 On this subject, see Mathias Schmoeckel, Die Großraumtheorie. Ein Beitrag zur Geschichte der Völkerrechtswissenschaft im Dritten Reich, insbesondere der Kriegszeit, Berlin 1994.

24 For more on the humanities in general, see Frank-Rutker Hausmann, 'Deutsche Geisteswissenschaft' im Zweiten Weltkrieg. Die 'Aktion Ritterbusch' (1940–1945), Dresden 1998. Regarding the role of history and historians, which is an area subject to particularly controversial debate at present, see: Winfried Schulze and Otto Gerhard Oexle, eds, Deutsche Historiker im Nationalsozialismus, Frankfurt 1999; Peter Schöttler, ed., Geschichtsschreibung als Legitimationswissenschaft 1918–1945, Frankfurt 1999; Ingo Haar, Historiker im Nationalsozialismus. Deutsche Geschichtswissenschaft und der 'Volkstumskampf' im Osten, Göttingen 2000.

25 On this subject, see Michael Fahlbusch, Wissenschaft im Dienst der nationalsozialistischen Politik? Die 'Volksdeutschen Forschungsgemeinschaften' von 1931–1945, Baden-Baden 1999; Mechthild Rössler and Sabine Schleiermacher, eds, Der 'Generalplan Ost', Berlin 1993; Bruno Wasser, Himmlers Raumplanung im Osten, Basel 1993; Czeslaw Madajczyk, ed., Vom Generalplan Ost zum Generalsiedlungsplan, München 1994.

tradition (with the exception of 'racial hygiene'[26]) which allowed science to develop concepts in these areas and bring them into play in the first place. This applies above all to the relationship between science and colonial rule, the area *par excellence* in which population economics had made its mark in the period before the outbreak of the Second World War;[27] and it applies particularly in the case of geography, which due to its general concern with exploration and the opening up of spaces was the quintessential imperial science. For the concept of space in particular, together with the concept of 'race', occupied a prominent position both in European colonialist ideology and in the Nazi policy of conquest. Both of these phenomena, European colonialism on the one hand and later the German policy and practice of occupation in the east, involved large-scale spatial economies (*Großraumwirtschaften*), and were characterised by efforts to open up a huge dependent territory to such activity.[28] For this reason alone, it is worthwhile to undertake a diachronic analysis of the relationship between academic geography and politics from the foundation of the colonial empire to the eastward expansion under the Nazis. There are, naturally, other lines of connection in the sciences apart from this one, notably in geopolitics. It is generally well known that the influence of geopolitics came to a climax under the Third Reich.[29]

This chapter, however, will not deal either with geopolitics or with the military research carried out independently by geographical institutions,[30] to name

---

[26] There is a relatively wide range of research into this question: Michael Burleigh, *Death and Deliverance. Euthanasia in Germany c.1900–1945*, Cambridge 1994; Weingart, Kroll and Bayertz, *Rasse*. For the international context, see Stefan Kühl, *Die Internationale der Rassisten. Aufstieg und Niedergang der internationalen Bewegung für Eugenik und Rassenhygiene im 20. Jahrhundert*, Frankfurt 1997.

[27] To date, there have only been two studies that have concerned themselves extensively with the lines of continuity between colonialism and Nazism: one is Wolfgang Eckart, *Medizin und Kolonialimperialismus*; and the other, on the institutional links, Stefan Wulf, *Das Hamburger Tropeninstitut 1919 bis 1945. Auswärtige Kulturpolitik und Kolonialrevisionismus nach Versailles*, Berlin 1994.

[28] For greater detail, see: Jürgen Zimmerer, "Colonialism and the Holocaust. Towards an Archaeology of Genocide", in A. Dirk Moses, ed., *Genocide and Settler Society: Frontier Violence and Stolen Indigenous Children in Australia*, New York 2004, pp. 49–76 (a revised version appears in this book as pp. 175–197).

[29] For an introduction to geopolitics, see the articles in the following collection: Irene Diekmann, Peter Krüger and Julius H. Schoeps, eds, *Geopolitik. Grenzgänge im Zeitgeist*, 2 vols, Potsdam 2000.

[30] In 1936 an Institute for General Military Studies (*Institut für Allgemeine Wehrlehre*), headed by the geographer Oskar Ritter von Niedermayer, was established at the Friedrich Wilhelm University in Berlin, where lectures on military geography were given. See Christoph Jahr, "Die geistige Verbindung von Wehrmacht, Wissenschaft und Politik: Wehrlehre und Heimatforschung an

only those subjects that are immediately related to geography. Rather, it will attempt to uncover the manifold historical connections between universities, the political world and the public, through the example of a single institution. The role of the University as a political adviser with an orientation towards practical applications that this brings to light did not, however, originate only with the establishment of the first German colony in 1884; rather, it contributed to a degree that is not to be underestimated to the kindling and spreading of enthusiasm for the colonial idea in Germany long before the founding of the German Empire. It is therefore necessary to first take a brief look back into the past.

'Armchair Explorers': Geography and the Educated Public in the 19th Century

To understand the way geography developed in the 19th century it is necessary to look beyond the universities, and to take note of the development within society of an enhanced interest in distant countries, in well-founded knowledge about them and in the men who acquired this knowledge; and perhaps most importantly, to be aware of the first institutions to focus on these far-off parts of the world: the Geographical Societies.

In a variety of ways, these societies brought together the different groups responsible for gathering geographical data and opening up the 'unknown' regions of the earth – adventurers, explorers and travelling researchers, scholars, social worthies and 'armchair explorers', whether bourgeois or aristocratic[31] – and they took on a key role in shaping colonial fantasies throughout the German-speaking world.[32] At a time when the boundaries between academic research and adven-

---

der Friedrich-Wilhelms-Universität zu Berlin 1933–1945", *Jahrbuch für Universitätsgeschichte*, 4 (2001), pp. 161–176.

31 I use this term in allusion to Jürgen Osterhammel and Susanne Zantop, who use the expressions 'armchair geography' (*"Lehnstuhl-Geographie"*) and 'armchair conquerors' (*"Lehnstuhl-Eroberer"*). By the former term Osterhammel means the compilation of geographical knowledge without any actual fieldwork, which culminated in (for instance) the work of Carl Ritter. Zantop for her part uses the second term to refer to the way readers might develop fantasies of colonial conquest simply by reading accounts of such undertakings within their own four walls. Osterhammel *Forschungsreise*, p. 167. Zantop, *Kolonialphantasien*, p. 31.

32 Scholars are beginning to get to grips with the fantasies of the geographers. See Alexander Honold, "Flüsse, Berge, Eisenbahnen: Szenarien geographischer Bemächtigung", in Alexander Honold and Klaus R. Scherbe, eds, *Das Fremde. Reiseerfahrungen, Schreibformen und kulturelles Wissen*, Frankfurt 2003, pp. 137–161. For an example of the repercussions of geographical conceptions on colonial ideology, here taking literature as an example, see John K. Noyes, "Landschafts-

turous exploration were still fluid, and when formal geography at university level was still in its infancy, it was the geographical societies that were the real breeding grounds of geographical research. In addition, they created the public climate in which the rise of geography became possible.

The story of the geographical societies had begun with the foundation of the 'African Association', or to give it its full name the 'Association for Promoting the Discovery of the Interior Parts of Africa', in London in 1788, out of which the 'Royal Geographical Society of London' was formed in 1830. On the continent, it took another 30 years before the geographical societies of Paris (*Société de Géographie*) and Berlin (*Gesellschaft für Erdkunde zu Berlin*) were established in 1821 and 1828 respectively. Other such societies soon followed, including those in Frankfurt (1836), Bombay (1838), Mexico City (1839), St Petersburg (1845), Darmstadt (1845), Delft (1851), New York (1852), Vienna (1856), Buenos Aires (1856), Geneva (1858), Leipzig (1861), Dresden (1863), Munich (1869) and Bremen (1870). In the early days after their establishment, these geographical societies consisted mainly of relatively small circles of people interested in exploration and the research conducted by 'explorers'; there was little resonance among the general public, and the societies were still only in loose contact with academic geography. After all, academics were not the only 'explorers': soldiers, diplomats, missionaries and adventurers in general all published their own reports on foreign lands. However, as they were all pursuing completely different objectives, their works were of only limited utility for scientific purposes. It was not until there was a shift towards the professionalisation of this area that such travels and travel accounts too became true 'tools of geography'. And some of the most prominent geography lecturers at the universities, such as the above-mentioned Ferdinand von Richthofen, had begun their careers as academic travellers.[33]

A general problem for expeditions of all kinds was the cost; expeditions were expensive and hardly any financial support was available in the German Confederation. German 'explorers', therefore, increasingly signed up to take part in expeditions organised by other countries. Although this promoted international exchange, at a time of growing German nationalism many people found it an unsatisfactory

---

schilderung, Kultur und Geographie. Von den Aporien der poetischen Sprache im Zeitalter der politischen Geographie", in Alexander Honold and Oliver Simons, eds, *Kolonialismus als Kultur. Literatur, Medien, Wissenschaft in der deutschen Gründerzeit des Fremden*, Tübingen/Basel 2002, pp. 127–142. For more on the various concepts of geographical space, as expressed not least in the form of maps, and their political implications, see Hans-Dietrich Schultz, "Raumkonstrukte der klassischen deutschsprachigen Geographie des 19./20. Jahrhunderts im Kontext ihrer Zeit", in *Geschichte und Gesellschaft*, 28 (2002), pp. 343–377.

33 Schulte-Althoff, *Studien*, pp. 17–19.

state of affairs, since precisely in the absence of a German colonial empire achievements in the area of 'discovery' were supposed to serve as a substitute. Consequently, in the academic sphere at least Germany was determined to play a part in the efforts of the European powers to divide the world up between them. With regard to Africa, Adolf Bastian put this credo into words in 1875:

> Guided by the conviction that the long series of African discoveries that German explorers have been actively and outstandingly involved in, and that with the utmost enthusiasm and commitment, is gradually approaching its end, Germany must not neglect to be a player in the competitive struggle, so that when in the future the names of the discoverers come to be written in the annals of the history of geography, the German people too will be represented.[34]

However, for many people this was not enough. They wanted the Germans to become officially active in their own right, and in the long term to create their own colonial empire. The factors behind this movement were not only nationalistic zeal and the romance of colonialism, but also the ambitions of the geographical fraternity to enhance the regard they were held in among the general public by demonstrating their practical utility, to gain more public funding and, in the long term, to become institutionally established in schools and universities.

A good example of the interaction between international experience and the attempt on the one hand to further German geographical research and at the same time on the other hand to secure one's own position can be seen in the life and work of the cartographer August (Augustus) Petermann. He went to London at the age of 23 and became a member of the Royal Geographical Society, where he advanced for a time to the position of Under-Secretary.[35] From London, he networked with leading German explorers and also linked them up with international expeditions. In 1854 he returned to Germany. There he founded the famous *Petermanns Geographische Mitteilungen* (Petermann's Geographical Communications), and as an initiator of expeditions and tireless fundraiser for them played a major role in ensuring that German expeditions too could play their part in the 'exploration' of the world – and that such expeditions were perceived as a 'national task' in Germany. The idea driving him in making his appeals was less that of creating a national school of geography than that of ensuring continuity of financial support for his discipline, using national pride in exploration and discovery as a key argument, so to speak.

From Germany's new global importance following unification and the establishment of the Empire there was thus immediately derived a 'duty' to participate

---

34 Adolf Bastian in *Petermanns Geographische Mitteilungen (Petermann's Geographical Communications)*, 1875, p. 6; quoted according to Schulte-Althoff in *Studien*, p. 55.
35 With regard to Petermann, see ibid., pp. 23–38.

in the 'exploration' of the world. And so the manner in which an *Afrikanische Gesellschaft in Deutschland* (African Society of Germany) formulated the abilities and aspirations of geography in its founding declaration of 1873 was demanding and beseeching in equal measure:

> The obligations incumbent upon a nation in the search for solutions to the challenges of its cultural mission are measured in terms of the political weight it carries. Now that Germany has regained its rightful place in the concert of nations, it must even more than ever before play a leading role in the cultivation of science. Above all it behoves it to take the lead in the organisation of geographical ventures designed to open up new fields of knowledge, because such advances will be inscribed in history under the name of the country that bravely and resolutely first blazed the trail to achieve them.[36]

It was only a short distance from here to the explicit demand for German colonies, which sections of the nationalistically-minded German bourgeoisie had been raising at least since 1848. The fact that such a statement of position is contained in the founding declaration of a geographical society demonstrates the close relationship and mutual complementarity between the enthusiasm outside academic circles for exploration, voyages of discovery and geographical research on the one hand, and the institutionalisation of geography on the other. Academic and extra-academic interest in geography continued to develop in parallel, since both experienced the upswing brought about by the unification of Germany to constitute the German Empire. Whereas only seven geographical societies had been founded in Germany between 1828 and 1871, nine more were added by 1884, and another five by the outbreak of the First World War. This development mirrored a world-wide trend.[37] The first German national geographical conference (*Deutscher Geographentag*) was held in 1881, and was well attended not only by representatives of the princely dynasties and by explorers and professors, but also by members of the educated bourgeoisie. Alongside the motivations of curiosity, the prospect of adventure and fantasies of German colonies fuelled by the reports of Stanley's crossings of Africa, considerable interest was also aroused in the economic sector, with many business people hoping to acquire practical knowledge concerning, for example, economic structures, transportation routes and the presence of raw materials in far-off countries.[38]

Thus business had at last taken on board the arguments that those lobbying for a strengthening of geography in Germany had been invoking for years; for as early as 1873 the *Correspondenzblatt der Afrikanischen Gesellschaft* had declared:

---

36 "Gründungsaufruf der Afrikanischen Gesellschaft in Deutschland", in *Petermanns Geographische Mitteilungen 1873*, p. 72; quoted according to Schulte-Althoff, *Studien*, pp. 50f.
37 Ibid., p. 43.
38 Ibid., pp. 47f.

> All the things that such efforts are able to achieve are equally beneficial to science on the one hand and to trade and industry on the other; for after all, geography stands at the point where the theoretical and practical aspects of life come together. The routes established by pioneering geographers lead, sooner or later, to new trading markets, which merchants will soon follow them to and where new sources of revenue will be opened up by busy exchange. The powerful force of global trade has grown out of the prudent utilisation of the resources offered by geography [...].[39]

The great opportunity afforded by the unification of Germany and the resulting changes in foreign trade relations were beneficial to the world of academic geography too. As already mentioned, in the year the Empire was founded there had been Chairs of Geography only in Berlin and Göttingen, and the subject was not taught as a separate subject in schools either. In 1871, however, a Chair of Geography was established in Leipzig, to which Munich, Halle, Strasbourg and Dresden were added two years later. In 1874 the Prussian government even adopted a measure to establish Chairs of Geography at all Prussian universities, though this could not be put into effect immediately, due, significantly, to a lack of suitably qualified personnel.[40] Finally, in the curricula for academic secondary schools (*Gymnasien*) adopted in 1882 and 1892 it was decreed that geography should be an independent subject, and thus 'freed' from its previous controversial link to history.[41]

When the German colonial empire began to be established in 1884, the specialist knowledge of geographers came to be even more in demand. The *Schutzgebiete* needed to be surveyed and their economic potential analysed, and the colonial administrative officers themselves needed to be trained. Furthermore, the colonialist movement in Germany was itself interested in obtaining an increasing amount of information. Geography was finally established in society and at the universities. It had been able to exploit the constantly growing demand for information about foreign countries and also the universal enthusiasm for colonial adventures among the bourgeoisie to establish itself as an independent academic discipline.

This was one reason why the vast majority of university geographers were proponents of Germany's colonial expansion. Another was no doubt the fact that the partitioning of the world between the colonial powers was beginning to restrict the free pursuit of research, so that the nation needed its own colonies as a 'substitute'. As the Berlin-based geographer Ferdinand von Richthofen expressed it in 1889, "the individual is increasingly being hampered in the free choice of his

---

39 *Correspondenzblatt der Afrikanischen Gesellschaft*, No. 1, 1873, 2; as quoted by Schulte-Althoff, *Studien*, p. 60.
40 Ibid., p. 41.
41 Ibid., p. 120.

field of research, because the colonial aspirations of the European states are restricting even scientific investigation to the national territories of the scientists concerned".[42]

A Devotee of Colonialism: Ferdinand Von Richthofen

Justified as this criticism may have been in individual cases, there is a certain irony in the fact that it was von Richthofen of all people who expressed it, since – as is documented by the quotation that opened this chapter – he had been among the most vehement supporters of the establishment of a German colonial empire from the very beginning. And thanks to his position as a professor at the Friedrich Wilhelm University in Berlin and his reputation as a great 'explorer', his voice carried no little weight within the discipline. And it was he in particular who was endeavouring to create close links to the colonial movement, thereby making the Geographical Institute in Berlin one of the more influential institutions in Germany in matters relating to colonialism.

Born in Carlsruhe in Upper Silesia, the young von Richthofen studied geology in Berlin between 1852 and 1856 under, among others, Carl Ritter. After carrying out research in Transylvania and Tyrol, he took part in the Prussian East Asian Expedition of 1860–1862. Having then investigated metal production in the gold mines of California between 1862 and 1868, he was commissioned to undertake the task that would establish his long-term reputation: between the years 1868 and 1872 he undertook a total of seven journeys across China on behalf of the European-American Chamber of Commerce, the results of which, published in five volumes under the title 'China: the findings of my own journeys of exploration and of studies arising out of them', together with the associated 'Atlas of China. Orographic and geological maps',[43] not only gave rise to a "new and more differentiated picture of China",[44] but also combined academic and practical work. For in his cartographic work von Richthofen was able not only to correct a series of

---

[42] Ferdinand von Richthofen, in "Verhandlungen des 8. Geographentages in Berlin", 1889, p. 12; quoted according to Schulte-Althoff, *Studien*, p. 121.
[43] Ferdinand von Richthofen, *China. Ergebnisse eigener Reisen und darauf gegründeter Studien*, i-v, Berlin 1877–1912; Ferdinand von Richthofen, *Atlas von China. Orographische und geologische Karten*, i: *Das nördliche China*, Berlin 1883; ii: *Das südliche China*, ed. Max Groll, Berlin 1912.
[44] Lothar Zögner, "Ferdinand von Richthofen – Neue Sicht auf ein altes Land", in Hans-Martin Hinz and Christoph Lind, eds, *Tsingtau. Ein Kapitel deutscher Kolonialgeschichte in China 1897–1914*, Deutsches Historisches Museum Berlin 1997, pp. 72–75, here p. 72. See also Gerhard Engelmann, *Ferdinand von Richthofen (1833–1905) und Alfred Penck (1858–1945). Zwei markante Geographen Berlins*, Stuttgart 1988, pp. 7–9.

erroneous depictions in previous Chinese and Jesuit maps, but also to give valuable pointers to how the country might be 'developed'. For example, coal deposits or suggestions for the route of the planned railway were marked in his maps, and he put forward detailed suggestions for the latter in his writings.[45] In his diary he expressed the hope that one day "the first railway in China might be built here".[46] And it was by no means by chance that he had selected China as his destination; it seemed to him, in his "partly Prusso-German, partly [...] comprehensively imperialistic sense of mission", that "the opening up of this, the last remaining huge country outside Europe that is still largely unexplored" still offered him the opportunity to make a name for himself.[47]

As he noted in his diary, von Richthofen recognised at an early stage the importance that might accrue to a German, or rather Prussian, outpost in China:

> As a free port in the hands of a power such as Prussia, Chusan would occupy a commanding position. The harbour can easily be fortified and a naval fleet would control traffic with northern China and Japan. It would achieve great importance as a trading post.[48]

Von Richthofen did not, however, stop at daydreams of colonial achievements; rather, as shown above, he wrote a letter to the Chancellor of the *Norddeutscher Bund* (North German Confederation), Otto von Bismarck, even while he was still in China, in order to draw his attention to the value such a naval base and trading post would have.

While von Richthofen's original principal was not interested in these results, August Petermann immediately recognised the significance of von Richthofen's investigations and played a part in getting them widely diffused in Germany in the following years.[49] The Prussian government then paid for the results to be properly compiled and documented.[50]

Only a few years later, von Richthofen's career took off in Germany. In 1875 he became a professor in Bonn, and in 1883 moved to Leipzig as the successor of Oscar Peschel.[51] Nonetheless, he was still not content: working exclusively as a

---

45 Zögner, "Ferdinand von Richthofen", pp. 72–75, here pp. 74f.
46 Von Richthofen, *Tagebücher aus China*, Berlin 1907, Vol. 1, p. 29, quoted according to Zögner, "Ferdinand von Richthofen", pp. 72–75.
47 Osterhammel, *Forschungsreise*, p. 172. Osterhammel also gives a vivid description of von Richthofen's arrogance and his conviction of the superiority of his own civilisation, which he demonstrated by taking European food and crockery with him on his travels, in order to be able to maintain his European standards.
48 Von Richthofen, "Tagebücher", Vol. 1, p. 44, as quoted by Engelmann, *Richthofen / Penck*, p. 10.
49 Zögner, *Ferdinand von Richthofen*, pp. 72–75.
50 Engelmann, *Richthofen / Penck*, p. 10.
51 Ibid., pp. 11f.

university teacher was not enough for him. As he wrote to the Prussian Minister of Education, Friedrich Althoff, he felt himself too "limited to my very narrow professional activity and cannot satisfy my desire to make myself useful in the interests of the Fatherland in general, as far as that is possible for a geographer."[52] This would change when he was appointed Professor of Geography at the Friedrich Wilhelm University in Berlin in 1885. Here a new Chair of Physical Geography was established for him, alongside Carl Ritter's original Chair of Geography, which was occupied at the time by Heinrich Kiepert.[53]

Von Richthofen's campaign for the establishment of a German trading and naval station in China was also ultimately successful: in 1897 the German Empire finally took possession of Kiaochow. Von Richthofen was able to declare with satisfaction: "This outcome naturally gives me a certain degree of pleasure, since all my efforts of the last 25 years have finally come to fruition."[54] He enthusiastically celebrated the establishment of a German colony in China with two monographs. 1897 saw the publication of 'Kiaochow. Its global situation and probable future importance'; this was followed one year later by 'Shantung Province and the Gateway to it: Kiaochow'.[55]

However, von Richthofen did not content himself with acting as a publicist for European colonial rule in general and German empire-building in particular: he was also active as a practical lobbyist and as a political adviser. He was one of the founder members of the *Association Internationale Africaine*, established in 1876 on the initiative of King Leopold II of the Belgians and appearing on the surface to be aimed more at the general promotion of European influence in Africa than at the direct establishment of a colonial empire. Von Richthofen apparently overlooked – as many others also did – that this association was essentially merely a propaganda instrument designed to camouflage Leopold's plans to build up his own private colonial empire in the Congo.[56] A German section of the Association was founded in the same year, with the involvement of high-ranking members of the German aristoc-

---

52 Letter to Althoff, Leipzig 1885 III 2; quoted according to Engelmann, *Richthofen / Penck*, pp. 12f.
53 Ibid., p. 13.
54 Letter to Hettner, Berlin 1897 XII 9; quoted according to Engelmann, *Richthofen / Penck*, p. 10.
55 Von Richthofen, *Kiautschou. Seine Weltstellung und voraussichtliche Bedeutung*, Berlin 1897; Ferdinand von Richthofen, *Schantung und seine Eingangspforte Kiautschou*, Berlin 1898.
56 On the atrocities in the Congo, see, for example, Samuel Henry Nelson, *Colonialism in the Congo Basin, 1880–1940*, Athens (Ohio) 1994. A useful overview of the Belgian involvement in the Congo and of the unparalleled publicity campaign undertaken to legitimise it in the eyes of the public is also given in the book by Hochschild that became an international best-seller: Adam Hochschild, *Schatten über dem Kongo. Die Geschichte eines der großen fast vergessenen Menschheitsverbrechen*, Stuttgart 2000.

racy, military officers and industrialists; this then merged in 1878 with the *Deutsche Gesellschaft zur Erforschung Äquatorialafrikas* (German Society for the Exploration of Equatorial Africa). The President of this body was the German ambassador in Vienna, Prince Heinrich VII Reuß, and Ferdinand von Richthofen was his deputy.[57] Between 1873 and 1878 and again between 1888 and 1905 he also officiated as Chairman of the *Gesellschaft für Erdkunde zu Berlin*.[58]

Though von Richthofen, through his activities outside the university, already stood at the interface between academic research and colonial involvement, this was still not enough for him. At the Friedrich Wilhelm University, as in his previous positions, he continued to seek ways to strengthen his own position and establish an institute of his own. Again, it was the requirements of a colonial Germany that served as arguments to justify him in this. Expansion in geographical research, he declared, had been made necessary by the "strengthening of colonial interests and the unparalleled increase in movements and interactions on a world scale". It was

> therefore in the interests of the economy and of the State, on the one hand to train people who are able to act in a strictly scientific way in researching the individual parts of a large and complex field and to disseminate through teaching the knowledge they have acquired; while on the other hand, it is also in the State's interest to create a central location where geographical work can be performed by trained staff under suitable and adequate conditions, and where the materials can be assembled in such a way, in accordance with a variety of categorisations, that they can be used at any time in the event of there being a requirement for information and processing.

This "central location", which would naturally be under von Richthofen's own direction, would, in addition to procuring information about far-off regions of the world, also be used to train scientists and travellers, as well as to

> provide training in geography to those officers and state civil servants who, in their work in the colonial service, as consular representatives, in the navy, or in any other way, have tasks assigned to them for the mastery of which an extensive knowledge of foreign countries and their economic situations is necessary.[59]

Such a "central location" was never actually established, but a year later von Richthofen put in an application, with very similar argumentation, for the estab-

---

57 Schulte-Althoff, *Studien*, pp. 64–73.
58 Engelmann, *Richthofen / Penck*, p. 16.
59 Von Richthofen, *Denkschrift betreffend die Erweiterung des Geographischen Instituts der Universität Berlin zu einer Lehr- und Arbeitsstätte der Geographie in ihren wirtschaftlichen Grundlagen und ihren praktischen Beziehungen*, 1898, reproduced in Engelmann, *Die Hochschulgeographie in Preussen 1810–1914*, Wiesbaden 1983, pp. 157–165, here pp. 157f.

lishment of an Institute of Oceanography, which was successfully implemented. Although the Ministry of Education, as before, was not prepared to set up the institute itself, it did support a scheme to cooperate with the Imperial Navy, which was planning at the time to establish a naval museum in Berlin. Von Richthofen headed the institute until 1905, but did not live to see the completion of the affiliated Museum of Oceanography.[60]

The training of specialist officers for the colonies is indeed likely to have been one of the most important areas of interaction between academic geography and the practical administration of the colonies, even though in the absence of any prosopographical research we are not able to give any precise information in respect of German colonial personnel. Among those of von Richthofen's students who entered into active colonial service, however, at least one attained to great prominence as a colonial propagandist: Paul Rohrbach. Having originally studied theology, he had soon realised that he would not be able to pursue an active academic career in either theology or history, so he chose to pursue geography. In Berlin he was accepted into von Richthofen's celebrated colloquium, where he was particularly valued because of his practical experience as an 'explorer'. He originally planned to undertake a major expedition through East Asia and India in preparation for writing his post-doctoral thesis in Overseas Economic Studies, a plan expressly approved by von Richthofen. Instead, however, he initially went out to German South West Africa as Commissioner for Settlement. This assignment ended unpleasantly for Rohrbach in a difference of opinion with the colonial administration on the spot; but this did not prevent him from coming to be regarded in public perception as one of the most important protagonists of colonial policy in that territory and, despite the fact that he actually dissented from the way it was practised, as one of the most prominent experts on colonial policy in general. Although he returned from Windhoek with the post-doctoral thesis that was intended to qualify him for a university appointment almost completed, his plans for an academic career came to nothing, as von Richthofen had died in the meantime and his successor Albrecht Penck refused to accept the thesis, considering that its topic belonged in the field of political economy and not in that of geography. The deeper reason behind this may well have been that Penck did not feel Rohrbach would make a good university teacher, and saw in him proof of the axiom that travelling did not in itself make a geographer.[61] As one of the most

---

60 Engelmann, *Richthofen / Penck*, pp. 18f.
61 Walter Mogk, *Paul Rohrbach und das 'Größere Deutschland'. Ethischer Imperialismus im Wilhelminischen Zeitalter. Ein Beitrag zur Geschichte des Kulturprotestantismus*, München 1972, pp. 63–66. Rohrbach also had great geopolitical ambitions in the Middle East: on these, see also Dominik J. Schaller, "Die Rezeption des Völkermordes an den Armeniern in Deutschland,

famous publicists in the German Empire, however, he continued to make an impact in popularising debate on issues of colonial economics.[62]

The physician Siegfried Passarge is to be regarded as a further university lecturer who was closely connected to German colonialism. He became a geographer under the influence of von Richthofen and ultimately held the Chair of Geography at the Hamburg Colonial Institute.[63]

Von Richthofen was also directly involved in German colonial politics as a member of the Colonial Council *(Kolonialrat)*. This body was set up in 1892 to advise the central colonial administration in Berlin on specific issues.[64] The Council was originally made up of 19 members, but it was expanded to 25 members, including Ferdinand von Richthofen, in 1895.[65]

When von Richthofen died in 1905, Albrecht Penck succeeded him at the head of both the university Department of Geography and the Institute of Oceanography. Like von Richthofen, he exerted influence going far above and beyond his own subject: he had been a professor in Vienna, and had made a name for himself above all in ice-age research and geomorphology. Like von Richthofen in the academic year 1903/04, Penck was even appointed Vice-Chancellor of the Friedrich Wilhelm University in 1917/18.[66]

Penck also continued the tradition of maintaining close links to both colonial research and practical colonial policy. He was a member of the Commission for Local Studies, Exploration and Research in the Colonies *(Kommission für die landeskundliche Erforschung der Schutzgebiete)* set up by the Colonial Council in 1904.[67] This commission had been specially established, once the German colonial administration in Berlin had recognised the value of geographical knowledge for

---

1915–1945", in Dominik J. Schaller and Hans-Lukas Kieser, eds, *Der Völkermord an den Armeniern und die Shoah*, 2nd edn, Zürich 2003, pp. 517–555.

62 Out of the multitude of his published works, only those that are most important for the colonial question are mentioned here: Paul Rohrbach, *Deutsche Kolonialwirtschaft*, I: 'Südwest-Afrika', Berlin 1907; Paul Rohrbach, *Deutsche Kolonialwirtschaft. Kulturpolitische Grundsätze für die Rassen- und Missionsfragen*, Berlin 1909; Paul Rohrbach, *Koloniale Siedlung und Wirtschaft der führenden Kolonialvölker*, Köln 1934; Paul Rohrbach, *Wie machen wir unsere Kolonien rentabel? Grundzüge eines Wirtschaftsprogramms für Deutschlands afrikanischen Kolonialbesitz*, Halle 1907.

63 Schulte-Althoff, *Studien*, p. 125. An (incomplete) list of von Richthofen's students can be found in: Engelmann, *Richthofen / Penck*, pp. 15f.

64 See Hartmut Pogge von Strandmann, "Der Kolonialrat", in Ulrich van der Heyden and Joachim Zeller, eds, *Kolonialmetropole Berlin. Eine Spurensuche*, Berlin 2002, pp. 32–34.

65 Schulte-Althoff, *Studien*, p. 126.

66 On the biography of Penck, see the overview by Engelmann, even though it is only very cursory in its treatment of the period after 1918: Engelmann, *Richthofen / Penck*, pp. 23–37.

67 Schulte-Althoff, *Studien*, p. 127.

the practical administration of the colonies, to coordinate and give expert support to scientific research activities that received government funding.[68] After the dissolution of the Colonial Council in 1907, the Commission was renamed the Local Studies Commission of the Imperial Colonial Office (*Landeskundliche Kommission des Reichskolonialamtes*). The publication "Reports from Explorers and Scholars in the German Colonies" *(Mitteilungen von Forschungsreisenden und Gelehrten aus den Deutschen Schutzgebieten)* acted as its journal; from 1907 onwards this appeared under the title "Reports from the German Colonies" (*Mitteilungen aus den Deutschen Schutzgebieten*).[69] The members of the Commission drew up expert opinions on colonial issues and carried out scientific expeditions. Penck himself was involved at least with the academic concept for an expedition to the South Seas, which was undertaken on the initiative of the Local Studies Commission as a continuation of the 1908 Sapper-Friederici Expedition to explore the Bismarck Archipelago.[70]

Even during the First World War, when there could be no question of sending out expeditions and all the German *Schutzgebiete* were either occupied by allied troops or, as in the case of German East Africa, were the scene of hostilities, the Commission carried on with its proceedings, and did not suspend its activities until 1919.[71]

Colonial Revisionism

For Penck and most of his colleagues, the issue of German colonies was by no means removed from the agenda with the ending of the First World War, when Germany lost its colonies under the Treaty of Versailles.[72] This was apparent from, among other things, the continued existence of the Berlin Chair of Colonial Geography, which had originally been established in 1911 as the first of its kind in

---

68 Markus Schindlbeck, "Deutsche wissenschaftliche Expeditionen und Forschungen in der Südsee bis 1914", in Hermann Joseph Hiery, ed., *Die deutsche Südsee 1884–1914. Ein Handbuch*, Paderborn 2001, pp. 132–155, here pp. 133–135.
69 Schulte-Althoff, *Studien*, p. 127.
70 The aim of the new expedition was supposed to be, among other things, to search for plants that yielded latex and to test whether the soil was suitable for the establishment of plantations. Schindlbeck, "Deutsche wissenschaftliche Expeditionen", pp. 150f.
71 Schulte-Althoff, *Studien*, p. 127.
72 On the topic of how colonial issues were dealt with in the Treaty of Versailles, see Jürgen Zimmerer, "Von der Bevormundung zur Selbstbestimmung. Die Pariser Friedenskonferenz und ihre Auswirkungen auf die britische Kolonialherrschaft im Südlichen Afrika", in Gerd Krumeich, ed., *Versailles 1919: Ziele – Wirkung – Wahrnehmung*, Essen 2001, pp. 145–158.

Germany. Endowed by the 'explorer', publisher and public benefactor Hans Meyer, it symbolises in the most direct manner possible the link between geography and colonialism. The holder of the Chair was to be head of the Department of Colonial Geography in the Faculty of Geography.[73]

The person appointed to this position was Fritz Jaeger, himself a former student of von Richthofen's. He had earlier completed his doctorate under another of von Richthofen's former students, Alfred Hettner, in Heidelberg, before going on to undertake numerous fairly large-scale exploratory expeditions to East Africa which were financed in part by the Imperial Colonial Office.[74]

In his inaugural lecture in Berlin, Jaeger placed himself very deliberately in the service of politics:

> In geography, and especially in colonial geography, you can immediately see the practical benefits. [...] It is the task of geography to draw a correct overall picture of a country. But a correct assessment of the nature of the land and its inhabitants is the crucial foundation for proper utilisation. The primary purpose of colonies is that they should be economically utilised and exploited to the benefit of the mother country. If no economic benefit is forthcoming, then colonies are a luxury that cannot be justified in terms of national economy. Thus colonial geography provides an important foundation for a rational colonial economy.[75]

As the German colonial empire was destined to survive only for a further three years, the concrete influence of the Chair of Colonial Geography on colonial politics was limited. The fact that it remained in existence after the end of the First World War shows the key role geography played in the colonial revisionism of the Weimar Republic.[76] This brought together rejection of the 'war guilt lie' and of the 'colonial guilt lie', that is to say, the accusations raised by the Allies in the

---

73 Carl Troll, *Fritz Jaeger. Ein Forscherleben*, Erlangen 1969, pp. 10f. A further privately endowed Chair in Colonial Geography was established in Leipzig as late as 1915, to which Hans Meyer was appointed.
74 On the biography of Jaeger, see Troll, *Fritz Jaeger*.
75 Fritz Jaeger, "Wesen und Aufgaben der kolonialen Geographie", *Zeitschrift der Gesellschaft für Erdkunde zu Berlin*, (1911), pp. 400–405.
76 Agitation against the loss of the colonial empire was not restricted to the field of academic geography. Those involved in such agitation saw the indoctrination of young people as being particularly important; the German Colonial Society (*Deutsche Kolonialgesellschaft*) for example, supported by geography teachers in the schools, worked hard to ensure that the special legal status of the former German colonies was explicitly noted in maps in school textbooks. This wish was granted by the Prussian Educational Committee in 1929 in the form of a provision that no books would be authorised for use in schools which did not show the former German *Schutzgebiete* as German possessions. Heinz Peter Brogiato, *Wissen ist Macht – Geographisches Wissen ist Weltmacht. Die schulgeographischen Zeitschriften im deutschsprachigen Raum (1880–1945) unter besonderer Berücksichtigung des Geographischen Anzeigers*, Part 1, text volume, Trier 1998, p. 405.

peace negotiations of 1918/19, as a justification for the confiscation of the German colonial empire, that Germany was unfit to rule over colonies. All those who were unhappy about the loss of the colonies, the abolition of the monarchy and Germany's loss of world power status gathered behind this rallying cry.[77]

When the assets of Hans Meyer's foundation melted away as a consequence of the economic and financial crises of the Weimar Republic, the Prussian state took over the financing of the professorship. At the same time, Jaeger expanded his activities in the field of ensuring that the academic world continued to pay attention to German communities abroad.[78] In 1928 he accepted appointment to the Chair of Geography at the University of Basel; he remained in Basel until 1947, when he was dismissed from his post without compensation because of the contacts he had had with the Third Reich and his work to promote the Nazi cause in Switzerland.[79]

A successor was appointed to his position in Berlin in 1930: this was Carl Troll, who had obtained his doctorate and post-doctoral qualification in geography in Munich. He too was a passionate colonial revisionist; indeed, the widespread commitment of many geographers to this cause was reinforced after 1933 not only by leading protagonists such as Fritz Jaeger and Albrecht Penck, but also by colleagues of theirs including Heinrich Schmitthenner, Erich Obst, Karl H. Dietzel and Franz Thorbecke.[80]

Already in 1931, the National Geographical Conference had adopted a resolution, proposed jointly by Troll, Thorbecke and Schmitthenner, that emphasised the importance of the colonies for geographical research.[81] At the 1936 Conference Troll pointed out explicitly once again

---

77 On colonial revisionism, see Jens Ruppenthal, *Die Kolonialfrage in der Politik der Weimarer Republik. Der Kolonialrevisionismus in der deutschen Außenpolitik von 1919 bis 1926*, University of Kiel 2002 (M.A. thesis); Jan Esche, *Koloniales Anspruchsdenken in Deutschland im Ersten Weltkrieg, während der Versailler Friedensverhandlungen und in der Weimarer Republik (1914 bis 1933)*, Hamburg 1989; for an exhaustive depiction of the relationship between colonial revisionism and the Nazi party, Klaus Hildebrand, *Vom Reich zum Weltreich – Hitler, NSDAP und koloniale Frage 1919–1945*, München 1969.
78 Troll, *Fritz Jaeger*, p. 18.
79 For an exhaustive account, see ibid., pp. 26–31. In a lengthy lawsuit, Jaeger was able to dispose of all the criminal accusations and to secure half of his pension. In the process he publicly affirmed his nationalistic political attitude. In 1963, he was awarded the Gustav Nachtigal Gold Medal, the highest distinction of the Berlin Geographical Society, in recognition of his research in Africa.
80 On this subject and for references to relevant publications of the persons named, see: Kost, *Einflüsse*, p. 213.
81 "Verhandlungen und wiss. Abhandlungen des 24. Deutschen Geographentages zu Danzig 1931", Breslau 1932, pp. 31f.; quoted according to Brogiato, *Wissen ist Macht*, p. 405.

in how many different ways colonial questions are intertwined with geographical science, [... which] will also form the core feature of National Socialist colonial policy in the future. [...] What we are striving for with the demand for colonies, above and beyond the reestablishment of our honour, is a lawfully acquired place in the sun, a field of activity in the wide world beyond the seas, where a genius then in charge of our foreign policy secured us a place while there was still time.

At the same time, Troll foresaw that colonial geography would be faced by a fundamental shift in the range of its tasks:

Unlike the situation in the middle of the last century, you are no longer confronted by the so-called 'dark' continent, but rather by an African world undergoing rapid transformation. [...] It is therefore no longer the task of European academia to send out expeditions to explore little-known areas; but rather to use scientific tools and scientific perspectives to intervene in the process of colonisation itself and its problems.[82]

The extent to which the political world's clinging to the idea of possessing colonies influenced the research opportunities of geographers can be seen in an eleven-month expedition to Africa undertaken by Carl Troll in 1933/34. The decision to finance this expedition was taken at a time when Germany was still suffering from the after-effects of the world economic crisis of 1929. The purpose of Troll's expedition was to

gain scientific and colonial knowledge of Africa on the basis of first-hand experience, which is essential to ensure the reliability and persuasive power of the assessment, but above all also through scientific study, on sound biological and geographical foundations, of living conditions and the possibilities of gaining a livelihood in the mountainous regions of Africa. These highland regions were chosen because they stand at the forefront of interest in respect of issues concerning the development of the tropics by whites. In Africa, the only region that came into question was the mountainous eastern half, where highland regions stretch across the whole of the equatorial zone, extending beyond the tropics both to the north and to the south.[83]

Financial support for the expedition into the highlands of the former German East Africa was provided by the Emergency Association of German Science *(Notgemeinschaft der deutschen Wissenschaft)*, the Cultural and Colonial Departments of the Foreign Office, the Prussian Academy of Sciences, the German Colonial So-

---

[82] Carl Troll, "Kolonialgeographische Forschung und das deutsche Kolonialproblem", in *GEO-Tag, 1936*, Jena/Breslau 1937, pp. 119–138, here pp. 122 and 135–136, quoted according to Kost, *Einflüsse*, pp. 195–197.
[83] Carl Troll, *Das deutsche Kolonialproblem auf Grund einer ostafrikanischen Forschungsreise 1933/34*, Berlin 1935, pp. 8–10.

ciety, the Charlottenburg Section of the German Colonial Society and the Bavarian Academy of Sciences.[84]

Troll politely expressed his gratitude for this financial support – the list of those approached for funding is in itself enough to give an idea of the political side-effects the expedition was expected to have – when he published his travel report (which had initially been presented as a lecture to the Colonial Society), dedicating it to "our fellow-Germans in East Africa". The introductory lines that Troll prefaced the text with are even more revealing:

> Since the unhappy outcome of the World War, by which our German land was cut back on all sides, leading to return migration from those territories that have been torn away from Germany, the issues of living space for the German people have become the most urgent ones facing our nation. So it is no coincidence that they rank foremost among the action plans and objectives of our new Reich.
>
> If one looks around to see where an expansion or deepening of German living space is possible, there are two completely different regions that primarily attract one's attention: the German East and the continents overseas. Among the latter there are again two continents that particularly attract our interest: South America and Africa. South America, because in contrast to North America nationalities are established there that are by nature foreign to Germans, so that the German will be able to keep himself purer in his national characteristics and culture than would be the case in North America, as is demonstrated by the areas of German settlement in southern Chile and southern Brazil; and Africa, because Germany has acquired a historical right to its own colonial possessions there, and we can hope that with German power and German people we will once again be able to work on German soil there, but also because in the German colonies tropical raw materials are produced that are very much needed by the German market.[85]

The new National Socialist rulers in Berlin would of course decide against seeking to regain the former German colonies in Africa in favour of a policy of conquest in the east. Troll, on the other hand, was a member of the circle of 'conservative' colonial revisionists. As such he hoped that Germany would acquire colonies in Africa too, at the latest after having won the Second World War. From his point of view, the academic world was ready for it:

> By taking up the German colonial question, the colonial sciences have also placed themselves at the forefront of public interest. Fortunately, through their years of quiet work, they have created perfect conditions for being able to deal with the many tasks that are now engulfing them as a result. For it is not simply a matter of 'applying' the methods and experiences of so and so many different disciplines to Africa. The reordering of the African

---

84 Ibid., p. 8.
85 Ibid., p. 7.

colonial world involves tasks that cannot be performed except out of a deepened understanding of the area and its problems.[86]

At the time when he wrote this Troll was teaching at the University of Bonn, where he had been since 1938 and would remain until his retirement, occupying the position of Vice-Chancellor in 1960/61.[87]

Like von Richthofen and Penck back in Imperial days, Troll did not restrict himself to purely academic research and teaching work; he too nurtured contacts to the field of political consultancy. Together with other colleagues such as Erich Obst, Walter Behrmann and Karl Heinrich Dietzel, he acted as an expert, a committee chairman and a specialist group chairman for the Colonial Science Department of the National Research Council *(Reichsforschungsrat)*, which cooperated closely with the Colonial Policy Office of the National Socialist Party and made half a million reichsmarks available for colonial research between 1937 and 1942.[88] As is commonly known, however, these endeavours were no longer able to attain to direct political importance.

Expansion in the East

While Troll's demands for the spatial re-ordering of entire continents were concentrated on Africa, and for that reason among others were never put into prac-

---

[86] Carl Troll, "Koloniale Raumplanung in Afrika", in *Das afrikanische Kolonialproblem. Vorträge, gehalten in der Gesellschaft für Erdkunde zu Berlin im Januar-Februar 1941*, Berlin 1941, pp. 1–41, here p. 1.

[87] After the Second World War Troll became one of the internationally best-known German geographers. Amongst other things he was President of the International Geographical Union from 1960 to 1964, and represented geography on the UNESCO Advisory Committee on Natural Resources Research and the International Council of Scientific Unions between 1964 and 1969. Later, under the auspices of the International Geographical Union, he headed the Commission for High Altitude Geo-Ecology. In 1960/61 he occupied the position of Vice-Chancellor at the University of Bonn. His particular field of interest was research into geographical problems in 'Third World' countries and research into 'developing' countries. See Wilhelm Lauer, "Carl Troll zum 70. Geburtstag", in Wilhelm Lauer, ed., *Argumenta Geographica. Festschrift für Carl Troll zum 70. Geburtstag*, Bonn 1970, pp. 11–17, here p. 12. It would be very worthwhile to investigate connections and continuities between colonial geography and research into 'developing' countries, including with regard to methodological and theoretical continuities: however, this is not the place to attempt this. Furthermore, with his review of the history of geography in the Third Reich, which appeared as early as 1947, Troll became one of the principal witnesses seeking to vindicate the honour of the discipline: Carl Troll, "Die geographische Wissenschaft in Deutschland in den Jahren 1933 bis 1945. Eine Kritik und eine Rechtfertigung", *Erdkunde*, 1 (1947), pp. 3–47.

[88] Kost, *Einflüsse*, p. 197 n. 7.

tice, other geographers were involved in planning for the revision of the changes brought about in Europe itself by the Treaty of Versailles, and for the economic and ethnic restructuring of eastern Europe. The points of departure for these considerations were firstly the question of the borders drawn in 1919, and secondly that of Germans living outside Germany. As has been described above, the Berlin Chair for Colonial Geography had been assigned responsibility for the care of Germans living abroad when it was taken over by the Prussian state. Apart from the traditional German minorities in South America, this now also included the inhabitants of the former German colonies, who had been turned into 'German expatriates' by the Treaty of Versailles, but also and above all those of the areas of eastern Europe now separated off from German territory, that is to say, of the newly re-established Poland. This was one of the most virulent and most easily emotionalised problems arising out of Versailles; it was also at the root of the later fixation – in fact, virtually an obsession – with issues concerning borders. In short, Germany had discovered, to its own disadvantage, what it had hitherto itself claimed as a self-evident right, for instance in the colonies: namely that it is the victor or victors who draw borders without any proper consideration of either the interests or ethnic composition of the indigenous population.

This in itself was reason enough for denunciations of three highly resented factors often to go hand in hand: the 'dictated peace' of Versailles, the surrender of German territory and the loss of its colonies. Like many others, Albrecht Penck, the holder of the Chair of Geography at the Friedrich Wilhelm University, had been a vehement supporter of the First World War. He had regarded himself as a combatant in spirit and lauded the 'healing' effect of the conflict and the purging of society through the patriotism that was on display everywhere. In a simple dualistic model, German troops were perceived as the bearers of civilisation and human rights, while the Entente was merely carrying on a 'base' and humiliating war of depredation.[89] All the greater, therefore, were the dismay and bitterness Penck felt when the war was lost; and he viewed the French use of African occupying forces as a deliberately humiliating crime committed against the "white masters".[90]

---

89 Ibid., p. 342. On the subject of 'intellectual mobilisation   in general, see: Jeffrey Verhey, *Der 'Geist von 1914' und die Erfindung der Volksgemeinschaft*, Hamburg 2000; Wolfgang J. Mommsen, ed., *Kultur und Krieg. Die Rolle der Intellektuellen, Künstler und Schriftsteller im Ersten Weltkrieg*, München 1996.

90 Quoted according to Kost, *Einflüsse*, p. 220. On the issue of African troops in general, see: Christian Koller, *'Von Wilden aller Rassen niedergemetzelt'. Die Diskussion um die Verwendung von Kolonialtruppen in Europa zwischen Rassismus, Kolonial- und Militärpolitik (1914–1930)*, Stuttgart 2001.

For Penck, the colonial question was positioned within the wider framework of the question of the future of the German people. He wanted to "stir the conscience of the world and preach that the German colonial issue is only part of a larger problem: what is the future of our race, what is the future of Europe?"[91] For Penck, the answer to this question had unambiguously racist and nationalistic undertones. The 'race' had to be protected and nurtured. In Africa, where "hitherto at least, the white man has not really been able to work consistently, but only to rule, administer or command", it was necessary to establish an unbroken "bloodline of the white race". This "did not necessarily need to be very large [...], but if it is interrupted or too much reduced, white domination will cease".[92]

For Penck, however, this problem existed in Europe as well, as in his opinion it was above all the Germans living here who had been treated unjustly, with millions now finding themselves living outside the new borders of the German state. Indeed, it was in the field of the propaganda battle against the 'Diktat von Versailles', in demonstrating the injustice done to the Germans and the legitimacy of territorial claims against the – in some cases only just newly created – countries of eastern and southern Europe that Penck's influence was most effective.

In this context, his most significant influence on nationalistic thinking and the ideology of *Lebensraum* stemmed from his investigations into "physical anthropogeography"[93] and research concerning 'the soil that yields the nation and its culture' *(Volks- und Kulturboden)*. The field of physical anthropogeography sought to rate the quality of the soil of a particular region or location by determining its ecological yield-bearing capacity, and could be enlisted – not without assistance from Penck – to justify the demand for new colonial possessions.[94] First and foremost, however, it supported the then prevailing social Darwinistic view that nations are engaged in a struggle for land and resources. According to Penck, the scientific research of the preceding decades had made it possible to view the world as a whole, with far-reaching consequences:

> We sense its size, and at the same time become aware of the narrowness of our own living space. In our own home place, we have only a narrow, constricted space, which is not par-

---

91 Albrecht Penck, "Das deutsche Kolonialproblem", *Petermanns Mitteilungen*, 83 (1937), pp. 261–263, here p. 263, quoted according to Kost, *Einflüsse*, p. 219.
92 Albrecht Penck, "Zur deutschen Kolonialfrage", *Zeitschrift der Gesellschaft für Erdkunde zu Berlin (1937)*, pp. 43–48, here pp. 46f., quoted according to Kost, *Einflüsse*, p. 224.
93 Albrecht Penck, "Das Hauptproblem der physischen Anthropogeographie", *Zeitschrift für Geopolitik*, 2 (1925), pp. 330–348. This is a reprint of an article first published a year previously, but which apparently did not gain a wide readership until after it had been published in the *Zeitschrift für Geopolitik*. See Kost, *Einflüsse*, p. 95.
94 Ibid.

ticularly large in terms of the whole earth. There are not only boundaries of peoples and states, but boundaries of humankind as well. We may have learned how to rise up into the air and to dive down into the depths of the oceans, and to dig shafts that penetrate the depths of the earth's crust. But no invention can enable us to free ourselves to any essential extent from the surface of the earth. Even though there is practically nowhere on it any longer that is inaccessible to us, we can still only bring about slight shifts in the boundaries of our living space. The human being, constantly multiplying, sits as it were in a fortress from which he cannot escape.[95]

The task of the geographer was to educate his fellow citizens in this respect: "No national study of geography can limit itself to those issues that concern its own people; rather, it must get to know all the forces of the earth and humanity, both effectual and dormant, and learn about the battle of humanity on earth for food and space".[96]

As regards Germany, this meant driving forward the efforts to regain the territories in eastern and south-eastern Europe that had been lost after the First World War. The instrument available to Penck as a professor was science, to which he attributed a distinctly national task:

> We regard science as the common property of humanity; in a system of supranational sciences there is no room for national sciences. But they do play a major role in the lives of nations. National geography is what a nation needs for itself.[97]

For Penck, as for other scientists of a nationalist inclination who worked with him at the *Deutscher Schutzbund* (German Protection Federation)[98] or in the *Grenzmarkenausschuß* (Prussian Borderland Committee),[99] the main factor was not the free exchange of different opinions; rather it was the determination to force through the adoption of certain political standpoints and to provide legitimation for political actions. Penck too shared the view that the methodological requirement for objectivity in scientific research should not be misunderstood in such a way as to countenance "smashing the windows of our own Fatherland", in a phrase coined by Wilhelm Volz.[100]

Penck used this latter argument to justify founding the *Mittelstelle für zwischeneuropäische Fragen* (Agency for Intra-European Issues) in Leipzig in 1923; this immediately developed into a think-tank for revisionist research in the field of *Volks-*

---

95 Albrecht Penck, *Nationale Erdkunde*, Berlin 1934 (a revised version of a lecture presented to the Geographical Society in Berlin, 21 October 1933), pp. 23f.
96 Ibid., p. 27.
97 Ibid., p. 3.
98 Rössler, *Wissenschaft und Lebensraum*, p. 53.
99 Haar, *Historiker*, p. 26.
100 Quoted according to Haar, *Historiker*, p. 37.

und Kulturboden. Its members deliberately offered themselves to the Foreign Office and the Ministry of the Interior as intermediaries between the academic world and the political arena. Above all though, it formed a central institution where the *Volks- und Kulturboden* theorem could be "established as a paradigm of nationalist science in the interwar period".[101] As was only logical, the Leipzig research association was renamed the *Deutsche Mittelstelle für Volks- und Kulturbodenforschung* (National Agency for Ethnic and Cultural Soil Research) in 1925, and a year later it was converted into a foundation[102] with Albrecht Penck as its first President.

The conceptional work, which at the same time also provided a framework for foreign policy, was based on the fundamental assumption that Germany was subject to 'population pressure' which was constantly increasing and needed to be relieved in a controlled and directed manner. By contrast to the time when imperialism was at its zenith in the 19th century, when it appeared possible to find a solution in the country's acquisition of colonial possessions of its own, the target region for prospective flows of German settlers was now eastern Europe. Penck's individual contribution to this cannot be overestimated. Apart from his above-mentioned research into the yield-bearing capacity of the soil, he also provided a definition of the term *Volks- und Kulturboden* in the central manifesto of early national ethnic research *(Volkstumsforschung)*: published under the patronage of the German *Schutzbund*.[103]

Under the term *Volksboden* (national or ethnic soil) Penck understood areas settled by Germans, where German was spoken and where the results of German industry and diligence were manifest. Only part of this 'ethnic soil' lay within the frontiers of Germany. The 'ethnic soil' was surrounded by 'cultural soil', because "wherever Germans live socially and work the surface of the earth, German culture appears, whether or not it leads to the development of an area of ethnic soil".[104] As *Kulturträger* (bearers of culture and civilisation), therefore, Germans could lay claim to territories far beyond the boundaries of their existing country.[105]

Penck described in more detail what he meant by this in 1934, at a time when the Leipzig-based foundation had already been dissolved following his retire-

---

101 Ibid., p. 31.
102 Ibid., pp. 26–37.
103 Albrecht Penck, "Deutscher Volks- und Kulturboden", in K. C. von Loesch, ed., *Volk unter Völkern. Bücher des Deutschtums*, i, Breslau 1926, pp. 62–73.
104 Penck, "Deutscher Volks- und Kulturboden", p. 69, quoted according to Haar, *Historiker*, p. 46.
105 For a discussion of this concept, see Haar, *Historiker*, pp. 46f.

ment, and had subsequently been replaced by other institutions after the Nazis came to power:[106]

> Germany can clearly be recognised by its unique cultural landscape. Anyone with a trained eye can easily recognise when he is on *German cultural soil* [emphasised by spacing in the original], by the loving way it is cultivated, by the way field, forest and meadow snuggle into the contours of the landscape. [...] German villages are prettily arranged: scattered like seeds on flat ground, nestling in the valleys in mountainous country and popping up in the midst of forests. The land is criss-crossed by clear paths. On German soil, raw nature is tamed by humanity; mankind really is the master of the land. [...]
>
> We can distinguish three different things: Germany with its German cultural soil in the German area of central Europe; within that, the German ethnic soil; and within that, reaching as far as the boundaries of the ethnic soil in only two places, the German *Reich*. The landscape shows us where we are in Germany; from the language we can hear where exactly we are on German soil; while the legislation and regulations tell us where we are within the *Reich*, the German state. Neither for the first nor for the second of the entities named does the German *Reich* form a core that could easily be laid bare. Rather, it is an administrative area; we cannot even say that it is a legal entity, because a very great deal of injustice has been done to it in the delineation of its boundaries. The Reich is the variable element that has undergone many changes in the course of historic time. Germany is the fixed pole within the flux of its manifestations.[107]

The ability to control the forces of nature and to reclaim land for cultivation or other economic use as the legitimation of possession: these are classic patterns of the legitimation of colonial rule. In Gustav Frenssen's *Peter Moors Fahrt nach Südwest*, for example, Germany's most important colonial novel alongside Hans Grimm's *Volk ohne Raum*, one of the protagonists justifies the 1904 genocide against the Herero in German South West Africa as follows:

> These blacks deserved death before God and before man, not because they murdered those two hundred farmers and rebelled against us, but rather because they did not build houses or dig wells. [...] God has allowed us prevail here, because we are the more noble and the ones striving to advance. That is not saying much in comparison with this black race; but we have to take care that it is us who become the best and most alert of all, before all other nations of the world. The world belongs to the most able and the freshest. That is the justice of God.[108]

---

[106] Ibid., pp. 65–69; pp. 110f. On the new Nazi institutions controlling the academic scene, see Fahlbusch, *Wissenschaft*.
[107] Penck, *Nationale Erdkunde*, pp. 5–8.
[108] Gustav Frenssen, *Peter Moors Fahrt nach Südwest. Ein Feldzugsbericht*, Berlin 1906, p. 200. On this subject, see also Medardus Brehl, "Vernichtung als Arbeit an der Kultur. Kolonialdiskurs, kulturelles Wissen und der Völkermord an den Herero", *Zeitschrift für Genozidforschung*, 2 (2000), pp. 8–28. Regarding the connection between the genocide against the Herero and the Nazi policies of conquest and extermination, see Jürgen Zimmerer, "Krieg, KZ und Völkermord in Süd-

One begins to get a feeling for the effect that such rhetoric had on the later National Socialist policy of conquest if one considers eyewitness accounts dating from the Second World War.[109] Heinrich Himmler's secretary, Hanns Johst, who travelled around conquered Poland shortly after that country's defeat, was no doubt also reflecting his boss's ideas when he described his impressions as follows:

> The Poles are not a state-building people. They lack even the most basic prerequi-sites. I have travelled all over the country at the side of the *Reichsführer* SS. A country which has so little feeling for the essence of settlement that it is not even up to the task of creating a village of any style has no claim to any sort of inde-pendent political status within Europe. It is a country crying out to be colonised![110]

Adolf Hitler too spoke of a "primeval world"(*'Urwelt'*) which one "only needed to see" in order to appreciate "that nothing happens here if one does not assign people the work they have to do. The Slav is a born slave, they are a mass crying out for a master."[111]

Even though it is still debatable to what extent the conceptual work of the Leipzig Agency for Intra-European Issues and the academics working there helped to give rise to the Nazi policies of conquest and extermination,[112] they undoubtedly prepared the ground for it in the sense of providing legitimation for Nazi revisionist and

---

westafrika", in Jürgen Zimmerer and Joachim Zeller, eds, *Völkermord in Deutsch-Südwestafrika. Der Kolonialkrieg (1904–1908) in Namibia und seine Folgen*, Berlin 2003, pp. 45–63.

109 For greater detail, see: Jürgen Zimmerer, "Colonialism and the Holocaust. Towards an Archeology of Genocide", in A. Dirk Moses, ed., *Genocide and Settler Society: Frontier Violence and Stolen Indigenous Children in Australian History*, New York 2004, pp. 49–76.

110 Hanns Johst, *Ruf des Reiches: Echo des Volkes!*, München 1940 p. 94, quoted according to: Michael Burleigh, *Die Zeit des Nationalsozialismus. Eine Gesamtdarstellung*, Frankfurt 2000, p. 515.

111 Hitler, 17 September 1941, in Adolf Hitler, *Monologe im Führerhauptquartier*, ed. Werner Jochmann, Hamburg 1980, p. 63. The similarity between the words *Urwelt* (primeval world) and *Urwald* (primeval forest) also points to a subconsciously generated association with the European penetration of the tropics, a point which could certainly sustain further research. The semantic field of the term *Urwald* as an antithesis to the orderly, disciplined and civilised European homeland of those sent out as pioneers, and the way it forms a central component of colonial justification ideology, are illuminated by Wirz: Albert Wirz, "Innerer und äußerer Wald. Zur moralischen Ökologie der Kolonisierenden", in Michael Flitner, ed., *Der deutsche Tropenwald. Bilder, Mythen, Politik*, Frankfurt 2000, pp. 23–48.

112 Fahlbusch sees a direct "line from the beginnings of national ethnic research to the policy of extermination"; Oberkrome is more sceptical. Fahlbusch, *Wissenschaft*, p. 796; Willi Oberkrome, "Geschichte, Volk und Theorie. Das Handwörterbuch des Grenz- und Auslanddeutschtums", in Peter Schöttler, ed., *Geschichtsschreibung als Legitimationswissenschaft 1918–1945*, Frankfurt 1999, pp. 104–127. Specifically with regard to Penck himself as a person, further research into his activities during the war seems to be necessary. There are no references to his wartime activities either in Fahlbusch, *Wissenschaft*; Rössler, *Wissenschaft;* Kost, *Einflüsse* or Haar, *Historiker*.

expansionist thinking. But this was also exactly what academics like Penck, who had made it to the top, perceived as being their primary task, namely to stir up support for policies that would lead Germany out of the depths of its 1918 defeat and resolve the seemingly inescapable demographic dilemma of the "nation without space".

Conclusion

Penck was no stranger to this kind of instrumentalisation of academic work, or to pandering to political trends in this way; after all, geography itself had used precisely such methods in respect of colonial expansion to pursue its own rise to being a respected university discipline. It is well known that this process was not confined to merely providing legitimation or to non-committal intellectual games. The German colonial empire became a reality in 1884, and the attempt to revise Germany's eastern borders by military force began in 1939. In both cases, geographers were closely involved in creating the specific forms of domination, exploitation and infrastructure development that were inevitably linked to these events.

A glance at the relationship between geography and German colonialism will reveal the closely interlocking relationship that existed between the two. Geography, represented by such luminaries as Ferdinand von Richthofen, made an all too willing contribution to the development of the German colonial empire and to the exploitation of the conquered territories. This points to rational aspects of colonialism that are often in danger of vanishing behind the images projected by romanticising or even mentally unstable colonial adventurers. Application-orientated political consultancy of the type that came to the fore was not limited to the period between 1884 and 1918, when a German colonial empire actually existed; rather, it was responsible to an extent that should not be underestimated for the kindling and spread of enthusiasm for colonialism in Germany long before unification in 1871, and remained a prominent voice in colonial revisionism after the First World War. By disseminating their fantasies in relation to German expansion and colonisation, popularising them and dressing them up in pseudo-scientific argumentation, academics – including some like Carl Troll, who subsequently even gained international renown – also created a willingness to pursue further expansion that was to target other regions of the world. Albrecht Penck advocated both: he railed against the Treaty of Versailles from the vantage point of one of the central institutions in the university system of the Weimar Republic, the Friedrich Wilhelm University in Berlin, pleaded for the recovery of the colonies and rendered a weighty contribution to ethnic and cultural soil research, one of the starting points for the later *Volkstumsforschung* (research into the character and 'soul' of the – German – people). He is therefore an important link between colonial revisionism and the *völkisch* eastward expansion.

Since the publication of Hannah Arendt's major study on 'The Origins of Totalitarianism',[113] the key issue of the fundamental relationship between colonialism and National Socialism has remained an open question without there having been (as yet) any systematic attempt to address it. This chapter would never have been able, and has not sought, to provide such an answer. If, however, the continuity of personnel and institutions demonstrated in it were to stimulate further research on the substantive connections, in the academic sphere and beyond it, between colonialism and the Nazi policies of conquest and extermination, then it would have fulfilled an important aim.

---

[113] Hannah Arendt, *The Origins of Totalitarianism*, New York 1951.

Mass Violence: A German *Sonderweg*?

No German *Sonderweg* in 'Race Warfare': The Genocide against the Herero and Nama (1904–1908)

> The crimes of the *Wehrmacht* represent a deep caesura, not just in German history. From an international perspective too, the effects of this radicalisation of warfare can scarcely be understated [sic]. Since 1945, more and more new variations have demonstrated the high degree to which things that are generally categorised as war crimes have come to shape, and to some extent replace, modern warfare. [...] The German-Soviet war was not the first and only, but was definitely the decisive, starting point for developments that have since increasingly determined the course of military events: the war of annihilation adopted as a deliberate strategy, the terrorisation of the civilian population and the uninhibited exploitation of occupied countries, partisan warfare and the indiscriminate measures taken to combat it, the systematic maltreatment of prisoners of war, and the impressment of former adversaries into forced labour.[1]

This summing up, a recent contribution to the continuing debate about the crimes of the German armed forces, is thoroughly typical of certain tendencies in both German and international World War research. It not only detaches the history of the Second World War from its prehistory, but also ignores the entire Asia-Pacific dimension of the conflict. As a result, the Second World War is turned into a European regional conflict, and no justification is apparent for the global significance attributed to it, which would require considering it in comparison with both earlier conflicts and simultaneous developments. Only the First World War is assigned a certain precursor role, as a result of which many of what are considered to have been breaches of taboos are moved forward thirty years. The Second World War – and we are not talking about the Holocaust here – and the way Germany waged it is afforded a pre-eminent role in world history, being presented, on the basis of the various breaches of taboos that took place during it, as an unprecedented event. In a disturbing analogy to the decontextualisation of the Holocaust,[2] the whole war is turned into an event without a history, an event lifted right out of history.

Furthermore: to regard this war as being unprecedented because of factors that it displays such as 'the war of annihilation adopted as a deliberate strategy',

---

[1] Christian Hartmann, Johannes Hürter and Ulrike Jureit, "Verbrechen der Wehrmacht. Ereignisse und Kontroversen der Forschung", in Christian Hartmann, Johannes Hürter and Ulrike Jureit, eds, *Verbrechen der Wehrmacht. Bilanz einer Debatte*, München 2005, pp. 21–28, here p. 27f.
[2] For more on this problem, see, for example, Götz Aly, *Macht – Geist – Wahn. Kontinuitäten deutschen Denkens*, Frankfurt 1999, pp. 185–196.

the 'terrorisation of the civilian population' and the 'uninhibited exploitation' of countries and people, not to mention the particular brutality of its partisan warfare, betrays an amazing level of ignorance of world history. The assertion that the waging of a partisan war, or, to use the modern terminology, asymmetric warfare, always requires the Second World War's Eastern Front as a role model, is based on pure Eurocentrism. Guerrilla fighters, or 'terrorists' as they are more often called nowadays, do not need the Second World War to inspire them; they have plenty of role models in their own history. The asymmetric wars of the present day are, as a rule, fought out in former colonial regions – one needs only to think of Vietnam, Iraq or Afghanistan.[3] And it is the colonial wars by which the histories of these countries have been shaped that ought to be investigated first and foremost in the search for precursors and as providing inspiration for the military tactics employed. Nor do the United States, the United Kingdom and Russia, to name just three countries that have taken the lead in major military actions since the beginning of the twenty first century, need the German *Wehrmacht* as a model to develop their fundamental tactics. All three countries have imperial traditions that include the copious use of massive levels of force.[4]

Nevertheless, the authors quoted at the beginning are not completely wrong, and this leads directly to the question of *Sonderwege* (specific national paths) and continuities. The Second World War, in the way it was conducted above all, if not exclusively – remembering Nanking or similar occurrences – by the German *Wehrmacht* does indeed show striking similarities to wars of the later colonial period and to neo-colonial wars. Not, though, because it led to the establishment of new traditions and strategies, even in the aspects mentioned, but because the Second World War itself displays considerable structural similarities to colonial wars of the past.[5] We can and must interpret the 'war on the Eastern Front' – and it is this that people in Germany are thinking of when they talk about the Second

---

[3] For an introduction to the asymmetric wars of the present day, see Herfried Münkler, *Die neuen Kriege*, Reinbek 2004.
[4] An initial overview of the topic of colonial wars is provided (in German) by Thoralf Klein and Frank Schumacher, eds, *Kolonialkriege. Militärische Gewalt im Zeichen des Imperialismus*, Hamburg 2006. A 'classic' handbook of anti-partisan warfare is Charles E. Callwell, *Small Wars*, London 1896, various editions since then. Having appeared in the nineteenth century, its publication date demonstrates the error of assuming it was the Second World War that acted as a trigger.
[5] However, this does not mean that army commanders and military theoreticians did not learn lessons from the past in terms of their strategies and doctrines, because ultimately armies tend to be among the institutions that are most capable of learning and adapting.

World War possessing a new quality – as a colonial war,[6] if we consider the structures lying behind the armies of tanks, the mechanisation of warfare and the dogfights in the skies.[7]

It is not a matter of monocausal explanations or one-dimensional lines of development, but rather of the fact that in many of its characteristic features the war demonstrates enough similarities with colonial conflicts to be interpreted using the instruments of (post-)colonial historiography. The question of what direct relationships with previous colonial conflicts exist is initially a subordinate one; although here too there are a number of indications that particular developments can be traced back to earlier conflicts. Research on this is however still in its infancy, as the academic world has up to now almost entirely failed to take account of the entire complex of questions concerning the colonial origins of twentieth-century conflicts, despite the forceful admonitions of people such as Hannah Arendt or Aimé Césaire. On the one hand, this has been a result of the blinkered nature of German and European/North American national historiography, both of which have equally ignored the role played by colonialism in shaping world history over the past half-millennium, while at the same time often trivialising and romanticising it. On the other hand, it also arose out of the Eurocentric, if not even racist, arrogance that leads many to believe that situations and developments that can be described in relation to Africa, Asia or the Americas could not possibly be applicable to 'developed' Europe with its 'higher level of civilisation'.

In fact, however, both the Nazi war aims and the methods with which the war was fought fit perfectly into a colonial template: conquest, control, exploitation and settlement have, after all, been among the fundamental aims of the European appropriation of the world since the early days of the Portuguese and Spanish expeditions of conquest. Above all, however, the Manichean logic of the binary distinctions on which Germany's manner of waging war was based provides almost an ideal type of colonialism. It goes beyond the friend/foe distinction that is fundamental to every military conflict, since the opponent is not merely the Other, but is transformed into the Absolute Other, even into a no longer human creature, who can then be annihilated or destroyed, to use the euphemisms frequently applied to the murder and slaughter of the defenceless in par-

---

6 The Germans conducted the war in the East in a markedly different way from that in the West. As an introduction, see the series published by the Militärgeschichtliches Forschungsamt, *Das Deutsche Reich und der Zweite Weltkrieg*, 10 vols, Stuttgart 1984ff.

7 On this subject, see Jürgen Zimmerer, "Die Geburt des 'Ostlandes' aus dem Geiste des Kolonialismus. Ein postkolonialer Blick auf die NS-Eroberungs- und Vernichtungspolitik", *Sozial.Geschichte. Zeitschrift für die historische Analyse des 20. und 21. Jahrhunderts*, 1 (2004), pp. 10–43 (English version: "The Birth of the 'Ostland' out of the Spirit of Colonialism", pp. 230–261 in this book).

ticular. A war of annihilation, however, is in the tradition of colonial warfare; and a colonial war is, in practice, almost always also a war of annihilation!

Pointing out the colonial dimension of the German war of annihilation in the East neither takes away its significance and its horror, nor does it diminish German responsibility. It does however help towards understanding both the mental and the discursive environment that gave rise to some of the underlying ideas, but also and especially to the willingness to implement them. Attempts are made again and again to discredit this approach[8] by claiming that other European states had even more extreme experiences with colonialism than the Germans had, but nevertheless did not commit any crimes comparable to those of the Third Reich. This argument on the one hand confuses continuity with causality; while on the other hand it overlooks the important distinction that the question is not how it came about that the Nazis came to power in Germany, which is primarily to be explained in terms of the immediately preceding events since the First World War; rather, it concerns the tradition their imperialistic programme of conquest stood in, and what models they were able to draw on once the decision to undertake a new attempt at colonialism had been taken. Even this does not mean that the 'archives' of colonialism were the only source available for them to draw on, and which they did indeed draw on; but only that these archives did exist and played an important role, in terms of both motivation and practical implementation, with regard to the war on the Eastern Front in particular.

Such a postcolonial and global approach also offers an explanation as to why so many Germans were quite prepared to participate in the crimes and why they did not offer resistance, or more determined resistance. Colonial conquest and administration and the waging of colonial wars were not perceived as anything new, as breaches of any taboo, but were rather recognised as familiar factors, as normal processes in the course of history. They also helped to give meaning to events, including on a personal level. This may not have applied to every individual soldier – convinced anti-Polish or anti-Russian racists had less need for such justification[9] – but it was true for a sufficiently large number to be taken seriously as an explanation.

The elite of the regime used colonial images and chains of association; and were themselves quite at home in the world of colonial discourse and attitudes. If

---

8 Most recently by Robert Gerwarth and Stephan Malinowski, "Vollbrachte Hitler eine ‚afrikanische' Tat? Der Herero-Krieg und der Holocaust: Zur Kritik der neuesten Sonderwegsthese", *Frankfurter Allgemeine Zeitung* (11 September 2007).

9 Here too, however, it would be worthwhile to go more deeply into the question of the extent to which the racism directed against Slavs bore and bears similarities to that directed against Africans. For more on racism, see Christian Geulen, *Geschichte des Rassismus*, München 2007.

Hitler could write that "the struggle for hegemony in the world will be decided in favour of Europe by the possession of Russia; this will make Europe the place that is more secure against blockade than anywhere else in the world. [...] The territory of Russia is our India, and just as the English rule India with only a handful of people, so too we will govern this colonial territory of ours.",[10] then this is to be taken seriously. The colonial dimension of Nazi policies in the East cannot be read out of this passage alone,[11] nor does it mean that Hitler would have created a one-to-one copy of the British style of colonialism; it does not even mean that he had any accurate picture of the actual state of affairs in India. Pointing out that the British colonial empire by no means corresponded to what the *'Führer'* imagined it to be misses the point of the argument completely, since whether Hitler had a correct understanding of British colonialism is irrelevant to determining whether he was influenced by colonialist concepts. What is important in this question is not so much any historical reality of colonialism, however that may be defined, but rather the perception of such colonialism prevailing in Germany and particularly in the corridors of power of the regime and among its expert advisers. Although there has been no detailed research into the matter, it seems that the colonial world as Germans – including Hitler – imagined it to be had been shaped by an author who did not possess any colonial experience and who, at least on the surface, did not even deal with the theme of colonialism in his work: Karl May.

The passage quoted above, at any rate, shows beyond all doubt that Hitler – like other leading representatives of the regime – was in the grip of an imaginary conception of the imperial world. He believed in a colonial world order in the sense of a 'racial state, divided into serving and ruling classes on the basis of constructed ethnic entities and of a social Darwinist interlinking of 'race' and 'space', that is to say on the connection between the biopolitical principle and the geographical one. And precisely that is a clear characteristic of settler colonialism.

However, the links to colonialism are not restricted only to the field of imagination. Numerous structural similarities also support a postcolonial approach to the Third Reich's policies of expansion and annihilation. This chapter can only

---

10 Hitler, 17 September 1941, in: Adolf Hitler: *Monologe im Führerhauptquartier*, ed. Werner Jochmann, Hamburg 1980, pp. 60–64.
11 Nor has anyone as yet attempted to do so, even if this is repeatedly alleged, with denunciatory intent, by those criticising the post-colonial perspective. See, for example, the contentious article by Gerwarth and Malinowski published in the *Frankfurter Allgemeine Zeitung*. For more detail, see Robert Gerwarth and Stephan Malinowski, "Der Holocaust als 'kolonialer Genozid' Europäische Kolonialgewalt und nationalsozialistischer Vernichtungskrieg", *Geschichte und Gesellschaft*, 33 (2007), pp. 439–466.

touch on these points briefly:[12] in many ways, for instance, the *Lebensraum* ('living space') concept follows the same internal logic as the colonial movement during the *Kaiserreich*. Thus Wilhelminian imperialism – just like its counterparts elsewhere in Europe – was nourished in a not insignificant measure by the social Darwinist understanding of the Nation as a biopolitical organism in permanent competition with other nations. The assumption was that this competition could only be won, and the survival of one's own collective thereby secured, if all resources, including the population, could be mobilised. Colonies were intended to act as Germanised retention cisterns for the massive flows of emigrants – which in the contemporary world of ideas otherwise had to mean a substantial loss for the collective body of the German people – at the same time as providing sales markets and being sources of raw materials. Thus space for settlement became an essential requirement; and in the logic of settler colonialism this meant that the space for the local population had to be limited, insofar as they were granted the right to stay or, in the last instance, even to stay alive at all in their homeland. This applied equally to Africa and to Ukraine. Accordingly, the ways the settlers, both in actual practice and in plans for the future, dealt with the populations originally occupying the conquered or to-be-conquered regions demonstrated deeply colonialist traits. According to Hitler, "The Slavic peoples [...] are not destined to lead independent lives of their own." And so he wanted to supply the Ukrainians with "headscarves, glass bead necklaces as jewellery, and all the other things that appeal to colonial peoples".[13]

More important than all utterances emanating from Hitler, however – and at this point I do not wish to discuss either the debate between 'functionalists' and 'intentionalists', or the dispute about Hitler's position and the importance of his personal role in the murderous policies of the Third Reich – are the structural similarities in the governmental and administrative utopia. Above all, these similarities are sufficient to provide the justification for making use of colonial and post-colonial instruments in analysing the Nazi politics of terror.

---

[12] For an extensive presentation, see Jürgen Zimmerer, "Holocaust und Kolonialismus. Beitrag zu einer Archäologie des genozidalen Gedankens", *Zeitschrift für Geschichtswissenschaft*, 51/12 (2003), pp. 1098–1119 (English version: "Colonialism and the Holocaust", pp. 125–153 in this book); Jürgen Zimmerer, "Geburt des 'Ostlandes'" (English version: "The Birth of the 'Ostland' out of the Spirit of Colonialism", pp. 230–261 in this book). This latter text also contains a more detailed analysis of the relevant literature. Such an analysis will be kept brief below for reasons of space.
[13] Hitler, 17 September 1941, in Hitler, *Monologe*, pp. 60–64. The mention of "glass beads" takes up one of the central motifs in the European history of expansion and contact; they are the classic symbol of 'underdevelopment' and of a quintessentially 'native' existence. It also demonstrates how the interweaving of colonial fantasies with the actual exercise of imperial rule was increasingly giving rise to practical effects.

Central to this are the concepts of 'race' and 'space', and the relationship between the two, which shaped both the colonial settlement and expansion programme and that of the Nazis. Both systems involved establishing patterns of domination based on a 'racial hierarchy' and extending these to other territories as well. With regard to National Socialism this is a familiar enough concept; but settler colonialism too, which is what we are concerned with above all when we refer to colonialism in this context, was necessarily based on the establishment of a hierarchy, understood in ethnic terms, among the elements of the population. The invasion and occupation of other continents were motivated and justified by the division of people into higher 'races', which were destined to rule, and lower ones who were doomed to be subjugated. Whether unashamed robbery or justified in terms of a 'civilising mission', it is only rarely that any acceptance of the 'indigenous' peoples as counterparts of equal status is to be found. Rather, almost everywhere the local peoples were degraded and disenfranchised. Whether it was the proselytising of the 'heathen', the 'White Man's Burden' or the 'Manifest Destiny': the legitimising concept might vary, but an emphasis on the colonisers' standing as guardians of the true faith or their 'chosen-ness' always played an important role in the ideological preparation of the expansion of colonial domination. Indeed, the enormous expropriation – theft – of land and the exploitation associated with settler colonialism could not have been justified at all except by invoking a fundamental inequality. All too often, at the lowest end of this imagined ranking system the colonisers placed groups that they thought to be doomed to destruction; helping along with the fulfilment of this 'destiny' was seen almost as a 'duty' within the wider context of world history, rather than the brutal mass murder that it actually was.[14] This binary encoding, this establishment of a 'racial hierarchy', also characterised the violence associated with settlement and the expropriation of land. The original population were considered to be 'racially inferior' or even less than human, so that their human rights did not have to be taken into account.

These are the same conditions that make the Second World War so shocking, above and beyond the number of the victims and the extent of the destruction, both of which were apocalyptic in scale. It is precisely the combination of the destructive power of high-technology weapons with the efficiency of modern bureaucracy and the racist ideology of the inferiority of the adversary that led to any attempts to contain the consequences of waging war, such as those provided for under international law, for example, remaining ineffective. Therein lies the root

---

14 For example, see Russell McGregor, *Imagined Destinies. Aboriginal Australians and the Doomed Race Theory, 1880–1939*, Victoria 1997; Saul Dubow, *Scientific Racism in Modern South Africa*, Cambridge 1995.

of the 'unrestrained violence' that is deplored by so many commentators. Such violence knows no limits, because the human rights of the adversary, which ought to place a limit on the violence, have been set aside. This is why colonial wars are 'unrestrained wars', as was the war of annihilation in Eastern Europe as well. Such wars are inherently different from so-called 'contained wars', that is to say wars in which attempts are made to protect the civilian population and also above all the combatants themselves, a form of warfare that characterised, for example, the Western Front in the Second World War, despite all the war crimes that took place there as well. The Hague Convention (1899/1907), for instance, attempted to achieve such containment, but it explicitly did not apply to colonial wars. So even contemporaries – at least the Europeans: the inhabitants of the colonies were not consulted – were aware of the differences in the natures of these two kinds of war; and to a large extent they accepted the situation. As is well known, the Hague Convention was not applied on the Eastern Front either; explicit legal instruments, such as the *Kriegsgerichtsbarkeitserlaß* (Decree on the Jurisdiction of Martial Law), and the *Kommissarbefehl* (Commissar Order), suspended it de facto. Thus this order and this decree transformed the war on the Eastern Front from a relatively contained (European) one into an unrestrained colonial war. In what is almost a classic argument from the sphere of colonialism, the other side was accused of conducting the war with a degree of cruelty that did not conform to European standards, and this was taken as justification for one's own unrestrained brutality. As the Commissar Order, for example, states: "In the battle against Bolshevism, it must be assumed that the enemy will not behave in a manner consistent with the principles of humanity or international law. Hate-filled, cruel and inhumane treatment of our prisoners is to be expected, especially from the political commissars of all kinds, who are those truly responsible for maintaining resistance. To give quarter or display clemency in accordance with international law" would therefore be "the wrong way to treat these elements". The "political commissars" were said to be "the originators of barbaric, Asiatic forms of combat". Thus it was necessary to undertake extreme measures against them, "summarily, unhesitatingly and with all severity. As a matter of routine, therefore, if captured in battle or when exercising resistance, they are to be shot dead immediately."[15]

The Decree on the Jurisdiction of Martial Law also empowered German troops to perform summary executions and to shoot hostages in large-scale acts

---

[15] Der Führer und Oberste Befehlshaber der Wehrmacht, "Erlaß über die Ausübung der Kriegsgerichtsbarkeit im Gebiet 'Barbarossa' und über besondere Maßnahmen der Truppe" [Kriegsgerichtsbarkeiterlaß], 13 May 1941, BArch MA, RW 4/v. 577, sheets 72–74; "Richtlinien für die Behandlung politischer Kommissare" [Komissarbefehl], 6 June 1941, BArch MA, RW 4/v. 578, sheets 42–44.

of retribution. Policies such as these were part of the standard repertoire of colonial warfare. The 'new' aspect was that these measures were applied to Europeans. Nazi anti-Slavic racism paired with anti-Bolshevism, which was associated with that racism in many ways, led to a process of 'Othering', as it is called in postcolonial theory,[16] in which images of 'the enemy' taken over from colonialist thinking were transferred to the enemy in the 'East'. These images, as the reference above to "Asiatic forms of combat" indicates, were in itself something taken out of the colonial archive. The Decree on the Jurisdiction of Martial Law and the Commissar Order are expressions of this transformation of the European war into a colonial war.[17]

In the twentieth century, the armies of tanks and fleets of bombers merely made it actually possible to destroy and kill on a scale unparalleled in history. It is this scale of the destruction that makes historians identify the First World War above all as a precursor event. And no doubt that war did play an important role. But just as the First World War, despite its name, was not the first globally fought war in history (the Seven Years' War at least is worth mentioning as a rival candidate), so too the contempt for humanity with which technological advances were used for the purposes of mass murder can be traced back well beyond that 'great seminal catastrophe of the twentieth century'. At the Battle of Omdurman, for example, British units and allied Egyptian troops killed up to 10,000 of the Mahdi's warriors and wounded 16,000 in a single day (2 September 1898), above all thanks to the use of the Maxim machine gun, while themselves suffering losses of only 48 dead and 382 wounded.[18] 'Soldiers of scientific war' was the term used by the young war correspondent Winston Churchill to describe the army that brought about this turning point in military and colonial history.[19]

The machine gun made it possible to carry out massacres on a completely new scale. Only a few years before, 14,000 Zulus had needed three hours to kill 900 British soldiers at Isandlwana. At Omdurman, moreover, it was the numerically stronger army that suffered such horrendous losses. The machine gun thus soon became the guarantor and symbol of European dominance, as was ex-

---

16 For an introduction to this complex of issues, see Bill Ashcroft, Gareth Griffiths and Helen Tiffin, *Key Concepts in Post-Colonial Studies*, London 1998.
17 This was a gradual process that presumably began during the Polish campaign, though it only became fully effective with Germany's attack on the Soviet Union. See Militärgeschichtliches Forschungsamt, *Das Deutsche Reich und der Zweite Weltkrieg*.
18 A general survey of the Battle of Omdurman can be found in John C. Pollock, *Kitchener. The Road to Omdurman*, London 1998.
19 Winston Spencer Churchill, *The River War: An Historical Account of The Reconquest of the Soudan*, 2 vols, London 1899, pp. 82–164.

pressed almost in the form of an aphorism by Hilaire Belloc: "Whatever happens, we have got the Maxim gun and they have not."[20]

The fact that military or administratively organised massacres had become technically feasible conjoined with the binary view of the nature of the world underlying colonialism. The adversary was not merely the 'Other' but was transformed into a thoroughly incompatible 'Absolute Other' with whom reconciliation or even coexistence was impossible. The view of the 'indigenous Other' as being nonhuman or subhuman contributed extensively to a willingness to use excessive violence. Such violence is unrestrained, since 'subhuman beings' are not granted the enjoyment of that moral protection that fellow human beings can still claim, even when they are adversaries in war. According to Helen Fein, however, this exclusion of certain people or groups from the community of those "whom we are obligated to protect, to take into account, and to whom we must account",[21] is a major prerequisite for the initiation of genocide; the ideological prerequisite, so to speak, for turning quite ordinary people into mass murderers. The effect that this had in everyday colonial life can be seen in an example from Australia, where young men sometimes spent their Sundays having fun hunting Australian Aboriginal people:

> There are instances when the young men of the station have employed the Sunday in hunting the blacks, not only for some definite purpose, but also for the sake of the sport.[22]

Murder as a sport became possible because the original inhabitants were not seen as being fully human:

> And, being a useless race, what does it matter what they suffer any more than the distinguished philanthropist, who writes in his behalf, cares for the wounded half-dead pigeon he tortures at his shooting matches. 'I do not see the necessity,' was the reply of a distinguished wit to an applicant for an office who remarked that 'he must live;' and we virtually and practically say the same to the blacks and with better reason.[23]

was an explanation given in a reader's letter printed in the newspaper 'The Queenslander'. The consequences of dehumanisation, the negation of what it means to be human, could not be expressed more clearly. And there was no softening of this attitude where women and children were concerned. Settlers hunted them deliberately in order to destroy the reproductive capacity of the enemy,

---

20 Hilaire Belloc, *The Modern Traveller*, London 1898, p. 41.
21 Helen Fein, "Definition and Discontent: Labelling, Detecting, and Explaining Genocide in the Twentieth Century", in Stig Förster and Gerhard Hirschfeld, eds, *Genozid in der modernen Geschichte*, Münster 1999, pp. 11–21.
22 Quoted according to Alison Palmer, *Colonial Genocide*, Adelaide 2000, p. 44.
23 The Queenslander, 8 May 1880, https://trove.nla.gov.au/newspaper/article/20332884, accessed 12 Jul. 2023, see Palmer, Genocide, p. 45.

who was understood to be the 'absolute Other'. In 1889, a report on so-called settler vigilante justice against 'cattle thieves' stated:

> He shot all the men he discovered on his run, because they were cattle killers; the women, because they gave birth to cattle killers; and the children, because they would in time become cattle killers.[24]

In the United States, one Colonel Chivington, a former Methodist minister and the commander of the Third Colorado Militia Regiment, expressed himself as follows: "My intention is to kill all Indians I come across"; and he ordered his men "[to] kill and scalp all, little and big", i.e. adults and children, because "Nits make lice",[25] a saying that was coined with regard to the 'Indians' during King Philip's War (1675–1677).

This same genocidal logic is also displayed in Heinrich Himmler's notorious Posen speech of 1943:

> The question arose: what of the women and children? Here too I have decided to find a very clear solution. I did not think I would be justified in eradicating the men – in other words, killing them or having them killed – while allowing their avengers, in the shape of their children, to grow up for our sons and grandsons to have to deal with. The hard decision had to be taken to remove these people from the face of the earth.[26]

Naturally, the perpetrators quoted above differ from one another in many respects. In view of the singularity of every historical event in terms both of the process and of the context, it would be senseless to consider them as identical. Nonetheless, it is impossible to overlook the fact that the colonial extermination logic was paralleled in Nazism.

So-called punitive expeditions such as were carried out by Chivington and others[27] were a tried and tested method of driving local populations out of certain regions or of making them amenable through terror. Other than in the case of criminal prosecution – in respect of which, incidentally, the issue as to whether it was legally legitimate for a European state to presume that it possessed the com-

---

24 Quoted according to ibid., p. 43.
25 Quoted according to Michael Mann, *Dark Side of Democracy*, Cambridge 2005, p. 98.
26 Himmler, 'Rede in Posen', 6 October 1943, quoted according to Bradley F. Smith and Agnes F. Petersen, eds, *Heinrich Himmler. Geheimreden 1933 bis 1945 und andere Ansprachen*, Frankfurt 1974, pp. 169f.
27 The murdering of 'Indians' even constituted the main raison d'être for these militias. When the Governor of Colorado was petitioned by an army officer to at least try to negotiate with the American Indians, he asked rhetorically what he should then do with Chivington's regiment. "They have been raised to kill Indians", he declared, "and they must kill Indians." Quoted according to Mann, *Dark Side of Democracy*, p. 98.

petence to impose criminal justice outside its sovereign territory (in Europe) would provide plentiful material for a protracted and controversial debate – in which a criminal who is alleged to have committed a particular crime is sought and if necessary punished, these 'punitive expeditions' were purely acts of revenge involving only summary punishment.

The bombardment of the Hermit Islands in the South Pacific, for example, arose out of a personal initiative of Chancellor Otto von Bismarck's. The inhabitants there had allegedly murdered a German sea captain, a European merchant and several workers. As a punishment the German gunboats *Carola* and *Hyäne* bombarded the islands and landed sailors on them; these combed the islands, murdering all the indigenous warriors and destroying "villages, plantations and canoes".[28]

Notable with regard to this action are not only the facts that it occurred two years before the islands were officially declared a German *Schutzgebiet*, or that Bismarck personally recommended that the campaign of extermination should be continued (whereupon the *Hyäne* resumed the murderous campaign that it had previously broken off), but also that it occurred in the South Pacific, which is generally presented even today, and even among academics, as an example of peaceful German colonial rule, differing – supposedly – from the excesses seen in Africa. While the number of victims in the South Seas may have been relatively low – which however is no surprise considering the smaller population of the area – the application of similar tactics in German East Africa at the end of the nineteenth century (that is, prior to the Maji Maji War, which claimed about 300,000 victims) led to tens of thousands of deaths.[29] These summary punishments, this form of terror, are to be found again in the form of the shootings of hostages carried out by the German *Wehrmacht* during the Second World War.[30]

The conduct of German troops gained worldwide notoriety through the repression of the so-called 'Boxer Uprising' in China. In his 'Hun Speech', as it became known, Emperor Wilhelm II explicitly issued the order for terroristic massacres:

---

[28] For more on this topic see Alexander Krug's book, *'Der Hauptzweck ist die Tötung von Kanaken'. Die deutschen Strafexpeditionen in den Kolonien der Südsee 1872–1914*, Tönning 2005. Krug fills page after page with accounts of German atrocities and clearly demonstrates the repressive character of German rule. The bombardment of the Hermit Islands is described on pages 33–49.

[29] Michael Pesek estimates the number of victims in the war against the Hehe at about 100,000. Particular brutality started to be used after the Hehe had attacked and annihilated a German patrol. Michael Pesek, *Koloniale Herrschaft in Deutsch-Ostafrika. Expeditionen, Militär und Verwaltung seit 1880*, Frankfurt 2005, pp. 191–196.

[30] On this subject, see Christian Gerlach, *Kalkulierte Morde. Die deutsche Wirtschafts- und Vernichtungspolitik in Weißrußland 1941 bis 1944*, Hamburg 1999, pp. 870–974.

> When you come face to face with the enemy, then he will be trounced, no quarter will be given, prisoners will not be taken. Those who fall into your hands shall be in your hand. Just as a thousand years ago the Huns under their King Attila won a reputation that still makes them appear mighty in stories that have lived on right down to today, so may the name of Germany be made known in China in such a way that no Chinese will ever again even dare so much as to look askance at a German.[31]

Not only did this make it a war aim to spread terror; more than that, the call to kill all prisoners was an explicit authorisation to wage war in a manner contrary to any spirit of restraint.

In the context of a different political ideology, Hitler had explained before the German attack on the Soviet Union that because Communism represented a "monstrous danger for the future", German soldiers needed to

> distance themselves from any standpoint of soldierly camaraderie. The Communist is not a comrade beforehand, and not a comrade afterwards. This is a battle of annihilation. If we do not view it as such, then we will still beat the enemy, but in thirty years' time we will find ourselves faced by the Communist enemy again. We are not waging this war in order to conserve the enemy.[32]

The term "comrade" implies a military adversary of equal stature, whose essential human dignity is recognised as being worthy of protection. Communists, on the other hand, were no more comrades than the Chinese or the Africans were; we referred above to the link made between Bolsheviks and 'Asiatics'.

In China, as is well known, the German Emperor's troops carried out his instructions to the letter. Having arrived too late to take part in the actual fighting, they acquired a reputation for extreme brutality through their draconian 'pacification policy' and their punitive expeditions, which resulted in large numbers of casualties. In this, however, they were not alone. The forces of the seven other powers taking part in the campaign also practised 'retaliatory justice', either on separate occasions or acting in concert.[33] In the view of the Commander of the American contingent, Adna R. Chaffee, "It is safe to say that where one real Boxer has been killed since the capture of Peking, fifty harmless coolies or laborers on

---

31 Quoted according to Bernd Sösemann, "'Pardon wird nicht gegeben!' Staatliche Zensur und Presseöffentlichkeit zur 'Hunnenrede'", in Mechthild Leutner and Klaus Mühlhahn, eds, *Kolonialkrieg in China. Die Niederschlagung der Boxerbewegung 1900–1901*, Berlin 2007, pp. 118–122, here p. 188.
32 Address by Hitler to military commanders dated 30 March 1941, transcript made by Franz Halder, Chief of the General Staff, quoted according to Michael Burleigh, *Die Zeit des Nationalsozialismus. Eine Gesamtdarstellung*, Frankfurt 2000, p. 597.
33 For an introduction to the German involvement in the 'Boxer War', see Leutner and Mühlhahn, eds, *Kolonialkrieg*.

the farms, including not a few women and children, have been slain." The 'Boxers' were "closely tied up with the broad mass of the population", so that if "a large number of people" were killed, then there would "also be Boxers among them".[34]

At about the same time, the U.S. military was waging a war in the Philippines that claimed large numbers of victims. Violence against the civilian population escalated especially after local resistance fighters initiated a phase of guerrilla warfare. In December 1900, General Arthur MacArthur imposed martial law on the islands. "In countless campaigns of devastation, the agricultural basis of entire districts was systematically destroyed, and the surviving population resettled into so-called concentration camps."[35] When the US 9th Regiment was then caught in an ambush on the island of Samar, the situation escalated even further. General 'Hell Roaring' Jake Smith was commissioned to devastate the entire province. He ordered that every man who would have been able to offer military resistance should be killed. His Order of the Day was to "burn, plunder and kill", in such a way as to transform the area into "a howling wilderness".[36]

---

[34] Quoted according to George Lynch, *The War of the Civilisations. Being the Record of a 'Foreign Devil's' Experiences with the Allies in China*, London 1901, p. 84.

[35] Frank Schumacher, "'Niederbrennen, plündern und töten sollt ihr': Der Kolonialkrieg der USA auf den Philippinen (1899–1913)", in Thoralf Klein and Frank Schumacher, eds, *Kolonialkriege. Militärische Gewalt im Zeichen des Imperialismus*, Hamburg 2006, pp. 109–144, here p. 122. This also includes an overview of the context and course of the war. As is well known, the 'Boers' in South Africa had to endure a similar experience during the South African War, when the British Army, as a measure to counter the guerrilla warfare directed against them, held tens of thousands of 'Boer' women and children captive in camps. On this subject, see Christoph Marx, "'Die im Dunkeln sieht man nicht': Kriegsgefangene im Burenkrieg 1899–1902", in Rüdiger Overmans, ed., *'In der Hand des Feindes' – Kriegsgefangenschaft von der Antike bis zum Zweiten Weltkrieg*, Köln 1999, pp. 255–276.

[36] Schuhmacher, "'Niederbrennen'", p. 122. Jan-Bart Gewald too has pointed out this and other contemporary parallels. A remarkable finding of his is that when the American civil administration found out about the excesses of their military in the Philippines, it intervened and put a stop to the war of extermination. This was however not the case in German South West Africa. On the contrary, von Trotha was explicitly given a free hand. Gewald, *Learning to wage and win wars in Africa: A provisional history of German military activity in Congo, Tanzania, China and Namibia*, African Studies Centre, ASC Working Paper no. 60, Leiden 2005, http://www.ascleiden.nl/Pdf/workingpaper60.pdf, accessed 12 Jul. 2023. Despite the fact that in German South West Africa too, the most brutal of von Trotha's orders were ultimately revoked, the authorities were so slow in doing so that the work of extermination can be regarded as having been largely completed by then. See Jürgen Zimmerer, "Das Deutsche Reich und der Genozid. Überlegungen zum historischen Ort des Völkermordes an den Herero und Nama", in Larissa Förster, ed., *Namibia-Deutschland. Eine geteilte Geschichte. Widerstand, Gewalt, Erinnerung*, Köln 2004, pp. 106–121 (English version: "The German Empire and Genocide", pp. 154–174 in this book).

The immediate shooting of all armed warriors was also the first order that General von Trotha issued, while he was still on board ship on his way to South West Africa. The war against the Herero had broken out in the German colony on 12 January 1904, and became the longest colonial war, with the highest tally of casualties, fought under the Wilhelminian Empire. Because the conflict was regarded in Berlin as being of the greatest importance, and because the authorities there did not trust the then Governor Theodor Leutwein to take radical enough measures to crush the resistance, the colonial war veteran Lothar von Trotha, well known for his brutality, was named Commander in Chief and sent to Africa. The timing of this first order is significant, because being issued while von Trotha was still far removed from any logistical problems or the turmoil of battle – factors which have been put forward in attempts to explain the radicalisation of policy in terms of the situation and to play down the ideological component[37] – it shows that von Trotha had set out to pursue his brutal strategy from the very start. The Emperor had given him a free hand, requiring him simply to crush the 'rebellion' using whatever means were necessary. This was his authority to pursue a war of annihilation, and ultimately also to commit genocide. Von Trotha, who had earned the bloody reputation which qualified him for the task in South West Africa during the war against the Hehe in German East Africa mentioned above and had also taken part in the suppression of the 'Boxer Uprising', clearly thought in the categories of 'race war'. He believed Africans would "yield only to force", and was determined to exercise this with "blatant terrorism and even with cruelty". In this way he intended to "annihilate the rebellious tribes with rivers of blood".[38]

This is genocidal rhetoric. It is only a small step from this point to the decision to completely drive the Herero out of the territory and to destroy them. In the background was the idea of South West Africa as a settler colony for Germans. Genocide needs two opposing groups or two groups defined as absolute opposites, one of which is willing and able to replace the other. Raphael Lemkin, the originator of the concept of genocide and 'father' of the UN Genocide Convention, knew this when he wrote the following in his fundamental work, *Axis Rule in Occupied Europe*:

> Genocide has two phases: one, destruction of the national pattern of the oppressed group: the other, the imposition of the national pattern of the oppressor. This imposition, in turn,

---

[37] On this subject, see the debate between Hull and Zimmerer in *Bulletin of the German Historical Institute*, 37, Washington 2005.
[38] Von Trotha to Leutwein, 5 November 1904, as quoted by Horst Drechsler, *Südwestafrika unter deutscher Kolonialherrschaft. Der Kampf der Herero und Nama gegen den deutschen Imperialismus 1884–1915*, 2nd edn, Berlin 1984, p. 156.

may be made upon the oppressed population which is allowed to remain, or upon the territory alone, after removal of the population and the colonization of the area by the oppressor's own nationals.[39]

Such were the categories von Trotha thought in too, and in his famous argument with Leutwein, who warned him not to destroy all the Herero as they were needed as labourers, he dismissed this argument completely, pointing out that South West Africa was a settler colony and that the Whites would just have to work for themselves. What then followed was the often-quoted Annihilation Proclamation of 2 October 1904, in which von Trotha decreed:

> The Hereros have ceased to be German subjects.
> They have murdered and robbed, have cut off the ears and noses and other bodily parts of wounded soldiers, and are now too cowardly to want to go on fighting. I say to that people: Whoever delivers one of their *Kapteins* to one of my posts as a prisoner will be given 1,000 marks; whoever brings Samuel Maharero will be given 5,000 marks. But the Herero people must quit this country. If they do not, I will compel them to do so with the *Groot Rohr* [cannon].
> Within the borders of German territory, any Herero, with or without a firearm, with or without livestock, will be shot; nor will I give refuge to women or children any more. I will drive them back to their people or have them fired upon.[40]

In an Order of the Day of the same date, he sought to clarify this by stating that for the sake of the reputation of the German soldier the order to "fire upon women and children" was "to be understood in such a way that shots were to be fired over their heads, in order to force them to run away". He "definitely assume[d] that this Proclamation would lead to no further male prisoners being taken", but would not degenerate "into atrocities against women and children". They would "doubtless run away, if shots are fired over their heads a couple of times".[41]

This proclamation sanctioned the ensuing mass murder. Survival in the Omaheke was not possible; the only Herero that could be shot at were those who were trying to escape from the semi-desert due to the life-threatening conditions there. Also, the explanation that women and children were to be 'spared' is to be thought of, at best, as potentially relieving German soldiers of a duty that von Trotha did not want to have to directly order them to undertake, namely that of actually shoot-

---

39 Raphael Lemkin, *Axis Rule in Occupied Europe: Law of Occupation, Analysis of Government, Proposals for Redress*, Washington 1944, p. 79.
40 Proclamation by von Trotha, Osombo-Wind[imbe], 2 October 1904, Federal Archives Berlin-Lichterfelde (BArch), Imperial Colonial Office R-1001/2089, Sheet 7af. This is a copy of the original document. Other copies of the Proclamation can be found in the Federal Archives, Military Archives Freiburg (BA-MA) and in the National Archive of Namibia in Windhoek (NAN).
41 Ibid.

ing women and children; for there was virtually no chance of their surviving if they were 'driven back' again. The need to camouflage the murder of women and children, even in the midst of general mass murder, arose again in the Second World War when Himmler ordered the massacre of the Pripet Marshes in his Order of the Day of 1 August 1941: "All Jewish men are to be shot, Jewish women driven into the swamps."[42] The intention was clear: that they too would perish there without a German soldier even having to raise his weapon.

The consequences of this policy in South West Africa, consequences which from the autumn of 1904 onwards also included the war of extermination against the Nama, are well known.[43] Up to 80 per cent of the Herero and half of the Nama lost their lives. Displacement, destruction of livelihoods and annihilation in the camps were applied so systematically that this war may well be designated as the first genocide of the twentieth century.[44]

Alongside the driving of the population out into the desert, a main feature of this German war of annihilation was the establishment of concentration camps, and these camps in particular distinguish it even from the colonial punitive expeditions of other nations. They serve as evidence of the will to exterminate which persisted within the German military, or at least within an influential section of the military, over a period of four years, and show up the cool, calculated nature of this policy of extermination. The murder of old people, women and children through neglect, such as is documented with regard to the concentration camp on Shark Island – statements about other camps are difficult to make due to inadequate research – had nothing to do with the tactical or strategic necessities of war. Moreover, at a time when there was no longer any military threat in the greater part of the country, this policy proved to be economically counterproductive: the people concerned could have been used as workers, for which there was an urgent requirement.[45] It is also this intentional extermination through neglect that distinguishes the German concentration camps from those in the Philippines or in South Africa. They were not, it is true, extermination camps in the Nazi sense, but they were places of annihilation through neglect, comparable to a number of the Ger-

---

42 Gerlach, p. 278.
43 For a summary of the war, see Jürgen Zimmerer and Joachim Zeller, eds, *Völkermord in Deutsch-Südwestafrika. Der Kolonialkrieg in Namibia (1904–1908) und seine Folgen*, Berlin 2003.
44 For more details of the reasoning behind this claim, see Jürgen Zimmerer, "Das Deutsche Reich und der Genozid" (English version: "The German Empire and Genocide", pp. 154–174 in this book).
45 With regard to the camp on Shark Island, see Jürgen Zimmerer, "Kriegsgefangene im Kolonialkrieg. Der Krieg gegen die Herero und Nama in Deutsch Südwestafrika (1904–1907)", in Rüdiger Overmans, ed., *'In der Hand des Feindes' – Kriegsgefangenschaft von der Antike bis zum Zweiten Weltkrieg*, Köln 1999, pp. 277–294; Caspar W. Erichsen, *'The Angel of Death Has Descended Violently Among Them'. Concentration Camps and Prisoners-of-War in Namibia, 1904–08*, Leiden 2005.

man camps for Soviet prisoners of war during the Second World War.[46] If Omdurman stands for the mechanisation of massacre, then Shark Island takes its place alongside it as a symbol of administrative mass murder. The ethnic cleansing of whole swathes of land, the clearance of large areas in order to then rebuild them as model economic areas, to create space for settlement, already bears a close resemblance to the goals later outlined in the *Generalplan Ost* during the Second World War.[47] Under this master plan, up to 80 million Russians were to be driven out of the newly established German colonial lands into the areas beyond the Urals, whereby the planners were well aware that several million (up to 30 million, to be more exact) would not survive this.

Refusing to acknowledge the colonial dimension of the Eastern Front is not only Euro-centric, but also obstructs a clear view of new perspectives on the most pressing issues of the history of the war in the East: and in particular the issue of how it came about, and why so many took part in it so willingly. By contrast, the predominating master narrative (especially in Germany) relating to the breach of taboos during the war in the East dehistoricises what actually happened. What, though, if the question as to why this breach of taboos occurred is the wrong question to ask, because the German soldiers did not even notice that they were breaking a taboo? What if they felt they were acting in accordance with a centuries-old colonial history that had been positively received? Taking colonial precursors and worlds of colonial imagination seriously does not construct any causalities. Of course there is no causality between colonialism and National Socialism in the sense that the Nazi crimes necessarily had to follow on from the events of colonialism. Nonetheless, the two are connected by the colonial discourse in which *Lebensraum* thinking seemed to be an entirely natural answer to the social Darwinist and therefore colonialist question of ensuring the survival of one's own biopolitical collective. The world of colonialist ideas offered a framework for explanation and legitimisation, allowing individual soldiers to make sense of their own actions. After all, the colonial 'development' and transformation of entire continents, the 'clearing away' of structures – and peoples – that

---

46 See the classic study on prisoners of war by Christian Streit, *Keine Kameraden: Die Wehrmacht und die sowjetischen Kriegsgefangenen 1941–1945*, Stuttgart 1978.

47 On the plans for the re-ordering of German South West Africa, see Jürgen Zimmerer, "Der Wahn der Planbarkeit: Vertreibung, unfreie Arbeit und Völkermord als Elemente der Bevölkerungsökonomie in Deutsch-Südwestafrika", in Michael Mann, ed., *Comparativ*, 13/4 (2003), Special Issue: Menschenhandel und unfreie Arbeit, pp. 96–113. (English version: "Planning Frenzy: Forced Labour, Expulsion and Genocide as Elements of Population Economics in German South West Africa", pp. 57–76 in this book). For a summary of the *Generalplan Ost*, see Mechthild Rössler and Sabine Schleiermacher, eds, *Der 'Generalplan Ost'*, Berlin 1993; Czeslaw Madajczyk, ed., *Vom Generalplan Ost zum Generalsiedlungsplan*, München 1994.

had existed beforehand and a restructuring 'from scratch' had been practices that had been commonly applied and had received recognition (among the colonial powers) in world history since the fifteenth century at the latest. Those who examined their own actions from within this perspective would feel themselves to be justified by world history.

But are these exclusively German continuities? Is this a *Sonderweg*, a special path and a uniquely German approach? The answer must be no, even though the prominent role of German colonialism in general and of the genocide committed against the Herero and Nama in particular need to be acknowledged, especially simply because of their temporal proximity. And both colonialism and the Herero and Nama War were very familiar to the German public, and enjoyed a popularity that is almost inconceivable today.[48] However, it should also be emphasised that on the one hand both colonialism (including German colonialism) and the Herero and Nama War form part of a global process, and on the other hand, that the mental 'archives' of colonialism also drew upon ideas and views from the colonial experiences of other colonial powers and other times.

The stage has now been reached at which the question of colonial genocide is being researched and openly debated from Sydney to San Francisco. The colonial wars waged by other countries were indeed often no less bloody or heavy in casualties. The German Empire, however, can claim the dubious honour of having picked up these tendencies and systematised them in a manner that had never been seen before. And this does indeed make the genocide in South West Africa a key event in both German history and in the universal history of genocide.

There is no specifically German *Sonderweg* in 'race warfare'; however, responsibility for the war in the East and the way it was waged cannot simply be laid to the charge of history in general. As the Second World War in Western Europe showed, a different approach would have been possible. The Commissar Order and the Martial Law Decree quite deliberately turned European adversaries into 'Natives', 'racially inferior' people whose extermination was not merely not forbidden, but was even demanded. It is high time to view the Second World War from a global perspective. Both German history and wider European history can only benefit from this.

For the concrete case of German rule in Eastern Europe during the Second World War, this means turning our attention to a previously neglected strand of tradition in German history. This will allow us to identify precursors and recognise

---

[48] See Zimmerer, "Geburt des 'Ostlandes'" (English version: "The Birth of the 'Ostland' out of the Spirit of Colonialism", pp. 230–261 in this book) for a detailed presentation of the ways in which colonial visions and experiences from imperial days were transferred to the Third Reich.

models of behaviour. Some elements that appear unique from a narrow perspective may turn out to be variants – admittedly ones carried to utter extremes – of practices previously applied in the colonial context. In this way, the Second World War and the colonial wars in Africa, Asia or America can be used as analytical building blocks for a global history of mass violence. And the writing of such a history is a task we are urgently called upon to undertake.

Archive Sources Referenced

German Federal Archives, Lichterfelde, Berlin (Bundesarchiv Berlin-Lichterfelde – BArch)

Imperial Colonial Office (Reichskolonialamt) (R-1001)

R-1001/1220	Confiscation of African Assets
R-1001/2057	Establishment of Local Self-Government in GSWA
R-1001/2059	Establishment of Local Self-Government in GSWA
R-1001/2087	General Matters in GSWA
R-1001/2089	Differences between Lieutenant General v. Trotha and Governor Leutwein on the relationship between political and military measures to end the war
R 1001/2119	Rebellion of the Herero 1904–1907
R 1001/2140	Rebellion in Namaland (Namaqualand) and the battle against it

National Archives of Namibia (NAN)

Zentralbüro des Gouverneurs – Central Office of the Gouvernor (ZBU)

ZBU F.IV.R.1.	Mixed marriages and their Progeny: Gen.
ZBU W.II.I.1. Vol. 1	Taxation of the Natives: Gen.
ZBU W.III.A.1 Vol. 1	Ordinances and Regulations concerning the Natives: Gen.
ZBU W.III.A.3. Vol. 1	Ordinances and Regulations concerning the Natives: District Office Reports on the Practical Implementation of the Native Ordinances
ZBU W.III.B.1.Vol. 1	Measures for the Surveillance of the Natives: Gen.
ZBU W.III.B.2. Vol. 1	Measures for the Surveillance of the Natives: Spec.
ZBU W.III.B.3. Vol. 1	Measures for the Surveillance of the Natives: Procurement of Employment Logbooks, Travel Passes and Registers
ZBU W.III.B.4. Vol. 1	Measures for the Surveillance of the Natives: Identification of operations with more than ten Native workers
ZBU W.III.B.5 Vol. 1	Measures for the Surveillance of the Natives: Desertion and Vagrancy of the Natives, Limitations on Freedom of Movement
ZBU W.III.K.1. Vol. 1	Pass Requirement and Pass Tokens for the Natives: Gen.
ZBU W.III.R.1. Vol. 1	Maltreatment of Natives by Whites: Gen.
ZBU W.IV.A.3. Vol. 1	Native Labour Relations: old files

∂ Open Access. © 2024 the author(s), published by De Gruyter. This work is licensed under the Creative Commons Attribution 4.0 International License.
https://doi.org/10.1515/9783110754513-013

ZBU Geheimakten – Confidential Documents

ZBU Geheimakten IX.A.Vol.1   Powers of the High Command of the Schutztruppe
ZBU Geheimakten IX.B. Vol. 1   Structure, Deployment and Auxiliary Units of the Schutztruppe

Archives of the Evangelical Church in the Republic of Namibia (ELCIN)

V.16.   Chronicle of Lüderitzbucht Municipality

Die Deutsche Kolonialgesetzgebung – German Colonial Legislation (DKG)

Die Deutsche Kolonialgesetzgebung. Sammlung der auf die deutschen Schutzgebiete bezüglichen Gesetze, Verordnungen, Erlasse und internationalen Vereinbarungen mit Anmerkungen und Sachregister (German Colonial Legislation. A Collection of the Statutes, Ordinances, Decrees and International Agreements relating to the German Schutzgebiete, with Notes and an Index, published in 13 volumes, Berlin 1893–1910.

Bibliography

Published Sources

Aly, Götz, *'Endlösung'. Völkerverschiebung und der Mord an den europäischen Juden*, Frankfurt 1995.
Aly, Götz, *'Final Solution': Nazi Population Policy and the Murder of the European Jews*, London/New York 1999.
Aly, Götz, "'Jewish Resettlement': Reflections on the Political Prehistory of the Holocaust", in Herbert, Ulrich, ed., *National Socialist Extermination Policies: Contemporary German Perspectives and Controversies*, New York 2000, pp. 53–83.
Aly, Götz, *Macht – Geist – Wahn. Kontinuitäten deutschen Denkens*, Frankfurt 1999.
Aly, Götz and Heim, Susanne, *Vordenker der Vernichtung. Auschwitz und die deutschen Pläne für eine neue europäische Ordnung*, Hamburg 1991.
Arendt, Hannah, *The Origins of Totalitarianism*, New York 1951.
Ashcroft, Bill, Griffiths, Gareth and Tiffin, Helen, *Key Concepts in Post-Colonial Studies*, London 1998.
Ayaß, Wolfgang, *'Asoziale' im Nationalsozialismus*, Stuttgart 1995.
Baer, Martin and Schröter, Olaf, *Eine Kopfjagd. Deutsche in Ostafrika*, Berlin 2001.
Bald, Detlef, "Afrikanischer Kampf gegen koloniale Herrschaft. Der Maji-Maji-Aufstand in Ostafrika", *Militärgeschichtliche Mitteilungen*, 19/1 (1976), pp. 23–50.
Balk, Norman, *Die Friedrich-Wilhelms-Universität zu Berlin*, Berlin 1926.
Barkan, Elazar, *Völker klagen an. Eine neue internationale Moral*, Düsseldorf 2002.
Barta, Tony, "Discourses of Genocide in Germany and Australia: A Linked History", *Aboriginal History*, 25 (2001), pp. 37–56.
Barta, Tony, "Relations of Genocide: Land and Lives in the Colonization of Australia", in Wallimann, Isidor and Dobkowski, Michael N., *Genocide and the Modern Age: Etiology and Case Studies of Mass Death*, 2nd edn, Syracuse 2000, pp. 237–251.
Barth, Boris and Osterhammel, Jürgen, eds, *Zivilisationsmissionen. Imperiale Weltverbesserung seit dem 18. Jahrhundert*, Konstanz 2005.
Barth, Boris, *Genozid. Völkermord im 20. Jahrhundert: Geschichte – Theorien – Kontroversen*, München 2006.
Bartov, Omer, *Murder in Our Midst. The Holocaust, Industrial Killing and Representation*, New York 1996.
Bartov, Omer, "Utopie und Gewalt. Neugeburt und Vernichtung der Menschen", in Hans Maier, ed., *Wege in die Gewalt. Die modernen politischen Religionen*, Frankfurt 2000, pp. 92–120.
Bauer, Yehuda, *Rethinking the Holocaust*, New Haven/London 2001.
Bauman, Zygmunt, *Modernity and the Holocaust*, Ithaca 1989.
Bauman, Zygmunt, *Modernity and Ambivalence*, Cambridge 1991.
Bayer, Maximilian, *Mit dem Hauptquartier in Südwestafrika*, Berlin 1909.
Becker, Felicitas and Beez, Jigal, eds, *Der Maji-Maji-Krieg in Deutsch Ostafrika, 1905–1907*, Berlin 2005.
Becker, Frank, "Kolonialherrschaft, Rassentrennung und Mission in Deutsch-Südwestafrika", in Becker, Frank, Großbölting, Thomas, Owers, Armin and Schlögel, Rudolf, eds, *Politische Gewalt in der Moderne*, Münster 2003, pp. 133–163.
Becker, Frank, "Soldatenkinder und Rassenpolitik. Die Folgen des Kolonialkriegs für die Mischlinge in Deutsch-Südwestafrika (1904–1913)", *Militärgeschichtliche Zeitschrift*, 63/1 (2004), pp. 53–77.
Belloc, Hilaire, *The Modern Traveller*, London 1898.
Benninghoff-Lühl, Sibylle, *Deutsche Kolonialromane 1884–1914 in ihrem Entstehungs- und Wirkungszusammenhang*, Bremen 1983.

Bergen, Doris L., "Rivalry, Indifference or Solidarity? Jews and 'Other Victims' in Studies of the Holocaust and Comparative Genocide", in Levy, Margot, ed., *Remembering the Future. The Holocaust in an Age of Genocide*, I: History, pp. 29–42.
Berghahn, Volker, *Europa im Zeitalter der Weltkriege. Die Entfesselung und Entgrenzung der Gewalt*, Frankfurt 2002.
Berman, Russell A., *Enlightenment or Empire. Colonial Discourse in German Culture*, Lincoln 1998.
Birn, Ruth Bettina, "Zweierlei Wirklichkeit? Fallbeispiele zur Partisanenbekämpfung", in Bernd Wegner, ed., *Zwei Wege nach Moskau. Vom Hitler-Stalin Pakt zum 'Unternehmen Barbarossa'*, München 1991, pp. 275–290.
Black History Resource Working Group in conjunction with the Race Equality Management Team, ed., *Slavery: An Introduction to the African Holocaust, with Special Reference to Liverpool, 'Capital of the Slave Trade'*, 2nd edn, Liverpool 1997.
Bley, Helmut, *Kolonialherrschaft und Sozialstruktur in Deutsch-Südwestafrika 1894–1914*, Hamburg 1968.
Blood, Philip Warren, *Bandenbekämpfung: Nazi Occupation Security in Eastern Europe and Soviet Russia 1942–45*, Cranfield University 2001 (Ph.D. Thesis).
Boemeke, Manfred F., Chickering, Roger and Förster, Stig, eds, *Anticipating Total War. The German and American Experiences, 1871–1914*, Cambridge 1999.
Brehl, Medardus, "'Das Drama spielt sich auf der dunklen Bühne des Sandfeldes ab.' Die Vernichtung der Herero und Nama in der deutschen (Populär-)Literatur", in Zimmerer, Jürgen and Zeller, Joachim, eds, *Völkermord. Der Kolonialkrieg (1904–1908) in Namibia und seine Folgen*, Berlin 2003, pp. 86–96.
Brehl, Medardus, "Vernichtung als Arbeit an der Kultur. Kolonialdiskurs, kulturelles Wissen und der Völkermord an den Herero", *Zeitschrift für Genozidforschung*, 2 (2000), pp. 8–28.
Brogiato, Heinz Peter, *Wissen ist Macht – Geographisches Wissen ist Weltmacht. Die schulgeographischen Zeitschriften im deutschsprachigen Raum (1880–1945) unter besonderer Berücksichtigung des Geographischen Anzeigers*, Part 1, text volume, Trier 1998.
Browning, Christopher R., *Ordinary Men. Reserve Police Battalion 101 and the Final Solution in Poland*, New York 1992.
Bühler, Andreas Heinrich, *Der Namaaufstand gegen die deutsche Kolonialherrschaft in Namibia von 1904–1913*, Frankfurt 2003.
Burleigh, Michael, *Death and Deliverance. Euthanasia in Germany c.1900–1945*, Cambridge 1994.
Burleigh, Michael, *Die Zeit des Nationalsozialismus. Eine Gesamtdarstellung*, Frankfurt 2000.
Burleigh, Michael, *Germany turns Eastwards. A Study of Ostforschung in the Third Reich*, Cambridge 1988.
Burleigh, Michael, *The Third Reich: A New History*, London 2000.
Burleigh, Michael, and Wippermann, Wolfgang, *The Racial State. Germany, 1933–1945*, Cambridge 1991.
Burkert, Martin, *Die Ostwissenschaften im Dritten Reich. Teil I: Zwischen Verbot und Duldung. Die schwierige Gratwanderung der Ostwissenschaften zwischen 1933 und 1939*, Wiesbaden 2000.
Callwell, Charles E., *Small Wars. Their Principles and Practice*, London 1896.
Chadha, S. K., ed., *Environmental Holocaust in Himalaya*, New Delhi 1989.
Chalk, Frank and Jonassohn, Kurt, "Genozid: Ein historischer Überblick", in Mihran Dabag and Kristin Platt, eds, *Genozid und Moderne*, i: *Strukturen kollektiver Gewalt im 20. Jahrhundert*, Opladen 1998, pp. 294–308.
Chalk, Frank and Jonassohn, Kurt, *The History and Sociology of Genocide. Analyses and Case Studies*, New Haven/London 1990.
Chiari, Bernhard, *Alltag hinter der Front. Besatzung, Kollaboration und Widerstand in Weißrußland 1941–1944*, Düsseldorf 1998.

Chickering, Roger and Förster, Stig, eds, *Great War – Total War, Combat and Mobilization on the Western Front, 1914–1918*, Cambridge 2000.
Chickering, Roger and Förster, Stig, eds, *The Shadows of Total War: Europe, East Asia, and the United States, 1919–1939*, New York 2003.
Churchill, Ward, *A Little Matter of Genocide: Holocaust and Denial in the Americas 1492-Present*, San Francisco 1997.
Churchill, Winston Spencer, *The River War: An Historical Account of The Reconquest of the Soudan*, 2 vols, London 1899.
Conrad, Sebastian, "Doppelte Marginalisierung. Plädoyer für eine transnationale Perspektive auf die deutsche Geschichte", *Geschichte und Gesellschaft*, 28 (2002), pp. 145–169.
Conrad, Sebastian, *Globalisierung und Nation im Deutschen Kaiserreich*, München 2006.
Conrad, Sebastian and Randeria, Shalini, "Einleitung. Geteilte Geschichten – Europa in einer postkolonialen Welt", in Conrad Sebastian and Randeria, Shalini, eds, *Jenseits des Eurozentrismus. Postkoloniale Perspektiven in den Geschichts- und Kulturwissenschaften*, Frankfurt 2002, pp. 9–49.
Corni, Gustavo, "Richard Walther Darré – Der 'Blut-und-Boden' Ideologe", in Smelser, Ronald, Syring, Enrico and Zitelmann, Rainer, eds, *Die braune Elite: 21 weitere biographische Skizzen*, 4th edn, Darmstadt 1999, pp. 15–27.
Davis, Mike, *Late Victorian Holocausts: El Niño famines and the making of the Third World*, London 2001.
Dedering, Tilman, "'A Certain Rigorous Treatment of All Parts of the Nation'. The Annihilation of the Herero in German South West Africa, 1904", in Levene, Mark and Roberts, Penny, eds, *The Massacre in History*, New York 1999, pp. 205–222.
Dedering, Tilman, "The German-Herero War of 1904. Revisionism of Genocide or Imaginary Historiography?", *Journal of Southern African Studies*, 19 (1993), pp. 80–88.
Diekmann, Irene, Krüger, Peter and Schoeps, Julius H., eds, *Geopolitik. Grenzgänge im Zeitgeist*, 2 vols, Potsdam 2000.
Diner, Dan, *Das Jahrhundert verstehen. Eine universalhistorische Deutung*, München 1999.
Drechsler, Horst, *Südwestafrika unter deutscher Kolonialherrschaft. Der Kampf der Herero und Nama gegen den deutschen Imperialismus 1884–1915*, 2nd edn, Berlin 1984.
Drescher, Seymour, "The Atlantic Slave Trade and the Holocaust: A Comparative Analysis", in Rosenbaum, Alan S., ed., *Is the Holocaust Unique? Perspectives on Comparative Genocide*, Oxford 1996, pp. 65–86.
Driver, Felix, *Geography Militant: Cultures of Exploration and Empire*, Oxford 2001.
Dubow, Saul, *Scientific Racism in Modern South Africa*, Cambridge 1995.
Ebeling, Frank, *Geopolitik. Karl Haushofer und seine Raumwissenschaft 1919–1945*, Berlin 1994.
Eckert, Andreas and Wirz, Albert, "Wir nicht, die Anderen auch. Deutschland und der Kolonialismus", in Conrad Sebastian and Randeria, Shalini, eds, *Jenseits des Eurozentrismus. Postkoloniale Perspektiven in den Geschichts- und Kulturwissenschaften*, Frankfurt 2002, pp. 372–392.
Eckert, Andreas, *Kolonialismus*, Frankfurt 2006.
Eckart, Wolfgang Uwe, *Medizin und Kolonialimperialismus. Deutschland 1884–1945*, Paderborn 1996.
Eckenbrecher, Margarethe von, *Was Afrika mir gab und nahm. Erlebnisse einer deutschen Frau in Südwestafrika*, Berlin 1907.
Ehmann, Annegret, "Rassistische und antisemitische Traditionslinien in der deutschen Geschichte des 19. und 20. Jahrhunderts", in Sportmuseum Berlin, ed., *Sportstadt Berlin in Geschichte und Gegenwart*, Berlin 1993, pp. 131–145.
Ehmann, Annegret, "From Colonial Racism to Nazi Population Policy: The Role of the so-called Mischlinge", Berenbaum, Michael and Peck, Abraham J., eds, *The Holocaust and History; The Known, the Unkown, the Disputed, and the Reexamined*, Washington 1998, pp. 115–133.

Eirola, Martti, *The Ovambogefahr. The Ovamboland Reservation in the Making – Political Responses of the Kingdom of Ondonga to the German Colonial Power 1884–1910*, Rovaniemi 1992.
Engelmann, Gerhard, *Ferdinand von Richthofen (1833–1905) und Alfred Penck (1858–1945). Zwei markante Geographen Berlins*, Stuttgart 1988.
Erichsen, Caspar W., *'The Angel of Death Has Descended Violently Among Them.' Concentration Camps and Prisoners-of-War in Namibia, 1904–08*, Leiden 2005.
Esche, Jan, *Koloniales Anspruchsdenken in Deutschland im Ersten Weltkrieg, während der Versailler Friedensverhandlungen und in der Weimarer Republik (1914 bis 1933)*, Hamburg 1989.
Essig, Rolf-Bernhard and Schury, Gudrun, "Karl May",in Etienne François and Hagen Schulze, eds, *Deutsche Erinnerungsorte*, Vol. 3, 2nd edn, München 2002, pp. 107–121.
Essner, Cornelia, *Die 'Nürnberger Gesetze' oder die Verwaltung des Rassenwahns 1933–1945*, Paderborn 2002.
Essner, Cornelia, "'Wo Rauch ist, da ist auch Feuer'. Zu den Ansätzen eines Rassenrechts für die deutschen Kolonien", in Wagner, Wilfried, ed., *Rassendiskriminierung, Kolonialpolitik und ethnischnationale Identität*, Münster 1992, pp. 145–160.
Essner, Cornelia, "Zwischen Vernunft und Gefühl. Die Reichstagsdebatten von 1912 um koloniale 'Rassenmischehe' und 'Sexualität'", *Zeitschrift für Geschichtswissenschaft*, 45/6 (1997), pp. 503–519.
Estorff, Ludwig von, *Wanderungen und Kämpfe in Südwestafrika, Ostafrika und Südafrika 1894–1910*, ed. Christoph-Friedrich Kutscher, Wiesbaden 1968.
Estorff, Ludwig von, *Wanderungen und Kämpfe in Südwestafrika, Ostafrika und Südafrika 1894–1910*, ed. Christoph-Friedrich Kutscher, Windhoek 1979.
Fabian, Johannes, *Out of Our Minds: Reason and Madness in the Exploration of Central Africa*, Los Angeles 2000.
Fahlbusch, Michael, *Wissenschaft im Dienst der nationalsozialistischen Politik? Die 'Volksdeutschen Forschungsgemeinschaften' von 1931–1945*, Baden-Baden 1999.
Fahlbusch, Michael, Rössler, Mechtild and Siegrist, Dominik, *Geographie im Nationalsozialismus. 3 Fallstudien zur Institution Geographie im Deutschen Reich und der Schweiz*, Kassel 1989.
Fein, Helen, "Definition and Discontent: Labelling, Detecting and Explaining Genocide in the Twentieth Century", in Förster, Stig and Hirschfeld, Gerhard, eds, *Genozid in der modernen Geschichte*, Münster 1999, pp. 11–21.
Fein, Helen, *Genocide: A Sociological Perspective*, London 1990.
Fein, Helen, "Genozid als Staatsverbrechen. Beispiele aus Rwanda und Bosnien", *Zeitschrift für Genozidforschung*, 1 (1999), pp. 36–45.
Fenske, Hans, "Ungeduldige Zuschauer. Die Deutschen und die europäische Expansion 1815–1880", in Reinhard, Wolfgang, ed., *Imperialistische Kontinuität und nationale Ungeduld im 19. Jahrhundert*, Frankfurt 1991, pp. 87–140.
Fenske, Hans, "Imperialistische Tendenzen in Deutschland vor 1866. Auswanderung, überseeische Bestrebungen, Weltmachtträume", *Historisches Jahrbuch*, 97/98 (1978), pp. 336–383.
Ferguson, Niall, *Empire: How Britain made the Modern World*, London 2003.
Finkelstein, Norman G., *The Holocaust Industry*, London 2000.
Finzsch, Norbert, *Late 18th Century Genocidal Practices in North America and Australia: A Comparison*, Canberra 2003 (Humanities Research Centre, Australian National University, Work in Progress Lecture), https://web.archive.org/web/20030731085250/http://www.uni-koeln.de/phil-fak/hist sem/anglo/html_2001/Finzsch/Lecture.pdf, accessed 12 Jul. 2023.
Fischer, Fritz, *From Kaiserreich to Third Reich*, London 1986.
Fischer, Fritz, *Germany's aims in the First World War*, New York 1967.
Fischer, Fritz, *Hitler war kein Betriebsunfall*, München 1998.

Fischer, Fritz, *War of illusions: German Policies from 1911 to 1914*, London 1975.
Förster, Stig and Hirschfeld, Gerhard, "Einleitung", in Stig Förster and Gerhard Hirschfeld, eds, *Genozid in der modernen Geschichte*, Münster 1999, pp. 5–10.
Förster, Stig and Nagler, Jörg, eds, *On the Road to Total War: The American Civil War and the German Wars of Unification, 1861–1871*, New York 1997.
Frenssen, Gustav, *Peter Moors Fahrt nach Südwest. Ein Feldzugsbericht*, Berlin 1906.
Friedberg, Lilian, "Dare to Compare: Americanizing the Holocaust", *American Indian Quarterly*, 24/3 (2000), pp. 353–380.
Friedländer, Saul, *Nazi Germany and the Jews*: i, *The Years of Persecution, 1933–1939*, New York 1997.
Friedrichsmeyer, Sara, Lennox, Sara and Zantop, Susanne, eds, *The Imperialist Imagination. German Colonialism and Its Legacy*, Ann Arbor 1998.
Fuhrmann, Wolfgang, "'Nashornjagd in Deutsch-Ostafrika' – Die frühe Kolonialfilmindustrie", in Heyden, Ulrich van der and Zeller, Joachim, eds, *Kolonialmetropole Berlin. Eine Spurensuche*, Berlin 2002, pp. 184–208.
Furber, David, *'Going East'. Colonialism and German Life in Nazi-Occupied Poland*, University of New York at Buffalo 2003 (dissertation).
Gerlach, Christian, "Deutsche Wirtschaftsinteressen, Besatzungspolitik und der Mord an den Juden in Weißrußland 1941–1943", in Herbert, Ulrich, ed., *Nationalsozialistische Vernichtungspolitik 1939–1945. Neue Forschung und Kontroversen*, Frankfurt 1998, pp. 236–291.
Gerlach, Christian, *Kalkulierte Morde: Die deutsche Wirtschafts- und Vernichtungspolitik in Weißrußland, 1941–1944*, Hamburg 1999.
Gerlach, Christian, *Krieg, Ernährung,Völkermord. Forschungen zur deutschen Vernichtungspolitik im Zweiten Weltkrieg*, Hamburg 1998.
Gerwarth, Robert and Malinowski, Stephan, "Der Holocaust als 'kolonialer Genozid' Europäische Kolonialgewalt und nationalsozialistischer Vernichtungskrieg", *Geschichte und Gesellschaft*, 33 (2007), pp. 439–466.
Gessler, Bernhard, *Eugen Fischer, (1874–1967). Leben und Werk des Freiburger Anatomen, Anthropologen und Rassenhygienikers bis 1927*, Frankfurt 2000.
Gessler, Myriam, *Die Singularität des Holocaust und die vergleichende Genozidforschung. Empirische und theoretische Untersuchung zu einem aktuellen Thema der Geschichtswissenschaft*, University of Bern 2000 (M.A. thesis).
Geulen, Christian, *Geschichte des Rassismus*, München 2007.
Geulen, Christian, "'The Final Frontier ...'. Heimat, Nation und Kolonie um 1900: Carl Peters", in Kundrus, Birthe, ed., *Phantasiereiche. Zur Kulturgeschichte des deutschen Kolonialismus*, Frankfurt 2003, pp. 35–55.
Gewald, Jan-Bart, "Colonization, Genocide and Resurgence: The Herero of Namibia 1890–1933", in Gewald, Jan-Bart and Bollig, Michael, eds, *People, Cattle and Land: Transformations of a Pastoral Society in Southwestern Africa*, Köln 2001, pp. 187–225.
Gewald, Jan-Bart, "Herero and Missionaries. The Making of Historical Sources in the 1920s", in Möhlig, Wilhelm J. G., ed., *Frühe Kolonialgeschichte Namibias 1880–1930*, Köln 2000, pp. 77–95.
Gewald, Jan-Bart, "Imperial Germany and the Herero of Southern Africa: Genocide and the Quest for Recompense", in Jones, Adam, ed., *Genocide, War Crimes & the West, History and Complicity*, London 2004, pp. 59–77.
Gewald, Jan-Bart, *Learning to wage and win wars in Africa: A provisional history of German military activity in Congo, Tanzania, China and Namibia*, African Studies Centre, ASC Working Paper no. 60, Leiden 2005, http://www.ascleiden.nl/Pdf/workingpaper60.pdf, accessed 12 Jul. 2023.

Gewald, Jan-Bart, *Towards Redemption. A Socio-political History of the Herero of Namibia Between 1890 and 1923*, Leiden 1996.
Gewald, Jan-Bart, *'We Thought we Would be Free ...'. Socio-Cultural Aspects of Herero History in Namibia 1915–1940*, Köln 2000.
Gliech, Oliver, "Wilhelm Faupel. Generalstabsoffizier, Militärberater, Präsident des Ibero-Amerikanischen Instituts", in Liehr, Reinhard, Maihold, Günther and Vollmer, Günter, eds, *Ein Institut und sein General. Wilhelm Faupel und das Ibero-Amerikanische Institut in der Zeit des Nationalsozialismus*, Frankfurt 2003, pp. 131–279.
Graichen, Gisela and Gründer, Horst, eds, *Deutsche Kolonien. Traum und Trauma*, München 2005.
Grimm, Hans, *Volk ohne Raum*, München 1926.
Grosse, Pascal, *Kolonialismus, Eugenik und bürgerliche Gesellschaft in Deutschland, 1850–1918*, Frankfurt 2000.
Gründer, Horst, ed., *'... da und dort ein junges Deutschland gründen'. Rassismus, Kolonien und kolonialer Gedanke vom 16. bis zum 20. Jahrhundert*, München 1999.
Gründer, Horst, "Genozid oder Zwangsmodernisierung? Der moderne Kolonialismus in universalgeschichtlicher Perspektive", in Dabag, Mihran and Platt, Kristin eds, *Genozid und Moderne*, i: *Strukturen kollektiver Gewalt im 20. Jahrhundert*, Opladen 1998, pp. 135–151.
Gründer, Horst, *Geschichte der deutschen Kolonien*, 3rd edn, Paderborn 1995.
Haar, Ingo, *Historiker im Nationalsozialismus. Deutsche Geschichtswissenschaft und der 'Volkstumskampf' im Osten*, Göttingen 2000.
Hartenstein, Michael A., *Neue Dorflandschaften: Nationalsozialistische Siedlungsplanung in den 'eingegliederten Ostgebieten', 1939–1944*, Berlin 1998.
Hartmann, Christian, Hürter, Johannes and Jureit, Ulrike, "Verbrechen der Wehrmacht. Ereignisse und Kontroversen der Forschung", in Christian Hartmann, Johannes Hürter and Ulrike Jureit, eds, *Verbrechen der Wehrmacht. Bilanz einer Debatte*, München 2005, pp. 21–28.
Hartmann, Wolfram, "'... als durchaus unerwünscht erachtet ...'. Zur Genese des 'Mischehenverbotes' in Deutsch-Südwestafrika", in Förster, Larissa, Henrichsen, Dag and Bollig, Michael, eds, *Namibia-Deutschland. Eine geteilte Geschichte. Widerstand, Gewalt, Erinnerung*, Köln 2004, pp. 182–193.
Hausmann, Franz-Rutker, *Deutsche Geisteswissenschaft im Zweiten Weltkrieg: Die 'Aktion Ritterbusch' (1940–1945)*, Dresden 1998.
Hegel, Georg Wilhelm Friedrich, *The Philosophy of History*, translated from the German by J. Sibree, New York 1956.
Heideking, Jürgen, *Geschichte der USA*, 4th edn, Tübingen 1999.
Henrichsen, Dag, "Heirat im Krieg. Erfahrungen von Kaera Ida Getzen Leinhos", in Zimmerer, Jürgen and Zeller, Joachim, eds, *Völkermord in Deutsch-Südwestafrika. Der Kolonialkrieg in Namibia (1904–1908) und seine Folgen*, Berlin 2003, pp. 160–168.
Henrichsen, Dag, *Herrschaft und Identifikation im vorkolonialen Zentralnamibia. Das Herero- und Damaraland im 19. Jahrhundert*, University of Hamburg 1997 (Ph.D. Thesis).
Herbert, Ulrich, *Hitler's Foreign Workers: Enforced Foreign Labor in Germany under the Third Reich*, Cambridge/New York 1997.
Herbert, Ulrich, ed., *National Socialist Extermination Policies: Contemporary German Perspectives and Controversies*, New York 2000.
Herbert, Ulrich, ed., *Nationalsozialistische Vernichtungspolitik 1939–1945. Neue Forschungen und Kontroversen*, Frankfurt 1998.
Herbert, Ulrich, "Traditionen des Rassismus", in Ulrich Herbert, ed., *Arbeit, Volkstum, Weltanschauung. Über Fremde und Deutsche im 20. Jahrhundert*, Frankfurt 1995, pp. 11–29.

Herf, Jeffrey, *Reactionary Modernism. Technology, Culture and Politics in Weimar and the Third Reich*, Cambridge 1984.
Hildebrand, Klaus, *Das vergangene Reich. Deutsche Außenpolitik von Bismarck bis Hitler*, Stuttgart 1995.
Hildebrand, Klaus, *Vom Reich zum Weltreich – Hitler, NSDAP und koloniale Frage 1919–1945*, München 1969.
Hillebrecht, Werner, "Die Nama und der Krieg im Süden", in Jürgen Zimmerer and Joachim Zeller, *Völkermord. Der Kolonialkrieg (1904–1908) in Namibia und seine Folgen*, Berlin 2003, pp. 121–132.
Hillesheim, Jürgen and Michael, Elisabeth, *Lexikon nationalsozialistischer Dichter. Biographien – Analysen – Bibliographien*, Würzburg 1993, pp. 211–222.
Hillgruber, Andreas, *Hitlers Strategie. Politik und Kriegführung 1940–41*, München 1982.
Hintrager, Oskar, *Südwestafrika in der deutschen Zeit*, München 1956.
Hipler, Bruno, *Hitlers Lehrmeister. Karl Haushofer als Vater der NS-Ideologie*, St. Ottilien 1996.
Hitler, Adolf, *Monologe im Führerhauptquartier*, ed. Werner Jochmann, Hamburg 1980.
Hochschild, Adam, *Schatten über dem Kongo. Die Geschichte eines der großen fast vergessenen Menschheitsverbrechen*, Stuttgart, 2000.
Hofer, Walther, ed., *Der Nationalsozialismus: Dokumente, 1933–1945*, new revised edn, Frankfurt 1982.
Honold, Alexander, "Flüsse, Berge, Eisenbahnen: Szenarien geographischer Bemächtigung", in Honold, Alexander and Scherbe, Klaus R., eds, *Das Fremde. Reiseerfahrungen, Schreibformen und kulturelles Wissen*, Frankfurt 2003, pp. 137–161.
Honold, Alexander and Simons, Oliver, eds, *Kolonialismus als Kultur. Literatur, Medien, Wissenschaft in der deutschen Gründerzeit des Fremden*, Tübingen/Basel 2002.
Hubatsch, Walter, *Grundriß zur deutschen Verwaltungsgeschichte 1815–1945*, xii: *Bundes- und Reichsbehörden*, Marburg 1983.
Huber, Hansjörg Michael, *Koloniale Selbstverwaltung in Deutsch-Südwestafrika. Entstehung, Kodifizierung und Umsetzung*, Frankfurt 2000.
Hull, Isabel V., *Absolute Destruction: Military Culture and the Practices of War in Imperial Germany*, Ithaca 2005.
Jacobsen, Hans-Adolf, *Karl Haushofer. Leben und Werk*, 2 vols, Boppard am Rhein 1979.
Jaeger, Fritz, "Wesen und Aufgaben der kolonialen Geographie", *Zeitschrift der Gesellschaft für Erdkunde zu Berlin*, (1911), pp. 400–405.
Jahr, Christoph, "Berthold von Deimling. Vom General zum Pazifisten. Eine biographische Skizze", in *Zeitschrift für die Geschichte des Oberrheins*, new version 142 (1994), pp. 359–387.
Jahr, Christoph, "Die geistige Verbindung von Wehrmacht, Wissenschaft und Politik: Wehrlehre und Heimatforschung an der Friedrich-Wilhelms-Universität zu Berlin 1933–1945", *Jahrbuch für Universitätsgeschichte*, 4 (2001), pp. 161–176.
Jahr, Christoph, "'Die reaktionäre Presse heult auf wider den Mann.' General Berthold von Deimling (1853–1944) und der Pazifismus", in Wette, Wolfram, ed., *Pazifistische Offiziere in Deutschland 1871 bis 1933*, Bremen 1999, pp. 131–146.
Jones, Adam, *Genocide. A Comprehensive Introduction*, London 2006.
Kaminski, Andrzej J., *Konzentrationslager 1896 bis heute: Geschichte-Funktion-Typologie*, München 1996.
Kaufmann, Stefan, "Der Siedler", in Horn, Eva, Kaufmann, Stefan and Bröckling, Ulrich, eds, *Grenzverletzer. Von Schmugglern, Spionen und anderen subversiven Gestalten*, Berlin 2002, pp. 176–201.
Kaufmann, Stefan, "Naturale Grenzfelder des Sozialen: Landschaft und Körper", in Fludernik, Monika and Gehrke, Hans-Joachim, eds, *Grenzgänger zwischen Kulturen*, Würzburg 1999, pp. 121–136.
Kaulich, Udo, *Die Geschichte der ehemaligen Kolonie Deutsch Südwestafrika (1884–1914). Eine Gesamtdarstellung*, Frankfurt 2001.

Katz, Steven T., *The Holocaust in Historical Perspective*, i: *The Holocaust and Mass Death before the Modern Age*, Oxford 1994.
Kelly, Robin, "A Poetics of Anticolonialism", *Monthly Review*, 51/6 (1999), http://www.monthlyreview.org/1199kell.htm, accessed 12 Jul. 2023.
Kennedy, Dane, "Imperial History and Post-Colonial Theory", *Journal of Imperial and Commonwealth History*, 24/3 (1996), pp. 345–363.
Kiernan, Ben, *Blood and Soil: A History of Genocide and Extermination from Sparta to Darfur*, New Haven 2007.
Kieser, Hans-Lukas and Schaller, Dominik J., eds, *Der Völkermord an den Armeniern und die Shoah*, Zürich 2002.
King, Richard H. and Stone, Dan, eds, *Hannah Arendt and the Uses of History. Imperialism, Nation, Race, and Genocide*, New York 2007.
Klee, Ernst, *'Euthanasie' im NS-Staat. Die 'Vernichtung lebensunwerten Lebens'*, Frankfurt 1983.
Klein, Thoralf and Schumacher, Frank, eds, *Kolonialkriege. Militärische Gewalt im Zeichen des Imperialismus*, Hamburg 2006.
Koller, Christian,*'Von Wilden aller Rassen niedergemetzelt'. Die Diskussion um die Verwendung von Kolonialtruppen in Europa zwischen Rassismus, Kolonial- und Militärpolitik (1914–1930)*, Stuttgart 2001.
Koselleck, Reinhart, "Zur historisch-politischen Semantik asymmetrischer Gegenbegriffe", in Koselleck, Reinhart, *Vergangene Zukunft. Zur Semantik geschichtlicher Zeiten*, Frankfurt 1989, pp. 211–259.
Kößler, Reinhart, "From Genocide to Holocaust? Structural Parallels and Discursive Conditions", *Africa Spectrum*, 40/2 (2005), pp. 309–317.
Kößler, Reinhart and Melber, Henning, "Völkermord und Gedenken. Der Genozid an den Herero und Nama in Deutsch-Südwestafrika 1904–1908", in Wojak, Irmtrud and Meinl, Susanne, eds, *Jahrbuch 2004 zur Geschichte und Wirkung des Holocaust*, Frankfurt/New York 1996, pp. 37–75.
Kost, Klaus, *Die Einflüsse der Geopolitik auf Forschung und Theorie der Politischen Geographie von ihren Anfängen bis 1945. Ein Beitrag zur Wissenschaftsgeschichte unter besonderer Berücksichtigung von Militär und Kolonialgeographie*, Bonn 1988.
Kotek, Joël and Rigoulot, Pierre, *Das Jahrhundert der Lager. Gefangenschaft, Zwangsarbeit, Vernichtung*, Berlin/München 2001.
Kotek, Joël and Rigoulot, Pierre, *Le siècle des camps*, Paris 2000.
Kriegsgeschichtliche Abteilung I des Großen Generalstabs, *Die Kämpfe der deutschen Truppen in Südwestafrika*, 2 vols, Berlin 1906/07.
Krug, Alexander, *'Der Hauptzweck ist die Tötung von Kanaken'. Die deutschen Strafexpeditionen in den Kolonien der Südsee 1872–1914*, Tönning 2005.
Krüger, Gesine, *Kriegsbewältigung und Geschichtsbewußtsein: Realität, Deutung und Verarbeitung des deutschen Kolonialkrieges in Namibia 1904–1907*, Göttingen 1999, pp. 126–135.
Kühl, Stefan, *Die Internationale der Rassisten. Aufstieg und Niedergang der internationalen Bewegung für Eugenik und Rassenhygiene im 20. Jahrhundert*, Frankfurt 1997.
Kühl, Stefan, *The Nazi Connection. Eugenics, American Racism, and German National Socialism*, New York 1994.
Kum'a N'dumbe III, Alexandre, *Was wollte Hitler in Afrika? NS-Planungen für eine faschistische Neugestaltung Afrikas*, Frankfurt 1993.
Kundrus, Birthe, "Grenzen der Gleichsetzung. Kolonialverbrechen und Vernichtungspolitik", *Informationszentrum 3. Welt* (iz3w), 275/March (2004), pp. 30–33.

Kundrus, Birthe, "Kontinuitäten, Parallelen, Rezeptionen. Überlegungen zur "Kolonialisierung" des Nationalsozialismus", *WerkstattGeschichte*, 43 (2006), pp. 45-62.
Kundrus, Birthe, *Moderne Imperialisten. Das Kaiserreich im Spiegel seiner Kolonien*, Köln/Weimar/Wien 2003.
Kundrus, Birthe, "Von Windhoek nach Nürnberg? Koloniale 'Mischehenverbote' und die nationalsozialistische Rassengesetzgebung", in Kundrus, Birthe, ed., *Phantasiereiche. Zur Kulturgeschichte des deutschen Kolonialismus*, Frankfurt 2003, pp. 110-113.
Kuß, Susanne, "Deutsche Soldaten während des Boxeraufstandes in China: Elemente und Ursprünge des Vernichtungskrieges", in Susanne Kuß and Bernd Martin, eds, *Das Deutsche Reich und der Boxeraufstand*, München 2002, pp. 165-181.
Laak, Dirk van, *Imperiale Infrastruktur. Deutsche Planungen für eine Erschließung Afrikas, 1880 bis 1960*, Paderborn 2004.
Lange, Werner, *Hans Paasches Forschungsreise ins innerste Deutschland. Eine Biographie*, Bremen 1995.
Lau, Brigitte, "Uncertain Certainties. The Herero-German War of 1904", in Lau, Brigitte, *History and Historiography – 4 Essays in Reprint*, ed. Annemarie Heywood, Windhoek 1995, pp. 39-52.
Lauer, Wilhelm, "Carl Troll zum 70. Geburtstag", in Wilhelm Lauer, ed., *Argumenta Geographica. Festschrift für Carl Troll zum 70. Geburtstag*, Bonn 1970, pp. 11-17.
Lemkin, Raphael, *Axis Rule in Occupied Europe: Law of Occupation, Analysis of Government, Proposals for Redress*, Washington 1944.
Lettow-Vorbeck, Paul von, *Heia Safari! Deutschlands Kampf in Ostafrika*, Leipzig 1920.
Leutwein, Theodor, *Elf Jahre Gouverneur in Deutsch-Südwestafrika*, 3rd edn, Berlin 1908.
Levene, Mark, *Genocide in the Age of the Nation State*, 2 vols, London 2005.
Levy, Daniel and Sznaider, Natan, *Erinnerung im globalen Zeitalter: Der Holocaust*, Frankfurt 2001.
Liebert, Eduard von, *Neunzig Tage im Zelt. Meine Reise nach Uhehe Juni bis September 1897*, Berlin 1898.
Lindqvist, Sven, *Exterminate all the Brutes*, London 1997.
Linne, Karsten, "Deutsche Afrikafirmen im 'Osteinsatz'", in *1999. Zeitschrift für Sozialgeschichte des 20. und 21. Jahrhunderts*, 16/1 (2001), pp. 49-90
Linne, Karsten, *Weiße 'Arbeitsführer' im 'Kolonialen Ergänzungsraum'. Afrika als Ziel sozial- und wirtschaftspolitischer Planungen in der NS-Zeit*, Münster 2002.
Liulevicius, Vejas Gabriel, *War Land on the Eastern Front. Culture, National Identity and German Occupation in World War I*, Cambridge 2000.
Loewen, James W., *Lies across America: What our Historic Sites Get Wrong*, New York 2000.
Lösch, Niels C., *Rasse als Konstrukt. Leben und Werk Eugen Fischers*, Frankfurt 1997.
Lower, Wendy, "A New Ordering of Space and Race: Nazi Colonial Dreams in Zhytomry, Ukraine, 1941-1944", *German Studies Review*, 25 (2002), pp. 227-254.
Lundgreen, Peter, ed., *Wissenschaft im Dritten Reich*, Frankfurt 1985.
Lundtofte, Henrik, "'I believe that the nation as such must be annihilated ...' – The Radicalization of the German Suppression of the Herero Rising in 1904", in Jensen, Steven L. B., ed., *Genocide: Cases, Comparisons and Contemporary Debates*, Copenhagen 2003, pp. 15-53.
Lynch, George, *The War of the Civilisations. Being the Record of a 'Foreign Devil's' Experiences with the Allies in China*, London 1901.
Madajczyk, Czeslaw, ed., *Vom Generalplan Ost zum Generalsiedlungsplan*, München 1994.
Mai, Uwe, *'Rasse und Raum'. Agrarpolitik, sozial- und Raumplanung im NS-Staat*, Paderborn 2001.
Mann, Michael, ed., Comparativ 13/4 (2003), Special Issue: *Menschenhandel und erzwungene Arbeit*.
Mann, Michael, *Dark Side of Democracy*, Cambridge 2005.
Mann, Michael, *Die dunkle Seite der Demokratie. Eine Theorie der ethnischen Säuberung*, Hamburg 2007.

Marx, Christoph, "'Die im Dunkeln sieht man nicht': Kriegsgefangene im Burenkrieg 1899–1902", in Overmans, Rüdiger, ed., *'In der Hand des Feindes' – Kriegsgefangenschaft von der Antike bis zum Zweiten Weltkrieg*, Köln 1999, pp. 255–276.

Marx, Christoph, "Entsorgen und Entseuchen. Zur Diskussionskultur in der derzeitigen namibischen Historiographie – eine Polemik", in Melber, Henning, ed., *Genozid und Gedenken. Namibisch-deutsche Geschichte und Gegenwart*, Frankfurt 2005, pp. 141–161.

Marx, Christoph, "Grenzfälle: Zu Geschichte und Potential des Frontierbegriffs", *Saeculum*, 54/1 (2003), pp. 123–143.

Marx, Christoph, *'Völker ohne Schrift und Geschichte'. Zur historischen Erfassung des vorkolonialen Schwarzafrika in der deutschen Forschung des 19. und frühen 20. Jahrhunderts*, Stuttgart 1988.

Mazower, Mark, "After Lemkin: Genocide, the Holocaust and History", *The Jewish Quarterly*, 5/Winter (1995), pp. 5–8.

Mazower, Mark, *Dark Continent: Europe's Twentieth Century*, London 1998.

McGregor, Russell, *Imagined Destinies. Aboriginal Australians and the Doomed Race Theory, 1880–1939*, Victoria 1997.

Melber, Henning, "How to Come to Terms with the Past: Re-visiting the German Colonial Genocide in Namibia", *Africa Spectrum*, 40/2 (2005), pp. 139–148.

Melber, Henning, "Kontinuitäten totaler Herrschaft. Völkermord und Apartheid in Deutsch-Südwestafrika", *Jahrbuch für Antisemitismusforschung*, 1 (1992), pp. 91–116.

Meyer, Theodor, *Reichs- und Staatsangehörigkeitsgesetz*, Berlin 1914.

Meyn, Rolf, "Abstecher in die Kolonialliteratur. Gustav Frenssens 'Peter Moors fährt nach Südwest'", in Dohnke, Kay and Stein, Dietrich, eds, *Gustav Frenssen und seine Zeit. Von der Massenliteratur im Kaiserreich zur Massenideologie im NS-Staat*, Heide 1997, pp. 316–346.

Militärgeschichtliches Forschungsamt, *Das Deutsche Reich und der Zweite Weltkrieg*, 10 vols, Stuttgart 1984ff.

Mogk, Walter, *Paul Rohrbach und das 'Größere Deutschland.' Ethischer Imperialismus im Wilhelminischen Zeitalter. Ein Beitrag zur Geschichte des Kulturprotestantismus*, München 1972.

Mommsen, Wolfgang J., ed., *Kultur und Krieg. Die Rolle der Intellektuellen, Künstler und Schriftsteller im Ersten Weltkrieg*, München 1996.

Mommsen, Wolfgang J., *Imperialismustheorien. Ein Überblick über die neueren Imperialismustheorien*, Göttingen 1980.

Mordekhai, Thomas, *Vessels of Evil: American Slavery and the Holocaust*, Philadelphia 1993.

Morlang, Thomas, "'Die Kerls haben ja nicht einmal Gewehre.' Der Untergang der Zelewski-Expedition in Deutsch-Ostafrika im August 1891", *Militärgeschichte*, 11/2 February (2001), pp. 22–28.

Moses, A. Dirk, "An Antipodean Genocide? The Origins of the Genocidal Moment in the Colonization of Australia", *Journal of Genocide Research*, 2 (2000), pp. 89–106.

Moses, A. Dirk, "Coming to Terms with Genocidal Pasts in Comparative Perspective: Germany and Australia", *Aboriginal History*, 25 (2001), pp. 91–115.

Moses, A. Dirk, "Conceptual Blockages and Definitional Dilemmas in the 'Racial Century': Genocides of Indigenous Peoples and the Holocaust", *Patterns of Prejudice*, 36/4 (2002), pp. 7–36.

Moses, A. Dirk, ed., *Empire, Colony, Genocide: Conquest, Occupation, and Subaltern Resistance in World History*, New York 2008.

Moses, A. Dirk, "Empire, Colony, Genocide. Keywords and the Philosophy of History", in Moses, A. Dirk, *Empire, Colony, Genocide: Conquest, Occupation, and Subaltern Resistance in World History*, New York 2008, pp. 3–54.

Moses, A. Dirk, "Structure and Agency in the Holocaust: Daniel J. Goldhagen and his Critics", *History and Theory*, 2 (1998), pp. 194-219.
Moses, A. Dirk, "The Holocaust and Genocide", in Dan Stone, ed., *The Historiography of the Holocaust*, London 2004, pp. 533-555.
Moses, John A., *The Politics of Illusion*, London 1975.
Müller, Rolf-Dieter and Überschär, Gerd, *Hitlers Krieg im Osten 1941-1945. Ein Forschungsbericht*, Darmstadt 2000.
Münkler, Herfried, *Die neuen Kriege*, Reinbek 2004.
Naimark, Norman M., *Flammender Hass. Ethnische Säuberungen im 20. Jahrhundert*, München 2004.
Nelson, Samuel Henry, *Colonialism in the Congo Basin, 1880-1940*, Athens (Ohio) 1994.
Novick, Peter, *The Holocaust in American Life*, Boston/New York 1999.
Noyes, John K., *Colonial Space. Spatiality in the Discourse of German South West Africa, 1884-1915*, Chur 1992.
Noyes, John K., "Landschaftsschilderung, Kultur und Geographie. Von den Aporien der poetischen Sprache im Zeitalter der politischen Geographie", in Honold, Alexander and Simons, Oliver, eds, *Kolonialismus als Kultur. Literatur, Medien, Wissenschaft in der deutschen Gründerzeit des Fremden*, Tübingen/Basel 2002, pp. 127-142.
Oberkrome, Willi, "Geschichte, Volk und Theorie. Das Handwörterbuch des Grenz- und Auslanddeutschtums", in Schöttler, Peter, ed., *Geschichtsschreibung als Legitimationswissenschaft 1918-1945*, Frankfurt 1999, pp. 104-127.
Osterhammel, Jürgen, "Die Wiederkehr des Raumes: Geopolitik, Geohistorie und historische Geographie", in *Neue Politische Literatur*, 43 (1998), pp. 374-396.
Osterhammel, Jürgen, "Expansion und Imperium", in Burschel, Peter, Häberlein, Mark, Reinhard, Volker, Weber, Wolfgang J. and Wendt, Reinhard, eds, *Historische Anstöße*, Berlin 2002, pp. 371-392.
Osterhammel, Jürgen, "Forschungsreise und Kolonialprogramm. Ferdinand von Richthofen und die Erschließung Chinas im 19. Jahrhundert", *Archiv für Kulturgeschichte*, 69 (1987), pp. 150-195.
Osterhammel, Jürgen, *Kolonialismus. Geschichte - Formen - Folgen*, München 1995.
Osterhammel, Jürgen, "Krieg im Frieden. Zu Form und Typologie imperialer Interventionen", in Osterhammel, Jürgen, *Geschichtswissenschaft jenseits des Nationalstaats. Studien zu Beziehungsgeschichte und Zivilisationsvergleich*, Göttingen 2001, pp. 283-321.
Osterhammel, Jürgen, "Raumerfassung und Universalgeschichte im 20. Jahrhundert", in Hübinger, Gangolf, Osterhammel, Jürgen and Pelzer, Erich, eds, *Universalgeschichte und Nationalgeschichten. Ernst Schulin zum 65. Geburtstag*, Freiburg 1994, pp. 51-72.
Osterhammel, Jürgen, "Wissen als Macht: Deutungen interkulturellen Nichtverstehens bei Tzvetan Todorov und Edward Said", in Auch, Eva-Maria and Förster, Stig, eds, *'Barbaren' und 'Weiße Teufel'. Kulturkonflikte in Asien vom 18. bis 20. Jahrhundert*, Paderborn 1997.
Palmer, Alison, *Colonial Genocide*, Adelaide 2000.
Penck, Albrecht, "Das Hauptproblem der physischen Anthropogeographie", *Zeitschrift für Geopolitik*, 2 (1925), pp. 330-348.
Penck, Albrecht, "Deutscher Volks- und Kulturboden", in K. C. von Loesch, ed., *Volk unter Völkern. Bücher des Deutschtums*, i, Breslau 1926, pp. 62-73.
Penck, Albrecht, *Nationale Erdkunde*, Berlin 1934.
Pesek, Michael, *Koloniale Herrschaft in Deutsch-Ostafrika. Expeditionen, Militär und Verwaltung seit 1880*, Frankfurt 2005.
Petersen, Johannes, *Der koloniale Gedanke in der Schule. Sinn, Aufgabe und Wege kolonialer Schularbeit*, Hamburg 1937.

Plumelle-Uribe, Rosa Amelia, *Weisse Barbarei. Vom Kolonialrassismus zur Rassenpolitik der Nazis*, Zürich 2004.
Pogge von Strandmann, Hartmut, "Der Kolonialrat", in Heyden, Ulrich van der and Zeller, Joachim, eds, *Kolonialmetropole Berlin. Eine Spurensuche*, Berlin 2002, pp. 32–34.
Pohl, Dieter, *Nationalsozialistische Judenverfolgung in Ostgalizien, 1941–1944: Organisation und Durchführung eines staatlichen Massenverbrechens*, München 1996.
Pollock, John C., *Kitchener. The Road to Omdurman*, London 1998.
Pommerin, Reiner, *Sterilisierung der Rheinlandbastarde. Das Schicksal einer farbigen deutschen Minderheit 1918–1937*, Düsseldorf 1979.
Pool, Gerhard, *Samuel Maharero*, Windhoek 1991.
Prein, Philipp, "Guns and Top Hats. African Resistance in German South West Africa 1907–1915", *Journal of Southern African Studies*, 20 (1994), pp. 99–121.
Pugach, Sara, *Afrikanistik and Colonial Knowledge. Carl Meinhof, the Missionary Impulse and the Development of African Studies in Germany 1887–1919*, Ph.D. thesis, University of Chicago, 2000.
Puls, Willi W., *Der koloniale Gedanke im Unterricht der Volksschule*, Leipzig 1938.
Rafalski, Hans, *Vom Niemandsland zum Ordnungsstaat. Geschichte der ehemaligen Landespolizei für Deutsch-Südwestafrika*, Berlin [n.d.].
Reichskolonialamt, ed., *Die deutschen Schutzgebiete in Afrika und der Südsee. Amtliche Jahresberichte*, iv (1912/13), Berlin 1914.
Reichsministerium des Inneren, *Handbuch für das Deutsche Reich 41*, 1914.
Reinhard, Wolfgang, *Geschichte der Staatsgewalt. Eine vergleichende Verfassungsgeschichte Europas von den Anfängen bis zur Gegenwart*, München 1999.
Reinhard, Wolfgang, *Kleine Geschichte des Kolonialismus*, Stuttgart 1996.
Renneberg, Monika and Walter, Mark, eds, *Science, Technology and National Socialism*, Cambridge 1994.
Reynolds, Charles, *Modes of Imperialism*, Oxford 1981.
Richthofen, Ferdinand von, *China. Ergebnisse eigener Reisen und darauf gegründeter Studien*, i–v, Berlin 1912.
Richthofen, Ferdinand von, *Atlas von China. Orographische und geologische Karten*, i: *Das nördliche China*, Berlin 1883.
Richthofen, Ferdinand von, *Atlas von China. Orographische und geologische Karten*, ii: *Das südliche China*, ed. Max Groll, Berlin 1912.
Rohrbach, Paul, *Deutsche Kolonialwirtschaft*, I: 'Südwest-Afrika', Berlin 1907.
Rohrbach, Paul, *Wie machen wir unsere Kolonien rentabel? Grundzüge eines Wirtschaftsprogramms für Deutschlands afrikanischen Kolonialbesitz*, Halle 1907.
Rohrbach, Paul, *Deutsche Kolonialwirtschaft. Kulturpolitische Grundsätze für die Rassen- und Missionsfragen*, Berlin 1909.
Rohrbach, Paul, *Koloniale Siedlung und Wirtschaft der führenden Kolonialvölker*, Köln 1934.
Roller, Kathrin, "Der Rassenbiologe Eugen Fischer", in Heyden, Ulrich van der and Zeller, Joachim, eds, *Kolonialmetropole Berlin. Eine Spurensuche*, Berlin 2002, pp.130–134.
Roller, Kathrin, "Mission und 'Mischehen', Erinnerung und Körper – geteiltes Gedächtnis an eine afrikanische Vorfahrin. Über die Familie Schmelen-Kleinschmidt-Hegner", in Förster, Larissa, Henrichsen, Dag and Bollig, Michael, eds, *Namibia-Deutschland. Eine geteilte Geschichte. Widerstand, Gewalt, Erinnerung*, Köln 2004, pp. 194–211.
Roller, Kathrin, "'Wir sind Deutsche, wir sind Weiße und wollen Weiße bleiben' – Reichstagsdebatten über koloniale 'Rassenmischung'", in Heyden, Ulrich van der and Zeller, Joachim, eds, *Kolonialmetropole Berlin. Eine Spurensuche*, Berlin 2002, pp. 73–79.

Rosenfeld, Gavriel D., "The Politics of Uniqueness: Reflections on the Recent Polemical Turn in Holocaust and Genocide Scholarship", *Holocaust and Genocide Studies*, 13/1 (1999), pp. 28–61.

Rössler, Mechthild, *'Wissenschaft und Lebensraum'. Geographische Ostforschung im Nationalsozialismus. Ein Beitrag zur Disziplingeschichte der Geographie*, Berlin 1990.

Rössler, Mechthild and Schleiermacher, Sabine, eds, *Der 'Generalplan Ost'*, Berlin 1993.

Rubinstein, Richard L., "Afterword: Genocide and Civilization", in Wallimann, Isidor and Dobkowski, Michael N., eds, *Genocide and the Modern Age: Etiology and Case Studies of Mass Death*, 2nd edn, Syracuse 2000, pp. 283–298.

Ruppenthal, Jens, *Die Kolonialfrage in der Politik der Weimarer Republik. Der Kolonialrevisionismus in der deutschen Außenpolitik von 1919 bis 1926*, University of Kiel 2002 (M.A. thesis).

Sadji, Amadou Booker, *Das Bild des Negro-Afrikaners in der Deutschen Kolonialliteratur (1884–1945). Ein Beitrag zur literarischen Imagologie Schwarzafrikas*, Berlin 1985.

Sandkühler, Thomas, *'Endlösung' in Galizien. Der Judenmord in Ostpolen und die Rettungsinitiativen von Berthold Beitz*, Bonn 1996.

Schaller, Dominik J., "Die Rezeption des Völkermordes an den Armeniern in Deutschland, 1915–1945", in Schaller, Dominik J. and Kieser, Hans-Lukas, eds, *Der Völkermord an den Armeniern und die Shoah*, 2nd edn, Zürich 2003, pp. 517–555.

Schaller, Dominik J., Rupen, Boyadjian, Scholtz, Hanno and Berg, Vivianne, eds, *Enteignet – Vertrieben – Ermordet. Beiträge zur Genozidforschung*, Zürich 2004.

Schaller, Dominik J., "Kolonialkrieg, Völkermord und Zwangsarbeit in Deutsch-Südwestafrika", in Schaller, Dominik J., Rupen, Boyadjian, Scholtz, Hanno and Berg, Vivianne, eds, *Enteignet-Vertrieben-Ermordet. Beiträge zur Genozidforschung*, Zürich 2004, pp. 147–232.

Schaller, Dominik J., "'Ich glaube, dass die Nation als solche vernichtet werden muss': Kolonialkrieg und Völkermord in Deutsch-Südwestafrika 1904–1907", *Journal of Genocide Research*, 6/3 (2004), pp. 395–430.

Schaller, Dominik J. and Zimmerer, Jürgen, eds, *Late Ottoman Genocides*: The Dissolution of the Ottoman Empire and Young Turkish Population and Extermination Policies, London 2009.

Schaller, Dominik J. and Zimmerer, Jürgen, eds, "Settlers, Imperialism, Genocide", *Journal of Genocide Research*, 10/2 (2008) (thematic issue).

Schaller, Dominik J. and Zimmerer, Jürgen, eds, *The Origins of Genocide. Raphael Lemkin as a Historian of Mass Violence*, London 2009.

Schindlbeck, Markus, "Deutsche wissenschaftliche Expeditionen und Forschungen in der Südsee bis 1914", in Hiery, Hermann Joseph, ed., *Die deutsche Südsee 1884–1914. Ein Handbuch*, Paderborn 2001, pp. 132–155.

Schmitt-Egner, Peter, *Kolonialismus und Faschismus: Eine Studie zur historischen und begrifflichen Genesis faschistischer Bewußtseinsformen am deutschen Beispiel*, Gießen 1975.

Schmoeckel, Mathias, *Die Großraumtheorie. Ein Beitrag zur Geschichte der Völkerrechtswissenschaft im Dritten Reich, insbesondere der Kriegszeit*, Berlin 1994.

Schmuhl, Hans-Walter, *Rassenhygiene, Nationalsozialismus, Euthanasie*, Göttingen 1987.

Schneider, Rosa B., *'Um Scholle und Leben'. Zur Konstruktion von 'Rasse' und Geschlecht in der deutschen kolonialen Afrikaliteratur um 1900*, Frankfurt 2003.

Schöning, Jörg, ed., *Triviale Tropen. Exotische Reise- und Abenteuerfilme aus Deutschland 1919–1939*, München 1997.

Schöttler, Peter, "Eine Art 'Generalplan West'. Die Stuckart-Denkschrift vom 14. Juni 1940 und die Planungen für eine neue deutsch-französische Grenze im Zweiten Weltkrieg", *Sozial.Geschichte. Zeitschrift für historische Analyse des 20. und 21. Jahrhunderts*, 3 (2003), pp. 83–131.

Schöttler, Peter, ed., *Geschichtsschreibung als Legitimationswissenschaft 1918–1945*, Frankfurt 1999.

Schröder, Martin, *Prügelstrafe und Züchtigungsrecht in den deutschen Schutzgebieten Schwarzafrikas*, Münster 1997.
Schubert, Michael, *Der schwarze Fremde. Das Bild des Schwarzafrikaners in der parlamentarischen und publizistischen Kolonialdiskussion in Deutschland von den 1870er bis in die 1930er Jahre*, Stuttgart 2003.
Schulte, Jan Erik, *Zwangsarbeit und Vernichtung: Das Wirtschaftsimperium der SS. O. Pohl und das SS-Wirtschafts-Verwaltungshauptamt 1933-1945*, Paderborn 2001.
Schulte-Althoff, Franz-Josef, "Rassenmischung im kolonialen System. Zur deutschen Kolonialpolitik im letzten Jahrzehnt vor dem Ersten Weltkrieg", *Historisches Jahrbuch*, 105 (1985), pp. 52-94.
Schulte-Althoff, Franz-Josef, *Studien zur politischen Wissenschaftsgeschichte der deutschen Geographie im Zeitalter des Imperialismus*, Paderborn 1971.
Schultz, Hans-Dietrich, "Raumkonstrukte der klassischen deutschsprachigen Geographie des 19./20. Jahrhunderts im Kontext ihrer Zeit", in *Geschichte und Gesellschaft*, 28 (2002), pp. 343-377.
Schulze, Hagen, *Freikorps und Republik, 1918-1920*, Boppard am Rhein 1969.
Schulze, Winfried and Oexle, Otto Gerhard, eds, *Deutsche Historiker im Nationalsozialismus*, Frankfurt 1999.
Schumacher, Frank, "'Niederbrennen, plündern und töten sollt ihr': Der Kolonialkrieg der USA auf den Philippinen (1899-1913)", in Klein, Thoralf and Schumacher, Frank, eds, *Kolonialkriege. Militärische Gewalt im Zeichen des Imperialismus*, Hamburg 2006, pp. 109-144.
Seitz, Theodor, *Vom Aufstieg und Niederbruch deutscher Kolonialmacht, iii*: Die Gouverneursjahre in Südwestafrika. Karlsruhe 1929.
Semelin, Jacques, *Säubern und Vernichten. Die politische Dimension von Massakern und Völkermorden*, Hamburg 2007.
Shaw, Martin, *What is Genocide?*, Cambridge 2007.
Simon, Thomas W., "Genocides: Normative Comparative Studies", in Margot Levy, ed., *Remembering the Future. The Holocaust in an Age of Genocide*, i: *History*, pp. 91-112.
Sippel, Harald, "'Im Interesse des Deutschtums und der weißen Rasse'. Behandlung und Rechtswirkungen von 'Rassenmischehen' in den Kolonien Deutsch-Ostafrika und Deutsch-Südwestafrika", *Jahrbuch für afrikanisches Recht*, 9 (1995), pp. 123-159.
Smidt, Karen, "'Germania führt die deutsche Frau nach Südwest'. Auswanderung, Leben und soziale Konflikte deutscher Frauen in der ehemaligen Kolonie Deutsch-Südwestafrika 1884-1920. Eine sozial- und frauengeschichtliche Studie", University of Magdeburg 1995 (Ph.D. Thesis).
Smith, Bradley F. and Petersen, Agnes F., eds, *Heinrich Himmler. Geheimreden 1933 bis 1945 und andere Ansprachen*, Frankfurt 1974.
Smith, Helmut Walser, *The Continuities of German History. Nation, Religion, and Race across the Long Nineteenth Century*, Cambridge 2008.
Smith, Helmut Walser, "The Logic of Colonial Violence: Germany in Southwest Africa (1904-1907); the United States in the Philippines (1899-1902)", in Lehmann, Hartmut and Wellenreuther, Hermann, eds, *German and American Nationalism. A Comparative Perspective*, Oxford 1999, pp. 205-231.
Smith, Woodruff D., *The Ideological Origins of Nazi Imperialism*, Oxford 1986.
Sösemann, Bernd, "'Pardon wird nicht gegeben!' Staatliche Zensur und Presseöffentlichkeit zur 'Hunnenrede'", in Leutner, Mechthild and Mühlhahn, Klaus, eds, *Kolonialkrieg in China. Die Niederschlagung der Boxerbewegung 1900-1901*, Berlin 2007, pp. 118-122.
Spoerer, Mark, *Zwangsarbeit unter dem Hakenkreuz. Ausländische Zivilarbeiter, Kriegsgefangene und Häftlinge im Deutschen Reich und im besetzten Europa 1939-1945*, Stuttgart/München 2001.

Spraul, Gunter, "Der 'Völkermord' an den Herero", in *Geschichte in Wissenschaft und Unterricht*, 39 (1988), pp. 713-739.
Stannard, David E., *American Holocaust. The Conquest of the New World*, Oxford/New York 1992.
Stannard, David E., "Uniqueness as Denial: The Politics of Genocide Scholarship", in Rosenbaum, Alan S., ed., *Is the Holocaust Unique? Perspectives on Comparative Genocide*, Oxford 1996, pp. 163-208.
Stoler, Anna Laura, "Rethinking Colonial Categories: European Communities and the Boundaries of Rule", *Comparative Studies of Society and History*, 31 (1989), pp. 134-161.
Stone, Dan, "White Men with Low Moral Standards? German Anthropology and the Herero Genocide", *Patterns of Prejudice*, 35/2 (2001), pp. 33-45.
Streit, Christian, *Keine Kameraden: Die Wehrmacht und die sowjetischen Kriegsgefangenen 1941-1945*, Stuttgart 1978.
Sudholt, Gert, *Die deutschen Eingeborenenpolitik in Südwestafrika. Von den Anfängen bis 1904*, Hildesheim 1975
Theweleit, Klaus, *Männerphantasien*, Frankfurt 1977.
Thornton, Russell, *American Indian Holocaust and Survival. A Population History since 1492*, London 1987.
Todorov, Tzvetan, *Die Eroberung Amerikas. Das Problem des Anderen*, Frankfurt 1985.
Troll, Carl, *Das deutsche Kolonialproblem auf Grund einer ostafrikanischen Forschungsreise 1933/34*, Berlin 1935.
Troll, Carl, "Die geographische Wissenschaft in Deutschland in den Jahren 1933 bis 1945. Eine Kritik und eine Rechtfertigung", *Erdkunde*, 1 (1947), pp. 3-47.
Troll, Carl, *Fritz Jaeger. Ein Forscherleben*, Erlangen 1969.
Troll, Carl, "Koloniale Raumplanung in Afrika", in *Das afrikanische Kolonialproblem. Vorträge, gehalten in der Gesellschaft für Erdkunde zu Berlin im Januar-Februar 1941*, Berlin 1941, pp. 1-41.
Trotha, Trutz von, *Koloniale Herrschaft. Zur soziologischen Theorie der Staatsentstehung am Beispiel des 'Schutzgebietes Togo'*, Tübingen 1994.
Verhey, Jeffrey, *Der 'Geist von 1914' und die Erfindung der Volksgemeinschaft*, Hamburg 2000.
Voigt, Rüdiger, ed., *Das deutsche Kolonialrecht als Vorstufe einer globalen 'Kolonialisierung' von Recht und Verwaltung*, Baden-Baden 2001.
Wächter, Katja, *Die Macht der Ohnmacht. Leben und Politik des Franz Xaver Ritter von Epp (1868-1946)*, Frankfurt 1999.
Walgenbach, Katharina, "Zwischen Selbstaffirmation und Distinktion: Weiße Identität, Geschlecht und Klasse in der Zeitschrift 'Kolonie und Heimat'", in Winter, Carsten, Hepp, Andreas and Thomas, Tanja, eds, *Medienidentitäten – Identität im Kontext um Globalisierung und Medienkultur*, Köln 2003, pp. 136-152.
Warmbold, Joachim, *'Ein Stückchen neudeutsche Erd' ...' Deutsche Kolonialliteratur. Aspekte ihrer Geschichte, Eigenart und Wirkung dargestellt am Beispiel Afrikas*, Frankfurt 1982.
Wasser, Bruno, *Himmlers Raumplanung im Osten*, Basel 1993.
Weingart, Peter, Kroll, Jürgen and Bayertz, Kurt, *Rasse, Blut und Gene. Geschichte der Eugenik in Deutschland*, Frankfurt 1988.
Weitz, Eric D., *A Century of Genocide. Utopias of Race and Nation*, Princeton 2003.
Wildenthal, Lora, *German Women for Empire, 1884-1945*, Durham 2001.
Wirz, Albert, "Innerer und äußerer Wald. Zur moralischen Ökologie der Kolonisierenden", in Flitner, Michael, ed., *Der deutsche Tropenwald. Bilder, Mythen, Politik*, Frankfurt 2000, pp. 23-48.
Wirz, Albert, "Missionare im Urwald, verängstigt und hilflos: Zur symbolischen Topografie des kolonialen Christentums", in Wagner, Wilfried, ed., *Kolonien und Missionen*, Hamburg 1994, pp. 39-56.

Wolfe, Patrick, "History and Imperialism. A Century of Theory, from Marx to Postcolonialism", *American Historical Review*, 102/2 (1997), pp. 388–420.

Wolters, Christine"Dr. Friedrich Hey, (1864–1960). Missionsarzt und Bückeburger Unternehmer", in Höing, Hubert, ed., *Strukturen und Konjunkturen. Faktoren in der schaumburgischen Wirtschaftsgeschichte*, Bielefeld 2004.

Wulf, Stefan, *Das Hamburger Tropeninstitut 1919 bis 1945. Auswärtige Kulturpolitik und Kolonialrevisionismus nach Versailles*, Berlin 1994.

Young, Robert, *White Mythologies. Writing History and the West*, London/New York 1990.

Zantop, Susanne, *Kolonialphantasien im vorkolonialen Deutschland, 1770–1870*, Berlin 1999.

Zeller, Joachim, *Kolonialdenkmäler und Geschichtsbewußtsein. Eine Untersuchung der kolonialdeutschen Erinnerungskultur*, Frankfurt 2000.

Zeller, Joachim, "Orlog in Deutsch-Südwestafrika. Fotografien aus dem Kolonialkrieg 1904 bis 1907", *Fotogeschichte. Beiträge zur Geschichte und Ästhetik der Fotografie*, 85/86 (2002), pp. 31–44.

Zimmerer, Jürgen and Zeller, Joachim, eds, *Völkermord in Deutsch-Südwestafrika. Der Kolonialkrieg in Namibia (1904–1908) und seine Folgen*, Berlin 2003.

Zimmerer, Jürgen, "Annihilation in Africa: The 'Race War' in German Southwest Africa (1904–1908) and its Significance for a Global History of Genocide", *Bulletin of the German Historical Institute*, 37/Fall (2005), pp. 51–57.

Zimmerer, Jürgen, "Colonialism and the Holocaust. Towards an Archeology of Genocide", in Moses, A. Dirk, ed., *Genocide and Settler Society: Frontier Violence and Stolen Indigenous Children in Australian History*, New York 2004, pp. 49–76.

Zimmerer, Jürgen, "Colonial Genocide: The Herero and Nama War (1904–1908) in German South West Africa and its Significance", in Stone, Dan, ed., *The Historiography of Genocide*, London 2007, pp. 323–343.

Zimmerer, Jürgen, "Das Deutsche Reich und der Genozid. Überlegungen zum historischen Ort des Völkermordes an den Herero und Nama", in Förster, Larissa and Henrichsen, Dag, eds, *Namibia – Deutschland. Eine geteilte Geschichte. Widerstand, Gewalt, Erinnerung* (Ethnologia Vol. 24), Köln 2004, pp. 106–121.

Zimmerer, Jürgen, "Der koloniale Musterstaat? Rassentrennung, Arbeitszwang und totale Kontrolle in Deutsch-Südwestafrika", in Zimmerer, Jürgen and Zeller, Joachim, eds, *Völkermord in Deutsch-Südwestafrika. Der Kolonialkrieg in Namibia (1904–1908) und seine Folgen*, Berlin 2003, pp. 26–41.

Zimmerer, Jürgen, "Der totale Überwachungsstaat? Recht und Verwaltung in Deutsch-Südwestafrika", in Voigt, Rüdiger, ed., *Das deutsche Kolonialrecht als Vorstufe einer globalen 'Kolonialisierung' von Recht und Verwaltung*, Baden-Baden 2001, pp. 175–198.

Zimmerer, Jürgen, "Der Wahn der Planbarkeit: Vertreibung, unfreie Arbeit und Völkermord als Elemente der Bevölkerungsökonomie in Deutsch-Südwestafrika", *Comparativ*, 13/4 (2003), pp. 96–113.

Zimmerer, Jürgen, "Der Wahn der Planbarkeit: Vertreibung, unfreie Arbeit und Völkermord als Elemente der Bevölkerungsökonomie in Deutsch-Südwestafrika", in Mann, Michael, ed., *Comparativ*, 13/4 (2003), Special Issue: *Menschenhandel und unfreie Arbeit*, pp. 96–113.

Zimmerer, Jürgen, *Deutsche Herrschaft über Afrikaner. Staatlicher Machtanspruch und Wirklichkeit im kolonialen Namibia*, Münster/Hamburg/London 2001 [English edition: *German Rule, African Subjects: State Aspirations and the Reality of Power in Colonial Namibia*, New York 2021].

Zimmerer, Jürgen, *Deutsche Herrschaft über Afrikaner. Staatlicher Machtanspruch und Wirklichkeit im kolonialen Namibia*, 3rd edn, Hamburg 2004.

Zimmerer, Jürgen, "Deutscher Rassenstaat in Afrika. Ordnung, Entwicklung und Segregation in Deutsch-Südwest (1884-1915)", in Brumlik, Micha, Meinl, Susanne and Renz, Werner, eds, *Gesetzliches Unrecht. Rassistisches Recht im 20. Jahrhundert*, Frankfurt 2005, pp. 135-153.

Zimmerer, Jürgen, "Die Geburt des 'Ostlandes' aus dem Geiste des Kolonialismus. Die nationalsozialistische Eroberungs- und Beherrschungspolitik in (post-)kolonialer Perspektive", *Sozial.Geschichte. Zeitschrift für die historische Analyse des 20. und 21. Jahrhunderts*, 19/1 (2004), pp. 10-43.

Zimmerer, Jürgen, "Environmental Genocide? Climate Change, Mass Violence and the Question of Ideology", *Journal of Genocide Research*, 9/3 (2007), pp. 349-352.

Zimmerer, Jürgen, "Holocaust und Kolonialismus. Beitrag zu einer Archäologie des genozidalen Gedankens", *Zeitschrift für Geschichtswissenschaft*, 51/12 (2003), pp. 1098-1119.

Zimmerer, Jürgen, "Im Dienste des Imperiums. Die Geographen der Berliner Universität zwischen Kolonialwissenschaften und Ostforschung", *Jahrbuch für Universitätsgeschichte*, 7 (2004), pp. 73-100.

Zimmerer, Jürgen, "Kein Sonderweg im Rassenkrieg. Der Genozid an den Herero und Nama 1904-08 zwischen deutschen Kontinuitäten und der Globalgeschichte der Massengewalt", in Müller, Sven-Oliver and Torp, Cornelius, eds, *Das deutsche Kaiserreich in der Kontroverse*, Göttingen 2008, pp. 323-340.

Zimmerer, Jürgen, "Kolonialer Genozid? Vom Nutzen und Nachteil einer historischen Kategorie für eine Globalgeschichte des Völkermordes", in Schaller, Dominik J., Rupen, Boyadjian, Scholtz, Hanno and Berg, Vivianne, eds, *Enteignet-Vertrieben-Ermordet. Beiträge zur Genozidforschung*, Zürich 2004, pp. 109-128.

Zimmerer, Jürgen, "Krieg, KZ und Völkermord in Südwestafrika", in Zimmerer, Jürgen and Zeller, Joachim, eds, *Völkermord in Deutsch-Südwestafrika. Der Kolonialkrieg (1904-1908) in Namibia und seine Folgen*, Berlin 2003, pp. 45-63.

Zimmerer, Jürgen, "Kriegsgefangene im Kolonialkrieg. Der Krieg gegen die Herero und Nama in Deutsch Südwestafrika (1904-1907)", in Overmans, Rüdiger, ed., *'In der Hand des Feindes'- Kriegsgefangenschaft von der Antike bis zum Zweiten Weltkrieg*, Köln 1999, pp. 277-294.

Zimmerer, Jürgen, "The Birth of the 'Ostland' out of the Spirit of Colonialism: A Postcolonial Perspective on the Nazi Policy of Conquest and Extermination", *Patterns of Prejudice*, 39/February (2005), pp. 197-219.

Zimmerer, Jürgen, "The First Genocide of the Twentieth Century: The German War of Destruction in South West Africa (1904-1908) and the Global History of Genocide", in Bergen, Doris L., ed., *Lessons and Legacies, viii: From Generation to Generation*, Evanston 2008, pp. 34-64.

Zimmerer, Jürgen, "Von der Bevormundung zur Selbstbestimmung. Die Pariser Friedenskonferenz und ihre Auswirkungen auf die britische Kolonialherrschaft im Südlichen Afrika", in Krumeich, Gerd, ed., *Versailles 1919: Ziele - Wirkung - Wahrnehmung*, Essen 2001, pp. 145-158.

Zimmerer, Jürgen, "Von Windhuk nach Warschau. Die rassische Privilegiengesellschaft in Deutsch-Südwestafrika — ein Modell mit Zukunft?", in Becker, Frank, ed., *Rassenmischehen—Mischlinge—Rassentrennung. Zur Politik der Rasse im deutschen Kaiserreich*, Stuttgart 2004, pp. 97-123.

Zimmerer, Jürgen, "Wissenschaft und Kolonialismus. Das Geographische Institut der Friedrich-Wilhelms-Universität vom Kaiserreich zum Dritten Reich", in Heyden, Ulrich van der and Zeller, Joachim, eds, *Kolonialmetropole Berlin. Eine Spurensuche*, Berlin 2002, pp. 125-130.

Zimmerman, Andrew, *Anthropology and Antihumanism in Imperial Germany*, Chicago 2001

Zimmermann, Michael, *Rassenutopie und Genozid. Die nationalsozialistische 'Lösung der Zigeunerfrage'*, Hamburg 1996.

Zögner, Lothar, "Ferdinand von Richthofen – Neue Sicht auf ein altes Land", in Hinz, Hans-Martin and Lind, Christoph, eds, *Tsingtau. Ein Kapitel deutscher Kolonialgeschichte in China 1897–1914*, Deutsches Historisches Museum Berlin 1997, pp. 72–75.

Newspaper Articles

Fröschle, Hartmut, "Ein normaler Kolonialkrieg, kein Genozid." *Frankfurter Allgemeine Zeitung* (11 November 2002).

Gerwarth, Robert and Malinowski, Stephan, "Vollbrachte Hitler eine 'afrikanische' Tat? Der Herero-Krieg und der Holocaust: Zur Kritik der neuesten Sonderwegsthese", *Frankfurter Allgemeine Zeitung* (11 September 2007).

"Herzog lobt die Beziehungen zu Namibia", *Frankfurter Allgemeine Zeitung* (5 March 1998).

"Herzog will Deutsch in Namibia stärken", *Süddeutsche Zeitung* (7 March 1998).

Horn, Hans-Rudolf, "Schwarze Legende vom Herero-Genozid" *Frankfurter Allgemeine Zeitung* (12 November 2002).

"Kein Pardon für Herero-Morde", *Die tageszeitung* (5 March 1998).

Marx, Christoph, "Kolonialapologetisches Sperrfeuer", *Frankfurter Allgemeine Zeitung* (23 November 2003).

Silvester, Jeremy, Hillebrecht, Werner and Erichsen, Casper, "The Herero Holocaust? The Disputed History of the 1904 Genocide", *The Namibian Weekender* (20 August 2001).

Statement of complaint by the "Herero People's Reparations Corporation" before the Superior Court of the District of Columbia, 18 Sept. 2001.

Transcript of the Prime Minister, the Hon. John Howard MP, Address to the Tasmanian Division, State Council Dinner, Burnie Civic Centre, Burnie, 6 November 1998, *Prime Minister of Australia, News Room*, https://pmtranscripts.pmc.gov.au/release/transcript-10972, accessed 12 Jun. 2023.

Willoughby, Brian, "PETA Sparks Outrage with Holocaust Comparison", 23 March 2003, https://www.alternet.org/2003/03/peta_sparks_outrage_with_holocaust_comparison, accessed 12 Jun. 2023.

Winkelmann, Ulrike, "Keine Entschuldigung, keine Entschädigung", Die Tageszeitung (10/11 January 2004).

Zimmerer, Jürgen, "Die Zeugen der Massaker. Ein Historikerstreit über die Aborigines in Australien", *Süddeutsche Zeitung* (24 February 2003).

Zimmerer, Jürgen, "Wir müssen jetzt 'krassen Terrorismus üben'. Von der Unterdrückung zur Ausrottung: Der Krieg gegen die Herero und Nama in Deutsch-Südwestafrika als Erbe der deutschen Kolonialzeit und die Klage auf Entschädigung", *Frankfurter Allgemeine Zeitung* (2 November 2002).

Zimmerer, Jürgen, "Warum nicht mal 'nen Neger? Menschenfresser und barbusige Mädchen: Ein ZDF-Film und ein Buch verkitschen und verharmlosen den deutschen Kolonialismus in skandalöser Weise" ["Why not put in a negro? Cannibals and bare-breasted girls: a ZDF film and book present a kitschy view of German colonialism that scandalously plays down its impact"], *Süddeutsche Zeitung* (23 November 2005).

Supplementary Bibliography

Axster, Felix, "Arbeit, Teilhabe und Ausschluss. Zum Verhältnis zwischen kolonialem Rassismus und nationalsozialistischem Antisemitismus", in Kundrus, Birthe and Steinbacher, Sybille, eds, *Kontinuitäten und Diskontinuitäten: der Nationalsozialismus in der Geschichte des 20. Jahrhunderts*, Göttingen 2013, pp. 121–133.

Bachmann, Klaus, "Germany's Colonial Policy in German South-West Africa in the Light of International Criminal Law", *Journal of Southern African Studies*, 43/2 (2017), pp. 331–347.

Bachmann, Klaus, *Genocide Empires. German Colonialism in Africa and the Third Reich*, Frankfurt 2018.

Baer, Elizabeth R., *The Genocidal Gaze. From German Southwest Africa to the Third Reich*, Windhoek 2018.

Bajohr, Frank, "Holocaust, Kolonialismus und NS-Imperialismus Forschung im Schatten einer polemischen Debatte", *Vierteljahrshefte für Zeitgeschichte*, 70 (2022), pp. 191–202.

Bajohr, Frank and Löw, Andrea, "Tendenzen und Probleme der neueren Holocaustforschung: Eine Einführung", in Bajohr, Frank and Löw, Andrea, eds, *Der Holocaust. Ergebnisse und neue Fragen der Forschung*, Frankfurt 2015, pp. 9–30.

Bajohr, Frank, "Holocaustforschung – Entwicklungslinien in Deutschland seit 1945", in Brechtgen, Magnus, ed., *Aufarbeitung des Nationalsozialismus. Ein Kompendium*, Göttingen 2021, pp. 122–42.

Bajohr, Frank and O'Sullivan, Rachel, "Holocaust, Kolonialismus und NS-Imperialismus: Forschungen im Schatten einer polemischen Debatte", *Vierteljahrshefte für Zeitgeschichte* 70 (2022), pp. 191–202.

Baranowski, Shelley, *Nazi Empire. German Colonialism and Imperialism from Bismarck to Hitler*, Cambridge 2010.

Baranowski, Shelly, Bergen, Doris L., Bauman, Zygmunt, Pergher, Roberta, Roseman, Mark and Zimmerer, Jürgen, "The Holocaust: A Colonial Genocide? A Scholar's Forum", *Dapim. Studies on the Holocaust*, 27 (2013), pp. 40–73.

Benz, Wolfgang, ed., *Erinnerungsverbot? Die Ausstellung 'Al Nakba' im Visier der Gegenaufklärung*, Berlin 2023.

Berghahn, Volker, "German Colonialism and Imperialism from Bismarck to Hitler", *German Studies Review*, 40/1 (2017), pp. 147–162.

Böcker, Julia, "Juristische, politisch und ethische Dimensionen der Aufarbeitung des Völkermords an den Herero und Nama", *Sicherheit und Frieden*, 38/1 (2020), pp. 50–54.

Conrad, Sebastian, "Rethinking German Colonialism in a Global Age" *The Journal of Imperial and Commonwealth History*, 41/4 (2013), pp. 543–566.

Conrad, Sebastian, "Rückkehr des Verdrängten? Die Erinnerungen an den Kolonialismus in Deutschland 1919–2019", *Aus Politik und Zeitgeschichte*, 40–42 (2019), pp. 28–33.

Conze, Eckart, *Schatten des Kaiserreichs. Die Reichsgründung von 1871 und ihr schwieriges Erbe*, München 2020.

Conze, Eckart, "'Fischer Reloaded?' Der neue Streit ums alte Kaiserreich", in Zimmerer, Jürgen, ed., *Erinnerungskämpfe. Neues deutsches Geschichtsbewusstsein*, Stuttgart 2023, pp. 80–104.

Čupić, Nenad and Fischer, Florian, *Die Kontinuität des Genozids. Europäische Moderne und der Völkermord an den Herero und Nama in Deutsch-Südwestafrika*, Berlin 2015.

Dedering, Tilman, "Compounds, Camps, Colonialism", *Journal of Namibian Studies*, 12 (2012), pp. 29–46.

Diner, Dan, Habermas, Jürgen, Friedländer, Saul, Frei, Norbert and Steinbacher, Sybille, eds, *Ein Verbrechen ohne Namen. Anmerkung zum neuen Streit über den Holocaust*, München 2022.

Eckl, Andreas, ed., *Krieg und Genozid in Deutsch-Südwestafrika*, (Zeitschrift für Genozidforschung, 20. Jahrgang, Heft 2 (2022)), Weilerswist 2022.

Erichsen, Casper W. and Olusoga, David, *The Kaiser's Holocaust. Germany's forgotten genocide and the colonial roots of Nazism*, London 2010.

Finlay, Frank, "'ein Holocaust, aber eben nicht meiner': The Armenian Genocide in the Works of Edgar Hilsenrath", *The Modern Language Review*, 115/ 3 (2020), pp. 618–638.

Funke, Hajo, "Der Streit um Achille Mbembe und die Frage der Deutungshoheit über die Geschichte", in Zimmerer, Jürgen, ed., *Erinnerungskämpfe. Neues deutsches Geschichtsbewusstsein*, Stuttgart 2023, pp. 310–319.

Geiger, Wolfgang and Melber, Henning, eds, *Kritik des deutschen Kolonialismus. Postkoloniale Sicht auf Erinnerung und Geschichtsvermittlung*, Frankfurt 2021.

Gerber, Jan, "Holocaust, Kolonialismus, Postkolonialismus. Über Opferkonkurrenz und Schuldverschiebung", *Hallische Jahrbücher*, 1 (2021), pp. 19–46.

Gordon, Michelle and O'Sullivan, Rachel, eds, *Colonial Paradigms of Violence. Comparative Analysis of the Holocaust, Genocide, and Mass Killing*, Göttingen 2022.

Habermas, Jürgen, "Der neue Historikerstreit", *Philosophie Magazin* 60 (2021), pp. 10–11.

Häussler, Matthias, "'Kultur der „Grausamkeit' und die Dynamik 'eradierender Praktiken'. Ein Beitrag zur Erforschung extremer Gewalt", *Sociologus*, 63/1–2 (2017), pp. 147–169.

Häussler, Matthias, *Der Genozid an den Herero. Krieg, Emotion und extreme Gewalt in Deutsch-Südwestafrika*, Weilerswist 2018.

Hillebrecht, Georg, *'S ist ein übles Land hier'. Tagebuchaufzeichnungen aus dem Herero-Krieg in Deutsch-Südwestafrika 1904–1905*, Bochum 2021.

Kakel, Carroll, *The Holocaust as Colonial Genocide: Hitler's 'Indian Wars' in the 'Wild East'*, Basingstoke 2013.

Klävers, Steffen, *Decolonizing Auschwitz? Komparativ-postkoloniale Ansätze in der Holocaustforschung*, Berlin 2018.

Kopp, Kristin, "Arguing the Case for a Colonial Poland", in Langbehn, Volker and Salama, Mohammad, eds, *German Colonialism. Race, the Holocaust, and Postwar Germany*, New York 2011, pp. 146–163.

Kößler, Reinhart, "Der Friedhof der Zwangsarbeit: Knochenfunde verweisen auf deutsche Kolonialverbrechen in Namibia", *iz3w*, 331 (2012), pp. 38–39.

Kößler, Reinhart, "Genocide in Namibia: The Holocaust and the issue of Colonialism", *Journal of Southern African Studies*, 38/1 (2012), pp. 233–238.

Kößler, Reinhart, "Kolonialismus, Völkerrecht und Krieg", *Peripherie*, 133 (2014) pp. 94–105.

Kößler, Reinhart, *Namibia and Germany: Negotiating the Past*, Münster 2015.

Kößler, Reinhart and Melber, Henning, *Völkermord- und was dann? Die Politik deutsch-namibischer Vergangenheitsbearbeitung*, Frankfurt 2017.

Kößler, Reinhart, "Postcolonial Asymmetry. Coping with the Consequences of Genocide between Namibia and Germany", in Albrecht, Monika, ed., *Postcolonialism Cross-Examin ed. Multidirectional Perspectives on Imperial and Colonial Pasts and the Neocolonial Present*, London 2020, pp. 117–134.

Kotek, Joël, "Le génocide des Herero, symptôme d'un Sonderweg allemand?", *Revue d'histoire de la Shoah*, 189/2 (2008), pp. 177–197.

Kreienbaum, Jonas, "'Wir sind keine Sklavenhalter' Zur Rolle der Zwangsarbeit in den Konzentrationslagern in Deutsch-Südwestafrika (1904 bis 1908)", in Jahr, Christoph and Thiel, Jens, eds, *Lager vor Auschwitz: Gewalt und Integration im 20. Jahrhundert*, Berlin 2013, pp. 68–83.

Kreienbaum, Jonas, *„Ein trauriges Fiasko". Koloniale Konzentrationslager im südlichen Afrika 1900–1908*, Hamburg 2015.

Kühne, Thomas, "Colonialism and the Holocaust. Continuities, Causations and Complexities", *Journal of Genocide Research*, 15/3 (2013), pp. 339–362.
Kundrus, Birthe, "German Colonialism: Some Reflections on Reassessments, Specificities, and Constellations", in Langbehn, Volker and Salawa, Mohammad, eds, *German Colonialism. Race, the Holocaust, and Postwar Germany*, New York 2011, pp. 29–47.
Kundrus, Birthe, "Einleitung", in Kundrus, Birthe and Steinbacher, Sybille, eds, *Kontinuitäten und Diskontinuitäten. Der Nationalsozialismus in der Geschichte des 20. Jahrhunderts*, Göttingen 2013, pp. 9–29.
Kundrus, Birthe, *"Dieser Krieg ist der große Rassenkrieg". Krieg und Holocaust in Europa*, München 2018.
Lausberg, Michael, *Deutsche Kolonialpolitik in Afrika*, Hamburg 2020.
Melber, Henning, „Genocide Matters – Negotiating a Namibian-German Past in the Present", *Stichproben. Wiener Zeitschrift für kritische Afrikastudien*, 33/17 (2017), pp. 1–24.
Mendel, Meron, *Über Israel reden. Eine deutsche Debatte*, Berlin 2023.
Moses, A. Dirk, "Hannah Arendt, Imperialism, and the Holocaust", in Langbehn, Volker and Salawa, Mohammad, eds, *German Colonialism. Race, the Holocaust, and Postwar Germany*, New York 2011, pp. 72–92.
Moses, A. Dirk, "The Holocaust and World History: Raphael Lemkin and Comparative Methodology", in Stone, Dan, ed., *The Holocaust and Historical Methodology*, New York 2012, pp. 272–289.
Moses, A. Dirk, "Weltgeschichte und Holocaust: Ein Blick in Raphael Lemkins unveröffentlichte Schriften", in Steinbacher, Sybille, ed., *Holocaust und Völkermorde. Die Reichweite des Vergleichs*, Frankfurt/New York 2012, pp. 195–213.
Moses, A. Dirk, *The Problems of Genocide: Permanent Security and the Language of Transgression*, Cambridge 2021.
Moses, A. Dirk, "Deutschlands Erinnerungskultur und der 'Terror der Geschichte'", in Neiman, Susan and Wildt, Michael, eds, Historiker Streiten. Gewalt und Holocaust – Die Debatte, Berlin 2022, pp. 199–242.
Moses, A. Dirk, "The German Catechism", Geschichte der Gegenwart (23 May 2021), https://geschichtedergegenwart.ch/the-german-catechism, accessed 11 Sept. 2023
Neiman, Susan and Wildt, Michael, eds., *Historiker streiten. Gewalt und Holocaust – die Debatte*, Berlin 2022.
O'Donnell, Krista Molly, *The Servants of Empire. Sponsored German Women's Colonization in Southwest Africa, 1896–1945*, New York 2023.
Osthues, Julian, *Literatur als Palimpsest. Postkoloniale Ästhetik im deutschsprachigen Roman der Gegenwart*, Bielefeld 2017.
Overy, Richard, *Blood and Ruins: The Great Imperial War, 1931–1945*, London 2021.
Perraudin, Michael and Zimmerer, Jürgen, eds, *German Colonialism and National Identity*, New York 2011.
Press, Steven, *Blood and Diamonds. Germany's Imperial Ambitions in Africa*, Cambridge 2021.
Redaktion der Beiträge zur Geschichte des Nationalsozialismus, eds, *NS-Geschichte als Herausforderung. Neue und alte Fragen*, Göttingen 2022.
Rivinius, Karl Josef, *"Wir sind Weiße und wollen Weiße bleiben". Rassismus in Deutsch-Südwestafrika*, Sankt Ottilien 2021.
Roos, Ulrich, "Im ‚Südwesten' nichts Neues? Eine Analyse der deutschen Namibiapolitik als Beitrag zur Rekonstruktion der außenpolitischen Identität des deutschen Nationalstaats", *Zeitschrift für Friedens- und Konfliktforschung*, 4/2 (2015), pp. 182–224.

Rothberg, Michael and Zimmerer, Jürgen, "Enttabuisiert den Vergleich!", *Die Zeit* (31 March 2021), https://www.zeit.de/2021/14/erinnerungskultur-gedenken-pluralisieren-holocaust-vergleich-globalisierung-geschichte/komplettansicht, accessed 11 Sept. 2023.

Sandler, Willeke, *Empire in the Heimat: Colonialism and Public Culture in the Third Reich*, New York 2018.

Sarkin, Jeremy, *Germany's Genocide of the Herero: Kaiser Wilhelm II., his General, his Settlers, his Soldiers*, Cape Town 2011.

Snyder, Timothy, *Black Earth: The Holocaust as History and Warning*, New York 2015.

Snyder, Timothy, *Bloodlands: Europe between Hitler and Stalin*, New York 2012.

Steinbacher, Sybille, "Sonderweg, Kolonialismus, Genozide: Der Holocaust im Spannungsfeld von Kontinuität und Diskontinuität der deutschen Geschichte", in Bajohr, Frank and Löw, Andrea, eds, *Der Holocaust: Ergebnisse und neue Fragen der Forschung*, Bonn 2015, pp. 83–101.

Stone, Dan, "Defending the Plural: Hannah Arendt and Genocide Studies", *New Formations*, 71 (2011), pp. 46–57.

Sznaider, Natan, *Fluchtpunkte der Erinnerung. Über die Gegenwart von Holocaust und Kolonialismus*, München 2022.

Terrero Gelhaus, Julian Alexander, *Deutsche Kolonialgeschichte – Die Kolonialfrage bei Bismarck und die Genozid-Debatte heute: Eine interdisziplinäre Studie anhand der ehemaligen Kolonie Deutsch-Südwest (heutiges Namibia)*, Hamburg 2020.

Wiedemann, Charlotte, "Über die Nakba sprechen lernen", *Geschichte der Gegenwart* (16 April 2023), https://geschichtedergegenwart.ch/ueber-die-nakba-sprechen-lernen/, accessed 11 Sept. 2023.

Wempe, Sean Andrew, *Revenants of the German Empire: Colonial Germans, Imperialism, and the League of Nations*, New York 2019.

Wildt, Michael, "Was heißt: Singularität des Holocaust?", *Zeithistorische Forschungen*, 19 (2022), pp. 128–147.

Zimmerer, Jürgen, "The Value of Genocide Studies", in Bate, Jonathan, ed., *The Public Value of the Humanities*, London 2011.

Zimmerer, Jürgen, "Lager und Genozid. Die Konzentrationslager in Südwestafrika zwischen Windhuk und Auschwitz", in Jahr, Christoph and Thiel, Jens, eds., *Lager vor Auschwitz: Gewalt und Integration im 20. Jahrhundert*, Berlin 2013, pp. 54–67.

Zimmerer, Jürgen, "Colonialism and Genocide", in Jefferies, Matthew, ed., *The Ashgate Research Companion to Imperial Germany*, Burlington 2015, pp. 433–453.

Zimmerer, Jürgen, *German Rule, African Subjects. State Aspirations and The Reality of Power in Colonial Namibia*, New York 2021.

Zimmerer, Jürgen, ed., Erinnerungskämpfe. Neues deutsches Geschichtsbewusstsein, Stuttgart 2023.

Zimmerer, Jürgen, "Der Völkermord an den Herero und Nama und die deutsche Geschichte", in Zimmerer, Jürgen, ed., *Erinnerungskämpfe. Neues deutsches Geschichtsbewusstsein*, Stuttgart 2023, pp. 55–79.

Zimmerer, Jürgen, "Erinnerungskämpfe. Wem gehört die deutsche Geschichte?", in Zimmerer, Jürgen, ed., *Erinnerungskämpfe. Neues deutsches Geschichtsbewusstsein*, Stuttgart 2023, pp. 11–37.

Index

Adorno, Theodor W. 20
Althoff, Friedrich 276
Amherst, Sir Jeffery 144–145, 148, 190, 193
Arendt, Hannah 5, 126, 236, 293, 299

Bastian, Adolf 271
Bauer, Yehuda 142, 178–179
Bauman, Zygmunt 20
Baumann, Ludwig 209, 220
Bayer, Maximilian 39, 163, 259
Behrmann, Walter 285
Belloc, Hilaire 306
Bismarck, Otto von 33, 106, 262, 275, 308
Boettcher, Viktor 252
Bülow, Bernhard von 167
Büttner, Carl Gotthilf 204–205, 207

Césaire, Aimé 4, 299
Chaffee, Adna R. 309
Charny, Israel W. 129, 181
Chivington, John Milton 146, 191, 307
Churchill, Winston 305
Clinton, Bill 128, 180
Cox, Oliver 4

Darré, Richard Walther 254
Deimling, Berthold von 47–48, 151, 170, 253
Dietzel, Karl Heinrich 282, 285
Drechsler, Horst 60
Du Bois, W. E. B. 4
Durkheim, Emile 178

Eckenbrecher, Margarethe von 259
Ehrhardt, Hermann 251
Eichmann, Otto Adolf 183
Engelhard, Georg 222
Epp, Franz Xaver Ritter von 251, 255
Estorff, Ludwig von 29–30, 33, 43, 48, 163, 170
Eulenburg, Botho zu 262

Faupel, Wilhelm 251
Fein, Helen 15, 130, 162, 182–183, 306
Fischer, Eugen 253–254

Fischer, Fritz 126
Fredericks, Cornelius 45, 167
Frenssen, Gustav 259, 290

Golinelli, Angelo 63, 66, 80
Göring, Heinrich 34, 63, 77, 106, 205, 211
Grimm, Hans 126, 260, 290

Hall, H. L. 51, 146, 191
Hegel, Georg Wilhelm Friedrich 3, 20, 23, 241
Herzog, Roman 128, 180
Hettner, Alfred 281
Himmler, Heinrich 54, 120, 135, 152, 187, 241, 249, 291, 307, 313
Hintrager, Oskar 63, 212–213
Hitler, Adolf 18, 119–121, 125, 135–136, 152, 183, 187, 227, 236–237, 241, 243, 249, 291, 301–302, 309
Horkheimer, Max 20
Howard, John 128, 155, 176, 180

Isaak, Samuel 47, 169

Jaeger, Fritz 281–282
James, C. L. R 4
Johst, Hanns 120, 135, 187, 241, 291

Kenyatta, Uhuru 24
Kiepert, Heinrich 276
Knickrehm, Sergeant 214–216
Koselleck, Reinhart 239
Krabbenhöft, Willy 208–209, 220
Kuhn, Philalethes 253

Laaf, Emil 46–47, 169–170
Langer, Major 201
Lemkin, Raphael 9, 14, 130, 154, 157, 175, 182, 311
Leopold II, King 276
Lettow-Vorbeck, Paul von 251–252, 259
Leutwein, Theodor 33–34, 36–37, 39, 63–67, 69–70, 79–80, 83, 88, 102, 107, 111, 121, 145, 150, 161, 194, 205–206, 211, 218, 311–312
Liebert, Eduard von 44, 166, 246

Open Access. © 2024 the author(s), published by De Gruyter. This work is licensed under the Creative Commons Attribution 4.0 International License.
https://doi.org/10.1515/9783110754513-015

Liedecke, Ewald 135, 187, 230
Lindequist, Friedrich von 45, 63–65, 71, 79–80, 83–84, 86, 109, 252

MacArthur, Arthur 310
Maharero, Samuel 34, 40, 45, 70, 107, 150, 159, 166, 195, 248, 312
May, Karl 260, 301
Meyer, Hans 281–282
Mkwawa, Chief 44
Mkwawa, Chief Sonderfall, kein Vorname 44, 166, 246
Mollison, Theodor 253

Nehru, Jawaharlal 24
Nyhof, Hermann 170

Obst, Erich 282, 285
Olpp, Johannes 99

Paasche, Hans 253
Padmore, George 4
Panzlaff, Wilhelm 112, 203
Passarge, Siegfried 279
Penck, Albrecht 257, 278–280, 282, 285–289, 292
Peschel, Oscar 275
Petermann, August 271, 275
Peters, Carl 119
Pizarro, Francisco 7

Reinhard, Wolfgang 233
Reuß, Prince Heinrich VII 277
Rhodes, Cecil 57
Richthofen, Ferdinand von 257, 262–263, 270, 273–279, 281, 285, 292

Ritter, Carl 274, 276
Rodenwaldt, Ernst 253
Rohrbach, Paul 252, 259, 278

Schlieffen, Alfred von 37, 43, 50, 164, 247
Schmitt, Carl 239
Schmitthenner, Heinrich 282
Schneidewind, Friedrich 222
Schuckmann, Bruno von 62
Schwerin, Hans Bogislav Graf von 99
Seitz, Theodor 98–99, 212
Smith, Jake 310
Stelzner, Feodor 214–216
Streitwolf, Kurt 98
Stuurman, Shepherd 45, 167

Tecklenburg, Hans 46, 63, 111–115, 137, 168, 202, 206–208, 211, 216–217
Thorbecke, Franz 282
Troll, Carl 282–285, 292
Trotha, Lothar von 7, 12, 22, 25, 29, 33, 37–46, 48–52, 54, 68–69, 121, 145, 147–148, 150–152, 158–168, 170–171, 190, 192–195, 206, 247–249, 311–312

Volz, Wilhelm 288

Wandres, Carl 114, 137, 210, 216
Weber, Max 20
Wilhelm II, Kaiser 36, 42, 49, 52, 160, 164, 308, 311
Winthrop, Wait 144, 189
Witbooi, Hendrik 34, 45, 47, 107, 165, 167, 169

Zülow von 170
Zürn, Ralf 35